The *Aztlán* Mexican Studies Reader, 1974–2016

AZTLÁN ANTHOLOGY SERIES

The *Aztlán* Mexican Studies Reader, 1974–2016

Edited by

Héctor Calderón

UCLA Chicano Studies Research Center Press

Los Angeles

2018

CSRC Director: Chon A. Noriega
Senior Editor: Rebecca Frazier
Business Manager: Connie Heskett
Manuscript Editor: Catherine A. Sunshine
Design and Production: William Morosi

"Folklore, Lo Mexicano, and Proverbs" © 1982 by Américo Paredes
"Historical Notes on Chicano Oppression: The Dialectics of Racial and Class
Domination in North America" © 1974 by Tomás Almaguer
"Mexican Muralism: Its Social-Educative Roles in Latin America and the United
States" © 1982 by Shifra M. Goldman
"No Te Me Muevas, Paisaje: Sobre el Cincuentenario del Cine Sonoro en México"
© 1983 by Carlos Monsiváis
"Origins, Form, and Development of the Son Jarocho: Veracruz, Mexico" © 1982
by Steven Loza
"Responses to Mexican Immigration, 1910–1930" © 1975 by Ricardo Romo
Front cover: José Villalobos, *Noche otomi*, 2013. Image courtesy of the artist.

Library of Congress Cataloging-in-Publication Data
Names: Calderón, Héctor, author.
Title: The Aztlán Mexican studies reader, 1974-2016 / edited by Héctor
    Calderón.
Other titles: Aztlán.
Description: Los Angeles : UCLA Chicano Studies Research Center Press, [2018]
    | Series: Aztlan anthology series ; volume 6 | Includes bibliographical
    references and index.
Identifiers: LCCN 2018047832 | ISBN 9780895511690 (pbk. : alk. paper)
Subjects: LCSH: Mexican Americans--Civilization. | Mexican Americans in
    literature. | Mexican-American Border Region--Civilization. |
    Mexico--Civilization.
Classification: LCC E184.M5 C29 2018 | DDC 973/.046872--dc23
LC record available at https://lccn.loc.gov/2018047832

UCLA Chicano Studies
Research Center
193 Haines Hall
Los Angeles, California
90095-1544
www.chicano.ucla.edu

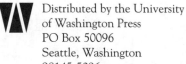
Distributed by the University
of Washington Press
PO Box 50096
Seattle, Washington
98145-5096
www.washington.edu/uwpress

CONTENTS

Introduction
Documenting Greater Mexico, from Chicano Studies to Mexican Studies

Héctor Calderón

The Chicano Studies Research Center (CSRC) at the University of California, Los Angeles, was founded in 1969 as the Mexican American Cultural Center, one of the first ethnic studies centers in the country. Its biannual publication, *Aztlán: A Journal of Chicano Studies*, has been the premier research journal in the field of Chicana and Chicano studies since 1970. CSRC director Chon Noriega has launched a series of readers for scholars, students, and the general public, drawing on some of the best writing in *Aztlán*, and I am pleased that *The Aztlán Mexican Studies Reader, 1974–2016* is part of this series. Throughout its history, *Aztlán* has always included a Mexican cultural presence. Some of the earliest articles in the disciplines of history and sociology assessed the origin, extension, and economic status of Mexican-origin populations in the United States. Over the years, the journal has published numerous essays on Mexican American and Mexican artistic cultures—literature, film, art, and music—including some in Spanish by well-known Mexican scholars. Indeed, beyond its reputation in the field of Chicana/o studies, *Aztlán* should also be considered a preeminent journal in Mexican studies, as for decades it has showcased cutting-edge research encompassing Mexican cultures on both sides of the border. No other journal in the United States has a similar publishing history in relation to Mexican culture.

As editor and reader, I began the research for this collection by surveying Mexico-related articles published in *Aztlán* since 1971. From these, I chose seventy to evaluate for possible inclusion in *The Aztlán Mexican Studies Reader*. I winnowed the group to fourteen that had withstood the test of time and were still topical in 2018. Some of these articles are by

1

noted scholars in Chicana and Chicano studies: Américo Paredes on folk genres, Shifra Goldman on muralism, Steven Loza on *son jarocho*, and Tomás Almaguer on a historical overview of race, caste, and class domination in North America. In the area of Mexican studies, I have included essays on *rock-en-español* founding band Maldita Vecindad, on transborder novelist Cristina Rivera Garza, and on violence in Mexico City in a noir novel by Patricia Valladares, along with an early film essay by Mexico's most well-known cultural critic, Carlos Monsiváis. Essays on feminism, gender violence, femicide, and Mexican internal racism lend currency to the field of Mexican studies. Three essays by young feminist scholars—Carolyn González, Audrey Harris, and Sandra Ruiz—were written specifically for this collection. All of the essays touch on major Mexican historical events that affected life on both sides of the border. The collection begins with two 1970s essays in Chicano studies and ends with four twenty-first-century essays in contemporary Mexican studies. The breadth of topics in multiple disciplines is unique to this collection of essays and establishes *Aztlán's* pre-eminence in the study of the Mexican cultural diaspora of North America.

Migration, Immigration, and Border Crossers in the Formation of Greater Mexico

The collection is framed by the writings of noted sociologist Tomás Almaguer and newcomer Carolyn González. In "Historical Notes on Chicano Oppression: The Dialectics of Racial and Class Domination in North America," Almaguer focuses on mestizos, *indios*, *negros*, and mulattos—the racial and ethnic groups that composed the laboring classes and the vast majority of inhabitants of New Spain, later Mexico, and the Southwestern United States. Written in 1974, the essay strongly suggests a cultural concept that would become critical to Chicano and Chicana studies beginning in the 1980s, namely Américo Paredes's "Greater Mexico," which is to say, Mexican cultural areas extending beyond the present political borders of the Mexican Republic. Chicanas and Chicanos in the twentieth century, argues Almaguer, have their origins in the cultural and racial history of conquest and colonization in North America that began in New Spain in the sixteenth century. That Almaguer in 1974 saw the racial mixtures of New Spain and Mexico as central to the history of North America placed him ahead of Mexican scholars writing on similar topics. It was not until 1984 that anthropologist Guillermo Bonfil Batalla published *México profundo: Una civilización negada*, reclaiming indigenous communities forgotten by the Mexican government and demonstrating that the exclusionary national project is due to Mexico's racial colonizing past. And not until 1992 did the Mexican government acknowledge that Mexican culture, traditionally seen as composed of European and indigenous elements, has a third root, the African presence, *la tercera raíz*. Mexico had erased the history of African slaves by alleging their "disappearance" into Mexico's racial and cultural mixtures. But of course, Mexico's *afrodescendientes* have not disappeared, as readers will understand in Kirstie Dorr's "Putting a Stamp on Racism," also selected for the collection.

Almaguer's work is especially timely when read with Carolyn González's "Fronteriza Writing in *Nadie me verá llorar:* Cristina Rivera Garza and Other Border Crossers of Yesterday and Today" (2016). A leading Mexican novelist, Rivera Garza was born in 1964 in Matamoros, Tamaulipas, across the Rio Grande from Brownsville, Texas, a hotbed of Texas Mexican scholars who were among the founders of Chicano and Chicana cultural studies. She is best known for her acclaimed novel *Nadie me verá llorar* (1999), which is set within Mexico City's insane asylum, el Manicomio General de la Castañeda, during the regime of Mexican dictator Porfirio Díaz, just prior to the Mexican Revolution of 1910. In depicting the domination and containment of prostitutes, the poor, the indigent, the indigenous, and mestizos in La Castañeda, the novel makes use of Rivera Garza's research for her 1995 PhD dissertation at the University of Houston, "The Masters of the Streets: Bodies, Power and Modernity in Mexico, 1867–1930." As González shows, Rivera Garza drew on Michel Foucault, Walter Benjamin, and Antonio Gramsci, as well as on US practitioners of critical anthropology writing in the 1980s, such as James Clifford and Michael Taussig, for her study of state repression and social control in the emergence of modern Mexico. González also presents convincing evidence for the influence of Sandra Cisneros's *Woman Hollering Creek and Other Stories* (1991b) and Américo Paredes's 1958 *"With His Pistol in His Hand"* (2010), mentioned by Rivera Garza in her dissertation. In her dissertation chapter titled "The Mad People's Portrait: A Dossier of Terror," she presents a composite portrait of the asylum inmates through photographs and files. Rivera Garza writes, "Yet, in the reduced space of the portrait, the pair of eyes, the mouth, the nose, the hair styles, the shoulders, hats and clothes, also constructed a social identity. The insane were dark-skinned, men often wore peasant hats while long-braided women wrapped themselves with the traditional *rebozo*. These objects and styles laid bare the class and ethnic traits of the insane and clearly delineated as well visual representations of the Mexican working poor" (1995, 306–7). In the novel, Rivera Garza takes up the title from her dissertation "masters of the streets" and transforms it in Spanish to *las insometidas*—intelligent, unsubmissive women who stage resistance within the prison. Moreover, in both the 1995 dissertation and the 1999 novel, Rivera Garza's inmates and characters return us to Tomás Almaguer's 1974 article on social and class domination in North America, though updated by González in 2016 with the issue of gender.

The northern Mexican cultural diaspora began in 1598 with the migration of settlers, of different racial castes, from small pueblos in Zacatecas, New Spain, to an unknown indigenous world. Juan de Oñate, born in Zacatecas in 1552, took possession of the land that would become la Provincia de la Nueva México. Following indigenous trails, Oñate established El Paso del Norte and, as capital of la Nueva México, San Juan de los Caballeros, just north of present-day Santa Fe, New Mexico. El Paso del Norte, now the binational border area of El Paso, Texas, and Ciudad Juárez, Chihuahua, has remained a physical and symbolic gateway to *el norte*.

Migrations have continued since that Oñate expedition of conquest and settlement, enabling Mexican populations to spread across the US Southwest. Writer Rivera Garza traces that history in her own family background, describing herself as a "granddaughter of migrant mine workers, agricultural workers, and deportees from the United States" (2017). She herself has crossed back and forth across the border, teaching at Mexican and US universities. Mexican immigrants, mainly laborers, have moved more or less freely throughout North America since the sixteenth and seventeenth centuries; only in the twentieth century, some fifty years after the US hostilities against Mexico and the creation of the international border, did these Mexican immigrants come to be seen as a problem. Historian Ricardo Romo's "Responses to Mexican Immigration, 1910–1930" (1975) focuses on three states: California, Arizona (part of the Territory of New Mexico until 1912), and Texas. His emphasis is on Los Angeles, which by 1925 had the second-largest Mexican population of any urban center after Mexico City. During this period, "push-pull" economic factors led to a million and half Mexicans residing in the United States by 1930. Though Mexican workers were preferred over Chinese and Japanese workers, they were not always welcomed. Indeed, the influx of Mexican laborers and war refugees, most by way of the El Paso border station, led to inevitable white nativist sentiments. Romo records calls to "save California for Californians." He relates, "Stories of the 'invading hordes' constantly appeared in the *Los*

Angeles Times during the years of the Mexican Revolution. Five thousand Mexican refugees crossed the 'International Line,' the *Times* reported one year, 'entice[d]' by 'three square meals.' The bill for feeding these refugees, the *Times* continued, would be sent to the Mexican government." These responses are not dissimilar to the current anti-immigrant sentiments against Central Americans and Mexicans expressed by Republicans in the Trump era. President Donald Trump's call for the Mexican government to pay for a border wall has its historical antecedent in the *Los Angeles Times* article quoted by Romo.

The history of Mexicans in the United States is the history of Mexican labor, of Mexicans who sought work and contributed to the development of the US economy in agriculture, railroads, and mining. Though exploited and underpaid, Mexican laborers, emphasizes Romo, served as the principal work force in agricultural industries throughout the Southwest. This component of the twentieth-century US economy is evident in Tomás Almaguer's critique on race and class domination in North America. In the twenty-first century, the agricultural workforce in California, traditionally composed of Mexican mestizos, now includes indigenous farmworkers from the states of Guerrero, Oaxaca, Puebla, and Chiapas. According to the California-based Indigenous Farmworker Study, these populations are estimated to total 165,000, including workers and family members; they speak twenty-three indigenous languages, with Mixtec, Zapotec, and Triqui predominating (Mines, Nichols, and Runsten 2010). Although cash wages in US employment are better than what a farm can provide in Mexico, indigenous farmworkers must face historical discrimination on both sides of the border.

Art, Muralism, Performance, and National Cultures

At the time of the Spanish Conquest, México-Tenochtitlan, now *la capital* of the modern Mexican state, was at the center of a multilingual, multicultural indigenous diaspora that reached from present-day Central America into what is now the US Southwest, the mythical Aztlán. Muralism as an art form was practiced throughout the Americas by these peoples. In what is now Mexico, archaeological sites bear witness to the importance of muralism as religious, social, and political memorialization of culture, and murals evidence the extent of artistic exchange that occurred. For example, murals at the archaeological site of Cacaxtla have similarities to the marvelous Mayan frescoes at Bonampak on the Mexico-Guatemala

5

border. Caczxtla, which is just sixty-eight miles to the east of present-day Mexico City, in the state of Tlaxcala, was inhabited by the Olmec-Xicalanca people. Probably Mayan settlers who had migrated from the Gulf Coast, they spoke Mayan and Náhuatl languages. After the destruction of México-Tenochtitlan by the Spanish in 1521 and the construction of a new political, social, and cultural order, the ruins of Mexico's indigenous cultures were transformed into the North American counterpart of Greek and Roman antiquities. The indigenous past was and continues to be a lasting influence on Mexican twentieth and twenty-first century art, as evidenced by the career of Oaxacan artist José Villalobos, who provided *Noche otomí* (2013) as cover art for this volume (see pages 35–36).

In Mexico City, following the Revolution of 1910 and the Constitution of 1917, Mexican intellectual leaders embarked on a project that was both political and artistic. José Vasconcelos, who was rector of the Universidad Nacional de México and secretary of public education, promoted public art in university buildings and at the Ministry of Public Education. The now famous 1920s murals by José Clemente Orozco in the Antiguo Colegio de San Ildefonso were available to administrators, professors, and students, since this building served as the *rectoría* for the university. The walls of the nearby colonial building that housed the education ministry served well for the murals by Diego Rivera. This was the beginning of *la escuela mexicana de pintura*, the Mexican school of art, a public art of personal genius that combined the indigenous past with the struggles of the Mexican Revolution and was influenced by the European avant-garde. In 1954 artists Juan O'Gorman, Diego Rivera, and David Alfaro Siqueiros participated in the indigenous-themed murals that grace the first buildings of the present-day Universidad Nacional Autónoma de México (UNAM): the Estadio Universitario (Rivera), the Rectoría (Siqueiros), and the Biblioteca Central (O'Gorman). These three large structures were planned with surrounding spaces to resemble indigenous plazas and stand as artistic tributes to mid-twentieth-century Mexican modernism.

From Mexico City's Aztec and colonial historic center, muralism spread throughout Mexico and into the United States. The political and artistic intentions of Mexican muralism are clearly evident in the art produced by exiled Mexican artists and artists who were shaped by the Chicano movement. As in Mexico, muralism in the United States was at the service of a national project. Noted art historian Shifra M. Goldman (1926–2011), in "Mexican Muralism: Its Social-Educative Roles in Latin America and the United States" (1982), examines the origins of this artistic movement in the 1920s and 1930s, describing its northward course. Well-known Mexican artists began painting murals in the Los Angeles area, which became an important art center for muralism as a consequence of the Chicano movement. José Clemente Orozco painted in fresco a monumental figure of Prometheus at Pomona College in 1930. In 1932 David Alfaro Siqueiros produced two politically subversive murals in Los Angeles, the infamous *América tropical* (Goldman campaigned tirelessly for its preservation) and *Mitin obrero*, depicting a multiracial and multigenerational meeting of workers; both were immediately covered. In 1946, Alfredo Ramos Martínez left unfinished a mural of indigenous women, *The Flower Vendors*, at Scripps College. From these Mexican masters, the torch passed to Chicana and Chicana artists.

Goldman wrote her 1982 article soon after receiving a doctorate in art history from the University of California, Los Angeles (UCLA) in modern Mexican art in 1977. A transplanted New Yorker and lifetime resident of East Los Angeles, Goldman had been a political activist since the 1950s and a student and teacher of Mexican and Chicano art prior to entering the graduate program at UCLA. Her scholarship centered on art and politics, with highly developed research on the art produced by the Chicano movement of the 1960s. In addition to the 1982 essay included in this volume, some of her major publications include *Contemporary Mexican Painting in a Time of Change* (1981); *Arte Chicano: A Comprehensive Annotated Bibliography of Chicano Art, 1965–1981* (1985), which she edited with Tomás Ybarra-Frausto; and *Tradition and Transformation: Chicana/o Art from the 1970s through the 1990s* (2015), edited and introduced by Charlene Villaseñor Black. In 1992 Goldman received the College Art Association's Frank Jewett Mather Award for distinction in art criticism, followed by the "Historian of the Lions" award from the Center for the Study of Political Graphics in 1996.

The common artistic and political thread throughout Mexican and Chicana/o muralism was to *mexicanizar el arte*. The Mexican artists who began the mural movement in the center of Mexico City envisioned a new art that would reflect Mexico, its history, its landscapes, and its indigenous people. The same can be said of Chicana/o art, which was produced by Mexican Americans searching for their Mexican roots. As Goldman writes in her contribution to this volume, "Among Chicanos . . . the recovery of Mexican muralism was part of a larger recovery of heritage and identity after a century of deliberate deculturalization by the dominant society."

7

Her 1982 article for *Aztlán* was derived from a lecture she gave at a 1980 conference titled "Arts and Music of Latin America for Pre-College Educators," held at the Institute of Latin American Studies, University of Texas, Austin. The article has historical significance because of its focus on Mexico *and* Chicana/os—probably the first time that an acknowledged expert on both Mexican and Chicana/o art presented these two traditions in a comparative context. It came some sixty years after the revolutionary period in Mexico and fifteen years after the beginning of the Chicano movement. One artistic moment is part of history; the other is history in the making. Indeed, Goldman did go on to write on many topics pertinent to Chicana/o art: rasquache aesthetics, border art, arts and AIDS, feminism, postmodernism, and art forms such as video and installation, for example. By the time of her death in 2011, she had seen major developments and changes in Chicana/o art, including the emergence of women artists and muralists. In her 1980 conference presentation, she assesses the Chicano muralism of the 1970s. Also, given the still-fledgling institutional programs with courses in the Chicano experience, Goldman offers a blueprint for comparative studies of these two traditions, noting common goals and topics and the misconceptions perpetuated in art history courses. Mexican and Chicana/o muralism had the common goals of transforming consciousness and educating, which made art pedagogically useful in history, sociology, and political science courses. It is evident that in 1980, Chicana/o studies had yet to develop in the direction of the humanities and the arts.

Goldman relates art to indigenism, mestizaje, revolution, historical conflict, and national and international politics—themes that were not easily accessible to Chicana/o artists at the time, given the reigning theories of art history in the United States, where the social and political were not "artistic" considerations. With the advent of Chicana/o studies programs and mural groups in the Southwest and Midwest, young Chicana/o instructors and artists revitalized the work of the Mexican muralists, extending Mexican revolutionary themes and heroes and indigenous motifs from Mexican archeological sites to diverse geographic, historical, social, and economic circumstances of Mexican Americans in the 1960s and 1970s—a new way to *mexicanizar el arte*. Certainly, Mexican intellectuals wanted to establish a new forward-looking Mexico that drew from the past. Chicana/os, through their widespread political awakening and activism, aspired to come together as a nation. As Texas novelist Tomás Rivera wrote of the 1970s and the Chicano artist, "Perhaps the single most important element of Chicano literature is that it was able to capture from the beginning of the decade this very wisdom of a very disparate and amorphous nation or kindred group" (1982, 9). The contribution of 1960s and 1970s Chicana/o art in the United States was to promote aesthetic, social, and political connections among art, artists, and the community.

Guillermo Gómez-Peña is one of the best-known Mexican-born performance artists in the United States, where he has lived since the late 1970s, residing in Tijuana–San Diego, New York City, and San Francisco. In his autobiographical performance piece "Multiple Journeys: The Life and Work of Gómez-Peña (A Performance Chronology)" (2009), he begins with a question from a (fictional) journalist who asks Gómez-Peña, "What do you do when a writer or a curator wishes to deport you from performance art history?" To which Gómez-Peña responds, "You write yourself back into it on your own terms. Chicanos taught me that." Gómez-Peña does exactly this in "Performance Chronology," a conceptual artwork in which he connects his life and family to his art, which in turn is embedded in a political and art historical context. The piece goes as far as 2008 and ends "TO BE CONTINUED."

This "Performance Chronology" has taken various forms, in addition to this text originally published in *Aztlán* in 2009. Diana Taylor, known for her theoretical work on hemispheres, presents another version on the website of her Hemispheric Institute of Performance and Politics (http://hemisphericinstitute.org/web-cuadernos/multiple-journeys). Here readers will find the text accompanied by visual images that reveal the transformations Gómez-Peña has undergone: from his middle-class origins, born Guillermo Liberio Gómez-Peña, followed by his early life and education in Mexico City, to the evolving selves in his performance tableaux over a thirty-year period. The online "Performance Chronology" was also presented for discussion at Taylor's Hemispheric Institute in New York City.

When he arrived on the US performance scene in 1978, Gómez-Peña found rich content for his pieces in the social and political experiences suffered by Chicana/os and Mexican immigrants for decades and addressed in visual art, murals, and performance. He speaks of his "Chicano-ization" and of becoming a "wetback . . . beaner . . . greaser." Life as he knows it on both sides of the border is informed by the relationships that Mexican Americans, Chicanas and Chicanos, and Mexican immigrants have had since the nineteenth century. Some of the concepts in his work are migration, hybridity, foreignness, barrioization. Most of his performance pieces feature the brown body in a clichéd religious ritual performance of sacrifice, martyrdom, confession, exhibitionism, and funeral. His work speaks to debates on cultural diversity, border culture, and US-Mexico relations. He has responded to significant historical events in the United States in his performance pieces, always from a border point of view. He states that he develops multicentric narratives and performative poetics from a border perspective. Gómez-Peña is yet another bordered identity in a Mexican North America, an identity that is played out and performed mostly in English. In 1991 he was awarded the prestigious MacArthur Fellowship, and in 1997 he received an American Book Award for *The New World Border* (1996).

Gómez-Peña attained dual nationality when he became a US citizen in 1999. This has allowed him to continue performing as a non-Mexican or post-Mexican, experiencing in a more acute way *desmexicanización*, *pochización*, and *chicanización*. Though his work has been published by Mexico's prestigious Fondo de Cultura Económica (*Bitácora del cruce*, 2006), only in 2017–18 did he have his first solo exhibition in Mexico City; titled *Guillermo Gómez-Peña: Mexican (IN)documentado*, it showed at the Museo de Arte Moderno from November 30, 2017, to April 22, 2018. In Mexico he offered, "A través de los chicanos descubrí que mi arte podía ser el medio idóneo para explorar y reinventar mis múltiples y cambiantes identidades (algo que hubiera sido impensable en el México de aquel entonces)" (quoted in *Reversos* 2018). Which is to say, in the United States he has been able to explore his multiple and changing identities, something that would not have been possible in Mexico.

Gómez-Peña is a citizen of North America with documents that allow him to freely cross the US-Mexico border. His is one immigrant's tale among others in 2017–18, when the border has become a place of terror with the separation of families and the imprisonment of children. The brown body—now including brown children—is the site of abuse and sexual exploitation. *La perrera*, the kennel-like chain-link prison that houses immigrants and refugees, is known by border crossers from Mexico and Central America, though it was only in 2018 that it came under scrutiny by the mass media. Deportations of parents without their children are now a fact of the border. And increasingly, as occurred in the 1930s, Mexicans are being deported in large numbers. We are witnessing a strange reversal of geographies. The map of indigenous Mexico, from north to south, is being superimposed on California—witness the Tarahumara, Huichol, Otomí, Purépecha, Náhuatl, Mixteco, Zapoteco, Triqui, Tzeltal, Chol, and Mayan farmworkers toiling in California agribusiness (Mines, Nichols, and Runsten 2010). And now the map of California is being superimposed on Mexico City. There is an area near the Monumento a la Revolución in Colonia Tabacalera that is now known as "Little LA" because it shelters thousands of people recently deported by the US government. With their English-language proficiency, some of these deportees have found work at call centers near the monument (*Wall Street Journal* 2018). Now English mixes with Spanish and indigenous languages in the postmodern geographies and national cultures of North America. Carlos Monsiváis wrote in 1995, "All Mexicans live on the border" (41), and this truth has even greater significance in 2018.

Mexican American Folklore, Corridos, and Cultural Struggle on the Texas-Mexico Border

Américo Paredes (1915–99) is acknowledged as one of the founders of Mexican American and Chicano cultural studies. His 1956 doctoral dissertation for the English Department at the University of Texas, Austin, established him as the leading scholar of Mexican studies in the United States at that time. Published in 1958 as *"With His Pistol in His Hand": A Border Ballad and Its Hero*, Paredes's study was a civil rights–era defense of Mexican culture on both sides of the border. In his creative contextual study of the border ballad, the corrido, he affirmed the key cultural difference between Mexican and Mexican American folklore, namely that Mexican American folklore was based on cultural conflict. Paredes chose one song, "El Corrido de Gregorio Cortez," to present a brief on behalf of Texas Mexicans. The song recounts the story of Mexican immigrant Gregorio Cortez Lira, who was wrongfully accused of horse theft and the murder of two Texas sheriffs in a 1901 case; after years of imprisonment, Cortez was pardoned in 1913. During his years as a professor at the University of Texas, Paredes continued his studies of Mexican American folklore from northern Mexico to Chicago. With the advent of the Chicano movement in the 1960s, he described this political and social fervor as the culmination of long historical struggle: "Mexican-Americans have been awake to their problems since the time of Cortina [1859]. They have also been quite preoccupied with questions of self-analysis and identity, ever since the Treaty of Guadalupe. The Chicano 'awakening' of the 1960s is the culmination of a long continuous struggle, spanning more than a century" (Paredes 1976, 27). In 1970, along with Chicano student activists, Professor Paredes was one of the principal organizers of the Center for Mexican American Studies at the University of Texas, Austin, becoming its first director.

With his study of the border corrido, Paredes noted the mutual influences between Mexican American and Mexican cultures through a concept first used in his 1956 dissertation: that of Greater Mexico. In 1976, he collapsed the inside-outside polarity that had been created by the border separating Mexico from the United States into his final definition: "'Greater Mexico' refers to all the areas inhabited by people of Mexican culture—not only within the present limits of the Republic of Mexico but in the United States as well—in a cultural rather than a political sense" (xiv). Late in his life, both the United States and Mexico acknowledged his scholarship. In 1989, the National Endowment for the Humanities awarded him the Charles Frankel Prize for his outstanding contributions to the public's understanding of the humanities. And in 1990 Paredes received La Orden Mexicana del Águila Azteca, the highest honor that Mexico presents to citizens of other countries.

Aztlán published Paredes's "Folklore, Lo Mexicano, and Proverbs" in 1982. It originated as a talk given to an American studies group in San Antonio, Texas, in 1970, at a time when Mexican American or Chicano studies was becoming institutionalized as an academic field. In his talk, Paredes explained that while it is not easy to define *lo mexicano*, folklore could be described as "the unofficial heritage of a people." This view of folklore was important to minority groups who speak a language that is different from the language used by the majority or national culture, the culture deemed "official." The dichotomy between unofficial and official language and culture has continued as a problem for Mexican Americans and Latinos in the United States today. The fact that many speak Spanish (though they may also speak English) has provided grounds for constant racist critiques against them. In *"With His Pistol in His Hand"* (which very few had read in 1970), Paredes skillfully used both the unofficial and the official to critique the official history of Texas and the atrocities committed against Mexicans, as well as the state-sanctioned, racist scholarship of two noted white Texas scholars, Walter Prescott Webb and J. Frank Dobie. Paredes used the satire and humor of the "unofficial heritage of a people" to make his case on behalf of Texas Mexicans.

His larger point was that context matters. In his brief piece for *Aztlán*, reprinted in this volume, we see him nimbly work through supposedly stereotypical Mexicans who appear dumb or stupid when seen from the viewpoint of a folklorist who ignores contextual clues. Without context, proverbs, or *dichos*, may be taken to mean the opposite of what they actually mean, especially if the folklorist relies solely on the written word, ignoring the voices and mannerisms of the informants. This was common in written folklore collections such as those that Paredes's American studies audience would have relied on in 1970. For Mexican Americans, folklore, as "the unofficial heritage of a people," can be an expression of identity. For those not knowledgeable about cultural and contextual clues in the informant situation, identities and interpretations of Mexican character based on racist stereotypes may arise. In his essay, as in his dissertation, Paredes uses folklorist-anthropologist J. Frank Dobie in several examples to make his point about folklorists who do not understand the culture they are studying, who do not read cultural cues in the oral performance of informants. Paredes contests the interpretations of Mexicans and Mexican Americans as lazy, fatalistic, cruel, and aggressive—some of the racist stereotypes that early Chicano historians, anthropologists, and writers in the 1970s had to combat—and he does so from the point of view of Mexican Americans. (This racism continues today, as candidate Trump made clear in 2015 when he described Mexicans as rapists and drug dealers.)

In "'¡Yo soy Gregorio Cortez!': Américo Paredes and the Mexican Immigrant" (2016), Audrey Harris sheds new light on the origins of Chicano literature by focusing on Paredes, a Mexican in South Texas who used his study of a border corrido and its hero to defend Mexican immigrants and their civil rights. She notes the racist attitudes that Paredes critiques in his early study of the 1901 corrido. But Harris also discusses attitudes toward immigration in the 1930s through the 1950s, when young Paredes began exploring the corrido tradition for his groundbreaking 1958 novel *"With His Pistol in His Hand."* Paredes never identified as a Chicano; he was a Texas Mexican, aware of the negotiation of identity given the situation of Mexicans in the history of Texas. In his 1970 talk, Paredes makes no mention of Chicanos: his focus is on providing cultural definitions of *lo mexicano* and folklore. *Lo mexicano* is what concerned Paredes, and Harris argues with her title ("¡Yo soy Gregorio Cortez!") that Paredes identified strongly with Gregorio Cortez. "I will show," writes Harris, "how Paredes brought his views of immigration, and of his own identity as a Mexican American who identified with Mexican immigrants from south of the border, to bear on *'With His Pistol in His Hand.'"* To make her case, Harris utilizes early studies of Mexican immigration published in English by Mexican anthropologist Manuel Gamio. His *Mexican Immigration to the United States* (1930) and *The Mexican Immigrant: His Life-Story* (1931) were little known in Mexico but well known in the United States, where his work was funded by the Social Science Research Council. Gamio is recognized in Mexico for his

1916 classic *Forjando patria*, a political tract arguing for assimilation of the indigenous into Mexican culture. Harris notes that "Paredes's study of 'El Corrido de Gregorio Cortez' both parallels and reflects the influence of Gamio's English-language studies conducted in Texas."

Gamio included a version of the Gregorio Cortez corrido in *Mexican Immigration to the United States*. Like Gamio, Paredes portrays the plight of Texas Mexicans and Mexican immigrants, but he does so with a much more creative version of "El Corrido de Gregorio Cortez." Harris argues that after collecting all available versions of the corrido, analyzing them, noting their folkloristic and lyrical merits, and then "polishing and recombining" them, Paredes produced a version that was more artistically and politically nuanced than the one recorded by Gamio decades earlier. The story of Cortez as a Mexican who refused to be treated like a Mexican was central to the 1950s dissertation, written at a time when the Mexican population in the United States had increased dramatically and faced pressure to assimilate. In "The Mexico-Texan Corrido," a essay published in *Southwest Review* in 1942, Paredes laid out the relationship between Mexican identity and the corrido tradition, noting that the corrido had "reached perhaps its most significant developments among the Mexicans living in South Texas who have not yet become Americanized" (1942, 470). Harris notes that in *"With His Pistol in His Hand,"* Paredes included a version of the ballad that had no historical antecedents but may have been formed by combining the most stirring verses of other versions. It is in this version that Gregorio Cortez shouts defiantly to Texas Rangers pursuing him, "Ah, so many mounted Rangers just to take one Mexican!" (2010, 13). Harris concludes, "In this shortened version, we can see Paredes inscribing himself into this lineage, not just of those who study and analyze folklore but also of the tellers themselves."

Harris also recalls the legal status of Mexican immigrants during the period when Gamio and Paredes were writing about the plight of the Mexican. In 1924, Congress established the US Border Patrol to enforce newly decreed immigration caps that rendered undocumented workers illegal. By the time of the Great Depression, the "push-pull" relationship between the US and Mexico referenced by Romo in his essay had given way to the US government–sponsored Mexican repatriation program (1929–36). Though Mexicans were encouraged to relocate voluntarily to Mexico, the reality was that some 500,000 Mexicans (some of them US citizens) were forcibly deported. During World War II, with the wartime US economy in need of labor, US and Mexican officials created the Bracero Program, which allowed temporary guest workers to work in US agriculture. Soon after the war, however, the Justice Department launched Operation Wetback, and in 1954 some 1,075,168 Mexicans were deported.

The Cortez incident of 1901 preceded these US government measures to limit the flow of documented and undocumented Mexican workers to the United States. Like others before him, Harris narrates, the child Cortez, born in 1875 on the border near Matamoros, had crossed the Rio Grande with his family to find work on the north side of the river. He had lived peacefully until the fateful day when the law came looking for a horse thief. By the time Paredes wrote his dissertation, however, the situation of Mexican immigrants and Mexican Americans in the United States was quite different, influencing Paredes's self-identity and his defense of his culture. (The other side of the coin, the assimilationist Mexican, is portrayed in Paredes's novel *George Washington Gómez*, written a quarter century before the dissertation and published in 1990.) What Paredes studied, now seen much more clearly because of Harris's essay, were the cultural identity choices available to Mexican Americans. Finally, Harris argues that one of the first Chicano films, *The Ballad of Gregorio Cortez* (1982), directed by Robert Young, had two writers. In the film credits Paredes is listed as the first writer—an unusual move in film, where authors of source material typically are listed after screenwriters. Harris suggests that Young had learned from Paredes's nuanced storytelling: "Indeed, Young availed himself of many of the cues from Paredes's book, to such a degree that the film can be seen as extending and providing a visual medium for Paredes's storytelling."

Mexican Musical Cultures, Rural and Urban

Steven Loza is a well-known scholar and professor in the Department of Ethnomusicology at UCLA. His contribution to this anthology, written in 1982 when he was a graduate student, examines the *son jarocho*, which in recent years has become as popular in California as it is in Veracruz, Mexico. Loza's "Origins, Form, and Development of the Son Jarocho: Veracruz, Mexico" (1982) describes this musical form's roots in colonial rhythms—the *coplas*, *coplillas*, and *letrillas* of the sixteenth, seventeenth, and eighteenth centuries—and its transformation to its more open present form on both sides of the US-Mexico border. According to Loza, the first documentation of the son jarocho dates back to 1776: "At that time, during the Spanish Inquisition, the son was often banned in Mexico and other regions of New Spain, most likely on grounds that it was immoral.

This was, after all, a period in which the authorities attempted to convert the masses to Catholicism." As Loza explains, the high-spirited son had always featured ribald commentary in its lyrics; letrillas in "bad taste" were criticized by the clergy and later banned.

The son jarocho as communal dance and singing of verses evolved shortly before and after independence from Spain. As early as 1840, Loza writes, the Spaniard Don José María Esteva observed performances of the son jarocho "La Bamba" as he traveled through Veracruz. Esteva describes the traditional *tablado*, or wooden platform, used for the *zapateado*, rhythmic dancing with the stamping of feet, as well as the witty repartee of verses among the singers. Independence from Spain had unleashed new forms of playing and dancing the son, with the *fandango* (communal dancing) enjoyed by the lower classes and the different racial castes in Veracruz. Citing the observations of ethnomusicologist Robert Stevenson on the son, Loza writes, "Verse forms such as the *copla* (couplet), *cuarteta* (quatrain), *quintilla* (five lines), and *décima* (ten lines), often with octosyllabic line length, frequently were picaresque, with double meanings, and usually had a romantic, sexual, or at times of topical (e.g., anticlerical) significance." The octosyllabic verse line is the traditional Spanish (Peninsular) form of oral composition, also noted by Américo Paredes in the oral performance of corridos. These verse forms were enjoyed at public events as well as within groups of guitarists or among families. Talented verse makers in the décima and corrido forms were well known along the Rio Grande Valley. The traditional instruments included the *jarana* (small guitar) and *requinto* (smaller five-string guitar), sometimes the violin, and the now well-known *arpa veracruzana*, which came later. Hence, an important regional "national" identity in music was being formed, the now-Mexican son jarocho.

In California, the son jarocho has enjoyed great popularity among musicians who desire to maintain the original communal aspects of the fandango. Los Angeles has become a center for son jarocho with *encuentros* (meetings) between Los Angeles and Mexican *jaraneros*. Around one hundred years after the son jarocho's description by Spaniard Esteva, Ritchie Valens's rock classic of 1958, "La Bamba," would lead to various fusions and transformations of the son jarocho. There is a recording of a young Mick Jagger singing "La Bamba" in 1961. Just three years after it was released in California, "La Bamba" was one of the founding songs for the young Londoners who would become the Rolling Stones. Bob Dylan acknowledges that he used Valens's "La Bamba" chord progression for the 1965 classic "Like a Rolling Stone." The son jarocho, in both its traditional string instruments and its fusion with rock and electronic music, has found a home in Los Angeles groups, including Los Lobos (indeed, that band began with high school friends playing traditional Mexican music), Ozomatli, Quetzal, La Santa Cecilia, and Las Cafeteras. Mexican rock groups Caifanes and Café Tacvba have recorded compositions of son jarocho. One of the most recent fusions is a CD by San Francisco–based producer Héctor "Hecdog" Pérez, *Sistema Bomb Presenta Electro-Jarocho*, which features well-known Mexican jarocho practitioners such as Patricio Hidalgo (Afrojarocho), Ramón Gutiérrez (Son de Madera), the late Andrés Flores, Liche Oseguera, the legendary Los Cojolites, Asdru Sierra (Ozomatli), and Maldita Vecindad vocalist Roco. This CD received the 2013 Grammy for Best Latin Rock, Urban, or Alternative Album. The Mexican mestizo son jarocho is now counted with *son jalisciense* and mariachi as among Mexico's national musical traditions.

Regional Mexican cultures, like that of Veracruz with its rich and diverse cultural history, can be defined by their music. Besides the son jarocho, Veracruz can also boast of its musical cousin, *son huasteco* (also *huapango*). In Mexico City, el Distrito Federal (DF), emerging youth cultures, decades of political activism, and a recording music industry led to the beginning of *rock en español*. From South America—Argentina and Chile—in the 1970s the torch passed to Mexico City. One of the organic "regional" musical contributions from el DF is rock, and Maldita Vecindad y los Hijos del Quinto Patio is one of the defining bands of Mexican rock. Formed in the 1980s by musicians from Mexico City, with origins in Oaxaca, San Luis Potosí, and Argentina, and produced by record labels RCA and BMG and a fledgling recording rock-en-español music industry in the United States, Maldita has continued performing its music for over thirty years. The band's longevity is due to its excellent musicianship and its Mexican working-class collective sense of music for the people. Maldita's followers know that they come to dance and listen to favorite Maldita compositions with a sense of social and political community.

In "The Mexico City–Los Angeles Cultural Mosh Pits: Maldita Vecindad, a Chilanga-Chicana Rock Banda de Pueblo" (2006), I make the case for the mutual cross-border influences between Chicano culture and Maldita Vecindad's rock music. Maldita has always been drawn to Chicano culture. In 1989 the band released its first album, one of the first digital recordings in Mexico, *Maldita Vecindad y los Hijos del 5° Patio*. It included "Mojado," which recounts the death of an immigrant in the United States and is one of the first compositions to deal with crossing both national and musical borders (with a mix of "rumba flamenca y cubana"). Shortly after the release of this first album, Maldita began a US tour, and in 1989 the band was invited to a MEChA Cinco de Mayo celebration in San Francisco. Maldita's members were among the first artist-intellectuals to express a kindred spirit with the Chicano movement. The band's *Gira pata de perro 93* (1993) is both a photographic essay of Maldita's 1993 world tour and a manifesto of their artistic and political goals. Maldita acknowledged for its own musical project the importance of redefined Mexican working-class cultural symbols popularized by the Chicano movement:

> En 1985, cuando comenzamos, muchos grupos en México tocaban en inglés o tenían nombres en ese idioma. Había una influencia musical muy fuerte del rock inglés o americano, se reproducían géneros como el blues, el punk o el heavy metal.
>
> En la cultura chicana había una redefinición de idea de mexicanidad y eso se reflejaba en la música de fusión, la pintura callejera con el graffiti, los íconos populares: Zapata, la Virgen de Guadalupe, la bandera, el teatro campesino, los pachucos o la presencia popular de la cultura prehispánica, por ejemplo.
>
> Nuestro trabajo en Maldita siempre ha tenido muchos puntos de contacto con esa búsqueda de la cultura chicana. (Maldita Vecindad 1993)

For inspiration, Maldita also reached back to the El Paso–Ciudad Juárez border music of the pachuco era, the 1940s. Pachucos were Mexican American youth who moved in their own bilingual, bicultural world. Originating in El Paso, the phenomenon spread throughout the Southwest. In a racially segregated Los Angeles, these youth were the objects of racial violence; the infamous Zoot Suit Riots of 1943 were dramatized in the Luis Valdez's 1981 *Zoot Suit*, the film adaptation of the Broadway play. Germán Valdés, the much-loved Ciudad Juárez radio personality who traveled to Los Angeles in the 1940s, created a recording and film-star character, a pachuco known as el Tin Tan. Hugely popular among generations of Mexico City youth, Valdés became Maldita's own Mexican cultural symbol through the song "Pachuco" on the album *Circo*. If there is one rock-en-español song that qualifies as an international rock anthem, it is Maldita's "Pachuco." Maldita also reached back to the pachuco-era founders of Mexican American–Chicano music, Arizonan Lalo Guerrero and Texan Don Tosti, performing Guerrero's "Los chucos suaves" and Tosti's "Pachuco Boogie." Maldita vocalist Roco (Rolando Ortega) always performs the role of the pachuco in a mashup of 1940s and 1950s attire—long goatee, hat, fingertip coat, baggy pants, chain, handkerchief, two-toned shoes—along with twenty-first-century Mexican rock styles of tattoos, long hair, earrings, Indian necklaces and bracelets.

In the quotation from *Gira pata de perro 93*, Maldita publicly acknowledged 1985 as the beginning for the band. Indeed, that year was a turning point for Mexico City. The earthquake of 1985 led to the emergence of a civil society based on mutual assistance. The young members of Maldita played at functions to raise funds for earthquake victims, often performing on a flatbed truck. Indeed, the earthquake proved life-changing for Mexico City residents. Maldita's members, who were nearing adulthood in 1985, also recall the student movement of summer and fall 1968 and the fateful student massacre at Tlatelolco on October 2 of that year. Maldita's members have a repertoire of socially conscious music. Bass player Aldo Acuña was a Mexico City street youth who survived by performing *nueva canción* with his folk group at *peñas*. I have heard Aldo, an Argentinian exile, play a folk song about the death of fellow Argentinian Ernesto "Ché" Guevara. Other members of Maldita who attended university, such as guitarist Pato (Enrique Montes), had professors who lived through the 1968 student massacre. In the album *Mostros*, released September 15, 1998, Maldita included song "2 de octubre."

The origins of Maldita are in the streets, in grassroots political organizing, and in the lives of the many street performers (musicians, jugglers, clowns) who are survivors of Mexico's social and economic inequalities. Maldita took its name from Mexico's Golden Age Cinema in tribute to the film and bolero *Quinto patio* (1950)—the "fifth patio" being a reference to the poorest of the urban poor. Maldita is the band of *música callejera*, music that amplifies street voices, telling of social problems. Despite a succession of governments promising change (Mexico City's slogan is "la Ciudad de la Esperanza," the City of Hope), Mexico has not seen the significant social and political changes that poor Mexicans hope for. For over thirty years, Maldita has remained the Mexican people's *banda*. To celebrate the twenty-fifth anniversary of their groundbreaking 1991 concept album *Circo*, Maldita returned to the same space where they first presented the album, under the big top. In 1991 the venue belonged to the well-known Circo Atayde Hermanos, a touring circus that has been Mexico's entertainment for the poor. In 2016, Maldita reprised its complete musical songbook with songs telling of the plight of punks, indigenous peoples, the urban poor, and street performers, including violence against gays and the death of immigrants.

"Conversación con Aldo Acuña" is based on a December 5, 2002, class meeting in my UCLA Spanish course on Mexican literature, culture, and society. Maldita bass player Aldo's visit came on the last day of the term, dramatically concluding the course section on *rock en tu idioma*. For over an hour and a half, Aldo fielded our questions. He offered insights into the band's transformation of punk culture into a contestatory musical project through a discussion of key songs from *Maldita Vecindad y los Hijos del 5° Patio* (1989), *Circo* (1991), and *Baile de Máscaras* (1996). The conversation presented here is faithful to the live performance of the class and includes lyrics of the music played during the discussion. At the end of the discussion, Maldita's fusion of art and politics is clearly evident in Aldo's assessment of the current state of artists, politics, and government in Mexico.

Mexican Cinema of the Golden Age and the Mexican Family Romance

During its Golden Age (1933–64), Mexican cinema was one of Mexico's important exports. Throughout Latin America, Mexican films enjoyed great success, as they also did in the United States among Mexican immigrant and Mexican American populations. Spanish-language movie theaters existed in the US Southwest, especially in border cities. Going to the movies in the 1940s and 1950s meant going to theaters such as Teatro Colón, Teatro Azteca, and in Los Angeles (also a border city), El Million Dollar on Broadway.

John Rechy (born Juan Francisco Flores Rechy), one of Mexican American literature's founding authors, based his early writings on Mexican values and cultural problems that were available to him in Mexican films. As a child, Rechy accompanied his mother to view Mexican film greats such as María Félix at the Teatro Colón in El Paso. His groundbreaking gay novel *City of Night* (1963), with a central Mexican American character, came a few years after his first published piece, a border autoethnographic essay that appeared in 1958 in the *Evergreen Review*. Titled "El Paso del Norte," the essay used the traditional historical name for the gateway to *el norte* established in 1598 by Juan de Oñate. El Paso del Norte meant for Rechy both El Paso and Ciudad Juárez, and he wrote on binational border neighborhoods in a satiric, fast-paced English vernacular. One of the most interesting cultural critiques in the essay is a humorous rendering of Mexico's sentimental films of the Golden Age and the Mexican family romance: "Mothers are a Grand Mexican thing. . . . Mexicans really love Mothers. Americans dont" (1958, 135). Rechy narrates the Mexican mother love plot in a fictional, but very real, Mexican Golden Age film:

Dig: A serious Mexican movie. The favorite theme. The son goes away. The little Old Mexican Mother stands at the dingy door with her black shawl sheltering her from the drizzling rain. Christ. The son goes away, and forgets about her. He becomes a Great Matador [. . .] The Little Mother in the Black Shawl wanders over Mexico, working for harsh people [. . .] She comes at last into a very rich home in Mexico City. Of course. It is her son's home. [. . .] He is gruff. "Old woman, look how much dust has accumulated on this my favorite table." [. . .] One day the Big Corrida comes on. The wife is digging it on television (she cant bear to go it live). The matador is gored. The shawled Mother screams, MI HIJO!!!! The wife knows now [. . .] They run out, get a cab, go to the bullring. There he is. Unconscious. Dying. The beautifully dressed wife pulls the shawl off the little old Mother and proclaims to the dying matador, "Die if God wills it—but not without knowing that—This—Is—Your—Mother!!!!" Everyone is crying, the unnatural son repents (as he must), and all three live happily ever after. (133–34).

What Rechy describes in the little Mexican mother plot was a staple of corny, melodramatic Mexican films. As the long-suffering woman who did everything for her family, and especially for her sons, the Mexican mother was the sweet counterpart to the Mexican macho.

Later, Sandra Cisneros in "Mexican Movies" (1991a) recalls a Spanish-language theater in Chicago in which Golden Age Mexican cinema is transported to the Midwest, with small children and parents all going to the movies even though the film may not be suitable for children. Cisneros turns the camera on the audience, where children are playing in the theater and a mother is afraid of rats under her feet. The young female narrator enjoys the films with a happy ending, where a male actor is singing on horseback, and dislikes the films of violence against women. The child narrator refers to the man who undresses the lady as "just plain dumb." Cisneros describes two male-dominated genres: the happy hacienda-rancho films with song, like *Allá en el rancho grande* (1936) with Tito Guízar, the first box office hit of the Golden Age; and films starring a tough male figure, like *El bruto* (1953) with Pedro Armendáriz, one of the era's last hits. Whether just across the Rio Grande on its north bank or in the more distant Midwest, Mexican films found a home with Mexican families.

Carlos Monsiváis (1938–2010) was one of Mexico's most important critics of Mexican popular culture of the twentieth and twenty-first centuries; since his passing he is also acknowledged as one of the defenders of gay rights in Mexico. As a journalist, film critic, and lover of art, music, and dance, he focused his accessible creative writing on Mexico City. His early publications include two books of essays, *Días de guardar* (1971) and

Amor perdido (1977). In 1983 he wrote the essay selected for this volume, "No te me muevas, paisaje (sobre el cincuentenario del cine sonoro en México)," commemorating the fiftieth anniversary of sound motion picture in Mexico. The essay presents a critical panorama of Mexico's Golden Age cinema, considering directors like Fernando de Fuentes and Emilio "el Indio" Fernández as well as much-loved film stars, including Pedro Infante. Coming some thirty years after the Golden Age, Monsiváis's essay is one of the first pieces of film criticism to assess Mexico's film industry in its golden decades, from the 1936 *Allá en el rancho grande* to the groundbreaking social realism of Luis Buñuel's *Los olvidados* (1950).

Monsiváis writes that Mexican cinema was grounded in the Mexican family: the nation was the family and the family was the most accurate representation of the nation. Though the Hollywood star system influenced Mexican cinema, the Mexican industry relied on archetypes such as la Sufrida Mujer (the suffering good woman), la Prostituta con Corazón de Oro (the prostitute with a heart of gold), el Macho Generoso (the generous macho), and el Hombre Primitivo que Aspira a la Justicia (the primitive male who seeks justice). Monsiváis presents actor Pedro Infante as the perfect multiple Mexican archetype. With a career of sixty-one films from 1939 to 1956, Infante was the virtuous son of the masses who held their attention with music and song. María Félix was the willful female who becomes strong like a man in order to survive and whose strength is also her beauty. Dolores del Río is the fragile, weak woman whose beauty is also her invincible strength. Del Río is perfect as the humble indígena in *María Candelaria* (1943), while Félix dominates as an upper-class *hacendada* in *Enamorada* (1946). In these two Emilio Fernández films, both female characters, from different ethnicities and social classes, are good women who are loyal to their men and to the ideals of the Mexican Revolution.

Monsiváis asserts that whether in comedy, urban melodrama, or the rural ranchero genre, Mexican films in general never presented any social or political criticism. Whether in laughter or in sentimentality, the state's hold on Mexicans persisted. Monsiváis was a lifelong critic of Mexico's hegemonic political party, the Partido Revolucionario Institucional (PRI). No director seriously intended to reject machismo, the morality of feudalism, class inequality, or internal racism. There was never any serious subversion of the state or the Catholic Church. Films of the Golden Age were produced by an industry still in thrall to the false modernity of the Mexican Revolution. *Allá en el rancho grande* (1936), a much-loved film of the musical ranchero genre, is also for Monsiváis a film against agrarian reform, one that presented a utopian view of landholders and praised the submission of the rural poor. Only with Luis Buñuel did Mexican films attain a level of artistry. With *Los olvidados* (1950), Buñuel exposed Mexico City's urban underclass left behind by the progress of the Mexican Revolution. For Monsiváis, Buñuel brought to Mexican cinema a much-lacking dimension, a liberating moral intensity.

The themes raised by Monsiváis continue in Juanita Heredia's "From Golden Age Mexican Cinema to Transnational Border Feminism: The Community of Spectators in *Loving Pedro Infante*" (2008). Heredia assesses the critical reception of Golden Age cinema north of the border as expressed in the novel *Loving Pedro Infante* (2001), by New Mexican Denise Chávez. In the novel, young women who are fans of Pedro Infante films begin to find fault with the films and the machista attitudes of the male figures, which have raised their awareness of women's roles within Mexican culture. For Monsiváis in "No te me muevas," Infante was "el Macho desbordado de simpatía que cautivaba y deslumbraba con canciones y actitudes. Hoy es una suerte de museo dinámico del México que desaparece." Once the perfect film archetype of the generous macho, who captivated audiences with his songs and attitude, he is now a museum piece, relic of a Mexico that is disappearing. Had Monsiváis read John Rechy's "El Paso del Norte," Sandra Cisneros's "Mexican Movies," and Chávez's *Loving Pedro Infante*, along with Heredia's essay, he would have discovered similar critical views of Mexican Golden Age films north of the border.

It is important to note that gay cultural critic Monsiváis in 1983 termed Infante a "macho," a consideration that comes to the fore in the characters' discussions in *Loving Pedro Infante*. Also noteworthy is the book's title. The masses loved Pedro Infante, the person and the actor. And loving means, within the Chávez novel, loving by both males and females: Infante is the object of gay desire. In the novel, Ubaldo Miranda is a gay Chicano member of the Infante fan club. According to Heredia, "Chávez incorporates the character of Ubaldo to complicate her transnational border feminism and also to contest the institutionalization of traditional masculinity." Denise Chávez is a New Mexican from the border area formed by Las Cruces, New Mexico, El Paso, Texas, and Ciudad Juárez, Chihuahua. She, like Rechy, writes about el Teatro Colón in El Paso. She is a border writer who decided to write a critical Mexican studies novel of a Mexican film great. She is, therefore, quite different from upriver New Mexicans who cling to the illusion of whiteness by tracing their roots to the Spanish conquerors and settlers of northern New Mexico. In the novel, Chávez includes two males of Spanish descent who hail from northern New Mexico and are condescending to border Mexican la Wirma (Irma), a member of the Infante fan club. That a community of women and a gay man, of various ages, has come together in the novel indicates not just the importance of Mexican films but also the importance of Mexican values that need to be reexamined critically in the novel's fictional border town, Cabritoville. Female characters Tere and la Wirma become Mexican social critics, like the author Chávez and like John Rechy, Sandra Cisneros, and Monsiváis.

Loving Pedro Infante is not just a critique of Mexican films; as Heredia argues, it also advances a progressive Chicana vision of the future. Chávez constructs a transnational border feminism by addressing romanticism and realism in relation to gender roles. From the darkness of the theater to the discussions of Infante films by the Pedro Infante Club de Admiradores Norteamericanos #256, a new form of community or *familia* emerges. Club members gradually distance themselves from the traditional values of the Golden Age films by not depending on men and by taking control of their own lives. This, then, is one of the great values of the discussion by women and men of the fan club in *Loving Pedro Infante*. Moreover, viewing Infante classics *Arriba las mujeres* (1943), *Angelitos negros* (1948), *Las mujeres de mi general* (1951), and *A toda máquina* (1951), we can return to Monsiváis's critique of Golden Age films: they accept and even celebrate machismo, a racist and classist society, and submission on the part of the rural poor. The characters in *Loving Pedro Infante* begin to understand the nature of gender, race, and class in the films in relation to Mexican culture and within the United States. Tere, the intellectual character, offers, "You can learn so much about Mejicano culture, class structure, the relationships between men and women, women and women, men and men, as well as intergenerational patterns of collaterality in Pedro's movies" (Chávez 2001, 51). Chávez, Heredia notes, "suggests that if people of color, especially women, are ever going to receive their due respect in society, they must become speaking and acting subjects of their destinies."

Women at the Border: Confronting Gender Violence, Reclaiming Public Spaces

Chávez and Heredia write on women's liberation on the north side of the border. South of the border, Mexican culture is patriarchal, with the lesser value of women a constant theme. Gender violence against women—verbal, sexual, and physical—occurs on a daily basis in Mexico, and most of the time no guilty party is punished. This is one of the tragic results of Mexico's misogynist culture and the negligence of its criminal justice system. It is the pressure of public opinion, families, activists, and journalists that has sometimes forced the authorities to take action. In the essays by Julia Monárrez Fragoso and Sandra Ruiz, we travel from Ciudad Juárez, Chihuahua, to la Colonia Roma in Mexico City, glimpsing the kind of violence against women that occurs throughout Mexico.

Julia Monárrez Fragoso produced one of the earliest studies by a woman of the femicides (a theoretical term first coined in 1976) in Ciudad Juárez. Her *Aztlán* essay, "Serial Sexual Femicide in Ciudad Juárez, 1993–2001" (2003), is adapted from "Feminicidio sexual serial en Ciudad Juárez: 1993–2001," first published in *Debate Feminista* in 2002. In her essay, Monárrez Fragoso analyzes the murders of young women on the border that have been attributed to serial sexual killers. Other works that have heightened international awareness of the Juárez murders include the activist journalism of Victor Ronquillo, whose investigations began in 1993 and were published as *Las muertas de Juárez* in 1999; the 2000 documentary rock music video "Invalid Litter Dept." by El Paso rock band At The Drive-In, from their album *Relationship of Command* (2000); Chicana filmmaker Lourdes Portillo's 2002 PBS documentary *Señorita Extraviada*; and Alicia Gaspar de Alba's murder mystery *Desert Blood: The Juárez Murders* (2005).

Seeking to explain the killings of predominantly young women on the border, Monárrez Fragoso turns to the theory of femicide, defined as motive-driven misogynist killing of women by men. Such crimes reflect the imbalance of power between the sexes in political, social, and economic spheres and the degree of tolerance that society shows toward these violent acts. They are also related to structural changes in society, and the author argues that Ciudad Juárez has undergone serious social stress as the international maquila industry has expanded on the border. Under the 1965 binational Border Industrialization Program, light industry largely replaced agricultural work and transformed the employment landscape, especially on the south side of the border. The maquilas, or assembly plants, in the Mexican border cities of Tijuana, Mexicali, Ciudad Juárez, and Nuevo Laredo were part of the Mexican government's efforts to integrate the border into Mexico's national economy. They rely on inexpensive labor, usually provided by young women. Historically, women on both sides of the border have been hired to work in the clothing industry, in the Farah company in El Paso, Texas, for example. In his *Generaciones y semblanzas* (1977), Texas writer Rolando Hinojosa writes of the Mexican women workers of the Suggs Clothing Manufacturing Company in fictional Klail City in the Rio Grande Valley. But the main overall impact of the maquila program has been to stimulate an increase in migration from the interior of Mexico to the border. Presenting her data in a series of graphs, Monárrez Fragoso concludes that young, poor, working-class women, many of them employed in the maquilas, are the primary targets of serial sexual killings in Ciudad Juárez.

In her "Reclaiming Mexico City: Feminist Spatial Justice in Patricia Valladares's *Tan frío como el infierno*" (2016), Sandra Ruiz turns to the issue of gender violence and measures that can be taken to improve the public safety of women. Patricia Valladares's *Tan frío como el infierno* (2014), its title taken from Dante's *Inferno*, is a feminist noir novel that spotlights Mexican women's continuous organizing to reclaim the right to their own city and nation. For over twenty-five years, Valladares has been a professor at the UNAM Iztacala campus in Estado de México and a clinical psychologist working with survivors of domestic violence. Long before the publication of her debut 2014 novel, she was an activist against gender violence. In 1988 Valladares created a research center, el Programa Interdisciplinario para la Atención de la Violencia (PIAV), where she has been able fund studies on gender violence. She has also worked with the Centro de Atención Múltiple and Centro al Maltrato Intrafamiliar y Sexual, both centers dealing with domestic violence. In 2002 she coauthored *Manuales de prevención de la violencia de género* (Manuals for Prevention of Gender Violence), now integrated into government manuals that can be found on the national website of Mexico's Comisión Nacional de Seguridad under the Secretaría de Gobernación. She has received several awards for her academic and clinical work.

Both Valladares's novel and Ruiz's essay have as their context recent events and discussions in Mexico on the security of public spaces for women. Certainly, femicides on the border are invoked, but Valladares and Ruiz make clear that violence against women also takes place in the center of the country. In Estado de México, where Valladares teaches, nearly one thousand homicides were identified as femicides between 2005 and 2010. Sandra Ruiz lists a series of measures that have been taken to counter gender violence. Viajemos Seguras was initiated in 2008 by the Instituto de las Mujeres de la Ciudad de México (Mexico City Women's Institute) to implement safe riding policies for women. More recently, in 2015, the government established the "alerta de género," or gender alert, under provisions of the Ley General de Acceso de las Mujeres a una Vida

Libre de Violencia (Law on Women's Access to a Life Free from Violence). Digital platforms such as Facebook and Twitter have also been used to organize against gender violence. Sunday, April 24, 2016, was declared Primavera Violeta (Violet Spring). Using the hashtags #24A and #Primavera Violeta, street protests against gender violence were mobilized on that day in twenty-seven Mexican cities, adding up to the largest feminist public protest in the nation's history. #NoTeCalles (Do Not Remain Silent) and #MiPrimerAcoso (My First Incident of Harassment) are social platforms with videos of women coming forward to expose sexual abuse and violence.

Through her fictional private investigator, Milena Ruiz, Valladares foregrounds discussions on the origin of gender violence, its extension throughout Mexico and internationally, and women's roles in combatting violence. Milena, with a master's in criminology, once worked for the government in units concerned with sexual crimes and homicides. Tired of the misogyny of government officers and of criticism for working on "cosas de mujeres" (women's matters), she decided to go it alone. Milena is a mestiza feminist with short punk-like purple-tinted hair; she is mentally and physically strong, having trained in martial arts in Israel and Palestine. She has immersed herself in a digital world (she uses an iPhone and reads newspapers on her iPad) in hipster Colonia Roma. Her training includes cyberactivism, and she knows how to hack into computers to gather information on cases. Milena's actions in solving the kidnapping of Eloísa Castellanos, a well-known war photojournalist, allow twenty-first-century women activists to support one another and articulate an educated women's perspective on violence. This 2014 novel advances strategies for grassroots organizing on violence, given the ineffectiveness of the government.

Through Milena, professor and psychologist Valladares uses statistics to refute the notion that violence against women in Mexico is mainly a problem of serial sexual killers. In her search for a culprit, Milena presents the short list of known killers in Mexico. According to Valladares, in an interview with Sandra Ruiz, the list in the novel is real and was compiled in 2006 by Valladares and co-researchers for Mexico's Cámara de Diputados (Chamber of Deputies). The list served to demystify the existence of serial killers and establish that violence against women is a structural problem, embedded within a misogynist society and exacerbated by the corruption in Mexican government institutions. As a practicing clinical psychologist with a private practice, Valladares knows well the extent of sexual violence and abuse within families, most often committed by fathers, husbands, boyfriends, and other male relatives.

Tan frío como el infierno is in the tradition of hardboiled detective fiction with the intelligent, independent, strong, hard-drinking, and risk-taking Milena; however, feminist Valladares also transforms the genre for service on behalf of women. It is a decolonial narrative that centers on twenty-first-century women who refuse to be victims and who assert their autonomy with regard to the city and its streets. Milena trains at a gym, practices kick-boxing, and runs through her Roma neighborhood past familiar signposts, through Chapultepec Park and along Reforma Avenue to the Monumento a la Independencia. The monument, which rises about 150 feet, is topped by a statue that is commonly known as el Ángel. It is the *genius loci* for Mexico City, a symbol of the city and of women's autonomy. The Angel is actually the statue of winged Nike, the Greek goddess of war, victory, and sport, poised for flight. It is a place for Milena to rest after her nine-mile run and consider the plight of women. She knows that there is no magical list of serial sexual killers in Mexico. Instead the problem lies elsewhere. She considers Eloísa Castellanos's war photographs of Afghan women in Pakistani prison camps and the photographer's conclusion that "el cuerpo de las mujeres es un territorio de guerra" (women's bodies are territories of war), a mantra that Milena will make her own. Given the history of colonialism and imperialism, the situation of women in Mexico is not that different from women's positions in war-torn countries. The war is embedded in Mexican culture and history. In a moment of feminist consciousness, Milena agrees with Eloísa's reasoning that all women are imprisoned: crushed by the burden of daily chores, dominated by evil husbands or authoritarian fathers, enclosed within walls of prejudice, subjugated by myths of love; sold, freely exchanged, tortured, enchained.

> Tienes razón, todas estamos cautivas. Y no solo las presas, las locas o las monjas. Avasalladas. Sometidas a los deberes cotidianos o a un mal marido, a un padre autoritario o a los hijos. Cercadas entre murallas de prejuicios. Subyugadas y rendidas a los mitos amorosos. Vendidas, inter-cambiadas, doblegadas, torturadas, encadenadas. (Valladares 2014, 40–41)

Valladares wrote her noir novel as a decolonial feminist narrative, noting the serious crimes being committed against women historically and in the twenty-first century. By demystifying the serial sexual killer, Valladares lays blame on patriarchy and colonialism. According to Valladares in her interview with Sandra Ruiz, women's bodies are a territory of war anywhere in the world, whether in Estado de México, Oaxaca, Palestine, or Pakistan. However, the novel, Valladares asserts, also has a subtext of women who refuse to be victims. These women struggle, organize, resist; they are activists. Sandra Ruiz ends her essay by emphasizing that Milena resists injustice. Milena's runs through her city are acts of defiance. According to Ruiz, Milena conditions her body and mind in acts of autonomy and agency every day. She reclaims women's rights to the city and exercises solidarity with those in disadvantaged positions.

Mexican Internal Colonialism and Racism: Yaquis, Afro-Mexicans, and Chinese

The indigenous Yaquis of Sonora are well known for their role in the national history of the Mexican Republic. Under the nineteenth-century Porfirian dictatorship, until the Mexican Revolution of 1910, the Yaquis were robbed of their lands and forcibly relocated to work on henequen plantations in Yucatán. This genocidal strategy did not end the Yaqui nation; many fled across the border to Arizona and other parts of the Southwest. Ariel Zatarain Tumbaga's essay, "Arraigamiento: Contesting Hegemonies in Alfredo Véa Jr.'s *La Maravilla*" (2013), traces the cultural, literary, and political presence of the Yaquis in Arizona in the work of Chicana and Chicano writers who identify as Yaqui. Tumbaga discusses the different representations of Yaquis in twentieth-century Mexican literature to explain the continuity of these portrayals in Chicana/o literature. Spanish and Mexican colonial epistemologies depict the Yaquis as senselessly violent warriors—what Tumbaga calls "the Yaqui warrior myth." According to the author, this colonizing perspective disconnected the Yaquis from their traditional origin stories that tell of their history of colonial invasion. Tumbaga resurrects Yaqui ancestral stories of resistance against the Spanish and Mexican colonizers of their homeland.

Tumbaga utilizes Alfredo Véa Jr.'s 1993 novel *La Maravilla* to explore a contestatory response to the colonizing discourses that informed racist depictions of Yaquis. He does so through the recovery of Yaqui knowledge, accomplished by reappropriating historical, ethnographic, and literary texts. In the Mexican Yaqui context, traditional knowledge (rites, dance, origin stories) is linked to what Tumbaga calls *arraigamiento*, a cultural rootedness that re-creates the link between Yaqui culture, territory, and resistance. Véa, an Arizona novelist and attorney who identifies as Yaqui, has, from the north side of the border, studied the Yaquis as historically a transborder culture spanning Sonora and Arizona. On the Arizona side, Véa presents Yaqui culture in opposition to US mainstream culture. The Yaquis, like other indigenous groups, have suffered under US rule. Tumbaga also highlights Véa's challenge to the use of Aztec motifs to represent Chicano nationalism, most notably the myth of Aztlán.

Along with Véa, Tumbaga mentions the Chicana/o Yaqui writers Miguel Méndez, Luis Valdez, and Alma Luz Villanueva. Their work in novels, poetry, and plays, he suggests, spring from a distinctly Yaqui epistemic register. They assert a Chicana/o identity and contest nonindigenous perspectives on Yaqui history and culture by adapting ethnographic texts and oral histories and depicting religious practices in their work. However, Véa stands out in confronting the legacy of colonialism on both sides of the border, which cast the Yaquis as "internal Others" who had to be incorporated and assimilated into Mexico's national culture. Véa's novel is written from a historically and culturally informed point of view that challenges hegemony. Tumbaga gives detailed evidence of how Véa has incorporated anthropological and literary discourse from both sides of the border, in English and Spanish, to depict a Yaqui-Chicano resistance against assimilation. In the end, the argument of resistance and continuity is used to question the iconography of a mythical Aztlán in favor of a living Yaqui borderless culture in Arizona and Sonora. Both Véa's and Tumbaga's visions of Yaqui indigeneity intervene in the continuing racism of discourses related to indigenous cultures in Mexico.

Contemporary white supremacy and racism in Mexican culture, specifically against Mexican *afrodescendientes*, or Afro-descendants, came to the fore in 2005 when the Mexican postal service issued a commemorative stamp depicting the popular comic book character Memín Pinguín. The black, monkey-faced figure on the stamp is a clearly racist caricature. The ensuing controversy is the subject of Kirstie Dorr's "'Putting a Stamp on Racism': Political Geographies of Race and Nation in the Memín Pinguín Polemic" (2014). Though Afro-descendants have contributed to the racial diversity and cultural richness of Mexico, they were not seen as included in the cultural and biological formation of the Mexican nation until 1992, when Africa was officially acknowledged as the third racial root, *la tercera raíz*, of Mexico. Father Glyn Jemmott, a Trinidadian Catholic priest serving in El Ciruelo, Oaxaca, began México Negro, AC, a Mexican nonprofit working on behalf of Afro-Mexicans' civil rights. In 1997 Father Jemmott began the Encuentros de Pueblos Negros (Meetings of Black Peoples), which have continued and will be held in Múzquiz, Coahuila, in November 2018. In 2015, the Mexican government census estimated the Afro-Mexican population at 1,381,000. Most Afro-descendants live on the

Costa Chica in the states of Oaxaca and Guerrero, as well as in Veracruz, which had the largest Afro-descendant population during the Viceroyalty of New Spain. The Afro-descendants of Múzquiz are descendants of Afro-Indian settlers, also known as Black Seminoles, who escaped US slavery and racism and migrated to Coahuila. Trafficking in black bodies and images has been a constant in the African diasporas of the Americas.

As Dorr notes, the stamp's character was created by Mexican artist Yolanda Vargas Dulché after her trip to Cuba in the early 1940s. So taken was Vargas Dulché with Afro-Cuban children that she imagined the child-like black character Memín Pinguín. She saw this as a novel idea, since it was widely believed that there were no *negritos*, no black people, in Mexico. This common misconception marked the classic Mexican films of the 1940s in which black rumba dancers and musicians were popular: they were not Mexican, they were Cuban. Even the much-loved film *Angelitos negros* (1948), whose theme was racism, cast Afro-Cuban actress Rita Montaner as the mother, Nana Mercé. The racially mixed child of the film was in black-face, which was also part of the Memín Pinguín controversy, as the character recalled the racist blackface minstrel shows put on by white performers.

The stamp ignited an international controversy that played out in the US and Mexican media. Mexican officials, President Vicente Fox among others, and intellectuals, including historian Enrique Krauze and writer Elena Poniatowska, as well as US African American leaders such as Al Sharpton and Jesse Jackson, all weighed in on the debate. Each group defended or condemned the stamp. For most Mexicans, the stamp was not racist, but showed a fondness for the black race. For African Americans, on the other hand, it was demeaning and insulting. The stamp in question is part of the history of colonialism, of the Mexican Republic's oppression and marginalization of Afro-Mexicans. Mexico is a racist state that for years defined its national essence as a racial mixture of Spanish and indigenous, to the exclusion of Afro-descendants. Differences of opinion between the United States and Mexico regarding the racism of the stamp also reflect the history of colonialism. Mexicans saw US involvement in the debate around a Mexican national (albeit racist) symbol as continuing the history of US cultural and economic imperialism in North America. How often does Mexico interfere in US cultural and political affairs?

Afro-Mexicans, meanwhile, remained largely on the sidelines of the cultural battles around Memín Pinguín. Unlike the United States, with its highly developed research on African American culture, Mexico has not had prominent Afro-Mexican intellectuals, Afro-Mexican studies centers, or university courses taught by Afro-Mexican professors, though Mexican anthropologists have contributed to the history of Afro-Mexico. Only recently, in 2013, did Mexico's Instituto Nacional de Antropología e Historia initiate the Programa Nacional de Investigación Afrodescendientes y Diversidad Cultural. Nonetheless, Dorr does note that an association representing 50,000 Afro-Mexicans living on the southern Pacific coast of Mexico submitted a letter to President Fox on July 5, 2005, demanding a recall of the stamp. In fact that group was México Negro, founded by Father Jemmott, who also signed the letter to Fox requesting an apology for the stereotypical and racist postage stamp. Memín carries heavy loads, is mentally unstable and uneducable, has doubtful family origins, and does not speak correctly (Universia México 2005). In this way, the stamp celebrates, typifies, and officially recognizes the diminished, distorted, and comical view of the black community that prevails in Mexico.

The controversy over the stamp was short-lived, writes Dorr, but the issue of race and colonization continues. In 2008, US retail chain Walmart started selling classic Memín comic books in California, Texas, and Florida, aiming at the Mexican immigrant market. The tragic history of Mexicans and African Americans is that both were subjected to white supremacy, including through lynchings and other types of racist violence, and white supremacy continues in both the United States and Mexico. But attitudes toward black Mexicans may be changing, albeit slowly. On August 10, 2018, the first full-length feature film on Afro-Mexicans was released in Mexico City at Cineteca Nacional de México. *La negrada* is directed by Jorge Pérez Solano with a cast (finally!) of Afro-descendants from the Costa Chica of Oaxaca who are not professional actors. The film is an effort to give voice and visibility to the Afro-Mexican community.

With Jayson Gonzales Sae-Saue's "Model or Menace? Racial Discourses and the Role of Chinese and Mexican Labor at the US-Mexican Border, 1900–1940" (2015), we return to the themes taken up earlier in the volume by Ricardo Romo. Chinese have labored in California and in Mexico since the nineteenth century, when they were known for their work in agriculture and the construction of railroads. The presence of Chinese immigrants in the United States led to the country's first state-supported discriminatory immigration practices, the Chinese Exclusion Act of 1882, which prohibited the entry of all Chinese laborers. In the following decades, the country's business elite, while discriminating against Asians, took a generally favorable view of Mexican laborers as Spanish and white. This eventually led to large numbers of immigrants from Mexico—the grandparents and parents of later generations of Mexican Americans, Chicanas and Chicanos. Sae-Saue examines the history of Chinese laborers on both sides of the border between California and Baja California in the early twentieth century. In Mexicali, Baja California, the history of the Chinese population includes not only laborers but also flourishing Chinese businesses that were influential in their communities.

Capitalist agribusiness came early in the twentieth century to the border area of California–Baja California. Twin border cities Calexico and Mexicali were made possible by a water diversion project that transformed an area of the northern Sonora desert into one of most productive agricultural regions in the Americas. Irrigation canals from the Colorado River gave both valleys, the Imperial Valley north of the border and the Mexicali Valley south of it, the water necessary for year-round agriculture. Sae-Saue writes that the Mexicali Valley was controlled from Los Angeles by the Colorado River Land Company, the booster for the water diversion project; the company was owned by a syndicate led by Harrison Gray Otis, publisher of the *Los Angeles Times*, and his son-in-law Harry Chandler. The land company offered land tenancy to Chinese immigrants. This was the beginning of large-scale cotton production on both sides of the border, using Mexican labor on the north side and Chinese labor on the south side. Chinese workers in Baja California competed for jobs as field workers and railroad workers. By 1921, Chinese were the largest foreign-born population in Mexico.

In the United States, meanwhile, additional immigration laws were passed to exclude Chinese. The Immigration Act of 1924, which barred Chinese from entering the United States, exempted Mexico and other Western countries from numerical quotas. This led to a flow of Mexican laborers into the Imperial Valley of California. US business leaders and government officials ascribed favorable profiles to Mexican workers, who were identified racially as "free white persons." In contrast, the Chinese were perceived as threats, socially and economically. In 1908 the US Department of Commerce and Labor described Mexicans workers in the stereotypical mold of docile, patient, obedient, somewhat intelligent workers who could provide cheap labor under supervision. However, at times Mexicans were also described as indigenous in origin and thus socially primitive.

The influx of Chinese immigrants into Mexico through Pacific ports (mainly Ensenada) was also driven by the policies of Mexican dictator Porfirio Díaz, who wanted to develop agriculture in the northern borderlands. But the increase in Chinese immigrants and the economic success of the Chinese in Baja California and elsewhere in northern Mexico led to anti-Chinese uprisings, or *movimientos anti-chinos*. This intensified after the Mexican Revolution of 1910 and the establishment of the Mexican ideal of national mestizaje, a mixture of Spanish and indigenous elements. Also important was the perceived lack of work for Mexicans, given that the Mexican Revolution was fought by and on behalf of Mexican laborers. Sae-Saue describes the infamous 1911 *massacre de chinos*, war atrocities by Mexican Revolutionary forces against Chinese residents in Torreón, Coahuila, another area of cotton production. Over 300 Chinese in Torreón were mercilessly murdered and disfigured in the xenophobic massacre. Finally, in the 1930s, the socialist agrarian reforms of Mexican President Lázaro Cárdenas shattered Harry Chandler's control of the Mexicali Valley, which was transformed into collectively controlled *ejidos*. However, Mexicali today still boasts a thriving Chinese community.

In his essay on the parallel yet divergent histories of these two important labor sources on the California–Baja California border, Sae-Saue argues for transnational studies of the Pacific Southwest that include both Chicana/o and Asian American studies. Sae-Saue writes:

> This interracial and transnational dynamic speaks to an important confluence between Chinese and Mexican labor histories. Although this entanglement lasted for nearly four decades of the early twentieth century, it remains underexamined in both Chicana/o and Asian American studies. In order to understand the era that saw one of the largest flows of Mexicans into the United States, we must examine how US industry and government managed Chinese social identities at and beyond the US-Mexico border. To this end, this essay bridges emergent critical interests in cross-racial and transnational formations in Chicana/o and Asian American studies.

The Future of Border Writing

In closing, we return briefly to Carolyn González's "Fronteriza Writing in *Nadie me verá llorar:* Cristina Rivera Garza and Other Border Crossers of Yesterday and Today." Like others in this Mexican studies collection, Rivera Garza has criss-crossed the border in her career. Born in Mexico, she has been a student in Houston, a writer and journalist in Mexico City, and a professor at the University of California, San Diego, most recently returning to the University of Houston as professor of Hispanic studies and director of the Creative Writing Center. In this position she is also heading up a new program, a PhD in Spanish with a concentration in creative writing (Concentración en Escritura Creativa en Español-PhD/ECE). This is a noble and original experiment in the Spanish language by a Mexican writer who has been increasingly tied to the northern side of the Mexico-US border since doctoral work at the University of Houston. Rivera Garza explores her changing identity in a recent essay, "Escritura creativa" (2016), in *Literal* magazine, which presents Latin American voices from Canada, the United States, and Mexico. I include Rivera Garza's original statement with a translation by Carolyn González:

> Tampoco nos dejamos engañar: para muchos de los bilingües contemporáneos que vivimos en los Estados Unidos, el español y el inglés van de la mano en nuestras vidas privadas y públicas. No hay razón alguna para que ese cruce constante, volátil, generativo, no forme parte también de la producción escritural de esos autores que, sin duda, serán los autores del siglo XXI.

> Let us not delude ourselves: for many of the contemporary bilingual people who live in the United States, Spanish and English go hand in hand in our private and public lives. There is no reason why this constant, volatile, generative crossing cannot also be a part of the written production of those authors that, without a doubt, will be the authors of the twenty-first century.

In a country that wants to seal linguistic, cultural, and political borders, Rivera Garza sees the advantages of embracing Spanish as well as English in our public and private lives. As a multicultural writer and professor, through her writing and her work at the university, she will have a hand in shaping the twenty-first-century writers who are transcending borders. Rivera Garza will enable a new generation of bilingual border writers in a United States where in the near future a significant population will speak both Spanish and English.

Noche otomí: Cover Art by José Villalobos

I am very pleased to have acclaimed Oaxacan artist José Villalobos provide his oil on canvas, *Noche otomí* (2013), as the cover for our collection of essays. Villalobos was born in 1950 in Ciudad Ixtepec, Oaxaca, on the Isthmus of Tehuantepec, and maintains his working studio in Zaachila, Oaxaca. He studied architecture at UNAM, after which he dedicated himself full-time to art. In Villalobos's art, abstract shapes and forms are given life by Oaxaca's landscapes and indigenous colors. The evolution from architecture to art began with his personal studies of the migrations of the

Mixtecs from Veracruz to Oaxaca, to the terrain known as the Mixteca Alta, the northern mountain range that separates the State of Oaxaca from the State of Puebla. The trope of the artist's walk lends titles to his exhibitions: *Las tierras altas* (1998), *Territorios* (2010), *Horizontes imaginarios* (2017), and his most recent, *Mirar la tierra* (2017).

As Villalobos began his artistic career, he traveled through the Mixteca Alta, viewing rock, wood, and rivers with a perceptive intensity. These close encounters with the natural material world give life to his play of form, light, and color. He notices minute details of form and movement, to be later revived in his studio in spectacular large works on canvas. As he showed me in his studio, a very small piece of rock is interesting for the movement it contains. Sunlight through the trees creates a surprising chiaroscuro, producing constant movement throughout the day. Change, movement, and migration are important to Villalobos, as they are to the essays in this volume. But he is a visual abstract artist; the memory of a color he once saw is reworked as he mixes traditional colors to attain in his imagination that precise previous moment. One could think of Villalobos using indigenous colors, but like the indigenous peoples of Mexico, who took their colors from the material world, he too rediscovers color on the canvas that is deceptively static but also displays a world of change and movement.

Works Cited

Chávez, Denise. 2001. *Loving Pedro Infante*. New York: Farrar, Straus & Giroux.

Cisneros, Sandra. 1991a. "Mexican Movies." In Cisneros 1991b, 12–13.

———. 1991b. *Woman Hollering Creek and Other Stories*. New York: Random House.

Gamio, Manuel. 1916. *Forjando patria*. Mexico City: Librería de Porrúa Hermanos.

———. 1930. *Mexican Immigration to the United States*. Chicago: University of Chicago Press.

———. 1931. *The Mexican Immigrant, His Life-Story*. Autobiographic documents collected by Manuel Gamio. Chicago: University of Chicago Press.

Gaspar de Alba, Alicia. 2005. *Desert Blood: The Juárez Murders*. Houston: Arte Público.

Goldman, Shifra M. 1981. *Contemporary Mexican Painting in a Time of Change*. Austin: University of Texas Press.

———. 2015. *Tradition and Transformation: Chicana/o Art from the 1970s through the 1990s*. Edited and introduced by Charlene Villaseñor Black. Los Angeles: UCLA Chicano Studies Research Center Press.

Goldman, Shifra M., and Tomás Ybarra-Frausto, eds. 1985. *Arte Chicano: A Comprehensive Annotated Bibliography of Chicano Art, 1965–1981*. Berkeley: Chicano Studies Library Publications Unit, University of California.

Gómez-Peña, Guillermo. 1996. *The New World Border: Prophecies, Poems, and Loqueras for the End of the Century*. San Francisco: City Lights.

———. 2006. *Bitácora del cruce: textos poéticos para accionar, ritos fronterizos, videografitis, y otras rolas y roles*. Mexico City: Fondo de Cultura Económica.

———. 2018. "Guillermo Gómez-Peña: Mexican (IN)documentado." *Reversos*, February 18. http://reversos.mx/guillermo-gomez-pena-mexican-indocumentado/.

Hinojosa, Rolando. 1977. *Generaciones y semblanzas*. Berkeley, CA: Justa.

Maldita Vecindad. 1993. *Gira pata de perro 93*. Mexico City: Maldita Vecindad.

Mines, Richard, Sandra Nichols, and David Runsten. 2010. *California's Indigenous Farmworkers: Final Report of the Indigenous Farmworker Study (IFS) to the California Endowment*. http://www.indigenousfarmworkers.org/index.shtml.

Monárrez Fragoso, Julia. 2002. "Feminicidio sexual serial en Ciudad Juárez: 1993–2001." *Debate Feminista* 13, no. 25: 279–308.

Monsiváis, Carlos. 1995. "Dreaming of Utopia." *NACLA Report on the Americas* 29, no. 3: 39–41.

Paredes, Américo. 1942. "The Mexico-Texan Corrido." *Southwest Review* 27, no. 4: 470–81.

———. 1976. *A Texas-Mexican Cancionero: Folksongs of the Lower Border*. Urbana: University of Illinois Press.

———. 1990. *George Washington Gómez*. Houston: Arte Público.

———. 2010. *"With His Pistol in His Hand": A Border Ballad and Its Hero*. Austin: University of Texas Press. First published 1958.

Rechy, John. 1958. "El Paso del Norte." *Evergreen Review* 2, no. 6: 127–40.

———. 1963. *City of Night*. New York: Grove.

Rivera, Tomás. 1982. "Chicano Literature: The Establishment of a Community." In *A Decade of Chicano Literature (1970–1979): Critical Essays and Bibliography*, edited by Luis Leal, Fernando de Necochea, Francisco Lomelí, and Roberto G. Trujillo, 9–17. Santa Barbara, CA: Editorial La Causa.

Rivera Garza, Cristina. 1995. "The Masters of the Streets: Bodies, Power and Modernity in Mexico, 1867–1930." PhD diss., University of Houston.

———. 1999. *Nadie me verá llorar*. Mexico City: Tusquets.

———. 2016. "Escritura creativa." *Literal: Latin American Voices*, July 4. http://literalmagazine.com/escritura-creativa/.

———. 2017. "The Cristina Rivera Garza Interview." By Scott Esposito. *Quarterly Conversation*, December 11.

Ronquillo, Victor. 1999. *Las muertas de Juárez*. Mexico City: Planeta.

Universia México. 2005. "Ofende a México Negro sello de Memín." July 7.

Valladares, Patricia. 2014. *Tan frío como el infierno*. Mexico City: Planeta.

Véa, Alfredo Jr. 1993. *La maravilla*. New York: Plume.

Wall Street Journal. 2018. "In 'Little L.A.,' U.S. Deportees Adjust to Life in Mexico." February 2. https://www.wsj.com/video/in-little-la-us-deportees-adjust-to-life-in-mexico/77540AB5-7EC5-421E-8E79-C5CF52FF7F50.html

Historical Notes on Chicano Oppression
The Dialectics of Racial and Class Domination in North América

Tomás Almaguer

This preliminary discussion of Chicano oppression attempts to schemati-
cally outline the development of racial and class domination in the North
American continent. The central concern is to historically trace the salient
aspects of this dual oppression as it has affected the Chicano and his historical forefathers. A second and equally important concern is to provide a
larger theme or perspective to the Chicano experience. All too often the
history of the Chicano has not been seen as an integral part of the larger
forces that have been at work in the shaping of the modern world. This
discussion views aspects of our history in a larger context, as part of that
historical reality that has spelled the similar oppression of colonized people
throughout the world. Lastly, since I do not pretend this discussion to be
either exhaustive or definitive, I hope to at least touch upon a number of
areas that are in need of more specific research.

In examining the history of Chicano oppression it is essential to examine both capitalist and colonial structures. It is through the institutional
apparatus of these structures that both racial and class domination has
unfolded. My discussion of capitalism and its class dynamics is set within
the context of several theoretical and historical studies by Marxist writers.[1] While there remains some question about the wholesale application
of a traditional Marxian analysis to the Chicano situation, Marxism must
remain today the most useful and insightful *method* that can be employed in
examining the dynamics of oppression in a capitalist society. A materialist
interpretation of society and the application of the dialectical method,

the central components of historical materialism, remain unquestionably important tools in analyzing the objective situation of oppressed people both inside the United States and throughout the Third World.

In addition to this methodological and theoretical approach, I will also rely on another body of literature that has attempted to grasp the dynamics of racial oppression and the distinctiveness of the colonial situation.[2] In examining the experience of the Indio, the Mestizo, the Mexicano, and the Chicano as a colonial experience—each with a common bond and common root—it will be useful to view colonization as a historical process. Colonization, be it "classic colonialism," "neocolonialism," or "internal colonialism," should be viewed as a historical process that has been "as significant an organizing principle of social and economic power in the modern world as the rise and spread of capitalism itself" (Blauner 1974).

Since its inception at the turn of the sixteenth century, European colonization has spelled the domination of people of color throughout the world. Everywhere the Western European or North American has ventured he has sought colonial super-profits through either new markets, new investment outlets, new territories and raw materials, or an exploitable supply of cheap labor. As a net result of this colonial expansion and conquest, the economic and social life of the colonized was to be totally disrupted and reorganized to fill the needs of the intruding European metropolis.

As these areas of the non-Western world fell into European hands, similar historical processes were at play. (1) In all cases the economic factor was primary—colonization was initiated by the need of the European or North American metropolis to economically expand and to bring within its web of domination the land, resources, and market potential of the dependent colony. (2) This metropolitan economic and territorial expansion was to also spell the total disorganization of traditional life in the colony and the transformation of the indigenous masses into colonized workforces. In nearly every instance those colonized were non-European people of color. (3) To rationalize and justify what was to become a racially defined class system of exploitation, there gradually developed an elaborate system of racial and, in some cases, religious ideology. Race not only provided the central source of ideological justification of the colonial situation, but it also became the central factor upon which classes in colonial society were to outwardly develop. (4) Accompanying and playing an integral role in the maintenance of this racial domination, European cultural chauvinism was to ravage indigenous cultures, values, traditions, and the distinctiveness of the non-Western way of life. (5) Finally, to consolidate control of the colonial situation, political and social institutions were erected to maintain the relationships of power and privilege that lay at the heart of the colonial situation.

The rise of capitalism and the expansion of colonial systems of domination have largely formed the histories of oppressed people throughout the world. While one system of exploitation dialectically led to and reinforced the development of the other, advanced monopoly capitalism is now the dominant mode of production that continues to systematically perpetuate the colonial domination of the non-European world.[3]

Outwardly, however, each system has manifested and maintained its own particular form of economic exploitation and social oppression. While both systems are based on the exploitation of a laboring class of people, be they slaves, peons, or wage laborers, the colonial situation was to differ from the capital/labor relationship in the maintenance of its exploitation on racial terms. For this discussion, it is the development of both racial and class oppression in the colonial situation of North América that provides us with one of the unifying threads that historically ties the Chicano experience with the Spanish colonization of México in the sixteenth century. The colonial and class relations that initially oppressed the *indigena* in México and those that oppress the Chicano today have shifted from a semifeudal precapitalist colonial base to the monopoly capitalist base found in the United States. These two colonial situations were part of the same historical process that characterized European and North American hegemony in the Américas.

Historical Roots of Chicano Oppression

The conquest of the non-Western world by the nation-states of Western Europe far exceeded that of any previous world empire. The scope and magnitude of this European web of domination over the land, labor, and resources of the peoples they encountered resulted in a world empire unparalleled in history.

> While the ancient world had known empires of great extent—such as the Roman, Chinese, Mongol, and Inca—with the growth of the postfeudal European states, empires of unprecedented proportions came to be formed. By the sixteenth century, the revolutionary development of gunpowder weapons, maneuverable sailing vessels, and navigational devices gave to the European states a marked technological superiority over most of the world's societies. With this new equipment the European states were able to overcome hitherto undreamed-of distances for the purposes of

state expansion. Within a few hundred years, Africa, North and South America, India, southeast Asia, part of China, central and northeastern Asia, Indonesia, Melanesia, Polynesia, and Australia were to become, with varying degrees of permanency, subject to European governments. (Wagley and Harris 1971, 13)

The advent of this European world hegemony was set in motion with the early colonial ventures of the Iberian axis. Symbolically, through a series of papal bulls in 1493, the "new world" was divided between Spain and Portugal: the west going to Spain and the east to Portugal. This was adjusted a year later when the Treaty of Tordesillas was enacted to permit Portuguese ownership of Brazil (E. Williams 1966, 3).[4] By the close of the fifteenth century the Américas had been "discovered," and the turn of the century was to signal a further escalation in the early European scramble for colonial possessions throughout the world.

It was the Iberians, particularly the Spanish, who became the initial European promoters of conquest and procurers of an early mercantile empire. Heir to an advanced Islamic technology, particularly that pertaining to oceanic navigation, and having mobilized all the moral energies of her people through the nearly eight centuries of struggle for emancipation from Saracen domination, Spain was by 1521 already establishing control over a large area of what is now central México. It was this early establishment of colonial domination over the indigenous people of "New Spain" that set the roots of European colonial relations within the North American context. Spurred on by the search for precious metals and by an intoxicating "salvationistic-mercantile" zeal, the Spanish intrusion and colonization of México not only helped mark the dawning of Europe's colonial domination of the Américas but more specifically spelled the beginning of what has been over 450 years of European domination of the Indio-Mestizo in North América.[5]

It was with the establishment of the early colonial relations set by an incipiently capitalist but still largely "semifeudal" Spain and Portugal that we see the beginning of a class system of domination that was to manifest itself principally in racial terms.[6] It is at this historical juncture that racial oppression and racism began to fully develop, as contact and subjugation of colonized people intensified. In this sense, then, racism and racial oppression are not forms of domination that have been with us since time immemorial, nor are they merely the by-products of a later capitalist development.[7] While there are traces of ethnocentrism and racial-cultural chauvinism in earlier epochs, it was not until the rise of European colonization that we see the wholesale racial domination of a group of people and the promulgation and elaboration of racial ideology.[8] In earlier empires, for example, racial factors were not nearly as important in making distinctions between people as was culture (in the Greek empire), estates (in the Alexandrian period), or citizenship (in the Roman Empire). While these distinguishing factors were not the fundamental source of oppression in these times, it is clear that racial antagonism and racial exploitation that we know today were largely unknown in these earlier empires. It was in fact possible for ethnically diverse people to integrate and assimilate into the higher strata of these societies (Cox 1964).

The early European colonization began a period in history in which race was largely used by one people (Europeans) to distinguish themselves from and oppress all others (non-Europeans). It was with this European contact and conquest of the "new world" that racial oppression and racism became an intrinsic part of the social order of modern society. Since racial differences were the most obvious distinguishing factor between the European colonizer and the colonized, they soon became the basis upon which economic exploitation and the social organization of colonial society took shape.

To justify this racially based class exploitation, the colonizing Europeans developed an elaborate system of racial—and in the case of Spain, also religious—ideology which was used to dehumanize the colonized and characterize them as an "inferior" and "savage" breed of people. Relegated to the lower levels of "humanity," the colonized had as their sole purpose in life to serve the private interests of the colonizer and his economic system. In Spain, for example, a debate continued throughout the sixteenth century on the question of whether or not the Indio in "New Spain" had a soul or was simply a beast or half-beast. In the colony, "The Indians were represented as lazy, filthy pagans, of bestial morals, no better than dogs, and fit only for slavery, in which state alone there might be some hope of instructing and converting them to Christianity" (MacNutt 1909, 83, quoted in Cox 1964, 334).

One of the basic features of the conquest and incorporation of México into the Spanish empire was the organization of colonial life on a system of racial hierarchy. The various forms of social, political, and, above all, economic relations in the colony were within a framework of European racial domination. According to Magnus Mörner (1967), "This colonial reality was characterized . . . by the dichotomy between conquerors and conquered, masters and servants or slaves. . . . People were classified in accordance with the color of their skin, with the white masters occupying the highest stratum. Theoretically, each group that could be racially defined would constitute a social stratum of its own" (54).

Similarly, Stanley Stein and Barbara Stein (1970) characterized colonial life in México, as well as in all of Latin América, as follows:

> The social heritage of colonial Latin America was not merely a rigid structure of an elite of wealth, income, and power at the apex and, at the bottom of a broad pyramid, a mass of poverty-stricken, marginal, powerless, and subordinate people. Such societies have flourished everywhere. The tragedy of the colonial heritage was a social structure further stratified by color and physiognomy—by what anthropologists call phenotype: an elite of Whites or near-Whites and a mass of people of color—Indians and Negroes, mestizos and mulattoes, and the gamut of White, Indian, and Negro intermixture called the castas. As North America has come to perceive, a society may perpetuate social inequalities far more effectively when the maldistribution of income is buttressed by phenotype. (60)

While there were actually a great number of identifiable racially mixed groupings of people that were to develop in the colony, the five major castas that came to characterize the social positions in colonial México can be outlined as follows (ranked in descending order):[9]

1. Peninsular Spanish
2. Criollos
3. Mestizos
4. Mulattoes, Zamboes, & Free Negroes
5. Indios

While the organization of the colonial economy was to produce well-defined social classes, the division in its social classes came to closely correspond to the racial differentiations that miscegenation was to produce in the colony. The size and relative position of each of these major groups was, of course, subject to some change as the colonial period progressed. Like the social organization of the society, the organization and division of its labor system came to be largely defined in terms of race. "The peninsulars then appear as the bureaucrats and merchants par excellence, the criollos as the large landowners, the mestizos as the artisans, shopkeepers, and tenants, the mulattoes as urban manual workers, and finally, the Indians as community peasants and manpower for different kinds of heavy, unskilled labor" (Mörner 1967, 61). Thus, racial differences not only were used in making social distinctions and in delineating certain social groups, but they were also used in the very organization of the economic structure of colonial society. The racial realities of the colonial situation in México had a material basis in the organization of the social relations of production in the colony. Manfred Kossok (1973) reminds us of the importance of these social relations of production in this "semifeudal" colony:

> Colonial economic and power relationships gave rise to a decided but not absolute congruence of ethnic and social differentiation. The social and political subordination of the conquered (or those imported as slaves) first expressed itself in form and outward appearance as ethnic diversity, including social-cultural and language differences. But it was the socioeconomic and political factor that gave real significance to ethnic differentiation, and not vice versa. Because it coincided with the prevailing pattern of exploitation, ethnic separation (segregation) contributed to the stability of the colonial power system. (22)

As the colonial period progressed, different forms of forced labor systems were contrived to better secure the economic privileges of the Spanish ruling class. In examining the economic and social structures that were erected in colonial México, one economist notes the changes that these forms of Indian-based labor took:

> The early period was marked by the enslavement of the Indian, which lasted from 1521 to 1533. This was followed by the *encomienda*—a system under which the Indian was obliged to provide labor or tribute to the *encomendero*. After a short time the labor *encomienda* was eliminated (although in colonial Chile it persisted for a long time and was impossible to extirpate). Between 1545 and 1548, there was a great epidemic which reduced the available labor supply at a time when the discovery of silver increased the demand for laborers. As a result of the increased need for labor and the diminished supply, the *encomienda* system was increasingly altered until it became what was called *el catequil*. (In Peru it was called *la mita*; the system was never established in Chile because it did not suit Chilean needs.) It lasted until about 1603, but after 1580 it was no longer the dominant method of utilization of labor. The predominance of the latifundium or hacienda, which increased after 1580, began as the result of another epidemic which further reduced the available labor supply, and consequently production in the mines as well . . . the modes of production which were employed and then replaced in Mexico . . . and the resulting transformation in the class structure responded to changes in the colonies' ability to serve metropolitan needs. (Frank 1972, 26–27)

For the Indio-Mestizo, the legacy of this colonial hegemony left its mark not only in central México but also in the northern regions of the

Spanish empire. In Nuevo México, for example, there developed a "semifeudal" set of social relations that were in one case to be distinguished by the dichotomy between the *patrón* and the *peón*. A few wealthy families came to wield tight control over the internal affairs of the colonized area. Primarily of Spanish criollo origin, the patrones were joined in their control of Nuevo México by Spanish aristocrats, officials, and the influential clergy of the Church. Subservient to this Hispanic elite were the peones—composed primarily of Mestizos and Indios. The economic relations of this village life were organized in such a way as to benefit the light-skinned European and deprive the Indio and Mestizo (Meier and Rivera 1972, 51).

Similarly, colonial California was characterized by a racial-class society based on the missions and later on the ranchos. Though not totally parallel to the social structures that developed in other territories, class stratification in California was again marked by the predominance of a small Spanish criollo elite—the so-called *gente de razón*. Like the patrones in Nuevo México, they controlled the lives of the Mestizos and Indios in the colonial territory. After the secularization of the missions, this ruling elite was estimated to number no more than forty-six landowners, and it retained a tight-fisted control over the affairs of California (Meier and Rivera 1972, 43–44).[10]

Overall, the Spanish control of México extended itself for a period of about 300 years, from the conquest in the early sixteenth century to the Mexican Independence in 1821. While she had become an early colonial power, Spain was by the time of the Mexican conquest well on its way to becoming economically subservient to England and to a lesser extent to Holland, France, and Northern Italy.[11] Despite Spanish creation and control of its overseas empire in the sixteenth century, by 1700 Spain had become a secondary power in Europe. Commenting on this fall of Spain as a world power, Andre Gunder Frank (1972) has written:

> Since the destruction of the Spanish Armada by the English in 1588 and the economic colonization and de-industrialization of Portugal by means of a series of commercial treaties . . . Great Britain had virtually eliminated the Iberian countries from participation in world capitalist development. This process was exemplified by the exchange of English textiles—an industrial product—for Portuguese wines—an agricultural product. . . . England and France until the defeat of Napoleon by the British had gradually achieved complete control of Spanish and Portuguese trade and colonies. (46)

While Spain still had a foothold in Central and North América, she increasingly shared her claim to the Américas with rising European rivals.

By 1700 the Russians were encroaching on Spanish territory in California, the greater Mississippi-Louisiana territory was in the hands of the French, and the English on the east coast were steadily pushing their way westward and south into Spanish Florida. With the demise of Spain as a colonial power, the forces of wealth and power in Europe moved north to England, France, and Holland. Accompanying this transfer in colonial supremacy was a shift in the main spheres of colonial activity from Brazil, Perú, Central América, and México to the Caribbean islands and later to Asia, Africa, and the Pacific.[12] Having secured the major advantages of the economic dependency of Spain and its colonial holdings, and having undergone a radical transformation in its own internal economic and political structure, England emerged as the major European power. With English emergence came the full maturation of commercial capitalism.

In contrast to earlier empires, the rise and expansion of commercial capitalism in Western Europe was tied to conquered colonial territories becoming an integral factor in the development of the metropolitan economy.[13] The postfeudal European economy was to become based on the development of commodity production (as opposed to a feudal or tributary economy). It became necessary to totally destroy the traditional social and economic organization in the colonies and to transform the colonized into a workforce that could be used to effectively exploit the natural resources needed by the metropolis. The economic development of the capitalist metropolis was directly based on the continued exploitation and under-development of the colony. The colony became merely an appendage of the mother country.

Spain contributed to the development of commercial capitalism through its expansion and conquest of the "new world," and its creation of the conditions and global framework in which the expansion of modern capitalism could take place. By providing a crucial source of capital accumulation for England, Holland, and France, Spain played an important role in Europe's rupture with feudalism and in the development of a capitalist mode of production. By being the first to harness and use the technological developments of the day, Spanish colonial domination was a transition from the early world empires of tribute and plunder to the empires maturing as commercial capitalist centers of power.

The economic, social, and political structures erected by Spain and Portugal in the Américas represented a special form of semifeudal colonialism. Kossok (1973) has characterized the context in which Iberian colonization took place:

Spain and Portugal "exported" to America a feudalism in decline, which on the European side was increasingly distorted by the growth of capitalism. However, developed capitalism was concentrated in Northwestern Europe (Netherlands and England) and, as a result, there took place a refeudalization of the original regions of early capitalism. Spain and Portugal were thus forced out into the periphery of capitalism at the decisive moment when the "true" history of primary accumulation was beginning with the burgeoning of merchant capital. The functional interdependence of capitalism and colonialism in the period of primary accumulation was distorted in a very special way in the case of Spain and Portugal. They served only as channels through which colonial profits flowed into rising capitalist countries. The part of the colonial riches that remained on the Iberian peninsula was, as a rule, not realized capitalistically but became feudal hoarding, and thus did not contribute to the disintegration of the feudal order. It was significant for Latin America that some rudimentary elements of capitalism were preserved in the metropolis, whereas no viable roots of autonomous capitalist development appeared in the colonies until the end of the eighteenth century. (14–15)

Incapable of developing an indigenous industrial infrastructure, Spain was to then fall outside of the center of capitalist development and play a transitional and intermediary role in its development. Spain's failure to develop into a mature commercial capitalist nation was largely due to its destruction of its crafts industry with the expulsion of the Muslims, its suppression of its nascent merchant strata with the expulsion of the Jews, and most importantly, its falling under the yoke of the already developing commercial capitalist centers.[14]

The "primitive accumulation" of capital to which Spain contributed conditioned the gradual development of capitalism and the world market economy.[15] Without the massive plunder of the Américas by Spain, and the eventual redirection of this wealth to England, Holland, and France, large-scale capitalist manufacture and industry would not have been brought about so successfully. This massive accumulation of capital was therefore a crucial prerequisite for the development of nascent capitalism and for the perpetuation of the colonial exploitation of the non-European world. Robert Allen (1972) notes the extent to which this accumulation of capital was to play in the development of Western Europe:

Internationally the emergence of capitalism resulted in the concentration of capital in a small part of the world—western Europe, and later North America. The early colonial plunder of the non-European world provided a global base for the accumulation of capital in Europe. These accumulations made industrial and cultural development possible. The development of the steam engine, heavy industry, shipbuilding, manufacturing and many modern financial institutions were all financed directly or indirectly by the slave trade and other forms of colonial exploitation. Indeed, it is no exaggeration to suggest that the Industrial Revolution, which enabled Europe and North America to leap far ahead of the rest of the world in material welfare, would have been delayed by several centuries if not for the capital yielded by colonialism. (9)

In a similar vein, Marx and Engels (1972), in the *Communist Manifesto*, noted the extent to which this early colonization influenced the development of the bourgeois epoch in Western Europe:

> The discovery of America, the rounding of the Cape, opened up fresh ground for the rising bourgeoisie. The East Indian and Chinese markets, the colonization of America, trade with the colonies, the increase in the means of exchange and in commodities generally, gave to commerce, to navigation, to industry, an impulse never before known, and thereby, to the revolutionary element in the tottering feudal society, a rapid development.
>
> The feudal system of industry, under which industrial production was monopolized by closed guilds, now no longer sufficed for the growing wants of the new markets. The manufacturing system took its place. The guildmasters were pushed to one side by the manufacturing middle class; divisions of labour between the different corporate guilds vanished in the face of division of labour in each single workshop.
>
> Meantime the markets kept ever growing, the demand ever rising. Even manufacture no longer sufficed. Thereupon, steam and machinery revolutionized industrial production. The place of manufacture was taken by the giant, Modern Industry, the place of the industrial middle class, by industrial millionaires, the leaders of whole industrial armies, the modern bourgeoisie. (31–32)

The development of the capitalist mode of production made possible the continuation and re-entrenchment of the basic form of social oppression and economic exploitation that Marx and Engels outlined. In asserting that the history of all hitherto existing society was the history of class struggle and class exploitation, it should also be made clear that world history was shaped by an equally powerful form of exploitation and oppression. Starting with the early colonization by the Iberians and intensifying with developing capitalist colonization, racial exploitation and racial oppression became leading forces in the shaping of the modern world. Since capitalist and colonial domination extended to worldwide proportions, it can be argued that both racial and class oppression have now become the two principal forms of social domination in the present epoch.

It is through the historical dialectic of colonial and capitalist development that racial and class oppression have become integrally bound. The
establishment of colonial systems of domination (be they either "classic,"
"neo-," or "internal") have dialectically fed into the development of capitalism from inception to its present monopoly stage, and capitalism has in turn
reinforced and perpetuated the colonial situation in all parts of the world.

The Development of US Capitalism and México

The rise of England as the imperial power of the eighteenth and nineteenth
centuries, and the birth of one of its former colonies, the United States,
as an imperial power in its own right, began the second major phase of
European colonization that was to affect the Indio-Mestizo in Northern
México. Initially a white settler colony of England, the United States began
its own imperialist thrust very early in the advanced stages of the European
colonial partition of world. Having secured its own national independence
in its revolutionary war with England, the United States was no sooner
an independent nation than it too began undertaking highly expansionist foreign policies and began developing its own colonial empire. An
heir to England's basic social and economic structure, the United States
wasted little time in establishing its place in the unfolding scenario of late
nineteenth-century European imperialism.[16]

The United States participation in this escalation of the colonial partition of the world occurred initially through continental expansion, then
through "overseas" colonial expansionism. After both "Northern capitalists
and Southern planters had joined hands in 1776 to win independence
from England," the United States very methodically moved its national
boundaries to the Pacific.[17] Having won its independence in 1821, México
was by midcentury wracked with internal political and economic turmoil,
and was unprepared to deal with the imperialistic foray that the United
States was to unleash in the usurpation of Texas in the 1830s and in the
Mexican-US War that was to follow.

To make sense of these United States aggressions against México,
they must be understood in the context of the rise and expansion of US
capitalism. The root of the US empire dates to the years from 1843 to
1857—the period that marked the "takeoff" stage of the US economy.[18]
The rapid maturation of the US industrial economy and the development of the United States as one of the two greatest forces in the world
occurred during this period. This period preceded the Mexican-US War

and concluded in the era just before the War for Southern Independence. It saw the dramatic shift of US political power from the Southern planters to the Northern and Eastern industrialists and financiers (LaFeber 1963, 6).[19] As industrial capital gradually gained predominance over the slave economy, it set the stage for the maturation of monopoly capitalism in the United States. The war with México and the usurpation of one-half of México's territory was to become a crucial component of the development.

It is clear that the development and expansion of industrial capital in the United States went hand in hand with territorial expansion and the conquest of new territories.[20] It was the acquisition of these lands that provided the crucial raw materials needed for industrialization and the maturation of a capitalist mode of production. Just as "the need of a constantly expanding market for its products chases the bourgeoisie over the whole face of the globe," as Marx and Engels (1972) wrote, so too at an earlier time did the development of capitalist production in the United States turn bourgeois interest inward (to the North American continent) in their unending search for sources of raw materials and future markets. The new lands of the West provided not only the resources needed for the expanding economy, but also the strategic locations (such as the ports on the California coast) from which to launch further searches for precious raw materials and new markets for US-made products.[21]

There were at least six stages in US westward expansion. Alonso Aguilar (1968) has outlined this expansion and absorption of new territories as follows:

> 1. In 1803, Louisiana was purchased from France, which lost Haiti at the same time; the expansionist designs of France in America thereby suffered a severe blow. The United States paid the ridiculous sum of $15 million for the vast territory of almost one million square miles.

> 2. The second step was taken in 1819. After repeated border incidents and long drawn out negotiations, Spain ceded her possessions east of the Mississippi and renounced her right to Oregon. As a result, the United States acquired the territory of Florida (38,700 square miles) for $5 million.

> 3. In 1846, it was Oregon's turn. The joint occupation by England and the United States ended under pressure from the latter and an agreement was reached whereby the United States added another 286,500 square miles to its already enormous territory, an area which today comprises the states of Oregon, Washington, Idaho, and parts of Wyoming and Montana.

4. In the same year war began against Mexico, a frankly unjust war which completely exposed the aggressiveness of United States policy and the violent character of its territorial expansion.

5. As a result of the aggression against Mexico, the United States first acquired Texas and shortly after, in 1848, another slice of territory. Altogether, the United States incorporated some 945,000 square miles—a vast area which today includes the states of Texas, Arizona, New Mexico, California, Nevada, Utah, and part of Wyoming. After appropriating these lands, to which it had no right whatsoever, the United States paid $26.8 million for them—as though this made the annexation legal.

6. Finally, in 1853, through the Gadsden Purchase, the United States acquired another small strip of border land of some 45,000 square miles in the Mesilla Valley for the absurd sum of $10 million.

To sum up, in the course of half a century, the United States increased its territory tenfold—not including Alaska. This is to say, nearly 2.3 million square miles were acquired by various means for the "reasonable" price of a little over $50 million. (32–34)

Having undertaken its continental expansion in the half century between 1803 and 1853, the United States was by the mid-1850s already moving to extend its "rising empire" into areas of the Pacific, notably Hawaii, as well as into Asia, Africa, and even further into Latin América. Instead of only seeking farmlands, grazing lands, and minerals, the United States also sought foreign markets for its increasing production of agricultural staples and industrial goods. To secure the economic base upon which to build its overseas empire, the United States "annexed a continental empire by undermining, economically and ideologically, British, French, Spanish, Mexican, and Indian control and then taking final possession with money, bullets, or both" (LaFeber 1963, 1–2).

As Walter LaFeber (1963) has convincingly shown, the United States built its new empire at the same time that its industrial economy was maturing. Between 1850 and 1900 this industrial complex evolved into one of the most dynamic of the expanding capitalist economies. United States foreign investment began spiraling, and "by the 1870's the staggering rise in exports changed the historically unfavorable balance of American trade to a favorable balance which would last at least through the first half of the twentieth century. . . . By 1893 American trade exceeded that of every country in the world except England" (18). The United States asserted itself as a principal participant in the world capitalist market and was becoming the undisputed leader of the world imperialist system.

This tremendous boom in US economic development was directly based in no small part on US exploitation of Mexican land, labor, and natural resources. The United States continued its economic stranglehold on México after 1848. México provided for the United States what one US newspaper termed an "almost virgin outlet for extension of the market of our overproducing civilization" (quoted in LaFeber 1963, 51).

After the absorption of one-half of México's territory, and the enlargement of the United States by one-fifth, Secretary of State James G. Blaine "neatly summarized one of the themes of the new empire, by officially informing Mexico that the United States desired no more land; it only wanted to use its labor and 'large accumulation of capital, for which its own vast resources fail to give full scope,' to exploit Mexico's 'scarcely developed resources.' Americans invested heavily in Mexican railroads, mining operations, and petroleum development. United States trade with Mexico had been $7,000,000 in 1860. It doubled to $15,000,000 in 1880, doubled again to $36,000,000 in 1890, and nearly doubled again to $63,000,000 in 1900" (LaFeber 1963, 51–52).[22]

The annexation and exploitation of the natural resources of the Southwest and the imperialist exploitation of México after the war were part and parcel of the rise of the US empire and its development of monopoly capitalism. As David Horowitz (1969) has succinctly put it,

> the basis of capitalist expansion is . . . the fact that capitalism develops a commodity market which "transcends the limits of the state" and that it extends capitalist relations with their monopolistic and dominative tendencies into the inter-state sphere. At the most basic level, therefore, *imperialism is capitalism which has burst the boundaries of the nation-state.* (37–38, emphasis in original)

The unfolding of this historical imperative of capitalist development was, in short, at the very root of the United States' dealings with México. The continental and extra-continental expansionism of the United States was not simply some aberration in foreign policy or some self-righteous means of "spreading democracy," but rather was a crucial requisite for the continued development and expansion of US capitalism.

The Internal Colonization of the Chicano

Although they were the victims of a classic colonial conquest, the colonization of the Indio-Mestizos in the Southwest did not take on the form of a "classic" colonial system, i.e., one in which the exploitive relationship is generally carried out between the metropolis and a spatially separated colony. Rather, as they became a numerical minority on their own land and had their lands "annexed" to the United States metropolis, the colonial situation in which the Mexicanos found themselves can be more correctly defined as an "internal colonial" one.[23] While the relationship of the Mexicano to the Anglo-American was indeed one of subordination and exploitation, the colonization of the Mexicano unfolded *within* the political boundaries of the colonizing metropolis nation.

Although US colonization of the Mexicano was carried out "internally," it was a case of colonial domination nonetheless. What happened to the Mexicano in the Southwestern United States was a reflection of the very same forces that were at work in the establishment of overseas or external colonial relations. The "annexation" of the land and natural resources of Northern México and the proletarianization of an exploitable Mexican labor force were to contribute four major elements to the development and stabilization of US capitalism.

One, the use of Chicano labor greatly contributed to the concentration and accumulation of capital needed to transform this region from a relatively underdeveloped area into an agricultural oasis. The extraction of surplus value from Chicano labor contributed to the development of this agricultural base, which in turn played a major role in the growth of advanced capitalism.

Two, the use of Chicano labor and technical skills provided for the development of the mining and railroad industries. Both of these sectors were crucial components of the "mineral-transport-communications" infrastructural base needed for future industrialization and modernization of the area (Blauner 1972, 62). By helping lay the foundation—or infrastructure—upon which the development of this region was based, Chicano labor played a central role in the development and spread of capitalism.

Three, as a largely mobile and seasonal workforce, Chicanos functioned as a "reserve army of labor." In times of intense labor needs they have been actively recruited in the Southwest to work in agriculture, mining, the livestock industry, or the railroads (circa 1900–30). Displaced by the Mexican Revolution at the turn of the century and by the intense US foreign investment that hastened the breakup of traditional social and economic life in México, thousands of Mexicanos became a highly exploitable workforce upon which the US capitalists were able to draw (Flores n.d.). The United States has been able to deport, repatriate, or simply disemploy this surplus labor with relative ease.[24] Capitalist interests have been able to overcome intensely racist feelings on the part of white labor in periods when Chicano labor is needed and have been all too happy to use anti-Mexican racial animosity when their labor is no longer expediently needed.

Four, the Chicano worker and his community have functioned as what Robert Allen has called a "shock absorber"—that is, any social or economic crisis that this society produces is generally felt most strongly and "absorbed" by Third World people within the United States.[25] As part of the Third World community, the Chicano is an important part of that sector of society that feels and carries the major brunt of the internal contradictions produced within society. The class contradictions that Marx insightfully described as being endemic to the capitalist mode of production have largely been muffled or smoothed over and have manifested themselves as racial contradictions. It is especially during times of crisis that "white-skin privilege" blunts any power that a developing "class consciousness" or "class struggle" could meaningfully exert. The social oppression and class contradictions of monopoly capitalism have found continuing expression in racial terms and fall on the backs of colonized people of color.[26]

There is a dialectical relationship at work in the development of monopoly capitalism in the United States and the development of internal colonialism in the Southwest. One force feeds and reinforces the development of the other. Ronald Bailey and Guillermo Flores (1973) have summarized it in this way:

> The colonial expansionism by which the U.S. absorbed vast territories paved the way for the incorporation of its non-white colonial labor force. This contributed in turn to the accelerated process of capital accumulation necessary for the development of modern capitalism . . . not only did internal colonialism and monopoly capitalism develop concurrently, but . . . both processes are intimately interrelated and feed each other. At the same time that the utilization of non-whites as a controlled, colonized labor force contributed to the development of the U.S. as a major metropolis of the international capitalist system, the attendant class system in the U.S. provided a means of reinforcing a racially and culturally defined social hierarchy. (150)

With the development of the dialectic between the rise of capitalism and the maintenance of systems of colonial domination, there is also a dialectical relationship between the forces of class and race. Similarly, as in the colonial-capital relationship, the forces of class and racial oppression interpenetrate and reinforce each other. They have become dual forms of social oppression, both equally a primary form of social oppression and a central contradiction of monopoly capitalism in the United States.

The Legacy of Class and Racial Oppression

Chicano oppression in the United States has not simply been the outgrowth of a "culture conflict" between the Anglo-American colonizer and the Chicano, nor the result of a virulent form of "manifest destiny" or "white man's burden." Unlike what some historians would have us believe, the economic exploitation and the many forms of social and political oppression that the colonized faced were not merely the result of conflicting styles of life or a vicious racist ideology.[27] Rather, these forms of oppression have a concrete basis in the working relationship between the two peoples. The conflicts that manifested themselves were grounded in the material conditions of life. *Both the class and racial oppression of the Chicano, and of other colonized people of color, have stemmed from the organization of the economic structure of US capitalism and from the labor relationships that arise from that particular mode of production.*

The foundation of Chicano oppression is the organization of the social relations of production. These are predicated on the need to secure profits at the expense of an exploited working class as defined by their relationship to the means of production and on the propensity to further intensify this basic exploitive relationship with respect to non-European racial minorities. Commenting on the role that race and colonized racial minorities have played in the organization of the economic structure of the United States, Robert Blauner (1974) has observed:

> *What has not been understood is the fact that racial realities have a material basis.* They are built into the economic structure as well as the culture of all colonial societies, including those capitalist nations which developed out of conquest and imported African slaves to meet labor needs. . . . From the very beginning race has been central to the social relations of production in America. The right to own property, the right not to become property, and the distribution of labor were all essentially matters of color. Southern slavery was a system of production based on race. But not only in the antebellum South, elsewhere and after, the racial principle continued to organize the structure of the labor force and the distribution of property. The free laborers, the factory proletariat, was largely recruited from white ethnic groups, whereas people of color (Mexicans, Asians, to a lesser degree Indians, and of course, Blacks) were employed

in various unfree labor situations. The ethnic labor principle appears to be a universal element of the colonial situation and this is why race and racism are not simply aspects of cultural "superstructure," but cut through the entire social structure of colonial societies.

Because the United States is "*concentrating people of color in the most unskilled jobs, the least advanced sectors of the economy, and the most industrially backward regions of the nation*," the material basis of racism and racial oppression has become structurally organized into the labor system of this society and more concretely into the very relation that workers (white and non-white) have to the means of production (Blauner 1972, 62, emphasis added). The social relations of production have been largely cast in racial and ethnic terms. Racism and racial oppression are more than just a ploy on the part of the bourgeoisie to "divide the working class," for the real basis of racial contradictions is grounded in the different relationship that white and nonwhite workers have to the means of production in the United States.

The organization of the economic structure of this capitalist society is crucial, for it is through this organization that all social-political structures and relationships essentially take their shape. The basic fabric of this society is built and organized around a capitalist mode of production, i.e., private ownership of the means of production (private property), the transformation of labor into "wage labor" (to be bought like any other commodity), free enterprise, rugged individualism, etc. All the social and institutional arrangements that maintain this society are built upon these basic precepts. The organization of the political system, the organization of systems of justice, the mandates of schooling institutions all reflect the premises upon which this society's economic structure is organized and maintained. As Marx (1969) was to so insightfully observe in this classic statement:

> In the social production of their life, men enter into definite relations that are indispensable and independent to their will, relations of production which correspond to a definite stage of development of their material productive forces. The sum total of these relations of production constitutes the economic structure of society, the real foundation, on which rises a legal and political superstructure and to which correspond definite forms of social consciousness. The mode of production of material life conditions the social, political and intellectual life process in general. It is not the consciousness of men that determines their being, but, on the contrary, their social being that determines their consciousness. (182)

The effects of a society based on such an economic system are pervasive. The daily lives of all people within its domain are greatly determined by the organization of the social structures that emanate from capitalist organization. For the internally colonized, for the Chicano, society's institutional structures have reflected the class and racial biases upon which they are built. While social institutions are purportedly organized to more systematically meet recurring human needs, they have primarily served as the structures through which social privileges are doled out (for whites) and through which colonial relations are mediated for people of color. As John O'Dell (1967, 8) puts it: "In defining the colonial problem it is the role of the institutional mechanisms of colonial domination which are decisive" (quoted in Bailey and Flores 1973, 154).

This institutionalization of dependent colonial relations and policy of racial containment became the principal mechanisms of domination and social control in the internal colonies of the United States. The colonized have become more dependent upon the "colonial-capitalist" institutions of society for their very existence. For example, the job market, social welfare programs (food stamps), financial assistance programs (both community and student), training programs, and dependence on unemployment benefits are but a few of the institutional structures that are now promoting a state of dependency in the internal colony. In addition, some of these institutions have also acted as mechanisms for controlling and containing the colonized in the internal colonies, e.g., law enforcement agencies (local, state, and national), prisons, jails, parole and probation departments, immigration departments, etc. Social control has been not only physical but also psychological in nature—especially as it is perpetrated through schooling institutions and the mass media. Moreover, it has become increasingly apparent that institutions not only maintain the colonial structure by promoting dependence and enforcing containment, but also are pivotal structures through which racism has become systematically woven into every area of this society.

Forms of racial oppression and racial exploitation have changed as the needs of the expanding metropolitan economy have changed. As Guillermo Flores (1973) and Jeffrey Prager (1972–73) have both noted, changes in colonial forms of racial exploitation have also caused shifts in the racial ideology (racism) that buttresses this system. Using Franz Fanon's (1967) classic insight into the nature of racism, we see how racial ideology has coincided and changed with shifts in the economic relations of the colony:

> The evolution of techniques of production, the industrialization . . . of the subjugated countries, the increasingly necessary existence of collaborators, impose a new attitude upon the occupant. The complexity of the means

of production, the evolution of economic relations inevitably involving the evolution of ideologies, unbalance the system. *Vulgar racism in its biological form corresponds to the period of crude exploitation of man's arms and legs. The perfecting of the means of production inevitably brings about the camouflage of the techniques by which man is exploited, hence of the forms of racism.* (35, emphasis added)

When Chicanos as a group toiled primarily with their hands, the type of racial oppression and exploitation they faced was physical in nature and the forms of racism they confronted were based on biological premises. In this period Chicanos labored primarily as captives of agriculture production and as exploited laborers in all facets of mining, the railroads, and the livestock industry.

In the period when the economy caused a large movement of the Chicano population out of the fields and into the cities, racial ideologies shifted from a biological to a cultural basis.[28] As social contact between the colonizer and colonized increased with Chicano entry into the urban setting as factory and urban-based manual laborers, Chicano "biological abnormalities" were increasingly replaced by "cultural" explanations for our "backwardness." The justifications for racist practices and poor living conditions were no longer merely that Chicanos had inherited "low-grade" biological traits; instead, it was said that the culture was "backward" or "traditional" and we were "culturally deprived."[29] The early 1940s saw a dramatic change in the Chicano social and economic relationship with Anglo-capitalist society and also a change in the view of Chicanos as an ethnically distinct people.

In the last thirty years another shift has taken place in Chicanos' social and economic relationship with the dominant society. As one social scientist put it:

During and after the Second World War blacks and browns from the rural backwaters of the South and Mexico came by the millions to northern and western industrial cities. But the era of increasing absorption of unskilled and semiskilled labor into the industrial system, and thereby into the mainstream of class society, was rapidly drawing to a close. Blacks and browns were relegated to employment in the most technologically backward or labor-intensive sectors (menial services, construction labor, corporate agriculture) and to unemployment, the squalor of ghetto life, and welfare handouts. Today, the black, Chicano, and Puerto Rican colonies remain indispensible sources of cheap labor for the technologically backward and labor-intensive sectors. They also provide a servant class to relieve the affluent of the chores of ordinary

living and to enhance their status and feeling of superiority. For the highly
technological corporate and the rapidly expanding public sectors which
require high skills levels, however, the minorities have become superfluous
labor. (Johnson 1972, 286)

The quality of life of the colonized is not improving as greatly as the
dominant ideology of "equal opportunity" would have us believe.[30] There
is, to be sure, a small sector of the Chicano population whose life situation
is improving, but such token "social mobility" is not without its costs. This
small rising Chicano middle class finds itself in the situation in which they
may be—or are now being—used to serve the interests of those who wield
power in the dominant society. It is no accident this "class integration" is
now developing, for it has always been part of colonial policy to develop
a "native elite" who will serve as an intermediary, buffer group between
the colonized masses and the politically and economically powerful. Both
corporate and governmental policies have been consciously at work in
the development of this Chicano middle class.[31] For the majority of the
colonized, the importance of the traditional role as unskilled laborer in the
economy is steadily diminishing.

As institutions become pivotal structures through which colonized
people are dealt with, we also find that the racism that this society breeds
is increasingly central to the institutional apparatus. Racism and racial
oppression are steadily being transformed from overt forms of expression
(biologically and culturally based racial ideology and widespread racial
exploitation of colonial labor) to covert, institutional forms of oppression
(institutional racism and institutionalized dependency and racial containment).[32] This is not to say that the Chicano is no longer being directly
exploited, but rather that the ways in which he is exploited and oppressed
are changing. It would be naive to think that all Chicano laborers will
someday soon be totally outside of the economy itself, but it is becoming
increasingly apparent that major upheavals in the economy are making
certain sectors of the Chicano workforce superfluous.[33] Oppression of
colonized racial groups will not suddenly come to an end but will merely
take on a new form. As long as the dominant society continues to derive
social and economic privileges from the oppression of the internally
colonized there will be forces at work to keep the colonial situation
intact. As long as Chicanos and other oppressed groups are exploited by
a capitalist and colonial structure there will be forces at work to destroy
the exploitive social order.

Conclusion

I hope that at least one point has been made clear: the relationship between racial oppression and class oppression, between internal colonialism and monopoly capitalism, in the United States has been a dialectical one in which each element has interpenetrated and reinforced the development of the other. In a capitalist society like this one, it is no longer realistic to talk about class or race alone as being the "central contradiction" of society. History is much too complex for simple, dogmatic analyses and solutions. Clearly, then, racial and class forms of oppression in North América have become inextricably intertwined, and the racial struggle in US society must become a class struggle as well.

This author believes that much work is needed in the ideological and theoretical battle that Chicanos face today. We must fight this ideological battle against the distortions of our past. This area of struggle is a crucially important front in the liberation of our people. It is essential that we begin developing a clearer understanding of the nature of our oppression if we are to contribute to the transformation of this society. To this end, the present discussion is a small contribution. These efforts at providing an analysis or perspective to the Chicano experience are only a point of departure—the task of joining theory and concrete political action is yet to be done.

Notes

Editor's note: From *Aztlán: Chicano Journal of the Social Sciences and the Arts*, volume 5, numbers 1–2 (Spring and Fall 1974). The original essay was lightly edited for this collection.

I am grateful to the following people, with whom I have had the opportunity to share ideas and receive critical comments on an earlier draft of this paper: Guillermo Flores, Armando Valdéz, Carlos Vásquez, Carlos Muñoz, Mario Barrera, Robert Allen, the editors of *Aztlán*, y mi esposa Clementina Duron Almaguer.

1. A few of the most helpful critiques of American society and in Marxian theory are those by Baran (1957, 1962), Baran and Sweezy (1966), Sweezy (1942), Miliband (1969), Kolko (1962), Dobb (1973), Cornforth (1973), Lenin (1965), Domhoff (1967, 1970), and Edwards, Reich, and Weisskopf (1972). The works by Marx and Engels, however, must remain the most valuable, seminal sources for grasping the dynamics of historical materialism. See especially Marx (1963, 1964, 1967, 1971) and Marx and Engels (1967, 1969).

2. For a list of some of the more useful of these sources, see Works Cited and Works Consulted.

3. According to Maurice Cornforth in *Historical Materialism* (1973), a "mode of production" can be defined as follows: "The way in which people produce and exchange their means of life is known as the mode of production. Every society is based on a mode of production, which is what ultimately determines the character of all activities and institutions . . . The mode of production involves two factors—the forces of production, consisting of instruments of production and people with production experience and skills, and the relations of production. The latter in their totality constitute the economic structure of society" (35–36, 46–47).

4. Characteristic of the mode of production are the way in which the means of production are owned and the social relations between people in society, which arise from their connections in the production process. Capitalism can then be defined as the particular mode of production in which the means of production (i.e., factories, manufacturing equipment, land, etc.) are privately owned by a small class in society, the bourgeoisie. Opposed to this class and exploited by them through their private appropriation of the means of production is a class of workers whose labor has been transformed into wage labor. The private ownership of property has forced workers in this economic system to sell their labor for a wage. Their labor has itself become a commodity to be bought and sold like any other. Capitalism is then a historically evolved economic system based on the private ownership of the means of production and the emergence of wage labor. It is this particular method of class exploitation in the capital-labor relationship that distinguishes capitalism from feudal or slave societies of the past. See Dobb (1973).

5. Also see Cox (1964, 332). The entire chapter entitled "Race Relations—Its Meaning, Beginning, and Progress" (321–52) offers an informative discussion of the origin and development of racial oppression.

6. See Ribeiro (1972, 55–56).

7. There continues to be a large debate (between Marxists and non-Marxists) on whether or not Spain and Portugal were either truly capitalist or feudal. Many strong arguments have been made both ways. For the sake of this discussion, I am more inclined to agree with the view that Spain was neither a truly capitalist nor a traditional feudal society. Rather, Spain and its colonies reflected a "semifeudal" (for lack of a better word) character and structure. This position, however, should not be seen as a hard and fast one, for there is clearly still much historical and theoretical work to be done on this important question. While it is beyond the purview of this article to discuss the theoretical arguments involved, a partial list of scholars active in this debate will be noted. For arguments that Spanish colonization was essentially a feudal or semifeudal undertaking, see Kossok (1973), Laclau (1971), Ribeiro (1972, 49–94), Stein and Stein (1970), and Genovese (1971a, chap. 18; 1971b, chap. 2). In Genovese (1973), see the lively discussion in part 3, "New World Slavery in the History of Capitalism," particularly the articles by Eric J. Hobsbawm, "The Seventeenth Century in the Development of Capitalism"; Lewis Cecil Gray, "Genesis of the Plantation System as an Agency for the Colonial Expansion of Capitalism"; and Jay R. Mandle, "The Plantation Economy: An Essay in Definition." Mandle's article is particularly noteworthy, since

he ties this debate to the larger debate in Marxian theory on the transition from feudalism to capitalism. For discussions by a few of those who have written in line with the argument that Spain and its colonial exploitation was essentially a capitalist undertaking, see Frank (1967, 1969, 1972), Vitale (1968), and Stavenhagen (1968). Also see Wolf (1953).

8. An example of the incorrect assertion that racism and racial oppression are merely by-products of capitalism can be seen in an old article by Paul M. Sweezy, "Capitalism and Race Relations" (1953). In his formulation, Sweezy sees race relations as merely "the product of capitalism" and sees the development of racism as part of the "purpose and strategy of the white ruling class. . . . This is . . . because the white ruling class is the architect and builder of the entire structure of American race relations" (149). For a criticism of this myopic view, see Prager (1972–73); Genovese, "Class and Nationality in Black America," in Genovese (1971a); and particularly the works of Robert Blauner in his *Racial Oppression in America* (1972). Blauner's book is among the best of the new works that try to develop a neoMarxian analysis of race relations in the United States.

9. See Cox (1964, 321–52). Also see Benedict (1940), Gossett (1963), Kovel (1971), Jordan (1968), and Frazier (1957).

10. For a similar ranking of the castas in México, see Mörner (1967, 60) and Van den Berghe (1967).

11. Also see Pitt (1970).

12. For an excellent discussion of the economic forces that were at play in this transference of power in Europe, see Stein and Stein (1970) and also Kossok (1973, 14).

13. For a brief outline of the manner in which European colonization historically unfolded, see the introduction to Nadel and Curtis (1964, 1–26).

14. See James O'Connor's (1971) discussion on the difference between mercantile exploitation and nineteenth-century imperialism.

15. See Ribeiro (1972, 53–58).

16. As Robert Allen (1972) has put it: "Mercantile capitalist accumulations were rapidly acquired in western Europe because (1) the geographical location of many European countries gave them the opportunity to develop maritime and river navigation and trade at an early date, and (2) such trade paradoxically was stimulated by Europe's relative lack of economic development and paucity of highly valued natural resources. Thus, European traders journeyed to the tropics in search of spices, tea, ivory, indigo, etc.; to Asia seeking high quality cloth, ornaments, pottery, etc.; and finally engaged in vicious plundering of gold, silver and precious stones from many parts of the world. In short, Europe's location at the cross-roads of trade routes between more economically developed civilizations and/or countries more highly endowed with natural resources, stimulated an explosive advance of trade and capitalist accumulation by European merchants. At the same time, the requirements of long-range navigation and trade fostered rapid development of scientific knowledge and weapons technology that enabled Europe to begin the colonial plunder and subjugation of other areas" (8).

17. The high stages of European colonial expansion and of the rise of imperialism—"the monopoly stage of capitalism"—are generally agreed to have occurred in the period from the 1880s to 1914. See Lenin (1965).

18. For a critical examination of this early period of American history, see Lemisch (1969) and Lynd (1969). Also see Van Alstyne (1960) and W. A. Williams (1966).

19. See especially LaFeber (1963). Also see North (1961, 1966), Beard and Beard (1927), Rostow (1960), and Van Alstyne (1960).

20. Also see Genovese (1965) and "Marxian Interpretation of the Slave South" in Genovese (1971a) and Bernstein (1969).

21. See Magdoff (1969, 27–66) and Horowitz (1969, 29–50).

22. For a discussion of this "expansionist thesis" and other views regarding causes of the outbreak of the Mexican-American War, see the brief collection of arguments in Ruiz (1963) and Vázquez de Knauth (1972). Also see the impressive discussion by Gómez-Quiñones (1971).

23. For an excellent discussion of the Porfiriato and the Mexican Revolution, see Cockcroft (1972).

24. For discussions of the view that Chicanos are a colonized people, see Almaguer (1971), Barrera, Muñoz, and Ornelas (1972), Flores (1973), and Bailey and Flores (1973).

25. For a brief discussion of this use of Chicano labor, see Almaguer (1971).

26. This discussion is primarily based on a lecture given by Robert Allen, "The Illusions of Progress," at the University of California, Berkeley, November 30, 1973.

27. This relationship that the Chicano community and other Third World communities now maintain to white capital is parallel to the relationship that "external colonies" have to the white metropolises of Western Europe and the United States. Throughout the Western world there has developed a privileged position on the part of white labor vis-à-vis colored labor in Third World colonies. This translation of privilege into racial terms closely parallels what Lenin saw developing at the turn of the century, i.e., an "aristocracy of labor." The development of this privileged stratum of the proletariat was only possible during the imperialist era of capitalism. As the class contradictions of Western Europe and North America passed on to the colonial situations of the Third World, the "class contradictions" of capital increasingly became national and "racial contradictions" as well. See Nicolaus (1970), Hobsbawn (1970), and Allen (1972, 12).

28. A recent example of the facile contention that the origin of the War with México was the result of a "culture conflict" can be seen in the following quote from Feliciano Rivera: "The Mexican War was merely an incident in a malignant conflict of cultures that arose some years before and survived long after the ratification of the Treaty of Guadalupe Hidalgo. Within the framework of this ancient conflict it is possible to discover the roots of the conflict that permeates the relationship between Anglo and Mexican American" (Meier and Rivera 1972, 72). Rivera's blaming Anglo-Chicano conflict on the spirits of the past (or as he puts it, on the "ancient conflict") does little to clarify this historical relationship. His simpleminded mystification of historical reality only serves to obfuscate and draw attention away from the political and economic dimensions that were involved in the conquest.

29. This relationship between ideological superstructure and the economic relations in society has been largely overlooked by many Chicanos who have done critical reviews of social science literature. Beginning with Octavio Romano's "The Anthropology and Sociology of the Mexican-Americans" (1973) and continuing through the recent misguided effort by Ray Padilla, "A Critique of Pittian History" (1973), the relationship between ideology and the material relations in which it has roots has not been critically examined. This oversight has led many to criticize the social sciences for the wrong reasons. Rather than engage in a discussion with Anglo counterparts and criticize their representation of the Chicano as "bad social science" (based on ethnocentrism, faulty methodology etc.), we must understand that this work done by traditional Anglo social science is really "good" sociology or anthropology. That is, the efforts that we have berated for the past five years have not really been bad social science; rather, this type of scholarship has done exactly what it has always been meant to do: distort history, mystify reality, and create a racial ideology that can be used to rationalize and justify the oppression of the Chicanos. Until we leave the defensive position of criticizing the social sciences, and for the wrong reasons no less, we run the risk of only adding to Anglo social science's mystification of reality. Anglo social science has, after all, never been objective (an assumption we sometimes overlook in our "objective" critique of this work), but instead has always been an ideological tool.

30. A careful reading of reviews of social science literature in the periods in which the Chicano was most extensively used as a "field hand" in agriculture, mining, or the railroads reveals that the social sciences primarily drew upon and spun biologically based racial ideology. As Nick Vaca (1970) has noted in his study of the portrayal of the Chicano in the social sciences: "In 1925 the House Immigration Committee published a report by Robert Foerster, then a Princeton economist, in which he made the point that over 90 percent of the Latin American population was racially inferior to Anglo American stock and asked for limitation of Latin American immigration. At about the same time Harry Laughlin, the eugenicist who served as biological expert to the House Committee from 1921 to 1924, testified to the same effect on the qualities of the Mexican immigrant[:] 'Stating that race should be the basic standard for judging immigrants, Laughlin urged that Western Hemisphere immigration be restricted to whites.' Representative John Box of Texas, another strong supporter of restriction of Mexican immigration, reported that Mexican immigrants were '. . . illiterate, unclean, peonized masses who stemmed from a mixture of Mediterranean-blooded Spanish peasants with low-grade Indians who did not fight to extinction but submitted and multiplied as serfs'" (10).

31. For example, recent government statistics (March 1971) show that proportionally there has not been an increase in the income of Chicano families when compared to gains made by Anglo families. In 1970, Chicano families earned only 70 percent of what Anglo families made in the same year. This figure is near the 1960 percentage given by Grebler, Moore, and Guzmán in *The Mexican-American People* (1970). In raw figures, the total average income of Chicano families in 1970 was $7,117, while Anglos made $10,236 in the same year. This figure is, of course, misleading, because all the income of Chicano families was computed in the total Anglo (or by their own definition, "white") figure, thus bringing down the true

mean income of all Anglo families. A better estimate would lie somewhere between $11,500 and $12,000, placing the true ratio of Chicano income to white at about 60 percent, or two-thirds of the average Anglo family income.

32. Using income again as a variable, another indicator shows that in the same year (1970), nearly 50 percent (49.7 percent) of working Chicanos over twenty-five years of age made less than $6,000. Nearly 95 percent (93.5 percent) of working Chicanas over twenty-five years of age made less than $6,000, and 61.9 percent made less than $3,000. Statistics from "Selected Characteristics of Persons and Families of Mexican, Puerto Rican, and other Spanish Origin: March 1971," Population Characteristics, US Department of Commerce, Bureau of the Census, Series P-20, No. 224, October 1971, pp. 5-6, cited in Flores (1973, 204–5).

33. For an excellent discussion of how this process is affecting the Black community, see chapter 5, "Corporate Imperialism vs. Black Liberation," in Allen (1969).

34. An elaboration of this point can be seen in Knowles and Pruitt (1969).

35. There is, on the other hand, a developing line of argument that points out the fact that while a certain sector of minority workers are being displaced, others are increasingly being centered in the most productive areas of the economy. Concentrated in the crafts and operative sector of the workforce, Chicanos are increasingly placed in the crucial areas of the economy that have the most potential for developing into a radical labor movement. For a discussion of this point as it relates particularly to Black workers, see Cherry (1973). For a discussion of this point as it relates to Chicano workers, see Flores (n.d.).

Works Cited

Aguilar, Alonso. 1968. *Pan-Americanism: From Monroe to the Present.* New York: Monthly Review Press.

Allen, Robert. 1969. *Black Awakening in Capitalist America.* Garden City, NY: Doubleday.

———. 1972. "Black Liberation and World Revolution." *Black Scholar* 3, no. 6: 7–23.

Almaguer, Tomás. 1971. "Towards the Study of Chicano Colonialism." *Aztlán: Chicano Journal of the Social Sciences and the Arts* 2, no. 1: 7–21.

Bailey, Ronald, and Guillermo Flores. 1973. "Internal Colonialism and Racial Minorities in the U.S.: An Overview." In *Structures of Dependency*, edited by Frank Bonilla and Robert Girling, 149–60. Stanford, CA: Nairobi Bookstore.

Baran, Paul M. 1957. *The Political Economy of Growth.* New York: Monthly Review.

———. 1962. *The Longer View.* New York: Monthly Review.

Baran, Paul M., and Paul Sweezy. 1966. *Monopoly Capital.* New York: Monthly Review.

Barrera, Mario, Carlos Muñoz, and Charles Ornelas. 1972. "The Barrio as Internal Colony." In *People and Politics in Urban Society,* edited by Harlan Hahn, 465–98. Urban Affairs Annual Reviews, vol. 6. Beverly Hills, CA: Sage.

Beard, Charles A., and Mary R. Beard. 1927. *The Rise of American Civilization.* New York: Macmillan.

Benedict, Ruth. 1940. *Race: Science and Politics.* New York: Viking.

Bernstein, Barton J., ed. 1969. *Towards a New Past.* New York: Random House.

Blauner, Robert. 1972. *Racial Oppression in America.* New York: Harper and Row.

———. 1974. "Marxist Theory, Nationality, and Colonialism." Unpublished manuscript.

Cherry, Robert. 1973. "Class Struggle and the Nature of the Working Class." *Review of Radical Political Economics* 5, no. 2: 47–86.

Cockcroft, James D. 1972. "Social and Economic Structure of the Porfiriato: Mexico, 1877–1911." In *Dependence and Underdevelopment: Latin America's Political Economy,* by James D. Cockcroft, Andre Gunder Frank, and Dale L. Johnson, 47–70. Garden City, NY: Doubleday.

Cornforth, Maurice. 1973. *Historical Materialism.* New York: International.

Cox, Oliver C. 1964. *Caste, Class, and Race.* New York: Modern Reader.

Dobb, Maurice. 1973. *Studies in the Development of Capitalism.* 3rd ed. New York: International.

Domhoff, G. William. 1967. *Who Rules America?* Englewood Cliffs, NJ: PrenticeHall.

———. 1970. *The Higher Circles.* New York: Random House.

Edwards, Richard, Michael Reich, and Thomas Weisskopf, eds. 1972. *The Capitalist System.* Englewood Cliffs, NJ: Prentice-Hall.

Fanon, Franz. 1967. *Toward the African Revolution: Political Essays.* Translated by Haakon Chevalier. New York: Grove. First published in French as *Pour la révolution africaine: Écrits politiques,* 1964.

Flores, Guillermo. 1973. "Race and Culture in the Internal Colony: Keeping the Chicano in His Place." In *Structures of Dependency,* edited by Frank Bonilla and Robert Girling, 189–223. Stanford, CA: Nairobi Bookstore.

———. n.d. "Radical Race Relations Models: A Review and Assessment of the Literature." Unpublished manuscript.

Frank, Andre Gunder. 1967. *Capitalism and Underdevelopment in Latin America.* New York: Monthly Review.

———. 1969. *Latin America: Underdevelopment or Revolution.* New York: Monthly Review.

———. 1972. *Lumpenbourgeoisie: Lumpendevelopment.* New York: Monthly Review.

Frazier, E. Franklin. 1957. *Race and Culture Conflicts in the Modern World.* Boston: Beacon.

Genovese, Eugene. 1965. *The Political Economy of Slavery.* New York: Random House.

———. 1971a. *In Red and Black: Marxian Explorations in Southern and Afro-American History.* New York: Random House.

———. 1971b. *The World the Slaveholders Made: Two Essays in Interpretation.* New York: Random House.

———, ed. 1973. *The Slave Economies,* vol. 1. Albany: John Wiley.

Gómez-Quiñones, Juan. 1971. "Toward a Perspective on Chicano History." *Aztlán: Chicano Journal of the Social Sciences and the Arts* 2, no. 2: 1–49.

Gossett, Thomas F. 1963. *Race: The History of an Idea in America.* New York: Schocken Books.

Grebler, Leo, Joan W. Moore, and Ralph C. Guzmán. 1970. *The Mexican-American People: The Nation's Second Largest Minority.* New York: Free Press.

Hobsbawn, Eric. 1970. "Lenin and the 'Aristocracy of Labor.'" In *Lenin Today*, edited by Paul M. Sweezy and Harry Magdoff, 47–56. New York: Monthly Review.

Horowitz, David. 1969. *Empire and Revolution.* New York: Random House.

Johnson, Dale L. 1972. "On Oppressed Classes." In *Dependence and Underdevelopment: Latin America's Political Economy*, by James D. Cockcroft, Andre Gunder Frank, and Dale L. Johnson, 269–304. Garden City, NY: Doubleday.

Jordan, Winthrop D. 1968. *White Over Black.* Baltimore: Penguin Books.

Knowles, Lewis L., and Kenneth Pruitt. 1969. *Institutional Racism in America.* Englewood Cliffs, NJ: Prentice-Hall.

Kolko, Gabriel. 1962. *Wealth and Power in America.* New York: Praeger.

Kossok, Manfred. 1973. "Common Aspects and Distinctive Features in Colonial Latin America." *Science and Society* 37, no. 1: 1–30.

Kovel, Joel. 1971. *White Racism: A Psychohistory.* New York: Vintage.

Laclau, Ernesto. 1971. "Feudalism and Capitalism in Latin America." *New Left Review*, no. 67 (May–June): 19–38.

LaFeber, Walter. 1963. *The New Empire: An Interpretation of American Expansion 1860–1898.* New York: Cornell University Press.

Lemisch, Jesse. 1969. "The American Revolution Seen from the Bottom Up." In Bernstein 1969, 3–45.

Lenin, V. I. 1965. *Imperialism: The Highest Stage of Capitalism.* Peking: Foreign Languages Press.

Lynd, Staughton. 1969. "Beyond Beard." In Bernstein 1969, 50–54.

MacNutt, Francis Augustus. 1909. *Bartholomew de las Casas.* New York and London.

Magdoff, Harry. 1969. *The Age of Imperialism.* New York: Monthly Review.

Marx, Karl. 1963. *Early Writings.* Edited by T. B. Bottomore. New York: McGraw-Hill.

———. 1964. *PreCapitalist Economic Formations.* Edited by Eric J. Hobsbawm. New York: International.

———. 1967. *Capital*, vols. 1–3. New York: International.

———. 1969. "The Preface to A Contribution to the Critique of Political Economy." In Marx and Engels 1969.

———. 1971. *The Grundrisse.* Edited by David McLellan. New York: Harper and Row.

Marx, Karl, and Friedrich Engels. 1967. *Basic Writings on Politics and Philosophy.* Edited by Lloyd D. Easton and Kurt H. Guddat. New York: Doubleday.

———. 1969. *Selected Works*, vol. 1. New York: International.

———. 1972. *Manifesto of the Communist Party.* Peking: Foreign Language Press.

Meier, Matt S., and Feliciano Rivera. 1972. *The Chicanos: A History of Mexican Americans.* New York: Hill and Wang.

Miliband, Ralph. 1969. *The State in Capitalist Society.* New York: Basic Books.

Mörner, Magnus. 1967. *Race Mixture in the History of Latin America*. Boston: Little, Brown.

Nadel, George H., and Perry Curtis, eds. 1964. *Imperialism and Colonialism*. New York: Macmillan.

Nicolaus, Martin. 1970. "The Theory of the Labor Aristocracy." In *Lenin Today*, edited by Paul M. Sweezy and Harry Magdoff, 77–90. New York: Monthly Review.

North, Douglass C. 1961. *The Economic Growth of the United States, 1790–1860*. Englewood Cliffs, NJ: Prentice-Hall.

———. 1966. *Growth and Welfare in the American Past*. Englewood Cliffs, NJ: Prentice-Hall.

O'Connor, James. 1971. "The Meaning of Economic Imperialism." In *Readings in U.S. Imperialism*, edited by K. T. Fann and Donald C. Hodges, 23–68. Boston: Porter Sargent.

O'Dell, J. H. 1967. "A Special Variety of Colonialism." *Freedomways* 7, no. 1: 7–15.

Padilla, Raymond V. 1973. "A Critique of Pittian History." In *Voices: Readings from "El Grito: A Journal of Contemporary Mexican-American Thought," 1967–1973*, edited by Octavio Ignacio Romano-V., 65–106. Berkeley, CA: Quinto Sol.

Pitt, Leonard. 1970. *The Decline of the Californios*. Berkeley: University of California Press.

Prager, Jeffrey. 1972–73. "White Racial Privilege and Social Change: An Examination of Theories of Racism." *Berkeley Journal of Sociology* 17: 117–50.

Ribeiro, Darcy. 1972. *The Americas and Civilization*. New York: E. P. Dutton.

Romano-V., Octavio Ignacio. 1973. "The Sociology and Anthropology of the Mexican-Americans: The Distortion of Mexican-American History." In *Voices: Readings from "El Grito: A Journal of Contemporary Mexican-American Thought," 1967–1973*, edited by Octavio Ignacio Romano-V., 43–56. Berkeley, CA: Quinto Sol.

Rostow, Walt W. 1960. *The Stages of Economic Growth: A Non-Communist Manifesto*. Cambridge: Cambridge University Press.

Ruiz, Ramon E., ed. 1963. *The Mexican War: Was It Manifest Destiny?* New York: Holt, Rinehart and Winston.

Stavenhagen, Rudolfo. 1968. "Seven Fallacies about Latin America." In *Latin America: Reform or Revolution?*, edited by James Petras and Maurice Zeitlin, 13–31. Greenwich, CT: Fawcett.

Stein, Stanley, and Barbara Stein. 1970. *The Colonial Heritage of Latin America: Essays on Economic Dependence in Perspective*. New York: Oxford University Press.

Sweezy, Paul M. 1942. *The Theory of Capitalist Development*. New York: Monthly Review.

———. 1953. "Capitalism and Race Relations." In *The Present as History*, 139–52. New York: Monthly Review.

Vaca, Nick C. 1970. "The Mexican-American in the Social Sciences, 1912–1970: Part 1: 1912–1935." *El Grito: A Contemporary Journal of Mexican American Thought* 3 (Spring): 3–24.

Van Alstyne, Richard W. 1960. *The Rising American Empire*. Chicago: Quadrangle Books.

Van den Berghe, Pierre L. 1967. *Race and Racism*. New York: John Wiley.

Vázquez de Knauth, Josefina. 1972. *Mexicanos y Norteamericanos ante la guerra de 47*. Mexico City: SepSetentas.

Vitale, Luis. 1968. "Latin America: Feudal or Capitalist?" In *Latin America: Reform or Revolution?*, edited by James Petras and Maurice Zeitlin, 32–43. Greenwich, CT: Fawcett.

Wagley, Charles, and Marvin Harris. 1971. "The Development of the Nation-State and the Formation of Minorities." In *Racial Conflict: Tension and Change in American Society*, edited by Gary T. Marx, 10–13. Boston: Little, Brown.

Williams, Eric. 1966. *Capitalism and Slavery*. New York: Capricorn Books.

Williams, William Appleman. 1966. *The Contours of American History*. Chicago: Quadrangle Books.

Wolf, Eric. 1953. "La formación de la nación: Un ensayo de formulación." *Ciencias Sociales* 4, no. 22: 146–71.

Works Consulted

Books

Acuña, Rodolfo. 1972. *Occupied America*. New York: Canfield.

Avineri, Shlomo. 1969. *Karl Marx on Colonialism and Modernization*. New York: Doubleday.

Césaire, Aimé. 1972. *Discourse on Colonialism*. New York: Monthly Review.

Chevalier, Francis. 1970. *Land and Society in Colonial Mexico*. Berkeley: University of California Press.

Cockcroft, Frank, Andre Gunder Frank, and Dale L. Johnson. 1972. *Dependence and Underdevelopment: Latin America's Political Economy*. Garden City, NY: Doubleday.

Cruse, Harold. 1968. *Rebellion or Revolution?* New York: William Morrow.

Fanon, Franz. 1963. *The Wretched of the Earth*. New York: Grove.

———. 1967. *Black Skin, White Masks*. Translated by Charles Lam Markmann. New York: Grove. First published in French as *Peau noire, masques blancs*, 1952.

Harris, Marvin. 1964. *Patterns of Race in the Americas*. New York: Walker.

McWilliams, Carey. 1964. *Brothers under the Skin*. Toronto: Little, Brown.

———. 1968. *North from Mexico*. New York: Greenwood.

———. 1971. *Factories in the Fields*. Santa Barbara, CA: Peregrine.

Memmi, Albert. 1965. *The Colonizer and the Colonized*. Boston: Beacon.

Rex, John. 1960. *Race Relations in Sociological Theory*. New York: Schocken Books.

Sierra, Justo. 1969. *The Political Evolution of the Mexican People*. Austin: University of Texas Press.

Spicer, Edward S. 1962. *Cycles of Conquest: The Impact of Spain, Mexico, and the U.S. on the Indians of the Southwest, 1533–1960*. Tucson: University of Arizona Press.

Tannenbaum, Frank. 1960. *Ten Keys to Latin America*. New York: Random House.

Woddis, Jack. 1967. *Introduction to Neo-Colonialism*. London: Lawrence and Wishart.

Articles

Balandier, Georges. 1966. "The Colonial Situation: A Theoretical Approach." In *Social Change: The Colonial Situation*, edited by Immanuel Wallerstein, 34–62. New York: John Wiley.

Gómez-Quiñones, Juan. 1972. "The First Steps: Chicano Labor Conflict and Organizing 1900–1920." *Aztlán: Chicano Journal of the Social Sciences and the Arts* 3, no. 1: 13–49.

González Casanova, Pablo. 1969. "Internal Colonialism and National Development." In *Latin American Radicalism*, edited by Irving Horowitz, Josué de Castro, and John Gerassi. New York: Random House.

Rocco, Raymond A. 1970. "The Chicano in the Social Sciences: Traditional Concepts, Myths and Images." *Aztlán: Chicano Journal of the Social Sciences and the Arts* 1, no. 2: 75–97.

Valdéz, Armando. n.d. "Communications Underdevelopment: A Synopsis." Unpublished manuscript.

Vásquez, Carlos. 1973. "Internal Colonialism: A Selected Bibliography." In *Structures of Dependency*, edited by Frank Bonilla and Robert Girling, 253–62. Stanford, CA: Stanford University Press.

Responses to Mexican Immigration, 1910–1930

Ricardo Romo

One of the most striking and persistent phenomena of the Southwest in the twentieth century has been immigration from México. Although well under way at the turn of the century, this immigration had its first major impetus during the period 1910–30. In 1900, perhaps 100,000 people of Mexican descent or birth lived in the United States; by 1930 the figure had reached 1.5 million (US Bureau of the Census 1932, 130). The 1910 Mexican Revolution sparked a large exodus of laborers to the Southwest, but this "push" factor only coincided with "pull" forces in the United States. Economic development in the Southwest, principally in California, Arizona, and Texas, was spurred by greater irrigation, extension of transportation systems, and the demands of World War I. Unsettled by social and economic conditions in their homeland, Mexican laborers were attracted by better wages in the United States; for unskilled occupations, Southwestern industries often paid common laborers five to ten times more than similar industries paid in México.

This influx of more than a million Mexican immigrants during 1910–30 led to a confrontation between Southwestern industries, which needed casual labor, and organized labor, which opposed Mexican immigration for economic and racial reasons. During three different years, 1917, 1921, and 1924, Congress curtailed "Oriental" and European immigration. However, agriculture, transportation, and mining industries successfully lobbied to prevent restriction of Mexican immigration. Throughout this era, Mexican laborers alleviated labor shortages in unskilled and skilled occupations in the Southwest and also in some industries in the Midwest. Immigration from México and the response accorded to these newcomers has not been sufficiently examined. This essay is a small contribution to that task.

Historians generally recognize three major immigration movements to the United States. The first two immigration waves occurred in the years 1815–60 and 1860–90, and were periods in which Germany, Ireland, and Great Britain contributed most heavily to the population growth of the country.[1] Mexican immigration was significant at the end of the third movement, which occurred between 1890 and 1914. Heavy northward migration of Mexican laborers began with the construction of Mexican railroads connecting US border towns with Mexico City and greatly increased with the completion of México's National Railroad to the border in the 1880s. Although the United States Immigration Service kept only partial records of Mexican immigration in the last half of the nineteenth century, the national census estimated that more than 50,000 Mexicans came to the United States between 1875 and 1900 (US Bureau of the Census 1932, 130).

Many of the Mexicanos recruited to work on the railroads during the 1880s settled in Los Angeles. Several California historians have estimated that the Mexican population in Los Angeles in 1887 numbered about 12,000, while another 15,000 were estimated to be residing in surrounding areas (McWilliams 1973, 69; Pitt 1970, 256). Chinese labor gangs built the extension of the Southern Pacific Railroad to Los Angeles, but when construction reached the San Fernando Valley, railroad supervisors recruited "Mexicans and Indians [to] join the work gangs" (Pitt 1970, 256).

The completion of the Transcontinental Railroad to Los Angeles gave birth to an economic boom. Between 1880 and 1890, the overall population of Los Angeles grew from 11,000 to more than 50,000 despite the exodus of thousands of residents after an economic recession in 1888. This population explosion created a dramatic change in the city's ethnic composition. According to one observer: "The boom made a permanent change in the city's character. The hybrid Mexican-American pueblo was no more" (WPA Writers Program 1941, 45). For the first time, the Mexican population in Los Angeles became a numerical minority.

While Mexican immigration to the United States before 1900 was less than 1 percent of the total immigration, by 1900 the Mexican population in dozens of Southwestern cities had doubled. The Mexican-born population of the United States in 1870, estimated at 42,435, increased to over 100,000 by 1900 (State of California 1930, 29). Ninety percent of the foreign-born Mexican population lived in three states: Texas, Arizona, and California. In 1900, Texas had the largest Mexican population, nearly 69.0 percent of the total, while 2.0 percent of the Mexican-born population lived in

California (31). The Mexican population of California grew rapidly over the next thirty years and by 1930 had increased fourfold, giving California 15.2 percent of the total Mexican population in the United States (31).

After 1900, most Mexicans entered the United States through Texas. Many, after having temporarily resided along the border, then traveled on to Arizona and California. In 1903, a Texas railroad official stated that Mexican immigrants had been recruited in El Paso for several years and that railroad employers had substituted them for Italians and Blacks in the Southwest (Clark 1908, 477–78). A few years later, a roadmaster working in Southern California reported that Mexicans had been employed in his division for "four or five years and were displacing other laborers." He observed that he preferred them to other available laborers, "especially the Japanese" (478).

At the turn of the nineteenth century, nativists in California had raised the issue of the "yellow peril," and thereby unwittingly aided the demand for Mexican laborers. The issue was later well summarized by Charles A. Thomson, a San Francisco minister, who wrote in 1926:

> The Mexican is the preferred of all the cheap labor available to the Southwest. On Oriental labor, Chinese and Japanese and Hindu, the verdict has already been cast; California has swung our national jury to an almost unanimous vote. (279).

Racially, Mexican laborers were more acceptable in California than Japanese or Chinese laborers.

During the period 1900–10, nearly 50,000 immigrants from Mexico officially crossed the international line. Mexican immigration represented 0.6 percent of the total immigration to the United States during this period (US Bureau of the Census 1932, 173). However, as one observer noted, they constituted one-sixth of the section hands and extra gangs on the railroads in the Western division. Railroad companies took Mexican laborers to work as far north as Illinois and Colorado. Given the seasonal nature of some track work, the companies often paid the expenses of any worker who wished to return to México (Jenks 1912, 212). Thousands of Mexican laborers during this period traveled back and forth across the border, but an increasing number began to settle during the off-season in cities such as Los Angeles.

During the decade of the Mexican Revolution, 1910–20, twice as many Mexicans entered the United States as in the previous decade. An analysis made in 1912 by journalist Samuel Bryan emphasized that immigration from Mexico "resulted from the expansion of industry both in Mexico and in the United States" (727). Moisés González Navarro, a Mexican historian, wrote that the United States acted as a "safety valve" for México, for in times of political and social unrest thousands fled across the border (1973, 735, 738). Bryan explained Mexican migration in a similar manner, noting that Mexicans were pulled to the north by the expansion of industries, drawing men from the farms and from the interior northward. This influx of immigrants, Bryan concluded, coincided with the economic expansion that took place in the Southwestern United States (1912, 727). The movement of immigrants to the border was facilitated by the use of the automobile and the railroad networks that connected the interior of México with the Southwest.

The railroad was the most common mode of transportation for the Mexican immigrant after 1910. Passage from central México to the US border during the Revolution cost ten to fifteen dollars per person. In 1911 the average number of passenger miles traveled on Mexican railroads was 346, and by 1920 this had increased to an average of 440 miles per passenger (DGE 1942, 1054–55; Cuellar 1935, 42–45). The increase in service and rail travel after the Revolution coincided with the general increase in Mexican immigration to the United States. Most of the immigrants going to California went by way of the Mexican border town of Juárez, across from El Paso, Texas. Others also went by way of Nogales, Arizona, and in the late 1920s through Calexico, California, and Mexicali, Baja California.

Another popular means of transportation was the automobile. Many Mexican immigrants bought automobiles in border cities and then sold them or returned with them to the interior of México, where United States automobiles were generally quite popular and always brought a good price. In one year alone, over five hundred Ford automobiles were taken back to México by returning Mexican laborers (Gamio 1930, 225). Automobile registration in México increased from over half a million in 1911 to over 8 million by 1920 and 17½ million five years later, in 1925 (DGE 1942, 1081–83). Frequently, immigrants bought automobiles in the United States in order to facilitate the migration of other members of their families, as did Ramón Lizárraga.

Lizárraga, a Mexican musician and an immigrant of the early twentieth century, utilized both the railroad and the automobile to emigrate to the United States. When Lizárraga first came to Los Angeles in 1903, he traveled by train. He returned to México in 1905 after having worked in Tucson and Los Angeles as a musician. In 1926, he again journeyed to Los Angeles by train, this time with enough money earned as a musician in México to enable him to purchase an automobile. He remained in the United States long enough to buy a "model T" Ford and returned shortly thereafter to México for his family. After selling their small farm in México, Mr. and Mrs. Lizárraga and their children loaded all their personal belongings into the old Ford and headed once again for Los Angeles.[2]

II

Unlike the Lizárraga family, the greatest number of Mexican immigrants streamed through the border station at El Paso, Texas. On occasion, as many as one thousand individuals per day went through the humiliating process of hot baths, medical examinations, and literacy tests in El Paso. Vera L. Sturges commented:

> Everything possible seems to be done to keep them clean and sanitary; but when five or six hundred steaming people, men, women and children, are crowded into the room at one time, sanitation becomes a farce. (1921, 470)

Seldom did the Mexican laborers emigrate with more than one or two family members, given the cost of $18 per person for visas and consular fees. In the 1920s, between 65 or 70 percent of the Mexican immigrants were males, the majority of them single (US Bureau of the Census 1932, 173). Those with large families often brought them across the border surreptitiously. Some immigrants left their families at the border on the Mexican side while the father found suitable and stable employment that would enable him to return for his family. Other immigrants, unable to pay or frustrated by long delays, crossed by night with the aid of a coyote.[3]

Once the immigrants crossed the border, labor agents or *enganchadores* competed vigorously to recruit them. These agents often made extravagant promises to induce immigrants to sign labor contracts with the companies they represented. One immigrant, now living in Los Angeles, recalled his crossing more than fifty years ago. He reminisced:

> They [the Texas Rangers] helped us cross [the Rio Grande] because they wanted workers from México. The companies perhaps gave them some money for allowing us to cross. The next day we found work [at the mines]. We were standing near the office when we were asked to go to work right away. But they did not pay very much—10 cents per hour, but not 10 cents in money, rather they gave us chits and you took them to the [company] store and bought your groceries.[4]

Enganchadores recruited workers according to instructions given to them by various employers. Helen W. Walker, a social worker in Los Angeles, observed that it was not uncommon for the *enganchadores* and employment bureaus to use "unscrupulous methods" to recruit Mexican laborers, since "their object [was] to get as many men as possible." The recruiters, Mrs. Walker found, gave "no guarantee of the length of employment," and rapid turnovers were common (1928, 57). Some farmers in Texas instructed their agents not to hire Mexicans who came without their families, while other farmers preferred immigrants coming across to the United States for the first time.

Workers often signed up with one firm in order to receive transportation to more favorable areas of employment. Ramón Terrazas, a resident of Los Angeles since the 1920s, left El Paso along with several hundred fellow Mexican laborers. Upon reaching the Imperial Valley in California, Terrazas jumped from the train as it stopped and proceeded to look for work on his own.[5] In earlier years, some workers transported to an area left their jobs before completing their contracts. One contractor complained that he "lost an entire gang, after paying $12.50 railway fare a head, before they reached the job to which they had been sent" (Clark 1908, 472).

III

In 1911 and 1912, nearly 80 percent of all emigrants who left México went to the United States (Departamento de la Estadística Nacional 1930, 149–55). In those two years Mexican immigration records show that some 144,308 Mexican immigrants, most of them single males, crossed into the United States, and interestingly, almost as many returned to México at the end of the year. In contrast, the United States census data reported only 40,785 Mexican immigrants during the same period (see table 1). The Mexican figures are perhaps more reliable because all persons entering México had to register at the border or face charges of illegal entry, a serious crime during the Revolution. Illegal entrants to the United States, on the other hand, were merely deported. It seems obvious that large numbers of Mexicans entering the United States crossed illegally. Jay S. Stowell, a close observer of border affairs, estimated that as many as 75 percent of the Mexican immigrants entered illegally (1938, 763).

As military activities intensified after the assassination of President Francisco Madero, movement across the border took on new and expanded dimensions. High loss of men through battle casualties and desertion

Table 1. Mexican Immigration to the United States, 1910–1930

	US data sources	Mexican data sources
1910	17,760	—
1911	18,784	59,198
1912	22,001	85,110
1913	10,954	50,105
1914	13,089	11,003
1915	10,993	10,123
1916	17,198	49,932
1917	16,438	25,758
1918	17,602	41,139
1919	28,844	55,162
1920	51,042	59,316
1921	29,603	22,117
1922	18,246	48,795
1923	62,709	100,562
1924	87,648	78,490
1925	32,378	65,336
1926	42,638	77,505
1927	66,766	87,979
1928	57,765	75,450
1929	38,980	—
1930	11,915	—

Sources: US data: US Bureau of Immigration 1913, 40, 54, 92. Mexican data: Departamento de la Estadística Nacional 1930, tables 47 and 48, 149–59. Mexican data for 1910, 1929, and 1930 are not available.

plagued Mexican armies. The US Department of Labor reported in 1914 that "approximately 8,000 panic-stricken aliens, mainly of the Mexican race, entered the United States at Eagle Pass, Tex., within a few hours" after fleeing from the Federal forces "who were reported about to attack the town of Piedras Negras" (US Bureau of Immigration 1914, 458). Countless hardships were related by immigrants who sought safety on the US side of the border. The *Los Angeles Times* reported one story that was not at all atypical of the refugees' experiences:

> Scores of women camp followers [of the civilian refugees] had lost their children in the scramble and were crying piteously in the corral provided for them on the American side. They were without clothing sufficient to protect them from the cold and all were drenched from wading through the river. The scene of disorder was almost as bad on the American side as on the Mexican.[6]

During the years that many Mexicans fled to the United States as war refugees, thousands of others left because of social and economic disruptions. Unlike the seasonal laborers recruited by industry and agriculture, these refugees came from the middle and upper classes of México and intended to remain in the United States for a longer period. J. B. Gwin (1917), an officer for the Red Cross, stated:

> The Mexican refugees have surprised all beholders with their healthy conditions, their quiet polite manners and especially with their failure to appear as half-starved, poverty-stricken people from a desolate land. . . . They probably represent the best element there is in Mexico today, the farmers and small business men who have taken no part in the wars. (621)

Most refugees generally preferred to work in communities with Mexican settlements. Many Mexican immigrants stayed in the Southwest to work, rather than travel on to the Midwest, in order to remain close to México where many of them had left relatives. In the Southwest, the immigrant also had the advantage of finding more places where his language was spoken and his culture persisted.

Many of the refugees who entered the United States—sometimes only slightly ahead of the advancing Mexican armies—found themselves confined for days and even weeks in United States Army processing camps. Few labor agents visited these camps to bid for laborers, thus giving the refugee camp immigrants limited employment options. In 1914 the *Los Angeles Times* reported that "the Mexican Federal soldiers in the custody of the United States border patrol forces at Presidio, Texas [would] be transferred to Ft. Bliss and [would be] interned there indefinitely."[7] In an article entitled "Making Friends of Invaders," J. B. Gwin (1917) wrote, "The camp is growing smaller rapidly. Over fifty have left with their families to go on the 'regancia' railroad work. Another forty have gone to the mines of New Mexico" (622). Stories of the "invading hordes" constantly appeared in the *Los Angeles Times* during the years of the Mexican Revolution. Five thousand Mexican refugees crossed the "International Line," the *Times* reported one year, "entice[d]" by "three square meals." The bill for feeding these refugees, the *Times* continued, would be sent to the Mexican government.[8]

IV

After the opening of the Panama Canal, boosters in California predicted "a large influx of South European immigrants by the way of the Panama

Canal" (Millis 1915, 125). The boosters had hoped to replace Mexican laborers with Southern European immigrants. However, the outbreak of World War I crushed their hopes. Southwestern employers interested in inexpensive labor continued to send labor agents to México. "Each week five or six special trains are run from Laredo," the *Los Angeles Times* stated in 1916, "carrying Mexicans who have been employed by labor agents, and similar shipments are being made from other border points." The demand for these laborers, concluded the *Times*, "is so great that they are employed as fast as they cross the Rio Grande. Men, women and children are gathered up and placed upon the trains and shipped to the fields."[9] The efforts of the labor agents in México proved to be very successful. In California, Mexican farm laborers had displaced other ethnic groups within a few years.

In 1917, the Immigration Restriction League pressured Congress to pass an immigration law over the objections of President Woodrow Wilson. The act doubled the head tax to $8.00 "and added chronic alcoholics, vagrants, and 'persons of constitutional psychopathic inferiority' to the list of excluded classes" (Jones 1960, 269–70). Most significantly, the act required immigrants to pass a literacy test that restrictionists knew would curtail non-English-speaking groups. For mining, agriculture, and railroad interests, the law did two things: first, it cut off the supply of cheap European labor, and second, it all but spelled an end to the surplus supply from México that had been activated after the outbreak of the Mexican Revolution. Railroad and agricultural interests lobbied in Congress for the exemption of Mexican labor from the Immigration Act of 1917 in order to ensure once again the availability of cheap labor from México. Their efforts did not go unrewarded.

Acting as special interest groups, railroad, agriculture, and mining companies employed several strategies in order to ensure the continued availability of Mexican laborers. One plan of action called for frightening the public about food shortages; proponents of this plan argued that the curtailment of Mexican farm laborers would bring about a serious decline in food production. The *Los Angeles Times*, whose owner employed hundreds of Mexicans, sided with those who acknowledged a need for cheap labor. In 1917, the *Times* carried an article that warned of serious consequences due to the "exodus" of Mexicans from Texas: "This remarkable exodus . . . has reached a serious phase, particularly as it relates to the growing of crops and attending to live stock interests upon many millions of acres of land upon the Texas border."[10]

A member of the California Fruit Growers' Exchange claimed in May 1917 that unless prompt action was taken to mobilize farm labor in California, a serious shortage of workers would hamper the harvest of bumper crops in Southern California.[11] During the same week, the Los Angeles Chamber of Commerce sent a telegram to Immigration Commissioner A. Caminetti in Washington requesting that Mexican laborers be excluded from Section 3 of the 1917 Immigration Act, which denied admission to aliens who could not read the English language. In the opinion of growers in Los Angeles, the law seriously restricted the necessary supply of agricultural workers from México.[12]

Within six months of the passage of the Immigration Act of 1917, Congress yielded to the pressure exerted by Southwestern industries and rescinded the decision to include Mexicans. in the restrictive clauses. Congress allowed the United States secretary of labor to suspend the literacy test, contract labor clause, and head tax of the 1917 law. Interest groups that had argued for suspension actually wanted permission to tap the reserve labor pool available in México; they used as a pretext the existence of a labor shortage created by the outbreak of World War I.

Conditions in the United States during World War I made extensive immigration from México expedient. J. B. Gwin (1926), an officer of the Red Cross, reported that after the Mexican Revolution of 1910, "the next impetus to immigration from Mexico came as a result of the scarcity of laborers in the United States during the World War." Indeed, almost twice as many Mexicans came during the period 1915–19 as in 1911–14 (328).

During the First World War Mexicans performed a valuable service to the United States and her allies. They manned railroads, helped construct new military bases, and picked cotton used in gunpowder and clothing. Mexicans who worked in mines of the Southwest also helped provide a steady flow of copper, lead, and other minerals needed in the war effort.

Thousands of Mexicans who entered the United States during the war years as temporary laborers remained after their six-month permission had expired. Of those remaining in California after the war, according to historian Robert G. Cleland, most of them settled in the Los Angeles metropolitan area, and by 1925 the former Spanish pueblo had become, next to Mexico City itself, the largest Mexican community in the world (1947, 251–52).

Those who used the war as a reason to hire Mexican laborers profited handsomely in return. Southwestern employers paid Mexican laborers low wages and provided them with poor housing. Vernon McCombs of the Home Council wrote in 1925:

On the tuberculosis chart for the city [Los Angeles] there is a black cloud about the Plaza region. The causes are clear: low wages, seasonal employment, high rent, overcrowding, and inadequate nourishment. The average family has five members and the average house has two rooms, for which exorbitant rents are charged. In Los Angeles, 28 per cent of these Mexicans' homes have no running water; 79 per cent have no bathrooms, and 68 per cent no inside toilets—in many cases six or eight families use a common toilet. (35)

Southwestern employers also violated the conditions of the immigration law under which Mexicans had been temporarily admitted. Mexican laborers were kept under employment longer than the government had sanctioned, as the law clearly called for only temporary admission of Mexicans. The United States secretary of labor later extended the length of time allowed in the United States for Mexican workers involved in all forms of mining and all government construction work in the states within the southern department of the United States Army (US Bureau of Immigration 1918, 692–93). Abuses of these immigration restrictions frequently occurred, but violators generally escaped penalties.

However, the end of the war caused a surplus of Mexican workers in urban areas. Four million men at the rate of over 300,000 a month returned to civilian life after the signing of the Armistice on November 11, 1918 (Soule 1968, chap. 4). The sudden return of so many men into civilian life put thousands of Mexican laborers out of work. Only in agriculture, transportation, and mining were Mexicans still in demand.

Moreover, successful pressure by interest groups in 1920 resulted in an extension of the "exclusion clause" of the 1917 Immigration Act, thus enabling a greater number of Mexican laborers to enter the United States. These workers, interest groups argued, were needed to keep pace with the increase in agricultural production. The cotton crop in California, for example, increased in value from $11,744 in 1909 to $9,237,182 ten years later. Arizona, whose irrigation works had been built by Mexican laborers, achieved even greater increases in cotton production, from an output valued at $730 in 1909 to $20,119,989 in 1919 (US Bureau of the Census 1932, 516; 1933, 674–75).

Massive migration of Southern blacks to the North forced some Southern and Southwestern labor recruiters to go south of the border for workers. Midwestern states also began to rely more heavily on Mexican labor and competed with Southwestern states in recruiting Mexican workers. Aggressive recruitment of Mexicans to the sugar beet fields in Colorado exemplified this competition. In 1918, the United States Department of Labor cooperated with Colorado beet growers in developing a plan for securing Mexican laborers who were considered "admirably adapted to this work," according to a department spokesman (US Bureau of Immigration 1918, 692). In fiscal year 1919, farmers recruited more than 10,000 of the 20,000 laborers admitted under the exclusion clause of the 1917 Immigration Act. Another 9,998 of these went to work on railroad maintenance (US Bureau of Immigration 1920, 7–8).

According to United States officials, 50,852 Mexican immigrants entered this country between 1917–1920, and about half of them found employment with the railroads. While the law required these Mexicans to return to México within six months, nearly half of them remained, and in 1920, nearly 23,000 were still employed in the United States (US Congress 1928, 89–91; US Bureau of Immigration 1920, 7–8).

V

After 1921, it became virtually impossible to hold back the influx of both legal and undocumented workers or "illegal aliens" from México. Gerald B. Breitigam, a journalist for the *New York Times*, reported in 1920 that since 1913 "more than five hundred thousand Mexicans [had] entered the Southwest."[13] Another writer estimated that over a period of seven months in 1920, "more than one hundred thousand Mexicans . . . had crossed into the United States, relieving our farm labor shortage."[14]

Mexican immigrants came to the United States because they expected to find a more stable existence there and earn higher wages as well. The "higher wages have been effective stimuli," wrote sociology professor Emory Bogardus. "Three dollars a day, for instance, in 1929, looked large to a Mexican accustomed to receiving the equivalent of fifty cents" (1934, 39). Economics professor Constantine Panunzio found that the average family income per year of one hundred nonmigratory Mexican wage earners' families was $1,337.35 for 1929–30 in San Diego, California (1933, 14–15). In the mid-1920s, Bogardus found that although wages varied greatly according to occupation and "the types of Mexicans employed," the median wage appeared to range between $2.75 and $3.25 a day (1927, 473). Some industries such as railroad and agriculture had high labor turnovers, despite relatively high wages, and working conditions that were far from suitable. The following corrido or ballad sung during the 1920s illustrates the disappointment over working conditions experienced by numerous Mexican laborers in the United States:

The Immigrants
(Los Enganchados—"The Hooked Ones")

On the 28th day of February,
That important day
When we left El Paso,
They took us out as contract labor.

We arrived on the first day
And on the second began to work.
With our picks in our hands
We set out tramping.

Some unloaded rails
And others unloaded ties,
And others of my companions
Threw out thousands of curses.

Those who knew the work
Went repairing the jack
With sledge hammers and shovels
Throwing earth up the track.

Said Jesus, "El Coyote,"
As if he wanted to weep,
"It would be better to be in Juárez
Even if we were without work."

These verses were composed
By a poor Mexican
To spread the word about
The American system. (Gamio 1930, 84)

Nonetheless, Mexican laborers served as the principal work force in the industrialization and development of agribusiness in the Southwest. Without Mexican labor, high profits and large-scale expansion in industries, transportation, and agribusiness would have been impossible. The commissioner general of immigration in the United States understood the role of the Mexican laborers, stating that while Mexican immigration was not very extensive, it played "an important part in the labor supply of the Southwest." In fact, the commissioner added, "much of the movement is made up of those whose coming and going is regulated by the demand for labor in the border States" (US Bureau of Immigration 1919, 61). As has been shown, economic interests were able to successfully modify immigration laws in order to meet the demands for a source of cheap labor. However, vociferous and sharp opposition to Mexican immigration developed within the United States and México.

VI

The continuous flow of emigrants across the border during the Mexican Revolution was not always viewed favorably by the Mexican government. The *Christian Science Monitor* reported in 1920, "The Mexican government threatens to prevent by military force the exodus of workmen to the United States and . . . nevertheless hundreds leave daily 'because of the unsettled conditions of the country.'"[15] The great loss of life during the Revolution, a drop in the birth rate, and a need for laborers to help rebuild the nation prompted México to restrict emigration. Toward the end of the Revolution, at a time when US laws favored the immigration of Mexicans, President Carranza "notified the [state] Governors of Northern México that they must prevent the increasing exodus of laborers to the United States" (Oxnam 1920, 21). President Carranza had every reason to be alarmed; one report stated that a recruiter for a sugar beet company from California had raided Carranza's army and returned to the United States with 1,400 Mexican soldiers (Martinez 1971, 46).

The Mexican government failed to keep citizens from leaving their villages and farms in México because the government could not provide jobs or political stability, something Mexicans hoped they would find in the United States. Nevertheless, Mexican officials made various attempts to persuade Mexicans to stay home. Citizens were warned of the difficulties that Mexicans encountered in the United States. The *Los Angeles Times* commented in March 1920 that the Mexican government had warned "the workmen not to leave Mexico, stating that they would receive no protection from the American government, that justice would be denied them, and that they would become victims of mob violence if they went to the United States." The *Times* stated that the exodus to the United States was causing alarm. Northern Mexican states sent news that there was "serious danger to numerous industries in that region through nonuse and to large areas of farm land through lack of cultivation."[16] In March 1920, the Federal government instructed the governors of Northern México "to wage a publicity campaign to stop the emigration" (Martinez 1971, 48). The campaign failed. Immigrants continued to cross into the United States, probably because conditions in México were still such that despite unfavorable publicity in the Mexican press, Mexicans preferred the risks of finding employment and housing in the United States to the hardships in México.

However, Mexicans did indeed encounter hardships in the United States. For example, they, like most US citizens, were adversely affected by the economic recession of 1921. But they survived and by the mid-1920s were working in Midwestern cities that twenty years before had never seen a Mexican. Thousands of Mexican laborers had entered the industrial labor force in the Midwest by completely bypassing the border areas. Recruitment of Mexicans to the Midwest helped draw them into urban areas of Illinois, Michigan, Kansas, and Indiana. For example, by 1930 the Mexican population of Illinois numbered 28,906, Michigan listed 13,336, while Kansas had 19,150 and Indiana 9,642 (US Bureau of the Census 1923, 731; 1933, 89–99). Important railroad connections from St. Louis and Kansas City to El Paso partially explained the movement of a large number of Mexicanos to those Midwestern cities. In 1930, Kansas City, Missouri, and Kansas City, Kansas, both claimed Mexican communities of more than 5,000 (US Bureau of the Census 1933, 98–99). Edwin A. Brown, a Baptist minister from Los Angeles, commented on the movement of Mexicanos to the Midwest:

> During the past fifteen years of revolution [in Mexico], no less than *five million Mexicans* have come into the United States, and of these, some two million have returned to Mexico. Each year now, from fifty to ninety thousand come north across the border so that today there are over three million Mexicans in the United States, scattered from the border northeast to Chicago and beyond. (1926, 192, emphasis in original)

As Mexican immigration grew, however, opposition from various elements of US society intensified.

The strongest opposition to unrestricted Mexican immigration came from organized labor. During the years before World War I, when Mexican immigration amounted to less than 1 percent of total immigration to the United States, organized labor all but ignored the influx of Mexican immigrants. In 1913, for example, the American Federation of Labor's (AFL) annual convention entertained a resolution by a San Diego labor organizer to solicit the membership of Mexican laborers in the area. The representative said that in cities in Southern California, "common labor is mostly performed by workers of Mexican nationality," and that these workers "are forced to work for wages below standard, thereby lowering the wages for all labor." He urged the international unions to admit Mexicans into their locals. The delegate also expressed a need for a Spanishspeaking organizer to assist him in working with Mexicanos (AFL 1913, 164).

In 1917 the AFL adopted the request of several of its delegates, including a Mexicano, C. A. Vargas, to work toward the organization of Mexican miners in the Southwest. Mexican miners already were organized in the Clifton-Morenci-Metcalf area in Arizona, with locals 80, 84, and 86 representing more than five thousand men. The delegates urged the AFL leadership "to do everything in their power . . . to organize the entire fourteen thousand Mexican miners" in Arizona, and throughout the Southwest (AFL 1917, 264). The outbreak of World War I dealt a blow to the efforts of the AFL members supporting the recruitment of Mexicans into their locals. As more Mexicans crossed the border, organized labor changed its position toward Mexican workers. The AFL came to view Mexican workers more as competitors for jobs held by native Anglos than as potential union members.

When World War I broke out, Samuel Gompers, head of the AFL, became concerned over the thousands of Mexican workers being admitted to the United States to replace workers engaged in combat. Harry W. Fox, a labor delegate to the AFL annual convention in 1919, perhaps best expressed Gompers's fear of Mexican immigration.

Fox reported to the AFL executive body that Mexicans in the sugar beet industry not only held down wages, but "accepted employment in different lines of effort [nonagricultural], to the detriment of labor standards" (AFL 1919, 247). The lowering of wages and the displacement of native labor were probably the main objections of the AFL to the admission of Mexican labor during the war. Gompers feared that Mexicans would not be content to remain in farm labor and would soon enter semiskilled and skilled trades. Fox believed the movement of Mexicans into other employment was "detrimental to the best interests of the nation" (247). The AFL executive body advised immigration officials to be careful to turn away those without proper permits. There was also a resolution introduced that criticized the use of Mexican laborers in construction crews at Fort Bliss, Texas. The delegate who brought up this resolution warned of the "necessity of employing red-blooded American citizens," for he found the Mexicans "not only un-American in their ways, and nonunion, but also aliens, owing their allegiance to another country" (242).

In addition to being seen as those who lower wages and displace native labor, Mexicans were also viewed as strikebreakers. For example, in the steel strike of 1919, steel companies in Chicago and Gary recruited labor from México. While it seems that some unwary Mexican workers became strikebreakers, they were but a small number and do not appear to have hindered union bargaining efforts. According to economist Paul S. Taylor, the number of Mexicans hired from 1916 to 1919 in the Chicago-Gary area was insignificant compared to the number of Southern blacks. In 1916, there were 18 Mexicans and 558 blacks employed in the two major steel plants in the Chicago-Gary area. Three years later, during the nationwide steel strike, only 142 Mexicans, alongside 2,699 blacks, worked in the two plants surveyed by Taylor in Gary, Indiana. By 1921, while organized labor pressed for the curtailment of European and Mexican immigrants, 49 Mexicans and 1,375 blacks labored in the previously mentioned steel mills (Taylor 1930, 614). Indeed, Mexicans and blacks suffered from the economic recession of that year, as well as from the successful campaign of organized labor to exclude them from industrial occupations.

Still, Mexican immigrants continued to arrive in large numbers. Their search for better work opportunities took them to states farther and farther away from the border. According to one observer, they were:

> probably recruited from the backway of the beet industry . . . there are now about 8,000 Mexicans employed in various industries in Detroit. There are many in the automobile industry employed as unskilled laborers chiefly in the Ford Rouge plant and the Briggs Mfg. Co. where parts are made for all cars. (McDowell 1926, 15)

Organized labor was not the only sector of society to oppose large-scale Mexican immigration.

During the 1920s dozens of articles critical of the admission policies of the Immigration Service appeared in the United States. The concern voiced by those in opposition to Mexican immigration was typically expressed by *The Survey* of April 10, 1920:

> Amid wild gestures and mutual accusations between Mexico City and Washington, Mexican laborers are leaving their own country for the United States in ever increasing numbers. . . . They do not come singly but en masse, not from adjoining districts but often long distances. Whole villages emigrate together.[17]

This increase in Mexican immigration led restrictionists to organize vicious campaigns to end the unrestricted flow of Mexicans to the United States.

In 1920, President Warren Harding signed into law the Johnson Act, the first immigration quota law in US history. This law limited the number of entrants admitted annually to three percent of the number of foreign born of that nationality already in the United States, according to the census of 1910. Mexicans, as well as Canadians and other immigrants from the Western Hemisphere, were protected from the Johnson Act through the efforts of strong special interest groups in the Southwest.

Those individuals favoring open Mexican immigration to the United States argued that it was relatively small compared to that of European nations. Mexicans represented less than 4 percent of total immigration to the United States between 1911 to 1921 (Bennett 1963, 61–62). Those who favored the exemption of Mexicans from the quota laws contended that they returned to México much like "homing pigeons." Others argued that the Mexican was less visible in the United States because he was geographically isolated and therefore did not present a racial problem to society. More than 90 percent of the Mexicanos lived in the three states of Texas, Arizona, and California, while the core of the restrictionist movement was on the East Coast and concerned itself with non-northern European groups such as Italians, Jews, Slavs, and Greeks.

After passage of the Immigration Act of 1924, the question of Mexican immigration became more complex. Opponents of Mexican immigration became adamantly concerned about the failure of Congress to include Mexicans on the quota list. As the restrictionists gathered strength, representatives from agriculture and railroad companies took an active role in defending the free flow of Mexican laborers into this country. A popular argument used by defenders of immigration from México rested on the premise that "white" men would not perform menial work. "White men" refused this work because of the "character of the toil, rather than the scale of wages" (Marvin 1928, 352). Another supporter of Mexican labor added a somewhat contradictory statement when he argued, "We can't get good white labor at our common labor rate, 35 cents an hour" (Taylor 1934, 81). In 1920, the Department of Labor conducted a survey to determine whether or not Mexican labor was in fact displacing Anglo labor. The department hoped to settle the issue by submitting the following:

> Our investigation proves beyond a reasonable doubt that white men are averse to accepting, and refuse to accept (as they have the right to do), employment as unskilled or common laborers. (US Department of Labor 1920, 1097)

Other strong opponents of Mexican immigration included those who considered Mexicans nonassimilable or undesirable as an ethnic group. A statement by Congressman Albert Johnson in 1929 serves as a good example of this sentiment. Speaking before a group in New York, Congressman

Johnson noted that "the time [had] come again when it [was] necessary for Congress to save California for Californians." To this statement, Roy Garis, writing in the *Saturday Evening Post*, added, "and the entire Southwest for Americans" (1930, 182). Remsen Crawford expressed similar views when he said that "in various localities of the Southwest, there [was] almost perfect unanimity on the main point—that these people can never be assimilated with white Americans" (1930, 904). A sociologist, W. Garnett, argued against the introduction of Mexican laborers into Texas: "Negroes and Mexicans, of course, constitute our main nonassimilable population elements" and would "bring racial complication to a section which heretofore [has] been blessed with freedom from this vexatious problem" (1925, 35). Other opponents of Mexican immigration warned the public of possible health problems, racial miscegenation, and displacement of Anglo workers.

Both organized labor and Immigration Restriction Leagues considered the exclusion of Mexicans from the quota laws a grave mistake. Kenneth L. Roberts, well known to *Saturday Evening Post* readers for his articles on European immigration, voiced the concern of the Restriction Leagues. Roberts wrote that since the restriction of European immigrants, "the brown flood of Mexican peon immigration—the immigration of Mexican Indians and Mexican mestizos, or halfbreeds—has risen from year to year" (1928b, 14). Aware of the congressional hearings regarding the admission of Mexicans into the United States, Roberts visited several cities to investigate the issue. In Los Angeles, Roberts reported, one can

> see the endless streets crowded with the shacks of illiterate, diseased, pauperized Mexicans, taking no interest whatever in the community, living constantly on the ragged edge of starvation, bringing countless numbers of American citizens into the world with the reckless prodigality of rabbits. (1928a, 43)

By the early 1920s organized labor's opposition to Mexican immigration had become unequivocal. Failing in its bid to have México included in the quota acts of 1921 and 1924, the AFL pursued the matter from another angle. Samuel Gompers, a longtime "friend" of México, called upon leaders of the Confederación Regional Obrera Mexicana (CROM), México's largest labor union, to attend a meeting in Washington (Levenstein 1971, 117).

Gompers hoped that he could convince México to restrict the emigration of her citizens in a manner similar to the Gentlemen's Agreement of 1905 with Japan. Little came of the negotiations with México, and Mexican labor leaders often used the sessions to express disapproval of the treatment of Mexicanos in the United States. CROM leaders argued that Mexican workers often worked for lower wages than native Anglos because the AFL would not allow Mexicanos into their unions. After the death of Gompers and the assassination of President Obregón in México, the two groups discontinued efforts to come to an understanding (Levenstein 1968, 212).

VII

Immigrants have always played an important role in United States history, and Mexican immigrants have proven to be no exception. From the early 1880s, railroad companies employed Mexican laborers in construction and maintenance of railroad lines throughout the Southwest. At the turn of the century, the entrance of Mexicanos into the United States increased significantly, and so did the number of industries dependent upon their labor. Beginning in 1910 and continuing to 1930, social and economic dislocations in México drove thousands northward while even stronger economic factors associated with the expanding Southwest lured those emigrants into the United States. Immigration from south of the Río Grande increased tremendously between 1900 and 1930 due to US requirements for labor during the war years. This influx, however, did not come without some opposition. Organized labor accused Mexicanos of taking jobs from US citizens. At the same time, other restrictionist organizations labeled Mexicans thriftless and prone to accept charity. Notwithstanding this opposition, Mexican laborers played an important role in the economic development of the Southwest. While debate in Washington, DC, over the restriction of immigration continued throughout the 1920s, perhaps a million Mexican immigrants entered the United States. Eventually not legislation but the economic Depression after 1929 finally caused a marked decrease in Mexican immigration. By 1929, Mexicanos, however, had firmly established themselves in urban and rural communities throughout the Southwest and Midwest.

Notes

Editor's note: From *Aztlán: International Journal of Chicano Studies Research* 6, no. 2 (1975): 174–94. The original essay was lightly edited for this collection.

1. I would like to thank my wife Harriett as well as Raymund Paredes, Stanley Coben, and Ruth Kennedy for their critical reading of my first draft of this essay.

2. See, for example, Jones (1960), chaps. 4 and 7, and Divine (1957), chaps. 1–4.

3. Ramón Lizárraga, interview by author, San Fernando, CA, November 1972.

4. Coyote: a person who engages in smuggling undocumented persons.

5. Valente S. Ramírez, interview by author, East Los Angeles, CA, December 1972.

6. Ramón Terrazas, interview by author, August 1972.

7. "Thousands of Refugees Cared for at Presidio," *Los Angeles Times*, January 12, 1914, I-1.

8. "Army Feeds Refugees, but Uncle Sam Means to Hand the Bill to Mexico," *Los Angeles Times*, January 13, 1914, I-2.

9. "'Three Square Meals' Entice the Mexicans," *Los Angeles Times*, January 17, 1914, I-1.

10. "Mexican Labor a Texas Need," *Los Angeles Times*, September 18, 1916, I-3.

11. "Many Mexicans Leaving Texas," *Los Angeles Times*, June 10, 1917, I-3.

12. "Must Have All Farm Workers," *Los Angeles Times*, May 19, 1917, II-8

13. "May Import Mexicans to Work on Our Farms," *Los Angeles Times*, May 30, 1917, II-1.

14. Quoted in *Literary Digest* 66 (July 17, 1920), 53.

15. Quoted in *ibid.*, 39.

16. "Mexican Immigrants," *The Survey* 44 (April 10, 1920), 81.

17. "Try to Halt Labor Hegira," *Los Angeles Times*, March 5, 1920, I-2.

18. "Mexican Immigrants," 81.

Works Cited

AFL (American Federation of Labor). 1913. *Report of Proceedings of the Thirty-Third Annual Convention of the American Federation of Labor*. Washington, DC: Law Reporter Printing.

———. 1917. *Report of Proceedings of the Thirty-Seventh Annual Convention of the American Federation of Labor*. Washington, DC: Law Reporter Printing.

———. 1919. *Report of Proceedings of the Thirty-Ninth Annual Convention of the American Federation of Labor*. Washington, DC: Law Reporter Printing.

Bennett, Marion T. 1963. *American Immigration Policies*. Washington, DC: Public Affairs.

Bogardus, Emory. 1927. "The Mexican Immigrant." *Journal of Applied Sociology* 11: 470–88.

———. 1934. *The Mexican in the United States*. Los Angeles: University of Southern California Press.

Brown, Edwin A. 1926. "The Challenge of Mexican Immigration." *Missionary Review of the World* 49 (March): 192–96.

Bryan, Samuel. 1912. "Mexican Immigrants in the United States." *The Survey* 28 (September 7): 726–30.

Clark, Victor S. 1908. *Mexican Labor in the United States*. Washington, DC: US Government Printing Office.

Cleland, Robert Glass. 1947. *California in Our Time*. New York: Knopf.

Crawford, Remsen. 1930. "The Menace of Mexican Immigration." *Current History*, no. 31 (February).

Cuellar, Alfredo B. 1935. *La situación financiera de los ferrocarriles nacionales de Mexico con relación al trabajo*. Mexico City: Universidad Nacional Autónoma de México.

Departamento de la Estadística Nacional. 1930. *Anuario de 1930: Estados Unidos Mexicanos*. Mexico City: Departamento de la Estadística Nacional.

DGE (Dirección General de Estadística). 1942. *Anuario estadístico de los Estados Unidos Mexicanos*. Mexico City: Dirección General de Estadística.

Divine, Robert A. 1957. *American Immigration Policy, 1924–1952*. New Haven, CT: Yale University Press.

Gamio, Manuel. 1930. *Mexican Immigration to the United States*. Chicago: University of Chicago Press.

Garis, Roy. 1930. "The Mexicanization of American Business." *Saturday Evening Post*, February 8.

Garnett, William Edward. 1925. "Immediate and Pressing Race Problems of Texas." In *Proceedings of the Sixth Annual Convention of the Southwestern Political and Social Science Association*, edited by Caleb Perry. Austin: Southwestern Political and Social Science Association.

González Navarro, Moisés. 1973. Unpublished manuscript. Mexico City.

Gwin, J. B. 1917. "Making Friends of Invaders: Mexican Refugees in Advance of the Returning Troops." *The Survey* 37 (March 3): 621–23.

———. 1926. "Social Problems of Our Mexican Population." In *Proceedings of the National Conference of Social Work, Fifty-Third Annual Session*. Chicago: University of Chicago Press.

Jenks, Jeremiah W. 1912. *The Immigration Problem*. New York: Funk.

Jones, Maldwyn Allen. 1960. *American Immigration*. Chicago: University of Chicago Press.

Levenstein, Harvey A. 1968. "The AFL and Mexican Immigration in the 1920s: An Experiment in Labor Diplomacy." *Hispanic American Historical Review* 48, no. 2: 206–19.

———. 1971. *Labor Organizations in the United States and Mexico*. Westport, CT: Greenwood.

Martinez, John R. 1971. *Mexican Emigration to the United States, 1910–1930*. San Francisco: R and E Research. Reprint of PhD diss., University of California, Berkeley, 1957.

Marvin, George. 1928. "Monkey Wrenches in Mexican Machinery." *Independent* 120 (April 14): 352–83.

McCombs, Vernon. 1925. *From Over the Border: A Study of the Mexican in the United States*. New York: Council of Women for Home Missions and Missionary Education Movement.

McDowell, John. 1926. *A Study of Social and Economic Factors Relating to Spanish Speaking People in the United States.* Report by the Commission on Social and Economic Factors. [New York?]: Home Missions Council.

McWilliams, Carey. 1973. *Southern California: An Island on the Land.* Santa Barbara, CA: Peregrine Smith. First published 1946 under the title *Southern California Country: An Island on the Land.*

Millis, Henry Alvin. 1915. *The Japanese Problem in the United States.* New York: Macmillan.

Oxnam, G. Bromley. 1920. *The Mexican in Los Angeles: Los Angeles City Survey.* [New York?]: Interchurch World Movement of North America.

Panunzio, Constantine. 1933. *How Mexicans Earn and Live.* Berkeley: University of California Press.

Pitt, Leonard. 1970. *The Decline of the Californios.* Berkeley: University of California Press.

Roberts, Kenneth L. 1928a. "The Docile Mexican." *Saturday Evening Post*, March 10.

———. 1928b. "Mexicans or Ruin." *Saturday Evening Post*, February 18.

Soule, George. 1968. *The Prosperity Decade: From War to Depression, 1917–1929.* New York: Holt, Rinehart & Winston. First published 1947.

State of California. 1930. *Mexicans in California: Report of Governor C. C. Young's Mexican Fact-Finding Committee.* San Francisco: California State Building.

Stowell, Jay S. 1938. "The Danger of Unrestricted Mexican Immigration." *Current History* 28, no. 5: 763–66.

Sturges, Vera L. 1921. "Mexican Immigrants." *The Survey* 46 (July 2): 470–71.

Taylor, Paul S. 1930. "Some Aspects of Mexican Immigration." *Journal of Political Economy* 38, no. 5: 609–15.

———. 1934. *Mexican Labor in the United States: Bethlehem, Pennsylvania.* University of California Publications in Economics, vol. 7, no. 2. Berkeley: University of California Press.

Thomson, Charles A. 1926. "The Man from Next Door." *Century Magazine*, no. 3 (January).

US Bureau of the Census. 1923. *Fourteenth Census of the United States, 1920: Abstract.* Washington DC: US Government Printing Office.

———. 1932. *Reports on Agriculture . . . Fifteenth Decennial Census, 1930.* Vol. 2, pt. 3. Washington DC: US Government Printing Office.

———. 1933. *Fifteenth Census of the United States, 1930: Abstract.* Washington DC: US Government Printing Office.

US Bureau of Immigration. 1913. *Annual Report of the Commissioner-General of Immigration to the Secretary of Labor, 1912–1913.* Washington DC: US Government Printing Office.

———. 1914. *Annual Report of the Commissioner-General of Immigration to the Secretary of Labor, 1914.* Washington DC: US Government Printing Office.

———. 1918. *Annual Report of the Commissioner-General of Immigration to the Secretary of Labor, 1918.* Washington DC: US Government Printing Office.

———. 1919. *Annual Report of the Commissioner-General of Immigration to the Secretary of Labor, 1919.* Washington DC: US Government Printing Office.

———. 1920. *Annual Report of the Commissioner-General of Immigration to the Secretary of Labor, 1920.* Washington DC: US Government Printing Office.

US Congress. 1928. *Restriction of Western Hemisphere Immigration.* Hearing before the Senate Committee on Immigration, 70th Congress, 1st Session. Washington DC: US Government Printing Office.

US Department of Labor. 1920. "Results of Admission of Mexican Laborers, under Departmental Orders, for Employment in Agricultural Pursuits." *Monthly Labor Review* 11, no. 5: 1095–97.

Walker, Helen W. 1928. "Mexican Immigrants as Laborers." Sociology and Social Research 13 (September): 55–62.

WPA Writers Program. 1941. *Los Angeles: A Guide to the City and Its Environs.* New York: Hastings House.

Mexican Muralism
Its Social-Educative Roles in Latin America and the United States

Shifra M. Goldman

Mexican muralism was originally created to play a social role in the postrevolutionary period of modern Mexico. It was clearly an art of *advocacy*, and in many cases it was intended to change consciousness and promote political action. (Whether or not it succeeded is a matter for sociological investigation.) Its other role was educative: to convey information about the pre-Columbian heritage—in the 1920s, a new and revolutionary concept; to teach the history of Mexico from the Conquest to independence; and to deal with national and international problems from the Reform to the contemporary period.

Since the muralists undertook to address a mass, largely illiterate audience in the 1920s, they chose a realistic style (often narrative) that would serve, as in the Renaissance, as a "painted book," and they contracted to paint their murals in accessible public buildings—government buildings, markets, schools, etc.

The argument for teachers today is that Mexican murals can still be used in an educative manner in schools. The same is true for the murals of other Latin American artists and for the Chicano murals of the 1970s, which were influenced by the Mexicans. However, some words of caution are necessary concerning the *method* of using art to teach other subjects in another time and another cultural framework.

First, artists are *not* historians. Some, like Diego Rivera, were encyclopedic in their research for the painted images they produced. Nevertheless, two points must be kept in mind: (a) the advocacy position already mentioned—meaning the interpretative function of the artist with his material according to his personal politics and ideology;

and (b) the poetic license that accompanies even the most "objective" presentation of the facts.

Second, a historical perspective is necessary. *When* a particular mural was painted is important, since the issues and attitudes toward them have certainly changed with time. It is also important to consider *where* and *for whom* a mural was painted, especially when different national, regional, and local issues and attitudes are addressed. I would argue that *all* art viewing is more meaningful and emotionally stimulating when considered within its historical and cultural context. I hold the still unpopular view that understanding and enjoyment of art is time- and culture-bound. The enduring works are those reinterpreted for each society's needs; the original context is invariably lost in a short time or across any distance. Art—except on a formal, decorative level perhaps—is neither eternal nor universal; it functions in a time-space continuum and is assigned a new meaning in a new framework.

These cautionary suggestions can work advantageously in an educational situation. Art—particularly that being considered here, which is especially accessible because of its original purpose—can be used, as novels and films are, in history, sociology, or political science classes. Art becomes accessory to the facts and theories; it gives a human dimension and a personal point of view. Most important, art provides insight into the complexities of the time as interpreted by an individual artist or an artistic group.

An idea can appear in one time framework serving a given historical function, then reappear later, transformed and charged with new meanings and implications. For example, the image of the Mexican revolutionary leader Emiliano Zapata had one meaning for José Guadalupe Posada, a Mexican engraver during the early revolutionary period; he was sympathetic, but at times satirical of a contemporary. For Diego Rivera, at a later date, Zapata represented the promises of the Mexican Revolution for agrarian reform and land distribution. Rivera treated Zapata as a historical heroic figure (he was assassinated in 1919 before Rivera returned from his European studies). For contemporary Mexicans in the United States, Zapata has become deified and sacrosanct. He has left history and become an abstract symbol. The fact that city-born youths from large urban ghettos in the United States transform a Mexican peasant leader into a hero image for their aspirations gives insight into the contemporary Chicano dynamic. Zapata has since been supplemented by more contemporary and relevant hero models: César Chávez, Che Guevara, and Rubén Salazar.

Indigenism

Diego Rivera in 1921 painted the first mural of what has become known as the Mexican Mural Renaissance.[1] Many of his murals precisely depict the great Indian civilizations that existed before the Spanish Conquest. Rivera, one of the earliest Mexicans to appreciate and collect pre-Columbian artifacts, carefully researched the history, culture, and art forms and represented them with great accuracy and detail.[2] Poetic license and substitutions of motifs and images can, however, be found in his paintings. After the Mexican Revolution Rivera was concerned with two issues, and these determined his artistic themes: the need to offset the contempt with which the conquistadores had viewed the ancient Indian civilizations, and the need to offset the anti-mestizo and anti-Indian attitudes of the European-oriented ruling classes during the Porfiriato (the dictatorship of Porfirio Díaz). Mestizo and Indian peasants formed the basic fighting forces of the Revolution, and their economic needs were to be addressed on the political plane. The role of the arts was to restore understanding of and pride in the heritage and cultures that the concept of Spanish superiority had subverted. Postrevolutionary *indigenista* philosophy appeared in the work of writers, musicians, filmmakers, sculptors, and painters as a facet of Mexican nationalism. In an advocacy position, the early *indigenistas* tended to glorify the Indian heritage and vilify that of the Spaniards as a means of rectifying a historical imbalance and advancing certain political ideas.

The Tres Grandes (Big Three) of the Mexican mural movement did not all agree in their interpretations of the indigenous heritage. Rivera idealized the Indian past, as seen in his depiction of the Toltec god Quetzalcoatl in the National Palace mural.[3] Except for the small Indian group engaged in warfare at the lower left of the painting, all is peace and harmony. This contrasts with the realities of the ancient past, especially the conflicts of empire-building cultures like the Olmec, Teotihuacano, Toltec, Maya, and Aztec, whose warring activities are reflected in their arts. Rivera shows ancient civilization almost without conflict: ideal and utopian like a lost Golden Age.

José Clemente Orozco had a very different view of history. He was a *hispanista*. As his paintings and writings make evident, he opposed Indian glorification, ancient or modern. However, he did add one ancient Indian to his pantheon of heroes: Quetzalcoatl. Orozco depicted him as a statesman, educator, and promoter of the arts and civilization, who, according to legend, was eventually exiled by the restored clergy of older gods he had replaced, after which he sailed away on a raft of serpents.[4] It is curious that

Orozco chose a mythological figure whom legend described as having been white-skinned, bearded, and blue-eyed—the very antithesis of the dark-skinned, dark-haired Indians. Orozco's heroes were often of Greek origin (Prometheus, the Man of Fire) or Spanish (Cortés, Franciscan monks, or the criollo Father Hidalgo), or were allegories of spirituality, education, human rationality, or rebellion. He did heroize modern Indian/mestizo leaders like Felipe Carrillo Puerto, Benito Juárez, and Zapata. For him, these—like Quetzalcoatl—were the exceptional men who stood above the crowd.

The notion of a white hero/god as savior and civilizer of dark-skinned peoples is not unique to Orozco; more recently the idea has been promulgated by diffusionist anthropologist Thor Heyerdahl in books on the Ra reed vessels he sailed from Africa to the New World in an attempt to prove that the ancient Egyptians brought pyramids and mathematics to the indigenous peoples of the Americas. Ironically, the Egyptian civilization evolved in an African context, and the Egyptians themselves can certainly not be classified as "white," although the hierarchy of Western civilization that rests on the Egyptian-Greek-Roman foundation has "sanitized" Egypt by conceptually separating it and its history from that of black Africa. Thus Orozco's Quetzalcoatl and Heyerdahl's Egyptians both underline a European ethnocentricity.

Rivera and Orozco again illustrate their dichotomy in differing treatments of the ancient Aztecs. Rivera's mural of Tlatelolco is an encyclopedic presentation of the multiple products, services, activities, and personages to be seen at the great Aztec marketplace.[5] Presided over by an enthroned official, all is calm and orderly in the market. In the background is a topographical view of the Aztec capital city Tenochtitlan, with its pyramids, plazas, palaces, and canals. The painting gives no hint of Aztec imperialism, which the market symbolizes. Tribute and sacrifice victims were brought to Tenochtitlan from the subject peoples.

Orozco, on the other hand, took a critical stance. He often painted the brutality and inhumanity of ancient Indian sacrifice. Aztec culture for Orozco was cruel, bloodthirsty, and barbaric. He illustrates a scene of priests holding a victim's body from which a priest is about to tear out the heart.[6] Spanish Conquest was also cruel and bloodthirsty, according to Orozco's images, but it brought the redeeming quality of a higher level of civilization and of Christianity, which Orozco compared favorably (in his Hospicio de Cabañas epic mural cycle) to the ancient religions.

Clearly neither Diego Rivera's unqualified *indigenista* idealization of Indian cultures nor Orozco's *hispanista* condemnation of Indian barbarism reflects historical accuracy. What teachers can extract from these representations are the *modern* interpretations of the past that accurately reflect a clash of ideologies in revolutionary and postrevolutionary Mexico.

Many of Rivera's murals show that his indigenism was not just historical. It was intimately tied to the interests of modern Indians and mestizos, who had been exploited and abused not only during the 300 years of the Conquest but also by large landowners, the Church, and commercial enterprises during the independence period up to the Revolution. Two of the most important planks of the 1917 Constitution dealt with agrarian reform and the rights of labor unions. Thus Rivera's mural in the Hospital de la Raza deals with modern medical treatment by the social security system as well as with the medicinal practices of the indigenist past.[7] Presided over by Tlazolteotl, goddess of creation, the earth, fertility, and carnal love, and recreated from the Codex Borbonicus, the indigenous section is an excellent index for teaching this aspect of pre-Columbian culture. The modern section shows medical care available to contemporary Mexicans who are both Indian and mestizo. But even this aspect has been idealized; the greater portion of the Mexican people today are not covered by social security, and thus care is not the norm, but the aspiration.

David Alfaro Siqueiros, youngest of the Tres Grandes, took a different approach to indigenist themes. He did not recreate archeologically accurate visions of the ancient world but used the indigenous motifs as allegories or metaphors for contemporary struggles. In two heroic images of Cuauhtemoc, the last of the Aztec emperors becomes a symbol of heroic resistance against invaders across time. These murals were painted in 1941 and 1944, during World War II; they were meant to indicate that even overwhelmingly powerful forces could be defeated through resistance. *Death to the Invader* makes reference to the invading Axis powers in Europe and Asia, while *Cuauhtemoc Against the Myth* refers to the myth of Spanish invincibility.[8] Though the original Cuauhtemoc was killed, Siqueiros shows him conquering the Spaniards. Not the historical Cuauhtemoc, but the symbolic one is important.

Mestizaje

The Conquest brought the mingling of the races; it produced the mestizo, who is referred to as the fusion of the Indian and the Spaniard. Actually mestizaje in Mexico (as in other American countries like Venezuela, Colombia, Brazil, the Caribbean countries, and the United States) included intermixture with Africans, who were brought in as slaves after the decimation of the Indians. Though modern murals do not often deal with this aspect, the colonial period produced a whole series of paintings that carefully delineated the various crossings, with appropriate names for each caste.

Rufino Tamayo in *Birth of Our Nationality* treats the merging of two peoples in a poetic manner.[9] His large Picassoesque horse of the Conquest with a multi-armed figure on its back (the Spaniard) is framed by a Renaissance column on one side (European civilization) and a pre-Columbian moon/sun symbol on the other. Amid broken blocks of buildings (the destroyed Indian civilizations), an Indian woman gives birth to a child that is half red and half white. Deep rich color and the mythic quality of the figures gives a mysterious and dreamlike quality to the event. It is nonnarrative, fixed in time like a fable from the past that has eternal verity.

Orozco deals with mestizaje in terms of known historical personages, Cortés and Malinche.[10] Malinche (Malintzin, or Doña Marina) was a Nahuatl- and Maya-speaking Indian woman who became Cortés's guide and translator and helped him conquer the imperial Aztecs. She was also his mistress; their son represents the mestizaje of the upper classes, the descendants of Spaniards and Indians who were often incorporated into the Mexican ruling class. In Orozco's image, the two nude figures—like the Adam and Eve of Mexican nationality, as Octavio Paz considers them—are seated together and are of equal size. White and brown color and European and Indian features are accentuated for contrast. Their hands are clasped in union, but Cortés is obviously dominant: his foot (and their union) rests on the fallen body of an Indian.

Rivera approaches the same theme in a more historical, narrative, and accurate vein that is neither poetic nor exalted. Within the context of the armed conflict of the Conquest, he picks out a small detail in which an anonymous Spanish soldier rapes an anonymous Indian woman. For the vast majority, this is how much mestizaje occurred.[11]

Revolutionary History

Among the educative concerns of the Mexican muralists were a reordering and revision of Mexican history from a revolutionary point of view. Like Mexican American scholars and artists today, who are revising US history by mandating the inclusion of Mexicans, Mexican Americans, and Native Americans as the original occupants and the bearers of culture, so too did Mexican intellectuals and artists in the 1920s challenge the

European-oriented historical view. History did not begin with the "discovery" of the Americas by Spaniards or Englishmen; they were simply the latest comers who chose, on the whole, to ignore or disparage the millennia of cultures and civilizations that had preceded them. By the same token, the Mexican muralists did not choose to represent Mexican history as a succession of colonial aristocrats or postindependence rulers, but as a series of insurgencies and revolutions by the Mexican people and their leaders against colonizers and dictators.

The central portion of Rivera's epic mural at the National Palace recreates conflicts from the Conquest to the revolutions of 1810 and 1910.[12] Though his theme is conflict, movement and violence are only in the Conquest scenes; the later periods are presented in a static manner with a dense, cubistically composed piling-up of human forms, many of them historical portraits in shallow space. Porfirio Díaz can be seen surrounded by his *científicos*, military men, and the clergy. Behind him are the haciendas of Mexican landowners and the buildings of the Pierce Oil Company of London, a reference to foreign capital exploiting Mexican natural resources during the Díaz dictatorship. The revolutionary opposition appears on the other side: among them are Pancho Villa, Zapata, Felipe Carrillo Puerto, members of the Serdán family who fired the first shots of the 1910 Revolution, Ricardo Flores Magón, Francisco Madero, and caricaturist José Guadalupe Posada.

Siqueiros's treatment of the same subject also shows the alliance between Porfirio Díaz, the Mexican upper class, and the military, but in a more dynamic composition that openly confronts the ruling with the working class.[13] His theme is a particular historical event: the 1906 strike by Mexican workers against the Cananea Consolidated Copper Company located in Sonora, Mexico, and owned by a North American, William Greene, known as the "copper king of Sonora." This event was one of several believed to have triggered the Mexican Revolution.

International Issues

The Mexican mural movement (which has been represented here only by the Tres Grandes, but which had a large following) did not limit itself to national issues; its view was international in scope. In the 1920s, Rivera and Siqueiros were members of the Mexican Communist Party. They had an unreserved admiration for the Soviet Union, whose revolution occurred seven years after the Mexican one. Rivera's views later underwent a major change as his friendship with Leon Trotsky and his anti-Stalinism grew. However, he and Siqueiros remained strong advocates of socialism—not an uncommon phenomenon in the 1920s and 1930s. Orozco was an iconoclast; he was critical but not unsympathetic in these early years. The contrasting views of Rivera and Orozco in the mid-1930s are instructive.

Rivera's *Man at the Crossroads* was originally painted in Rockefeller Center, New York, under the sponsorship of Nelson Rockefeller.[14] The inclusion of Lenin's portrait was too upsetting for Rockefeller and the tenants of the center. The mural was covered and then destroyed, so Rivera repainted it in the Palace of Fine Arts in Mexico City. Surrounding the central motif of a Russian workman at the controls of the universe are the worlds of capitalism (soldiers with gas masks, unemployed strikers attacked by the police, the rich gathered around festive tables) and of socialism (joyous youth, Lenin as a symbol of world brotherhood). In this mural, Rivera reflects the realities and horrors of World War I, which were still fresh in memory, and the Depression, during which the mural was painted. Nevertheless, Rivera applies the same utopian vision that informed his treatment of indigenist themes to this new work. By 1933 Lenin was dead, and Trotsky, after disagreements with the Stalin government, had been exiled. The only indication of this rift is the pointed inclusion of Trotsky's portrait and the exclusion of Stalin's beside the figures of Marx and Engels in the socialist half of the mural.

Orozco's New York murals of the same period feature three heroic leaders with their followers: the assassinated Mayan governor of Yucatan, Felipe Carrillo Puerto; the assassinated Lenin; and the Indian leader Mahatma Gandhi in his confrontation with British imperialism.[15] With Gandhi was one of the few women Orozco placed in a heroic light, Madame Sarojini Naidu. Though Carrillo Puerto and Lenin occupy similar spaces and elevation in the mural, individualized followers surround Carrillo Puerto while Lenin appears above robotized masked soldiers with ranks of sharp bayonets. Through this subtle difference, Orozco could heroize the individual without necessarily accepting the society he constructed. This illustrates Orozco's philosophy in general; he distrusted masses of people and looked in a Nietzschean manner to individual supermen for social reform or salvation.

After Siqueiros returned to Mexico from the Spanish Civil War, he painted a complex mural on the walls, windows, and ceiling of a staircase in a trade union building.[16] For him, the world scene looked bleak. Spain had been the proving ground for Nazi and fascist militarism; the Spanish Civil War presaged World War II. While the Axis consolidated its power in Europe and Asia, the Western nations adhered to a "neutrality" and appeasement policy, which brought down the Republican government in Spain and allowed Hitler access to European conquest. Siqueiros had no sympathy for either the Axis or the Allies. Beneath a huge steel-plated eagle/dive bomber in his mural, he painted an anthropomorphic machine that turns human blood from war victims into gold coins (profits from munitions on both sides). On one side are the British, French, and US allies; on the other are the Japanese, Germans, and Italians. On the left wall, a parrot-like demagogue waves a fiery torch while masses of soldiers march; on the right, as a symbol of opposition, is a powerful figure of the people's resistance.

For US historians and teachers, Siqueiros's mural highlights a moment in time that tends to be overshadowed by the subsequent unity of World War II: namely, the period between the fall of Spain to Franco in 1939 and the attack on Pearl Harbor in 1941 that finally brought together the United States, the Soviet Union, England, France, and many other countries (including Mexico) against fascism. For artists, the mural is a fascinating study of the new artistic technology developed by Siqueiros (synthetic paints, spray-gun application on a wall, documentary photography incorporated into painting) and new formal methods (filmic movement on a static painted surface, illusionistic destruction of architectural space, creation of a containing "environment"). Many of these means presage artistic directions explored in the United States in the 1960s.

For all their power and command of pictorial means, Rivera and Orozco used methods and expression were far more traditional, though all three artists shared revolutionary social content. Perhaps this is one reason why Rivera and Orozco were the major influences on US and South American artists until World War II, and Siqueiros was the most admired and copied by the US street mural movement of the 1960s and 1970s.

Before leaving Mexican terrain, one must note that issues and attitudes change and are reinterpreted with time. In the aftermath of the Mexican Revolution, the muralists and other cultural workers were aware of the need to create a new formal and thematic language in the interests of social change. New aspects of history were to be emphasized, new heroic figures to be given prominence, and new views of social relationships to be advanced. This language would reflect political concepts that emerged from the revolutionary process: agrarian reform, labor rights, separation of church and state, Mexican hegemony over natural resources, defense against foreign economic penetration, and literacy and education for the masses.

Sixty years have passed since the termination of the Revolution. The Mexican state, economy, political structure, and international role have changed. Much revolutionary oratory has become rhetoric in the speeches of government functionaries. Younger generations of artists have reexamined and are revising concepts of the traditional heroes. For example, two murals on revolutionary themes face each other in a salon of the National History Museum in Chapultepec Park, Mexico City. One, by Jorge González Camarena, is a mannered, heroicized portrait of Venustiano Carranza, revolutionary general and early president of Mexico.[17] Carranza at one stage fought against Zapata and was responsible for his assassination. Zapata had accused him of deceit and hypocrisy for preaching and not practicing agrarian reform. Directly opposite the Camarena mural is one by a much younger artist, Arnold Belkin.[18] He confronts the Carranza portrait with one of Zapata and Pancho Villa derived from a famous Casasola photograph. The irony of the placement has not escaped Belkin. In addition, the figures of Zapata and Villa have the flesh stripped away as if the artist intends to demythologize them as well as Carranza.

In a similar vein is Felipe Ehrenberg's easel painting/collage of Carranza and Zapata.[19] In it Carranza appears twice: once as a general with the Mexican flag substituted for his face, as though his true features were hidden behind his patriotism, and again as president, where he is superimposed over the body and face of Zapata. Carranza destroyed the man, but he absorbed his legendary aura. Beneath each figure is a ruler to take anew the measure of history and mythology.

The Mexican muralists accepted the role, as Jean Franco said in her book *The Modern Culture of Latin America*, of "guide, teacher and conscience of [their] country," and produced an art that played a social role. The very choice of means—muralism—underscores their consciousness of this role, since the technique and form is public and not conducive to the expression of subjective or introspective material. It served the needs of the time objectively. It created a new plastic language, a new ideology, and a new iconography. For the first time, the anonymous peoples of Mexico appeared in art, not as quaint or exotic subjects for genre paintings, but as heroes taking control of their own destinies: Orozco's villagers marching off to the Revolution; Rivera's masses of farmers receiving the divided lands of the great estates; Siqueiros's workers creating unions in order to benefit from the riches of their own lands. With them are the leaders who aligned with them or came from their own ranks.

South America

The 1920s, a period of reassessment and reevaluation of European values, followed the devastation and slaughter of World War I. Until then, these values had been considered the acme of civilization. Europeans (and some Latin Americans) turned to Dada, a self-mocking, iconoclastic movement that questioned existing mores, customs, and the nature of culture itself. The Americas, from the United States to South America, turned inward upon their own resources in an exuberant expression of nationalism and regionalism and sought values indigenous to their own continent. In the United States, this took a politically isolationist form and spurred an artistic celebration of varied regions of the nation known as Regionalism. Among Afro-Americans from the Caribbean, Brazil, and Harlem came the celebration of "negritude" and the search for a national identity. In Mexico, Guatemala, and the Andean area, nationalism took the form of indigenism—ancient and modern—tied to contemporary social reform. Artists and writers sought to cut their dependence on European models and develop their own artistic vocabulary and themes; they naturally turned to the Mexican muralists, particularly Rivera, who was known internationally, for inspiration. Many traveled to Mexico to study. However, with the exception of US artists who worked in Mexico and those who assisted with or studied the murals done by Rivera, Orozco, and Siqueiros in many cities of the United States during the 1930s, few artists had the opportunity to do murals. The social conditions, including government commissions and support, conducive to monumental public art existed only in Mexico and in the United States of the New Deal. In other areas, relatively few murals were executed, and no opportunity existed for a national mural movement as in Mexico. Primarily, the Mexican influence can be seen in easel paintings, sometimes monumental in size. To my knowledge, no thorough study of modern Mexican influence on Latin American art has yet been compiled; a similar study of the Mexican influence in the United States has only just gotten underway. At this stage, any conclusions must be tentative. Nevertheless, stylistic, thematic, and some documentary evidence exists on Mexican influence in South America.

Two easel paintings by Cuban artists illustrate this influence. Abela's *Guajiros* and Carreño's *Sugar Cane Cutters* deal with rural workers.[20] Abela's work echoes Rivera's stocky, simplified, and static figures, and Carreño's is influenced by Siqueiros stylistically and in the use of Duco, an automobile lacquer that Siqueiros adapted to fine art use in the 1930s.

Cândido Portinari, universally recognized as Brazil's greatest modern artist, was among several young artists in the 1930s committed to dealing with Brazilian social problems and contemporary life. His large painting *Coffee* brought him international recognition.[21] The use of space, the simplification of figures, compositional devices, and the exaggeration of bodily proportions show Rivera's influence. Portinari painted many important murals at the Ministry of Education in Rio de Janeiro, the Library of Congress in Washington, DC, the Pampulha Church in Belo Horizonte, and the United Nations. He continued to paint sugar and coffee workers, slum dwellers, Negroes, mulattos, whites, Indians, and other typically Brazilian subjects. *Burial in a Net* is part of a series of paintings dealing with a terrible drought in northeastern Brazil during the 1940s; it has elements of Picasso as well as the tragic expressiveness of Orozco.[22]

In 1933 Siqueiros visited Buenos Aires, where, assisted by several local artists, he painted an experimental mural called *Plastic Exercise*. Among the artists was Antonio Berni, whose huge oil paintings, such as *Unemployment* of 1935, express his social realist concerns, though the style is not indebted to Siqueiros.[23] In 1946, Berni was one of a group of artists who did frescoes in an arcade in Buenos Aires (the others were Colmeiro, Urruchúa, Spilimbergo, and Castagnino).[24] Berni's monumental images in his two murals at this location owe a debt to Orozco and to the Italian Renaissance. Muralism, however, did not flourish in Argentina. There were no opportunities to do murals. As Berni stated in 1979, no revolution had taken place and there was no interest in public art. The immense size of his canvases seems to express a frustration with the lack of walls.

In Peru, with a larger Indian population, Mexican indigenism and social realism flourished. In 1922 José Sabogal visited Mexico, where the impact of the muralists turned him into an ardent indigenist and nationalist. His influence produced a school of painters, among them Teodoro Núñez Ureta, who shows the distinct influence of Orozco in his *Transmission of the Seed* and that of Siqueiros in *Allegory of Production and Work*.[25] Núñez's heroic treatment of indigenist and working-class themes places him in the social realist tradition of the Mexican School.

César Rengifo of Venezuela has been a social realist since the 1930s. He did one tile mural in Caracas on an indigenous theme, but realistic public art had few patrons in Venezuela. One exception is the case of Héctor Poleo, who studied mural painting in Mexico in the late 1930s. He was influenced by Rivera, and executed a mural for the new University City in Caracas. Since the 1950s, Venezuelan art has been dominated by geometric abstraction and kineticism, thoroughly cosmopolitan art forms that reflect the urban-industrial development of Caracas resulting from the discovery of large oil deposits in 1938 and 1973. Both Poleo and Rengifo dealt with the desolate life of the rural hinterlands (in contrast to the capital city, Caracas), primarily in easel paintings like Rengifo's *Settlement of Peons* and *What Petroleum Has Left Us: Dogs.*[26]

Chicano Muralism of the 1970s

Between the 1940s and the 1960s, public muralism in the United States suffered an eclipse. The New Deal art projects were terminated in the 1940s, and artists turned to other pursuits for the duration of World War II. In the complacent, prosperous, and individualistic 1950s—overshadowed by the Cold War and McCarthyism—introspective easel painting flourished, dominated by abstract expressionism. New York became the art capital of the world and centralized arbiter of taste in the United States. Critics fulminated against "narrative, propagandistic" art and attacked "literary content" in painting. Representational art in general faced lean times. Art history was revised as the Mexican School, South American social realism, US Regionalism, and New Deal art were written out of the history books. Only in the mid-1970s were these movements reassessed and reintegrated into art history as a number of authors began to publish books on the New Deal and as regional exhibitions of New Deal art took place. The issue of regionality in art, of the validity of artistic pluralism in the United States, and of resistance to the absolute dominance of New York's establishment over the nation has now come into focus.[27]

One of the key factors promoting this new decentralizing of artistic focus, reevaluating of the 1930s, and burgeoning interest in the art of Latin America and Latinos in the United States is the street mural movement, in which Chicano muralism has played a quantitative and qualitative part. The outdoor muralists turned to the Mexicans as an important source of knowledge, technique, concept, style, and inspiration. Nowhere was this more culturally important than among Chicanos, for whom the recovery of Mexican muralism was part of a larger recovery of heritage and identity after a century of deliberate deculturalization by the dominant society. Looking at this last statement with a finer lens, however, research still in its initial stages suggests that the deprivation of Mexican models for Mexican American artists is only two decades old, and applies to those artists who came to their calling during the hegemony of abstract expressionism and the "art for art's sake" dictums of the art schools. The process of revitalizing the work of the Mexican muralists (as well as that of younger artists) in the United States and making it available to artists of the 1960s and 1970s was the result of efforts by Chicano studies programs and mural groups in the Southwest and Midwest, along with the establishment of alternative Chicano cultural structures that researched and disseminated information about Mexican art.

In this brief consideration of Chicano muralism as influenced by the Mexican mural movement, there are examples of the transformation of themes that were important to the Mexicans at an earlier date and that were charged with new meanings and implications within the context of contemporary Chicano concerns. For example, the initial cultural-nationalist phase of Chicano consciousness in the mid-1960s produced a wave of neo-indigenism like that of the Mexicans in the 1920s but with certain important differences. First, the Americanist indigenism of the 1920s was part of an isolationist-nationalist wave following World War I. It was exercised not necessarily by the indigenous peoples themselves but by intellectuals on their behalf. Present neo-indigenism has made links with people of color throughout the developing Third World, and it is being promoted by the affected groups: Chicanos, Puerto Ricans, and Native Americans. Second, Rivera's indigenism responded to a largely agricultural nation where the landless or small farmers, Indian and mestizo, made up a great part of the population, and where agrarian reform was a major plank of the Revolution. Though Chicanos in the Southwest also include a large rural or semirural population, and the unionization struggles of the United Farm Workers were a focal point in the development of Chicano culture, agrarianism is in a highly industrialized country and even agriculture is a big business. Therefore, little probability exists that Chicanos would or could be the small farmers the Zapatistas aspired to be.

One of the earliest and strongest proponents of neo-indigenism was Luis Valdez of Teatro Campesino. He drew upon his interpretation of pre-Columbian religion to provide a non-European spiritual base for Chicano life. However, Valdez turned to this source at the point when he began to address urban Chicanos as well as farmworkers. He himself was urbanized through long residence in big California cities. The same is true of Chicano poets Alurista of San Diego and Rodolfo "Corky" Gonzales of Denver, important figures in the popularization of neo-indigenism.

Another point of differentiation was the exclusively pre-Columbian focus of the cultural-nationalist phase; the fraternity between mestizo

Chicanos and Native Americans based on a commonality of "race" and oppression within Anglo-dominated society did not occur until later. Mexico, on the other hand, has been a mestizo and Indian nation since the Conquest; indigenism in the 1920s served to emphasize that national fact. Mestizos and Indians were the *majority*, not the minority, and artists addressed their present problems.

Two Chicano murals, one from Los Angeles and the other from Denver, are taken directly from pre-Columbian sources; they are copied uncritically without concern for historical context. Charles Félix recreates in color a sacrifice scene from a ball court relief sculpture at El Tajín, Veracruz.[28] Al Sánchez reproduces the single figure of the goddess Tlazolteotl—the same used as a central figure by Rivera in his Hospital de la Raza mural on ancient and modern medicine.[29] Rivera related pre-Columbian to modern medicine in a continuum, the patients being Indians of the past and present. The murals by Félix and Sánchez are essentially decorative and unselective about content—surely Félix did not intend to glorify human sacrifice.

La Mujer, an enormous, collectively painted mural in Hayward, California, uses a variety of motifs that mingle the pre-Columbian with contemporary urban problems.[30] The central female figure with tripartite head and powerful outthrust arms is adapted from Siqueiros's 1944 *New Democracy* in the Palace of Fine Arts, Mexico City. On one side of the Hayward mural are the evils of the big city: contaminated food, arson, violence in the streets, drug abuse, and others. One of the great arms holds a destructive hammer over these scenes. The other arm terminates in a wheel incorporating the four elements; the Puerto Rican, Mexican, Cuban, and Pan-African flags; and Native American peace symbols. Pre-Columbian figures intertwine with death and destruction on the left, and with corn, peace, and growth on the right. Thus the indigenous motifs are selectively chosen and thematically enhancing.

Another elaboration of this kind that creatively adapts motifs and formal elements from indigenous sources and the Mexican muralists is *Song of Unity* in Berkeley, California.[31] Its point of departure is contemporary social song (called *nueva canción* in Latin America) in North and South America, and therefore its central motif is a double image of eagle and condor. The mural has an irregular billboard-like cutout surface. One side of the mural pictures North American musicians and songwriters like Daniel Valdez, Malvina Reynolds, and jazz musicians; the other side features the peoples of Latin America, particularly the Andean Indians. All the figures are dramatically foreshortened in space and seem to thrust from the surface

109

in a manner typical of Siqueiros's paintings. Also adapted from Siqueiros's sculpture-painting technique is the dominant figure of the mural, which is modeled three-dimensionally and projects in relief from the surface. This is an image of Chilean songwriter Víctor Jara, who was killed by the military junta during the fall of the Allende government in 1973. His severed hands continue to play a guitar, while the peoples of South America with their regional instruments march through his transparent mutilated arm.

In Houston, muralist Leo Tanguma painted an enormous mural called *Rebirth of Our Nationality.*[32] A Chicano man and woman emerge from a large red flower that rests in a bleak landscape on a platform of skulls. They are under the banner "To Become Aware of Our History Is to Become Aware of Our Singularity." From either side, brown-skinned figures, who represent the multiplicity of Mexican peoples and the complexity of their history and struggles in Mexico and the United States, drive toward the central inspiration of their rebirth. The dramatic thrust of the composition and the violent expressionism of the figures owe a debt to Siqueiros and Orozco, whom the artist has long admired. The social responsibility of the artist to his community is a philosophy Tanguma derived from Siqueiros, whom he had met personally.

Marcos Raya of Chicago has borrowed figures from Orozco and the major composition of Rivera's *Man at the Crossroads* for his mural *Homage to Diego Rivera.*[33] He has substituted Mayor Daly of Chicago for the central figure of the worker in the original mural and surrounded him with images of corruption and violence.

Chicano murals exist in all states of the Southwest, as well as the Midwest/Great Lakes region. California has more than 1,000, scattered in cities and some rural areas. Texas has murals in Austin, San Antonio, Houston, Crystal City, El Paso, and other locations. No single style unites them; their commonalty, to the degree that it exists, derives from thematic factors and what might be called "the Chicano point of view," a difficult thing to define and one that, even now, is undergoing transformation. Their commonalty derives from life experiences common to Chicanos living in the United States during the second half of the twentieth century, those Mexicans who are expressing a growing awareness of their long history on both sides of the present border. Murals also include the process of redefining and changing that history, and education has played no small role in that process.

Notes

Editor's note: From *Aztlán: International Journal of Chicano Studies Research* 13, nos. 1-2 (1982). The original essay was lightly edited for this collection.

This paper is adapted from a lecture given as part of the Arts and Music of Latin America for Pre-College Educators Conference, Institute of Latin American Studies, University of Texas, Austin, April 1980.

1. Diego Rivera, *Totonac Civilization*, 1950–51, second floor, National Palace, Mexico City.

2. Rivera, *Feather Arts*, 1945, second floor, National Palace, Mexico City.

3. Rivera, *The Ancient Indigenous World*, 1929–30, staircase, National Palace, Mexico City.

4. José Clemente Orozco, *Coming of Quetzalcoatl*, 1932–33, Baker Library, Dartmouth College, Hanover, New Hampshire.

5. Rivera, *Great Tenochtitlan*, 1945, second floor, National Palace, Mexico City.

6. Orozco, *Ancient Human Sacrifice*, 1932–33, Baker Library, Dartmouth College, Hanover, New Hampshire.

7. Rivera, *Ancient and Modern Medicine*, 1952–54, lobby, Hospital de la Raza, Mexico City.

8. David Alfaro Siqueiros, *Death to the Invader*, 1941, Mexican School, Chillan, Chile; David Alfaro Siqueiros, *Cuauhtemoc Against the Myth*, 1944, presently at the Tecpan of Tlatelolco, Mexico City.

9. Rufino Tamayo, *Birth of Our Nationality*, 1952, Palace of Fine Arts, Mexico City.

10. Orozco, *Cortes and Malinche*, 1926, National Preparatory School, Mexico City.

11. Rivera, *History of Mexico: The Conquest*, 1929–30, staircase, National Palace, Mexico City.

12. Rivera, *History of Mexico: The Present*, 1929–30, staircase, National Palace, Mexico City.

13. Siqueiros, *Revolt Against the Porfirian Dictatorship*, 1957–65, National History Museum, Mexico City.

14. Rivera, *Man at the Crossroads*, 1934, Palace of Fine Arts, Mexico City.

15. Orozco, *Struggle in the Occident* and *Struggle in the Orient*, 1930–31, New School for Social Research, New York.

16. Siqueiros, *Portrait of the Bourgeoisie*, 1939, Electricians Union, Mexico City.

17. Jorge González Camarena, *Venustiano Carranza*, 1966, National History Museum, Mexico City.

18. Arnold Belkin, *Emiliano Zapata and Pancho Villa*, 1979 (unfinished), National History Museum, Mexico City.

19. Felipe Ehrenberg, *Carranza and Zapata*, 1979, easel painting/collage.

20. Eduardo Abela, *Guajiros*, 1942, oil on canvas; Mario Carreno y Morales, *Sugar Cane Cutters*, 1943, Duco on wood.

21. Cândido Portinari, *Coffee*, 1935, oil on canvas.

22. Portinari, *Burial in a Net*, 1944, oil on canvas.

23. Antonio Berni, *Unemployment*, 1935, oil on canvas.

24. Berni, untitled mural, 1946, Galería Pacífico, Buenos Aires.

25. Teodoro Núñez Ureta, *Transmission of the Seed*, oil on canvas; Núñez, *Allegory of Production and Work*, 1958, Ministry of Agriculture, Lima.

26. Cesar Rengifo, *Settlement of Peons*, 1956, oil on canvas; Rengifo, *What Petroleum Has Left Us: Dogs*, 1963, oil on canvas.

27. Three issues of *Art in America* reflect this new consciousness: the July–August 1972 special issue on the American Indian; the May–June 1974 issue dealing with public art, women's art, and street murals (hitherto an "invisible" category) across the country; and the July–August 1976 "Art Across America" issue, whose cover is dominated by Texas artist Luis Jimenez's sculpture and whose perspective is epitomized by Donald B. Kuspit's article "Regionalism Reconsidered."

28. Charles Felix, *Sacrifice Scene from El Tajín*, 1973, Estrada Courts housing project, Los Angeles.

29. Al Sánchez, *Tlazolteotl*, ca. 1980, Denver.

30. Rogelio Cardenas and Brocha de Hayward, *La Mujer*, 1978, Hayward, California.

31. Ray Patlan, Osha Neumann, O'Brien Thiele, Anna DeLeon, *Song of Unity*, 1978, La Peña Cultural Center, Berkeley, California.

32. Leo Tanguma, *Rebirth of Our Nationality*, 1973, Continental Can Co., Houston.

33. Marcos Raya, *Homage to Diego Rivera*, 1973, Chicago.

Multiple Journeys
The Life and Work of Guillermo Gómez-Peña (A Performance Chronology)

Guillermo Gómez-Peña

Journalist: What do you do when a writer or a curator wishes to deport you from performance art history?
GP: You mean someone like RoseLee Goldberg? . . . You write yourself back into it on your own terms. Chicanos taught me that.
Journalist: What do you do to avoid being typecast and confined to a one-liner in the history of art?
GP: You have to constantly remind the art world that you work in multiple terrains and that some are invisible to them.

This performance chronology is a conceptual artwork in progress. It includes information and projects that connect my life and family to my art, which I embed in a political and art historical context. The project is inspired by the archival work that Diana Taylor and the Hemispheric Institute of Performance and Politics are doing, by Amelia Jones's and Suzanne Lacy's reflections on performance documentation, and by the work that Carolina Ponce de León is carrying out with the visual histories of Galería de la Raza in San Francisco. I also feel a strong conceptual connection with the project Documenting Live, generated in the United Kingdom by the Live Art Development Agency. That project was conceived as an intervention into the historical discourses of performance art. At the same time, it provides an invitation to Chicano/Latino historians to incorporate our multiple parallel histories in the discourse of contemporary art and for performance artists to engage in similar genealogical projects.

In the process of writing this Proustian text, I have asked several colleagues to help me rebuild the bizarre edifice of my memory. I particularly wish to thank Gretchen Coombs, Lisa Wolford Wylam, Linda Burnham, and Roberto Sifuentes for helping me prepare the manuscript; Emma Tramposch for archiving the extensive photographic material; and my *jaina* Carolina for designing the amazing PowerPoint that accompanies the live version. Many names and projects are still missing and I hope that future versions will be more thorough.

* * *

No-nato (prior to my birth): I wish to share two facts about my ancestors. Like so many Mexican families, mine has been migrating to the United States since the mid-1800s. If you review my family photo album from the late 1800s to the present, you'll see my forebears always had a highly developed sense of theatricality and an unselfconsciously baroque aesthetic. I'm just following suit.

1955: Born Guillermo Lino Liberio Gómez-Peña in the Sanatorio Español of Mexico City on September 23 at 11:10 p.m. My hairy face and bizarre intensity shocked my father. He was a gallant sportsman and civil engineer who devoted his life to bringing electricity to the Mexican countryside, putting food on our table, and playing jai alai. My mother was a fundraiser for social causes, a hostess extraordinaire, and the irrefutable nerve center of the family. Now, at eighty-six, she is still gorgeous and socially active. We are currently working on a couple of performance projects.

1961–66: I study at the Colegio Vanguardias elementary school, play guitar and *futbol* soccer, and travel constantly to the Mexican countryside with my family.

1967–72: Jesuits and Marista priests provide my *secundaria* and *preparatoria* education. I make surrealistic drawings and cheesy collages that I hope never to publish. Mexico is fairly stable and the United States a mythical northern place—a place to vacation, access modernity, and dream of the future. My sister Diana and brother Carlos migrate to Southern California.

1968: The Mexican student movement erupts like magma out of the Popocatépetl volcano. My older brother's and sister's friends are part of it. Some end up in jail; others disappear for good. Tanks surround my neighborhood. The Tlatelolco student massacre takes place five minutes away from my home.

1970: I write *El hombre de la coladera*, my first self-conscious performance, about a young activist who becomes a misanthrope and chooses to live beneath the city, inside the sewer system. The piece is presented in my Catholic high school with spoken word and slides. After the performance, a priest sends me to the school psychiatrist.

1971: The Normal de Maestros student massacre takes place a few blocks away from my home. I write and perform *Smogman*, a sci-fi piece based on one of my first alteric selves, an activist superhero who fights against pollution in Mexico City. The third act includes a museum of "things past" with purified water, plants, and taxidermied extinct animals. These ideas will resurface in my work years later.

1974: I form my first collective, a group called Anarquía SA. We produce ritual happenings and bad atonal music and practice "ritual drugs and sex." Gurdjieff, Artaud, Nicanor Parra, and Carlos Castañeda are our masters and inspiration. I join Swami Pranavananda's ashram in Tepoztlán, Mexico.

1974–78: I study *letras*, philology, and linguistics at UNAM, the Universidad Nacional Autónoma de México, in Mexico City. The campus is an open laboratory of radical politics and student activism. We read about the Latin American literary "boom" and liberation movements and discover the French symbolists and the Beat poets. Everyday life feels like a Goddard movie.

I engage in a series of "involuntary performance art pieces" using the streets of Mexico City as a gallery without walls. I still don't have a name for what I do. My main accomplices are my cousin Eugenio and the Argentine poet Mari Carmen Copani. My conceptual godfather is Felipe Ehrenberg (bless his tattooed heart), and my guru is Alejandro Jodorowsky.

1978: I receive a scholarship to study at the California Institute of the Arts. I cross the US-Mexico border in search of artistic fresh air and my lost Chicano family. I suddenly become . . . brown, a "wetback," a "beaner," a "greaser." I do not know the implications of these words. I begin my process of Chicano-ization with the unsolicited help of the Los Angeles police.

1978: I walk from Tijuana to Cal Arts in two and a half days, my head covered with gauze. I wear my father's suit and carry a briefcase containing my passport, talismans, and a diary.

1979–82: At Cal Arts, conceptualists Douglas Huebler and Jonathan Borofsky take me under their wing. My best friend is painter Ashley Bickerton. I explore the LA performance art scene. I am lucky. I hook up with the

High Performance magazine crowd, meeting Linda Burnham, Steve Durland, Paul McCarthy, Chris Burden, Bob & Bob, Rachel Rosenthal, and Asco.

1979: *The Loneliness of the Immigrant, Part I.* I decide to spend twenty-four hours in a public elevator wrapped in batik fabric and rope, a metaphor for a painful birth in a new country, a new identity as "the Chicano," and a new language, intercultural performance. It's my first performance "documented" by the art world.

1979: *The Loneliness of the Immigrant, Part II.* I spend twelve hours lying on the downtown LA streets as a Mexican homeless person. Despite the fact that I am wrapped in a serape and surrounded by candles, most people ignore me. I discover that as a Mexican (and a "homeless" person), I am literally invisible to the Anglo Californian population. Performance is my strategy for becoming visible.

I am trying to find my place and voice in a new country. One evening, I bring my audience to the edge of Interstate 5 and scream at the cars to "stop and save me from cultural shipwreck." When I am first busted by the California police for "looking suspicious"—in other words, for being Mexican—my response is to make a performance in which I burn a photo of my mother while screaming at the top of my lungs, "Madre, hazme regresar a la placenta!" (Mother, bring me back to the womb).

1979: *Spanglish Poetry Reading in a Public Bathroom.* For a whole day, I sit on a toilet and read epic poetry aloud, describing my journey to the United States. My audience is composed strictly of people who want to piss, shit, or wash their hands. Through these types of experiments, I become interested in the notion of performing for "involuntary audiences."

1980: *Mexiphobia: Post-revolutionary Situations.* I begin to experiment with fear of the Mexican other. My friends and I start showing up at various public places dressed as "typical drug dealers," caricatured "illegal aliens," and stylized "banditos," yet we behave in ways that contradict the stereotypes. Once we show up at a restaurant dressed as "typical Latino terrorists." The place empties out within five minutes of our arrival. I wonder what would happen if I were to re-create this performance today.

1980: At Cal Arts, choreographer Sara-Jo Berman and I form an interdisciplinary arts troupe named Poyesis Genetica (from the Spanish word *pollo*, a derogatory term for a migrant worker, and the Greek *genesis*). The members are newly arrived immigrant students from Latin America, Europe, the

Middle East, and Canada, bound by a shared sense of cultural displacement. Our objective is "to develop syncretic languages capable of articulating our condition of cultural outsiders and aesthetic freaks" (Poyesis Genetica flyer). Poyesis becomes a revolving door for rebel students.

We develop an artistic strategy of fusing various cultural traditions utilizing performance as a syntactic thread. We mix indigenous rituals from various parts of the world (or rather our romanticized perception of them) with installation and video art, combining sexual and political imagery, personal pathos, and pop culture. We perform in art spaces and theaters as well as in the street, and we often use live animals on stage. We also experiment with "altered states of consciousness" induced by fasting, alcohol, or lack of sleep. Though extremely important in our development as artists, these performances are more interesting to us than to our poor audiences.

1982: I graduate from Cal Arts and spend six months touring Europe with Sara-Jo and a few Poyesis members. It's our first tour ever. We begin performing in small theaters and artist's lofts and end up working the streets. I lose my virginity as a performance artist. At the end of the tour, I am hypoglycemic and hungry and weigh just sixty kilos. I write a book titled "The Misadventures of Mr. Misterio and Salome." The manuscript gets lost. Only a few performance poems survive.

The first Mexican financial crack occurs and our family's savings evaporate. My father advises me not to return to Mexico. "Stay in Southern California and wait for better times," he says. The wait turns out to be the rest of my life. I am still waiting . . .

1983: Poyesis Genetica relocates to the Tijuana–San Diego border region, where we find an ideal terrain to explore intercultural relations and become more overtly political. Sara-Jo and I reconstitute the troupe with local artists. We perform on both sides of the border as political praxis, making an average of $50 per performance, enough to buy props, tacos, and an occasional drink.

One day I receive a phone call in San Diego: my beloved cousin Alfonso, who grew up with me, has been murdered in Mexico City, stabbed twenty-two times. The murderer, a bodyguard of pop celebrity Enrique Guzmán, spends only one month in jail.

1983: I run the cultural section of *La Prensa San Diego*. I also work as a correspondent for *La Opinión* and *High Performance* magazine. Journalist

117

Marco Vinicio González and I begin to publish a border arts magazine, *La Línea Quebrada/The Broken Line,* connected to its Mexico City twin publication *La Regla Rota/The Broken Rule.*

1984–90: With visual, performance, and conceptual artists, we form BAW/ TAF, or Border Arts Workshop, a binational arts collective involving Chicano, Mexican, and Anglo artists. Our objective is to explore US-Mexico relations and border issues using performance, installation art, video, and experimental poetry. We proclaim the border region "a laboratory for social and aesthetic experimentation" and propose "the artist as a social thinker and binational diplomat." Similar activist groups are forming in other parts of the country, including the Guerrilla Girls, Group Material, ACT UP, and the Los Angeles Poverty Department. Performance, political activism, and community concerns are completely intertwined in the spirit of the times.

1985: BAW/TAF's strictly artistic activities help protect our backs and legitimize our more activist work. In addition to art shows, publications, radio programs, and town meetings, we organize performance events right on the borderline, where the US meets Mexico in the Pacific, literally performing for audiences in both countries. When the border patrol gets too close, we cross to the Mexican side. During certain performances, we invite our audiences to cross "illegally" to the other side. We exchange food and art "illegally," caress and kiss "illegally" across the border fence, and confront the border patrol in character. We are protected by the presence of journalist friends and video cameras. The political implications of the site and the symbolic weight of these actions garner immediate attention from the international media. These are the origins of the border arts movement.

1985: I begin *The Velvet Hall of Fame,* a long-term collaboration with painters of traditional velvet tourist art from Tijuana who reinterpret my performance characters. The process is very matter-of-fact; the more I pay, the better the painting is, period. They don't care about reviews or openings, but they get a kick out of my madness. My "conceptual velvet art" project will last for a decade, during which time I get to exhibit these paintings at the Walker Art Center, the Detroit Institute of Arts, the Corcoran Gallery of Art, and MACBA (Barcelona). When I see these paintings hanging within walking distance of a Gauguin or a David Salle, I somehow feel historically vindicated. I love to cross the border between "high" and "low" art.

1985: Within twenty-four hours, two major earthquakes destroy entire sections of Mexico City, killing more than 100,000 people. Poet Ruben Medina and I return immediately to DF. Most artists and intellectuals participate in the rescue efforts. My nephews, neighbors, and I form a humble brigade. We carry corpses from a police station to the morgue. The city will never be the same. A powerful civic society and a new culture emerge out of the debris. Superbarrio, Rock en Español, and the *nuevo periodismo* and radical cartoon movement are born. Felipe Ehrenberg declares the reconstruction of the barrio of Tepito his ultimate art project.

1986: I become interested in the interface between performance and photography. I work with artist/theorist Emily Hicks on a series of performances titled *Documented/Undocumented*, playing on the double meaning of the terms vis-à-vis immigration status and as an art piece. The performances are staged for the camera and documented in photojournalistic style. My interest in what I term "photo-performance" will continue until the present day.

1987: My collaborators and I stage several "performance pilgrimages" in different border cities. In *Tijuana-Niagara*, Emily and I spend a month working along the US-Canadian border, between Ontario and New York state, using New York's Art Park as a base of operations. We travel in a mobile temple created from pseudo-indigenous souvenirs and religious kitsch purchased in Tijuana and Niagara Falls. We carry out fifteen "performance actions," including the auctioning of border art, spiritual consultation "for tourists," begging for money in costume, photo sessions with "authentic border shamans and witches," and broadcasting bilingual poetry with a huge megaphone from one shore of the Niagara River to the other.

That same year, several Tijuana performance artists and I gather at the municipal cemetery of Tijuana and attempt to cross the US-Mexico border checkpoint in costume. From 1987 to 1990, I attempt several times to cross the border in costume. I am rejected three times, and those rejected personas never find their way into my performances.

1988: Emily and I stage our "performance wedding" right on the Tijuana–San Diego borderline, with poets and musicians performing on both sides, and family and friends crossing "illegally" into each other's countries during the ceremony. The media label the event "a masterpiece of symbolic politics." Emily is seven months pregnant.

My only son Guillermo Emiliano is born in San Diego. A few months later, my beloved father dies in Mexico City. Both events accelerate my process of Chicano-ization. I can no longer afford to think that one day I will return to Mexico (my place on the Chicano Olympus will continue to be contested by Chicano essentialists until the mid-1990s). I wear my father's clothes for one year. I inherit my family's oldest house, which soon becomes "Chicano Central" in Mexico City, a gathering place and party den for *chilango* and Chicano artists and writers.

1988: The performance monologue movement is officially born. Many performance artists, including Tim Miller, Karen Finley, Eric Bogosian, Spalding Gray, and me, feel that performance has become so artificial and technically complex that we need to go back to basics and recapture the power of the spoken word. The result is a low-tech, language-based type of performance that literally fits in a suitcase. This art movement provides us with incredible geographic mobility (we can travel with our entire production inside of a suitcase) as well as disciplinary mobility (we can present our work in the contexts of art, theater, literature, activism, radio, and film). The "performance field" expands to include spoken word poets, radical theorists, and weird stand-up comedians. We all share an interest in the transformative power of the live word and a desire to explore the flaming intersection of personal identity and social issues.

1988–89: My main contribution to the performance monologue movement is *Border Brujo*, a spoken word monologue dealing with border identity. The script is written in English, Spanish, Spanglish, gringoñol, and various made-up "robo-languages." My portable altar, which functions as set design, as well as my handmade costumes are composed of "pseudo-ethnic" objects, tourist tchotchkes, and cheap religious souvenirs.

With *Border Brujo* I become a migrant performance artist, spending two years on the road, going from city to city, from country to country and back, reproducing the migratory patterns of the Mexican diaspora. As I travel, I incorporate new texts, props, and costumes into the piece. The project is documented in two videos by filmmaker Isaac Artenstein. The Brujo and I end up back at the US-Mexico border in late 1989, where I bury his costume and props and stage his performance funeral. I receive both a New York "Bessie Award" and the Prix de la Parole from the Theater Festival of the Americas in Montreal. I am suddenly propelled into the center of the art world, and my personal life becomes extremely complicated.

1989: A group of artists, including Linda Burnham, Tim Miller, Steve Durland, Susanna Dakin, and me, jumpstart Highways Performance Space in Santa Monica. I begin ongoing collaborations with Tim Miller, Elia Arce, Keith Antar Mason, and Rubén Martínez. The LA art scene is imbued with a utopian spirit of collaboration and polyamorous hedonism.

Glasnost and perestroika spread like wildfire throughout the Soviet bloc. The right perceives this phenomenon as the defeat of socialism. I want to see this for myself. I travel to Russia with a binational human rights commission, presenting my performance art as a form of radical diplomacy.

1990: The United States experiences yet another seasonal "Latino boom," and border art becomes fashionable. The original Border Arts Workshop is invited to the Venice Biennale; after this event, we feel it's time to dismantle the group to avoid becoming a parody of ourselves, "the Grateful Dead of border art." But, as so often happens, the only Anglo male in the group appropriates the project, copyrighting the name and turning it into an art maquiladora.

It's time for me to search for a new place from which to speak. I begin a series of collaborations with writer and artist Coco Fusco, the first a multimedia installation titled *Norte/Sur*. Nola Mariano becomes my long-term manager, art bodyguard, and macabre accomplice.

1991: I move to New York to live with Coco and work on the first part of my trilogy, *The Re-discovery of America by the Warrior for Gringostroika*, at the Brooklyn Academy of Music's Next Wave Festival. One day, during rehearsal, I get the magical phone call announcing that I am a "MacArthur genius." Two months later, my ex-wife sues me, taking half of my fellowship in court, and some of the original members of BAW/TAF suggest that I split the other half among the group. I ask myself: "Is this my true birth ritual into the American art world?"

1992: Artists such as Fred Wilson, Adrian Piper, James Luna, and Jimmy Durham begin to interrogate the way museums represent cultural otherness and start a dialogue with radical anthropologists.

I begin to experiment with the colonial format of the "living diorama." My collaborators and I create interactive "living museums" that parody various colonial practices of representation, including the ethnographic tableau vivant, the Indian trading post, the border curio shop, the porn window display, and their contemporary equivalents. These performance/

installations function both as a bizarre set design for a contemporary enactment of "cultural pathologies" and as a ceremonial space for people to reflect upon their attitudes toward other cultures.

1992–93: During the heated debates surrounding the Columbus Quincentenary, Coco Fusco and I decide to remind the US and Europe of "the other history of intercultural performance," the sinister human exhibits and pseudo-ethnographic spectacles that were so popular in Europe from the seventeenth century until the early twentieth century. At the turn of the century in the United States, they transformed into more vulgar exhibits like the dime museum and the freak show.

In *The Guatinaui World Tour*, Coco and I live for three-day periods inside a gilded cage as "undiscovered Amerindians" from the fictional island of Guatinau ("what now") in the Gulf of Mexico. I am dressed as an Aztec wrestler from Las Vegas and Coco as a *taina* straight out of Gilligan's Island. We are hand-fed by fake museum docents and taken to public bathrooms on leashes. Taxonomic plates describing our costumes and physical characteristics are placed next to the cage. We tour the United States, Europe, Australia, and Argentina. Sadly, over 40 percent of our audiences believe the exhibit is real, yet they do nothing about it. The most drastic audience response is from an Argentine military man who throws acid on me during the performance in Buenos Aires. The tour is chronicled in the film *The Couple in the Cage*.

1992–93: Coco and I tour *New World (B)order*, a sci-fi piece based on the following metafiction: border culture and hybrid identities become official culture as Anglo Americans become a minority culture. We begin to practice "reverse segregation" of our audiences as they enter the art space, with members of "minorities," immigrants, and bilingual audience members entering the space first. The idea is to assume a fictional center and force monolingual/monocultural Americans to feel like foreigners and minorities in their own country, even if only for an hour or two. Coco leaves the project in the middle of the tour and Roberto Sifuentes replaces her. To continue the tour, we are forced to reconstitute the entire performance in less than a week. It somehow works. To this day, Roberto remains my main collaborator.

1993: Roberto and I become interested in Spanglish pirate radio. We stage our first pirate radio project in a performance festival in Hull, England. With a low-tech radio transmitter, we broadcast from the top of a ten-story building. Local radio pirates explain to us that it will take twenty minutes for the police to locate the source of our transmission and get to the site. As the police are circling the building, Roberto and I escape through the back door.

1993: The backlash era begins as multiculturalism gets a bad rap. I move back to LA and reconnect with the Highways performance scene. The LA earthquake transforms the city into a compassionate place. We see racial, social, and generational borders break down in front of our eyes as people help each other and speak with each other as never before. Sadly, this only lasts for a few months.

1993: I start a long-term collaboration with Native American artist James Luna. In *The Shame-man Meets El Mexican't at the Smithsonian Hotel and Country Club*, Luna and I share a diorama space at the Smithsonian's Museum of Natural History. I sit on a toilet dressed as a mariachi in a straightjacket with a sign around my neck announcing, "There used to be a Mexican inside this body." I unsuccessfully attempt to get rid of my straight-jacket while James paces back and forth, changing identities. At times he is an "Indian shoe-shiner," at other moments he becomes a "diabetic Indian" shooting insulin directly into his stomach. He then transforms into a janitor of color (like most janitors in US museums) and vacuums the diorama floor. Hundreds of visitors gather in front of us. They are sad and perplexed. Next to us, the "real" Indian dioramas speak of a mute world outside of history and social crises. Next to us, they appear much less "authentic."

While rehearsing the second part of our project, James lights up some sage. The security guards phone the DC police and we get busted in the dressing room for "smoking pot." Furious with such a ludicrous claim, curator Aleta Ringlero calls museum administration to demand an apology on our behalf. For James and me, such a situation is just a good anecdote. As James put it, "simply one more day in the life of an Indian and a Chicano." We reenact the bust in a series of photos.

1994: NAFTA comes into effect. The Zapatista insurrection takes the world by surprise. Organized crime makes its home in Mexico. To exorcise my own fear of losing the streets of Mexico City to the new culture of fear, I engage in a series of street performances in downtown Mexico City.

Grandma Carmen, the moral center of my family, dies in our Mexico City home. My relatives and I surround Grandma's bed as her soul tenderly leaves her body.

1994: Roberto Sifuentes and I crucify ourselves for three hours on sixteen-foot crosses at Rodeo Beach, in front of San Francisco's Golden Gate Bridge. The piece is designed to protest the xenophobic immigration politics of California governor Pete Wilson. Inspired by the biblical myth of Dimas and Gestas, the two petty thieves crucified next to Jesus, Roberto and I decide to dress as "the two contemporary public enemies of California." I am the "undocumented bandito" (mariachi) crucified by the Immigration and Naturalization Service, and Roberto is the generic "gang member" crucified by the Los Angeles Police Department. Using a flyer, we ask our audience "to free us from our martyrdom as a gesture of political commitment," but we miscalculate. Paralyzed by the melancholy of the image, it takes audience members over three hours to figure out how to get us down without a ladder. By then, my right shoulder has become dislocated and Roberto has passed out. The media pick up photographs of the Cruci-Fiction Project and the piece becomes international news.

1994: Graywolf Press (St. Paul, MN) publishes my first book, *Warrior for Gringostroika*, a collection of writings and photographs from 1979 to 1992. It's my "border art period." With this book, my work slowly begins to be embraced by academia.

1994: Roberto and I create the interactive pirate television project Naftaz-tec TV in collaboration with Adriene Jenik and Branda Miller (from the iEAR Studio at Rensselaer Polytechnic). This simulacrum of a pirate TV intervention is broadcast to hundreds of cable television stations across the country, as well as over computer networks via early broadband technology. The content is a strange blend of radical politics, autobiographical material, and parody of traditional TV formats gone bananas. We demonstrate a "Chicano virtual reality machine" that can turn collective and personal memories into video footage. The project is rebroadcast nationally in 1995 and becomes a cult hit. An edited version circulates in film and video festivals. I cannot help but wonder, what does it mean for a pirate TV intervention to be rebroadcast and embraced by the art world? Isn't this a contradiction in terms?

1994: Colombian ballerina-turned-radical-performance-artist Michele Ceballos joins the troupe.

1994–present: My colleagues and I begin to take our personas out of the museum or theater and into the streets, often crashing politically charged sites in costume. Our idea is as follows: if our personae survive the tough involuntary audiences of the street, they will definitely survive the harshness of the art world. Though these types of interventions are central to our performance praxis, they often go unnoticed by critics and art historians, who concentrate almost exclusively on work that takes place within the confines of the art world. This is why I have written extensively about these adventures in my books.

1994–96: Roberto and I tour *Temple of Confessions*, a performance/installation combining the format of the ethnographic diorama with that of the religious dioramas found in colonial Mexican churches. For three-day periods, we exhibit ourselves inside Plexiglas boxes as "end-of-the-century saints." Those visitors who wish to "confess" their intercultural fears and desires to us have three options: they can either confess into microphones placed on kneelers in front of the boxes (their voices are recorded and altered in post-production to ensure their anonymity), or, if they are shy, they can write their confessions on cards and deposit them in an urn. If they are extremely shy, they can call an 800 number.

The "confessions" are quite emotional and intimate. They range from confessions of extreme violence and racism toward Mexicans and other people of color to expressions of incommensurable tenderness and solidarity with us, or with our perceived cause. Some are filled with guilt or fear—fear of cultural/political/sexual invasion, violence, rape, or disease. Other confessions are fantasies about escaping one's identity: Anglos wanting to be Mexican or Indian or vice versa, self-hating Latinos wanting to be Anglo or simply "blond." There are also many descriptions (both real and fictitious, but equally revealing) of intercultural sexual encounters.

By the end of the third day, we leave the Plexiglas boxes and are replaced by human-size wax effigies. The *Temple of Confessions* remains as an installation piece for eight weeks, and written and phone confessions continue to be accepted. The project is documented in a Public Broadcasting Service documentary, a radio documentary for National Public Radio, and a book by the same title (powerHouse Books, Brooklyn, NY). The last performance of the tour takes place at the Corcoran Gallery of Art in Washington, DC.

1995: I move to San Francisco and begin the long-term project of tattooing my torso and arms. Nola Mariano and I found La Pocha Nostra. The objective is to create a loose interdisciplinary association of rebel artists interested in collaboration. Inspired by Zapatismo, our collaborative model of concentric and overlapping circles functions both as an act of civic diplomacy and as a means to create "ephemeral communities" of like-minded artists. We are more of a conceptual laboratory than a company, a strategic gathering of politicized artists thinking together, exchanging ideas and aspirations.

We begin a fruitful binational exchange project with Mexican performance artists titled *Terreno Peligroso/Danger Zone*. It's a good time for Mexican and Chicano artists to collaborate. We create a Free Art Agreement, an ongoing exchange of ideas and artwork, and begin to collaborate across the border.

1995: I begin my long-term association with the National Public Radio program *All Things Considered*. I write and record a monthly commentary from the position of a performance artist. I suddenly have a national voice in a society in which the mainstream media cover artists as celebrities, human-interest stories, or social monsters, but rarely as intellectuals.

1995–97: Roberto and I tour *Borderama*, a proscenium piece that subverts and parodies pop cultural formats such as the talk show, the self-realization seminar, the hypnotist's lounge act, the anthropologist's lecture, and the ethnic fashion show. In the press release, we invite the audience to "come to the show in costume, dressed as your favorite cultural other, and express those interracial fantasies we all have inside of us." We invite "special guests" from the local communities to participate in the show, bringing in street performers, drag queens, Mexican wrestlers, and small-town eccentrics. At the end of the piece, Roberto and I auction ourselves as "sexy, AIDS-free Third World performance artists."

1996: Like many Chicano artists at the time, Roberto and I visit the Zapatista area of southern Mexico. We travel through various military checkpoints posing as "eco-tourists."

1996: City Lights (San Francisco) publishes my next book, *The New World Border*, a collection of writings and photos from 1992 to 1995. In this book, perhaps my most experimental, I develop my thesis of hybridity and my critique of global culture. The whole book reads like a hypertextual performance script. It receives the American Book Award. Luis Valdez forgives my aesthetic sins. That same year, I begin a three-year collaboration with Nuyorrican maestro Miguel Algarín.

1996: I become interested in the politics of new technologies. I write extensively about "racism in the net" and develop the concept of "poetic and imaginary (or rather useless) technologies," meaning technologies with strictly aesthetic or ritual purposes. My colleagues and I begin to construct "Chicano cyborgs" with lowrider prosthetics and braces. The basic idea is: if we don't have access to this technology, we have to imagine it.

1997: The art world begins to talk about "relational aesthetics." Together with radical choreographer Sara Shelton Mann from the dance troupe Contraband, Roberto and I jump-start a three-year project titled *El Mexterminator*. The idea is to use the internet as a tool of "reverse anthropology" to research America's psyche regarding Anglo/Latino relations, then to develop an ever-evolving repertoire of performance personae based on this research. For this purpose, we develop "confessional" websites asking individuals to suggest how we should dress as Mexicans and Chicanos and what kind of performance actions and social rituals we should engage in.

The internet confessions are much more explicit than those gathered during live performances such as *Temple of Confessions*. Scholars help us select the most striking and representative confessions so we can use them as source material for performance. As performance artists, we embody this information and reinterpret it for a live audience, thus refracting fetishized constructs of identity through the spectacle of our artificially constructed identities on display. A gorgeous photo-portfolio by Mexican photographer Eugenio Castro is made out of the Mexterminator personae. At least 500 of these images haven't yet been printed or published.

1997–present: Chicana writer Sandra Cisneros invites the Latino MacArthur Fellows to form the "MacArturos" or the "MacCabrones." Part ombudsmen and part cultural instigators, the group meets once a year, each time in a different city with a sizeable Latino community in turmoil. These gatherings are designed as informal think tanks and as a means to insert a Latino perspective into current national debates. We strategically use our name to empower local communities, generate public dialogue, and confront local authorities. Our presence in the host city involves town meetings, panels, performances, and public debates. Besides Sandra and me, participants include activists Baldemar Velásquez, Maria Varela, and Joaquin Avila; writers Luis Alfaro, Ruth Bejar, and Alma Guillerprieto; radio entrepreneur Hugo Morales; and others.

1998: I team up with producer Michael Milenski and theater director David Schweizer to create a Chicano-ized version of *The Indian Queen*, a seventeenth-century opera by composer Henry Purcell and poet John Dryden. In collaboration with Elaine Katzenberger, I rewrite the original script in Spanglish. In our version, the Indian Queen is a fallen Hollywood starlet and her throne is a lowrider car shaped as a red stiletto.

1998: Enrique Chagoya, Felicia Rice, and I publish a book/art piece, *Codex Espangliensis*, first as a limited edition of fifty books printed in amate paper for collectors (Moving Parts Press, Santa Cruz, CA), and then in paperback form (City Lights). The Codex describes with performance texts and "post-Columbian" comic book imagery the history of NAFTA, from the conquest of Mexico to the present.

1998: La Pocha tours *Borderscape 2000*. Described by critics as a "high-tech Aztec Spanglish lounge operetta," the performance critiques the corporate appropration of multiculturalism, attempting to reintroduce the political discourse absent since the backlash against multiculturalism began, when audiences grew tired of "political" art. One image lingers in my mind: a stylized gang member clubbing a chicken to the tune of "Hotel California." We cross the PC border. The performance is heavily criticized by theorists for contributing to the fetishization of extreme Latino imagery. It's clear to La Pocha that we have reached a dead end and that we need to open a new door.

1998: I become obsessed with trying to understand X-treme pop culture. What ten years ago was considered fringe "subculture" is now mere pop. The insatiable mass of the so-called "mainstream" has finally devoured all "margins," and the more dangerous, thorny, and exotic these margins become, the better. In fact, sensu stricto, we can say that there are no margins left. "Alternative" thought, fringe "subcultures," and so-called "radical" behavior, as we knew them, have actually become the mainstream. Stylized racism and sexism are now daily spectacle. This poses all kinds of questions for us. If we choose to mimic or parody the strategies of the mainstream bizarre in order to develop new audiences and explore the zeitgeist of our times, what certainty do we have that our high-definition reflection won't devour us from inside out and turn us into the very stylized freaks we are attempting to deconstruct or parody? And if we are interested in performing for nonspecialized audiences, what certainty do we have that these audiences won't misinterpret our "radical" actions as merely spectacles of stylized radicalism? We risk these possible misinterpretations by embodying these personae in live performance and find that each context delivers different reactions, which keeps us developing new strategies to reach these complex audiences.

1998–89: We gradually begin to surrender our will to the audience, allowing them to shape the content of our work by manipulating us in tableaux and joining us in performing composite identities dictated by the fears and desires of museum visitors. The *Mexterminator* project becomes even more participatory, encouraging audience members to interact with us in various modes. They can touch us, smell us, hand-feed us. They can spray-paint our bodies, point fake weapons at us, braid our hair, change our makeup, or put different wigs and headdresses on us, using the performers as life-size paper dolls. They put dog leashes on us, engaging in consensual power games. Some people decide to get rough while holding the leash, especially the most conservative-looking ones. Wherever we go, we invite local artists, curators, intellectuals, or activists to stage their own dioramas within the larger piece.

1999: I marry gorgeous Colombian curator and writer Carolina Ponce de León. Our loft in San Francisco becomes an informal roadside museum, salon, and hostel for Mexican, Colombian, US, and European artists who pass through. A local TV station does a reportage on the house, calling it "the Smithsonian of the barrio."

1999: Filmmaker Gustavo Vazquez and I create *The Great Mojado Invasion*, a mock documentary that presents an ironic twenty-first-century reversal of US-Mexican relations, as "dastardly mustachioed bandits" reconquer the United States and impose their own language and culture upon Anglo Americans.

1999: There is major internal turmoil in the group. Roberto Sifuentes and Sara Shelton Mann step out for personal reasons, while Juan Ybarra and Michele Ceballos join on a more permanent basis. All projects must be reconfigured overnight.

1999–2002: The new Pocha Nostra troupe tours *The Living Museum of Fetishized Identities* internationally. The next step in our performance research is to develop large-scale interactive performance/installations that function as "intelligent raves and art expos of Western apocalypse." Every "living museum" is site-specific and involves a different group of local artists. Live music, video and computer projections, cinematic lighting, taxidermied animals, and twisted ethnographic motifs help enhance our high-tech "robo-baroque aesthetic." In these intoxicating environments, we exhibit ourselves on platforms as intricately decorated "ethno-cyborgs" and "artificial savages" for three to five hours a day. The structure is open and noncoercive, allowing the audience to walk around the dioramas designing their own journey. They can stay for as long as they wish, come in and out of the space, or return later, fully participating in our performance games or keeping to the sidelines as voyeurs.

In the first hour, the experience is typically voyeuristic. The "ethno-cyborgs" create slow-motion tableaux vivants that sample and combine radical political imagery, religious iconography, extreme pop culture, fashion, and theatricalized sexuality. The audience members are confronted with a stylized anthropomorphization of their own postcolonial hallucinations, a kind of cross-cultural poltergeist in which the space between self and other, "us and them," fear and desire, becomes blurry and unspecific. As the evening evolves, the experience becomes increasingly participatory. We include a diorama station where audience members can choose a "temporary ethnic identity" and become "their favorite cultural other," using makeup and costumes provided by us; after this, they are encouraged to integrate themselves into our living dioramas. Both audience members and performers make political, ethical, and aesthetic decisions on the spot. In this sense, the performance becomes an exercise in radical democracy. In the last hour, we step out of the dioramas and cede total control to the audience, as the postcolonial demons dance all around us.

2000: While touring in Brazil, I catch a mysterious parasite and experience a total "liver crash." My recovery takes eight months. The doctors forbid me to perform and rehearse. My mother and Carolina take care of me. During this time I write *Califas 2000* and *Brownout*, two of my darkest and most personal performance scripts ever. Also during my recovery, my new book comes out. *Dangerous Border Crossers: The Artist Talks Back* (Routledge) is a collection of writings and photos from 1997 to 2000.

2001: I begin touring my solo performance *Brownout*, using Spanglish, acid Chicano humor, and hybrid literary genres as subversive strategies. The script intertwines two discourses. One is a poetic/political account of the times. A parallel discourse recounts my inner hell during the recovery from my liver crash. I often broadcast live from the theater to a local radio station.

Gustavo and I re-edit *The Great Mojado Invasion* with newfound footage.

2001: The United States experiences on its own soil its worst terrorist attack ever. The neocons in power rapidly transform the country into a closed society ruled by paranoid nationalism and fear. An unprecedented era of censorship for artists and intellectuals begins. This climate forces La Pocha to spend more than half of the year outside the country, becoming Chicano expatriates abroad.

We begin to compare notes with Arab and Persian artists based in the US and the UK regarding the demonization of the brown body.

2002: In response to the challenges of 9/11, we create "re:group," a San Francisco–based performance laboratory dedicated "to re-conquer[ing] the artistic freedoms being taken away by the Bush administration." The group lasts for two years. A documentary of re:group is commissioned by PBS and later on censored by them. Their version of re:group is very tame. With the original footage, we edit our own version.

I publish my first book entirely in Spanish, titled *El Mexterminator: Antropología inversa de un performancero postmexicano* (Editorial Océano, Mexico City).

2002–4: La Pocha begins to incorporate workshops as part of every project we tour. It's like a nomadic performance workshop. We resume the exploration of ceding our will to the audience, begun in the *Mexterminator* project, with a performance titled *Ethno-techno* or *Ex-Centris* in which we completely reverse the gaze and step out of our dioramas. We create tableaux vivants with audience members, manipulating their body positions and decorating them with costumes and props. We then invite them to create their own imagery. We call this experiment "performance karaoke." It's our response to the extreme culture of mindless audience participation and role playing created by talk shows and reality TV.

2003: La Pocha performs *Ex-Centris* at the Tate Modern, a humongous coup for us brokered by performance curator Lois Keidan. A few months later, the troupe is confronted with harsh reality as Juan Ybarra steps out due to serious health issues and Michele Ceballos's father is kidnapped in Colombia. Roberto Sifuentes returns, Violeta Luna becomes a full-time collaborator, and Emiko R. Lewis joins in. All of our upcoming presenters are perplexed by the abrupt changes. It takes half a year for La Pocha to settle into the dynamics of the new troupe.

2004: I become interested in the search for a radical spirituality that can emerge from living against the backdrop of war and censorship. Emiko and I begin workshopping *Mapa/Corpo* as a response to the invasion of Iraq.

The performance/installation is a poetic, interactive ritual that explores neocolonization/decolonization through "political acupuncture" and the reenactment of the post-9/11 "body politic." It's clearly an antiwar performance and, for the first two years, we are only able to present it in Latin America, Europe, and Canada. Only after mid-2005 do US presenters dare to book it.

Michele Ceballos's passport gets confiscated as we are trying to catch a plane to Argentina for a project titled *Tucumán-Chicano*. It will take four years for Michele to recover it.

2004–present: I begin a long-term project with Spanish curator Orlando Britto Jinorio, a series of "photo-performance" portfolios created specifically for the camera. The initial portfolios are shot in Mexico City, San Francisco, Madrid, and the Canary Islands. It is the first time in my life that I have made art objects strictly for the gallery. My hope is that they function as a prosthetic extension of my live performances.

2005: As I approach my fiftieth birthday, my then eighty-three-year-old mother and I collaborate in a performance ritual "to prepare me for the second part of my life." She tenderly washes my body in an old-fashioned bathtub, then dries me with a towel and dresses me up with my father's clothes. The site is the garden of her Mexico City home. The audience is composed of forty relatives and neighbors who were alive and around during my earliest days of life, including my nanny and my first friends ever. The next morning my family takes me to the airport and sends me to the next stop in my tour. A film of the ritual bath by filmmaker Gustavo Vazquez is in the works.

2005: I publish *Ethno-Techno: Writings on Performance, Activism, and Pedagogy* (Routledge), a collection of writings from 2000 to 2005. Despite the fact that it may be my best book to date, the book is priced so high that it does not receive the distribution I expect. My literary heart is broken.

2005: We begin to conduct a yearly Pocha Nostra summer school of radical performance art in the state of Oaxaca in Mexico. Artists come from all over the world to collaborate with indigenous Oaxacans working in experimental art forms. We offer two seven-day intensive workshops on "the human body as a site for creation, reinvention, memory and activism." The first workshop is for young artists and the second for established artists, culminating in a public performance at MACO (Museum of Contemporary

Art of Oaxaca). The Pocha summer school becomes an amazing artistic and anthropological experiment in how artists from three generations and many countries, from every imaginable artistic, ethnic, and subcultural background, begin to find common ground. Performance becomes the connective tissue and lingua franca for our temporary "glocal" (local/ international) community of rebel artists.

2005–2007: Violeta Luna, Roberto Sifuentes, Gabriela Salgado, and I workshop and tour *Mapa/Corpo 2: Interactive Rituals for the New Millennium*. Violeta's nude body lies on a surgical table covered by the flag of the United Nations. Above the body, an acupuncturist dressed in a lab coat prepares for surgery, laying out forty needles. A small flag is attached to the tip of each needle, each representing a nation of the "coalition forces." As I deliver a multilingual poem dressed as my *chamán travesti* persona, the acupuncturist peels the UN flag from Violeta's body, working from the feet up, exposing her. The acupuncturist methodically inserts the forty needles into the body/ map, leaving the audience to ponder the after-image of a "colonized" female body/world. I ask the audience to "decolonize the Mapa/Corpo" by carefully removing the flags with the assistance of the acupuncturist. One by one, each flag is lifted, completing the ritual. Parallel to this, at a second station, a curator ritually shaves and washes the body of Sifuentes as if preparing it for burial, representing the brown body of the "universal immigrant." As the ritualized washing ends, Roberto's exposed skin becomes a canvas for the audience members to write upon his body a "poetics of hope." Those who accept the invitation also create tableaux vivants with his body, bringing tenderness and humanity to an objectified image. Different versions of *Mapa/Corpo 2* are performed in fifteen different countries. Sometimes Violeta is replaced by Colombian performance artist María Estrada. The piece becomes our main contribution to the performance field since *El Mexterminator*.

2006: I premiere a new solo performance titled *El Mexorcist: America's Most Wanted Inner Demon*. Shifting between languages and performance personae, I reflect on the post-9/11 condition, the "war on terror," the new anti-immigration hysteria, and the impact of all three on our notions of identity, community, nationality, and activist politics. Americans of all ages and ethnicities are finally fed up with the war and with the Bush administration.

2006: *Bitácora del Cruce* is published by El Fondo de Cultura Económica (Mexico City). The book contains a selection of my border diaries and performance texts from 1970 up to the present. It starts in 1970 in Mexico City (in Spanish), and as I move north the text slowly incorporates more Spanglish. The last chapters are in English and "robo-esperanto." It is the first time a major Mexican publishing house has published a book of this multilingual nature. Sadly, after an exhaustive internal controversy within the institution, FCE decides not to distribute it outside of Mexico. Their claims are that the book does not represent the ethos of FCE, that it is "too weird" and has "too much Spanglish." Eventually a letter campaign by Pocha associates and sympathizers forces them to begin its international distribution.

2006: My Chihuahua "son" Babalu is born in Northern California. He will soon become a regular troublemaker on YouTube. His performance series is titled *The Chihuahua Diaries*.

2007: I complete the first part of my tattoo project: my torso and arms are all connected in a sort of total "skin mural." I work as "image consultant" and "performance adviser" for the campaign of Krissy Keefer, a San Francisco activist lesbian dancer who runs for Congress on the Green Party ticket. My job is to produce provocative photo-portfolios for the media and suggest performative strategies for her campaign. The Green Party campaign officers are weirded out by my suggestions.

2007: Because of the militarization of Oaxaca, the Museum of Contemporary Art in Tucson invites La Pocha summer school to temporarily relocate to Arizona. They provide us with a huge warehouse for the month of August, where we hold workshops for artists from eight different countries as well as indigenous Arizonians. We continue to nurture multinational communities of rebel artists that ignore the existence of borders.

2007–present: James Luna and I reconnect to begin working on *La Nostalgia*, last in the series *The Shame-man Meets El Mexican't*. The project researches the symbolic and iconographic dimensions of nostalgia in both the Native "reservation" and the Chicano "barrio" through a series of live performances and photo shoots. We launch it with two performances. First, we stage our own ritual deaths inside coffins in a piece titled *The Shame-man Meets El Mexican't at a Funeral Parlor*, and then we engage in a poetic dialogue while Luna cooks an Indian stew and I play roulette.

2007: Video Data Bank (Chicago) publishes *Border Art Clásicos*, a collection of my collaborative video art works from 1988 to the present. The "conceptual box" contains four DVDs with twelve video art pieces and an accompanying catalog with critical writings by Amelia Jones, Richard Schechner, Carol Becker, and others. The goal is to use this box as a teaching tool in multiple university departments.

2007–2008: We jump-start *El Corazón de la Mission*, a unique bus tour guiding the audience through history, vernacular anthropology, and social reality into the heart of the Mission District of San Francisco, a place that expends a lot of energy dreaming of a better future. The passengers on this performance tour ride the legendary "Mexican bus" and are invited to participate in a processional, as if they were characters on a parade float. They witness "the creative neighborhood" and the city as a bohemian theme park, using the windows of an immigrant bus as a vantage point from which to view the streets. Meanwhile, they eavesdrop on my mind as they listen to a prerecorded tour commentary and engage with Violeta Luna performing live. People on the street become involuntary performers on the stage of my 'hood and living metaphors of a border zone. This poetic journey across a mythical Mission District invokes the pantheon of collective gods and goddesses buried by globalization and urban hipsterism.

2007: La Pocha premieres *The New Barbarian Collection*, commissioned by Arnolfini on the two hundredth anniversary of the abolition of slavery in the United Kingdom. Working with an international troupe of fifteen performance artists and a fashion designer, we appropriate the format of "an X-treme fashion show." We engage the audience with a variety of fashion-inspired stylized performance personas stemming from problematic media representations of foreigners, immigrants, and social eccentrics as both enemies of the state and sexy pop-cultural rebels. The "show" explores the bizarre relationship between the post-9/11 culture of xenophobia and the rampant fetishization of otherness by global pop culture. It is about politicized human bodies far more than about clothing. In this politicized fashion show, new designer hybrid identities are put up for sale. The piece ends with the disturbing auction of Abu Ghraib–like imagery and couture.

2008: La Pocha premieres *Divino Corpo* at the New Moves International festival in Glasgow. As part of our ongoing Mapa/Corpo series, this new work continues to examine the brown body as a site for radical spirituality, memory, penance, activism, and corporeal reinvention. We pose as living saints and Madonnas of unpopular causes (border crossers, undocumented migrants, bohemians, the infirm, and the displaced invisible others). At one station, Roberto's body is covered with leeches. At another station Violeta is wrapped on a pole with black rope as if getting ready to be burned by the audience. At a third station, I construct "pagan saints" with audience members. In a sense, we create a performative temple where the sacred and the profane intertwine with racy contemporary issues. Our goal is to invite audience members to embrace a new form of radical faith—faith that the art process can serve as a personal and political force and that the human body can becomes a site of change against a backdrop of global despair and war.

2008: Gustavo Vazquez and I premiere *Homo Fronterizus*, a video project in two parts. *One-on-one* includes reinterpretations of some of my classic performance pieces as well as "homages" to other performance artists who have influenced my work (Roi Vaara, Marina Abramovic, Stelarc, Melquiades Herrera, and James Luna). In *Duelos*, we explore the unspoken tension between performance and video, asking: Who is the real author? The performance artist who creates the concept and offers his body/identity/map/arte-facto in sacrifice to the camera, or the video artist who filters it, frames it, and in doing so, inevitably re-creates it?

2008: *La Nostalgia Remix*: James Luna and I continue our exploration of the cultural and political implications of nostalgia, both on the Native American "res" and in the Chicano barrio. We deal with nostalgia as style, resistance, false identity, and reinvention, in a series of reenactments of our "best hits and outtakes for an imaginary bar." We also create a digital mural with photographer RJ Muna. We tour Alaska in November.

TO BE CONTINUED

Editor's Note: From *Aztlán: A Journal of Chicano Studies* 34, no. 2 (2009). The original essay was lightly edited for this collection.

Folklore, Lo Mexicano, and Proverbs

Américo Paredes

The definition of *lo mexicano* has preoccupied Mexican philosophers on both sides of the border. This almost indefinable essence, making a Mexican or a Mexican American what he is, has been described in a number of ways. Another concept that has been given varying definitions is *folklore*. I will not attempt to define lo mexicano this evening, but I will make a stab at identifying folklore. For our purposes folklore may be described as "the unofficial heritage of a people." Defined in this way, folklore becomes especially important to minority groups, especially to groups that speak a language different from that of the majority. In such cases the national culture is the "official" culture, expressed in the majority language, while the minority culture becomes a "folk" culture, expressing itself in its own language.

In other words, folklore is of particular importance to minority groups such as the Mexican Americans because their basic sense of identity is expressed in a language with an "unofficial" status, different from the one used by the official culture. We can say, then, that while in Mexico the Mexican may well seek lo mexicano in art, literature, philosophy, or history—as well as in folklore—the Mexican American would do well to seek his identity in his folklore. If the Mexican American will not do it, others will do it for him, as they have done in the past. North Americans have sought clues to the Mexican character (both north and south of the border) by studying the Mexican's folklore. Let me give you an example, from the pen of a man who is considered by some as one of our greatest folklorists, J. Frank Dobie.

In 1957 Mr. Dobie published a little article called "Br'er Rabbit Watches Out for Himself in Mexico." The article analyzed a folktale collected in Mexico about a rabbit who outwits a series of animals stronger than him, fixing things so that each animal is killed by a successively stronger one, while the rabbit profits from each encounter. "The tales people tell reveal the tellers," Mr. Dobie stated. And he went on to conclude that this tale showed how ruthlessly competitive Mexicans were. Their philosophy of life was expressed in the saying "No te dejes." Mr. Dobie, with the help of an American businessman living in Mexico City, described this philosophy as a desire to get ahead of everybody else without any regard for ethics or fair play. His American friend told about a Mexican friend of his who was sending his son to study in the United States. The Mexican friend had been raised by his own father according to the philosophy of "no te dejes." But then he had gone to college in the United States, where a professor told him on the first day of class, "You are here to acquire knowledge, but you must never forget the principle of fair play. . . . Success is something more than just getting ahead of everybody else." This had been a revelation to the Mexican friend. Now he wanted *his* son to go to school in the United States, "where the idea of fair play is in the air," instead of letting him be educated in Mexico, where his mind would be warped by the "no te dejes" philosophy.

One can easily see the truth of Mr. Dobie's analysis of the Mexican character. Compared to North Americans, we Mexicans are a ruthless, aggressive, and extremely pragmatic people. That is why the center of world industry and finance is in Mexico City. That is why North Americans have to go begging hat-in-hand to the Mexican government for economic aid; and why North American business and industry is run by Mexicans who own villas in Florida and work in office suites in New York City, from which vantage point they can make casual assessments of the North American character. Need we say more? Perhaps not, except to note—somewhat sadly—that this was written not by some right-wing reactionary but by the leading Texas liberal of his time, a man who is still one of the father figures for the white liberals of this state.

Obviously there is something lacking in Mr. Dobie's interpretation since it is contradicted rather than supported by data from other sources. This is not to say that his little story may not tell us a great deal about the way Mexicans think and feel. The feelings and attitudes expressed in folklore, however, are not always lying on the surface to be picked up by the most casual observer. Finding them may require not only patience and wisdom but some real knowledge of the people and their culture. Compounding the problem is the matter of texture or complexity in such genres as folk narrative. There is such a wealth of elements in a folktale (plot, characters, setting, diction, performing style) that the "message" may be hard to spot. It may even be argued that the whole intricate structure is meant to entertain rather than to instruct, so that looking for a "message" is beside the point.

Still, there are many folktales—especially stories about animals—in which a dominant idea or "message" is clearly expressed, usually in a short and terse form: for example, "No te dejes," or "Un bien con un mal se paga." Such phrases exist independently, as proverbs. *Refranes*, we would call them in bookish Spanish, but our people call them simply *dichos* sayings. Dichos are simple little things, if one compares them with the complexities of a folktale that may take a whole night in the telling. But they are not devoid of structure by any means, even if it takes just a single breath to utter them. Take, for example, the "true" proverb, as it is called by folklorists—a dicho that is always a complete statement, a sentence. It is also a complete little poem, using the same kinds of effects that are found in other poetry. One of the simplest poetic effects, and one of the oldest, is balanced structure—the balancing of the two parts of the dicho on either side of a center, like two weights on an old-fashioned type of scale, for example: "Arrieros somos / y el camino andamos." This is the same type of structure used in the Old Testament, in the Psalms: "The Lord is my shepherd; / I shall not want."

Contrast may be added to balanced structure, and the effect is even more pleasing to one's sense of form. Notice how in the following dichos two words are contrasted against each other: "*Mucho* ruido / y *pocas* nueces." "A *buena* hambre / no hay *mal* pan." A more familiar effect is the use of rhyme, as in most poetry we know: "Cada oveja / con su pareja." "A Dios rogando / y con el mazo dando." Some dichos use alliteration, the repetition of the first sounds of words—a poetic adornment more commonly found in the Germanic languages than in Spanish: "*r*ough and *r*eady," for example. Assonance, the matching of the vowel sounds at the end of phrases, is much more common in Spanish. In the following dicho, both assonance and alliteration are used: "Quien da pan a perro ajeno / pierde el pan y pierde el perro."

Another kind of dicho is known as a "proverbial comparison." It is not a complete sentence but a phrase beginning with the word *como* (like): "Como agua pa' chocolate," "Como calcetín de a nicle," "Como el que chifló en la loma." Dichos of this kind usually have stories behind them, stories everybody knows, so that when somebody says, "I was left there like the man who whistled on the hill," everybody knows just how the speaker was left—holding the bag.

The use of dichos or proverbs is extremely old. Proverbs are found in the Old Testament, but some of them go back to earlier civilizations in Egypt and Mesopotamia. It has been said that proverbs are "the wisdom of many and the wit of one." They are the "wit of one" because it was some one person, at some particular time and place, who put the thought of each proverb into just the right words. And they are "the wisdom of many" because they are supposed to express the feelings and attitudes of whole groups of people rather than just the feelings of an individual poet. They should be useful then in analyzing the character of a people. The "thought" or "message" of each proverb is clear.

Working on the assumption that people do accept their own proverbs as containing wisdom, and that they quote them as expressive of their values, some anthropologists have attempted, if not to establish the "Mexican character," at least to identify important values held by specific Mexican groups, through the analysis of their proverbs. "As a man's speech mirrors his thoughts, so do a people's proverbs reflect dominant attitudes and patterns," we are told (Raymond 1954). Folklorists of the old school have objected to this use of dichos. Proverbs, say the old-fashioned scholars, are not only ancient but universal. All nations, for example, have believed that you tend to resemble the people you associate with. In English you say, "Birds of a feather flock together," and in Spanish you say, "Dime con quien andas y te diré quien eres," but the result is the same. These sayings tell us nothing about people today; they only tell us what somebody probably thought many, many years ago. People keep repeating proverbs out of habit, that is all. Furthermore, proverbs are often contradictory. Take a famous pair of proverbs in English: "Look before you leap" and "He who hesitates is lost." They advise you to do opposite things, so how can you believe that proverbs really mean anything.

Now, there was a time when most people believed that folklore was colorful but meaningless. Mexicans, for example, sang their corridos because they were happy (or drunk, perhaps). It was a quaint habit of theirs, inherited from their forefathers; but they did not mean anything by it. Today, we no longer accept the idea that there is no meaning at all to the way people behave. Telling dichos, narrating stories, and singing songs are all forms of behavior. If people persist in telling their children, generation after generation, "El que con lobos anda, a aullar se enseña," they must mean something by it. This certainly makes sense, but then, why are so many dichos contradictory?

"Entre menos burros, más olotes," the Mexican will say. "The fewer donkeys, the more corncobs." In other words, the fewer there are to share, the more there will be to go around. But the same person will also say, "Más vale pobre que solo"—"It's better to be poor than to live alone." Share what you have with others, even if there isn't much to share. There is another very Mexican dicho commenting on how difficult it is to change what is to be: "El que nace pa' tamal, del cielo le caen las hojas." If you're born to be a tamal, heaven will send you the cornshucks. So why try to be something else? Talk about the fatalistic Mexican, sleeping against an adobe wall in the sun! But the same people who use that dicho also have another one that says, "Todo cabe en un jarrito, sabiéndolo acomodar." That is to say, nothing is impossible. So where is our fatalistic Mexican now?

It seems that we are right back where we started from. How can dichos have any real meaning if they support both sides of the same question? Social scientists, however, are resourceful people. They point out—and rightly—that dichos do not contain absolute truths. They are not a set of rigid rules telling us exactly how to behave at all times. Instead, they are a storehouse of good advice, to be used according to specific situations. Obviously, people will have recourse to dichos that give all kinds of advice, depending on their mood and the situation they are in. But they do have sets of dominant values, which will be expressed in their choice of proverbs. The question then is, "Which proverbs do people prefer?" What we need—to borrow from the physical sciences—is quantitative analysis. Mr. Dobie's error was in trying to deduce the Mexican character from *one* Mexican folktale, which included *one* Mexican dicho. What must be done is to take a large number of dichos, since they do offer typical advice, and see what percentages are derived from them. We would get a small percentage that give advice contradicting the actual values of the people, while the greater proportion will reflect a people's actual values and behavior.

Scholars are beginning to do precisely that. They collect all the dichos told by a Mexican or a Mexican American group and analyze them according to the values expressed. Their results are extremely instructive. In all cases, it has been found by our Anglo social scientist friends, the great majority of Mexican dichos fall into easily recognizable groups. Preponderant are dichos such as the following:

¿A dónde ha de ir el buey, que no ha de seguir arando?
Where can the ox go that he will not have to plow?
(Where can a poor man go, that he will not be given the hardest kind of jobs for the lowest pay?)

El perro que come huevos, aunque le quemen el pico.
You can't make a dog stop stealing eggs, even if you burn his mouth.
(You can't change human nature. Things are the way they are going to be, and change is impossible.)

Others on the same theme:

El que ha de ser barrigón, aunque lo fajen.
El que nace pa' tamal, del cielo le caen las hojas.
El que tiene más saliva, traga más pinole.
Quien da pan a perro ajeno, pierde el pan y pierde el perro.
Un bien con un mal se paga.
Vale más mal conocido, que mejor por conocer.

Now, if you put these very popular Mexican dichos together and analyze them, you come up with the following picture of the Mexican:

1. He is quietistic.
2. He takes a fatalistic attitude toward life.
3. He is interested in the present or the past rather than in the future.
4. He is not interested in change.

So there we are again, with the usual stereotype of the Mexican—a much more familiar one than that of the ruthless, aggressive self-server Mr. Dobie talks about. We have ended up again with the peon, asleep with his back against an adobe wall, his ragged serape wrapped around him, and his hat over his eyes.

If we object that this is not a true picture, the social scientist will tell us we are being emotional and subjective about the whole thing. We are too close to it to really know what is going on. They, on the other hand, have applied an objective kind of analysis; and this is the picture their figures give them. If proverbs are a guide to the accepted behavior of a group, then the attitudes most frequently expressed in proverbs are those most highly valued by the group. And the majority of Mexican proverbs reflect a sense of fatalism and a resistance to change. So there you are—if you believe in figures. And we will have to admit—whether we like it or not—that any conclusions reached on the basis of a couple of hundred Mexican proverbs (where the message comes through loud and clear) are more convincing than Mr. Dobie's diametrically opposed conclusion based on one story accompanied by one dicho, "No te dejes."

But does the message come through loud and clear? Do the words we say always mean what they seem to mean? Let us return to Dobie and his

Mexican Br'er Rabbit, with its picture of the Mexican as living in a ruthless, dog-eat-dog society, while the North American believes in fair play. There is no doubt that in the United States the idea of fair play is always uppermost in our minds. Teachers and preachers are always expounding on the subject; yet we live in a highly competitive society, where making it is a high goal, and where nice guys always come in last.

Our answer is obvious, of course: principles that are honored more in the word than in the deed must be enunciated over and over again, in hopes that they will "take." If all the peoples in the world were one big, happy family, we would not have to spend so many, many words extolling the brotherhood of man. Dichos, proverbial or otherwise, may indicate social situations that are the opposite of what the dichos express. A reason for this may be an awareness, conscious or unconscious, that we are not living up to certain ideals we have set up for ourselves. Among the greatest exponents of fair play and good sportsmanship have been the British. This was not back during the Middle Ages, or during the Renaissance when English ships were challenging the might of Spain. It was in relatively recent times, when Britannia ruled the waves, when the British were building an empire at the expense of weaker peoples who were conquered and exploited without too much attention to such silly things as sportsmanship and giving your opponent a fair shake. Rudyard Kipling, himself the poet of imperialism, puts the whole thing into words when writing about the way British troops cut down spear-wielding Sudanese with their Martini-Henry rifles: "We sloshed you with Martinis, and it wasn't hardly fair." Fair play, indeed!

"No te dejes," then, may represent a desired state of affairs; but it does not tell us too much about what people actually do. We do not, therefore, know what the expression really means to the people who use it. We can find its true meaning only if we know *how* and *when* it is used. Words of themselves have no meaning; their meaning is given to them by the particular context in which they are used. So to study *verbal content* without a thorough knowledge of *performance context* is a futile exercise indeed. But nobody knows this better than the social scientists who should know all there is to know about studying social data in context. Social scientists, however, are not exempt from the human failing of not practicing what they preach. Those who run a quantitative analysis on hundreds of proverbs are still making the same mistake Frank Dobie made when he drew his conclusions from only one, except that they disguise their error with a lot of figures. They still are analyzing groups of words outside their context.

Let us take as an example a dicho mentioned earlier, "El que nace pa' tamal, del cielo le caen las hojas." No doubt, it owes a great deal of its currency to the fact that it is a nice little poetic construct. It says what it has to say so very well, and in the fewest words possible. Yet it would be difficult to find a choicer expression of all the weaknesses Mexicans are accused of having. What fatalism! What supreme distrust of the future! What an eloquent statement of the futility of any effort to improve ourselves!

But let us reconstruct a typical situation where this particular dicho may be used. A young man—let us say—is being persuaded by a parent or by an older friend to take a certain course of action. The advice may be "Try harder to do a good job," or "Stand up for your rights, you are being cheated," or "Demand what is your due," or some similar bit of advice requiring action or change. The young man, however, does not respond. He is timid, or lazy, or just unconvinced. He would rather leave things as they are. Finally, the older person becomes exasperated, and he may say, "¡Ah, es por demás hablar contigo! ¡El que nace pa' tamal, del cielo le caen las hojas!"

Nobody aware of the situation would even dream that the speaker means what his words seem to say. He is not counseling inaction or resistance to change, on the grounds that we will be what we are born to be and that is all we'll ever be. On the contrary, he is making a final attempt to goad his hearer into action by shaming him with this proverb. Far from advising that we accept things as they are, the proverb is a harsh call to action. It means exactly the opposite of what it says. But our field collector, avidly filling his little notebooks with Mexican dichos, rarely encounters such situations. He works with informants. He asks his informants for dichos; they tell him some dichos, and he enters them in his little notebook.

Proverbs may mean the opposite of what they say in still another fashion. The statements they make may give voice to bitter protest about the situations they portray. They express not the speaker's personal scale of values but his idea as to the values of his oppressors. It may be worthwhile to take another look at the great number of Mexican proverbs dealing with injustice, cruelty, and inequality—not as expressions of acceptance but as forms of social protest. It is ironic that they should be persistently interpreted as quietistic fatalism. Then, when the limits of human endurance are reached, when violence erupts, we do not know what to blame it on. And we must have recourse to still other stereotypes about the Mexican—such as machismo—in attempting an explanation.

I have been interested this evening in using proverbs as examples of what has been done, and what may be done, in using folklore to understand lo mexicano, because proverbs seem so simple, with such little possibility of being misunderstood. If explanations can be so far off the mark with proverbs—which seem to be all "message"—this is even truer of the more complex forms of folklore, such as legends, corridos, customs, or beliefs. We must know the situation in which this folklore is performed; and we must know the language and the people as well.

Editor's note: From *Aztlán: International Journal of Chicano Studies Research* 13, nos. 1–2 (1982). The original essay was lightly edited for this collection.

Works Cited

Dobie, J. Frank. 1957. "Br'er Rabbit Watches Out for Himself in Mexico." In *Mesquite and Willow*, ed. Mody Boatright, 113–17. Publications of the Texas Folklore Society, no. 27. Dallas: Southern Methodist University Press.

Raymond, Joseph. 1954. "Attitudes and Cultural Patterns in Spanish Proverbs." *Americas* 11: 57–77.

"¡Yo Soy Gregorio Cortez!"
Américo Paredes and the Mexican Immigrant

Audrey A. Harris

In his landmark work of Texas-Mexico border studies, *"With His Pistol in His Hand"*: *A Border Ballad and Its Hero*, Américo Paredes (1915–99), the pioneering writer and folklorist, creatively reimagines the story of one turn-of-the-century Mexican immigrant, updating it for a contemporary audience. Many critics have read the book as a study of the border ballad "El Corrido de Gregorio Cortez" and the man who inspired it. According to legend, Gregorio Cortez, the sharecropper son of Mexican immigrants in Karnes County, Texas, was wrongly accused of stealing a horse by the county sheriff, W. T. "Brack" Morris, who rode out to Cortez's land to question him and his brother Román. In a case of mistranslation, Gregorio Cortez replied to the sheriff that he had not acquired a horse (*caballo*), but rather had traded a mare (*yegua*); the resulting confusion led to a gun battle in which his brother was shot and Cortez killed the sheriff in self-defense. This triggered an epic manhunt by the Texas Rangers in which Cortez was chased by hundreds of men across the Texas desert until he was finally betrayed by an acquaintance, Jesús González. Though sentenced to fifty years, he ultimately spent twelve years in jail, having been granted his freedom by an official government pardon after the facts of the case came to light in court. Cortez famously pleaded to be granted the same right to a fair trial that is guaranteed to any American instead of being automatically criminalized for being Mexican.

Although Paredes's book is widely acclaimed as a milestone in border studies, little has been made of the fact that Gregorio Cortez was what we would today call a Mexican immigrant. Born on June 22, 1875, between Reynosa and Matamoros on the Mexican side of the border, Cortez moved with his family to Texas in 1887, at the age of twelve, and spent most of his adult life in the United States. In the 1930s, decades after Cortez's famous flight from the Texas Rangers, the Mexican immigrant population came to national academic attention in the work of anthropologist and sociologist Manuel Gamio. A Mexican national, Gamio is known in the United States for his studies *Mexican Immigration to the United States* (1930) and *The Mexican Immigrant: His Life-Story* (1931), written in English and supported by the Social Science Research Council. He is best known in Mexico for *Forjando patria* (1916), a tract arguing for the cultural assimilation of indigenous people into the post–Mexican Revolution nation under the constitution of 1917. *Forjando patria* was a point of departure for later Mexican anthropological studies and seminal in the founding of Mexico's Instituto Nacional Indigenista in 1948. Paredes's study of "El Corrido de Gregorio Cortez" both parallels and reflects the influence of Gamio's English-language studies conducted in Texas. It also voices Paredes's awakening ethnic consciousness, shaped by his experience in Japan following World War II and by his later activism alongside fellow Mexican American scholars at the University of Texas, Austin, where he helped found the Center for Folklore Studies and the Center for Mexican American Studies.

By focusing on the topic of immigration in the work, we can access a new reading of Paredes's telling of immigrant Cortez's life story. In this essay, I will show how Paredes brought his views of immigration, and of his own identity as a Mexican American who identified with Mexican immigrants from south of the border, to bear on *"With His Pistol in His Hand."* I also take into account his novel *George Washington Gómez*, written in the 1930s but not published until 1990, which presents an assimilationist narrative. Through the two works, Paredes indicates two possible paths for immigrants, assimilation versus assertion of a more traditional Mexican identity, and implicitly advocates for the latter.

"With His Pistol in His Hand" began as a doctoral thesis that Paredes wrote in 1956 for the Department of English at the University of Texas, Austin. It was published two years later, in 1958, by University of Texas Press. (In this essay I reference the 2010 reprint.) Paredes was not the first to publish the corrido of Gregorio Cortez or to include it in anthropological research. A simpler version of the corrido appears in Manuel Gamio's *Mexican Immigration to the United States* (1930), which like Paredes's dissertation is a study of Mexican immigrants in Texas alongside Texas Mexicans (or Tejanos—residents of the state of Texas who are descendants of the original Spanish-speaking settlers of Texas). Although he noted this popular song of a heroic Mexican immigrant, Gamio did not study its importance for Texas

Mexicans' cultural identity. Paredes, however, by collecting all available versions of the corrido of Gregorio Cortez, analyzing them for their lyrical merits, and then polishing and recombining them, produces a version that is more nuanced and more stirring than the one Gamio reproduces in his text. By highlighting certain aspects of Cortez's story and downplaying others, Paredes inscribed himself into the myth. When read in conjunction with earlier printed versions of the corrido such as Gamio's, Paredes's efforts to update and magnify the story become clear, as does his intention to present Cortez's defiance in the face of pressures to assimilate to the North American way of life (Gamio 1930, 96–98). Mexican immigration to the United States had ballooned in the decades since the corrido first appeared, and the definition of what it meant to be a Mexican in America had changed significantly.

Paredes's definition of the corrido is important for understanding the role he plays in telling the story of "El Corrido de Gregorio Cortez" and how he positions the narrative within the conflicted territory of South Texas, where Mexicans and white settlers have lived side by side since the annexation of Texas by the United States in 1845. Paredes provides context in his article "The Mexico-Texan Corrido." Written when he worked for the *Brownsville Herald* as an independent journalist before attending the University of Texas, the article was published in 1942 in *Southwest Review*.

> The Mexican *corrido* is, like the British ballad, a song of the people, composed by the people as a folksong in their moments of relaxation, and records past events of interest. Its prime quality is simplicity and lack of artistry; it flows from the singers as if it were a spontaneous product, and often new verses are added as it is sung. It has such a medieval flavor that a first thought might indicate that it could not flourish outside a country where primitive conditions are found. Yet, the *corrido* has reached perhaps its most significant developments among the Mexicans living in South Texas who have not yet become Americanized. Cut off from the folkways of their own country by international boundaries, hostile to the culture of the rulers of the land which was once theirs, these people are in a sense culturally adrift . . . their only genuine expression, their main artistic outlet, then, is in the *corrido*; in it they use their language, their own typical expressions; it is based on their own themes, on situations and happenings particular to themselves. (Paredes 1942, 470)

He goes on to explain how the corrido combines two traditional ballad forms, the British ballad and the Spanish *romance*: "The verses of the corrido are composed of eight syllables, corresponding perhaps to the old Spanish romance. However, the lines are grouped in quatrains, each completing a thought, more like the English ballad than the Spanish romance" (471). In the article, Paredes analyzes the corrido in the kind of minute detail that indicates that he was a craftsman of the genre as well as a scholar.

As Héctor Calderón points out in *Narratives of Greater Mexico* (2004), Paredes was a creative writer who wrote poems, short stories, and novels that dated from the 1930s but were published much later in his career. He also sang and played popular music on the radio in his youth and joined a circle of writers of poetry and balladry on the Brownsville-Matamoros border. The influence of his creative pursuits is clear throughout "*With His Pistol in His Hand*," particularly in the second chapter, where he narrates the legend of Cortez in the dialect of the Texas-Mexico border, and in the sixth and seventh chapters, where the author uses his intuition and extensive study of border balladry to write Variant X of "El Corrido de Gregorio Cortez." The book demonstrates the interdisciplinary confluence of Paredes the novelist and poet with Paredes the ethnographer, as he mixes extensive research, social theory, and literary analysis with his own creative rewritings of the legend.

In chapter 2, "The Legend," Paredes re-creates the legend as a story of the sort that might be told by old-timers after listening to a performance of the ballad. In this retelling, Paredes employs a technique that, in his analysis of the legend, he describes as common to its telling: Cortez was, the narrator relates, someone who "looked just a little bit like me" (2010, 34). According to José R. López Morín's biography of Paredes, *The Legacy of Américo Paredes* (2006), as a child, Paredes

> remembered spending hours recreating the stories he heard from the old men or making up his own, imagining he was Gregorio Cortez fighting against the *rinches* (Texas Rangers). Daydreaming allowed him to project himself as a hero of his people and helped him relieve his anger and frustration with the reality of the Mexico-Tejano border folk. (35)

In "*With His Pistol in His Hand*," Cortez is simultaneously the historical figure himself and a double of the author, crying out against the unjust treatment of his people. He embodies the spirit of the proud Mexican American who refuses to forget his homeland.

How is this spirit defined in the corrido? Cortez is a peaceful man, provoked to fight a "just war" in defense of his human rights. In contrast to white writers' racist portraits of Mexicans as lazy (as in the works of Charles F. Lummis), Cortez is a prodigious and indefatigable worker.[1] He is also, again in contrast to outsiders' image of Mexicans as sullen and common, always polite—a *caballero* in the true sense of the word. Like the medieval Spanish hero El Cid, he has given more to his community than he has received, and for this reason his entire community jumps to assist and protect him on his journey, despite his outlaw status. Writes Paredes, "That was Gregorio Cortez, and that was the way men were in this country along the river" (2010, 45). Here he mythologizes and elevates not just a man but a whole way of life that from the outside had always been depicted as uncivilized and poor.

Paredes's version of the legend draws from folktales of Cortez's exploits, deliberately morphing the name Karnes County into "El Carmen" (though he refers to it by its correct name elsewhere in the text) as many ballad versions do. Treating the story as a tall tale, he inflates accounts of Cortez's bravery and the cowardliness of the white sheriffs and Texas Rangers. Jumping off from the ballad line "so many mounted Rangers, just to take one Mexican," he describes the apprehension of Cortez, who rides alone, by "twenty or twenty-five" American men, who decide to let him pass rather than trying to take him on (2010, 41). He also describes a pack of three hundred men on his trail, another exaggeration that further raises Cortez's tale to the level of myth. He recounts that Cortez, on the point of being caught, shouts, "¡Yo soy Gregorio Cortez!" and fires a shot in the air (236). As Paredes explains, this trope also comes from the medieval *romance* tradition: El Cid shouts his name as a rallying cry as he heads to battle. When Cortez utters this famous cry, he is asserting his identity and his worth in the face of forces that would, on the one hand, imprison him or, on the other, assimilate him. Paredes reads Cortez as a hero not just of the Texas-Mexican border but also of the greater Mexican American immigrant community, just as El Cid was a border figure who came to symbolize the struggle of an entire people.

Paredes presents and analyzes eleven variations of "El Corrido de Gregorio Cortez" in chapters 6 and 7. In Variant X, he combines the best of many versions of the ballad to imagine its original content and form— something he admits that, in all his years of searching and research, he was never able to find. He takes a critical approach to several other variants, showing that the omission of certain elements detracted from the story's telling. His aim is particularly sharp when he describes the publication of the corrido in Mexico City as a broadside in which the border ballad is converted into a national hymn and the border hero Cortez is transformed into a symbol of Greater Mexico—a man who "honored his flag" (2010,

182). The broadside makes generalizations based on Cortez's story, stating for example that white Americans "wanted to exterminate our people" (162). This line exaggerates and muddies the actual tensions of border life, which had much more to do with law, order, and land grabbing than with a Nazi-style extermination plan. In fact, the border became a place of intermarriage, and tensions were multifaceted ones in which Americanized Texas Mexicans were positioned against those who resisted assimilation and in which many whites developed sympathies and affinities for Mexican culture. Paredes's criticism of the Mexico City broadside makes clear that, while Cortez was not an American, neither did he symbolize the average Mexican. As a Mexican living in the United States, he was something in between, and something different. He became an early standard bearer for Mexican Americans who began to seek their own mythology and heroes.

Another version of the ballad, apparently of Paredes's own crafting, appears immediately before the beginning of part 1. This version does not claim to be the original. Instead, it appears to be another distillation, in which Paredes again combines the best lines of all the versions into a stirring song, this time in considerably shortened form. Here we have the line "trying to catch Cortez was like following a star," and Cortez calling out, "his voice . . . like a bell, 'You will never get my weapons till you put me in a cell'" (2010, 12). We also have the bitter line, which shows Cortez, and a people, in capitulation to North American force: "Ah, so many mounted Rangers just to take one Mexican!" (13). As Paredes notes, this verse is found only in later versions of the ballad that appear in the period in which telling after telling and teller after teller distilled and winnowed the ballad into its most economical and emotional form. In this shortened version, we can see Paredes inscribing himself into this lineage, not just of those who study and analyze folklore but also of the tellers themselves.

Border Legality and Mexican Immigrant Status, from 1901 to 1958 and Beyond

Much changed politically and socially in the decades that intervened between Cortez's famous ride and Américo Paredes's landmark career at the University of Texas. Within the Mexican American community, one notable change was the huge growth of Mexican immigration and the ensuing US efforts to curtail it. In an interview with Héctor Calderón and José R. López Morín that Paredes gave shortly before his death, he commented, "Brownsville and Matamoros were different when I was young. What we see now is wave after wave of poor people in Matamoros, waiting to come into the States, trying to make a better life" (Paredes 2000, 203).

In 1848, the United States won the Mexican-American War and gained ownership of Mexico's lands north of the newly established border. It is clear that, in Paredes's view, this loss is still quite fresh, especially as he reflects back to the time of Cortez's ride. In *"With His Pistol in His Hand,"* he articulates a vision of "an organic Texas-Mexican pastoral society under siege from Anglo-Texan invaders," as Morán González notes (2009, 130). This view flips the paradigm of ownership, belonging, and exclusion that formed the basis of later US border laws, throwing the validity of border laws into question.

Significant changes in immigration practices and policy took place between 1901 and the 1950s. Immigration increased in 1910 with the advent of the Mexican Revolution; by 1920, between 50,000 and 100,000 Mexican workers migrated north every year looking for jobs, and the United States government invited their labor, particularly during World War I (Young 2015). Then, when the public began to grow concerned that the migrant workers were taking jobs from citizens, the US government sponsored a Mexican repatriation program (1929–36) that was intended to encourage people to voluntarily move to Mexico. Instead, thousands were deported against their will. Between 300,000 and 500,000 Mexicans were forced out of the United States in the 1930s. In the postwar era, the US Department of Justice launched Operation Wetback, through which 3.8 million Mexicans were deported between 1954 and 1958 (Public Broadcasting System 2013).

Another important change that occurred between Cortez's day and Paredes's concerns the legal status of Mexican migrants. In 1924, Congress established the US Border Patrol to enforce newly decreed immigration caps that rendered undocumented workers illegal. In Cortez's day, it was not illegal for an undocumented worker to live in Texas, and crossing the border was not an illegal act. However, by the time Paredes wrote *"With His Pistol in His Hand,"* a man in Cortez's situation was considered illegal, and the discriminatory practices against him had been institutionalized.

When the United States entered World War II in 1941, Mexican migrant labor was again in demand. In 1942, US and Mexican officials agreed to establish the Bracero Program, which allowed temporary guest workers (or braceros) to work in the United States without any of the labor protections extended to US workers. This program, which lasted until 1964, was active when Paredes wrote *"With His Pistol in Hand."* The antecedents of the braceros, Paredes writes, were peons (a *peón* is, literally, a man on foot), who came to the border to work (2010, 10–11). Exploitation, and what José Limón (1998) might describe as the erotic dance between the United States and Mexican immigrants—on the one hand, wanting their labor, and on the other, rejecting their legitimacy as citizens—are also important themes in Paredes's writings.

In early poetry, Paredes reflected on the exploitation of Mexican workers, writing in one poem, "The Mexico-Texan" (first published in the *Brownsville Herald* in 1936),

> For the Mexico-Texan
> he gotta no country, he gotta no flag,
> he gotta no voice, all he got is the han',
> to work like the burro; he gotta no lan' (Paredes 1991)

This dialectic of labor without adequate compensation is clearly present in *"With His Pistol in His Hand."* Underlying the skirmish over the horse, which is the catalyst for Cortez's flight from the Texas Rangers to Mexico, are the Cortez brothers' fear of injustice and their disillusionment with the poor life they and their family lead in the States, despite their hard work for US ranchers.

This discourse points to broader trends of institutionalized racism in the United States that extended throughout the twentieth century. Nonwhiteness or "otherness" was a category in which Mexicans, among other groups, were included. According to a 1911 report for the US Immigration Commission titled *Dictionary of Races or Peoples*, "Spanish American, Mexican and West Indian . . . 'Natives of the Western Hemisphere,' together with American Indians and Negroes, are included with the Magyar, Turkish, and Armenian races in the term 'All others,' the sixth grand division of immigrant races as classified by the Bureau of Immigration" (np). The government systematically classified immigrants into "white" and "nonwhite" groups and also carefully distinguished between people of "pure blood" and those of mixed racial inheritance. These categories were used to justify discrimination through laws such as the Jim Crow segregation laws, which continued in effect until the Civil Rights Act of 1964 and the Voting Rights Act of 1965 overruled them. The exclusion and deportation of Mexicans were reinforced by legislation enacted in the early twentieth century that broadly curtailed immigration and barred it from some countries altogether. All these measures of institutionalized racism reflected the attitude that Americanness was to be defined and limited by a principle of "whiteness" related to Anglo and Aryan ancestry. The laws also promoted an ethos of assimilation among immigrant groups, who seized the chance to be included in the white category, even if it meant sacrificing their own customs, music, and food (Roediger 2005, 3).

Amid these determinants of racial inclusion and exclusion, Mexican Americans, as a so-called in-between group that fell on the racial spectrum somewhere between "white" and "black," found themselves in a peculiar position that forced them either to accede to the dominant white society through assimilation or to suffer at the hands of a US legal and economic system highly prejudiced against racial outsiders. The *Dictionary of Races or Peoples* indicates this divide by breaking Mexicans into three groups: those of pure Iberian or "pure white blood," who made up less than 20 percent of Mexican society; those of "pure Indian blood," at 40 percent (these people were counted in the category of Indian rather than Mexican, because Indians, like "Negroes," were listed separately regardless of nativity); and those of mixed blood, at 43 percent (96). Meanwhile, according to Cybelle Fox and Thomas Guglielmo, "the white racial boundary at times expanded to include Mexicans, then contracted to exclude them" (2012, 335). Moreover, "whether Mexicans, as a category, fell on the white or on the non-white side of the racial divide could vary by location, time period, or the institutional field in question . . . [or] by an individual's generational status, skin color, or class" (336). Thus, unlike African Americans under Jim Crow laws, Mexicans were not universally considered one color. In order to preserve their culture they had to defend themselves from pressures to assimilate as well as from the negative legal and economic consequences of difference.

Beginning in the early twentieth century, Mexican American writers and ethnographers began to implicitly contest the facile racial categorizations and the exclusionary and dehumanizing language used to describe Mexicans by undertaking more nuanced investigations of Mexican American identity. Many of these writers also sought to identify cultural forms that could be considered uniquely Mexican American. Among them were traditional songs and stories, often passed down orally, that recorded their history and defined their identity. This provided a response to dominant US cultural forces that sought to oppress and negatively classify Mexican culture. The scholarship published between 1900 and 1950 by a number of academics profoundly influenced Paredes's own academic work. José R. López Morín has noted the importance of Arthur Campa, who, writing in the 1920s and 1930s, provided the following definition of Southwest

Mexican Americans: "Legally and nationally they are Americans; linguistically, Spanish; Spanish American, geographically; culturally, Mexican; native by birth, and New Mexican by State boundaries" (quoted in López Morín 2006, 29). Campa, like Paredes after him, emphasized the Mexican element of this identity, as opposed to the historic conception of Hispanic New Mexicans as cultural descendants of Spain. Perhaps an even more important influence on Paredes was Jovita González, who wrote about the social transformation that occurred in South Texas because of US expansionism (López Morín 2006, 30). She also produced an important model for *"With His Pistol in His Hand"* by reading the *Tragedia de Juan Nepomuceno Cortina*—Cortina was a *vaquero* outlaw who was the most famous precursor to Gregorio Cortez—as an exploration of conflicts between Mexicans and whites of the South Texas border (31).[2]

Paredes has since reflected that the element of protest was an important aspect of his choice of "El Corrido de Gregorio Cortez." This theme, present in Cortez's day, was also alive in mid-1950s when Paredes rewrote the "outlaw's" story for his doctoral dissertation. Although the term *Chicano* was not yet in currency, many view Paredes as a precursor of the movement. In an interview with Ramón Saldívar, Paredes says of himself,

> When I was in my twenties I was a fiery, loud radical. When I returned to the States in 1950s, I was still a radical, but I had learned in my work as a journalist in Japan that understatement and irony . . . can hit harder than loud words. The work I did later between 1950 and 1980—*With His Pistol in His Hand* and *A Texas-Mexican Cancionero* (1976), in particular—found initial disfavor with publishers because of their subject matter and because of their tendency toward irony and satire. (Saldívar 2006, 121)

Although Paredes was descended from an old Texas Mexican family, he witnessed the effects of US immigration laws firsthand in 1950, when he returned to the United States with his Japanese Uruguayan wife, whom he had married in 1948 while working in Japan. Not allowed to enter the United States on a permanent basis, his wife, Amelia, received a six-month visitor's visa with the option to renew for another six months. Amelia was granted permanent residency in 1951. Their experience with the racial discrimination of US immigration policies undoubtedly informed Paredes's opinion of the struggles of Mexican immigrants to obtain US citizenship and of the discriminatory treatment they received once they arrived.

Extending the Legacy, from the Page to the Screen: *The Ballad of Gregorio Cortez*

In 1982 a film version of *"With His Pistol in His Hand"* was released on PBS and for wide distribution. Titled *The Ballad of Gregorio Cortez*, it was directed by Robert M. Young, who had directed *Alambrista!* in 1977 but was best known as a documentary filmmaker. The film version extends Paredes's experimentation with and interrogation of storytelling in the context of border crossings and conflict. Young builds on his experience as a documentarian to create a cinéma verité style. He also experiments with point of view by incorporating testimonies from various characters, each of whom casts Cortez (played by Edward James Olmos) in a different light. Thus the narrative builds on Paredes's exploration of the importance of orality and language to the story and its telling.

Throughout the film, Young stresses the importance of language, both spoken and written. Reports are read aloud, and the reporter for the *San Antonio Express News* has a primary role. Visuals of telephone cables and hurried and otherwise botched conversations, often among men obviously predisposed to think the worst about nonwhites, illustrate how stereotypes are disseminated. The absence of subtitles emphasizes the underlying cause of Cortez's flight—the interpreter's inability to distinguish between a horse and a mare—and leaves English-only viewers at a disadvantage. The use of a handheld camera (which alternates with a dolly camera) and natural lighting heighten the documentary feel. All these elements pay homage to the ethnographic style of Paredes's book. Young focuses as much on the process of legend making—the various sources of Cortez's story and the manner in which it was told—as on the tale itself. The heroic nature of the tale is captured in the opening sequence, in which Cortez rides alone through the desert, pursued by lawmen.

Indeed, Young availed himself of many of the cues in Paredes's book, to such a degree that the film can be seen as extending and providing a visual medium for Paredes's storytelling. To begin with, Paredes is listed as the first writer on the film (often book authors are listed after other screenwriters in film credits). Second, the film's screen credits indicate that it is Paredes, who was also a musician, who sings the lyrical version of "El Corrido de Gregorio Cortez," one of two interpretations of the song that play throughout the film. By incorporating the corrido into the score (music for the film was composed and adapted by W. Michael Lewis and Edward James Olmos), the film performs an important service of extending the book. The instrumental version, with its galloping rhythms, encourages the audience to sympathize with the film's nontraditional hero, who, seated proudly astride his horse, provides a striking visual reminder that the heroes of the American West came from both sides of the racial/ethnic divide.

The Ballad of Gregorio Cortez, though now thirty-five years old, voices attitudes toward Mexicans that ring as true today as they have at any time over the past century. In one scene, a law enforcement official boards a train to announce, "I want every damn Mexican on the train arrested." This reminds the contemporary viewer that the practice of targeting Mexicans for legal persecution and the privation of liberty solely on the basis of race has persisted across the decades—from when Cortez made his actual ride to when Paredes wrote the book, to when Young filmed the movie and, finally, up to the present, with the passage of Arizona SB 1070 (the "show me your papers" law) and similar legislation. Donald Trump's sweeping denunciation of Mexicans as rapists and criminals during his presidential campaign continues to resound in the nation's collective consciousness. Trump infamously issued the following statement on Mexican immigrants during his presidential announcement speech on June 16, 2015: "When Mexico sends its people, they're not sending their best. They're not send-ing you. They're not sending you. They're sending people that have lots of problems, and they're bringing those problems with us. They're bringing drugs, they're bringing crime. They're rapists." Instead of retracting these remarks following outrage from Latino groups, he defended them on a number of occasions, including during a July 6, 2015, speech in which he stated, "What can be simpler or more accurately stated? The Mexican Government is forcing their most unwanted people into the United States. They are, in many cases, criminals, rapists, etc." In response to further pressing by reporters, he was able to point only to an isolated incident involving a San Francisco–based undocumented immigrant and repeat felon who was later acquitted of murder charges against him but indicted on gun possession.[3] According to statistics from the Congressional Research Service (CRS) published in the *Washington Post*,

> The vast majority of unauthorized immigrants do not fit in the category that fits Trump's description: aggravated felons, whose crimes include murder, drug trafficking or illegal trafficking of firearms. CRS also found that non-citizens make up a smaller percentage of the immigrant popula-tion in state prisons and jails, compared to their percentage in the total U.S. population. (Ye Hee Lee 2015)

Marc Rosenblum, former deputy director of the US Immigration Policy Program at the Migration Policy Institute, argues that evidence shows that first-generation immigrants are in fact less likely to commit crimes than the rest of the population. "Immigrants in general—unauthorized immigrants in particular—are a self-selected group who generally come to the U.S. to work. And once they're here, most of them want to keep their nose down and do their business, and they're sensitive to the fact that they're vulnerable" (quoted in Ye Hee Lee 2015). Rather than being based in any kind of fact, then, Trump's remarks painting Mexican immigrants as criminals are merely the latest iteration of an age-old practice of race-based discrimination against Mexicans that justifies racial profiling and other policies of exclusion and containment. Trump himself would fit in perfectly with the bigoted characters in Young's film, deliberately misinterpreting and inventing false facts against Mexican immigrants to suit his nationalist and white-centric agenda.

A Long-Forgotten Novel and a Road Not Taken: *George Washington Gómez*

George Washington Gómez, written twenty-five years before *"With His Pistol in His Hand,"* tells the story of the son of poor Tejano and Mexican immigrants who name him after the US president in the hope that he will achieve success in the United States. The book plays with the idea of split identity: for example, everyone calls Gómez "Guálinto," which is the closest his grandmother could come to pronouncing his name. Later, he claims that the name has indigenous Mexican roots, eliding the North American provenance of it altogether. After witnessing the death of his father at the hands of the Texas Rangers, Gómez capitalizes on his light skin and Anglo name to join the ranks of power in the nation's capital in a bittersweet fulfillment of his parents' dreams for him. He marries a white woman, and, describing her pregnancy, predicts that their children will be blond and blue-eyed and speak only English. In short, Gómez comes to represent an assimilationist attitude that is the polar opposite of Gregorio Cortez's defiant assertion of his Mexican identity. Such assimilation was promoted by LULAC, the League of United Latin American Citizens, which encouraged Mexicans to climb the ranks in US society by promoting English-only education and encouraging other assimilationist practices.[4] By contrast, Paredes depicts Cortez as refusing to adopt North American customs or to intermarry: "He did not like white bread and ham; it makes people flatulent and dull" (2010, 46). When President Lincoln's daughter asks to marry him, he refuses: "He could see himself already like a German, sitting on the gallery, full of ham and beer, and belching and breaking wind while a half-dozen little blond cockroaches played in the yard. And he was tempted. But then he said to himself, 'I can't marry a Gringo girl. We would not make a matching pair'" (63).

In *George Washington Gómez*, the hero witnesses discrimination in Texas in the 1930s that bears many similarities to Cortez's treatment years before by US law enforcement officials, including the sheriff of Karnes County, the judge who sentences Cortez to ninety-nine years for horse theft, and the Texas Rangers. The Rangers, known as *los rinches*, are a frequent target of Paredes's contempt. In the novel, they kill Guálinto's father; in *"With His Pistol in His Hand,"* the sheriff, a former Ranger, hastily shoots Gregorio's brother, Román. The sheriff is depicted as a man who, like the Rangers, shoots first and asks questions later. Furthermore, as Paredes notes, he was "out looking for wrongdoers"—in other words, he was seeking targets to fill his quota, and went looking in the Mexican part of town (110).

The vindictive attitude of seeking out and imprisoning or deporting Mexicans on any possible charge is one we see also in *George Washington Gómez*, this time on the part of an immigration officer. In his interview with Ramón Saldívar (2006, 136), Paredes commented, "Mexicans included under the rubric *rinche* almost all law enforcement officers, since they were all apparently out to kill Mexicans or beat them up whenever they could. The immigration officers were also always known as *rinches*. In fact, some of them were retired Rangers. So I think that the idea of the checkerboard of identities emerged from the experiences of my daily life, learning to live with both sides of the divide." In the same conversation, he alludes to the thematic connection between *George Washington Gómez* and *"With His Pistol in His Hand,"* although he says he was initially unaware of it: "When I started working on '*With His Pistol in His Hand*,' I never thought of *George Washington Gómez*. It was in a different compartment of my consciousness, covered up" (136–37).

The two works address different aspects of the immigrant experience and of Paredes's own identity as a Mexican American. Guálinto is a good student who finds success in a gringo world, while Cortez is a defiant Mexican, proud of his own country and critical of US hegemony, who will risk his life and reputation to defy North American rule. On his connection with Gómez, Paredes has said, "I may have thought that I was writing a novel that was much more autobiographical than it turned out to be, since

Guálinto in *George Washington Gómez* does not take the path in life that I finally chose" (Saldívar 2006, 120). Instead, Guálinto, who marries a white woman and becomes a lawyer, takes a path that Paredes could have chosen. According to the author, "I began Guálinto's story, I suppose, by basing it on my own experiences in school. But then I expanded his story and took it in a different direction than my own life had [gone]" (120).

In retrospect, it is not surprising that Paredes allowed *George Washington Gómez* to languish unpublished in a desk drawer for decades and instead established his career with his treatment of the story of the Mexican "outlaw" Gregorio Cortez. While *George Washington Gómez* tells the story of a road not followed by Paredes, the writer, folk teller, and scholar never relinquished his affinity for Gregorio Cortez, whom he had dreamed of emulating from boyhood. In *"With His Pistol in His Hand,"* he articulates Cortez's story as a powerful and heroic alternative to Mexican assimilationist practices in the United States. In the process, two defiant figures emerge from the book: Cortez and Paredes himself, who through words, song, and his impeccable scholarship continues to fight Cortez's immigrant cause and that of the Mexicans who have come after him. Employing the romantic, defiant, and independent vision of his *vaquero* forefathers, Paredes advocates for racial justice and for adherence to a more traditional ethnic Mexican identity. Under the spell of Paredes's folk telling, nothing could seem more revolutionary.

Notes

1. *Editor's note:* This essay was commissioned for this collection.

Charles F. Lummis in 1892 in *A Tramp across the Continent*, writes of Mexicans, calling them Greasers: "twice as dark as an Indian, with heavy lips and noses, long straight, black hair, sleepy eyes, and a general expression of ineffable laziness" (quoted in Calderón 2004, 9).

2. Juan Nepomuceno Cortina was a Mexican rancher, soldier, and politician from Brownsville, Texas, who in 1859 led one of the first rebellions of Mexicans against white Texan authority. The series of armed conflicts that followed are known as the Cortina Wars.

3. According to Michelle Ye Hee Lee (2015), writing for the *Washington Post*, the case he referred to is that of Juan Francisco López Sánchez, a seven-time felon who has been deported five times to Mexico and who in 2015 fatally shot a woman during a random shooting.

4. LULAC made a point of distinguishing between Mexican American citizens and immigrants in its quest for civil rights. According to an article in *Lulac News*: "the greatest care should be exercised to distinguish between this character of citizen [U.S.-born or naturalized Texas Mexicans] and the alien of latin extraction" (Morán González 2009, 101).

Works Cited

Calderón, Héctor. 2004. "Redefining the Borderlands: From the Spanish Southwest to Greater Mexico, from Charles F. Lummis to Américo Paredes." In *Narratives of Greater Mexico: Essays on Chicano Literary History, Genre, and Borders*. Austin: University of Texas Press.

Fox, Cybelle, and Thomas Guglielmo. 2012. "Defining America's Racial Boundaries: Blacks, Mexicans, and European Immigrants, 1890–1945." *American Journal of Sociology* 118, no. 2: 327–79.

Gamio, Manuel. 1916. *Forjando patria*. Mexico City: Librería de Porrúa Hermanos.

———. 1930. *Mexican Immigration to the United States*. Chicago: University of Chicago Press.

———. 1931. *The Mexican Immigrant, His Life-Story*. Autobiographic documents collected by Manuel Gamio. Chicago: University of Chicago Press.

———. 2002. *El inmigrante mexicano: La historia de su vida: Entrevistas completas, 1926–1927*. Edited by Devra Weber, Roberto Melville, and Juan Vicente Palerm. Mexico City: M. A. Porrúa.

Limón, José. 1998. *American Encounters: Greater Mexico, the United States, and the Erotics of Culture*. Boston: Beacon.

López Morín, José R. 2006. *The Legacy of Américo Paredes*. College Station: Texas A&M University Press.

Morán González, John. 2009. *Border Renaissance: The Texas Centennial and the Emergence of Mexican American Literature*. Austin: University of Texas Press.

Paredes, Américo. 1942. "The Mexico-Texan Corrido." *Southwest Review* 27, no. 4: 470–81.

———. 1990. *George Washington Gómez*. Houston: Arte Público.

———. 1991. "The Mexico-Texan." In *Between Two Worlds*. Houston: Arte Público.

———. 2000. Interview by Héctor Calderón and José R. López Morín. *Nepantla: Views from South* 1, no. 1: 197–228.

———. 2010. *"With His Pistol in His Hand": A Border Ballad and Its Hero*. Austin: University of Texas Press. First published 1958.

Public Broadcasting Service. 2013. "Latino-Americans: Timeline of Important Dates." PBS.org. http://www.pbs.org/latino-americans/en/timeline/.

Roediger, David. 2005. *Working toward Whiteness: How America's Immigrants Became White: The Strange Journey from Ellis Island to the Suburbs*. New York: Basic Books.

Saldívar, Ramón. 2006. *The Borderlands of Culture: Américo Paredes and the Transnational Imaginary.* Durham, NC: Duke University Press.

Young, Julia. 2015. "The History of Mexican Immigration to the U.S. in the Early 20th Century." Interview by Jason Steinhauer. *Insights* (Library of Congress blog), March 11. https://blogs.loc.gov/kluge/2015/03/the-history-of-mexican-immigration-to-the-u-s-in-the-early-20th-century/.

US Immigration Commission. 1911. *Dictionary of Races or Peoples.* Washington, DC: Government Printing Office.

Ye Hee Lee, Michelle. 2015. "Fact Checker: Donald Trump's False Comments Connecting Mexican Immigrants and Crime." *Washington Post,* July 8. https://www.washingtonpost.com/news/fact-checker/wp/2015/07/08/donald-trumps-false-comments-connecting-mexican-immigrants-and-crime/?utm_term=.f0b5b4cb719f.

No Te Me Muevas, Paisaje

Sobre el Cincuentenario del Cine Sonoro en México

Carlos Monsiváis

No cedamos ante la adversidad. Algún caso tendrá el estudio del cine mexicano, así todos insistan (con razones) que el interés es más sociológico que artístico. A lo largo de sus tres o cuatro mil películas, el cine mexicano ofrece —cálculo muy aproximado— seis o siete obras maestras, ochenta o cien buenos films, técnicos excelentes, buenos actores y un panorama de fracasos voluntarios e involuntarios, de exaltación del machismo y la intolerancia, de racismo interno y de elogio a la sabiduría de Dios que dividió eterna y justamente al mundo en clases. ¿Pero por qué ese cine ha preservado y determinado a tal grado a su público, las masas reverentes o suspirantes que le confieren en conjunto y aisladamente, el papel de Gran Intérprete de las Pasiones Familiares y los Fatalismos de la Raza? Poco se gana, así sea inevitable, con la mera descalificación de una industria que, con cinco décadas de vida sonora a cuestas, sigue siendo —los años no pasan por su virginidad artística— espectáculo en donde lo que menos interesa es el respeto a los espectadores.

Es cierto: la industria cinematográfica se ha desarrollado aprovechando el descuido y la ineptitud gubernamentales, el celo eclesiástico, los miedos empresariales, el atraso de sus espectadores. Pero la suma de estos elementos no explica por sí sola un poder de atracción al que también aclaran distintas razones: el asombro reverencial ante la tecnología, la fuerza de la cultura oral, el analfabetismo real y/o funcional (que impedía, por ejemplo, seguir con la rapidez debida los subtítulos en español). Todo se centra en un punta: la satisfacción de necesidades básicas. A su clientela, el cine (de ninguna manera considerado un "arte") la ha provisto del estímulo fundamental: la garantía del entendimiento divertido del mundo.

Atmósferas: La Sacralización de la Técnica

El primer encontronazo fue con la técnica. De alguna manera, el asombro sistemático ante las "maravillas de la técnica" ha sido una definición nacional, el *shock of recognition* de las limitaciones. Las monjas al oír al superior de la orden hablar por teléfono, suponen a este "instrumento maléfico" un vocero del demonio. Las multitudes rodean al fonógrafo buscando al enano oculto que genera estos sonidos. El tren se lanza sobre la cámara y los espectadores del cine mudo huyen de sus asientos. Los revolucionarios de la Convención de Aguascalientes al ver los noticieros le gritan y le disparan al Venustiano Carranza de la pantalla con la esperanza de liquidarlo físicamente. En los años treintas, una multitud intenta linchar a la actriz Emma Roldán por lo que su personaje hace en una película. Si algo, con el paso del cine mudo al cine sonoro se acrecienta la certidumbre: lo que sucede en pantalla es la realidad más real. No nos rechaza, no permite la identificación instantánea, protege nuestro amor a la familia, se dirige en primera instancia a nosotros, nos hace compartir su nacionalismo. Y la televisión hereda esta indistinción entre producto tecnológico y realidad.

En la década de los ochentas, los cambios en México han sido extraordinarios, han desaparecido muchísimos residuos feudales. Ya no estremecen supersticiones como la honra. El machismo es casi siempre término injurioso, pero se va al cine de todas maneras: por la reafirmación de las mínimas certezas, las escalas valorativas directas. Tú, espectador, sigues entendiendo lo que sucede a tu alrededor. Tu estilo de vida es lo suficientemente importante como para que el cine lo tome en cuenta. Sigues viviendo en un país devoto del patriarcado y temeroso de Dios; sigue vigilada tu propiedad (así no exista) y tu lenguaje y trato son tan graciosos y afortunados como los de tus padres y tus abuelos.

Lugar Común: El Cine, Fábrica de Sueños

La educación insustituible. En la novela *Myra Breckinridge* Gore Vidal cita al crítico Parker Tyler: "Durante los años treintas y cuarentas, todas las películas que Hollywood produjo fueron significativas. No hubo una sola película insignificante." Algo similar puede decirse de la "Época de Oro del cine mexicano" (de mediados de los treintas a principios de la década del cincuenta), donde todos los films son significativos, porque todos son creíbles, todos enriquecen la experiencia. Si algo demuestra este poderío (que transformó literalmente los hábitos de un país, a imitación de la renovación mundial del cine norteamericano) es la falsedad de la frase: "El cine, fábrica de sueños."

Queremos advertir en el melodrama la vía de acceso a los secretos de las clases medias. No acudieron al cine a soñar, sino a conocer, a enriquecer como pudieran su experiencia, a averiguar su propio aspecto y el reflejo de los dominadores. De esta escuela en la oscuridad se derivaron los modelos de vida, las readaptaciones de la apariencia, las condiciones sicológicas para el tránsito a la masificación. Novedosamente, se aceptó que la eternidad de la tradición radicaba en su mutación incesante y, sin faltarle el respeto al pasado, las masas reorientaron su comportamiento, sus costumbres y su habla. Aceptaron como anécdota entrañable la imposición histórica y política: la pertenencia a una nación.

En esa larga primera etapa, los trabajadores del cine —productores, actores, directores, argumentistas, camarógrafos, técnicos— no creyeron hacer arte o cultura. Lo suyo eran faenas artesanales, espectáculos en serie que —sin paradojas— lograsen que la multitud no se sintiese sola. El éxito no les sorprendió porque venían del triunfalismo de Hollywood; no otra era su inspiración cotidiana y su única formación. Quienes habían sido carpinteros o electricistas devienen directores; los fotofijan reaparecen convertidos en camarógrafos; los jóvenes de buena presencia son galanes y estrellitas. En estudios muy precarios, malamente iluminados, con muy deficientes equipos de sonido, no tiene caso intentar la competencia con el cine norteamericano. Para cautivar un público de analfabetos sólo se necesita darles escenas y situaciones que sientan muy suyas, y para eso nada más se precisa "nacionalizar" las fórmulas de Hollywood, ya sea traducirlo todo en la medida de las muy escasas posibilidades económicas y técnicas.

Urge retener a esos millones de espectadores de pueblos y ciudades, hechizados ante el glamour y la técnica. Si el término "fábrica de sueños" no persuade, sí exhibe una convicción: a estas sombras cantantes o llorosas les correspondió mediar entre las apetencias y las resignaciones, entre la ignorancia y la intuición. Las diosas y los dioses de la pantalla proponían modelos de vida naturalmente inalcanzables, pero al democratizarse las ilusiones, crearon el lenguaje común del deseo y la frustración.

Género Culminante: La Comedia Ranchera

El gran invento, la comedia ranchera. Fernando de Fuentes dirige en 1936 *Allá en el Rancho Grande*, Gabriel Figueroa fotografía, Tito Guízar y Lorenzo Barcelata cantan, Emma Roldán y Carlos López ("Chaflán") divierten,

Esther Fernández conmueve y René Cardona representa a la autoridad. La trama es simplísima: la vida en una hacienda "típica" en los años veintes y treintas, el destino de niños que crecen para que la diferencia de clase los separe, la nobleza alícuota del patrón y los campesinos, la sombra malévola de una alcahueta, el duelo de canciones, el desafío por el honor personal y familiar, la carrera de caballos y un final feliz. Pero de este conjunto elemental el cine mexicano desprende su destino y advierte que su porvenir no es la eficiencia técnica o artística sino el candor de los espectadores mexicanos y latinoamericanos.

En un previsible examen ideológico de *Allá en el Rancho Grande* y su secuela se notarán de inmediato la carga reaccionaria, su odio implícito a la reforma agraria cardenista, su utopía latifundista, su elogio de la sumisión rural. Pero en el tiempo del estreno, a la crítica no le indigna ese vasallaje, sino, en todo caso, la trama pueril. Si Fernando de Fuentes dirige, en el mismo año, la muy épica *Vámonos con Pancho Villa* y la muy antiépica *Allá en el Rancho Grande*, es debido también a la falta de status del espectáculo intrascendente que no puede complacer a las élites. En 1936, pese al empuje del nacionalismo revolucionario, pocos discuten seriamente la visión clasista como hecho cotidiano. Se habla, sí, de lucha de clases y hay devoción por Stalin y las masas invaden las calles, pero a nadie le acongoja la presencia diaria del prejuicio clasista y racista.

La crítica cultural no evita la asistencia masiva. A un público naturalmente ingenuo, la película le ofrece arquetipos y estereotipos, una idea divertida de la vida campirana, un esquema "romántico" y frases que compendian estilos de vida.

Mitos: La Oferta Indispensable

Para que el cine mexicano consolide su público requiere de los mitos (Jorge Negrete, Dolores del Río, Pedro Armendáriz, María Félix, Mario Moreno "Cantinflas" y Pedro Infante) y de los Personajes Entrañables o, si se quiere, de los estereotipos que de tanto repetirse se vuelven personajes hogareños. Para la cuarta película David Silva o Pedro Infante son ya los personajes David Silva o Pedro Infante. David Silva o Pedro Infante asumen una realidad cuya eficacia proviene de la fusión armónica de un actor y un estereotipo. Mitos y personajes recurrentes le son indispensables a un público formado en la comprensión *personalizada al extremo* de la política, la historia y la sociedad.

En su "Época de Oro" el cine nacional cuenta con el apoyo de una concurrencia que lo sigue, lo imita, le confía el manejo de su habla y de sus gestos, le reconoce la prioridad en el estilo, le transfiere buena parte de sus devociones religiosas. En rigor, es la Edad de Oro no del cine sino del público anheloso de poseer a sus ídolos, de entender el poderío de una María Félix, de reproducir la simpatía de un Pedro Infante, de reconstruir la madurez humana de la Voz de Arturo de Córdova. Poco queda hoy de lo aparente de esta "Edad de Oro" y uno la contempla por razones fundamentales arqueológicas. Es un cine a semejanza e imagen de los caciques y sus sentidos de la diversión, la unidad familiar, el honor, la sexualidad y la belleza de la foto fija. Pero le queda semioculto el ánimo y las transformaciones de verdadero hacedor, ese público que se "nacionalizó" de nuevo y compulsivamente gracias a esos dramas, a esas comedias y a estos rostros.

Lugar Común: El Cine, Elemento de Unión Nacional

Un Estado laico, una secularización cuya última etapa sangrienta es la guerra de los cristeros, un cine que se ofrece como espacio de unidad donde las convicciones profundas del auditorio conviven con las creencias que la modernidad impone. Concedámoslo: el Estado fuerte es dueño de toda la representación revolucionaria. Está al frente de la educación escolar y de los niveles de interpretación de política, economía y sociedad. Sólo deja fuera, para quien se interese, la vida cotidiana. De las esperanzas ultraterrenas se encarga la Iglesia: de las ilusiones terrestres, el cine, la radio, la industria del disco, los comics y luego, la televisión. Es una repartición de labores. El control de la conducta social del pueblo (el trabajo y la política) es asunto del Estado; el sentido final de la vida (lo que le pasa al Pueblo cuando se muere) es privilegio de la religión; lo que haga el Pueblo cuando está desocupado, es coto de caza de la industria cultural. Por eso el cine es elemento decisivo en la integración nacional. Su importancia aumenta por su condición de intermediario entre un Estado victorioso y masas sin tradición democrática que hallan su unidad más visible en la educación sentimental. Si no hay vida política, que fluyan en vez risas y lágrimas. Si la Buena Sociedad nos excluye, que el cine, la radio, las historietas forjen una sociedad que nos acepte. Si no hay hábitos de lectura, que existan hábitos visuales. Un público iletrado o que lee con dificultad no le encomienda a las películas norteamericanas, con subtítulos, la representación de sus experiencias. Confía en una cinematografía propia que le allega lo insustituible: los *giros familiares* del idioma, los escenarios de pobreza, los rostros —como espejo—, las peripecias del melodrama, la iluminación y la música sin sofisticación posible.

La tierra firme del cine mexicano es una idea implícita y explícita: la *nación* prolonga a *la familia. La familia* es la representación más cierta de *la nación.* Este nacionalismo es, a la vez, útil y lamentable, real y calumnioso, falso y verdadero. Expresa a un Estado autocrático y se explica por la debilidad política y social de una mayoría que acepta lo que lo unifique.

Atmósfera: La Revolución Mexicana

Un punto de vista preferido de la industria es la compasión teatral del "civilizado" ante el "primitivo." Los espectadores, que se saben no muy lejanos de ese "primitivismo" observado tan despreciativamente, caen en la trampa y se aferran a él. Se identifican con lo rechazado o lo observado conmiserativamente. Nada mejor entonces que aplicar esa técnica a la reconstrucción histórica. Al cine no le conviene olvidarse de lo que aconteció en los campos de batalla entre 1910 y 1917. Las cargas de caballería, las tomas de ciudades, el arrojo de las soldaderas, el desplante de los generales, la conmoción cuyo mayor sentido fue el servirle de prólogo a la calma. La revolución todavía es rentable, tiene características muy aprovechables. ¡Qué agasajos visuales en esa conjunción de polvo y sangre, de fusilamientos y perdones, de trenes villistas y adioses porfiristas! So pretexto de homenaje, la hipocresía promueve al machismo, adecenta el pasado y convierte a una explosión social en paisaje de western.

Un gran apoyo para el escamoteo con todas las ventajas se obtuvo en la figura de Pancho Villa. No es héroe fácilmente sacrilegiado. En él se confunden en demasía leyenda y verdad. No fundó instituciones como Carranza, ni estabilizó como Obregón y Calles. No es mártir puro como Zapata. Por si fuera poco, invadió a Columbus, lloraba en los entierros, mandaba fusilar primero y averiguar después, suscitó el fanatismo en su tropa, tenía un nombre sonoro, fue bandolero social, era brutal y justiciero, concentró por figura y desplantes la atención mundial. Gracias a Villa y al villismo, el cine usa la Revolución Mexicana sin comprometerse en lo mínimo.

Mitos: Los Pies de Barro Que No Terminan Nunca

Dice Gilbert Seldes: "Si uno ha creído que los cultos y las idolizaciones populares son expresiones aisladas de una clase especialmente estúpida, será inevitable el enfoque satírico. . . . Pero si uno toma esos cultos y movimientos como anormalidades estrechamente ligadas a la vida normal, parte de la existencia ininterrumpida de la nación, uno necesitará tan sólo describirlos y ponerlos en su verdadera perspectiva." La estética del cine mexicano se funda en su semejanza con la vida ideal de sus espectadores, lo bonito y lo divertido se parece a sus sueños elegidos y cultivados, sus lugares comunes, sus prejuicios, sus arrogancias, su idea del sexo y de la violencia. No debe adelantarse, no debe diferenciarse.

A la industria la sirven magníficamente los arquetipos: la Sufrida Mujer, la Prostituta con Corazón de Oro, el Macho Generoso, el Hombre Primitivo que aspira a la Justicia. Lo perfecto es el arquetipo múltiple: Pedro Infante, quien más persiste y quien más arraiga, la gran figura no susceptible de exportación (fuera del mercado latinoamericano). El Hijo del Pueblo cuyas limitaciones son su mayor virtud y cuyo intenso localismo evita cualquier expropiación. Infante es resultado del cine como medio de la voluntad de las masas, del propósito popular de elegir símbolos e interlocutores. Al principio, fue el Macho desbordado de simpatía que cautivaba y deslumbraba con canciones y actitudes. Hoy es una suerte de museo dinámico del México que desaparece. Jorge Negrete es ya plenamente anacrónico. Pedro Armendáriz es figura de época y su energía corresponde cabalmente a la idea de la ira de un general villista. Infante, más actual, representa de cualquier modo un país donde la gente se conocía, se representaba individualmente, vivía sentimientos que sus antepasados hubiesen identificado con facilidad.

Atmósferas: La Pobreza

El cine mexicano hace de la pobreza su razón de ser. No por razones políticas sino escenográficas y presupuestales. Si es inútil competir con Hollywood, mejor basarse en las carencias: escenarios lamentables, improvisación, torpeza de edición, de fotografía y sonido, falta de profesionalismo por parte de las estrellas, etcétera. No importa la inexperiencia o la torpeza de los argumentistas y guionistas. En caso de duda, recúrrase a la música. Esta llena tiempo, disculpa las fallas narrativas y satisface a raudales. De esta miseria surge una estética ardorosamente vivida por millones de espectadores en México y en América Latina. La pobreza de los escenarios los acerca al cine, suspende cualquier intimidación cultural o social.

Por eso voluntaria o involuntariamente, el cine mexicano copia las estructuras de Hollywood y evita la exhibición de recursos. Que se note la falta de dinero, la incapacidad que nunca erigirá escenarios majestuosos. Ni tenemos ni podemos disponer de un Cecil B. DeMille, de miles de extras o de la escenografía babilónica de *Intolerancia*, por D. W. Griffith. Nos corresponde imitar y nacionalizar géneros, formatos, técnicas de presentación de las primeras figuras, tramas inolvidables. La verdad está en la repetición. A fuerza de ver los mismos sets, el espectador los siente absolutamente genuinos. Conoce que éstos han permanecido al cabo del desfile de rostros y situaciones, han sobrevivido a tragedias temáticas y a carreras artísticas malogradas. Lo que se repite es emotivo. Al reiterarse los tres o cuatro argumentos básicos, los espectadores encuentran su identidad memorizando sus propias reacciones. Lloro porque soy sentimental; me indigna porque soy muy hombre; río porque sé reconocer lo que es chistoso. La estrategia del mismo diálogo ante el mismo escenario engendra confianza. Lo que no varía, es digno de crédito, es *espectáculo para familias.* Y en la expresión *espectáculo para familias* culmina un falso juego de espejos: la familia mexicana cree que el cine refleja su eterna unidad y la industria considera inmóvil para siempre a la familia, atada a semejanza con la pantalla. Ni siquiera deshace el ensueño la convicción de que el cine adelanta la moral de la época (es su vanguardia obligatoria). Sólo el auge de la televisión independizará al cine de sus cuidados hogareños.

Mito: La televisión Desplazó al Cine

Sí, en un sentido. No, de manera esencial. En los treintas y los cuarentas, su público demanda del cine nacional lo que el norteamericano no concede: las imágenes de virtudes públicas y vicios privados, la reafirmación de las ideas de *virtud* y de *vicio.* Hoy en día, los espectadores exigen de su cine algo fuera del alcance de la TV: un panorama de vicios públicos y virtudes privadas. Si el país ha tomado el aparente rumbo de la modernidad (en donde no encajan las mayorías), justo es que los espectáculos celebren los defectos de sus clientes: son mujeriegos, borrachos, irresponsables, ignorantes. Les gusta hablar con "malas palabras." Les encanta proclamar su hambre sexual. La TV, espectáculo clasista para todas las edades desde el recinto familiar, no complace estas peticiones.

La industria, pese a su enconada defensa de la ideología burguesa, nunca se aleja de los sentimientos de sus espectadores. Los ricos en el cine son una nebulosa, la abstracción arrogante y casi siempre canallesca. Los pobres son *nobles* o si se dejan llevar por sus instintos, son *auténticos.* Sólo una salvedad: ese "tomar partido" por los de abajo no implica la mínima complicidad con las mujeres, audiencia cautiva a la que no se le conceden derechos ni representaciones prestigiosas ajenas al heroísmo silencioso y la abnegación.

La burguesía usa implacablemente al cine. En la ideología de la explotación se entrenan multitudes que exaltan su condición dominada, y celebran limitaciones del Pueblo, como si pertenecieran a una abstracción remota. La televisión recurre de moda ortodoxo al melodrama. El cine lo disfraza con mujeres desnudas, explosión de palabras antes prohibidas, desfile de situaciones tremendas. La televisión obedece a las imágenes de la docencia reaccionaria. El cine escenifica pobremente lo que los productores suponen son los estallidos del inconsciente colectivo. Los dos medios no se enfrentan, se complementan.

Mito: Emilio "El Indio" Fernández

El nacionalismo cultural en el cine deriva su repertorio épico de imitaciones de Eisenstein y del western y lo enriquece con recuerdos confusos de la escuela primaria y las fiestas cívicas. Así resulta la Nación Inventada en donde nos escondemos de la Nación Real. La cumbre de este nacionalismo cinematográfico es Emilio "el Indio" Fernández, quien está seguro de que existe algo perfectamente codificable, la Mexicanidad: paraíso perdido con tramas donde la tragedia reina, los paisajes y las canciones ejercen violencia sentimental, las mujeres humilladas y los hombres muy hombres forman parejas clásicas. Durante unos años, su fuerza lírica y la admirable fotografía de Gabriel Figueroa, consiguen hacer creíble estas "catarsis atávicas." El público (y los críticos extranjeros) lo creen: así son los mexicanos, así viven el paisaje, así quieren, así se enfrentan al destino ya sea bajo la forma de un pelotón de fusilamiento o de una mujer. Todo es externo y la tradición enlista rostros, seres y escenarios. En pocos años, de este nacionalismo cultural no quedan restos. Pero con él se entierra la confianza de una crítica de cine internacional que, apegada al turismo, sólo aplica el criterio de realidad del "exotismo."

Mitos: María Félix y Dolores del Río

La belleza cruel y la belleza irreprochable. La mujer que exige su lugar de preferencia y al sometimiento que encumbra. La devoradora y el ave del paraíso. Doña Bárbara y María Candelaria. Si Dolores del Río es la fragilidad que encuentra en la belleza a su fortaleza invencible, María Félix es la hembra que se vuelve macho para sobrevivir y garantizar la humillación de las demás mujeres, las que no son hermosas, carecen de personalidad, no pueden imponerse ni manejar el látigo. Ambas definiciones de la mujer hermosa ocultan y posponen a todas las demás.

De Dolores del Río y María Félix atrae el carácter irrepetible de sus figuras y de sus facciones, son parte de una época donde el cine magnificó y encauzó el ánimo religioso, aniquiló las dudas. En un siglo formalmente laico, el cine ha representado una persistencia mística que abarca adoración de vírgenes y santos, la transformación catedralicia de héroes y heroínas y la canonización de la Pareja. Además, la asunción y resurrección del Rostro, la piedad para cortesanas y bufones, el estremecimiento beatífico ante la presencia del mal y del horror que, desde las butacas, se revelan como Milagros Travestidos, las Apariciones de Nuestra Señora Sedienta de Sangre.

"We had faces then," aclara con orgullo la diva del cine mudo Norma Desmond (Gloria Swanson) en *Sunset Boulevard* de Billy Wilder, la película que marca la transición de Hollywood de iglesia onírica a pasión cultural. Sí que disponían de rostros entonces, rostros concesión de la naturaleza, recreados en los estudios, mantenidos por el espíritu implacable de las propietarias . . . y por un esfuerzo conjunto de maquillistas, modistas, iluminadores, fotógrafos, los varios expertos en el trasvasamiento de luces y sombras en donde el close-up minimiza nuestra incredulidad y libera y exige nuestro candor. Por eso Dolores y María son las mujeres mas bellas de este siglo mexicano, y la *belleza*, aquí, es término donde se funden la hermosura evidente, el arte de la apariencia y la voluntad de una industria. Ninguna nativa ha sido tan definitiva (e irreal) como Dolores del Río en *What Price Glory?* o *Flor silvestre*; nunca cacica alguna alcanzó el esplendor de María en *Doña Bárbara*. Son ellas, indistinguiblemente, mito y realidad, la leyenda que persuade por su enorme demostración de méritos. Su condición de arquetipos las mantiene en la prudente o excesiva distancia, que humaniza calladamente nuestro entusiasmo. Son deslumbramientos transformados en ideas; son ideas que nos persiguen como deslumbramientos.

Atmósferas: La Comicidad

En el cine la mecánica de aceptación y consagración de los cómicos conoce escasísimas variantes. Un cómico cinematográfico necesita las siguientes características.

1) Pertenecer desde el aspecto a las clases bajas y expresarlas verbal y socialmente, ser simpático pero obediente, lascivo pero dominable, pícaro pero honesto.

2) Representar no el conflicto de clases sino las limitaciones de los desposeídos, su timidez o su falsa arrogancia o su mitomanía. Lo principal es convertir al rencor social en folclor agradecido, hacer del humor técnica que amortigüe impulsos rebeldes o levantiscos.

3) Vivir los conflictos amorosos de modo que se vea en la comicidad una prolongación del sentimiento. El chiste es un paréntesis de la emotividad y las risas ocultan al llanto (aunque no a la inversa).

4) Mantener su principal atractivo, es decir, su personalidad anterior, la que lo condujo al cine desde el teatro o la carpa o la televisión. No se ha dado hasta hoy un cómico *originado en el cine*. Sus recursos nacionales (expresiones, voz, sobrenombre, modales) serán sus recursos finales en un medio incapaz del gag o chiste visual.

5) Permanecer, pase lo que pase, en el mismo ámbito. Del arrabal al arrabal al arrabal (con una estancia en la riqueza, obligadamente breve).

6) Aceptar el uso abyecto de sus talentos. Con la excepción de Cantinflas y Tin Tan, todos los demás han sido empleados como alivios o apuntamientos del halo romántico de la Pareja Inmaculada o del close-up borrascoso de la Pareja Trágica. Lo quiera o no, el cine mexicano es incapaz de generar a un Groucho Marx o, siquiera, a un Bob Hope. El humor es, para la sociedad, función degradada y auxiliar, y el cine —instrumento de conquista— que actualiza y educa a la fuerza a un país, es magia atenta al melodrama, el único genero significativo.

7) Ser vehículo de puerilidades idiomáticas que consagran, por métodos invertidos, el terrorismo cultural de la Academia de la Lengua.

8) Atender a la principal regla de juego: en la diversión popular, el chiste es el reducto más prestigioso. Lo otro, las imágenes hilarantes, o el ingenio del instante traducido en frases, apodos y gritos oportunos, no es considerado humor sino —lo que nunca es lo mismo— *relajo*, la falsa subversión del orden, la tontería que se ríe a partir de nada y se queda en nada. El chiste, en su turno, es la capacidad (autodescubierta) de reírse con algo que es *en sí* gracioso, ya que se le puede memorizar y transmitir fielmente.

9) Resignarse a la falta de desarrollo humorístico por la ausencia de estímulos. Si el público y los productores se saben incapaces de competir con Hollywood o con Cantinflas, un cómico de éxito podrá llenar teatros y cines, será un ídolo pero en la mecánica identificatoria nunca será un mito porque no representa al Pueblo (la entidad con mayúsculas) sino a variantes de lo popular. A tal grado monopoliza Cantinflas la representación del Pueblo que inclusive Tin Tan, por famoso y admirado que sea, nunca obtendrá esa fuerza complementaria que hace que el público de cine se

divierta *por lo que sabe*, por los chistes que oye y *por los que se imagina*, por el humor que le consta y por el que narrará extasiado al día siguiente.

Metamorfosis Que No Lo Es Tanto: El Melodrama

Sin el melodrama, no hay cine mexicano. En un ámbito negado al humor y a la crítica, tienen segura resonancia las catarsis a domicilio, la degradación de las pasiones que ordenan su metamorfosis a pedido de las clases medias. De la ortodoxia sufridora de los cuarentas (el horror de la bastardía, el temor del adulterio, la caída en el vicio y el hampa) se transita al horror de la soledad, el temor de la monogamia, la caída en el vicio y el hampa. Desde los sesentas, el melodrama de clases medias busca desesperadamente el tono, quiere ser europeo y transmitir el vacío de la vida, la infinita pesadumbre del tedio; quiere norteamericanizarse y aceptar la libertad corporal. Pero el salto de *Ave sin nido* o *El derecho de nacer* a *La otra virginidad* y *Amor libre* nunca es completa, porque sigue siendo mecánica y machista la visión de la mujer, porque no provoca sino halaga a los espectadores.

De escuela de costumbres a paisaje de la velocidad imprimida al cambio de costumbres. En los cuarentas, el melodrama exaltó verbalmente a los Altos Valores Morales y, al conceder el atractivo de la ruptura y el pecado, exhibió su debilidad. Desde los setentas, el panorama se invierte y va de la condena verbal y exaltación visual a la condena visual y exaltación verbal. La pregunta ¿Para qué defender la virginidad hasta la muerte? se trueca por la desesperada interrogante: ¿Para qué seguir creyendo en la felicidad en un mundo promiscuo? July, la chava alivianada de *Amor libre* de Jaime Humberto Hermosillo es contundente: "Eso del hogar dulce ya pasó a la historia mi hijita" o "Los hombres son como klenex, desechables." Pero su tono vindicativo es función de la época no de la cinematografía y por eso el melodrama continúa invicto. Respeta las falsas costumbres libres con el tono con que acató las buenas costumbres. Es un género oportunista que entre lágrimas fingidas exhibe con fruición los nuevos hábitos colectivos sabiendo que en lo fundamental, nunca amenazan la moral de la clase dominante.

Una Obra Singular: Luis Buñuel

En 1950, en el momento de *Los olvidados*, Luis Buñuel ya es leyenda surrealista (*Un perro andaluz* y *La edad de oro*) y, en México, ha dirigido películas solo rescatables por la burla subterránea que se les atribuye: *Gran casino* y *El gran calavera*. Su primera obra maestra, *Los olvidados*, supera con facilidad el final declamatorio impuesto por la censura, aísla las condiciones sicológicas y sociales de la miseria, crea personajes e imágenes de fuerza perdurable, asimila a los clásicos españoles y las provocaciones surrealistas. "Para mí —declaró Buñuel—, lo sentimental es inmoral. Odio la dulcificación del carácter de los pobres." Buñuel le añade al cine mexicano una dimensión: la intensidad moral. Y por ésto entiendo una limpieza narrativa atenta a (pero no servidora incondicional de) sus propias obsesiones.

Si la influencia de Buñuel es enorme pero no asimilable se debe a que su formación cultural y su pasado heroico le permiten creer en las otras funciones del cine (simbólicas, poéticas, morales, liberadoras), en una etapa de comercialismo desenfrenado. Buñuel no es naturalista, ni costumbrista, ni le interesa complacer. Si fracasa (el caso de *Susana, carne y demonio*, *La hija del engaño*, *Una mujer sin amor*, *El bruto*, *Abismos de pasión*), no es en el orden de los entretenimientos convencionales. Sólo Alejandro Galindo, en *Una familia de tantas* y *Doña Perfecta*, se indigna de modo lúcido ante la represión moral. Pero Galindo, narrador tradicional, no maneja elementos poéticos que su realismo costumbrista deposita en las estampas gremiales. (Para el Indio Fernández, lo poético es aquello que Gabriel Figueroa fotografía a semejanza de los muralistas, un decálogo del ser nacional). Buñuel, en sus films significativos, entreverá el relato lineal con la audacia cultural, la crítica con el hallazgo poético: *La ilusión viaja en tranvía*, *Ensayo de un crimen*, *Nazarín*, *Simón del desierto*. Y esto se potencia en las obras maestras: *Los olvidados*, *Él*, *Viridiana*, *El ángel exterminador*.

¿Qué es la moral burguesa? Buñuel no lo dice, lo demuestra con rencor irónico. El no se propone "denunciar" en el sentido judicial sino mostrar, develar las visiones masturbatorias que hacen posible a las buenas conciencias. Entre repeticiones y esclarecimientos, Buñuel localiza un centro de conflictos: la opresión de la ética judeo-cristiana en su escenario ideal: la sociedad capitalista. En *Él*, la voluntad de posesión de un burgués católico se reduce y amplifica patológicamente; en *Viridiana*, la caridad ridiculiza con crueldad la pobreza; en *El ángel exterminador*, la vida social se condena angustiosamente en un relato que desborda todas las interpretaciones y cuya mejor exégesis es la descripción. Siempre a contracorriente, se filtran el poder y la esclavitud del erotismo.

La Influencia de la Crítica

No le fue difícil a la crítica de cine advertir, a principios de los sesentas, el atraso contaminador de la industria. La condena fue instantánea: he aquí la fábrica de la enajenación, los envilecedores de una colectividad finalmente indefensa que acepta lo que le dan. Acertada en el diagnóstico, la crítica no entendió su dimensión política y a conformarse con el dictamen artístico, prosiguió implícitamente su condena del público zafio, ávido de basura. Algo se consiguió. Alejó del cine mexicano a una clase media aculturada, feliz de huir de productos que la humillaban, que la enfrentaban al candor de sus padres, y a su propia inocencia reciente. Si, insólitamente, la clase media creyó en la crítica fue porque requería de argumentos sacralizados para justificar su disgusto ante una falta de prestigio. El concepto del cine, como expresión artística y cultural, se impuso y trajo consigo un aumento de la cultura cinematográfica y una considerable dependencia de las modas.

En los cuarentas, Xavier Villaurrutia en la revista *Hoy* no creía preciso trabajar sus notas. Eran quehaceres mecanográficos necesarios para vivir. Ni el cine era un arte ni la crítica una responsabilidad cultural. Desde los sesentas, la crítica del cine mexicano se escribe para quienes, de cualquier modo, no frecuentan estas películas. Y la falsa paradoja explica el desastre cultural y la felicidad económica de una industria.

Los Mitos: ¿Pero Hubo Alguna Vez "Época de Oro" del Cine Mexicano?

En países regidos en gran medida por el analfabetismo funcional, el cine sigue siendo (no obstante la influencia todopoderosa de la TV) el gran adelanto que es también la confirmación en el atraso. Por eso, la "Época de Oro" es tan sólo la etapa de confianza general en un espectáculo. Nadie seriamente pensó en rechazar el machismo, el moralismo feudal, el clasismo, el racismo interno. El sentido de la industria era la adulación de su audiencia y la "Edad de Oro" exaltó el primitivismo, las supersticiones, el falso carácter de oráculo sentimental de un cine que explicaba y orientaba la vida cotidiana. El cine enterró y prolongó una moral, confirmó y aplazó un sentido de nación a base de sus metamorfosis. A las costumbres que desaparecían, se les alababa; a la modernidad en verdad promovida, se le criticaba. Por reaccionario y clerical que fuese el mensaje ostensible, el mensaje visual era muy distinto. Por audaces que fuesen las imágenes, el peso ideológico las neutralizaba.

Agréguese a esto la falta de originalidad: trama y diálogos de tal modo inscritos en la memoria colectiva que funcionan a modo de páginas en blanco donde cada espectador halla lo que quiere ver. La censura gubernamental ha actuado para proteger a la familia, garantizar a la Iglesia la fidelidad del Estado, certificar la eterna minoría de edad de los espectadores. ¿Por qué no? El cine (se pensaba y se piensa) no es arte, ni instrumento de consolidación estatal. Es, en el mayor de los casos, un espectáculo genial e intrascendente que le toca en suerte a la industria capitalista. Así, la idea prosiguió, destruyó esfuerzos costosísimos y evitó la presencia de un *nuevo cine* (así se den obras individuales importantes). Todo sigue igual porque se mantiene el punto de vista sobre el público, y su necesidad de tutela. Que todo se confine en las mitologías, allí no existen las realidades culturales, políticas, morales. El Estado no cree en el cine como recurso expresivo y la industria vierte sin riesgos su odio a lo subversivo, su antiintelectualismo sin línea del menor esfuerzo, su baratura.

Esta fue y sigue siendo la gran ventaja de los productores privados: la esencia del cine mexicano ha sido, hasta la fecha, las relaciones de dominio entre un aparato industrial y un público que siente natural y justo el desprecio a su inteligencia y a sus capacidades de renovación, gracias a que ve satisfecha o saciada su gana de sensaciones.

¿Qué va de ayer a hoy, de un cine de tremendismo verbal y puerilidad moral? Que el espectador de ficheras y prófugas de la monogamia ya se sabe no frente a la realidad sino frente al séptimo arte, y lo divierte no la vida sino el choteo de la vida. La realidad lo espera en casa, contenida o enmarcada por una caja. Del cine de familias al cine para individuos o grupos que se creen a salvo de la mirada de las familias. El resultado: antes se solía creer que lo ocurrido en pantalla era cierto, porque ni la fotografía ni el estado de ánimo mentían. Hoy, ya más enterado, elige la realidad fílmica. Y sin embargo, de algo le ha servido este cine a sus espectadores, les ha dado lazos de unión, los ha modernizado en alguna medida, ha conjugado la impotencia y las aspiraciones heroicas de una colectividad sin salidas públicas. Si ese cine quiere ser un instrumento efectivo de liberación, deberá empezar por traicionar a su pasado, a las esperanzas de su público, a su destino impuesto, a sus tradiciones, a su oprobiosa historia, no exenta con todo de momentos muy agradables y recuperables.

Editor's note: From *Aztlán: International Journal of Chicano Studies Research* 14, no. 1 (1983). The original essay was lightly edited for this collection.

From Golden Age Mexican Cinema to Transnational Border Feminism

The Community of Spectators in *Loving Pedro Infante*

Juanita Heredia

At the beginning of the twenty-first century, Chicana writers have joined other US Latina writers in expressing a transnational vision of the United States, Mexico, and Latin America, specifically with respect to cultural production. In the novel *Loving Pedro Infante* (2001), Chicana author Denise Chávez critically portrays the fictional town of Cabritoville, New Mexico, a community on the US-Mexican border populated mainly by Anglo Americans, Chicanos, and Mexicanos. What may appear upon first glance to be a superficial portrait of small-town USA (with gossipy women, jealous friends, and extramarital affairs) is in reality a dialogue between US and Mexican cultural discourses.[1] This dialogue centers on a critique of Mexican cinema of the so-called Golden Age, specifically with respect to its gender roles. Chávez's protagonist forms her feminism by negotiating values of the past (influenced by Mexican cinema and popular culture) with a more progressive Chicana vision of the future (informed by her community of peers and her life experiences). The result is the formation of what I call a transnational border feminist culture. In a broader sense, this transcultural critique advances Chicana/o studies by engaging in a critical dialogue with Mexican studies with respect to feminism, film studies, cultural studies, and literary studies.

A number of Chicana feminist critics have contributed to theoretical paradigms about feminist consciousness. In *Feminism on the Border* (2000), Sonia Saldívar-Hull explores connections between the narratives of Chicanas (Gloria Anzaldúa, Sandra Cisneros, and Helena María Viramontes) and testimonials of women in Latin America (Rigoberta Menchú, Domitila

Barrios de Chungara). By comparing and critiquing specific histories and geographies, Saldívar-Hull helps form a border feminism that crosses national boundaries. In "Traddutora, Traditora: A Paradigmatic Figure of Chicana Feminism" (1994), Norma Alarcón constructs a Chicana feminist theory rooted in the translating skills of the trilingual indigenous woman known as Doña Marina or La Malinche. Alarcón's transnational feminism uses historical texts from sixteenth-century colonial Mexico as well as circumstances of the twentieth-century United States to define a model for Chicana subjectivity:

> Since Chicanas have begun the appropriation of history, sexuality, and language for themselves, they find themselves situated at the cutting edge of a new historical moment involving a radical though fragile change in consciousness. . . . Moreover, such subjectivity is capable of shedding light on Chicanas' present historical situation without necessarily, in this newer key, falling prey to a mediating role but, rather, catching stunning insights into our complex culture by taking hold of the variegated imaginative and historical discourses that have informed the constructions of race, gender and ethnicities in the last five hundred years and that still reverberate in our time. (127)

Chávez's novel depicts a transnational border feminism that is manifested through the transcultural experiences of the protagonist, evoking both Saldívar-Hull's critical paradigm of border feminism and Alarcón's historical account of the minoritarian position of Chicanas who are continually transforming Chicana subjectivity. However, Chávez's approach differs in that she engages the medium of film.[2] Compared to the oral *cuentos* recuperated by Saldívar-Hull or the historical memory Alarcón recovers in the figure of La Malinche, cinema is visually accessible to a larger public inside and outside Mexico and the United States.[3]

Pedro Infante was a legendary Mexican actor, singer, and sex symbol of the Golden Age of Mexican film (roughly 1936–56). Although he died suddenly in an airplane crash in 1957, his fandom persisted as a transnational cultural phenomenon that spread from Mexico to the United States. *Loving Pedro Infante* focuses on the female members of a fan club for the actor, one that serves as a microcosm of a Chicano/Mexican American community. It is thus the response by spectators, mainly women, that gives meaning and significance to this cultural era, just as much as the actual films.[4] Chávez faithfully depicts the cult of admiration that emerged around this popular male figure, but she also demonstrates the emergence of a critical response among the spectators.[5]

In the transnational reception of Golden Age Mexican cinema, among the most affected spectators are contemporary Chicanos/US Mexicans.[6] Although Chávez's apparent admiration for films of this era may seem like a nostalgic gaze at culture, viewing the construction of masculinity and femininity in cinema has played a pivotal role in gender identity formation for generations of US Mexican men and women. In an interview, Chávez elaborates:

> History is very important for me. I grew up with Pedro Infante's movies. The romantic dreams and types of relationships I saw in those movies were part and parcel of who I was, what I wanted in life, or so I thought. Those films have influenced generations of men and women in Mexico and the United States, as well as all around the world. I am only now beginning to understand the dreams of my ancestors and the women and men of my world. The questions I ask myself are, Are my dreams my mother's and father's dreams? Or my grandparents' dreams? What are the contemporary dreams? What does it mean to love someone? In my novel I explore the nature of real love, as opposed to the illusion of love, a celluloid phantasmal love. (Quoted in Kevane and Heredia 2000, 43)

Chávez explains that films represent ideal relationships as dreams, as an escape from the strains of quotidian life and the burdens of reality, but she also reflects on the difference between romanticism and realism with respect to gender roles in society. The Chicana women in her novel must struggle at various levels—in relation to film culture and the realities of their own lives—to understand their past, present, and future and construct their transnational border feminism. One can infer that the power of Mexican film culture over generations can be viewed historically as part of a "celluloid nationalism" achieved through melodrama.[7]

The Golden Age of Mexican Cinema

To understand the significance of the film references in *Loving Pedro Infante*, it is useful to locate this cinema production in its historical context.[8] In many ways, Mexican film functioned in the 1940s and 1950s much as Mexican literature did in the decades after the Revolution of 1910. Like Mexican writers of the period—Rosario Castellanos, Carlos Fuentes, Octavio Paz, Juan Rulfo, and José Vasconcelos, among others—filmmakers were concerned with the construction of a national identity in the twentieth century. By examining the past, both filmmakers and writers were able to fashion a cultural nationalism and affirm an identity based on a dialectical relationship between the past and present. However, Mexican critic Carlos Monsiváis (1995) suggests that film, more than literature, was able to capture the popular imaginary because it is accessible to spectators of different educational levels.[9]

Chávez's explicit and multiple references to scenes in Mexican cinema in *Loving Pedro Infante* demonstrate that film played an influential role in the perception of gender relationships among men and women in Mexico and other Latin American countries in the 1940s and 1950s, particularly in the *arrabales* or working-class neighborhoods of Mexico City. Mexican cinema of this period also provided an alternative image of Latinos by dismantling tropicalized Hollywood representations (such as Desi Arnaz and Carmen Miranda) that often exoticized Latinos.[10] Furthermore, Mexican films of the Golden Age offered a range of representations, from people living in the countryside to those in urban spaces, as Monsiváis points out, but these people were not marginalized and stereotyped the way Latinos were in the US films of the same period.

When Mexican cinema of the Golden Age crossed national borders into the United States, it gained magnified popularity as a commodity encompassing the local, the national, and the global. In *Mexico's Cinema* (1999), film critics Joanne Hershfield and David Maciel explain:

> The producers of the Golden Age went beyond giving the people what they wanted. Their films reflected the desires, social structures, morality, and popular culture of the period [1945–55]. These producers not only met with great success in building up the film industry to become one of the ten most important economic enterprises of the country, but they also captured important distribution markets throughout Latin America, Spain, and the United States. At the height of the Golden Age, in the United States alone there were three hundred movie theaters in the Southwest, Midwest, and East that exclusively showed Mexican cinema. (35)

This process illustrates José David Saldívar's *transfrontera* theory, described in *Border Matters* (1997). Since popular culture materials such as Golden Age Mexican films readily cross borders, they have an impact on the real lives of Chicana/os and other Latina/os in the United States. Chon A. Noriega further explains, "Whether through the classroom, the movie theater, or the television set, Mexican cinema continues to circulate as a cultural presence in the United States" (1994, 1). Thus, one can argue that Chicana/os are developing a transnational identity in part as a consequence of their exposure to Mexican films of this period. Furthermore, cinema yields a kind of freedom that allows spectators, men and women alike, to explore their unconscious, whether through dreams, fantasies, or illusions. When Chávez refers in *Loving Pedro Infante* to the spectator experience in the Colón Theatre in El Paso, Texas, she states, "We are all children in the darkness. In here, no one watches us or tells us how we feel" (2001, 14).[11]

Women at the Border of Film and Reality

Born and raised in Las Cruces, New Mexico, Denise Chávez holds a special position in Chicano/US Latino literature as she synthesizes her roles of novelist, playwright, actress, community activist, and professor. She is one of the first US Latina writers to have her novels published by a mainstream East Coast literary press to national acclaim. While Chávez has also written narratives, short stories, and plays and has produced one-woman shows, the novel *Loving Pedro Infante* is the feminist Mexican Revolution of her literary career, to borrow a metaphor from the novel (199). It is a fearless manifesto on Chicana feminist consciousness, desire, and liberation. Chávez is also probably one of the few writers in the American literary tradition to demonstrate an extensive knowledge of Golden Age Mexican cinema and to use this knowledge to link Chicano/Mexican cultural discourses across national lines.[12] While clear about her Chicana identity, Chávez is deeply committed to the study, incorporation, and critique of Mexican culture and history in her works.[13]

In *Loving Pedro Infante*, Chávez constructs a community of the star's US admirers, the Pedro Infante Club de Admiradores Norteamericanos #256. It consists of a multigenerational group of Chicanas/Mexicanas and a gay Chicano, illustrating the diverse cultural makeup of the border town, Cabritoville. The protagonist, Teresa, says, "The only real family I have, besides Albinita and Irma, are the members of the Pedro Infante Club de Admiradores Norteamericano #256. And the characters of Pedro's movies, whom Irma and I know as well as or better than we do our own kin" (50). The community's ties to the film actors and to each other thus transcend biological family relationships in Chávez's new definition of the term *familia*.

The temporal framework of the novel shifts between the contemporary lives of the club members, the life of Pedro Infante in Mexico City in the 1940s and 1950s, and the world of the Golden Age silver screen with its various temporal modes, including nineteenth-century Mexico in a film such as *Cuando lloran los valientes* (1945). Chávez compares growing up in Mexico in the 1940s and 1950s with living in Cabritoville in the 1950s and 1960s (153–54); Teresa describes the town as "twenty years behind the times" (27). Chávez further experiments with spatiality as she switches between reality and film contexts to show the effects of dreams and (dis)illusions in the characters' lives and the changing values of a border community in transition to modernization. In *Hybrid Cultures* (1995), Néstor García Canclini observes a disjuncture between different developing cultures in border places like Tijuana that may clash as a consequence of capital's influence. Cabritoville may compare on a smaller scale as it evolves from a farming community of goats (*cabritos*), roosters, and chickens to a modern town of "fences or barbed wire, or tall houses" (D. Chávez 2001, 318).

Loving Pedro Infante also focuses on a community of friendships formed through bonding, betrayal, and secrecy. The relationship between the Chicana protagonist Teresa Avila (also called La Tere) and her best friend Irma Granados (La Wirma), who appears to be named after Mexican actress Irma Dorantes, one of Pedro Infante's wives, is crucial in understanding the complexity and evolution of friendships between women who represent different philosophies regarding romance and men. Even though Tere and Wirma differ radically in personality, Chávez shows that there is more depth to this friendship than meets the eye. While Wirma analyzes situations and develops her intellectual life, Tere prefers to expand her spiritual life by communicating through her dreams or through those of the children with whom she works as a teacher's aide. Rather than resort to the traditional paradigms of womanhood available to Chicanas of earlier generations, Chávez is concerned with the alternatives that are offered to independent and intelligent women in their thirties like Tere and Wirma, who often find themselves at the interstices of modernity (thinking independently and critically) and tradition (obeying or living in the shadow of patriarchy). Irma maintains:

> Woman does not live by Man alone. You've always had the wrong attitude, Tere, that's all there is to it. It's the way most women think, and that's what gets them in trouble. We've got to have the right man or no man. But who's the right man? And what about this idea: maybe some women don't even need a man. Or at least in the way that cripples them. (19)

Through the characters of Tere and Wirma, Chávez critiques the development of women who are in the midst of finding their identities as participants in their cultures, as women with liberating impulses, and as socially engaged activists who care about the welfare and future of the community without having to depend on a man.[14] But what motivates these individuals to take control of their lives and act this way?

The novel highlights the bonding between the younger and older generations of women, the latter including Albinita, Tere's mother, and Nyvia Ester, Wirma's mother. When Teresa becomes physically ill after she is abandoned by her lover, it is her mother, Albinita, who comes to her rescue and nurses her (221). Although the older women initially followed the conventional paths set forth for them by marrying and having children, they learned through experience to lead independent lives. For example, Albinita needed to work when her husband passed away unexpectedly while Tere was still a child. Irma's mother, an immigrant woman with limited skills in English, had to support her eight children when her husband left them, shirking his responsibilities as a father. Even though these women belong to an older generation with a different set of values, they did not follow the archetypes of dependent women featured in Mexican films of the Golden Age.[15] Though the older generation of Mexican women in the novel may be enamored of a cultural icon like Pedro Infante, they are gradually distancing themselves from the traditional values of the Golden Age films by not depending on men. Rather, they have learned to think for themselves and to act on their own decisions out of necessity, rejecting patriarchal authority. Albinita passes down wisdom to her daughter: "I have no respect for women like that, Tere. Women who run after men, women who chase men down when they don't want to be found and then try to stay with them when the staying is nearly impossible" (240–41). Both Tere's and Wirma's mothers begin by leading traditional lives, but then they discover that they have to depend on themselves as women, as single heads of households, as matriarchs to a certain extent, to organize and control their own lives. In addition, they hold governing positions in the Pedro Infante fan club, which means they know how to organize a community, an extended family. Chávez makes these mothers their daughters' best friends because, as Tere observes, mothers are not given credit in culture and history.

Doña Meche, a spiritual healer who belongs to the older generation, passes down words of wisdom to awaken Tere to the reality of her love affair, saying, "We can't always be with the people we want to love" (203). Chávez, like many other Chicana writers, emulates neither the Anglo nor the Chicano/Mexican forms of patriarchal domination but insists on carving out a space for Chicana subjectivity, psychologically as well as physically. For the younger generation of women, seeing their mothers as film critics helps the daughters develop more critically because they are the beneficiaries of their mothers' experiences, which serve as lessons in life.

Loving Pedro Infante does not present an obedient Chicana protagonist who conforms to conventional social roles. Chávez prefers to explore the negative stereotypes that surround "fallen" women.[16] She constructs the character of Tere as a divorced elementary school teacher's assistant who has an affair with a married part-time salesman, Lucio Valadez. The relationship between the nonconformist Tere and this traditionally assimilated, perfectionist man becomes a catalyst for Tere as she changes from an easy-going, happy-go-lucky individual to a more cognizant and critical woman who thinks for herself. In the end, she leaves him. Lucio serves as a vehicle for Tere's self-confidence, and he admires her because she never loses her spirituality or her faith in people, a characteristic of many of the female protagonists in Chávez's works. Lucio tells her, "You don't understand. I like the fact that you have faith. I mean, just listen to you. And I do, believe me. You're like a child. You believe the best about people. What more can I say?" (178–79). Lucio may seem to be condescending to Tere by comparing her to a child, yet he also seems to compliment her positive outlook on life and her ability to trust people, a quality that most people, like Lucio, lose as adults.

In her spiritual characterization of Tere, Chávez further alludes to Santa Teresa de Avila, the character's *tocaya*, or namesake. The renowned Spanish poet and nun of the sixteenth century was a reflective and spiritual savior of her community. Moreover, Santa Teresa was talented in the arts; she played musical instruments and enjoyed singing, as does Tere, who delights in performing songs like the ranchera "Mi Tenampa." Yet Tere is well aware of the fact that she herself is not a saint, nor a virgin, nor sexually repressed as women of those times were, and she parodies herself in comparing a list of her values and philosophies with Santa Teresa's (71). Tere's community considers her affair with Lucio Valadez to be immoral behavior and consequently she is dismissed from work, a harsh economic punishment for a single woman. But as secretary of the Pedro Infante Club de Admiradores and a recorder of history, Tere does not allow this conservative judgment by the citizens of Cabritoville to control her life. While she may have compared her life's experiences to those of the characters in Golden Age Mexican cinema before her relationship with Lucio, she rapidly learns that she must differentiate between reality and film. As she becomes aware that she must rise above the limitations placed on women in her community, Teresa brings a transnational border feminist consciousness to bear on the politics of gender roles, both in her own life and in film. In becoming a critic of Golden Age Mexican cinema, she learns as much about her feminism as about the films themselves.

Dialogues with Golden Age Mexican Cinema

By incorporating specific films of the Golden Age in *Loving Pedro Infante*, Chávez bridges Chicano and Mexican cultural discourses and creates a transnational community of film spectatorship. Throughout the novel, but especially in the chapters "Minutes of the Pedro Infante Club de Admiradores Norteamericano #256" and "Another Pedro-athon," Chávez forms a cultural critique of a body of films to gain a better understanding of Pedro Infante's role as a hero of the people in various cinematic contexts. It is the inequality of power between the female and male characters in most of the twenty-six films Chávez mentions that has the greatest impact on the Chicana/o communities in the novel.[17] In particular, the films *Las mujeres de mi general*, *Angelitos negros*, and *A toda máquina* play influential roles in shaping Tere's awareness of gender, race, and socioeconomic status in both the United States and Mexico. She says, "You can learn so much about Mejicano culture, class structure, the relationships between men and women, women and women, men and men, as well as intergenerational patterns of collaterality in Pedro's movies" (51). By examining these films in a transnational context, Chávez critiques patriarchal domination and other social inequalities. The reader gains a better understanding of the relationship between male and female characters in the Golden Age films, but the heart of the novel is the response of the Chicana/o and Mexicana/o spectators and the transference of their responses from the films to their own lives. Miriam Hansen (1991) contends that the bonding between audience members, especially women, and screen characters enables the spectators to form a new concept of their own roles in society. Jacqueline Stewart (2005) agrees with this sentiment, but she adds that the relationship between spectators and the films they view is a fluid process subject to negotiation.

Throughout the novel, Chávez invites the reader to witness the formation of Tere's critical consciousness in response to her critical study of the films (153). What began as an innocent social club among friends suddenly turns into a school of criticism of Golden Age Mexican cinema. Irma says, "You and I should have a Ph.D. from watching Pedro's movies, Tere. We know more about Raza than Raza. If I ever go back to school, it's to get a degree in Mejicano culture. Then we could teach little Mejicanitos with brown faces who can't speak Spanish and little gabachitos who do, what it means to be Mejicanos. And Mejicanas. And, in turn, to be human" (51). The fan club members are educating themselves, learning to comment critically on a history of their Mexican heritage that is available to them via film—a form of culture that is accessible to a mass audience, literate or not. Furthermore, Chávez suggests that this tradition must be passed down to younger generations; otherwise, they will lose a sense of their cultural heritage and identity. Spectators on both sides of the US-Mexico border transform themselves from passive audience members into critical thinkers when they take film experiences that are relevant to their own lives and use them to reflect on their own actions and relationships.

Chávez critiques films in which strong women are on the verge of liberating themselves from patriarchal domination and becoming conscious of their subjectivity but fail to do so because they are dependent on male figures in moments of crisis. For example, Tere comments on the archetype of the *soldadera*, or soldier woman, in the historical film *Las mujeres de mi general* (My General's Women, 1950). It is the story of La Adelita, a soldier who struggles to keep her man and child in the political turmoil of the Mexican Revolution. This woman fights alongside her man to defend the rights of the provincial working class to their land. Although the film portrays the female protagonist as an active revolutionary agent, she does not exist independent of her revolutionary man, portrayed by Pedro Infante. Also, the female protagonist is perceived as the "other woman" when an upper-class literate woman attempts to seduce and finally conquers Infante, signaling a competition among women of different social classes. In her own life, Tere is also perceived as the "other woman," a rival to Lucio's legitimate wife. Tere identifies with the Adelita character as she struggles to keep the relationship with Lucio in the face of moral condemnation by society (199). While the Adelita character struggles to command a formal Spanish, Lucio always tries to improve Tere's vocabulary so she will speak more acceptable and formal English. Similar to the soldier woman, Teresa needs to attain a degree of legitimacy (in relation to career, language, and social status) before she can be accepted by society. Even in the film *Arriba las mujeres* (Go Women, 1943), which tracks women's migration from the countryside to Mexico City, Chávez sees the potential for women to be liberated, but in the end she observes that women lose out to men (124). Unlike the female protagonists in both films, especially in *Las mujeres de mi general*, whose title connotes a man's possession of women as objects, Tere takes control of her situation and learns to educate herself for her own self-improvement, not to win a man's acceptance. By transgressing the US-Mexico cultural borderlands, Tere begins to form her transnational border feminism.

Since the characters of Tere and Wirma are quite savvy and conscious of their working-class ethnic backgrounds, it is no surprise that questions of race and class—exemplified in the hierarchy of the Mexican class system in the film *Angelitos negros* (*Little Black Angels*, 1948), chosen as movie of the month by the fans—attract their attention. Chávez explicitly notes that this film was racist in its selection of actors as well as in its ideological message. Only one black actor was cast; the rest had painted faces, a result of the discriminatory policies against hiring dark-skinned people in Mexico in that period (244–45). Despite the different cultural and historical contexts of the film and novel, Chávez complicates border feminism by not only critiquing the role of privileged and light-skinned women in twentieth-century Mexico but also focusing on the identity of the most marginalized woman, the black woman, in this highly stratified society.

In *Angelitos negros*, the protagonist is a conflicted daughter who knows only her light-skinned father. Her mother is the black maid/housekeeper in the father's household, a fact of which the daughter is unaware. Master and servant were never married and hid their liaison; the mother gave birth out of wedlock and allowed the child's father to raise her. The unacknowledged relationship between the parents is important because of the power imbalance, which implies possible sexual abuse and perhaps rape. The mother decides to hide her daughter's hybrid identity as a *mulata*, a mixture of black, indigenous, and European heritage, to protect her from downward social mobility and shame. But the mixed-heritage daughter, who works as a teacher in a privileged school, develops a deep hatred and overt racism toward those not of her own perceived white racial and class background, including toward her own daughter, who is born black-skinned. At first she blames her husband, a performer/singer played by Pedro Infante, for this shameful outcome, accusing him of having "contaminated" blood in his genealogy. Furthermore, he associates with black and mulatto performers, jeopardizing her dreams and future by mixing with what she considers the "wrong crowd." Chávez uses the film to condemn racism with respect to questions of legitimacy, racial purity, and acceptance into an appropriate class (153). She further suggests that if people of color, especially women, are ever going to receive their due respect in society, they must become speaking and acting subjects of their destinies.

As Tere and Wirma, themselves culturally hybrid women, critically discuss the nature of race and class in this film, they realize that more is at stake regarding the politics of gender, race, and class, in both Mexico and US societies. By crossing national borders between the film and their own realities, they become aware of the significance of cinema as a projection of constructed images or celluloid fantasies: these may be incompatible with their own reality but they are crucial in the formation of their transnational border feminism. Ultimately they realize that they must transcend the limitations of the silver screen as they become more educated women who learn from their own life experiences.

In terms of masculinity, Chávez constructs the character of Lucio Valadez, Tere's married lover, to illustrate a hegemonic form of patriarchal domination. He lies to his wife Diolinda every time he secretly meets Tere at the Sand Motel, where she is symbolically sinking in this extramarital affair. He criticizes Tere's physical appearance and eating habits, evidence that he is yearning to control her body and mind (148). Facing the fact that she is involved with the antithesis of a Prince Charming, Tere compares her own experiences with those of the characters in Golden Age Mexican movies, transforming her real relationship, an extramarital affair, from a fairy tale ending into a disappointing emotional disaster. In drawing this relationship, Chávez moves from representing Pedro Infante as a cultural icon of mythic proportions to pointing out his flaws as a man, one who is a cheater, liar, and womanizer like Lucio. In the end, Tere ceases depending on him as a model of masculinity and starts to rely on herself as a critical thinker in control of her life and relationships.

Chávez offers an alternative model of masculinity in the relationship between Tere and her gay Chicano friend, Ubaldo Miranda, also a member of the Pedro Infante fan club.[18] A victim of childhood sexual abuse by an older male cousin, Ubaldo has experienced a different side of patriarchal domination. He prefers to sing romantic songs, like the Pedro Infante classic "Amorcito corazón," and reveals his feelings more than men are expected to do. Ubaldo also follows an unconventional path as he forms friendships with women in the fan club, especially with Tere. Essentially, she is his best friend.[19] Since Tere was raised in a predominantly matriarchal household and prays to a female God, she does not fear patriarchal control over her life, and perhaps that is why she treats Ubaldo as an equal. She is quite open and direct about her body and sexuality, neither "a repressed virgin nor nun" (150). Ubaldo and Tere also bond because they are both considered outsiders in their small-town community, castigated as *putos* (prostitutes) or "sexual outlaws" for their nonconventional behavior or sexual orientation. They therefore form a community of their own, a "familia from scratch," as Cherríe Moraga would say. Unlike the domineering male character of Lucio Valadez, Ubaldo is not afraid to admit that he admires a male actor—in this case Pedro Infante, an embodiment of physical beauty and the perfect male body. Infante's sensuality and physique, though marketed for the masses, encouraged women and men alike to explore their own bodies, leave behind sexual repression, and accept their sexual orientation and freedom. Chávez incorporates the character of Ubaldo to complicate her transnational border feminism and also to contest the institutionalization of traditional masculinity exemplified by the patriarchal Lucio Valadez. Chávez asks us to consider a new form of masculinity both in Mexican cinema and in *Loving Pedro Infante*.

In constructing the character of Ubaldo, Chávez alludes to certain myths surrounding the real Pedro Infante. When Ubaldo disappears in the novel, a climactic moment, the search for his body is ambiguous because nobody is certain whether he is dead or alive. Rumor has it that he left for Mexico to find a Pedro Infante look-alike boyfriend or "the real thing" (141). This incident is reminiscent of the disappearance of the real Pedro Infante after his death. According to Anne Rubenstein (2001), nobody saw Infante's face or body the day of his burial, leading his fans to doubt his death. Even today, many people, like the fan club members in the novel, believe that he never really died but must be hiding somewhere, like Elvis: "The King is not dead, but lives on forever." Also, Chávez intimates through Ubaldo that Pedro Infante was as meaningful to men, especially gay Chicano/Mexican men, as to women. She believes Infante opened a venue for men to feel comfortable about having male companions in public, as Ubaldo did, and about having other men as intimate, noncompetitive friends. Because of the character of the policeman that Infante portrays in the film *A toda máquina* (*Full Speed Ahead*, 1952), film critics like Sergio de la Mora have read the film as having a homoerotic subtext underneath the patriarchal competitive friendship on the surface (1998, 56–57).[20] Interestingly, the Mexican police were a strong presence at Infante's funeral, playing mariachis in his honor because he valued them as human beings, not just as violent fighters for justice. In the novel, Chávez states, "What about all the mariachis who still love him and all the men from the Police Motorcyclists Union? They respected Pedro for the work he did in *ATM: A Toda Máquina*, in which he played a stunt-riding motorcycle cop" (2001, 137). Ubaldo also follows this troop of admirers and chooses to become part of a transnational border community of the Pedro Infante fan club.

In the chapter "One Little Girl," Chávez begins a critique of the role of women who were subjected to patriarchal domination in the Pedro Infante films of the Golden Age. At the same time, Tere is changing her views on men, romance, and relationships. As a spectator, Tere realizes that she admires the exterior qualities of Pedro Infante (his physique, devotion to carpentry, and singing) but no longer the characters he plays in the films. Tere takes a journey from celluloid melodrama to her real life. By accepting the real life of Pedro Infante, she also learns to accept herself (320). Chávez claims that this conditioning begins in childhood as she observes the young actresses portraying young heroines in films such as *Los tres huastecos, Angelitos negros,* and *Nosotros, los pobres.* It is no small coincidence that Tere wishes to become an elementary school teacher who can help innocent children follow their dreams. She can also serve as a mentor who teaches them about gender equality after having learned from her own life experiences and from viewing Mexican films. As the novel progresses, Tere identifies less and less with the women in the Pedro Infante films (195). She begins to sympathize with them, wishing to form coalitions across national borders, but she is aware that she must break with the tradition of the victimized woman and confront her reality as a transnational border feminist (196).

Several scenes show the changes in Tere. For example, she rewrites orthodox Catholicism as she prays to a female God. She also acknowledges and accepts her abusive relationship with Lucio. Symbolically and literally, Tere finds a voice in her talkative self and in her singing; this annoys Lucio because he feels silenced, an inferior role for a traditionally dominant man. She also realizes that she must break with certain values of the past, with the history of women loving men as opposed to women loving themselves first (254). By burning the clothes she used to attract men at the Tempestad nightclub, Tere breaks with her dependency on men and asserts her identity as a self-motivated woman in control of her life, a border feminist. She states, "All to me now was meaning, and at the expense of sense" (262). Chávez allows Tere to think critically and analyze situations without letting her emotions—or the overpowering melodrama of the Mexican cinema—get the best of her.

Chavez further situates Mexican cinema as a response to the growing dominance of American mainstream culture and of institutionalized Hispanic culture in the United States. At one point, Tere and Wirma meet two proud men of Spanish descent who hail from northern New Mexico, an area known for preserving and speaking "100% pure Castillian Spanish." But La Wirma is not a victim of the cultural amnesia surrounding the history of Spanish colonization, and she does not allow the men to condescend to her. Instead she defends and legitimizes Mexican popular culture by recounting pivotal moments in Mexican history:

I'm the ambassador for Mejicano culture. My culture. I have to be. It's because too many people both here and elsewhere think that Mejicanos are uncultured. . . . What about the Mayan civilization? What about the pyramids? What about Monte Albán? What about Pedro Infante? Maria Felix? What about Cantinflas? Dolores Del Rio? It doesn't matter if we're in or out of Mejico, we're always Mejicanos, with roots as deep as the cottonwoods near the Rio Grande. (191)

Here Chávez reclaims a Mexican cultural legacy by invoking both official history and popular culture, ranging from pre-Columbian icons to the superstars of Mexican cinema—Pedro Infante, Maria Felix, Cantinflas (portrayed by Mexican comic Mario Moreno), and Dolores del Rio. These stars offer an alternative to the familiar Hollywood Latinos (notably Rudolfo Valentino and Rita Hayworth) who denied the reality of mestizaje. Chávez further exhibits her transnational consciousness of history when she refers to the Rio Grande, a geographic and political border between Mexico and the United States. The river is a metaphor for the cultural as well as physical crossings by Mexicans and Mexican Americans that take place despite attempts by border patrol and other law enforcement agents to prohibit this kind of cultural exchange.[21] In this example, Chávez cleverly alludes to the historical period before the Treaty of Guadalupe of 1848, when the ancestors of Mexican Americans were working the land they owned before the American conquest took place (J. Chávez 1984). La Wirma has become a cultural ambassador, a cultural translator of the legacies of cinema and history.[22] While borders, geographic or metaphorical, may conquer and divide communities, Chávez demonstrates her transnational border feminism by using literature and film to bridge communities on both sides of the US-Mexican border.

The Legacy of Pedro Infante and the Transnational Community of the Twenty-First Century

I began the research for this article on a trip to Mexico City in summer 2003, where I investigated Golden Age Mexican cinema and criticism at the Filmoteca (National Film Archive) of the Universidad Nacional Autónoma de México (UNAM) and at Cineteca Nacional. I ended it on April 15, 2007, at a celebration of the fiftieth anniversary of Pedro Infante's death at the Panteón Jardín in Mexico City.[23] At one point in her novel, Chávez notes, "Irma Granados suggested we should think about raising money for the annual pilgrimage to El Panteón Jardín de la Capital de la

República for the anniversary of Pedro's death on April 15" (2001, 107). Life imitates art, or rather, literature. On both occasions I posed questions to a cross-section of people, from taxi drivers and waiters to journalists, academics, and a film director (the son of Ismael Rodríguez, who worked closely with Pedro Infante) regarding the importance of Pedro Infante for them and for the nation.[24] Most people still spoke of this cultural icon as if his spirit lived on in their minds and hearts. In other words, Pedro Infante "no ha muerto"—he has not died (see Rubenstein 2001).

In 2005 I attended the Border Book Festival in Las Cruces, New Mexico, organized by Denise Chávez. She appeared to possess much Pedro Infante memorabilia at the Cultural Center de Mesilla. One could see, for example, posters of plays involving a fan club of women who are obsessed with Pedro Infante and light candles in his memory. Chávez herself holds Pedro-athons (Infante film marathons) for those interested. Infante's spirit is present for me as well as I recall my years growing up in California: my parents would take me to view Mexican movies at movie houses in the Mission District of San Francisco. Those theaters are long gone, but all is not lost. Today, films of the Mexican Golden Age are shown on Spanish-language television, and novels like *Loving Pedro Infante* are taught to younger generations. Infante's legacy lives on, in the United States and beyond.

In *Loving Pedro Infante*, Chávez has created a bridge between Golden Age Mexican cinema and the wider transnational community of spectators, readers, receptors, and listeners, a broad audience that spans national spaces and temporalities. The dreams and illusions constructed by the media—by films, magazines, and other forms of popular culture—give men and women a sense of gender relationships across different kinds of borders. Like today's television soap operas, Golden Age films constitute part of the transnational imaginary in the US-Mexico borderlands. But as Chicana women become empowered by education and social activism, they develop a feminist consciousness that allows them to decide which road to take in seeking social justice and liberation for themselves and their communities. In "The Emergence of the Chicano Novel," literary critic Héctor Calderón (2004) demonstrates that the community of readers of Chicano literature has given as much meaning to the text as is found in the text itself. I would like to extend that argument to claim that in *Loving Pedro Infante*, Chávez's community of spectators has given as much meaning to Golden Age Mexican films as the films have themselves. They have done so through the development of a transnational border feminism, one that crosses and bridges the US-Mexico borderlands.

Notes

Editor's Note: From *Aztlán: A Journal of Chicano Studies* 33, no. 2 (2008). The original essay was lightly edited for this collection.

I would like to extend my gratitude to the anonymous readers and editorial staff of *Aztlán* for their helpful comments in revising this article. Denise Chávez and my parents provided the inspiration to write this piece. Lisbeth Gant-Britton, Erlinda Gonzales-Berry, Irene Matthews, and Ralph Rodriguez read earlier versions of this work and provided important insights. Barbara Curiel and I held many stimulating conversations and she gave wonderful feedback on a later version. I also thank Susan Deeds for suggesting significant Mexican cultural production criticism for this article. The first research trip to the Filmoteca at UNAM and to Cineteca Nacional in Mexico City would not have been possible without the support of Dean Laura Huenneke of the School of Arts and Sciences at Northern Arizona University (NAU) in 2003. At the Filmoteca, I am grateful to the director, Ivan Trujillo, and the staff for helping me gain access to films and criticism not readily available in the United States. I also received an Intramural Summer Grant in 2004 from the Office of the Vice Provost at NAU to fund the writing of this article. Lastly, I am grateful for the hospitality of Héctor Calderón during my trip to Mexico City in 2007, when I was able to visit El Panteón Jardín and complete the last part of this article.

    1. On the presence of gossip (*chismes*) in Chicana narratives, see the chapter on Sandra Cisneros in Mary Pat Brady's *Extinct Lands, Temporal Geographies* (2002).

    2. See Claire Fox's *The Fence and the River* (1999) to understand how the different mass media have represented the US-Mexican geographic border since the Treaty of Guadalupe in 1848 (70, 94, 130–32).

    3. In my formation of transnational border feminism, I draw some distinctions with Gloria Anzaldúa's concept of mestiza consciousness set forth in *Borderlands/La Frontera* (1987). Anzaldúa maintains that Chicanas owe much to their indigenous roots and in particular to Aztec history and mythology, notably the concept of Aztlán, which informs their hybrid identity. Chávez, in her novel, is more concerned with the transnational consciousness that develops in response to two separate, already formed nations, Mexico and the United States, that are separated by a national boundary. Also, Chávez's engagement with Golden Age films is basically a realistic portrayal of contemporary cultural conflicts and relationships while Anzaldúa takes a more idealist, utopian, and somewhat nostalgic view of Aztlán.

    4. In *Cinemachismo* (2006), Sergio de la Mora discusses the importance of the fan clubs in both Mexico and the United States that paid homage to Pedro Infante and his films. In fact, the Club de Admiradores, the title Chávez uses in her novel, was the first Infante fan club in Mexico, but she emphasizes the large number of clubs by giving it a high number, 256.

    5. Jacqueline Stewart (2005) develops a concept of reconstructive spectatorship that "draws on the notions of fluidity, negotiation, heterogeneity, and polyphony." She observes that "by placing movie theaters in this constellation [as a reconstructive process], we can imagine how the cinema as a public space functioned as an important corollary (or alternative) to other spaces in which modern Black

life was experienced" (100–1). Chávez's fictional characters must also negotiate and reconstitute the space of cinema in their lives as Chicanos/Mexicanos.

6. For critical explorations of the role of Chicana/o, immigrant, and women spectators of film, see Miriam Hansen's *Babel and Babylon* (1991), Rosa Linda Fregoso's *The Bronze Screen* (1993), and Vicki Ruiz's "Star Struck" (1993). Hansen details the response by immigrants and women to films at the beginning of the twentieth century, noting that they were in search of an alternative public space and some degree of conformity to the mainstream. But the audience in Chávez's novel is only partly composed of immigrants; the majority are Chicanas who refuse assimilation to the dominant Anglo culture. In this sense the spectators in *Loving Pedro Infante* perform the oppositional discourse put forth by Fregoso and Ruiz.

7. In *Celluloid Nationalism*, Dever (2003, 79) says that "melodrama, as a rhetorical strategy, relies on excess, exaggeration, and a seemingly unending reiteration of its world view. Its history [since the French Revolution] as a modern genre illuminates how it could become such an effective tool in Mexico's post-revolutionary forge." Furthermore, melodrama could bring Mexico to "national unity," and like the muralists, Mexican cinema would render "the terms of citizenship in this new nation."

8. The Golden Age of Mexican cinema (the 1940s and 1950s) should be understood in terms of cultural politics and the formation of the Mexican nation-state. During this time, Mexico was undergoing a rapid process of modernization as it nationalized its economic and cultural assets, everything from oil to cinema (see Fein 2001, Fox 1999, Monsiváis 1995, and Rubenstein 2001). After a period of relative economic stability in the 1930s under the auspices of President Lázaro Cárdenas, the Mexican government negotiated with the US government and cultural curators (Rockefeller and Whitney) to promote its nationalism in culture and the arts. As the United States attempted to enforce the rhetoric of its Good Neighbor policy before and during World War II, it used its economic power to favor nations like Mexico. Among other things, this meant supporting the development of Mexican cinema while remaining indifferent to Argentina (which was neutral during the war) and the decline of its cinema project. The United States offered capital and technology to Mexican cinema directors, producers, and artists to help build the Mexican cinema industry. In reality, this transnational economic flow continued the neocolonial and imperialist relationship between the United States and Latin America. Mexico became an important ally due to its geography: as the closest Spanish-speaking neighbor of the United States, it could use its cinema to control and manipulate other audiences in Latin America who were disappointed with Hollywood's portrayal of Latin culture (see Fein 2001). Historian Seth Fein has argued that Pedro Infante became instrumental in selling a certain image of Mexico; in the films of this era, he appeared as a defender of social justice and patriotism in the face of evil and tyranny, which in the World War II period meant Germany and the other Axis powers.

9. Monsiváis elaborates on the function of Mexican cinema of this period. In "Mythologies," he states, "Mexican cinema, above all in the period 1939–55, makes great use of what is stored in the cultural memory of the people: expressions of love, forms of horror and catharsis, dishonour and excess, shared ideas about poverty and wealth, religious certainties, new forms of sexual appetite and hunger, songs, a sense

of humour petrified in jokes and amusing, theatrical ways of evoking tradition. . . . A modest but implacable cultural revolution is replacing literature as the centre of mass veneration, promoting at the same time, and without contradiction, both literacy and opening up a new space for a new audience, that draws its inspiration both from old customs and from the demands of modernization" (1995, 81).

10. See Frances Aparicio's introduction and definition of tropicalization in terms of the representation of Latinos and Latinas in both literature and popular culture. The rhetoric of tropicalization was not enough for global Spanish-speaking audiences. It was and is too formulaic as far as the role of the Latin lover is concerned (Aparicio and Chávez-Silverman 1997). For more on the Latin lover, see Hansen's (1991) chapters on Rudolph Valentino. This cultural exploitation of Latina/o images by Hollywood can be considered a colonial phenomenon similar to European fetishism of Asian/Indian cultures critiqued by Edward Said in *Orientalism* (1979).

11. In *A Taco Testimony* (2006), Chávez states that for the research on her novel she visited the Colón Theatre on the Texas/Mexico border; it is now a restaurant.

12. A number of works by Chicana/o authors refer explicitly to Pedro Infante and/or Golden Age Mexican culture. Examples include Norma Cantú's *Canicula* (1997), Sandra Cisneros's short stories "Mexican Movies" and "*Bien* Pretty" in *Woman Hollering Creek* (1991) and Cisneros's novel *Caramelo* (2002), Francisco Jiménez's *The Circuit* (1997), and John Rechy's *Miraculous Day of Amalia Gómez* (1994). Chávez actually makes this cultural production a central topic of her novel.

13. Chávez elaborated on her identity and motivation in a 2003 telephone interview with the author.

14. See Erlinda Gonzales-Berry and David Maciel's *Contested Homeland* (2000) for a historical account of the growing community and contributions of Chicanos in New Mexico and possibilities for the future.

15. See Rubenstein (2001) for a vivid discussion of gender roles in Pedro Infante films and the reception among audiences, both men and women. Also, de la Mora (1998) elaborates on the role of gender in the construction of masculinity in Pedro Infante films. The grandmother (often portrayed by legendary Mexican actress Sara García), the "fallen" woman or femme fatale, the "good" woman who is a virgin, and the religious woman are just a few examples of the female archetypes who played opposite Pedro Infante in his films.

16. Since the Chicano movement of the 1960s, Chicana writers have responded to the negative image of fallen women in various ways. Such women appear frequently in Golden Age Mexican cinema, including in the classic Pedro Infante film *Nosotros, los pobres* (1947). In Mexican film culture of this period, the figure of the fallen woman is ostracized and castigated, or death befalls her as punishment for her sins, which may range from drunkenness to sexual bravado to the shame of having a child out of wedlock. Once again, this archetype resembles the image of the *vendida/traidora*, alluding to Malinche in colonial Mexican history, as critics like Alarcón and Cherríe Moraga have theorized. See Alarcón's "Traddutora, Traditora" (1994) and Moraga's "A Long Line of Vendidas" in *Loving in the War Years* (1983) on betrayal of the community and the role of translator and traitor.

17. Recent works by Sergio de la Mora (2006) and Theresa Delgadillo (2006) make passing reference to Chávez's *Loving Pedro Infante*, but they mainly

analyze Pedro Infante and focus on specific films of his. I am more interested in how Chávez engages with Golden Age Mexican cinema to delineate its effects on Chicana/o spectators. In examining the Pedro Infante fan club as a critical school of thought, Chávez refers to approximately twenty-six films starring Pedro Infante. This legendary actor enjoyed sustained popularity among the communities of the US-Mexican borderlands, due in part to his physical appearance and working-class origins, and he exhibited great versatility in the cinematic roles he undertook. For example, he played a *charro/revolucionario* (cowboy/revolutionary) in historical films such as *Cuando lloran los valientes* (*When the Brave Cry*, 1945), *Dicen que soy mujeriego* (*They Say I Am a Womanizer*, 1945), *Las mujeres de mi general* (*My General's Women*, 1950), and *La vida no vale nada* (*Life Is Not Worth Anything*, 1955). But he also played an urban carpenter in the melodramatic trilogy *Nosotros, los pobres* (*We, the Poor*, 1947), *Ustedes, los ricos* (*You, the Rich*, 1948), and *Pepe, el toro* (*Pepe, the Boxer*, 1951); a nightclub performer in *Angelitos negros* (*Little Black Angels*, 1948); an orchestra conductor in *Sobre las olas* (*Above the Waves*, 1950); and a police officer in *A toda máquina* (*Full Speed Ahead*, 1952) and its sequel *Qué te ha dado esa mujer?* (*What Has That Woman Done to You?*, 1952). His last role was that of a Oaxacan indigenous man in *Tizoc* (1956), for which Infante was awarded posthumously the International Berlin Bear Award for best actor. Other films that Chávez mentions in her novel include the technically experimental *Los tres huastecos* (*The Three Huastecos*, 1948); *La mujer que yo perdí* (*The Woman I Lost*, 1949); *Los gavilanes* (*The Sparrowhawks*, 1954); *El enamorado* (*The Boyfriend/Lover*, 1951); *Gitana, tenías que ser* (*You Had To Be a Gypsy*, 1953); *Arriba las mujeres* (*Go Women*, 1943); *La oveja negra* (*The Black Sheep*, 1949); *No desearás la mujer de tu hijo* (*You Will Not Desire Your Son's Wife*, 1949); *Los hijos de María Morales* (*The Sons of Maria Morales*, 1952); *Un rincón cerca del cielo* (*A Corner Near Heaven*, 1952); *Ahora soy rico* (*I Am Rich Now*, 1952); *El inocente* (*The Innocent*, 1955); *Vuelven los García* (*The Garcías Return*, 1946); *El gavilán pollero* (*The Rooster*, 1950); and finally, *Islas Marías* (*María Islands*, 1950).

18. In Chicano literature, we see the representation of the gay man and gay sexuality in the works of Arturo Islas, John Rechy, Richard Rodriguez, and Michael Nava. Two feminists of color, Cherríe Moraga and Gloria Anzaldúa, also discuss, complicate, and elaborate the interstices of identity, race, gender, and sexual orientation in their groundbreaking collection *This Bridge Called My Back: Radical Writings by Women of Color* (1981).

19. Friendships between gay men and straight women, as alternatives to conventional man-woman relationships, have featured recently in US popular culture, for example in the hit TV comedy *Will and Grace*.

20. See the chapter on buddy movies in *Cinemachismo* (de la Mora 2006).

21. For an understanding of the im/migrant experiences in Chicana/o fiction, consider Helena María Viramontes's *Under the Feet of Jesus* (1994) and Francisco Jiménez's *The Circuit* (1997) as example narratives.

22. See Fox's last chapter in *The Fence and the River* (1999), where she discusses the role of a cultural ambassador in cautionary terms.

23. I met fans from all over the world at this event, including from Germany, Venezuela, and the United States, as well as, of course, native Mexicans. Some

played Pedro Infante songs, while others dressed up as memorable characters from films such as *Tizoc* and *A toda máquina*.

24. For a more contemporary understanding and reading of the impact of Pedro Infante, see historical film critic Gustavo Garcia's *La época de cine de oro* (1997) and *No me parezco a nadie* (1998).

Works Cited

Alarcón, Norma. 1994. "Traddutora, Traditora: A Paradigmatic Figure of Chicana Feminism." In *Scattered Hegemonies*, edited by Inderpal Grewal and Caren Kaplan, 110–33. Minneapolis: University of Minnesota Press.

Anzaldúa, Gloria. 1987. *Borderlands/La Frontera: The New Mestiza*. San Francisco: Aunt Lute.

Aparicio, Frances, and Susana Chávez-Silverman, eds. 1997. *Tropicalizations: Transcultural Representations of Latinidad*. Hanover, NH: University Press of New England.

Brady, Mary Pat. 2002. *Exctinct Lands, Temporal Geographies: Chicana Literature and the Urgency of Space*. Durham, NC: Duke University Press.

Calderón, Héctor. 2004. "The Emergence of the Chicano Novel: Tomás Rivera's . . . *y no se lo tragó la tierra* and the Community of Readers." In *Narratives of Greater Mexico: Essays on Chicano Literary History, Genre, and Borders*, 65–84. Austin: University of Texas Press.

Canclini, Néstor García. 1995. *Hybrid Cultures: Strategies for Leaving and Entering Modernity*. Minneapolis: University of Minnesota Press.

Cantú, Norma. 1997. *Canicula*. Albuquerque: University of New Mexico Press.

Chávez, Denise. 2001. *Loving Pedro Infante*. New York: Farrar, Straus & Giroux.

———. 2006. *A Taco Testimony: Meditations on Family, Food and Culture*. Tucson, AZ: Rio Nuevo.

Chávez, John. 1984. *The Lost Land*. Albuquerque: University of New Mexico Press.

Cisneros, Sandra. 1991. *Woman Hollering Creek*. New York: Random House.

———. 2002. *Caramelo*. New York: Random House.

de la Mora, Sergio. 1998. "Masculinidad y mexicanidad: Panorama teórico bibliográfico." In *Horizontes de la investigación*, edited by Julianna Burton-Carvajal, Angel Miguel, and Patricia Torres-San Martin, 45–63. Mexico City: Guadalajara/Instituto Mexicano de Cinematografía.

———. 2006. *Cinemachismo: Masculinities and Sexuality in Mexican Film*. Austin: University of Texas Press.

Delgadillo, Theresa. 2006. "Singing 'Angelitos Negros': African Diaspora Meets *Mestizaje* in the Americas." *American Quarterly* 58, no. 2: 407–30.

Dever, Susan. 2003. *Celluloid Nationalism and Other Melodramas: From Post-Revolutionary Mexico to Fin de Siglo Mexamérica*. Albany: State University of New York Press.

Fein, Seth. 2001. "Cultural Imperialism and Nationalism in Golden Age Mexican Cinema." In *Fragments of a Golden Age: The Politics of Culture in Mexico since*

1940, ed. Gilbert Joseph, Anne Rubenstein, and Eric Zolov, 159–98. Durham, NC: Duke University Press.

Fox, Claire F. 1999. *The Fence and the River: Culture and Politics at the US-Mexico Border*. Minneapolis: University of Minnesota Press.

Fregoso, Rosa Linda. 1993. *The Bronze Screen: Chicana and Chicano Film Culture*. Minneapolis: University of Minnesota Press.

García, Gustavo. 1997. *La época de cine de oro*. Mexico City: Clío.

———. 1998. *No me parezco a nadie: La vida de Pedro Infante*. Mexico: Clío.

Gonzales-Berry, Erlinda, and David Maciel, eds. 2000. *The Contested Homeland*. Albuquerque: University of New Mexico Press.

Hansen, Miriam. 1991. *Babel and Babylon: Spectatorship in American Silent Film*. Cambridge, MA: Harvard University Press.

Hershfield, Joanne, and David R. Maciel, eds. 1999. *Mexico's Cinema: A Century of Film and Filmmakers*. Wilmington, DE: SR Books.

Jiménez, Francisco. 1997. *The Circuit: Stories from the Life of a Migrant Child*. Albuquerque: University of New Mexico Press.

Kevane, Bridget, and Juanita Heredia, eds. 2000. *Latina Self-Portraits: Interviews with Contemporary Women Writers*. Albuquerque: University of New Mexico Press.

Monsiváis, Carlos. 1995. "Mythologies." In *Mexican Cinema*, edited by Paulo Antonio Paranaguá, Ana M. López, and Ignacio Durán Loera, 117–27. London: British Film Institute in association with Consejo Nacional para la Cultura y las Artes de México.

Moraga, Cherríe. 1983. *Loving in the War Years: Lo que nunca pasó por sus labios*. Boston: South End Press.

Moraga, Cherríe, and Gloria Anzaldúa, eds. 1981. *This Bridge Called My Back: Writings by Radical Women of Color*. New York: Women of Color Press.

Noriega, Chon A., ed. 1994. *The Mexican Cinema Project*. Los Angeles: UCLA Film and Television Archive.

Rechy, John. 1994. *The Miraculous Day of Amalia Gómez*. New York: Arcade/Little Brown.

Rubenstein, Anne. 2001. "Bodies, Cities, Cinema: Pedro Infante's Death as Political/Spectacle." In *Fragments of a Golden Age: The Politics of Culture in Mexico since 1940*, edited by. Gilbert Joseph, Anne Rubenstein, and Eric Zolov, 199–233. Durham, NC: Duke University Press.

Ruiz, Vicki. 1993. "'Star Struck': Acculturation, Adolescence, and the Mexican American Woman, 1920–1950." In *Building with Our Hands: New Directions in Chicana Studies*, edited by Adela de la Torre and Beatríz M. Pesquera, 109–29. Berkeley: University of California Press.

Said, Edward. 1979. *Orientalism*. New York: Vintage.

Saldívar, José David. 1997. *Border Matters: Remapping American Cultural Studies*. Berkeley: University of California Press.

Saldívar-Hull, Sonia. 2000. *Feminism on the Border: Chicana Gender Politics and Literature*. Berkeley: University of California Press.

Stewart, Jacqueline. 2005. *Migrating to the Movies: Cinema and Black Urban Modernity*. Berkeley: University of California Press.

Viramontes, Helena María. 1994. *Under the Feet of Jesus*. New York: Dutton.

Serial Sexual Femicide in Ciudad Juárez, 1993–2001

Julia Monárrez Fragoso

> In memory of Guillermina Valdés-Villalva

> It is not the final moments of this child's life that we are talking about.
> We are talking about a slow, long death. We may never know what
> those final moments were, and maybe that's a kindness. But we don't
> need to know . . . this was a crime of power.
> —Alice Vachss, *Sex Crimes*

> The appropriation of women's bodies, for sexual gratification or as a
> symbol of "victorious conquest," is a common theme in the literature
> on violence against women in war or other situations of conflict.
> —Monica McWilliams,
> "Violence Against Women in Societies under Stress"

I wouldn't be so interested in serial sexual femicide if not for the series
of murders of women and girls that has taken place in Ciudad Juárez.[1]
Nor would it be the subject of this paper if not for the impunity that has
prevailed and the meager information available about the killings. For
these reasons, I have researched the literature on femicide in Mexico and
discovered that in Latin America few feminist theorists, with the exception
of Ana Carcedo and Montserrat Sagot, have explored and investigated the
phenomenon of femicide.[2] This is not so in other countries.

The murders of more than 200 women in Ciudad Juárez since 1993,
and the torture and rape of almost 100 of them, are painful testimony to
the vulnerability of girls and women on the border and to the male violence
perpetrated against them. The media and the judicial agencies in charge of
solving the murders refer to them as homicides of women, serial killings,
and sex crimes. On the other hand, the police investigations have created

more doubts and problems than solutions. The information gathered remains insufficient and vague. Patricio Martínez, governor of the state of Chihuahua, declared:

> I ask the people of Chihuahua how they can today demand that we solve these crimes when all we got from the previous administration was twenty-one bags of bones. We don't know their names. We don't know what the circumstances were for those acts. The files are poorly put together. . . . How do we investigate these homicides?[3]

And the crimes continue.

The lack of a comprehensive strategy by the authorities charged with the administration of justice can be seen on various levels.[4] First, access is not allowed to the files on the murdered women to corroborate the exact number of women killed, the type of violence used to kill them, and whether the murderers have actually been convicted. Second, foreign and national criminologists who have come in to assist do not agree on the profile of the so-called serial killer, or they say that one does not exist, or that there are various copycats.[5] Third, a special prosecutor's office for the investigation of homicides against women was set up, but its personnel has changed four times.[6] Fourth, aspersions have been cast on the moral character of the victims.[7] Finally, questions have been raised and posed to the authorities regarding the men detained for these crimes against women. All this points to the inability of the police forces to deal with the problem, and above all it casts doubt on the capacity of the judicial institutions responsible for public safety, because the crimes continue.[8]

Insecurity and violence seem to be endemic in Ciudad Juárez. Its location on the border gives it certain characteristics not found in other cities of Mexico. The seat of a drug cartel, it is known as a violent place (Sánchez 1999, 44); men as well as women die violently here.[9] Nonetheless, the deaths of women express a gendered oppression and the relations of inequality between men and women; they are manifestations of domination, terror, social extermination, patriarchal hegemony, social class, and impunity.

Theoretical Reflections

> But if there is no compelling reason to use the same definition as that used by those with whom one disagrees, then it makes sense to define a phenomenon in a way that best fits feminist principles.
> —Diana E. H. Russell, *Making Violence Sexy*

Even though feminist criminology has made its way into mainstream criminology, its most important contribution has centered on the victimization of women, that is, on the kinds of crimes of which women are most frequently the victims. Sociological studies concerning violence and women's sexuality have especially focused on rape and personal assault (Britton 2000, 8). It could be said that feminist criminology started in 1976 with publication of the book *Women, Crime and Criminology: A Feminist Critique*, whose author, Carol Smarts, considers issues ignored by the criminological establishment, such as the experiences of women as offenders and as victims of crime (Britton 2000, 2).

In the 1980s feminist academics started questioning other areas of criminology, such as the murder of women. One of the chief contributions of this new incursion of gender into mainstream criminological studies was the analysis of sexual killings, in which all of the serial sexual killers are men and a majority of their victims are women.[10]

Jane Caputi, Deborah Cameron, and Elizabeth Frazer were the first to systematically analyze sexual killings from a gender perspective. However, Diana E. H. Russell coined the theoretical term *femicide* in 1976.[11] It is defined as the misogynist killing of women by men, and represents a continuation of sexual assault; in identifying femicide one must take into account the violent acts, the motives, and the imbalance of power between the sexes in the political, social, and economic spheres. Femicide occurs in direct proportion to the structural changes taking place in a society and in direct relation to the community's degree of tolerance of these acts and their level of violence (Vachss 1994, 227). All of the circumstances and all of the policies that end the lives of women are tolerated by the state and other institutions (Radford and Russell 1992).

In *The Age of Sex Crime*, Jane Caputi addresses the serial sexual murder of women by men.[12] She states that crimes of lust, rape-murder, serial killings, and recreational killings are new terms for a new kind of crime. This kind of murder by no means should be seen as lacking motives, since rape, torture, mutilation, and finally extermination speak to us of "'sexual murder' as sexually political murder, as functional phallic terrorism" (Caputi 1987, 2).

Nor can serial sexual murder be explained as an eruption of evil forces, as the "aberrant behavior of mysterious sexual maniacs," or as the work of "psychopaths," Caputi says (109).[13] She continues the line of reasoning set forth by Mary Daly and Andrea Dworkin, who portray these crimes as a logical consequence of the patriarchal system that maintains male supremacy through what Daly calls "gynocide" and Dworkin defines as "the systematic crippling, raping, and/or killing of women by men . . . the relentless violence perpetrated by the gender class men on the gender class women" (1976, 16, 19).[14]

The killing of women is usual in the patriarchy. Still, the twentieth century has been marked by a new class of crimes against women, one that includes torture, mutilation, rape, and the murder of women and girls. The upsurge in frequency of these acts has led Caputi to call our times "the age of sex crime." This epoch started with Jack the Ripper, the still-unknown London killer who in 1888 murdered and mutilated five prostitutes. The Ripper and his crimes established a tradition of sexual murders and sexual murderers whose purpose is "to terrorize women and to empower and inspire men" (Caputi 1989, 445).

Consequently, serial sexual murder is a ritualistic mythic act in the contemporary patriarchy where sex and violence meld, where an intimate relationship between manliness and pleasure is established:

> The murders of women and children—including torture and murder by husbands, lovers, and fathers, as well as that committed by strangers—are not some inexplicable evil or the domain of "monsters" only. On the contrary, sexual murder is the ultimate expression of sexuality as a form of power. (39)

Although the causes of violence are not found in the "pathological" characteristics of offenders, they do relate to the social status of the victims (Andersen 1983, 196).[15] When a society faces the extermination of women on a daily basis, it makes no sense to ask why one individual kills another. The question should be, rather, "why members of some *groups* kill members of others" (Cameron and Frazer 1987, 30, emphasis in original). In seeking an answer, we need to interrelate the motives and the violent acts of the criminals and place them within the framework of the social structures of a particular region and the inequalities in the hierarchy of sexual power (30).

However, Cameron and Frazer, in their book *The Lust to Kill*, go beyond the concept of male violence as a phenomenon derived from patriarchy. They explore the irrational fusion of sex and violence and ask why *some* men find killing the objects of their desire—whether men or women—to be "erotic."[16] They conclude that such brutal acts reflect not only misogyny and sadistic sexuality, but also the social construction of masculinity as a form of supremacy over others, both female and male, because the victims can be men as well as women. What is constant is the gender of the victimizer:

male. Therefore, these authors conclude that the presence of rape or sexual assault is neither a necessary nor a sufficient condition to label a crime as sexual. What is important is the "eroticization of the act of killing." Sexual murder is defined as and includes all cases in which the killer is motivated by sadistic sexual impulses, by "the lust to kill." This too is the product of a certain social order (Cameron and Frazer 1987, 18–19, 33).

Pornography, with the violence and degradation of women it portrays, can be and is a cause of rape. But in considering rape and femicide other causative factors should also be taken into account, such as men's socialization, men's experiences of sexual abuse during their childhood and adolescence, and the ease of purchasing firearms (Russell 1993, 257–58). It should be noted, though, that most sexual abuse is committed against girls and women, and by no means do these experiences turn *them* into sexual killers.

The analysis of crimes against women and girls inevitably takes us to the theoretical construct of femicide. This social phenomenon is tied into the patriarchal system that, to a greater or lesser degree, sets up women to be murdered, whether for the simple fact of being women or for not "behaving properly" as women. The latter presumes that the woman has "stepped out of line" and gone beyond established limits of accepted female behavior.[17] Accordingly, the authorities in Chihuahua state in reference to the victims:

> It is important to note that the behavior of some of the victims is not consistent with the guidelines of the established moral order, given that there has been excessive frequenting during the late night hours of entertainment places not appropriate for their age in some cases, as well as inadequate care and abandonment of the families with whom they have lived.[18]

Femicide comprises a progression of violent acts that range from emotional, psychological, and verbal abuse through battery, torture, rape, prostitution, sexual assault, child abuse, female infanticide, genital mutilation, and domestic violence—as well as all policies that lead to the deaths of women, tolerated by the state.

Religious institutions are not far behind. On December 16, 2001, the Catholic Church held an event in Juárez titled "Light and Justice for the Women of Our City," in which it called the murdered women angels in the presence of God, singing "Holy, Holy" to the good God. For its part, the Evangelical Ministerial Alliance of Ciudad Juárez sponsored on December 4 of the same year a forum on violence against women, during which the deaths of women were referred to as the work of a satanic cult that will last twelve years. Therefore, there are still four more years for the production of angels to be dragged to heaven by Satan.

In reality, the motive for femicide can be hatred, pleasure, anger, malice, jealousy, separation, arguments, robbery, or simply the sensation of possessing and dominating the woman and ultimately exterminating her. The victimizer can be a father, lover, husband, friend, acquaintance, stranger, or boyfriend, among others. In all cases these are violent men who believe they have the right to kill women.

But to leave the social class of the murdered women out of the analysis is to forget that sexuality is configured through subjectivity and society (Weeks 1998, 40). By killing certain women and girls who appear especially vulnerable, the murderers seek to control all women by ensuring that they internalize the threat and message of sexual terrorism (Caputi 1987, 118). This, together with the violence prevention campaigns, places restraints on women, on their mobility, and on their conduct in public and in private.

Prevention campaigns in this city have centered on making women responsible for any aggression that might befall them, especially if they go out at night or walk down a deserted street. Warnings have been sent out about attending parties, staying out until the early morning hours, walking alone, and, most important for the woman who is a worker, dressing provocatively and consuming alcoholic beverages; her guardian angel, it is said, will not always be there to take care of her. Men have been called upon to show their manliness and machismo by watching over their women and the activities in which they participate. These statements, as Tabuenca Córdoba asserts, are classist, misogynist, and heterosexist (1998, 10). Without a radical goal of eliminating sexual violence rather than just simply responding to it, prevention becomes an effort directed toward the victims or potential victims (Kelly and Radford 1998, 72).

Murders of women are also closely related to the structural changes taking place in a given society, and to the degree of tolerance that the society shows toward the killings and their level of violence (Vachss 1994, 227). Arturo González Rascón, attorney general for the state of Chihuahua, explains:

> What's going on is that we are all focusing right now on Ciudad Juárez, and perhaps if something like this happens in Chihuahua it isn't noticed, and if it happens in Torreón it isn't noticed, or in Durango or in the state of Sinaloa, where since January there have already been 96 homicides and it hasn't been noticed.[19]

205

It is important to note that, while all of the studies cited establish gender as a key construct in analyzing the murder of women, the social class system or other power structures or material conditions that can influence male violence against women are merely mentioned, not analyzed. Nonetheless, certain authors, including Monica McWilliams, affirm that societies under stress are particularly prone to violence against women. She defines these as societies that are undergoing a process of transformation, which may be modernization, civil unrest, war, or terrorism. Such experiences are not the only determining factors; religious systems and ideologies must also be understood as contributing to the escalation and legitimization of violence. Yet, *"attitudes toward the perpetrators and victims as well as the strategies available to prevent and combat [violence] may be dependent on both the political and ideological 'forces' that exist"* (McWilliams 1998, 112; italics mine).

Ciudad Juárez, located on the border, has certain peculiarities that are not found in other Mexican cities. There is a constant influx of migrants, both men and women, who find this a good place to settle or to cross over into the United States. Drug cartels operate here as well.[20] Because channels to US consumer markets are more accessible in this area, conditions are favorable not only for drug trafficking but also for the industrialization process that attracts men and women to jobs. The social relations and networks of these migrants—their families, friends, and relatives—have been altered as a result of the transformations taking place in the country.[21]

I assume that all these factors are closely related to the violence being committed against women. Even though violence against women existed long before the current processes of change taking place in the city, the continuing murders of women—raped, killed, and dumped into vacant lots and deserted areas—are a phenomenon not seen before the 1990s.[22]

Nevertheless, it should be emphasized that any investigation of the killing of women and girls in Ciudad Juárez that does not take into account the perspective that gender "is a constitutive element of social relationships based on perceived differences between the sexes [and] a primary way of signifying relationships of power" (Scott 2000, 289)—as well as the perspective of social class—will not succeed in explaining what has happened on this border. Indeed, the murder of women and girls who were born submerged in structures of inequality is directly related to these same structures.

Using the concept of sexual femicide as an analytical tool, this study seeks to analyze the crimes in Ciudad Juárez from the perspective of social class, since the social category of "female" is shaped by—among other influences—the class structure of society. Failure to take social class into account "would make it more difficult for [women] to identify and challenge the basis of the inequality which they experience" (Skeggs 1997, 6).

Marxist theory defines social classes as "groups of social agents, of men defined *principally* but not exclusively by their place in the *production process*, i.e. by their place in the economic sphere" (Poulantzas 1977, 96; italics in original). Marx was not interested in gender; therefore, sexual oppression is not a prominent theme in his analysis. For him, human beings are defined in relation to the means of production: they are peasants, workers, laborers, and capitalists, without distinguishing between men and women (Rubin 1999, 18).

However, the concepts of gender and class should be analyzed as "historically situated, not universal" (Bellhouse 1999, 960). No analysis centered on the reproduction of the workforce can explain "foot binding, chastity belts, or any of the incredible array of Byzantine, fetishized indignities, let alone the more ordinary ones, which have been inflicted upon women in various times and places" (Rubin 1999, 21). Andrea Dworkin calls these practices "culturally normalized violence against women" (1997, 20).

Nonetheless, violence can be understood not only as taking different forms, but also as occurring within very concrete and specific circumstances. In his *Economic and Philosophic Manuscripts of 1844*, Marx examines the male-female relationship within the framework of the theory of alienated labor, bourgeois society, and private property. Although the relationship between the sexes enters into this only accidentally, rather than being formally articulated, the analysis has the merit of situating the topic in a *concrete and historical field* in which the interpersonal relations between human beings unfold (Manieri 1978, 145).

When Marx and Engels speak of violence, in addition to relating it to social class, they refer to the hegemony of the state: "Violence is the political power of one class organized against another" (1980, 1: 129–30), but it is also "the power of the state [that] as such, is an economic power" (3: 522).

State officials attempt to justify violence against women based on their own stereotypes of class, gender, and appropriate spaces reserved for women. For example, the Chihuahua attorney general, Arturo González Rascón, has said:

> Unfortunately, there are women who because of the circumstances of their lives, the places where they go about their activities, are at risk; because it would be very difficult for anyone going out into the street when it is raining, well, it would be very difficult for them not to get wet.[23]

Rather than spotlight only the behavior of women, as the attorney general does, we need also to analyze the desire of men to kill them. There is no point in examining the behavior of prostitutes, factory workers, youth, students, or women in general, because to do so would ignore the poverty in which they live and, above all, would fail to scrutinize the violence on the part of some men, demanding instead that women themselves prevent rape and murder (Cameron and Frazer 1987, 110). While it is true that we women must take responsibility for ourselves, what happens when conditions of poverty force some women to work night shifts? What happens when women live in areas with little urban infrastructure and no electric lights? When there is neither private nor public transportation to drop women at their doors? And what about young girls? Marcia Pally argues that the key is neither sex, nor position, nor custom, but force, whether psychological, physical, or economic. This is the real root of the problems women experience. Men who rape do so because it hurts women, and a society that wishes to reduce that kind of violence must direct its attention to finding the reasons that men inflict such harm. Toward that end a society must enable women to develop the emotional capacity to know what their desires really are and the economic means to be able to say no to sexual violence and all forms of intimidation (Pally 1997, 25, 28).

On the other hand, violence is learned as a social model that lacks a social conscience to eradicate it (Fisas 1998b, 16). In violence there is an aggressor who seeks to benefit by subjecting another person to his aggression; irrespective of whether the violence is legal or illegal, it damages the physical and psychic well-being and the bodily integrity of the person who suffers it (Asensio Aguilera 1998, 19). In addition, in an act of violence, whether physical or verbal, a person is forced against her will to do what she does not want to do (Cortina 1998, 28). Violence requires an object, an object to which contrasting values can be applied, such as inferiority versus superiority. This way, the person who is the object is first dehumanized and their spirit broken by other factors such as poverty, or any other difference, whatever it may be. The object is a faceless being who is subjected to terror in all its raw brutality (Devalle 2000, 22). "We are facing a kind of violence in which the cause of aggression is neither ideological differences nor the possession of something valued, whether a position of power or a concrete material object—but the woman herself, her body and her life" (Sau 1998, 169).

The study of the body and criminology is central to the works of Foucault. The body, he says, is the territory of history, of biology, of physiological investigation, but also of society, of productive processes, and of ideologies. The body is a political field, pulled taut between competing powers that act and leave their mark on it, restrict it, and subject it to torture, punishment, and rituals. Violence is one of the mechanisms through which bodies with lesser power are taught agonizing lessons by those with greater power (Foucault 1998, 32, 35).

Foucault analyzes the production and redistribution of criminality as a kind of economy of illegalities, and as a crucial element in the rise and the construction of justice of the new ruling class—the bourgeoisie (277–78). This places the emphasis on its economic and class character (Bellhouse 1999, 959). In this context we may recall the statements made by Juan Carlos Olivares Ramos, president of the Asociación de Maquiladoras de Ciudad Juárez (AMAC):

> It is a very small number [of deaths], and yet we had people from the entire world interviewing us. . . . The fact that the authorities informed the general public that most of these women worked at the various factories, it taints the reputation not only of the city, but of the industry in general.[24]

Thus the continuing murders of women are a kind of permissible illegality, as criminality is constituted "in ways that are contingent on and serve to reinforce new bourgeois constructions of 'proper' and 'improper' gender identity" (Bellhouse 1999, 959). Melissa Wright maintains that the practices of the maquiladora industry toward its women workers add up to a cycle of *consumption and disposal.* It is a system sustained by the reproduction of disposable women, so it is no wonder that government authorities and industry officials share the same discourse concerning the murdered women (Wright 2001, 11). But the industry also helps create the gendered identities of working-class women using a discourse based on the material conditions in the maquila industry. Although the killers target only a few women, the most vulnerable, the message is for all women. The obligatory question asked by anyone visiting Ciudad Juárez has to do with the murders. As for female visitors, the city terrifies them; when they go out, they are warned of the risks they are taking. But men also tell them, "Don't worry, you are not the prototype; you're no longer young, you're not seventeen years old, you're not dark-skinned." Obviously this all has different meanings for women and for men: the men have nothing to fear (Caputi 1990, 2–3).

Although "crime is not a virtuality that self-interest or passion have instilled in the hearts of all men, but rather the *almost* exclusive undertaking of a certain social class" (Foucault 1998, 281; italics mine), men are no different from any other social class that resists losing its monopoly on power. Just as the whites of South Africa sought to suppress the blacks who chipped away at the base of the racial power structure, so men react to the liberation of women. As more women gain access to jobs, higher incomes, and professional success, violence by men against women increases, *although not necessarily against those who are successful* (Russell 1993, 258; italics mine).

Moreover, one has to take into account that "in the courts the society as a whole does not judge one of its members; rather, the social category responsible for order sanctions another that is responsible for disorder" (Foucault 1998, 281). That is why the authorities in Ciudad Juárez have assigned responsibility for the killings to the murdered girls and women themselves, accusing them of sexual misbehavior and of frequenting nightclubs at late hours (CNDH 1998, 3). The authorities explained to the National Human Rights Commission that since the women working at the maquila were not making enough money they were also prostitutes, and that this was the reason for the killings (5). It is not men's criminal atrocities, nor low wages, nor exploitation under economic globalization that is blamed, but women's behavior, and more specifically, women's sexual behavior. Sexuality itself is the object of punishment.

This leads to a denial of women's diverse aspirations, which, according to Selva, have been subjected to male sexual desire, with an additional value: productivity. That is, the expression of female sexuality is confined to that which is consistent with the demand for productivity and the satisfaction of male desire. "Without this, any free display of female sexuality appears as chaotic horror. It is never the other way around, because then disorder is established and chaos appears, which seems to be what is happening at the turn of this century" (Selva 1998, 177).

For that reason, when one speaks of the killing of women, the lives and actions of the victims are described but not those of the killers. The violence cannot be understood without taking into account the dominant class that is behind its organization, protecting its interests and privileges through a political system permeated by violence (Tecla Jiménez 1999, 83). Therefore, human violence is a destructive and annihilating force that erases or maintains a contradiction and prevents the development of opponents or destroys them (93). For the dominant classes, violence is a necessary value that helps to maintain the existing order; it is the right of the powerful (Devalle 2000, 22).

In this context, illegal acts are immensely useful. "This can be the case in relation to other illegal activities: independent but connected to them, turned back on their own internal organizations, concentrating on a violent criminality whose primary victims are usually the poorer classes" (Foucault 1998, 283). Critical feminism, and the feminism of cultural studies, tells us that the experience and prevalence of gendered violence, including rape, are related to and vary according to social class, race, country, and other sociohistorical distinctions. In addition to focusing on male domination and oppression, therefore, one must analyze the patriarchal hegemony as it relates to the capitalistic hegemony, and to other hegemonies that arise depending on the historical and geographic context in which the gendered violence takes place (Steeves 1997, 13).

Crime, with all the surveillances it implies, guarantees submissiveness, and it becomes a proxy for the suppressed criminality of the dominant groups (Foucault 1998, 283–84). One must also analyze the impact and consequences of individual assaults and repeated rapes of women and men, as well as the cultural significance of the victimization of women and girls, in and between different cultures. Nonetheless, there is a level of frequency and continuity of violence that cuts across all cultures: women and girls are held responsible for male sexuality, even though variations exist in the forms of violence and in how it is constructed and how it is contested (Kelly and Radford 1998, 68).

On May 5, 1999, Governor Patricio Martinez declared in a radio interview:

> We have something that was deplorable—*fortunately now past*. It is something we can see now as a nightmare from which we are just waking up, a huge number of homicides of women in Ciudad Juárez such as has never been seen before in any part of the country. . . . In that killing spree that overwhelmed Chihuahua and has now ended, almost 190 women were murdered in a period of five years.[25]

Delinquency administers and exploits illegalities and molds the exercise of power around them. The dominant class uses the delinquent class to its own advantage. That is why "crime functions as a political observatory" (Foucault 1998, 285, 287). The special prosecutor, Suly Ponce, made the following statement in November 2000: "There is a psychosis in Ciudad Juárez: half an hour's delay in a woman returning home is enough for her family to ask for help finding her."[26] At that moment, three young women were missing; the body of one of them was found later that year, and two were said to be found on November 6, 2001. Currently Suly Ponce is acting as coordinator for the agencies of the Public Ministry of the Northern Region, which means complete control of the administration of justice.[27] Observing this pattern of injustice, we can affirm that the least privileged, those at the bottom of the ladder, usually are the most oppressed, with little or no protection against the most flagrant local injustices (Frank 1999, 54).

The hierarchy of sexual exploitation that includes race, gender, and class

> is ultimately enforced through violence. Exploitation, torture, and murder that come down through this structure are, for the most part, distorted or ignored in "mainstream" educational curricula and the "mass" media. (Domingo 1992, 199)

Practice and Method

The analysis presented in this paper is based on secondary sources, which could be seen as invalidating the effort. One could ask, moreover, why it is necessary to repeat what the newspapers have been saying for years (Cameron and Frazer 1987, xii). Nevertheless, these secondary sources cease to be secondary and become "primary" when they deal with the experiences of women who are concerned about the massacre of other women (Daly 1990, 27). Using these analytical and information resources, I have been able to understand and quantify sexual femicide against the girls and women of this city.

On July 28, 1998, Esther Chávez Cano provided me with a list of women murdered between 1993 and 1998.[28] Other sources I obtained that document the murders of women during this period include two published reports: the first by the assistant prosecutor's office for the northern region, and the second by the state attorney general's office.[29] It is important to note that these reports were the result of pressure exerted by women's groups to end the femicide. Using this information and a database that I developed, I calculated 110 victims of serial and non-serial sexual femicide through December 2001 (see table 1).

The classification of "serial sexual femicide" was based on, one, the location where the victim was found, generally a deserted area; and two, a statement in the coroner's report that a rape had occurred. When the latter information was not available, the fact that the body was nude, the way in which the body was disposed of, and the various tortures or mutilations the body had been subjected to were all taken into account.

Table 1. Sexual Femicide in Ciudad Juárez, 1993–2001

Year	Cases	Serial killings	Cases solved	Offender(s) arrested	Non-serial killings	Cases solved	Offender(s) arrested
1993	8	6	0		2	2	4 men*/ son
1994	7	5	0		2	2	2 men/ neighbor
1995	17	15	3	Shariff/ Rebeldes	2	1	stepfather
1996	19	16	6	Rebeldes	3	3	2 men**
1997	16	11	0		5	5	uncle***/ 3 youths/ 2 men/ godfather/ lover
1998	16	15	3	Tolteca/ Choferes	1	0	
1999	9	6	4	Tolteca/ Choferes	3	2	stepson/ client
2000	6	6	0		0	0	
2001	12	9	8	Ruteros	3	0	
Total	110	89	24		21	15	

Source: Compiled by the author based on the "Femicide 1993–2001" database at El Colegio de la Frontera Norte.
* Four men took part in the murder of a minor.
** One of the offenders killed two young women but did not receive a prison term because he was also a minor.
*** This offender is serving a sentence.

Eighty-nine serial killings were recorded from 1993 to 2001, and several men identified as the physical and intellectual perpetrators are in custody. In 1995 Omar Shariff Latiff and the "Rebeldes" gang were detained.[30] In 1999 the gang known as "El Tolteca y los Choferes"[31] was apprehended, followed by Víctor Javier García Uribe and Gustavo González Meza in 2001.[32] With the exception of Omar Shariff Latiff, who was sentenced to thirty years in prison, no other prison terms have been handed down. However, in the year 2000 it became known that the body thought to be that of Elizabeth Castro García, whom Shariff was convicted of killing, does not belong to her. All this adds up to 24 cases "presumed solved"; of the remaining 65, nothing is known. In addition, 39 victims remain unidentified.

As for the victims of non-serial sexual femicide, the same classification criteria were used. A significant fact is that some of these crimes were committed in the home. It is worth asking whether there are any meaningful

213

differences between serial and non-serial sexual femicide. No, they have the same significance: the complete destruction and subjugation of the woman (Caputi 1987, 7). These non-serial sexual crimes totaled 21, with one or more arrests made in 15 of the cases. But even if we really believe that the so-called serial and non-serial killers are in fact the men who have been arrested, still only 35 percent of the cases have been "solved," while 65 percent remain unsolved.[33]

As to the origins of the girls and women, 35.5 percent of the victims remain unidentified; 40 percent have been identified but their origin is unknown. The remaining 24.5 percent are distributed as follows: 10 from Chihuahua (of whom 7 from Ciudad Juárez), 5 from Zacatecas, 4 from Durango, 3 from Veracruz, 3 from Coahuila, 1 from Puebla, and 1 from Sinaloa.

Although the number is too small to serve as a basis for conclusions, we can assume that the 39 unidentified women, along with the 20 women known to have come from places other than Ciudad Juárez, reflect the migratory character of this city of 1.2 million inhabitants. According to the 2000 census, 58.9 percent of the city's residents were born here, 32.0 percent elsewhere in Mexico, and 2.6 percent in another country; the origin of 6.5 percent is not known. The numbers are similar when they are disaggregated by sex: in 1995, 33.8 percent of women in Juárez came from another locality or country, and 59.6 percent were native to the city.[34]

The women, whether they are adults or girls, are raped, prostituted, and murdered, or murdered and then raped. This degradation is so common that the victims, their names, and the places where they were murdered are forgotten from one day to the next (Dworkin 1997, 188–89). Forgetting is the privilege of those who remain as observers or of those who carry out the aggression. By contrast, the victim's emotions and body are imprinted with everything she has to remember.

Their ages range from 10 to 42 years old (see table 2). The age group in which women are most likely to be murdered is 10–22, representing an aggregate percentage of 72.7 percent. Young women 17 years of age account for the greatest number of victims: 11. Although we only have age data on 77 cases, in the remaining 12 cases all the victims are described as very young women.

The ideology of the patriarchy claims to be against rape, yet legitimizes it when it sustains the myths of male sexuality as uncontrolled and aggressive and female sexuality as passive and receptive. However, in all social contexts, rape is a violent act in which sex is used as a weapon (Steeves

Table 2. Serial Sexual Femicide by Victim's Age, 1993–2001

Age	Incidents	Percentage of total	Aggregate percentage
10	3	3.9	3.9
13	5	6.5	10.4
14	1	1.3	11.7
15	8	10.4	22.1
16	7	9.1	31.2
17	11	14.3	45.5
18	5	6.5	51.9
19	5	6.5	58.4
20	5	6.5	64.9
21	1	1.3	66.2
22	5	6.5	72.7
23	4	5.2	77.9
24	3	3.9	81.8
25	1	1.3	83.1
28	2	2.6	85.7
29	1	1.3	87.0
30	3	3.9	90.9
33	2	2.6	93.5
34	1	1.3	94.8
35	2	2.6	97.4
42	2	2.6	100.0
Total	77	100.0	

Source: Compiled by the author based on the "Femicide 1993–2001" database at El Colegio de la Frontera Norte.

1997, 10–11, 13). For that reason, certain forms of sexual assault have been legitimized by the state. The normalization of this policy makes one wonder about the risk of sexual assault relative to the value accorded different categories of women, such as adult women, women with special needs, women of different ethnic groups, poor women, and so on (Kelly and Radford 1998, 74–75) (see table 3).

Tecla Jiménez states, "In an environment of violence, it is necessary to look for an explanation having to do with private property, the distribution of wealth, and ideology. Other aspects such as the physical characteristics of the population, the level of industrialization, and the educational level of the society must be left out of the analysis" (1999, 79). This statement is completely erroneous, however, because it does not take into account the hierarchy of sexual exploitation, which involves race, gender, and class.

Table 3. Serial Sexual Femicide by Victim's Occupation/Description, 1993–2001

Occupation	Incidents	Percentage
Homemaker	1	1.1
Bar employee	2	2.2
Drug addict	1	1.1
Worker	1	1.1
Domestic employee	2	2.2
Worker/student	3	3.4
Student	5	5.6
Sought work/maquiladora	4	4.5
Homeless	1	1.1
Maquiladora	14	13.5
Maquiladora/student	2	2.2
Secretary	1	1.1
Prostitute	1	1.1
Supermarket employee	1	1.1
Occupation not specified	50	58.4
Total	89	100.0

Source: Compiled by the author based on the "Femicide 1993–2001" database at El Colegio de la Frontera Norte.

In modern Western society, differences of sex, gender, social class, and race are facts that are used to make social inequality seem biologically determined and natural. This ideological process is used to overcome the inherent contradictions of a class-based society, and manifests itself most strongly when there are conflicts, contradictions, and tensions in the system. These are neutralized as the victims themselves are blamed for their own inferiority (Stolcke 2000, 42).

The young women who appear to be at greatest risk and most vulnerable to attack are those who work in the maquiladoras or seek work in this industry—20.2 percent of victims, the highest share of any single occupation. In addition to being women, they are migrants; they walk for long distances and at late hours of the night. We should be cautious in interpreting this figure, however, given that the maquila sector employs a higher proportion of the economically active population of the city than any other sector, and so would be expected to employ a large proportion of the victims.[35] Moreover, the occupations of 50 victims are unknown. Nonetheless, the available occupational data confirm that working-class women, many of them maquila workers, are the targets. This supports the conclusion that male violence against women has an immediate cause, the difference in physical strength between men and women, and a mediate cause, the social inequality of women (Izquierdo 1998, 77).

Conclusion

Serial sexual femicide in this city is a social problem that is real. The damage is irreparable: the killings stand as an unsettled debt and an ongoing story. Women, as the objects of male violence, are made to suffer because of their gender identity and their position in the class system. And although as feminists we avoid using the term *victim*, it is certainly a fact in femicide.

This sanctioned criminality comes with a series of discourses that derive meaning and direction from the material conditions that support the violence. As the city confronts a wave of femicide, with its diverse forms of subjugation of the victims, the statements made by judicial officials, business spokespersons, and churches allow us to see how the limits of tolerance are defined and managed. Most frightening of all is that moment when the accumulation of unsolved crimes becomes in itself a power, sending the message that those entrusted with enforcing the law are not interested in catching those who break it by killing girls and women.

Notes

Editor's note: From *Aztlán: A Journal of Chicano Studies* 28, no. 2 (2003). The original essay was lightly edited for this collection.

I wish to thank Ana Luisa Arredondo Escárzaga for her assistance in the development of this study. This work was supported by a grant from the Consejo Nacional de Ciencia y Tecnología—Sistema Regional de Investigación Francisco Villa, for the project titled "Feminicidio: El caso de Ciudad Juárez, 1993–1999. Perfiles de vulnerabilidad de las mujeres asesinadas y políticas públicas para mujeres en riesgo." This article originally appeared in Spanish in *Debate Feminista* (año 13, vol. 25, April 2002). It was translated from the Spanish by Octavio Rosales and Alicia Santo, Rosanto Traducciones, Alchete, Alicante, Spain, and was further edited for publication in *Aztlán* by Cathy Sunshine. Unless otherwise noted, translations of quotations from Spanish-language sources are by Rosanto Traducciones.

1. In the first place, I would like to establish *femicide* (*feminicidio*) as the correct term for referring to these murders of women. This term must be used because of the need to make women visible with respect to the crimes committed against them and, equally important, in terms of the language used to describe these crimes. For feminists, femicide is one of the most "harrowing and sensitive areas of male violence . . . to address" (Radford and Russell 1992, 5).

2. Carcedo and Sagot are feminist scholars working on the scourge of femicide in Costa Rica from 1990 to 1999.

3. Leoncio Acuña Herrera, "Me dejaron 21 bolsas con huesos: gobernador," *Norte*, June 20, 1999, 10b.

4. "A comprehensive strategy against crime must be based not only on an apt diagnosis of the deficiencies in institutional structures, but also on the social problems facing specific regions. The reason is clear: the better we understand the reality of a region, the better we can identify its problems; we will be able to differentiate more clearly between underlying problems and situational problems and we will better understand the causes and the effects of a specific problem" (Fuentes, Brugués, and Cortez 1998, 18).

5. There are no official documents or reports that would enable us to review the analyses by the various criminologists. Their conclusions are made known through the media. Interview with Lic. Jorge Ostos, director of the Police Academy of Ciudad Juárez, February 12, 1999.

On March 15, 1999, the state attorney general's office, the assistant prosecutor's office for the northern zone, and the "special prosecutor for the investigation of women" [*sic*] sent out to the media the following information about the presence of investigators from the National Center for the Analysis of Violent Crime of the US Federal Bureau of Investigation, relating to the crimes against women: "After reviewing, together, 78 files of these cases, [the investigators found that] 23 were of major interest, but they stated that it would be premature and irresponsible to speak of a serial killer. For them, the majority of these cases are isolated homicides."

Criminologist Robert K. Ressler believes that a multiple killer is responsible for at least six to twelve of the murders of women (Rafael Nuñez, "Mató Reséndez a 12 en Juárez," *Norte*, July 10, 1999, 7b). For Spanish criminologist José Antonio Parra Molina, this city is a laboratory culture dish with conditions that breed psychotic or habitual murderers, and he believes that serial killings have indeed taken place (Armando Rodríguez, "Gana criminólogo español dos mil 500 dólares al mes," *El Diario de Juárez*, August 21, 1998, 10c; Alejandro Gutiérrez, "September 30, 1998, 2a).

Criminologists Oscar Defassioux Trechuelo and Eduardo Muriel Melero alleged that the staff of the attorney general's office denied them any type of help in their investigation, and they predicted that the murders would continue due to the inadequacies of the investigation ("Criminólogos se fueron sin presentar renuncia. Nahúm," *Norte*, February 28, 1999, 6b).

6. The first special prosecutor was Lic. Ma. Antonieta Esparza; next came Lic. Silvia Loya and two temporary attorneys, Lic. Manuel Adolfo Esparza Navarrete and Lic. Marina Aspeitia de Meléndez. Lic. Suly Ponce Prieto became the third special prosecutor in 1998 (*Norte*, September 10, 1998, 1h; *El Diario de Juárez*, September 9, 1998; *Norte*, October 21, 1998). On July 28, 2001, Lic. Zulema Bolívar was sworn in.

7. The two main newspapers in the city, *Norte* and *El Diario de Juárez*, have documented such statements from 1993 to the present.

8. On March 30, 2001, five members of the so-called "Choferes" gang were arrested and charged with seven murders. It was said that with these arrests, the killings of women were ending.

218

9. From 1985 to 1997, a total of 1,677 people in the city died violently. Of these, 198 were women, according to mortality statistics from the Instituto Nacional de Estadística y Geografía (INEGI). To date, however, no one has undertaken a serious investigation of how many men have died in the city and the circumstances of their deaths.

10. The use of violence in general is greater among men than among women. For men, violence is enmeshed in a web of physical and cultural experiences; male culture uses it as an easy and available resource. Violence is a man's activity, and men are both more prone to using it and more capable of doing so (Dobash and Dobash 1998b, 164–66).

11. The Spanish term *femicidio* is used by Victoria Sau: "When we use the word 'man' to refer to men and women and even to humanity in general, this makes us incapable of differentiating between men and women and of making women visible in their labors and in their death. We use the word 'homicide' to refer to the killings of women, 'parricide' when a daughter is killed, as if the father were the victim, and 'fratricide' when a sister is killed. The correct terms are femicide [*femicidio*], filicide, and sororicide" (1993, 64). But it is Marcela Lagarde who uses the term *feminicidio* (1997, 10–12; 1999, 58–62). See also Monárrez (2000).

12. Robert K. Ressler is considered an authority on sex crimes; to him we owe the term *serial killer*, coined in the 1970s (Ressler and Shachtman 1993, 32). However, Jenkins states that the concept, if not the term, has existed for more than a century. It was disseminated during the 1980s by the Behavioral Science Unit of the Quantico, Virginia, office of the US Justice Department and the FBI's National Academy, a unit established during the 1970s to create profiles of violent aggressors. The media were responsible for popularizing the term. Nevertheless, the language and theory of the serial killer were developed at Quantico (Jenkins 1994, 7–8, 21, 55–56).

The concept of serial murder can be distinguished from several other types of multiple homicide, based on the intervals between attacks. These other types are known by other terms. For example, *mass murder* is a large number of murders committed in one place in a brief period of time. Murders carried out over a few days or weeks are called *spree killings* (an unusual number of killings committed in a limited period of time). By contrast, *serial murder* consists of crimes carried out and multiplying over several months or years, including periods when they disappear (21).

13. On the other hand, there are schools of thought that define the behavior of multiple killers as insanity or as a psychiatric or genetic oddity, or as resulting from possession by an evil spirit, satanic cults, or witchcraft. These explanations erase all blame, placing the crimes beyond personal responsibility. If the perpetrators are mentally ill, how is it that their clinical symptoms go undetected by society? And if we say that anyone who commits murder has lost all sanity and reason, this position is essentially a moral one and does not move us to investigate objectively the causes and meaning of such acts (Leyton 1995, 21).

14. "The notion of a universal patriarchy has been widely criticized in recent years for its failure to account for the workings of gender oppression in the concrete cultural contexts in which it exists" (Butler 2002, 6). Nevertheless, whenever

patriarchy is mentioned, the conception of theorists of violence is respected, especially those theorists dedicated to the analysis of femicide.

15. Gender violence is a reality that kills and injures millions of women and girls around the world. Even those who are not directly affected remain in constant fear of this violence (Steeves 1997, 96).

16. I take issue with this statement, since the term *erotic* refers to "sexually suggestive or arousing material that is free of sexism, racism, and homophobia, and respectful of all human beings" (Russell 1993, 3).

17. All of the theorists mentioned agree with this perspective.

18. Subprocuraduría de Justicia del Estado Zona Norte, "Informe de homicidios en perjuicio de mujeres en Ciudad Juárez, Chihuahua, 1993–1998," February 1998.

19. *El Diario de Juárez*, February 24, 1999, 9c. Arturo González Rascón was attorney general of the state of Chihuahua from 1998 to January 2002.

20. The Amado Carrillo cartel came from Sinaloa; a power struggle is reported to be underway between Carrillo's people and the Arellano Félix brothers from Tijuana.

21. As of November 1995, the municipality of Juárez reported a population of 1,011,786, of which 98.4 percent was concentrated in Ciudad Juárez (the city proper). The average age was 22, with 33.1 percent of the population younger than 15 and 3.4 percent 65 or older. One-third of the population was in the 15–29 year age group. Of residents overall, 35 percent were immigrants, while 22 percent of children aged 14 or younger were born out of state. The greatest immigration is among young people between 15 and 24 years of age, who make up 39.1 percent of all immigrants.

According to the *Encuesta sobre Migración en la Frontera Norte de México*, carried out by the El Colegio de la Frontera Norte, approximately 67,962 people settled in Ciudad Juárez between 1994 and 1995. The main migratory flows came from the state of Chihuahua, with 26 percent of the total, followed by Durango at 15 percent, Sonora at 9.7 percent, and Coahuila at 9 percent. It is interesting to note the trend in migration flows from Veracruz, which were 1.9 percent and 1.8 percent in 1994 and 1995 but increased to 7.6 percent in 1996–97, according to the *Encuesta*. At this time this survey cannot measure the migration flows of a large portion of the migrants who arrive from the states of Oaxaca, Chiapas, and Veracruz, because these people are brought to the border in contracted trucks for the express purpose of working in the maquiladora industry.

I have no data on the percentage of maquiladora workers who have come from other areas of the country, but it is estimated at around 80 percent. The Asociación de Maquiladoras de Ciudad Juárez (AMAC) says it does not have that information. According to AMAC, the maquiladora industry in the city had generated 245,000 jobs as of 1999; 55 percent of the workers are women and 45 percent are men.

22. Giving an exact number of women who have been killed in this way always triggers a debate. However, drawing on the "Femicide" database at El Colegio de la Frontera Norte, I can say that of 258 killings of girls and women between 1993 and 2001, 110 are sexual femicides; I believe that 89 of them fit the scenario described above.

23. *El Diario de Juárez*, February 24, 1999, 9c.

24. *Norte*, May 19, 2001, 3b.

25. Interviewed by Pedro Ferriz de Con in "Para empezar," May 5, 1999, Mexico City. Italics mine.

26. *Norte*, November 15, 2000, 1a.

27. Lucy Sosa and Alex Quintero, "Remueven a fiscal de mujeres," *El Diario de Juárez*, July 29, 2001, 1a.

28. Esther is a feminist activist from Grupo 8 de Marzo, and is well known both nationally and internationally for her struggle against the killing of women. Currently she is the director of the Casa Amiga crisis center, the first center to help victims of sexual assault in this city. The chronology she gave me uses information provided by the newspaper *El Diario de Juárez* and was developed by the gender study groups of the Universidad Autónoma de Ciudad Juárez, the Comité Independiente de Chihuahua de los Derechos Humanos, and the Grupo 8 de Marzo. Esther Chávez Cano is currently in charge of compiling data on the murders of women.

29. Subprocuraduría de Justicia del Estado Zona Norte, "Informe de homicidios en perjuicio de mujeres en Ciudad Juárez, Chihuahua, 1993–1998," February 1998; and Procuraduría General de Justicia del Estado/Subprocuraduría Zona Norte, "Homicidios cometidos en perjuicio de mujeres en Ciudad Juárez, Chihuahua, en el periodo de 1993–1998," preliminary hearings.

30. One murder was attributed to Shariff and eight to Los Rebeldes (Salvador Castro, "Orden de aprehensión contra violador en serie," *Norte*, September 27, 2001, 9; Armando Rodriguez, "Otra vez Sharif en la mira," *El Diario de Juárez*, November 4, 2001, 6).

31. Accused of seven murders.

32. Accused of eight murders.

33. As of this writing a series of protests, demonstrations, and other activities are underway in Juárez, demanding evidence that these men are truly guilty. The national and international press are present at every one of these events.

34. Instituto Nacional de Estadística, Geografía e Informática, *Perfil sociodemográfico de Chihuahua*, 1995.

35. According to the 1990 census, 50 percent.

Works Cited

Andersen, Margaret L. 1983. *Thinking about Women*. New York: Macmillan.

Asensio Aguilera, José María. 1998. "El ayer no nos hace violentos." In Fisas 1998a, 19–26.

Bellhouse, Mary L. 1999. "Crimes and Pardons: Bourgeois Justice, Gendered Virtue, and the Criminalized Other in Eighteenth-Century France." *Signs* 24, no. 4 (Summer) : 959–1010.

Britton, Dana M. 2000. "Feminism in Criminology: Engendering the Outlaw." *Annals of the American Academy of Political and Social Science* 571, no. 1: 57–76.

Butler, Judith. 2001. *El género en disputa: El feminismo y la subversión de la identidad*. Translated by Mónica Mansour and Laura Manríquez. Mexico City: UNAM/PAIDÓS/PUEG. First published as *Gender Trouble: Feminism and the Subversion of Identity* (New York: Routledge, 2002); quotations are from this edition.

Cameron, Deborah, and Elizabeth Frazer. 1987. *The Lust to Kill*. New York: New York University Press.

Caputi, Jane. 1987. *The Age of Sex Crime*. Bowling Green, OH: Bowling Green State University Popular Press.

———. 1989. "The Sexual Politics of Murder." *Gender & Society* 3, no. 4: 437–56.

———. 1990. "The New Founding Fathers: The Lore and Lure of the Serial Killer in Contemporary Culture." *Journal of American Culture* 13, no. 3: 1–12.

CNDH (Comisión Nacional de Derechos Humanos). 1998. *Caso de las mujeres asesinadas en Ciudad Juárez y sobre la falta de colaboración de las autoridades de la Procuraduría General de Justicia del Estado de Chihuahua: Recomendación No. 44/98*. Mexico City.

Cortina, Adela. 1998. "El poder comunicativo: Una propuesta intersexual frente a la violencia." In Fisas 1998a, 27–41.

Daly, Mary. 1990. *Gyn/Ecology: The Metaethics of Radical Feminism*. Boston: Beacon.

Devalle, Susana B. C. 2000. "Violencia: Estigma de nuestro siglo." In *Poder y cultura de la violencia*, edited by Susana B. C. Devalle, 15–31. Mexico: El Colegio de México.

Dobash, Rebecca Emerson, and Russell P. Dobash, eds. 1998a. *Rethinking Violence against Women*. Thousand Oaks, CA: Sage.

———. 1998b. "Violent Men and Violent Contexts." In Dobash and Dobash 1998a, 141–68.

Domingo, Chris. 1992. "What the White Man Won't Tell Us: Report from the Berkeley Clearinghouse on Femicide." In Radford and Russell 1992, 195–202.

Dworkin, Andrea. 1976. *Our Blood: Prophecies and Discourses on Sexual Politics*. New York: Harper and Row. Quoted in Caputi 1987, 3.

———1997. *Life and Death: Unapologetic Writings on the Continuing War against Women*. New York: Free Press.

Fisas, Vicenç, ed. 1998a. *El sexo de la violencia: Género y cultura de la violencia*. Barcelona: Icaria.

———. 1998b. Introduction to Vicenç 1998a.

Frank, Andre Gunder. 1999. "A Testimonial Contribution to the Twenty-fifth Anniversary Issue of Social Justice." *Social Justice* 26, no. 2 (summer): 1–15.

Foucault, Michel. 1998. *Vigilar y castigar*. Translated by Aurelio Garzón del Camino. Mexico: Siglo XXI.

Fuentes, Noé, Alejandro Brugués, and Willy Cortez. 1998. "Inseguridad pública en la frontera norte." *Ciudades* 40 (October–December): 18–24.

Izquierdo, María Jesús. 1998. "Los órdenes de la violencia: Especie, sexo y género." In Fisas 1998a, 61–91.

Jenkins, Philip. 1994. *Using Murder: The Social Construction of Serial Homicide*. New York: Aldine de Gruyter.

Kelly, Liz, and Jill Radford. 1998. 'Sexual Violence against Women and Girls: An Approach to an International Overview." In Dobash and Dobash 1998a, 53–76.

Lagarde, Marcela. 1997. "Identidades de género y derechos humanos: La construcción de las humanas." VII Summer Course. "Educación, democracia y nueva ciudadanía." Universidad Autónoma de Aguascalientes, 7–8 August.

Leyton, Elliott. 1995. *Hunting Humans: The Rise of the Modern Multiple Murderer*. Toronto: McClelland and Stewart.

Manieri, Rosaria. 1978. *Mujer y capital*. Translated by Benito Gómez. Madrid: Tribuna Feminista.

Marx, K., and F. Engels. 1980. *Obras escogidas*. 3 vols. Moscow: Editorial Progreso.

McWilliams, Monica. 1998. "Violence against Women in Societies under Stress." In Dobash and Dobash 1998a, 111–40.

Monárrez Fragoso, Julia E. 2000. "La cultura del feminicidio en Ciudad Juárez, 1993–1999." *Frontera Norte* 12, no. 23: 87–117.

Pally, Marcia. 1997. "Pornography Does Not Cause Sexual Violence." In *Sexual Violence: Opposing Viewpoints*, edited by Mary E. Williams and Tamara L. Roleff, 24–28. San Diego: Greenhaven.

Poulantzas, Nicos. 1977. "Las clases sociales." In *Las clases sociales en América Latina*, edited by Raúl Benitez Zenteno, 96–126. Mexico City: Siglo XXI. First published as "On Social Classes," *New Left Review*, no. 78 (1973); quotations are from this edition.

Radford, Jill, and Diana E. H. Russell. 1992. *Femicide: The Politics of Woman Killing*. New York: Twayne.

Ressler, Robert K., and Tom Shachtman. 1993. *Whoever Fights Monsters*. New York: St. Martin's.

Rubin, Gayle. 1999. "El tráfico de mujeres: Notas sobre la 'economía política' del sexo." In *¿Qué son los estudios de mujeres?*, edited by Marysa Navarro and Catharine Stimpson, 15–74. Mexico City: Fondo de Cultura Económica. First published as "The Traffic in Women: Notes on the Political Economy of Sex" (1975); quotations are from this edition.

Russell, Diana E. H., ed. 1993. *Making Violence Sexy: Feminist Views on Pornography*. New York: Teachers College Press.

Sánchez, M. Vicente. 1999. "Delincuencia en la frontera norte." *Ciudades* 40 (October–December): 44–51.

Sau, Victoria. 1993. *Ser mujer: El fin de una imagen tradicional*. Barcelona: Icaria.

———. 1998. "De la violencia estructural a los micromachismos." In Fisas 1998a, 165–73.

Scott, Joan W. 2000. "El género: Una categoría útil para el análisis histórico." In *El género: La construcción cultural de la diferencia sexual*, edited by Marta Lamas, 265–302. Mexico City: PUEG/UNAM. First published as "Gender: A Useful Category of Historical Analysis," *American Historical Review* 91, no. 5. (1986); quotations are from this edition.

Selva, Marta. 1998. "Violento masculino singular: Un modelo mediático." In Fisas 1998a, 175–83.

Skeggs, Beverley. 1997. *Formations of Class and Gender*. Thousand Oaks, CA: Sage.

Smarts, Carol. 1976. *Women, Crime and Criminology: A Feminist Critique*. London: Routledge & Kegan Paul.

Steeves, H. Leslie. 1997. *Gender Violence and the Press: The St. Kizito Story*. Athens: Ohio University Center for International Studies.

Stolcke, Verena. 2000. "¿Es el sexo para el género lo que la raza para la etnicidad . . . y la naturaleza para la sociedad?" *Política y Cultura*, no. 14 (Autumn): 25–60.

Tabuenca Córdoba, Maria Socorro. 1998. "La imagen de víctimas y victimarios en las campañas de prevención." Paper presented at Seminario de Conmemoración del Día Internacional de la Mujer, Universidad Autónoma de Ciudad Juárez, Mexico, 9 March.

Tecla Jiménez, Alfredo. 1999. *Antropología de la violencia*. Mexico City: Ediciones Taller Abierto.

Vachss, Alice. 1994. *Sex Crimes: Ten Years on the Front Lines Prosecuting Rapists and Confronting Their Collaborators*. New York: Owl.

Weeks, Jeffrey. 1998. *Sexualidad*. Mexico: PUEG/UNAM/PAIDOS.

Wright, Melissa W. 2001. "A Manifesto against Femicide." *Antipode* 33, no. 3: 550–66.

Reclaiming Mexico City
Feminist Spatial Justice in Patricia Valladares's *Tan frío como el infierno*

Sandra Ruiz

On March 8, 2016, Mexico City–based journalist Andrea Noel was sexually accosted while walking in the popular capital city neighborhood of Hipódromo Condesa. She publicly denounced her assault on Twitter (@metabolizedjunk), where she also posted security video footage documenting the attack.[1] The video shows Noel walking down a sidewalk as a man runs up from behind, lifts her dress, and physically assaults her. Noel is seen falling down, getting up, and gesticulating as the man runs away. The journalist's news organization, Vice Media's Mexico City office, denounced the attack and published an article reflecting on Noel's case as an example of the current state of gendered violence in Mexico: "Nos parece prioritario establecer un diálogo constante en torno a la violencia de género que se vive en este país, y éste sin duda es un ejemplo más de la persistencia diaria del fenómeno en México" (Vice Media 2016). Noel's experience exemplifies the cultural and systemic issues Mexican women encounter in their everyday lives.

The online news organization also acknowledges that Noel, unlike many Mexican women, has been able not only to denounce the attack on social media but also to report it to the local authorities, which has garnered her national and international attention. National Public Radio's program *All Things Considered* interviewed the journalist, who left Mexico City for the United States after death and rape threats were posted on her social media accounts. During the interview, Michel Martin asks Noel if she believes that the reason her case has received so much attention is because she is a light-skinned, blonde American woman. Noel does not directly answer Martin's question but acknowledges that "it doesn't really matter to me why people would want to speak to me about this issue. What matters is that the issue has been brought up. What happened is what I had hoped for, that the focus would shift towards the thousands of other women who suffer similar aggressions every single day . . . women have it tough, have it very tough, in Mexico and in Latin America" (Noel 2016). Unlike Noel, the large majority of Mexican women who suffer violent and predatory attacks do not have the means or resources to leave the country.

In the summer of 2015, the Mexican government issued an "alerta de género" (gender alert) under the provisions of a law known as La Ley General de Acceso de las Mujeres a una Vida Libre de Violencia. The effect was to publicly declare institutional support for women's safety in the Estado de México.[2] The gender alert serves as a platform to interrogate how Mexican women confront, negotiate, and challenge issues of gender violence in Mexico. What are the alternatives to waiting for governmental interventions to take place? What have been some of the institutional interventions against gender violence in the city? Are there current examples of women who seek, perform, and reclaim spatial justice in their own city?

Patricia Valladares's debut novel, a feminist crime narrative titled *Tan frío como el infierno* (2014), serves as an example of Mexican women's ongoing work to reclaim rights in their own city and nation. Valladares creates an intricate narrative that is at once insular and transnational. She employs multiple geographies like Mexico and Palestine/Israel, along with the geography of the Mexican female body, to represent literal and symbolic "territorios de guerra" (territories of war). Her novel connects the struggles of those marginalized by the Palestine/Israel conflict to the struggles of contemporary Mexican women, who confront and survive a misogynist culture and country in twenty-first-century Mexico City. By categorizing *Tan frío como el infierno* as a novel that promotes feminist spatial justice in Mexico City, I argue that the narrative defies and critiques the effects of global capital. The novel's noir element is an embodied and emblematic experience, unveiling the contradictory consequences of urban modernization and issues such as gender violence and women's agency, the use of technology, and spatial injustices. In response to this reality, Mexican women have mobilized and organized through the use of social media platforms to counter these gender-based attacks. Later on in this essay, I will discuss the ways in which Mexican women have confronted and brought to the forefront their demands for women's rights.

Valladares is a native of Mexico City who earned her bachelor's and master's degrees in psychology at the Universidad Nacional Autónoma de

México in Iztacala. For the past twenty-five years she has worked as a professor of clinical psychology at her alma mater, focusing on issues surrounding gender violence, specifically sexual violence against women. In 1988 she created a research center, the Programa Interdisciplinario para la Atención de la Violencia (PIAV), where she has been able to fund and study the effects of gender violence in Mexican society. By 1994 she had founded the first national center for survivors of domestic violence in Mexico, the Centro de Atención Múltiple (CAM) in Tlalnepantla, Estado de México. She also established the Centro de Atención al Maltrato Intrafamiliar y Sexual in 1997 with the support of the Mexican government's Procuraduría General de Justicia del Estado de México.

Her academic and clinical work has garnered awards such as the Medalla de la Mujer Tlalnepantlense in Education (2005) from the city of Tlalnepantla. She also received the Medalla al Mérito por su Trayectoria (2004), honoring her work in her field. To increase public awareness of gender violence, in 2002 she coauthored a series titled *Manuales de prevención de la violencia de género*; these are now integrated into governmental manuals and can be found on the website of Mexico's Comisión Nacional de Seguridad under the Secretaría de Gobernación.[3] She participated in a major regional study funded and organized by the Cámara de Diputados, LIX Legislatura, titled *Violencia feminicida en Sonora*. Published online by the Instituto Nacional de las Mujeres, it served as a case study of femicides occurring throughout the Mexican nation (Soto-Elízaga 2006).

Valladares earned a doctorate in creative writing and literature in 2013 at Mexico City's well-known cultural institution, Casa Lamm. Her doctoral project "Mujeres de agua" (2013) served as a foundation and precursor to *Tan frío como el infierno*. Valladares's academic work and activism provide an important foundation for her creative literary production, and the link between her professional career and the literary world she creates in *Tan frío* is palpable. Her character Milena Ruiz, a former federal police officer turned private investigator, has established a career dedicated to bringing justice to survivors of gender violence. The character acknowledges the heavy stigma that comes with her choice of career path, as early on in the narrative she recalls:

> Me acuerdo cuando llegué por primera vez comisionada a Delitos Sexuales; fue cuando empezaron las agencias especializadas. Creía que podía cambiar al mundo, puras pendejadas idealistas. Luego terminé el máster en criminología, me mandaron a Homicidios y luego a Feminicidios. "Solo te gusta investigar cosas de mujeres", me dijo mi jefe de entonces.

227

Mira si yo lo sabré; las mujeres no matamos, ni hacemos la guerra, pero siempre nos toca la peor parte. Mierda, a ver con qué me encuentro. (Valladares 2014, 22)

Milena's experiences during her career reflect the misogynist resistance Mexican women encounter when investigating and working on what are labeled "cosas de mujeres." The male superior she quotes sees crimes such as femicides as matters that solely concern and affect women. Therefore he, as a male subject, can remove himself from such issues: he does not and cannot concern himself with them, as they do not directly involve his gender or challenge his male privilege. Milena remains unfazed by such critiques, as she along with other female characters in the novel continue their passionate dedication in working toward gender equality and equity.

Hay muertos porque tenemos éxito: Mexico City in the Twenty-First Century

Milena is introduced to the reader when she is on her way to meet her first client. She has recently returned from a long stay abroad and has opened her own private detective agency in Mexico City. The encounter begins at a Starbucks close to el Ángel de la Independencia, formally known as El Monumento a la Independencia and popularly called el Ángel. The monument, which rises about 150 into the air, is topped with a golden statue of the winged Greek goddess Nike.[4] This important monument was commissioned by dictator Porfirio Díaz to commemorate Mexico's one hundredth anniversary of freedom from the Spanish Empire.

Ironically, during Díaz's thirty-three-year regime, the country was anything but independent, with an oligarchy suppressing civil liberties and foreign economic investments draining the nation's capital. Middle-class debt outweighed the generation of new wealth for the country. Díaz's gift to Mexican citizens was an artificial one at best, as historians suggest that his motivation for a major celebration in September 1910 was not to mark Mexico's independence but rather to stage a grandiose eightieth birthday celebration for himself; the "cost of the centennial exceeded the nation's education budget for 1910" (Kandell 1988, 386). Díaz's attempt to present Mexico as a modern nation had spurred urban development, with new public buildings, hotels, and theaters rising in the western part of the city. Over one hundred years later, two hundred years after independence, Valladares depicts a twenty-first-century city whose identity is shaped by foreign investments and global capital. Detective Milena Ruiz's interactions with the city's architecture and monuments serve as launching points in discussing the evolution of feminist spatial justice in early twenty-first-century Mexico.

The Angel serves as an important and constant focal point in the novel. Valladares takes Milena across a postcard Mexico City—hotels Nikko, Four Seasons, Intercontinental, and María Isabel, residential areas Polanco and Las Lomas, and Corporativo Santa Fe—only to return to el Ángel, where Milena sometimes pauses to reflect on her current cases as well as her personal life. The Angel, at the intersection of Paseo de la Reforma and Río Tíber, also functions as a marker of changes to the larger urban landscape. When Díaz erected the memorial, Mexico City's modernized spaces were to the west, toward Las Lomas de Chapultepec, Condesa, and Polanco. Mexico historian Jonathan Kandell (1988) describes the transformations that occurred in the nation's capital:

> Paseo de la Reforma, which spearheaded the city's westward expansion, led to the emergence of working-class neighborhoods northwest of the central district. Newspapers dubbed them instant slums, and noted that the authorities were maintaining a double standard for the wealthy and poor. Reimbursed by the government, real estate developers provided the new neighborhoods for the affluent with electricity, running water, sewage pipes, and asphalted streets graced with trees. But the poorer districts received none of these amenities because the developers could expect no public subsidies. (387)

While the Mexico City of the 1950s and 1960s was working toward modernization, it did so at the expense of the poor and working-class citizens who formed the backbone of the city's transformation and success. Milena Ruiz and Mexico City represent two feminine entities in constant transformation within a globalized urban context. The giant metropolis is in relentless motion, evolving in the name of progress and modernity. Like the city, Milena too is in constant motion.

Milena's Mexico City of the early twenty-first century has become a spatial realm struggling with its own paradoxical post/modern advances. Over the decades, the buildings surrounding the monument have taken on new identities. Change has come to the neighborhoods surrounding the Angel, traditionally working-class areas that have been transformed by the influence of global capital. In the mid-twentieth century, meeting someone in the city often meant going to Sanborns, one of the most popular department stores and cafés in the nation. Sanborns, founded by American businessmen brothers Frank and Walter Sanborn, was established in Mexico

City during the early 1900s and by midcentury had become an institutional staple of Mexican urban life. Carlos Fuentes's novel *La muerte de Artemio Cruz* (1962) contains a scene in which Catalina and Teresa Cruz shop for a wedding dress. To calm her daughter's nerves about the marriage, Catalina suggests they go to Sanborns for lunch and afterwards shop around the city for a bit (10–11). While the scene is brief, the significance here is that two wealthy women from Las Lomas select shopping and dining establishments in neighborhoods that do not figure in Valladares's story. Comparing the two novels speaks to the movement of wealth and capital in the city. The older southern areas of Coyoacán, San Ángel, Chimalistác, and Tlalpán are sectors that Artemio Cruz, Fuentes's main protagonist, presumably moved through, since he lived in Coyoacán. These neighborhoods do not appear in *Tan frío como el infierno*, set in the Mexico City of 2014.

Milena decides on a different establishment for her meetings. The contemporary private investigator does not meet her clients at Sanborns, taken over in the 1980s by the wealthiest Mexican citizen, Carlos Slim. Instead she meets him at a US-owned business, the internationally popular Starbucks. The average reader may not make note of this difference, since Starbucks has become central to everyday living, not only for US residents but for Mexicans as well. When the first Starbucks opened in Mexico City in 2002, skeptics were unsure of its brand.[5] Ten years later, in 2012, Alsea, Mexico's largest branding corporation and operator of American fast food restaurants, published a study announcing Starbucks's economic impact in Mexico.[6] According to Alsea's data, Starbucks is the second-largest coffeehouse chain in Mexico and number one in total gross income, with a 35 percent share of the market. Its existence has altered Mexicans' coffee-drinking habits, city life, and culture: "La marca vino a revolucionar la forma de tomar café en México, no sueles citar a los amigos en Vips o el Toks sino en el Starbucks, incluso tratas negocios ahí. Creo que Alsea y Starbucks Coffee Internacional (SCI) nunca se imaginaron el éxito que iba a tener" (quoted in Ugarte 2012).

The Starbucks example illustrates how foreign investment has decisively shaped not only the economy in Mexico but the culture as well. Starbucks cafés are present in hotels, hospitals, and department stores. In the novel, Milena meets clients in a Starbucks at the well-known María Isabel Hotel and Towers, a renovated luxury hotel owned by the US-based Sheraton Starwood Group. If one were to walk around the area, tracing Milena's steps in the narrative, one would encounter all the buildings she does. Valladares produces a literary picture of the real everyday life of Mexico City natives. In an interview conducted by email in 2014, the author affirms: "De hecho, yo vivo en la calle principal de la Colonia Roma y uno puede hacer un recorrido literal por los lugares por donde transcurre la novela, lo que le da verosimilitud y la hace muy cercana para los chilangos de cepa como yo."[7] Her original intent when writing this narrative was to create mimesis between fiction and the reality of contemporary Mexican urban life. Paying homage to her city, Valladares allows the reader to experience real-time Mexico City, seeing it from Milena's perspective as a woman and as a citizen.

The Angel, aside from ironically representing freedom and independence from a nineteenth-century European colonial power, symbolizes the transference of powers in the twenty-first century. A visual analysis of the surrounding architecture makes clear that the transference does not lie in Mexican hands. In addition to Starbucks and the Sheraton hotel, that stretch of Paseo de la Reforma also contains the United States Embassy and La Bolsa Mexicana de Valores, Mexico's powerful stock exchange. These four entities overlook the Angel, overpowering a space where historically the average Mexico City resident has gone to physically and vocally protest political, economic, and social injustices. The corporations are in control from above, their towering buildings looking down on the rest, representing a physical, economic, and symbolic domination of the city and ultimately the nation.

Urban planning scholar Edward Soja has researched and interpreted urban social spaces in Los Angeles. His study *Seeking Spatial Justice* (2010) discusses the importance of adopting a "critical spatial perspective" (2) when analyzing city spaces. In doing so, one will uncover "a consequential geography" (1), or intentional geographies, which help explain the symbolic purposes certain spatial realms possess along with the effects they may have on the populace—in the case of the Valladares novel, on Mexican women. The four entities previously discussed, the Sheraton, Starbucks, the US Embassy, and Bolsa Mexicana de Valores, stand like soldiers along Reforma, covertly watching the national symbol of Mexican independence and autonomy and waiting to take action if anyone moves out of line. And in fact, armed soldiers almost always surround the area where the Angel resides: the US Embassy is always protected with barricades and security forces. Soja's study helps us read the geography as one of spatial injustice, a location where economic, political, and social power lies not with the Mexican people but in global capital, principally US transnational capital. His study also creates a space from which to analyze "actions on the ground"—events experienced by Mexico City residents.

While the Angel symbolizes Mexican autonomy, its surrounding build-ings suggest a different narrative: one of Western cultural homogenization that replaces Mexican-owned businesses with multinational corporations like Starbucks and Sheratons. The resulting heightened sense of security creates a "hierarchy of security," meticulously selecting those who are secure versus those who are not. Community scholar and Los Angeles historian Mike Davis has studied the urban phenomenon in which certain social strata become obsessed with controlling their environments through security devices. He argues that strategies such as gated communities and the employment of high-powered cameras that function as a sort of "digital vigilante" provide a false sense of security and that their real purpose is deeper. According to Davis, "As a prestige symbol—and sometimes as the decisive borderline between the merely well-off and the 'truly rich'— 'security' has less to do with personal safety than with the degree of personal insulation, in residential, work, consumption and travel environments, from 'unsavory' groups and individuals, even crowds in general" (2006, 224).

In Mexico, personal insulation or security provides an artificial sense of safety, especially in a city where a staggering number of kidnappings, extor-tions, and violent acts against women occur, but the city's ultra-wealthy and political elite continuously perpetuate their own anxieties by creating a two-tiered system between the haves and the have-nots. As money is funneled away from social and economic necessities such as health care, mandatory minimum wage, affordable housing, and so on, the urban poor and the working class are left to fend for what little is left behind. The practice of economically and physically displacing the urban poor is not new. As Mexico historian Mauricio Tenorio-Trillo (2012) notes, during the early 1900s the Porfirio Díaz administration "wished to eliminate the presence of the poor so close to the corridors of power and wealth and feared the problems of health and morality" (12–13). Its actions created a divided and two-tiered city: the urban poor were pushed into the western part of the metropolitan space, which was severely underdeveloped, while the upper-class elite enjoyed modern amenities such as paved roads, electricity, and clean running water.

One modern-day example of Mexico's persistent economic gap is the controversial presidential airplane and airport hangar. Felipe Calderón's and Enrique Peña Nieto's administrations had proposed the purchase of a new presidential plane at a staggering cost. As reported by Mexican news outlets, President Calderón initiated the contract with Boeing, a US aero-space corporation, to design and build the plane. The reported estimated cost was nearly 7.5 billion pesos for the aircraft alone, not including the planned presidential hangar at the Benito Juárez International Airport or the maintenance cost, which brought the total to over 1 billion pesos (Delgado 2014c). *Latin Times* also reported on the controversial purchase by the Mexican government, calling it "the most expensive plane of its kind, more costly than planes belonging to presidents of the United States, China, Russia or Germany" (Lopez 2014). When the information was made public and Mexican citizens learned that public funds would pay for the aircraft, there was an indignant outcry at the absurdity of the transaction, made behind closed doors and without citizen approval by Calderón's administration and taken on by Peña Nieto's presidency. Public protest did not dissuade the government, which took delivery of the plane in 2016. Critics of this lavish governmental aircraft have dubbed it a "palacio flotante," or flying palace (Delgado 2014b), while also calculating the economic and social impact of this luxury expenditure on the average Mexican citizen.

Mexican newspaper *Proceso* put the astounding cost in perspective. "Con esta cantidad podrían construirse por lo menos ocho hospitales como el del IMSS que, apenas el 22 de abril, inauguró Peña en Hermosillo, Sonora, y que, a un costo de mil millones de pesos, tiene 189 camas, 11 quirófanos, dos salas de partos y una sala de urgencias para atender a 240 mil derechohabientes" (Delgado 2014a).[8] Hunger Project México reported in 2012 that over 28 million Mexican citizens suffer food insecurity and 11 million live in extreme poverty; the majority of citizens presently suffering from hunger are indigenous people, women, and children. Mexico as a nation-state claims to embrace one of the foundational elements of the Enlightenment and modernity: democracy. Yet its governing authorities neglect to practice democracy at the most basic level, with the very citizens who voted them into power, and instead they make secret deals with multinational corporations like Boeing. Here is where the modern paradox lies, as Terry Eagleton (1997) explains: "What China and other 'emergent' societies need is less Lyotard than civil liberties, full individual autonomy, material well-being, a democratized public sphere, in short all of the advantages which European Enlightenment promised to bring the West, however dismally it has failed to deliver" (5–6).

Along with hunger, gender violence has become endemic in Mexico. The Comisión Mexicana de Defensa y Promoción de los Derechos Humanos (CMDPDH) reports that from 2005 to 2010, nearly one thousand homicide cases were identified as femicides in the state of Mexico (el Estado de México).[9] While Mexico's wealthy assuage their security anxieties by creating carceral enclaves such as gated communities, with twenty-four-hour bodyguards and personal drivers, to control their safety and push out the undesirables, Mike Davis's study questions these acts. He asks the reader to consider those who exist outside of the protected communities, the everyday Mexican citizens whose insecurity comes from unjust living conditions and who survive without the basic human necessity of personal safety. How then, do a *novela negra* like *Tan frío como el infierno* and a character like Milena defy the urban spatial injustices found in her city? To understand the strategies employed, the reader must turn to the feminist detective character of Milena for answers.

Resistencias: Mexican Nike Seeks Spatial Justice

In *Tan frío como el infierno*, Mexico City is Milena's constant companion. She goes to the streets whenever she needs an escape from her apartment or her own thoughts. Unlike the wealthy who retreat to live in their guarded and gated homes, she physically interacts with her urban concrete jungle. When describing her neighborhood and all its amenities—fruit juice station, taco stand, and pharmacy—Milena expresses great adoration for it: "Amo esta puta colonia. La Roma es el ombligo del mundo. Álvaro Obregón resuelve casi todas mis necesidades primarias" (Valladares 2014, 37–38). Immediately after this declaration, she reads a newspaper report that discusses cuts in governmental funding for investigations of femicides in Juárez. She states out loud: "Pura violencia reprimida. No me extraña que la secuestraran en México. Por lo menos sabrá cómo lidiar con los malosos" (39). Milena is referring here to Eloísa Castellanos, a Mexican photojournalist who has been kidnapped in Milena's neighborhood. Kidnappings in the city are not a rare occurrence, which allows Milena to strangely find comfort in knowing that Eloísa, a Mexico City native and resident, knows how to handle herself in her unfortunate situation. Though the detective character does not directly state it, her comment illustrates the dangers that Mexico City women constantly deal with: gender violence in the city exists, and very few institutional structures have been implemented to safeguard the city's female residents.

To understand the limits and shortcomings of systemic responses to violence against women, one only has to see the signs, literal and figurative, within the cityscape, such as on the Metro underground train system. In 2008, the Instituto de las Mujeres de la Ciudad de México initiated a program called Viajemos Seguras, which implemented safe riding policies for women throughout the capital.[10] While the program's intent is commendable—to prevent and sanction sexual violence against female commuters who use the city's public transportation system—it does not address the issue directly. Rather, it requires men and women to use public transportation separately during heavily trafficked rush hours. Special train cars and buses have been designated as women-only safe cars in which female passengers can "securely" ride to and from work. Milena and her best friend, Congresswoman Silvia Plata, discuss the system and offer a critique of the security provisions for Mexico's most vulnerable: "—Sí, pues, pero podrían andar en un cuatro cilindros. Vi que hay autobuses rositas sólo para mujeres, ¿no? —Sí, pero no son suficientes. —¿Cuál es el mensaje? Que las personas se encierren en sus casas para que no les pase nada. No mames, no way" (2014, 27). This scene illustrates the degree to which women are subjugated by the violence in Mexico City. They have to resort to separating themselves from their male counterparts in order to be able to safely ride public transportation, and even when they do ride in the designated safe spaces, there are not enough subway cars for everyone. Milena ridicules the idea, as she perceives the segregation of females, whether in special subway cars or imprisoned in their own homes, as an unrealistic and weak government response to this social issue.

Milena and Silvia's conversation counters the Mexican government's master narrative regarding women's safety, deeming it impractical. Valladares's novel produces a feminist discourse on spatial justice when her characters critique this particular public policy and safety program. Viajemos Seguras places the responsibility for women's safety on women themselves rather than on a systematic approach that includes both men and women. By separating the sexes and creating specially designed Metro cars and color-coded buses for women travelers, the Instituto de las Mujeres overlooks the larger issues at hand. Addressing and solving gender violence in Mexico City's public transportation system is more complex than adding special riding hours for women and painting security buses pink. The program reinforces a patriarchal discourse in which the responsibility lies solely with the female rider and not the male. It is *she* who must follow the Viajemos Seguras program in order to "guarantee" her safety; it is not a communal effort but an individual one, and a gendered one. Valladares's novel exposes and challenges government discourses and practices in present-day Mexico, allowing alternative discourses to emerge, especially within femicide and gender violence narratives.

In the novel, Milena narrates a historical rundown of the short list of known Mexican serial killers, and while all of them have been involved in murdering women, what she clearly sees is that serial killing is not common in Mexico. In our interview, Valladares stated that the serial killers list is real, as she and her co-researchers compiled it for the 2006 Cámara de Diputados report on the nation's femicides. She said that with the major research findings "desmitificamos la hipótesis de asesinos seriales (está en la novela) para explicar que la violencia de las mujeres es un problema estructural, que está entreverado en la cultura misógina y la corrupción del Estado mexicano y sus instituciones. . . . Diez años después sabemos más del tema, pero sigue siendo un problema grave de salud pública y social en México" (email interview 2014). Valladares's conclusion echoes Arthur Asa Berger's interpretation of Fredric Jameson's use of postmodernism in urban spaces: "We have changed the way we relate to architectural spaces much more quickly than we have changed our psyches and our social systems" (2003, 71). The Mexican government's inadequate response to this grave social issue contradicts the modern and progressive image it presents on the international stage. It has spent over a billion dollars on an ostentatious airplane while its own female citizens cannot get to work or return home without being sexually accosted or harassed.

Spatial justice conceivably exists for those who can pay for it, trade it, or sell it, and yet security flaws exist even for those who choose selective imprisonment. In the novel, when Milena stakes out the safe house where Eloísa is being held captive, located in the middle-class suburban neighborhood of Ciudad Satélite, about ten miles northwest of el Ángel, she observes the lack of community in the area and the easy access she and her crew will have to the house when saving Eloísa:

> No tendremos problemas. Los suburbanos ni locos caminarían por las amplias aceras de sus colonias, ni se les ocurriría tampoco detenerse para que algún peatón ingenuo cruce la calle. Los satelucos prefieren circular a gran velocidad en sus autos de lujo, que compran a plazos con sus tarjetas de crédito, y por las noches penetran a sus casas por puertas automáticas. Pasan días sin encontrarse con los vecinos. La mayoría de las casas tiene grandes bardas que impiden ver lo que pasa adentro. ¿Será que viven cagados de miedo por los secuestros? Eso les pasa por aparentar lo que no tienen. (Valladares 2014, 162)

Milena's comments align with Mike Davis's observations on Los Angeles, a city rapidly losing public spaces to the privatization of redevelopment and gentrification. The city becomes a carceral space: "Even as the walls have come down in Eastern Europe, they are being erected all over Los Angeles" (Davis 2006, 228). Milena's expressed disdain mocks the false sense of security she observes in the suburban neighborhood. Her description produces the image of a ghost town, its dwellers too concerned with their own safety to live outside of their walls, walk their streets, and get to know their neighbors. And yet, with her military-style training, and having lived previously in a similar neighborhood, she knows all the flaws of the suburban, cookie-cutter tract homes. Milena refuses to allow the perpetual cycle of patriarchal and misogynist culture to imprison her in her own home and her own city, where spatial justice is scarce and insufficient; the Mexican feminist detective subverts the narrative of security as imprisonment by running free throughout the metropolis.

Reclaiming Mexico City

When we meet Milena, she has just finished a quick run through the city that ended up at el Ángel de la Independencia. She is heading over to Starbucks to meet with her first client, Mauricio Fuentes, secret lover of Eloísa Castellanos and the first person to report her missing and possibly kidnapped. Milena rates her run as being "not bad at all," but she has a preference when running in Mexico City's climate: "No me gusta el sol, prefiero correr cuando las aceras exhalan humedad que deja la lluvia" (Valladares 2014, 15). Milena determines when to run not by a governmental decree letting the public know when it is "safe" or "not safe" for a woman to be running in the city, but rather through something practical: she does not like to run in the sun.

Milena's location after her run is significant. Throughout the novel, Milena is always near or under the Angel—that is, Nike, the Greek goddess of war, victory, and sport, who holds a crown of laurels representing victory and in the other hand grips a broken chain symbolizing freedom. While Nike is a significant goddess in classical Greek mythology (her Roman counterpart is Victoria), her relationship with Milena can be read in a contemporary Mexican feminist context. Milena, like Nike, is a woman in constant motion. When she is not running she is at the gym, training, exercising, kick-boxing; when she self-exiled to Israel/Palestine, she registered for a self-defense course in the Israeli martial art of *krav maga*. Milena's physical conditioning allows the character to begin establishing her right to urban public spaces while reflecting on the limitations female citizens encounter in the capital city.

237

The second time Milena is at the Angel, she has once again just finished a run and is now sitting on the steps at the monument's base, reflecting on her kidnaping case: "Estoy sentada en las escalinatas del Ángel, mirando hacia la calle de Tíber. Me arden las plantas de los pies (no entiendo, si solo fueron quince kilómetros y los tenis tiene suela de aire)" (Valladares 2014, 69). As a contemporary woman, Milena wears clothing by Nike, the multinational clothing and shoe corporation. She mentions putting on "tenis Air Pegasus 25 y me largo a correr en Chapultepec" (91). Her T-shirt with "tecnología *dry-fit*" (36) is another reference to Nike, the creator of Dri-FIT exercise clothing, which works to evaporate sweat when a person is training. Milena's body reinterprets the fixed Angel/Nike of the Mexican monument, who appears poised to move, about to take flight, but not quite doing so yet. Milena, almost like a runner in a relay race, takes the Angel's place and physically embodies movement and action. Intriguingly, Nike's unfinished act parallels a conversation shared by Silvia and Antonio Pineda, a politician, in which both characters describe Mexico as "el país del ya merito" (Valladares 2014, 331).[11]

After saving Eloísa from her kidnappers, the two colleagues lament some of their losses, specifically not being able to bring to justice the corrupt governor of Oaxaca, which would have allowed Antonio to run for the southern state's gubernatorial seat. Instead the fraudulent government will continue its prolonged exploitation of indigenous populations in the state. Reflecting on these setbacks, Antonio says, "Pero ya ves, Silvia, vivimos en el país del ya merito, ya merito ganamos, quizás pa' la próxima, ya merito desaforamos al gobernador de tercera, ya merito se organizaba una nueva revolución" (231). Nike may represent victory, but victories are few and far between for those who seek to correct political and social injustices in Mexico. Yet Silvia's and Antonio's resiliency emerges, as they both believe Mexico, "el país del ya merito," and its people deserve better: "—Hay que seguir insistiendo. Si quieres cambiar las cosas, hay que estar adentro —aseguró la doctora diputada. —Para mí, hoy es el momento de volver a empezar —reflexionó Antonio Pineda—. Del pasado solo quedarán cicatrices. Mañana nadie recordará nada" (233). Whereas Antonio and Silvia will continue fighting from inside the government, with their progressive politics and social justice agendas, Milena endures the battle outside the governmental walls. The detective is the embodiment of a twenty-first-century Mexican Nike, a Mexican mestiza feminist who figuratively and literally exercises her own spatial justice in Mexico City.

By running, Milena converts an inhospitable city into her own. Running becomes a public performance that she does freely in an urban culture preoccupied with confinement, security, and vigilance. As Milena runs, she exercises her right as a woman to move freely in Mexico City, her urban space. Running is thus transformed into an act of defiance. She runs every day, conditioning her body for not only physical battle but also figurative battles for her autonomy and agency, her right to a place in a city that alienates, violates, and negates Mexican women. Milena practices what urban theorist Henri Lefebvre identified as the right to the city, a "stirring call to everyone disadvantaged by the conditions of urban life under capitalism to rise up to take greater control over how the unjust urban spaces in which they live are socially produced" (quoted in Soja 2010, 83). Once an intelligent woman like Milena becomes acutely aware of the social, political, and cultural structures built to oppress and dominate citizens, she can strategize alternative methods to subvert "los territorios de guerra" in her urban context. By running as a free woman throughout Mexico City, Milena demonstrates her control over a geographic space that has been uncontrollable for decades. Mexico City indeed is a monster metropolis, its expansion marked by gross injustices, from the displacement of poor residents to the disappearance of student protesters. Nevertheless, this petite woman with a 1980s punk-style haircut and purple highlights, this contemporary Mexican Nike, is able to find her own sense of being, her own autonomous control in an overpowering space through the act of running.

As a runner, she controls her own body and refuses to allow the expansion of global capital and its consequences, such as extreme security measures taken by the rich or the lack of security for the poor, to determine how she connects with her urban space. Without a doubt, Mexico City for most of its inhabitants is a territory of war: political war, economic war, cultural war, and racial war. Yet Milena wins a self-defined victory by freely exercising her body as she runs the city streets. She challenges the government's legal policies of forcing women to use the infantilized pink buses, which only further marginalizes Mexican women and trivializes the violence against them.

Milena as the Mexican feminist Nike extends her battles to include other narratives when solving urban crimes of gender violence, for she connects with territories outside, as well as inside, Mexico. While Milena works to find Eloísa and safely bring her back to her loved ones, the private investigator has constant flashbacks to her time spent in Israel/Palestine, where she met Yossi Levy, an ex–Israeli soldier turned political activist who becomes her lover. With Yossi, Milena also becomes a political activist, critiquing Israel's occupation and exploitation of the Palestine people. She compares what she witnesses in Israel to what she sees in Mexico, especially in terms of the struggle for access to the most basic necessity: water. Milena prefers to run in the rain, and yet water is not available to all citizens in different hemispheric spaces:

> parece un pipa de agua con las que hacen el reparto en las colonias depau-
> peradas de *Mexico City*. . . . Pienso en las elegantes colonias de la Ciudad
> de México y en las zonas marginadas que sobreviven as su lado. Casi
> siempre la historia es que primero vivían allí los pobres, luego les expro-
> pian o les mal compran sus terrenos y como arte de magia las colonias se
> transforman en viviendas de lujo para ricos. (Valladares 2014, 170–71)[12]

Milena's experiences abroad, along with her personal and professional experiences in Mexico, produce a hemispheric dialogue by taking foreign subjectivities, such as the Palestine experience, and linking them to Mexican urban life. Therefore, Valladares's work produces hemispheric solidarity between two groups who on the surface would seem unlikely to connect. The narrative also includes Mara, an *indigenista* activist living and working in Oaxaca. She has organized an exhibition in Mexico City to raise money for a poor Oaxacan orphanage; the exhibition highlights Eloísa's photographs taken in various war-torn countries abroad. The novel provides the reader with three distinct areas that women experience as "territorios de guerra": Mexico City, Oaxaca, and Palestine.

"Somos territorios de guerra"

While Milena diligently works to recover Eloísa from her captors, she decides to investigate Eloísa's life story while also consciously not allow-ing herself to get too close to her subject. Milena uses nicknames in order to assure herself some distance, not wanting to become too involved and possibly overlook potential clues to the case: "Fracciono a la gente como estrategia para mantener cierta distancia emocional. Si pensara en las víctimas o en los asesinos como si fueran personas completas, sentiría tanta conmiseración o tanta rabia que no podría actuar con objetividad" (Valladares 2014, 19). She names Eloísa "Ojos Brillantes," as her eyes are the first feature Milena admires when she sees a photograph of the female photojournalist. Milena gains access to the hard drive of Eloísa's computer and downloads the data onto her personal computer. She hacks into every password-protected file, demonstrating her aptitude for modern-day technology. In fact, Milena's apartment is a technophile's dream, as she has every up-to-date gadget imaginable and of high quality as well. She appears to use only Apple products, narrating that she sends emails via her "iPhone" (233) and reads the newspaper on her "iPad" (36) to do research for her case. Milena's use of twenty-first-century technology reflects the impact it has had in contemporary Mexico. Her hacking skills, which she uses to help solve the crime, could be considered part of a current movement throughout Latin America known as *ciberactivismo*, the use of modern-day technology and social media to bring to light injustices produced by capitalism, corruption, and oppression. Media studies scholar Tommaso Gravante (2012) defines *ciberactivismo* in Mexico as "la apropiación y uso de los medios digitales . . . es parte de una práctica cultural y política que encuentra espacio en el portaequipaje de toda la sociedad 'otra,' por otro lado, podemos añadir que la práctica de ciberactivismo además de ser un fenómeno social y político es también un laboratorio de innovación y experimentación de medios y modelos sociales" (51). For Milena the use of technology is indispensable, as it allows her to reflect on her case from a different perspective. Her private investigator skills continue to include those of the classic hard-boiled detective—asking questions, speaking to people, going into prohibited areas—but what makes Valladares's novel innovative is its depiction of technology as a tool for justice, replicating a contemporary practice in present-day Mexico.

Mexican writers, journalists, and activists have employed the social media platform Twitter to reach a wide audience in real time with messaging on sociopolitical issues occurring in Mexico. What does this mean? The average Mexican citizen can tweet about what is happening at local political protests and events, posting video or photographs before the traditional press gains access to its audience and publishes its own reports. Novelist and historian Paco Ignacio Taibo II and journalists Lydia Cacho and Sanjuana Martínez are known to employ their Twitter accounts to share information and provide real-time accounts with their followers. Martínez retweets requests from the family members of missing women and children who want to share digital flyers with photographs and personal information in the hope of finding their family members and loved ones. Politicians are using Twitter as well: when former Mexico City mayor Andrés Manuel López Obrador opened a Twitter account, news outlets like *El Universal* (2009) reported it, noting that López Obrador was using the medium as a cyber town hall to respond to questions and issues from his constituents.

While technology in Mexico appears to be a democratic tool, it does come with its own complex issues. In mid-2014, Enrique Peña Nieto's presidential administration passed a law popularly known as the "Ley Telecom" but officially titled La Ley Federal de Telecomunicaciones y Radiodifusión. It claims to reform current federal telecommunications policies into a more democratizing medium while giving the Mexican government full control over access to the internet, especially radio waves and outgoing cell phone messages. Paco Ignacio Taibo and Elena Poniatowska have taken to Twitter and Facebook to discuss what they call cyber censorship. In 2012, they joined forces to create and promote a socio-technological movement known as Movimiento Regeneración Nacional (MoReNa), which describes itself as a social network that works to democratize the flow of information in all twenty-first-century telecommunications formats. The president's bill has not discouraged Mexico's citizens from using Twitter—quite the opposite. Indeed, the platform has been used in organizing national street protests, such as the demonstration against *machista* violence in April 2016.

On Sunday, April 24, 2016, women across twenty-seven Mexican cities, including Guadalajara, Juárez, and Mexico City, declared the day as marking Primavera Violeta, or "Violet Spring." Borrowing the name from the 2011 Arab Spring, activists and organizers used the hashtags #24A and #PrimaveraVioleta to mobilize women and their allies, keep people up to date, and document the urban street protests. Mexico's Comisión Ejecutiva de Atención a Víctimas (CEAV) has reported that nearly 1,700 Mexican women are sexually assaulted every day, with an average of seven women killed per day (NoTeCalles 2016). While it is too soon to assess how the protest is going to influence future cultural, political, and social negotiations in relation to sexual violence and femicides in Mexico, news outlets such as *La Jornada* reported the April 24 protest as historic: it was the largest feminist women's protest in the nation's history (Juárez 2016).

Many activists have begun the discussion about what the next moves will be, as revealed by scrolling through the multiple photographs, videos, reports, and artworks that are linked by the Violet Spring hashtags. The nonprofit organization SocialTIC (2016) declared that along with public space and public policy, the Violet Spring should also consider "una Revolución Violeta en Internet" (a Violet Internet Revolution), working to create a feminist internet that is secure and inclusive of all. Slogans like "Vivas nos queremos" (We want each other alive) and "Los cuerpos de las mujeres no son campos de batalla" (Women's bodies are not battlefields) appeared not only on protest signs but also painted on women's bodies, which were then photographed and the photos uploaded to social media. One Twitter user who attended the women's protest march in Mexico City documented such a protest sign on her Twitter page, @axisaas.[13] Interestingly, the common slogan used to denounce the Juárez femicides, "Ni una más" (not one more), was inverted during the Primavera Violeta to "Ni una menos" (not one less), which implies refusal to allow another woman to disappear, be kidnapped, or be sexually assaulted.

In *Tan frío como el infierno*, Milena's use of the internet and other technological tools mimics what is happening on the ground in contemporary Mexico, where tools marketed as consumer products are being transformed into instruments for social and spatial feminist justice—a change driven by twenty-first-century Mexicanas. Valladares's inclusion of a modern female character who is skilled in these particular technologies expands the canon of Mexican detective fiction. Milena's character captures how deeply technology has infiltrated everyday life, as one does not have to step outside her own home to know what has occurred in the world throughout the day. As a staple of the developing world, technology allows for some areas of life to become more efficient and secure. But the modern-day paradox exists: one can order books online and have them securely delivered the next day; at the same time Mexican women repeatedly experience acts of gender violence, subjugation, and oppression. Although society has progressed in one area, its female citizens have yet to witness progress that addresses and solves issues of safety in their own city.

As Milena researches online information about Eloísa/Ojos Brillantes, she comes across Eloísa's book, a collection of photographs depicting Afghan women in a Pakistani refugee camp. Along with the pictures is an interview Eloísa gave discussing her experiences:

> En la segunda entrada del buscador, aparece un catálogo de fotografías de mujeres afganas en un campo de refugiados pakistaní; hay una larga entrevista en la que un reportero le pregunta a Eloísa por qué se convirtió en corresponsal de guerra: ". . . Van por la vida mirando el mundo a través de las rejillas de tela como si fueran jaulas coloridas. Como ellas, no puedo elegir. Siempre regreso a los lugares donde el cuerpo de las mujeres es un territorio de guerra."
>
> ¿Qué le pasa a esta dama? Me levanto, me sirvo otro trago, escribo en automático en el pizarrón: *El cuerpo de las mujeres como territorio de guerra*. (2014, 18, emphasis in original)

Milena, intrigued by Eloísa's mantra "women's bodies as territories of war," adds the phrase to a large diagram, mounted on the wall, that links facts related to the case. Later on in the narrative, Milena goes back to this phrase when she learns that Eloísa spent many years documenting women in different war-torn regions of the world. She continues reading Eloísa's book about her experiences in distant lands. At one point, in a bout of frustration, Milena asks out loud why Eloísa would travel so far to document issues that are prevalent in their home country of Mexico:

> ¿Cuándo te nació la conciencia? Por qué te fuiste tan lejos, Ojos Brillantes. Si no se necesita ser talibán para joder mujeres. Podrías haberte ido a Oaxaca, a Chiapas o aquí nomás a Chimalhuacán . . . , qué sé yo; en cualquier lado de este bendito país. Tampoco se necesita llevar un burka para estar presa. Tienes razón, todas estamos cautivas. Y no solo las presas, las locas o las monjas. Avasalladas. Sometidas a los deberes cotidianos o a un mal marido, a un padre autoritario o a los hijos. Cercadas entre murallas de prejuicios. Subyugadas y rendidas a los mitos amorosos. Vendidas, intercambiadas, doblegadas, torturadas, encadenadas. (40–41)

Milena's monologue reveals the multiple ways in which patriarchy is experienced in women's daily lives. Focusing on Mexico, the detective does not hold back in listing inequities and unjust treatment of women, subtlety alluding to Mexico's colonial "mito amoroso": the story of Malinche and Hernán Cortés. Indigenous chiefs gave adolescent slave Malinche, along with twenty other young women, to Cortés and his men. From Cortés's letters to King Carlos I, readers know that she was constantly at his side during the conquest of Mexico. He mentions her twice briefly in his letters of 1520 and 1526 as his *lengua*, or translator, and the Tlaxcala Codex often depicts her next to Cortés, translating on his behalf. Literary scholar Héctor Calderón (2004) documents the changes in Malinche's image: from the noble and powerful indigenous mother Doña Marina, as illustrated by Bernal Díaz del Castillo's *Historia verdadera de la conquista de la Nueva España* (2009), to "La Chingada," the despised figure in "Los Hijos de la Malinche," by mid-twentieth-century writer Octavio Paz (2004). Calderón identifies the point of transition as the 1826 publication of *Jicoténcal*, an unsigned historical novel that depicts the transfiguration of the indigenous noblewoman.[14]

In the Valladares novel, writes Calderón,

> Marina's fate is sealed as "la Malinche," traitor to her people. The conquest is seen as an allegory of the newly born patria, the Republic of Mexico, trying to rid itself of Spanish influences. Marina is characterized as an accomplice to evil, foreign influences that can corrupt and divide the nation. She uses her feminine guile to bring down the Indian nations. She becomes the Mexican Eve and her original sin is betrayal. (2004, 119–20)

Octavio Paz's portrayal of Malinche extends to Mexican (and by diasporic connection, Chicana) women, as they all become disposable and transferrable objects. He uses misogyny and patriarchy to explain Mexican modern nationalism and gender identity politics through a narrative of distrust of "los hijos de la Chingada," but in fact the most distrusted are "las hijas de la Chingada." Chicana feminist writer Cherríe Moraga, dialoguing with Paz's work in her seminal collection of essays, *Loving in the War Years: Lo que nunca pasó por sus labios* (1983), asserts that "slavery and slander is the price she must pay for the pleasure our culture imagined she enjoyed" (118). The narrative of the willing, submissive female in Paz's work oversimplifies a complex situation. Paz's patriarchal couple is disputed by the founding mother of Mexican detective fiction, María Elvira Bermúdez. In her sociological study *La vida familiar del mexicano* (1955), she dismantles Paz's colonial family and produces a new decolonial Mexican woman and man.[15] The writer shifts from the patriarchal lens to center on the Mexican family, one of the most important cultural institutions in the nation, allowing her to expose gendered inequities from a familial focal point. Bermúdez's study and body of creative fiction provides Valladares with a long-running legacy of Mexican women writers devoted to addressing the historical and cultural gender inequalities of their time period. With *Tan frío como el infierno*, Valladares brings the representation of new Mexican women and men into the twenty-first century through the strong and independent female characters of Milena, Silvia, and Eloísa.

Reading Eloísa's book about lives destroyed by acts of war, Milena sees that the photojournalist perceives a silver lining in the form of activism and solidarity among women, who are the most vulnerable during these instances. "Sin embargo, en medio del horror, aflora a ratos lo mejor de las personas: las mujeres se ayudan entre sí, cuidan a los hijos de otras como si fueran suyos. Resisten, hablan, no se dan por vencidas" (Valladares 2014, 40). The collective resistance gives Eloísa hope that women can uplift one another and resist together even under the most dire circumstances. Valladares explains that although the present situations are difficult real-life experiences, women have always resisted: "El cuerpo de las mujeres es un territorio de guerra en cualquier lugar del mundo: ya sea Tlalnepantla, Oaxaca, Palestina, Pakistán. Dicho sea en mexicano 'En donde quiera se cuecen habas.' Pero el otro subtexto de la novela es retratar a las mujeres que se niegan a ser víctimas. Ellas luchan, resisten, se organizan, son solidarias o activistas" (email interview 2014). Valladares's novel allows for an alternative and decolonial narrative when speaking of women's bodies as territories of war. A long historical legacy of resistance has endured from the era of the indigenous Malinche, to María Elvira Bermúdez's midcentury Mexico, with its resistance to the colonial father and family, to twenty-first-century women like Milena and Eloísa. The novel's proposal of a collective resistance is not farfetched, as affirmed by the Violet Spring protests throughout Mexico and the use of activist hashtags such as #NoTeCalles and #MiPrimerAcoso.

The collective bond between women is represented in *Tan frío como el infierno* by Milena and her best friend Silvia. The two women, who depend on each other for support throughout the novel, have a long, shared history in the fight for women's rights in Mexico. Their relationship is captured in a background report on Milena that is requested by Antonio Pineda, Eloísa's spouse: "Según las averiguaciones de su jefe de seguridad, Milena Ruiz es una criminóloga experta en feminicidios. Fue una alta funcionaria en el sexenio anterior. Con Silvia Plata resolvió algunos casos importantes. Ambas son muy conocidas en su campo y tienen fama de cabronas" (Valladares 2014, 35). The report's assessment is correct: Milena and Silvia are unapologetic *cabronas*. They represent the woman who refuses to back down, refuses to subjugate herself to the deplorable patriarchal culture—a woman who physically and metaphorically battles through her own wars, carving out public spaces for her right to exist and live, healing her scars as she continuously prepares, conditions, and builds her strength for the future.

Notes

Editor's note: This essay was commissioned for this collection.

1. Andrea Noel, Twitter post, March 8, 2016, https://twitter.com/metabolizedjunk/status/707394805471404032.

2. See the Seguridad y Justicia page of the Edoméx Informa website, http://edomexinforma.com/seguridadyjusticia/alertadegenero/.

3. The manuals can be found on the website of Mexico's Comisión Nacional de Seguridad (CNS) under "Compendio de Documentos de Prevención Social de la Violencia y la Delincuencia," http://www.cns.gob.mx/portalWebApp/wlp.c?__c=ea63.

4. Interestingly, Mexicans commonly refer to the Angel in the masculine, "el Ángel," even though her physical appearance clearly indicates that she is a woman. According to the rules of Spanish, the masculine article (*el*) is required here in place of the feminine article (*la*) in order to avoid a prolonged "a" sound ("laangel"). Because of this, the female Greek goddess is masculinized in everyday speech.

5. Interestingly, Starbucks did not open a store in Tijuana until a half-decade later, mainly due to the presence of its direct copy D'Volada, the "Mexicanized Starbucks . . . part of the sadness of Starbucks Tijuana is the threat it poses to D'Volada, a 'glocal' success story now tightly woven into Tijuana's urban fabric. Even worse, D'Volada shops are franchised by a family-run company; the Starbucks outlets in Mexico are part of the empire of Carlos Slim" (Kun 2007).

6. Alsea operates outlets in Mexico for a number of US-based fast-food and casual dining chains, including Starbucks, Domino's Pizza, Cheesecake Factory, Burger King, California Pizza Kitchen, and Chili's.

7. Patricia Valladares, email interview by Sandra Ruiz, September 2, 2014 (hereafter cited as "email interview 2014).

8. Instituto Mexicano del Seguro Social (IMSS) is one of the largest public health and social services hospitals in Mexico and Latin America.

9. See "Alerta de Género en el Estado de México: Línea de tiempo" on the CMDPDH website, http://cmdpdh.org/temas/violencia-contra-las-mujeres/alerta-de-genero-edomex/.

10. The website of the Instituto de las Mujeres de la Ciudad de México (http://www.inmujeres.cdmx.gob.mx/) contains the full program of Viajemos Seguras. In 2015, the institute introduced El Programa de Apoyo a las Instancias de Mujeres en la Entidades Federativas (PAIMEF), defined as "un programa social que instrumenta el Gobierno Federal para combatir la inequidad de género y desigualdad social que se traduce en diversas manifestaciones de violencia hacia las mujeres." Much of the program's work consists of distributing posters, stickers, and postcards around the city showing women and female children under the slogan of "Vida sin violencia" and "Esta es mi ciudad, tengo derecho a moverme con seguridad." See http://data.inmujeres.cdmx.gob.mx/conoce-tus-derechos/por-una-vida-libre-de-violencia/paimef/.

11. This Mexican colloquialism translates loosely as "the country of almost," as in almost there but not quite. It usually connotes a failure to complete something.

12. "Pedir pipa" means to request water service from a truck equipped with a water tank and a pipe. The water truck is for the poorest Mexico City neighborhoods that are not part of the "sistema de aguas," or those where water service is not working or has been terminated.

13. In a direct message conversation I had with Twitter user @axisaas, she revealed that she was a journalist documenting the protests and had taken the photograph of the sign that read "Los cuerpos de las mujeres no son campos de batalla." The image can be seen at https://twitter.com/axisaas/status/724667193481252866.

14. *Jicoténcal*, written anonymously and in Spanish, is now widely attributed to Félix Varela, a Cuban priest and political liberal. The novel was translated into English by Guillermo I. Castillo-Feliú and published as *Xicoténcatl* in 1999. By 1826 most of Latin American had gained independence from the Spanish and Portuguese. Cuba and Puerto Rico continued under Spanish rule until the resolution of the Spanish-American War in 1898.

15. Bermúdez was the first woman to earn a juris doctorate in Mexico and was later appointed as a judge to the nation's Supreme Court. Along with her professional accomplishments, Bermúdez has been touted as the founding mother of modern Mexican detective fiction. J. Patrick Duffey in *Latin American Mystery Writers: An A-to-Z Guide* describes her as "the most prolific female detective fiction author in the Spanish-speaking world, one of the most innovative practitioners of the genre in Mexico and one of its most perceptive critics" (2004, 24).

Works Cited

Berger, Arthur Asa. 2003. *The Portable Postmodernist*. Walnut Creek, CA: Altamira.

Bermúdez, María Elvira. 1955. *La vida familiar del mexicano*. Mexico City: Antigua Librería Robredo.

Calderón, Héctor. 2004. *Narratives of Greater Mexico: Essays on Chicano Literary History, Genre, and Borders*. Austin: University of Texas Press.

Davis, Mike. 2006. *City of Quartz: Excavating the Future in Los Angeles*. New York: Verso.

Delgado, Alvaro. 2014a. "El capricho de Peña: Avión de 7 mil millones." *Proceso*, June 2. http://www.proceso.com.mx/373709/el-capricho-de-pena-avion-de-7-mil-millones.

———. 2014b. "Llegó a México el 'palacio flotante' del presidente." *Proceso*, October 9. http://www.proceso.com.mx/384313/llego-a-mexico-el-palacio-flotante-de-pena-nieto.

———. 2014c. "Multimillonario avión presidencial, hasta septiembre del 2015." *Proceso*, June 5. http://www.proceso.com.mx/373915/multimillonario-avion-presidencial-hasta-septiembre-del-2015-sct.

Díaz del Castillo, Bernal. 2009. *Historia verdadera de la conquista de la Nueva España*. Barcelona: Linkgua Ediciones.

Duffey, J. Patrick. 2004. "María Elvira Bermúdez (1916–1988)." In *Latin American Mystery Writers: An A-to-Z Guide*, edited by Darrell B. Lockhart, 24–28. Santa Barbara, CA: Greenwood.

Eagleton, Terry. 1997. "The Contradictions of Postmodernism." *New Literary History* 28, no. 1: 1–6.

El Universal. 2009. "López Obrador abre cuenta de *Twitter*." October 15. http://archivo.eluniversal.com.mx/notas/633356.html.

Fuentes, Carlos. 1962. *La muerte de Artemio Cruz*. Mexico City: Fondo de Cultura Económica.

Gravante, Tommaso. 2012 "Ciberactivismo y apropiación social: Un estudio de caso: La insurgencia popular de Oaxaca." *Sociedade e Cultura: Revista de Pesquisas e Debates em Ciências Sociais* 15, no. 1: 51–60.

Hunger Project México. 2014. "Reporte Anual/Annual Report 2012." http://www.thp.org.mx.

Jicoténcal. 1826. Philadelphia: William Stavely. Translated into English by Guillermo I. Castillo-Feliú as *Xicoténcatl: An Anonymous Historical Novel about the Events Leading up to the Conquest of the Aztec Empire* (Austin: University of Texas Press, 1999).

Juárez, Blanca. 2016. "Estamos hartas de la violencia machista." *La Jornada*, April 25. http://www.jornada.unam.mx/2016/04/25/politica/015n1pol.

Kandell, Jonathan. 1988. *La Capital: The Biography of Mexico City*. New York: Random House.

Kun, Josh. 2007. "Starbucks Goes to Tijuana, Finally." *Los Angeles Times*, August 6.

Lopez, Oscar. 2014. "Enrique Peña Nieto to Become First President in World with Presidential Plane Valued at \$580M." *Latin Times*, June 3.

Moraga, Cherríe L. 1983. *Loving in the War Years: Lo que nunca pasó por sus labios*. Cambridge: South End Press.

Noel, Andrea. 2016. "An Assaulted Woman Takes Her Case Public—and Gets Threatened for It." Interview by Michel Martin. *All Things Considered*. National Public Radio, March 19. http://www.npr.org/2016/03/19/471113945/an-assaulted-woman-takes-her-case-public-and-gets-threatened-for-it.

No Te Calles. 2015. "Women in Mexico Stand Up against Sexual Violence." YouTube video, April 14. https://www.youtube.com/watch?v=3EXCe_5T-v0.

Paz, Octavio. 2004. *El laberinto de la soledad*. Mexico City: Fondo de Cultura Económica.

SocialTIC. 2016. "Hacia una revolución violeta en internet." April 26. https://socialtic.org/blog/hacia-una-revolucion-violeta-en-internet/.

Soja, Edward W. 2010. *Seeking Spatial Justice*. Minneapolis: University of Minnesota Press.

Soto-Elízaga, Renata, ed. 2006. *Violencia feminicida en Sonora*. Mexico City: H. Congreso de la Unión, Cámara de Diputados, LIX Legislatura. http://cedoc.inmujeres.gob.mx/lgamvlv/CAMARA/son.pdf.

Tenorio-Trillo, Mauricio. 2012. *I Speak of the City: Mexico City at the Turn of the Twentieth Century*. Chicago: University of Chicago Press.

Ugarte, Jesús. 2012. "Starbucks: 10 años despertando a México." *Expansión CNN*, October 12. http://expansion.mx/negocios/2012/10/11/starburcks-10-anos-despertando-a-mexico.

Valladares, Patricia. 2014. *Tan frío como el infierno*. Mexico City: Editorial Planeta.

Vice Media. 2016. "Sobre Andrea Noel, periodista agredida sexualmente en la Condesa." March 11. http://www.vice.com/es_mx/read/sobre-andrea-noel-la-periodista-agredida-sexualmente-en-la-condesa.

Origins, Form, and Development of the Son Jarocho
Veracruz, Mexico

Steven Loza

The *son jarocho* is a song and dance form that developed in Mexico during colonization in the seventeenth and eighteenth centuries. The emergence of this genre was a result of the intercultural and interracial interactions and relationships among Africans, the indigenous population, and Spaniards/Europeans. Literally translated, *son* means "a sound that is agreeable to the ear." The textual roots of son are in the popular Spanish forms called *coplas*, *coplillas*, and *letrillas* of the sixteenth, seventeenth, and eighteenth centuries. Their short verses usually featured ribald commentary within musical text and form. Even in the sixteenth century these letrillas were criticized by the clergy for being in "bad taste." The first documentation of the son dates back to 1776.[1] At that time, during the Spanish Inquisition, the son was often banned in Mexico and other regions of New Spain, most likely on grounds that it was immoral. This was, after all, a period in which the authorities attempted to convert the masses to Catholicism.

An important event in the eighteenth century was the arrival from Spain of a minor musical play called the *Tonadilla Escénica*. It was performed in the Coliseo de México, in the capital, and in other major Mexican cities. Various forms of Spanish song and dance accompanied the troupe, such as the *tirana*, *fandango*, *seguidilla*, *tonada*, *bolero*, and *copla*. Rural inhabitants traveled miles to see the *Tonadilla Escénica* and would return to their home villages inspired by its music. They used it as a model for composing their own *sonecitos del país*, or little sones of the country.

Eventually, mixed-race mestizos, as well as Indians and blacks, performed their own public spectacles, imitating the Spaniards in their own way. *Sonecitos regionales*, or regional little sones, such as "La Bamba," "El Besuquito," and "La Indita Valerosa," became very popular. The sonecito still exists today in the son jarocho, as well as in the *jarabe*, another song and dance form of similar ideological significance.

The sonecitos continued to be sung even with the passing of the Spanish *tonadilla*, and the dances continued to evolve among the mixed-blood and non-Spanish population. The Inquisition still condemned much of the art form, for the dances seemed to be sexually suggestive and the texts were often considered obscene or anticlerical. The following is an example of a sonecito censored during the Inquisition in 1808. It obviously pokes fun at the priesthood, referring to Latin words used in Catholic ritual:

El bonete del cura	The priest's bonnet
va por el río	goes in the river
y le clama diciendo	and he whines at it saying
bonete mío.	my bonnet.
Qué no, no, no, no,	No, no, no, no,
qué yo le diré	I will tell it
bonete mío, yo te	my bonnet, I will
compondré.	restore you.
Asperges me hisopo,	*Asperges me hisopo,*
mundabo lvabis me.	*mundabo lvabis me.*
Qué le den	Give it to him
qué le den	give it to him
con el *vitam venturi seculi*	with the *vitam venturi seculi*
amen.	amen.[2]
(Saldívar 1937, 255)	

It is possible that the repression of sexually suggestive texts led to the widespread use of double entendres in son texts, as in this *son jalisciense*:

Ay ay ay ay ay	Ay ay ay ay ay
yo vide pelear un oso	I saw a bear fighting
ay ay ay ay ay ay	ay ay ay ay ay ay
con una garza morena.	with a dark heron.

Among the Mexican Indians there seems to be a cultural attachment to indigenous animals. This is seen in the animal themes used in their songs. Many sones are named for animals, such as "La Calandria" (the lark), "El Gavilán" (the hawk), and "El Caimán" (the alligator).

In the following example, *El Palomo*, a sarcastic tone is evident, as in previous sones.

La paloma y el palomo	The female dove and the male dove
se fueron a misa un día	went to mass one day
la paloma reza y reza	she prayed and prayed
y el palomo se reía.	and he was laughing.

When Spanish rule was rejected during the Mexican Wars of Independence (1810 to 1821), the tyranny of Spanish culture was also rejected; this included the music. In the aftermath of independence, a frantic quest ensued for a true Mexican identity, especially among the mestizo population. In most cases they considered themselves neither exclusively Indian nor Spanish. Mexican nationalism was beginning to take form as miscegenation continued. It is among the mestizos, therefore, that we find the most intensive cultivation of popular forms such as the jarabe, the *romance*, and the son, even to the present day.

In his thesis on speech deviation in jarocho music, Daniel Sheehy refers to the Spaniard Don José María Esteva, who during a trip in 1840 through Veracruz, the jarocho region, observed a local jarocho dance and recorded the following:

> Las jarochitas bailan con mucha gracia, y algunas veces en ciertos sones como la bamba, admira la agilidad con que taconean y hacen mil movimientos, llevando un vaso lleno de agua en la cabeza sin que se derrame una sola gota, o formando de una banda que tienden en el suelo, unos grillos que ajustan a sus pies y que desatan luego sin hacer uso ninguno de sus manos. Comúnmente, cuando empieza la música a tocar un son, se levantan de sus asientos ocho o diez bailadoras, se ponen de pie sobre un tablado a algunas pulgadas del suelo, dan una vuelta y comienzan a bailar. Una de ellas (y muchas veces todas, según lo requiere el sonecito) canta, contestando a los versos de alguno de los músicos, y estos diálogos son las mas veces graciosísimos. (Campos 1928, 107, quoted in Sheehy 1974)

> The little jarochitas dance with much grace, and sometimes in certain sones like "La Bamba," one admires the agility with which they *taconean* (literally, beat noisily with the heels) and do a thousand movements, carrying a glass filled with water on the head without spilling a single drop, or forming from a band which they lay on the floor, some shackles which they adjust to their feet and then untie without using their hands at all. Commonly, when the music starts to play a son, eight or ten (women) dancers get up out of their seats, they stand up on a stage a few inches off the ground, turn and start to dance. One of them (or many times all

of them, according to what the sonecito requires) sings, answering the verses of one of the musicians, and these dialogues are in most cases very graceful (or witty).

Sheehy points out that our knowledge of the son's performance became more complete from this period of quest for Mexican identity, largely through the writings of travelers such as Don José María Esteva.

Improvisation within son verses has special significance in the regional cultures of Mexico. Real-life themes such as love or matrimonial intentions inspired competitive inventions of son texts through vivid metaphoric verses. The skill of text improvisation has declined in the jarocho region in this century, but occasional heated exchanges of verse at a rural dance may still occur.

Robert Stevenson (1952) makes a number of observations regarding the early musical and textual characteristics of the son. He notes that the son was rhythmically distinctive, usually 3/4 or 6/8 meter. It was played at a relatively fast tempo, and harmony mainly consisted of the tonic-dominant variety. Also, instrumental sections were alternated frequently. Verse forms such as the *copla* (couplet), *cuarteta* (quatrain), *quintilla* (five lines), and *décima* (ten lines), often with octosyllabic line length, frequently were picaresque, with double meanings, and usually had a romantic, sexual, or at times topical (e.g., anticlerical) significance. Stevenson also points out that the son was accompanied by guitar-type instruments, violins, and the diatonic harp. In addition, the son was most often paired with dancing, which possibly changed according to the particular son being performed, and which at times involved sexually suggestive gestures.

With respect to the different forms of dance accompaniment throughout Mexico, it is interesting to read the statement that appeared to forbid dancing of the jarabe during the 1802 Inquisition in Mexico City:

> Latterly there has been introduced amongst us another type of dance called the *jarabe gatuno* so indecent, lewd, disgraceful, and provocative, that words cannot encompass the evil of it. The verses and the accompanying actions, movements, and gestures, shoot the poison of lust directly into the eyes, ears, and senses. That lascivious demon, Asmodeus himself (Tobit 3.8), has certainly inspired this dance, so destructive is it of all Christian morals; but not only of religious virtue, even of the most elementary decencies. Its obscenity would shock even the most debased Sybarite. . . . We are obliged by the character of our sacred office, which pledges us to the salvation of souls by the blood of Jesus Christ, to prohibit, banish, and extirpate this dance. (Reprinted in Stevenson 1952, 184)

With the assimilation of the son into Mexican culture, regional cultural distinctions began molding the genre. The differentiating factors included ethnic background, degree of urbanization, climate, history, geography, and economy. In addition to regional preferences, patriotic identification with one's hometown in rural Mexico began to be an essential element of the son.

Today, the son is in a sense more standardized, but at the same time somewhat more varied than before, as Sheehy explains:

> (1) The formats of performance are often predetermined and set; (2) there are many "standard" arrangements of sones; (3) the son is more often identified with certain types of musical ensembles; and (4) textual material is often quite consistent. It has become more varied insofar as early son characteristics have been shaped or changed to accommodate regional preferences. Consequently, several main regional categories of sones exist in Mexico today, including the *Son Jalisciense*, the *Son Huasteco*, and, of course, the *Son Jarocho*, each identified by their corresponding region—Jalisco, the Huasteca, and Jarocho areas, respectively. It is, of course, the latter regional culture which is the most relevant to this study, in that it is the jarocho *culture* which has shaped the early son into a "Son Jarocho." (Sheehy 1974, 15)

The Son Jarocho

In Mexico today, the term *jarocho* refers to the Atlantic Seaboard of the state of Veracruz, or to someone or something from that area. This area of the state was probably so named because of the characteristics of the inhabitants. The word *jarocho*, still used in parts of Spain, has the meaning of "brusk, out of order and somewhat insolent."

The jarocho region encompasses a portion of the southern coastal area of Veracruz and extends somewhat inland (fig. 1). It is a tropical lowland zone with humid climate and dense vegetation. The inhabitants often wear loose white clothing to repel the intense heat. The Papaloapan River provides resources for the basic economy, and the region it occupies is considered to be the heart of jarocho culture.

North of the jarocho region lies the city of Veracruz. It is Mexico's largest seaport, and over the years it has been continuously exposed to Spanish and Caribbean cultural influences. Cuba in particular has influenced jarocho culture, which has become quite distinct from that of other regions of Mexico.

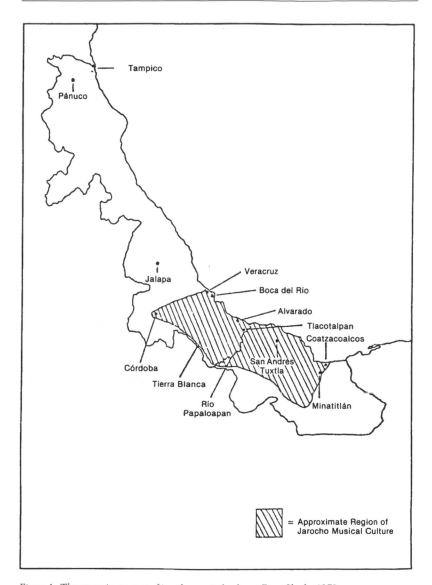

Figure 1. The approximate area of jarocho musical culture. From Sheehy 1979.

The jarocho area was colonized with the landing of Hernán Cortés in 1519 during the first expedition to Mexico. There was much Spanish influence on the region's music; however, the historical developments that did most to shape jarocho music were the arrival of African slaves and the subsequent formation and evolution of the mestizo race and culture.

255

African slaves were used in Mexico for various reasons, the most compelling being that they were a source of cheap, strong labor. The highland Indians proved to be poor laborers, so Africans were imported in large numbers. During colonization, as noted by Stevenson (1952, 96), there were more black slaves than Spaniards in New Spain. Since Veracruz was primarily black, the African influence in the area is strongly evident in its musical tradition.

Upon Mexico's independence from Spain, the mestizos, who would eventually make up 70 percent of Mexico's population, began molding their cultural heritage into the identity of Mexico as a nation. Each region developed its own music. Thus, the development of different regional styles occurred throughout Mexico, each style retaining individual characteristics.

The jarocho style of music today is considered to be one of Latin America's most unique forms. Its improvisations and rhythmic variations contrast markedly with other Mexican regional styles. In recent years, however, jarocho music has seemed to be on the decline, due in large part to the cosmopolitan development of the port of Veracruz and the exposure to various international mediums, such as imported commercial music, as well as other regional musics of Mexico such as mariachi.

Jarocho music is still popular, however, especially outside Veracruz. Jarocho conjuntos and/or jarocho ensembles have spread into far northern Mexico and the United States. Many recordings exist, and a good number of them have been performed by the Conjunto Lindo Veracruz, which has recorded the following example of son jarocho.

El Gavilancito
(Conjunto Lindo Veracruz)

Por esa calle derecha	Through that straight street
el gavilancito volar, volar	the little hawk flies, flies,
anda un gavilancito perdido	there is a little lost hawk,
volando viene, volando va	he comes flying, he goes flying,
volando viene, volando va	he comes flying, he goes flying
el gavilancito volar, volar.	the little hawk flies, flies.
CORO	CHORUS
Por esa calle derecha	Through that straight street
volando viene, volando va.	he comes flying, he goes flying.
Anda un gavilán perdido	There is a lost hawk
volando viene, volando va	he comes flying, flying he goes
volando viene, volando va	flying he comes, flying he goes
el gavilancito volar, volar.	the little hawk flies, flies.

Dicen que se va de sacar
volando viene, volando va
la paloma de su nido
volando viene, volando va
volando viene, volando va
el gavilancito volar, volar.

CORO
Dicen que se va de sacar
volando viene, volando va
la paloma de su nido
volando viene, volando va
volando viene, volando va
el gavilancito volar, volar.

Dicen que en el mar
se junta el gavilancito
volar, volar
agua de todos los ríos
volando viene, volando va
volando viene, volando va
gavilancito volar, volar.

Que volando viene, volando va
tus amores con los míos
volando vienen, volando van
volando vienen, volando van
gavilancito volar, volar.

CORO
Como no se han de juntar.[3]

They say that he is going to take
flying he comes, flying he goes
the dove from its nest
flying he comes, flying he goes
flying he comes, flying he goes
the little hawk flies, flies.

CHORUS
They say that he is going to take
flying he comes, flying he goes
the dove from its nest
flying he comes, flying he goes
flying he comes, flying he goes
the little hawk flies, flies.

They say that at the sea
the little hawk gathers
flying, flying
waters of all the rivers
flying he comes, flying he goes
flying he comes, flying he goes
the little hawk flies, flies.

How he comes flying, goes flying
your loves with mine
flying they come, flying they go
flying they come, flying they go
the little hawk flies, flies.

CHORUS
How can they not unite?

Instrumentation of the Son Jarocho

Instrumentation accompanying the son jarocho includes from one to four of the following instruments: *arpa veracruzana* (Veracruz harp), *jarana* (a small guitar-type instrument), *requinto jarocho* (a small, four-stringed guitar-type instrument, plucked with a large plectrum), and sometimes the violin (figs. 2, 3. When only one instrument is used, the jarana is played because by itself it can supply rhythmic-harmonic accompaniment. The most common grouping is the arpa, jarana, and requinto jarocho. Occasionally, the violin will replace the requinto jarocho. The most common of the instruments are the jarana and the arpa, which are examples of the rhythmic structure and harmonic limits of son jarocho. The different groupings of the conjunto

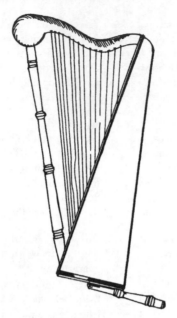

Figure 2. *Arpa veracruzana. Illustration by Robert Loza.*

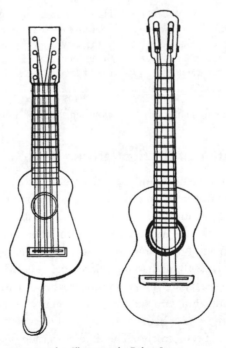

Figure 3. *Jarana and requinto jarocho. Illustration by Robert Loza.*

jarocho tend to characterize regional substyles within the jarocho area of Veracruz.

The arpa veracruzana is the unique element of jarocho music. Unlike a standard concert harp, it stands only four to five feet tall, with thirty-five strings spanning five octaves in range. It was introduced in Veracruz with the arrival of the Spaniards. Its limitations in tuning procedures have inhibited change in harmony of the son jarocho, for in order to change keys, the harpist must retune five strings, one in each octave. With the advent of more precise instruments, its use is gradually declining.

The jarana, a small guitar-type instrument, was also introduced by the Spaniards, and its name implies "noisy entertainment of ordinary people." The jarana has from five to ten strings set in five courses, similar to a twelve-string guitar, each course being tuned either in unison or in an octave. It is played in a struck style referred to as a *golpeado*. It yields a highly percussive sound, thus providing the rhythmic and chordal base for the son.

Harmony of the Son Jarocho

Harmony of the son jarocho is confined primarily to the voicing of Western music. Its limitations are reinforced by the basic nature of the traditional instruments used in son jarocho.

Most harmonic progression centers around the tonic and dominant chord positions. The IV chord is sometimes incorporated, and in a few cases the V of V or V of IV chords are used. The D-A^7 pattern occurs repeatedly, and a block, almost chorale form of harmonic progression is evident. In most sones, horizontal movement is caused not only by this tonic-dominant relationship, but also by a driving, ostinatolike repetition of one harmonic scheme. This can be observed in the eight-note patterns (fig. 4).

Rhythm of the Son Jarocho

The son jarocho is distinguished from other regional forms by its rhythm. Its distinctive rhythm is defined through the concepts of meter—*compás* and *contratiempo*. Son meter was derived from Spanish secular music. Initially, most sones had meters of 3/4 or 6/4. Today, more duple meter sones exist than before.

Compás also incorporates harmonic rhythm, using a repeated harmonic scheme on the ostinato premise mentioned above. Generally, the word compás refers to measure or the time period in which a musical phrase is

Figure 4. An example of jarabe jarocho. From Sheehy 1974.

marked. Within a son, compás can signify the smallest measure of rhythm, both harmonically and metrically. Over this repetitive measure of rhythm, a melody is superimposed. Different hand patterns in striking the strings of the jarana result in slightly varying sounds for each pattern. Consecutive combinations of these patterns result in a compás. In defining the hand pattern forming a compás, a typical example might resemble the illustration of the hand in upward and downward directions, as shown in figure 5 (> denotes emphasis of accents).

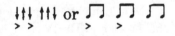

Figure 5. Hand pattern used in a compás.

The grouping of strokes, along with the accents, complies with the meter of a particular piece (e.g., 3/4, 2/4, etc.). Other groupings of stressed strokes would conflict with this metrical scheme. When this occurs, the rhythmic concept of contratiempo exists.

Literally, contratiempo means "against the beat." In other words, what we have here is syncopation. However, contratiempo includes more than syncopation. It forms, within the context of a metrical pattern, a temporary conflicting pattern. Not necessarily formed only by rhythmic variation and syncopation, this contradictory pattern can also be expressed through rhythm, pitch, or both. What develops is something of a rhythmic ambiguity. One common example would be a superimposition of the time signature 6/8 over 3/4. The combinations become quite complex in many cases, especially when a downbeat is not accented.

Performance of the Son Jarocho

Most sones jarocho begin with a section of music played instrumentally in which the tempo and compás are stated. Then come verses sung with subdued accompaniment. The number of verses ranges from two to seven or more; the average number is three. Instrumental technique is often displayed, and a verse section usually closes the son.

Lawrence Saunders makes an interesting observation about the son in relation to performance and the role of women:

> Only men are musicians in the son tradition. Some mestizo genres like the *Canción Ranchera* or *Corrido* in the Jalisco area allow for the participation of women in the role of vocal soloist. Most mestizo forms, however, including the son, are performed only by men. The presence of a female singer in some of the sones used for this study, therefore, is unusual and constitutes a break from traditional practice. (1976, 64)

Melody of the Son Jarocho

Narrow pitch range and strophic repetition most notably characterize the melody of son jarocho. Melodies rarely extend more than an octave in pitch. There seems to be a recitative nature within the melodies, emphasizing one pitch and embellishing melodically within a range of no more than a fifth.

Sheehy states that many of these melodies not of a recitative nature present an arc-shaped contour. Such a melody begins on its lowest pitch level, rises to its highest pitch near the center of the verse, and then falls, returning to its lowest pitch again. Sheehy notes a predominance of this contour pattern of melody in most mestizo music from the various regions of Mexico.

The Status and Future of the Son Jarocho

In Mexico today, the folkloric tradition of son jarocho persists strongly, especially in the preservation of the jarocho dance repertory, one of the most colorful styles in the vast spectrum of Mexican regional folk dance. Musically, the jarocho style has changed somewhat through the lesser use of improvisatory variations due to constant demand for performance of the most popular sones and dances. Economics and commercialization have affected the folkloric jarocho style, not only in musical terms but with respect to the traditional practices and motivation of the professional musician. In lieu of

261

playing for lodging, food, and other in-kind incentives, the jarocho musician now demands a monetary payment for performances; he is also a more versatile musician, adept at other musical styles as well. Changes in society have gone hand in hand with changes in the musical culture of Veracruz.

Interest in jarocho is firmly maintained both in Mexico and throughout the Mexican population of the United States. A rebirth of *folklóricos* has brought incessant references to the jarocho style of Veracruz. The social, historic, and artistic components of the son jarocho are the basis of its vividly important and exciting nature—one that must be preserved, maintained, and documented for its cultural significance as well as its inherent beauty.

Notes

Editor's Note: From *Aztlán: A Journal of Chicano Studies* 13, nos. 1–2 (1982). The original essay was lightly edited for this collection.

1. Published research on the son jarocho is almost nonexistent. There is, however, much information to be gleaned from the music itself. Daniel Edward Sheehy has compiled a significant amount of material while doing his master's thesis (1975) and PhD dissertation (1979). He also conducted extensive fieldwork in Veracruz under the auspices of a Fulbright-Hays research grant. His two studies constitute the main sources for this article.

2. Translation of these and other verses is by Sheehy (1974).

3. Anonymous text extracted from *Alegría Jarocha*, by Conjunto Lindo Veracruz (Discos Torre: SN-19050, Capitol Records, Hollywood, CA).

Works Cited

Campos, Ruben M. 1928. *El folklore y la música mexicana*. Mexico City: Secretaría de Educación Pública.

Saldívar, Gabriel. 1937. *El Jarabe: Baile Popular Mexicano*. Mexico: Talleres Gráficos de la Nación.

Saunders, Lawrence Ira. 1976. "The Son Huasteco: A Historical, Social, and Analytical Study of the Mexican Regional Folk Genre." Master's thesis, University of California, Los Angeles.

Sheehy, Daniel Edward. 1974. "Speech Deviations as One of the Determinants of Style in the Son Jarocho of Veracruz, Mexico." Master's thesis, University of California, Los Angeles.

———. 1979. "The Son Jarocho: The History, Style, and Repertory of a Changing Musical Tradition." PhD diss., University of California, Los Angeles.

Stevenson, Robert. 1952. *Music in Mexico: A Historical Survey*. New York: Thomas Y. Crowell.

The Mexico City–Los Angeles Cultural Mosh Pits

Maldita Vecindad, a Chilanga-Chicana Rock Banda de Pueblo

Héctor Calderón

A la memoria de Lalo Guerrero

Maldita Vecindad y los Hijos del 5° Patio had just completed another concert in the greater Los Angeles area, this one on February 4, 2002, at JC Fandango. The club's mosh pit had steamed up to a frenzy, especially after Maldita had answered the call for "Pachuco." By the end of the concert, bathroom mirrors were fogged up, and young men and women were nursing bruises from nonstop dancing. The clubgoers were dressed in the usual concert rock-punk-gothic attire: black outfits and Doc Martin boots, and, for the more adventurous, tattoos, piercings, black lipstick for both male and female, colored hair, and T-shirts with political messages. Props included a sombrero, huaraches, a Mexican flag, and a silver mask, like the one worn by El Santo, Mexico's popular wrestler.

Maldita's fans are products of recent demographic changes. They are mostly children of recent immigrants, working-class young people who are bilingual and bicultural and who remain close to their Mexican roots. They are similar in culture, class, and dress to their counterparts in Mexico City, the young crowds at the rockero Saturday flea market, el Tianguis del Chopo (fig. 1).

On this night in February, the crowd had come to an Orange County mini-mall, where JC Fandango is located, dressed and ready to have a good time. Before Maldita's appearance, the audience had danced to rock-en-tu-idioma hits from south-of-the-border bands. In anticipation of

Figure 1. Mexico City's rockero flea market, el Tianguis del Chopo, in 2005. Photo courtesy of author.

the main act, the crowd had begun the Maldita concert chant: "¡Maldita! ¡Maldita! ¡Maldita! ¡culeros! ¡culeros! ¡culeros!" The Malditos were already pumped up as they arrived through the side door entrance. Bass player Aldo Acuña came over to say hello to me, then ran upstairs with his bandmates to backstage dressing rooms to prepare. Later, when the dance floor was darkened, a roar from the crowd announced that the band had just hit the stage, with vocalist Roco grabbing the microphone and jumping high in the air. "¡Orale, raza de Califaztlán," he greeted the audience. "A ver quién brinca más alto, raza!" Thus begins the ritual that is reenacted by touring Mexican bands: band members and young Southern Californians reaching out to one another in the common languages of rock and español (fig. 2).

This essay examines the twenty-year career of Mexico City rock band Maldita Vecindad y los Hijos del 5° Patio. Although reviews, brief articles, and interviews on Maldita abound, I do not know of another study that chronicles the band from its inception to the present. With Maldita as the focus, I aim to move beyond scholarly, linguistic, and political borders. Chicana and Chicano studies as practiced in the United States has become, especially in literary scholarship, almost exclusively an English-language study of the US Southwest. US scholars engaged in "border studies" more often than not stop at the border. The same is true of Mexican scholars engaged in the Mexican version of border studies. For

Figure 2. Post-concert party at JC Fandango, February 4, 2002. From left, unidentified, Héctor Calderón, Yaotl from Aztlan Underground, Roco, Christine Calderón, Nicole Leiva. Photo courtesy of author.

many scholars on both sides, a clear political and disciplinary borderline divides the greater Mexican cultural diaspora that has existed in North America since the sixteenth century. As a group of artist-intellectuals, Maldita Vecindad has sought to build a bridge with Mexican America. Indeed, through Maldita's artistic-political statements, Mexican working-class cultural icons boldly taken up by the Chicano movement of the 1960s have returned to the center of Mexican identity, Mexico City. Along with a companion piece, "Conversación con Aldo Acuña," my study seeks to establish a dialogue between friends and scholars across languages and borders in a new pan-Mexican studies.

Haciendo Puentes: Cross-Border Musical Fusions

La Maldita is a trailblazer, one of the widely recognized leaders of the rockero movement on both sides of the border. It was the first Mexican rock band to tour the Mexican United States: its first US tour, in 1989, began with a MEChA Cinco de Mayo celebration in San Francisco and continued through California, Arizona, Texas, and Illinois. Since then the band has made several US visits each year. Maldita's members were also among the first Mexican rock artist–intellectuals to express a spirit of kinship with the

Chicano movement. *Gira pata de perro 93*, a photographic essay with text documenting Maldita's 1993 world tour, serves as a manifesto of the band's artistic and political goals. In it, Maldita acknowledged the importance of redefined Mexican working-class cultural symbols popularized by the Chicano movement:

> El movimiento chicano siempre nos llamó la atención.
>
> En 1985, cuando comenzamos, muchos grupos en México tocaban en inglés o tenían nombres en ese idioma. Había una influencia musical muy fuerte del rock inglés o americano, se reproducían géneros como el blues, el punk o el heavy metal.
>
> En la cultura chicana había una redefinición de idea de mexicanidad y eso se reflejaba en la música de fusión, la pintura callejera con el graffiti, los íconos populares: Zapata, la Virgen de Guadalupe, la bandera, el teatro campesino, los pachucos o la presencia popular de la cultura prehispánica, por ejemplo.
>
> Nuestro trabajo en Maldita siempre ha tenido muchos puntos de contacto con esa búsqueda de la cultura chicana. (Maldita Vecindad 1993)

In its first recordings, *Maldita Vecindad y los Hijos del 5° Patio* (1989) and *Circo* (1991), the band focused upon the migration of people and culture back and forth across the US-Mexico border. Hits included "Mojado" (1989), "Pachuco" (1991), and "Pata de perro" (1991). After the world tour of 1993, when Maldita visited over seventy cities in fourteen countries including Mexico, the United States, and European countries, the band played a return concert at Mexico City's Auditorio Nacional, captured live on the CD *En vivo: Gira pata de perro* (1993). Roco introduced "Mojado": "Esta va para todos los hermanos en todo el mundo que andan dispersos, en especial para los chicanos." This sense of a cultural family beyond borders was affirmed again eight years later in Los Angeles on a KJLA television interview. Guitarist Pato referred to the United States as "un país que no es el nuestro y sí es el nuestro a la vez, con toda esa contradicción enorme que existe" (Maldita Vecindad 2001).

In the publication *Gira pata de perro 93*, the page listing the redefined Mexican symbols of the Chicano movement included a photograph of Mexican film actor Germán Valdés, el Tin Tan. As a radio announcer for station XEJ in Ciudad Juárez, Chihuahua, in the 1940s, Valdés became one of the first significant cross-border personalities, taking the Mexican American pachuco from neighboring El Paso, Texas, and transforming him into a Mexican counterpart who also defied his society's rules. Having gained fame on Mexican radio, he later joined an itinerant tent theater company owned by Paco Miller. Valdés performed under his chosen stage name, El Pachuco Topillo Tapas. Sometime in 1943, while touring with the Miller company, Valdés crossed the border and in Los Angeles encountered the world of pachucos. Miller eventually renamed the Valdés stage character "el Tin Tan."

As Tin Tan, Valdés appeared in the 1945 film classic *El hijo desobediente*, which tells the story of a young Mexican who is sent by his father to study in the United States and returns a pachuco. The film captures the bilingual, bicultural pachuco in conflict with traditional Mexican middle-class values. In *El hijo desobediente*, Tin Tan, much to his father's dismay, dances both mambo and boogie and throws English slang into his Spanish in the style of his US counterparts.[1]

As Valdés was taking the pachuco south, Mexican American composers Don Tosti (Edmundo Martínez Tostado) and Eduardo "Lalo" Guerrero directed their music to post–World War II Mexican American working-class youth, who, while mostly US-born, were asserting their Spanish language and Mexican traditions. Don Tosti, from El Paso's El Segundo Barrio, the birthplace of the pachuco phenomenon, released "Pachuco Boogie" in 1948, and the Tucson-born Guerrero followed with "Los chucos suaves" in 1949. Both numbers were accented with pachuco slang in Spanish, accepting and glorifying this new youth culture while mixing musical genres from Mexico, Cuba, and New York. "Pachuco Boogie," a jump blues number with scat singing, featured a Tosti rap in Spanish. A chuco from El Paciente (El Paso), who has arrived in Los Ca (Los Angeles), sings, "Me vine a parar garra / porque aquí está buti de aquélla, ése. / Aquí se pone buti alerta todo, ve." On the other side of the cultural musical divide, Guerrero sang in his guaracha "Chucos suaves": "Carnal póngase abusado / Ya los tiempos han cambiado . . . Los chucos suaves bailan rumba, / bailan rumba y le zumban / Bailan guaracha sabrosón, el botecito / y el danzón."

In their musical compositions, Tosti and Guerrero and their band members drew on a variety of styles—boogie-woogie, swing, mambo, rumba, son montuno (Varela 2002, 5–6, 9). In his recent autobiography, *Lalo: My Life and Music*, Guerrero recalls the "pachuco years" in Los Angeles as a blending of musical styles: "The Latin music scene in Los Angeles after the war was very diverse and very exciting. . . . Groups from Mexico like Mariachi Vargas de Tecalitlán and Luis Arcaraz and his orchestra were very popular in Los Angeles. From New York City, we got the high-energy

Caribbean sounds of Música Tropical, the pachanga, the cha cha cha, and the mambo. The bands of Pérez Prado, Tito Puente, Machito, and Noro Morales played at The Trocadero, Coconut Grove, Ciro's" (Guerrero and Montes 2002, 97). Besides "Chucos suaves," Guerrero wrote the pachuco songs "Vamos a bailar," "Chicas patas boogie," and "Marijuana Boogie." "It seemed natural to write boogie-woogie and swing with caló [pachuco slang] lyrics" (99). In the 1950s, these fusions from north and south—jazz, R&B with Cuban rhythms—would find their way into the beat of R&B and rock pioneers Johnny Otis, Bo Diddley, and Fats Domino. And by the last decades of the twentieth century, Tosti and Guerrero would be influential in the musical development of Maldita Vecindad (fig. 3).[2]

The postwar years offered the first glimpses of cultural and musical fusions that traveled between two key Mexican centers, Los Angeles and Mexico City, via the border cities of Tucson, El Paso, and Ciudad Juárez. Valdés, with his Tin Tan character, headed for the Mexican capital, where he established himself as one of the great comedic actors of Mexico's golden age of cinema. Don Tosti and his Boogie Boys and Lalo Guerrero y Sus Cinco Lobos were recorded in studios in Los Angeles, the city that had become the site of Mexican American resistance, the pachuco in conflict with Anglo American society, epitomized by the so-called Zoot Suit Riots of 1943.

Maldita, with its cultural, political, and artistic fusions, continues these cross-border traditions. The band's "Pachuco," the first cut on *Circo* (1991), is introduced through sampling by Tin Tan, a mariachi musical intro with

Figure 3. Maldita Vecindad backstage with Lalo Guerrero at the John Anson Ford Theatre, Los Angeles, October 4, 2003. From left: Aldo, Roco, Sax, Lalo Guerrero, Javier Sosa, Jesús Méndez, Pato, and Daniel Infanzón. Photo courtesy of Mark Guerrero.

a mariachi shout, followed by "¡Golfas, ya llegó su pachucote!" Maldita's pachuco song is a playful take on the Champs' "Tequila," according to bassist Aldo Acuña. In a nod to inspiration, "Pachuco" includes a sampled rap in a bar: "un tequila antes de que empiecen los trancazos." As Aldo told me in an interview (2002), he did not know how the song could be danceable with its ska-punk, very high energy, fast-paced beat, "pero la gente encontró su manera de hacerlo y ya cuando eso sucedió ya no había vuelta para atrás y hacer ese tema más tranquilo."

In 1993, los Malditos could not have foreseen the reaction to the *Gira pata de perro 93* graphics showing Tin Tan in his pachuco outfit alongside comments on the value of the Chicano movement for their music. The acceptance of Tin Tan and the Chicano movement was by then a far cry from the classic interpretation of US pachucos by Octavio Paz in *El laberinto de la soledad*, first published in 1950. In the first chapter, "El pachuco y otros extremos," Paz interpreted the Los Angeles pachuco phenomenon as a rejection of Mexican identity. For Paz, these Angelinos were "clowns"—he used the English word in his Spanish text—who had rejected Mexican culture, language, religion, customs, and beliefs (1959, 14). However, as is well known, in the 1960s and 1970s the pachuco became for the Chicano movement a figure of resistance and the symbol of an emerging Mexican American bilingualism and biculturalism. That change was already under-way in the late 1940s and is clearly identifiable in the CD compilation *Pachuco Boogie*, which brings together the music of that era.[3]

Today, classic works of the Chicano movement have resurrected the pachuco of a bygone era for a new generation in Mexico. José Montoya's "El Louie" (1972) is a bilingual elegiac poem on the death of a pachuco from California's San Joaquín Valley. Maldita's Roco has in his extensive music collection an audio recording of "El Louie," given to him by Culture Clash's Ricardo Montoya, José Montoya's son. Luis Valdez's 1978 play *Zoot Suit*, presented by the Los Angeles Center Theatre Group, is based on the 1942–43 violence against pachucos on Los Angeles streets. The play and Valdez's 1981 Universal film *Zoot Suit* were influential in reintroducing the pachuco and Mexican American music of the 1940s to Mexico.[4]

In 2003 I witnessed Maldita play Guerrero's classic "Los chucos suaves" at a post-concert party at Universal Amphitheater. Roco, whose father wore the pachuco outfit, has taken the pachuco into the twenty-first century. His dress combines styles of the 1940s and 1950s—long goatee, hat, fin-gertip coat, baggy pants, chain, handkerchief, and two-toned shoes—with twenty-first-century Mexican rock styles of tattoos, long hair, earrings,

Indian necklaces and bracelets. If there is one Maldita song that has crowds jumping and slamming to a frenzy, it is "Pachuco," on *Circo*, which recalls the rebellion of a previous generation captured in *El hijo desobediente*. At the end of the twentieth century, a pachuco father is startled by his punk rockero son: "No sé cómo te atreves / a vestirte de esa forma / y salir . . . así. / En mis tiempos todo era elegante / sin greñudos y sin rock . . . En mis tiempos todas las mujeres / eran serias no había punk." And the new generation's reply: "Hey pa fuiste pachuco, / también te regañaban. / Hey pa bailabas mambo, / tienes que recordarlo" (*Circo*).

Since 1991, "Pachuco" has been *the* Maldita crowd pleaser, an international rock anthem. It is evidence of how in a post–Chicano movement world Maldita has become a Mexican borderless cultural institution influencing a generation of *mexicanos* on both sides of the international divide. Years after Maldita's music has ceased to be played on US rock-en-tu-idioma radio stations, this Mexican touring dance band continues to enjoy a multigenerational following of loyal fans. As in Orange County's JC Fandango in 2002, older and younger fans will dance and sing to the Maldita repertoire; so much in consonance with the world of Mexican immigrants in the United States, it is shaped by migration, mojados, repression, poverty, and struggle.

Maldita and Rock en Tu Idioma

In 1985, four of the present band members formed Maldita Vecindad y los Hijos del 5° Patio. Roco, Sax, Pacho, and Aldo (and later, Pato) came together because of similar tastes in musical genres such as punk, ska, and reggae and a similar interest in foreign rock bands, including the Clash, Sex Pistols, Pretenders, Police, the Specials, and XTC—that is, in the New Wave rock of the 1970s and 1980s (Acuña 2001). Before joining Maldita, Aldo, born in Jujuy, Argentina, to parents who later sought exile in Mexico, had a Guadalajara punk band, Madres y Comadres. However, unlike previous Mexican rock generations, this generation developed original material.

During the 1960s and 1970s, the "rock mexicano" documented in published studies on both sides of the border was a movement that coincided with early US rock and, politically, with the counterculture of the 1960s. It borrowed much from English-language rock.[5] This was a period of emulation, with Spanish-language covers of almost every major US rock hit. Names of rocanrolero bands, such as Los Teen Tops, Los Rockin Devils, Los Sinners, Peace and Love, Dangerous Rhythm, Crazy Boys, and

Mad Lads, are indicative of the enormous US influence on Mexican rock during this period.

The 1980s witnessed the beginning of a new era in Mexican rock. By the mid-1980s, Mexican youth in the large urban centers had already formed a well-defined rockero culture of dress styles, bands, clubs, slam dancing, and mosh pits. After joining Maldita, Aldo recalls (2002), he played at a variety of venues, including traditional Afro-Caribbean, bolero, and danzón dance clubs such as the well-known Salón Los Angeles, Salón Colonia, and Salón California. The band also played at labor demonstrations to raise funds for any number of social causes. The 1985 Mexico City earthquake was a catalyst for many concerts where Maldita performed to raise funds for the homeless survivors of the disaster. Aldo also recalls the first important rock clubs: the legendary Rockotitlán, El Nueve, and later, during the early 1990s, La Ultima Carcajada de la Cumbancha, known as El LUCC. El LUCC was a forum for jazz, blues, Afro-Caribbean music, rock, and theatrical performances. Aldo informed me that El LUCC was the first club to have rubber-covered walls for "el eslam." El LUCC also provided Maldita with important infrastructure that began the band's technical development and the consolidation of its sound for future concert tours.

Since its beginnings, Maldita understood that it was part of this new age of rock, a truly multilingual international movement in which bands from the Third World found an international audience.[6] "Somos parte de un movimiento en México y parte también de una actitud Mundial. En México como en otras partes del mundo se reproducían los estereotipos del rock, ya sólo como géneros. Ahora creemos que todo lo que llamamos el Tercer Mundo (Africa, Asia, y Latinoamérica), está desarrollando propuestas propias y concretas retomando al rock desde su propia tradición cultural como un elemento de cultura contemporánea" (Maldita Vecindad 1993).

Maldita is, indeed, a homegrown band, a banda de pueblo. The band's name, Maldita Vecindad y los Hijos del 5° Patio, is a reference to Mexico City's recent urban past and to a film and bolero of the same title. After the Mexican Revolution of 1910, the great mansions in Tepito, Lagunilla, and Morelos—las casonas—were abandoned by the wealthy for the then-growing Mexico City. They were converted into multifamily dwellings with a series of central patios around which daily life revolved for the urban poor—births, quinceañeras, marriages, seasonal celebrations, and deaths. Within the vecindades, Saturdays were reserved for the patio dance, where all enjoyed danzón, rumba, guaracha, and bugui-bugui. This gave rise to the label "quinto patio" for the fifth patio, the one in the rear and therefore the poorest, and "roto quintopatiero" for the urban working class.[7]

The golden age of Mexican cinema produced humorous, melodramatic, and tragic chronicles of these patios and their surrounding neighborhoods. The Luis Arcaraz and Mario Molina Montes classic bolero "Quinto patio" and the 1950 film *Quinto patio*, starring Emilio Tuero, gave this young urban band a logo and a clear vision as late twentieth-century troubadours of Mexico City's street life and urban underclass. At one time, young Mexicans danced to recorded music in the urban patios and neighborhood ballrooms like Salón Los Angeles to bands like Danzonera Dimas, to Acerina y su Danzonera, to the Arcaraz big band with a vocalist singing "Quinto patio": "Por vivir en quinto patio desprecias mis besos / un cariño verdadero sin mentiras ni maldad. / El amor cuando es sincero se encuentra lo mismo / en las torres de un castillo que en humilde vecindad."[8] Maldita Vecindad, whose members write lyrics and music collectively, is also a child of the poorest patio. With its name, logo, and music, Maldita laid claim to a working-class Mexican quintopatiera tradition represented in music and film.[9]

Música del Quinto Patio, Sonidos de la Calle

In its four original CDs to date, Maldita has not strayed from its purpose: to chronicle Mexico City's street life. The streets of Mexico bear the imprint of history, the accumulation of unsolvable problems. To survive, chilangos join the country's informal economy. Street children in clown outfits perform for auto passengers on Paseo de la Reforma; Indian women with children beg on trendy Zona Rosa sidewalks; in the metro, sellers hawk any number of items that passengers might need, from batteries and electrical cord to T-shirts and pirated CDs. A hungry musician with guitar in hand boards a bus to sing for his lunch; the street-corner knife sharpener turns his stone with bicycle pedals. This urban landscape of misery is, however, countered by life, by the sound of the Spanish language, by stall vendors selling newspapers and magazines and all the imaginable foods eaten by mexicanos, from hot cakes to the traditional grilled corn on the cob. Music is everywhere, blaring from stalls, from the metro, from strolling musicians, and from organ grinders playing "Viva mi desgracia" (Here's to My Misfortune).

Los Malditos have been articulate spokesmen in their music and interviews for Mexico's urban survivors. In *Gira pata de perro 93*, one page depicts a well-known image by José Guadalupe Posada (1853–1913), "Gran fandango y franchela de todas las calaveras." Maldita presents a fiesta of the dead and living, female and male skeletons in traditional Mexican dress (sombreros, sarapes, and long skirts) enjoying themselves with food, music, and dancing. Two literary citations add to the humorous visual rendering of a Mexican attitude toward life. From Nietzsche, the Malditos frame the Mexican graphic: "El animal que sufre más es el que inventó la risa." And from Mexico's Spanish colonial period, from Fray Servando Teresa de Mier: "Mi genio es festivo, el asunto trágico."

The Malditos are deadly serious about their musical project as live performers and as a studio group. Like the festive skeletons in the Posada graphic, the Maldita crowds come to have fun. They are urged on by vocalist Roco playing circus master in "Un gran circo," which depicts the harsh realities of street life in Mexico City: "Difícil es caminar / en un extraño lugar / en donde el hambre se ve / como un gran circo en acción; / en las calles no hay telón / así que puedes mirar / como rico espectador— / te invito a nuestra ciudad." When Roco continues, "También sin quererlo puedes ver / a un flaco extraño gran faquir / que vive y vive sin comer," the crowd will echo Roco's "¡Lanzando fuego!" Maldita displays great showmanship in its concerts. It's also known for its very tight performances. These are highly skilled musicians who have honed their music with a high degree of technical support so that the live sound is as good as the one recorded. This artistry evident in live performance is also reflected in their CDs. This post-punk, rock-alternativo band is responsible for music, lyrics, and production as well as artwork and design for each CD. Each of Maldita's four CDs has a high level of argument and thematic unity; each, like the Posada graphic, is a literate political and artistic statement on issues relevant to Mexicans on both sides of the border.

The cover of their first CD, the eponymous *Maldita Vecindad y los Hijos del 5° Patio* (1989), depicts the urban landscape of Mexico City after the devastating 1985 earthquake. The band, composed of six chavitos—Roco, Sax, Pacho, Aldo, Lobito, and Ticky—poses in front of a vecindad. This album, one of the first CDs produced in Mexico, combines the old and the new: a tinted photograph of shattered and weathered adobe walls contrasts with the new punk Mexicans—earrings, long hair, high-top shoes, and a variety of dress styles.

The album features eight songs depicting a Mexico nearing the end of the twentieth century. This is a view of Mexico from the bottom, not of the marketable commodity promoted by Mexican television (Televisa) and the commercial mass media. Already Maldita had begun its own interpretation of difference. "Apañón," the opening cut, speaks of a new group, rockeros and punks, suffering repression at the hands of the police: "—Hey tú / que haces aquí / caminando en la calle / vestido así." "Morenaza," "Rafael," and "Mojado," with their edgy themes and Afro-Caribbean rhythms, merengue and rumba, have remained relevant into the twenty-first century. "Morenaza" is a tribute to the dark Mexican woman: "No te enojes mi prieta / de lo que oyes hablar. / Enojona y coqueta / te queremos aún más." "Rafael" is a tragic story of Rafael, "vestido de mujer," who has lost his lover, Carlos. Rafael "está bien," meaning the tragedy is not that he dresses as a woman but that he has lost his love. In "Mojado," the Spanish rumba introduction counters the lyrics telling of the death of a border crosser. The lyrics were inspired by a tragic incident in Texas in 1987, when eighteen Mexicans died of asphyxiation in a railroad boxcar. Despite hardship and death, "el otro lado" is the solution for many Mexicans: "Yo me voy de aquí, / me voy de aquí. / No tengo nada / que darte a ti. / El otro lado es la solución / por todas partes / se oye el rumor: / 'Yo me voy de aquí.'" The band, like other Mexicans, has also crossed borders. Aldo recalls having to hawk their new and unknown album in the United States on radio stations during the first tours through Chicago and other Midwest cities.

The late 1980s were years of a new openness, especially with regard to sexuality. In 1993 Maldita acknowledged, among other differences, the freedom of sexual preference in *Gira pata de perro 93*:

> En nuestras letras profundizamos la posibilidad de disfrutar un mundo maravilloso en donde todos somos distintos al mismo tiempo, no importa el color de la piel, ni la religión que practiquemos, ni la preferencia sexual que tengamos, el lugar donde hayamos nacido, el idioma que hablemos, la forma de vestirnos; no importa lo que nos hace distintos, lo que importa es lo esencial que nos hace a todos los humanos, animales y plantas de todo el planeta. Lo que nos hace igual es precisamente la diferencia.

Mexicans could dress as they saw fit, in punk costume, or, as in the case of "Rafael," even in women's clothes for a male. During this period Mexicans from both north and south began to rethink traditional gender roles, a trend reflected in the populist feminist work of director María Novaro in her 1991 film *Danzón* and in the writing of Sandra Cisneros, whose short story "Little Miracles, Kept Promises" appeared the same year. Novaro, in her interrogation of femininity, depicts "las artistas," males dressed as women, in a cabaret in Veracruz. In her short story, Cisneros records young Mexican Benjamín T., from Del Río, Texas, who enters a church to pray for the person he loves, Manny Benavides, a soldier overseas (1991, 122–23). Maldita, too, was giving expression to a variety of identities available to Mexicans.

The band's rise from obscurity to international phenomenon was rapid. *Circo* (1991) was the first concept album of Mexican rock and was considered one of the top international albums of the 1990s. The circus has been a popular form of entertainment for Mexico's working class. With this album, Maldita captured the festive ambiance of the Mexican working-class circus, which includes both musical entertainment (the vaudeville tent or carpa tradition) and circus performers' acts. At the same time, the album addresses pressing urban issues of violence, poverty, and congestion. The cover, a painting with a Mexican Indian border motif, features the band as circus oddities (it includes new member Pato; Ticky and Lobito were no longer with the band). The album opened with the soon-to-be-classic "Pachuco," asserting that the band represents a new generation but draws inspiration from the past. "Un poco de sangre" focuses on class struggle on Mexico City streets as played out in an auto accident. A new car driven by Junior, symbolizing the power and wealth of the upper class, strikes José, a child who makes his living cleaning car windows. The song ends with "demasiada sangre / en esta ciudad." The history of Mexico City has been one of bloody sacrifices; the band used this song to recall the 1968 student massacre in Mexico City's Tlatelolco plaza. Mexico City is, indeed, like a great circus without a curtain, where "como rico espectador" one can enjoy child jugglers and clowns and fire-eaters: thus the lyrics of "Un gran circo" are sung by ringmaster Roco. "Pata de perro" with its fast-paced punta beat tells of Mexicans who must board ships looking for work. "Mare" is a Yucatecan rap. A provinciano from Yucatán, after visiting relatives in Mexico City, flees the violence, noise, and overpopulation: "Mucha tonta violencia. / Mucho ruido y mucha gente. / Yo mejor me regreso a Yucatán." The album ends with Maldita's ska-punk cover of Juan Gabriel's "Querida," in homage to the popular composer-performer raised in Ciudad Juárez.

In *Circo*, Mexico City comes alive with its many personalities: the punk-rockeros in "Pachuco," the street trumpeter in "Toño," the gran faquir in "Solín," the drunk in "Crudelia." We witness the daily tragedies of street children in "Un poco de sangre" and "Un gran circo," visit neighborhood cabarets in "Kumbala," and hear from those who escape in "Pata de perro" and "Mare." Years before the appearance of the new "world-class Mexican cinema" that chronicles Mexico City's tough urban street life, with films such as *Amores perros* (2000) and *De la calle* (2001), this chilanga banda had already provided a virtual visual soundtrack. *Circo*, described by Maldita as

275

a disco-novela, along with these recent films, resituates at the end of the twentieth century an urban genre of the Mexican golden age of cinema. The shanty neighborhood of Luis Buñuel's 1950 classic *Los olvidados* finds new life in Maldita Vecindad's postmodern *Circo*.

The 1996 *Baile de máscaras* appeared in a changing political climate. The ruling political party, the Partido Revolucionario Institucional (PRI), no longer held absolute political power in Mexico, and in 1994 an unexpected challenge to the Mexican state had emerged in the southern border state of Chiapas in the form of the Ejército Zapatista de Liberación Nacional (EZLN). *Baile de máscaras* is an ambitious album, Maldita's most self-consciously artistic and political effort.

The album notes include a quote from Octavio Paz's last book, *La llama doble* (1993), a play on what is seen and what is hidden: "¿Qué hay detrás de la máscara, qué es aquello que anima al personaje?" (129). The mask, as a symbol of personal and social alienation, was central to Paz's interpretation of Mexican identity in his "Máscaras mexicanas" in *El laberinto de la soledad*. Following the appearance of the masked Subcomandante Marcos at the head of the EZLN, Maldita presented its own politicized version of máscaras mexicanas. The computer-generated cover of the Maldita festive musical masque features a circle of four masks taken from some of Mexico's contributing cultures: máscaras de africanos, blancos, indígenas, y moros. These masks represent five hundred years of mestizaje in las Américas. On the inside of the album notes, beyond the lyrics barely visible in the background, is a village brass band—men in traditional straw hats and campesino white cotton. Maldita thus carries on the banda de pueblo tradition.

In "El dedo," with its folkloric instrumentation, Maldita criticizes the PRI political institution, known as "el dezado," started by Plutarco Elías Calles in 1929. In this system, each president chooses his own successor, whose identity remains hidden and who is known as "el tapado." The lack of political democracy of the dedazo is discussed in a conversation between two villagers with symbolic names: Juan Charrasqueado, taken from a popular corrido, and Don Emiliano, from the history of the Mexican Revolution. "—Uno no gana / para puro sustos, / cada seis años / vuelve a empezar. Con cada dedazo / todos se van a formar. / El que se mueve no sale en la foto, / con el tapado hay que esperar." "Saltapa'trás" critiques the racist Spanish colonial caste system, the seventeen ethnic types represented in the famous eighteenth-century casta family paintings: "Barzino con india / —calpamulato / mestizo con blanca / —castizo . . . Sangre con sangre, / mujeres y hombres. / Poder necesitas de nombres, / temor, divi-siones. / Colores y castas: / herencia de segregaciones." As Maldita notes, the powerful still maintain these divisions. The popular "Don Palabras," with a Moroccan beat, praises the street poet, the living memory of Mexico City's streets: "Miles de historias / en cada barrio. / Por la calle de Vieyra / viene ya Don Palabras / recitando poesías, / viene canta que canta . . . El tiempo vive en la memoria." *Baile de máscaras* is framed by transborder tracks, the first a sampling from a Mexico City street organ grinder playing "Viva mi desgracia," and the finale "Lamento," a Native American chant offered in Lakota.

Mostros was released in 1998, thirty years after one of the most tragic events of the twentieth century in Mexico, the student massacre in Tlatelolco on October 2, 1968. This album displays Maldita's retro, kitschy, darker musi-cal side. The title is a reference to horror genres of an earlier period, the 1950s through the 1960s, in which the masked wrestler El Santo, first a fotonovela character (1948) and later a film star (1952), battled evil. In the album notes, El Santo, who fought villains of every kind, from demons to vampires to mad scientists, is asked: "¿Y seguirás combatiendo contra los monstruos, vampiros y demonios?" He replies: "Pues, contra quien me pongan."

The title is also a reference to the internal monsters that menace the nation of Mexico. Indeed, Maldita rephrases on the album's interior the title of Francisco de Goya's famous etching, Capricho Núm. 43, *El sueño de la razón produce monstruos*, which depicts the artist slumped over his desk while the evil bird of night flutters behind. Maldita's personal satire, "El sueño de la razón crea monstruos," is directed toward the beasts of organized state crime, the dreams of reason that, according to a statement by Subcomandante Marcos, terrorize Mexico: el político-zarigüeya, el intelectual-ratón, el banquero-serpiente, el clérigo-demonio, el militar-hiena. The album includes "2 de octubre," commemorating the student massacre and demanding "que nunca vuelva a pasar."

"El barzón" rewrites a 1930s popular corrido of the same title. This song is recalled for the central lyric: "Se me reventó el barzón / y sigue la yunta andando" (the yoke strap is broken / but the team keeps moving)—which is to say, hardship continues. Both songs address land distribution and the plight of a campesino who suffers the life of an indentured servant at the beck and call of the hacendado. But there may be change; the last eighteen verses are different in the Maldita update, because the campesino is now aware of "pura manipulación / y mentiras del gobierno" and "Zapata ahora cabalga de nuevo." Maldita refers to the historical moment, certainly the neozapatismo of Chiapas but also the barzonista movement that emerged in the 1990s in opposition to the Salinas de Gortari administration's efforts to privatize communally held lands.[10] "El barzón" combines folkloric guitar strumming with a rap political delivery stressing citizen rights and self-governance against state manipulation by the PRI: "la revolución civil / viva el autogobierno."

"El cocodrilo" recalls a happier time through musical and lyrical references to a Pérez Prado mambo, "El mambo del ruletero." Maldita repeats the Pérez Prado refrain: "El Icuiricui / El Sacalacachimba / El Icuiricui / El Sacalacachimba." The ghost of a pachuco haunts Mexico City's center, cruising in his long green taxi ranfla, his cocodrilo: "¿De quién es esa ranfla? / Cuántos recuerdos trae . . . Una viejita / le dice a su nieta: 'en uno igual a tu abuelo conocí.'" It is impossible to cruise in Mexico City's fast-paced street scene with the ubiquitous green and white Volkswagen Beetle taxis. Mexico and Mexico City are, indeed, haunted by the past. However, after the last listed cut, "Mostros," "a tale of horror" with its demons and vampire bankers, the album hits a rousing, rocking funky high point with "Sirena," a hidden track not listed on the album. After almost two minutes of silence, the song begins with a symphonic opening. Here the symbol of the siren song serves as the promise of deliverance, a counter to the repressive Mexican monsters: "tú naciste con escamas en la piel / distinta a las demás / . . . hermosa sirena lejos del mar / cuando te oí cantar te soñé / que la ciudad es como el mar / un lugar que todo lo borra sin cesar . . . libre serás de la prisión de tu cuerpo / sirena, triste cantas al viento / sirena, te espera el mar."

Following the example of Chicano movement writers, Carlos Fuentes ended his 1995 *La frontera de cristal* with a call for a new mexicanidad unifying both north and south. For Fuentes, Chicano literature would be crucial in shattering the crystal border, the silence that separates Mexicans. In the last cuento, "Río Grande, Río Bravo," Fuentes invents José Francisco, a Chicano character who carries contraband across the El Paso–Ciudad Juárez border: "Su moto iba y venía por el puente sobre el Río Grande, Río Bravo, cargado de manuscritos chicanos a México y manuscritos mexicanos a Texas, la moto servía para llevar rápidamente palabras escritas de un lado a otro, ése era el contrabando de José Francisco, literatura de los dos lados, para que todos se conocieran mejor, decía, para que todos se quisieran un poquito más, para que hubiera 'un nosotros' de los dos lados de la frontera" (281). Like José Francisco and like many Chicana and Chicano writers, Maldita Vecindad too has been shattering la frontera de cristal. Through affiliation with the Chicano movement's fusion of politics and art, through travels throughout Greater Mexico (Mexico and Mexican United States), through lyrics and music, Maldita Vecindad has also redefined that unity formed out of diversity. In 1996, in "Saltapa'trás" from *Baile de máscaras*, Maldita sings of the colonial past and a present where power is used to divide Mexicans because of perceived differences between "chilangos, cholos, pochos, jotos." But the band ends by asserting, "Nuestras diferencias somos, / no hay pureza. / No hay pureza." We are our differences.

Maldita at Twenty

As I complete this essay in Mexico City in 2005, Maldita Vecindad is celebrating twenty years of existence (fig. 4). The passing decades have brought changes to these distinct personalities, now in their late thirties and beyond, now all parents with families. Drummer Pacho (José Luis Paredes Pacho) has left the band and works for the Oficina de Difusión Cultural at the Universidad Nacional Autónoma de México. Described by Aldo as the intellectual of the group, Pacho published what was probably the first book on the new Mexican rock, *Rock mexicano* (1993), and for years wrote a column for Mexico City's *Reforma* newspaper, "Ruidos de la calle," on new musical forms from throughout the world.

Figure 4. Maldita Vecindad after receiving the Walk of Fame award at the G. Martell School of Music, Mexico City, August 20, 2003. From left: Sax, Aldo, Pato, Rubén González of G. Martell, Roco, and Pacho. Photo courtesy of author.

The rest of the bandmates remain. Bassist Aldo Acuña records in his Colonia Condesa music studio and writes scores for short films. His fifteen-year-old son now has his own rock band and has also joined Maldita on vocals in concerts. Guitarist Pato (Enrique Montes), originally from Oaxaca, is a photographer and collector of classic lowrider cars. Maldita's "El cocodrilo," the cruising song set to a mambo rhythm, is based on Pato's long green cocodrilo lowrider. San Luis Potosí–born Sax (Eulalio Cervantes) is a virtuoso on alto, tenor, and soprano saxophones and other instruments such as trumpet, clarinet, Moroccan gaita, Indian shanai, Australian didjeridoo, and PVC pipe. He also has a studio and has recorded and produced other groups.

Vocalist Roco (Rolando Ortega), the only chilango in the group, remains the focal point on stage, a high-energy performer who dances and jumps through the ninety-minute concerts. Roco brings a great Mexican vitality to the rock performing tradition reminiscent of el Tin Tan. Like el Tintanazo, Roco is singer, actor, and mime with a comedic flair, offering social and political messages between songs. Roco has also ventured in new directions. He collaborated with filmmaker Alberto Cortés on a 2004 documentary, *Otros nosotros*, looking at Mexico City's hip-hop culture (fig. 5), and he provided the musical production for Manuel Márquez's film *Ni muy, muy . . . Ni tan, tan . . . Simplemente TIN TAN*. Roco also performs with DJ Aztek 732 (Adrián Peña), a member of La Vieja Guardia,

Figure 5. Roco, at right, during the filming of Otros nosotros, *2004. Photo courtesy of author.*

Figure 6. Roco with members of La Vieja Guardia in Colonia de Tlalpan, Mexico City, at "A 10 Años del Levantamiento Indígena en Chiapas" concert, August 29, 2003. From left: Flaco, Chivo, Chac Mool, DJ Aztek, Roco, Elmo, and Gordo (kneeling). Photo by Christine Calderón.

a Mexico City rapper and graffitero collective (fig. 6). Roco's Pachucote Sound System has Roco as MC backed by Aztek on turntables.

Now joined by Javier "Funky" Sosa on drums, Jesús Méndez on percussion, and Jesús "Kino" Domínguez on keyboards, Maldita has never sounded better. Recently I saw the band perform at the Hard Rock Café in the swanky Polanco district, at the legendary Rockotitlán in its new location in southern Mexico City, and at the Miramar, a traditional dance hall in the city center. Maldita fans still sing along with the Maldita repertoire, with some adventurous couples climbing the stage to dance. Whatever the venue, fans still come to have a good time, and Maldita continues committed to its evolving twenty-year, politically engaged artistic project with new material played at these Mexico City concerts.

Maldita Vecindad y los Hijos del 5° Patio appeared in a moment of transition from the age of vinyl to the digital age of the compact disc and the internet. As the band succeeded artistically, it fused the punk attitude with the artistic rock concert, the touring dance band with the neighborhood dance hall, and new rock idioms with traditional Mexican and Caribbean rhythms. Through the end of the twentieth century, Maldita continued with its música de fusión, representing Mexico's working classes, street people, campesinos, indígenas, marginals, and mojados, that is, those who have suffered the most political repression and who have remained outside of the supposed progress of the Mexican nation. A group that began by invoking the music of Pérez Prado, Tin Tan, Lalo Guerrero, and Don Tosti fused the past with rock, punk, ska, Algerian, and Moroccan rhythms to end up playing "un funky mambo, o la cumbia punk o el chacha reggae." These new musical genres emerged in a changing Mexico, both within and outside the national borders. This Mexican musical group has brought issues of political empowerment and cultural and sexual diversity to its audiences while at the same time making everyone dance. The rebellious spirit of Mexican rock and the circus ambiance of mosh pits now builds bridges across Mexican America. And an investigation of Maldita's twenty-year musical project illustrates how a progressive Chicano studies can take up a productive dialogue with greater Mexican cultural diasporas.

Notes

Editor's Note: From *Aztlán: A Journal of Chicano Studies* 31, no. 1 (2006). The original essay was lightly edited for this collection.

This essay was completed in 2005 during my stay in Mexico City, in Colonia Villa de Coyoacán, while I was serving as director of the Mexico Study Center of the University of California's Education Abroad Program. I would like to thank the members of Maldita Vecindad, especially Pato, Aldo (three interviews), and Roco (many conversations), and my dawgs DJ Aztek and Luis Manuel Márquez Briseño, whose friendship and knowledge contributed to the wide range of references from south of the border.

1. In 2005, Mexico City filmmaker Luis Manuel Márquez Briseño released a documentary titled *Ni muy, muy . . . Ni tan, tan . . . Simplemente TIN TAN*. The film chronicles the life of Tin Tan from his early Ciudad Juárez border years to his contemporary influence on rock en español. Márquez ends the film by interviewing members of Maldita Vecindad, Café Tavuba, El Gran Silencio, and Panteón Rococó. Márquez and his film expanded my knowledge of Valdés's early years and of his travel to Los Angeles. Moreover, the film demonstrates that Valdés with his pachuco character is no longer a cultural embarrassment to Mexicans. As Carlos Monsiváis states in the film, Tin Tan is "el primer mexicano del siglo XXI."

2. Mark Guerrero, Lalo's son, and I arranged for Maldita Vecindad to meet Lalo at the John Anson Ford Theatre on October 4, 2003, on the occasion of a tribute to Lalo (see fig. 3). For the story behind the meeting, see Mark Guerrero's "Maldita Vecindad: Bridging Mexican and Chicano Rock" (2005).

3. *Pachuco Boogie*, the original historic recordings featuring Don Tosti. Historic Mexican-American Music, vol. 10, Arhoolie Records, 2002.

4. The play resurrected Guerrero's music of the 1940s for new audiences thanks to UCLA ethnomusicologist Philip Sonnichsen, who had collected and

taped Guerrero's records. Valdez consulted Sonnichsen on music for his play (Guerrero and Montes 2002, 101). Aldo Acuña was introduced to Lalo Guerrero's "Chucos suaves," "Chicas patas boogie," "Marijuana Boogie," and "Vamos a bailar" through Valdez's 1981 film. *Zoot Suit* remains an influential film in Mexico: it is screened in Chicano and Mexican film courses at the Universidad Nacional Autónoma de México and is invoked by film students, young filmmakers, and all of Maldita's members for its seminal themes, dramatic techniques, and música de fusión. Maldita members have copies of the 2002 compilation of historic recordings, *Pachuco Boogie* (see note 3), and some of Maldita's members have a side band, Los Suavecitos, that plays music of the 1940s.

5. See, for example, Federico Arana's four-volume *Guaraches de ante azul: Historia del rock mexicano* (1985). Arana recently updated this work to include the new rock mexicano in his discographies (2002).

I should also note Eric Zolov's recent work lest there be some confusion between our respective views of Mexican rock. In *Refried Elvis* (1999), Zolov makes the case for what he calls "La Onda Chicana" and the Avándaro concert of 1971 as possible antecedents for the new rock mexicano. He overstates the case for this "Onda Chicana," which for Mexican critics is simply "La Onda." The period of music he describes lasted only a few years, 1969–71. Zolov's "La Onda Chicana" was not Chicana, nor were the lyrics political; the music was mostly a middle-class phenomenon that drew its inspiration from US rock and had lyrics in English. The culmination came at a music festival just north of Mexico City, in Avándaro, that drew middle-class jipiteca (hippie) types to what was, by all accounts, an imitation of the 1969 Woodstock. Carlos Monsiváis, in his "La naturaleza de La Onda" (1977), describes La Onda and Avándaro as apolitical movements inspired by US counterculture, quite different from the left-wing Mexican student movements of the late 1960s that responded to Mexican politics and culminated with the student massacre in Tlatelolco in 1968. Zolov continues his argument in his recent "La Onda Chicana: Mexico's Forgotten Rock Counterculture" (2004). It should be clear from my essay that Maldita's origins lie elsewhere, in other musical fusions taken from Afro-Caribbean, Mexican, and Mexican American musical cultures.

6. On the north side of the border, Los Angeles journalist Rubén Martínez was the first to write on the then-emerging 1980s rock en español in "El corazón del rocanrol" (1992). Martínez had this to say about Maldita: "Their look—resonances of James Dean, Tin Tan (a Mexican comedic great of the 1940s and 1950s, who popularized a Chicano/Pachuco swing style), U2." When Martínez wrote his piece, Maldita had not yet released "Pachuco" and had yet to realize its full cross-border potential. Josh Kun (1997) also includes a brief discussion of Café Tavuba and Maldita Vecindad.

7. Jesús Flores y Escalante, in his *Imágenes del danzón* (1994), offers a detailed description of these vecindades: "Ya desde principios del siglo, el término quintopatiero era bien popular entre las tropas de Tepito, la Lagunilla y la colonia Morelos. El agresivo término proliferó gracias a que los predios y las viejas casonas de estos lugares, después de la Revolución, fueron convertidas en vecindades. Cuarterías gigantescas divididas . . . que albergaban mundo incomensurable de gente, ropa tendida, lavaderos, música de todo género, macetas, trebejos y excusados comunes para varias familias . . . escenario inamovible de las consabidas pachangas y jolgorios

que iban (o van) desde el bautizo y los quince años, hasta las bodas o las rumbosas posadas navideñas . . . lo más importante para el vecindario eran los patios" (67).

8. For a written and photographic history of these neighborhood dance halls, see Jara Gómez, Rodríguez Yeyo, and Cedillo Castillo (1994, 59–113).

9. Lalo Guerrero, originally from Arizona, recalls living in a Mexico City vecindad in 1934 as one of the formative experiences in his life (Guerrero and Montes 2002, 51–56). He learned of popular Mexican musical personalities as well as another earthier musical tradition "from three old men who used to go from house to house begging for coins." These men would "take turns and they'd make up verses right on the spot. Everything rhymed, and some of them were really clever. I enjoy playing with words so, from that time on, I started making up funny verses" (55). Guerrero concludes of the three months in Mexico City: "Although our sojourn in Mexico City was a hardship in some respects, those three months were very important to my career. My music would never be the same" (56). The lively quintopatiera tradition, with all its humorous and serious cultural nuances, traveled north with this seventeen-year-old upon his return home. It would return years later to Mexico through Maldita Vecindad.

10. For an examination of the political contexts out of which the two versions of "El barzón" emerged, see Hernández (2001).

Works Cited

Acuña, Aldo. 2001. Interview by author, Mexico City, December 13.

———. 2002. Interview by author, Mexico City, September 5.

Arana, Federico. 1985. *Guaraches de ante azul: Historia del rock mexicano*. 4 vols. Mexico City: Editorial Posada.

———. 2002. *Guaraches de ante azul: Historia del roc mexicano*. Madrid: María Enea.

Cisneros, Sandra. 1991. "Little Miracles, Kept Promises." In *Woman Hollering Creek and Other Stories*, 116–29. New York: Random House.

Flores y Escalante, Jesús. 1994. *Imágenes del danzón: Iconografía del danzón en México*. Mexico City: Asociación Mexicana de Estudios Fonográficos.

Fuentes, Carlos. 1995. *La frontera de cristal: Una novela en nueve cuentos*. Mexico City: Alfaguara.

Guerrero, Lalo, and Sherilyn Meece Montes. 2002. *Lalo: My Life and Music*. Tucson: University of Arizona Press.

Guerrero, Mark. 2005. "Maldita Vecindad: Bridging Mexican and Chicano Rock." Guerrero personal home page, http://markguerrero.com/misc_27.php.

Hernández, Mark A. 2001. "Remaking the *Corrido* for the 1990s: Maldita Vecindad's 'El Barzón.'" *Studies in Latin American Popular Culture* 20: 101–16.

Jara Gómez, Simón, Aurelio Rodríguez Yeyo, and Antonio Cedillo Castillo. 1994. *De Cuba con amor . . . El danzón en México*. Mexico City: Grupo Azabache/CONACULTA-Culturas Populares.

Kun, Josh. 1997. "Against Easy Listening: Audiotopic Readings and Transcultural Soundings." In *Everynight Life: Culture and Dance in Latin/o America*, edited by Celeste Fraser Delgado and José Esteban Muñoz, 288–309. Durham, NC: Duke University Press.

Maldita Vecindad. 1993. *Gira pata de perro 93*. Mexico City: Maldita Vecindad.

———. 2001. Interview by LATV Live, KJLA-TV, Los Angeles, October 31.

Martínez, Rubén. 1992. "El Corazón del Rocanrol." In *The Other Side: Fault Lines, Guerrilla Saints, and the True Heart of Rock 'n' Roll*, 148–64. London: Verso.

Monsiváis, Carlos. 1977. "La naturaleza de la Onda." In *Amor perdido*, 225–62. Mexico City: Ediciones Era.

Montoya, José. 1972. "El Louie." In *Aztlan: An Anthology of Mexican American Literature*, edited by Luis Valdez and Stan Steiner, 333–37. New York: Random House.

Paredes Pacho, José Luis. 1993. *Rock mexicano: Sonidos de la calle*. Mexico City: Aguirre y Beltrán.

Paz, Octavio. 1959. *El laberinto de la soledad*. Mexico City: Fondo de Cultura Económica.

———. 1993. *La llama doble: Amor y erotismo*. Barcelona: Seix Barral.

Varela, Chuy. 2002. Introduction to *Pachuco Boogie*, the original historic recordings featuring Don Tosti. Historic Mexican-American Music, vol. 10, Arhoolie Records.

Zolov, Eric. 1999. *Refried Elvis: The Rise of the Mexican Counterculture*. Berkeley: University of California Press.

———. 2004. "La Onda Chicana: Mexico's Forgotten Rock Counterculture." In *Rockin' Las Américas: The Global Politics of Rock in Latin/o America*, edited by Deborah Pacini Hernandez, Héctor Fernández L'Hoeste, and Eric Zolov, 22 42. Pittsburgh: University of Pittsburgh Press.

RECORDINGS BY MALDITA VECINDAD Y LOS HIJOS DEL 5° PATIO

Baile de máscaras. 1996, BMG Ariola.
Circo. 1991, BMG Ariola.
En vivo: Gira pata de perro. 1993, BMG Ariola.
Maldita Vecindad y los Hijos del 5° Patio. 1989, BMG Ariola.
Mostros. 1998, BMG Ariola.

FILMOGRAPHY

Amores perros. 2000. Directed by Alejandro González Iñárritu. Lions Gate.
Danzón. 1991. Directed by María Novaro. IMCINE.
De la calle. 2001. Directed by Gerardo Tort. IMCINE.
El hijo desobediente. 1945. Directed by Humberto Gómez Landero. Laguna Films.
Los olvidados. 1950. Directed by Luis Buñuel. Clasa Films Mundiales.
Ni muy, muy . . . Ni tan, tan . . . Simplemente TIN TAN. 2005. Directed by Luis Manuel Márquez Briseño. Angel Márquez and Manuel Márquez in association with Carlos Valdés.
Quinto patio. 1950. Directed by Raphael J. Sevilla. Producciones Argel.
Zoot Suit. 1981. Directed by Luis Valdez. Universal.

Conversación con Aldo Acuña de Maldita Vecindad

Héctor Calderón

In December 2002, Maldita Vecindad once again toured the Los Angeles area. Between concert dates, on December 5, bass player Aldo Acuña was kind enough to accept my invitation to meet with my Spanish 144: Mexican Literature, Culture, and Society class at the University of California, Los Angeles. Aldo's visit came on the last day of the term, dramatically concluding the course section on rock en tu idioma. For over an hour and a half, Aldo fielded questions from students and me. He offered insights into the band's transformation of punk culture into a contestatory musical project through a discussion of key songs from *Maldita Vecindad y los Hijos del 5° Patio* (1989), *Circo* (1991), and *Baile de máscaras* (1996). At the end of the interview, Maldita's fusion of art and politics is clearly evident in Aldo's assessment of the current state of artists, politics, and government in Mexico.

The interview below is faithful to the live performance of the class and includes lyrics of the music played during the discussion (in italic). I would like to thank student Sara González, who provided the audiotape transcription later edited by me, and I extend my deepest appreciation to Aldo for finding time to visit UCLA after a late night concert in Anaheim.

Héctor Calderón: Empecemos con el primer disco, del '89, *Maldita Vecindad y los Hijos del 5° Patio*. Explícanos un poco de ese momento y, de nuevo, gracias por venir.

Aldo Acuña: ¿Gracias por venir? Yo creo que el más honrado soy yo. Nunca pensé estar en la escuela como los alumnos. No tuve mucho chance porque desde muy chiquito empecé a hacer música. No tuve una niñez como la mayoría de nosotros. También, dentro del grupo hay muchas historias, somos personajes diferentes, tenemos vidas comunes y corrientes. Gracias por invitarme.

HC: En la portada del CD, estabas muy chavito.

AA: ¿Héctor, qué insinúas?

HC: ¿Puedes recordar esos momentos, Aldo?

AA: Bueno, pues, no existía mucho de la industria del rock en español, de la nueva música, no sólo en México, sino en Latinoamérica, salvo las excepciones, Brasil por ejemplo, o la Argentina que ya hacía tiempo el rock manejaba el español, sus letras. No existía tanto la infraestructura del rock y no era un vehículo, no era un negocio todavía. Y cuando grabamos este disco era un experimento más. Nosotros grabábamos en pequeños estudios caseros y también grabábamos en estudios de radio cuando podíamos entrar a la radio y grabar algunos temas. Y ésos eran nuestros demos, nuestro material de promoción. Con el tiempo, llegaron algunas propuestas de algunas compañías, algunas independientes, algunas grandes como Sony, BMG. Y pues, decidimos hacer un disco con BMG, una compañía internacional. Hicimos un contrato, así nomás; nomás lo firmamos y ya; por eso estoy donde estoy. Fue una padre experiencia porque fue enfrentar nuestros trabajos a los leones de la industria. Con este primer disco, no vimos gran apoyo de la compañía. Simplemente, fue como una especie de trámite, digamos.

En este disco, nosotros planteamos nuestra primera propuesta como grupo. Nuestra propuesta consistía en el juego, el baile. Tomamos la música como vehículo y también como vehículo de contar historias cotidianas, quizá algo que entre nosotros había pasado o que le había sucedido a algunos amigos y era un poquito más una realidad con el apoyo de una compañía grande. Con el tiempo, ese disco se hizo una especie de clásico porque es muy raro. Casi no se encuentra. Y bueno, allí también empezamos a plantear la idea de hacerlo nosotros, es decir, las fotos. La mayoría de las fotos las tomamos nosotros, las fotos de promoción, el diseño de las portadas. El color que tiene la portada también es nuestro, es decir, trabajamos sobre los negativos, pintándolos con colores pastel. En general, lo hacemos todo nosotros. Llegamos a la compañía con un proyecto ya muy claro, muy definido. Ellos sólo tuvieron que grabar, meternos a grabar en un estudio. Y bueno, eso fue el principio de una serie de cuestiones. Fue de los primeros discos compactos que salió en México. Había uno o dos anteriores, pero fue una de las primeras grabaciones rock, bueno, o sea, que es la prehistoria.

HC: ¿Y de las composiciones, empezando con "Apañón"?

—*Vamos Juan / no lo dejes ir / va en la esquina / quiere huir. / Es un punk / míralo bien / y "panchito" ha de ser. / —Hey tú / qué haces aquí / caminando en la calle / vestido así. / —Pues discúlpeme señor / pero yo no soy doctor / y yo camino aquí / pues no tengo un "Gran Marquis."*

AA: "Apañón" es un intento de punk, punk con son montuno, le decimos. Tiene una serie de aportes rítmicos poco debido a la falta de pericia de algunos de los músicos y también a la inventiva. Es decir, hay cuestiones allí que son búsqueda musical y hay hallazgos, descubrimientos para nosotros. La letra es una pequeña crónica sobre una situación común y corriente en los barrios, en las ciudades de México, no sólo en el Distrito Federal, sino también en los estados de la República. Habla sobre la marginación. Habla sobre pequeñas historias sobre la relación de los chavos, de la gente joven, con la autoridad misma. Y también, lleva una propuesta contestataria, digamos. De alguna forma, habla sobre un apañón, donde van a agarrar un chavo, lo golpean y le sacan el dinero y lo dejan sin nada y el que ha hecho el atraco es la autoridad, es la policía. Es una escena que todos nosotros en algún momento llegamos a vivir, a pasar como jóvenes y como gente que no estábamos insertos directamente en la cuestión productiva o no estábamos solamente metidos en la escuela, sino que también estábamos haciendo otras cosas. Nos gustaba el cine, nos gustaba leer, nos gustaba mucho la música que venía de todos lados del mundo y a la que teníamos acceso sólo a través de ciertos amigos o, a veces, programas de radio.

"Apañón" es una canción que empieza un poco fuerte. Esa es la idea: poner algo fuerte en ese disco, en esa propuesta. De lo que recuerdo de esta producción, era una de las primeras veces que íbamos a un estudio profesional y nuestro encuentro con ese estudio fue la primera vez que empezamos a entenderlo como un instrumento más, es decir, somos varios músicos, todos trabajando en el proyecto, pero a la vez, el estudio se transforma en la posibilidad de manipular sonidos, cortar las frases, pegarlas, meterlas donde quisiéramos y hacerlo más o menos como nos imaginábamos. Y mucho de eso también pasó con las letras. Al entrar al estudio, descubrimos que quizá nuestra historia estaba contando, estaba diciendo algo pero que con una pequeña edición de mis amigos podríamos extender la historia, contar más detalles, pero a la vez, al hacer el disco, tuvimos que hacer una reducción de lo que pasaba. Eso es un poquito de la historia de esta canción, primer tema que se llama "Apañón" que queríamos llevar pero con energía.

HC: ¿Podrías contarnos un poco del movimiento musical punk, los chavos y las chavas de México en los '80?

AA: Era en 1988. "Apañón" habla de "panchito." "Panchitos" les decían a una banda de maleantes, era una banda de chavos. Los chavos de banda son los marginados de ciertas zonas, en ese tiempo, de ciertas zonas del Distrito Federal, de la Cuidad de México. "Panchito" era cualquiera que trajera los pelos parados o que se pusiera botas y jeans pegados, entonces, era punk, era panchito. Este estigma duró mucho tiempo, sobre todo, en Guadalajara. En ese tiempo, en la Ciudad de Guadalajara había una vigilancia que llevaba una patrulla de los azules, después llevaba una patrulla de tránsito, después llevaba una de los judiciales y al final iba una camioneta de policías armados con gases, con todo. Entonces, no había forma de huir porque si tenías una cosa con tránsito, se iban sobre ti o si había alguna otra infracción, pues, siempre tenían manera de hacerlo.

Hubo un tiempo en donde mi grupo de amigos que éramos punks y yo, a veces, nos detenían dos veces al día, las mismas personas, las mismas zonas, simplemente por la forma en que estábamos vestidos. En ese tiempo no había mucho tatú, no había mucho "piercing," no había muchos aretes y era un poquito complicado, muy cerrada esa ciudad. En ese tiempo, la cuestión del punk venía pegando ya un poco tarde. Todos escuchábamos The Clash, escuchábamos Sex Pistols y también oíamos New Wave. También escuchábamos otro tipo de cuestiones. El reggae, por ejemplo, calypso empezaban a llegar muy fuerte. Había una serie de programas interesantes en la radio de la U de G [Universidad de Guadalajara] en donde había dos horas de música. Había música del mundo, no sólo era rock, punk o reggae o ska, había, a veces, jazz. Era una fuente importante de información, sobre todo, en ese tiempo que no existían la Internet y la computadora tanto. Eran tiempos, por un lado duros, y por otro, muy divertidos. Había muchas cosas que hacer. Había casi todo que hacer como todavía sigue siendo en México, sobre todo.

HC: ¿Aldo, y "Mojado"? ¿Y las "intros"? La introducción musical es importante para todos los temas de Maldita Vecindad, ¿no?

Yo sabía que te ibas a ir / hoy por fin te vi partir. / Yo temía que te ibas a ir / hoy tu voz la oí decir: / "Yo me voy de aquí / me voy de aquí. / No tengo nada / que darte a ti. / El otro lado es la solución / por todas partes se oye el rumor: yo me voy de aquí." / Te vi partir. / Ahora estoy sola / sola sin ti. / Yo te vi partir, / partir, partir, partir.

AA: El mojadito. Sí, aquí hay una fusión al principio, sobre todo. Hay una fusión de rumba flamenca, música de España con música del Caribe.

HC: En México, en tu estudio en la Colonia Condesa, Aldo, me hablaste del origen de la canción.

AA: Bueno, en realidad, la idea de hacer un tema de la emigración también surgió porque muchos amigos nuestros tenían la experiencia de haber venido a Estados Unidos y regresarse y contar las historias, las maravillas del primer mundo y todo eso. Y también tuvimos noticias que aún hoy siguen llegando y cada vez más, la situación de los emigrantes, la gente que cruza ya solamente buscando, mucha gente que viene a encontrar y encontraron que estaba cada vez más difícil, cada vez más duro. Encontramos una noticia en el periódico, como tantas otras, el montón de gente que se muere en un vagón, y en función de eso, encontrar una letra que contara esa historia, un poquito quizá de manera burda y cruda, pero presente porque era así como nos llegaba a nosotros. Era muy fuerte leer en el periódico que treinta personas habían muerto asfixiadas en un vagón del tren, como tantos otros, y un poco de eso, nos llevó a inventarnos esta historia del personaje que va a pasar y que no regresa nunca. Y bueno, algunos no vuelven porque encuentran lo que buscan o siguen buscando. Y algunos otros se quedaron en el camino, como muchos miles.

Trae en la mano un diario gris / hay una nota perdida entre mil / que habla de ti. / Habla de ti: / "MOJADO MUERTO, AL INTENTAR HUIR."

Era difícil congeniar que pudiera existir en un solo tema, una idea, la posibilidad de bailar como está planteada la rumba flamenca y en una historia triste, una historia aguda, pero decidimos jugar. Jugar es mucho lo que hacemos, jugar con las palabras, es un juego de tonos y sonidos, de expresión también, y es una forma de afrontar también nuestro trabajo. Decidimos jugar en el terreno de la frontera entre lo triste y lo vital, y eso es un poquito la idea de "Mojado," la historia de muchos connacionales y latinoamericanos que cruzan y que quieren cruzar y siguen viajando y siguen llegando.

Estudiante: ¿Estarías de acuerdo como yo en que Gustavo Santaolalla ha sido el productor?

AA: Gustavo Santaolalla es un personaje que nosotros conocimos a través de la industria. El y su mancuerna en ese tiempo, Aníbal [Kerpel], venían de la música de Argentina, venían de una experiencia que ellos tuvieron y que, bueno, ellos son mis mayores. También fue muy importante porque hubo mucha cooperación, la oportunidad de plantearnos nuestro trabajo a gente que sí tenía bastante idea de cuál era la propuesta. Ellos se involucraron más, desde luego, cuando supieron que se trataba de nosotros y cuando supieron de qué se trataba esto que nosotros estábamos haciendo. Yo creo que como estaba diciendo al principio, lo más importante para estas producciones es que nosotros llegamos al estudio con el trabajo avanzado, es decir, con gran parte de la producción ya concluida, ya terminada.

El trabajo de ellos en este caso, sobre todo en *Circo*, fue pulir las aristas musicales, digamos, los picos de la métrica, de la letra, cuestiones así. Los detalles de la producción son muchos y hay muchos factores que intervienen en una producción discográfica de la misma manera que intervienen en un evento colectivo y son las mismas, los mismos planteamientos, la idea de llevar la energía de la música al pequeño grid de laser para que suene caliente. Es complicado, es a grandes rasgos querer, no sé, plasmar en hielo algo que puede dispersarse pero que hay un pequeño margen en donde va a perder forma y va a perder energía, brillo. No podemos reproducir en disco lo que sucede exactamente en vivo. Su trabajo fue importante y sigue siendo importante, no sólo para nosotros sino para todos los demás músicos que trabajaron con él después, otros grupos mexicanos y colombianos y españoles. Ellos tienen mucha experiencia en trabajar con fusión y con nuevas ideas. Fue importante y ellos tuvieron visión porque trabajaron con mucha confianza con nosotros y nosotros aprendimos también a trabajar de la mano con la industria allí con ellos. Fue importante eso y tanto como lo fue en el *Circo*. Creo que en *Circo* es donde más ellos hacen lucir su trabajo.

E: ¿Cómo usted veía que reaccionaba la gente cuando oía esta música ya diferente a la clásica?

AA: Aún ahora la gente sigue oyendo nuestra música. Hay mucha gente que nos va a ver a shows y son chavos que nunca nos habían visto. Habían escuchado nuestra música, saben nuestra historia quizá un poco, pero aún ahora se siguen sorprendiendo, igual que nosotros, con su reacción.

E: ¿Con los grandes mensajes?

AA: Es sorpresa, es una gran sorpresa. Es una comunión, los eventos en vivo. El show en vivo es único y cuando uno ejecuta, a menos que lo grabes, no vas a tener otra visión igual, nunca va a suceder igual. Yo jamás voy a tocar una nota y jamás va a durar lo mismo aunque sea la misma nota y mi compañero esté tocando lo mismo y el otro también. Siempre va a haber una diferencia y la diferencia la hace, yo creo, la mayor parte del tiempo, la hace la gente, la gente que escucha y que retroalimenta. Para nosotros es importante esa retroalimentación. Siempre fue una cuestión importante el baile, el movimiento, porque el baile libera, como el fútbol, como otras actividades físicas, el yoga. El baile libera muchas tensiones y libera también la mente. Si uno se puede abandonar a la música, puede también imaginar, y al imaginar o al bailar, estamos, simplemente, haciendo formas y marcando los tiempos de la música. De alguna manera, estamos haciendo música.

HC: Ahora *Circo* de '91 y el primer tema, "Pachuco," que se ha convertido para toda una generación de rockeros en el himno nacional de México y Estados Unidos.

AA: Allí hay una cuestión. Allí es donde más nos decidimos a jugar. Este disco empezó como el juego que teníamos pendiente, que habíamos empatado con el otro equipo. Era una especie de reto pero también, como le decía a ella, la amiga estudiante, el factor más importante para este disco es la situación del país, de México y de la calle y de las historias cotidianas. Esto es lo más importante de este disco para mí en términos de la letra, de la lírica. El siguiente elemento es la fusión de la música. Encontramos que queríamos hacer bolero, queríamos, a veces, danzón. Queríamos experimentar con diferentes patrones de ritmo y de tiempo. Cada una de las canciones es una historia, partes inclusive como la que se llama "Otra" es una broma de nosotros. En *Circo* es donde empezamos un poquito a jugar con "samplers." Nosotros fuimos de los primeros que incorporamos el "sampler" en la producción discográfica en México, bueno, en el rock y también de esta generación. Y lo buscamos y lo experimentamos de muchas maneras. Hay un pedacito que dice "otra, otra, otra" y es una broma para nosotros un poco personal de cómo nos vemos nosotros como público, es decir, uno que pide "otra, otra, otra" y otro que dice "¡ya bájense!" y otros "una cerveza" y otros "agua," "n'ombre, tóquenla de nuevo." Entonces era poquito jugar con eso. Y también metimos allí una porra de fútbol al revés. Si ustedes pudieran tocar su CD al revés, sería escuchar una palabra antisonante que sólo se oye en el estadio o en las tocadas de Maldita Vecindad, como "¡culero! ¡culero! ¡culero!" y no la pueden censurar.

HC: ¿Y "Pachuco"?

AA: Pues sí, en "Pachuco" es otro ejemplo del uso del sampler. El sampler es una copia casi fiel del sonido ambiental, de un sonido x, de un sonido cualquiera. "Pachuco" empezó como un juego un poco rudo, una especie de "eslam" entre nosotros solos en el ensayo. Hacía tanto frío que necesitábamos algo de acción y entonces empezamos a jugar con "Pachuco." Eran dos acordes, por horas, horas, horas. Entonces uno entra en una especie como de mantra, como que ya está pegando allí, y entonces, ¿qué contamos con esta cosa tan frenética, no? Pues un baile loco, un baile loco como lo era en sus tiempos el danzón o el chachachá y el mambo, era un poco estigmatizado, sobre todo, por la gente, los adultos, por la "gente bien," y que decían que esos bailes eran sacrílegos. Y resulta que encontramos en la historia de un hijo que le dice al padre: "Oye, no me estés dando lata sobre si uso aretes o si me tatúo o si la greña o si la ropa. Tú te vestías así, el pantalón de tirilón, te vestías de pachucote, te salías de fiesta, bailabas mambo, ¿no?" Y eso es lo que me dice mi hijo ahora. Es algo muy divertido, es algo interesante ver como las nuevas generaciones descubren esa canción, descubren como tiene relación con ellos, con su "abismo generacional." Ya, tal vez, otro tono más pequeño porque la gente tiene hijos más chiquitos, como niños teniendo niños. No sé sabe cuál es la generación.

HC: Y Darío, tu hijo, tiene un grupo rockero, ¿no?

AA: Ah, bueno, tiene su grupo y toca y yo no le puedo decir "Oye, regresa temprano," como papá. Es una experiencia muy padre, muy divertida, ver crecer a alguien y poderle contar estas cosas, tener eso que contarle, eso que darle. Bueno, ya todos estamos muy contentos con nuestros hijos, bueno, los que tenemos.

HC: ¿Y la figura del pachuco tal como la interpretó en los '40s Germán Valdés, el Tin Tan?

AA: Tin Tan es un aporte bastante invaluable. Yo creo que es generador en gran parte de la filosofía que nosotros en algún momento llegamos a manejar. Es como el personaje que escogimos un poco para explicarnos a nosotros mismos, también por qué hacemos esto. Así como Tin Tan, existen muchos músicos y grandes artistas de la carpa. Ellos son artistas de carpa. La carpa en México es una tradición que tiene, bueno, por tradición, los espectáculos populares que se llevaban a los pueblos, a la ciudades, en diferentes lugares de las ciudades, artistas, cómicos, payasos, rumberas, músicos, no.

Contaban historias que hacían mofa, hacían burla de cuestiones políticas. Era muy politizada la gente que iba a la carpa. Podían quejarse de su nivel, podían hacer bromas sobre el regidor que estaba en el gobierno y al mismo tiempo de contarse historia, convivir allí. Tin Tan venía de allí, de la carpa. Tin Tan nos llenó después de cultura y de humor a través de sus películas, de sus canciones, de todo lo que él propuso: una forma relajada, divertida y lúdica, de transmitir, de contar historias, de contar cuentos. Fue uno de los básicos, pero hay muchos otros, la música de Pérez Prado, la música de Agustín Lara y muchos otros, el cantautor [Salvador] "Chava" Flores como cronista, digamos, de las cuestiones urbanas en la Ciudad de México y es parte de lo que encontramos. Yo creo que Tin Tan fue el más claro, el personaje que más claramente definió lo que queríamos hacer nosotros. Queríamos representar, queríamos jugar con él. El ya lo había hecho antes y nuestra búsqueda era ésa: buscar y encontrar este personaje que definiera nuestro trabajo. Por eso es tan fuerte la presencia de Tin Tan en nuestro trabajo.

HC: Voy a tocar la introducción a "Pachuco."

—*¡Golfas, ya llegó su pachucote!* / — *No sé cómo te atreves* / *a vestirte de esa forma* / *y salir . . .así* / *En mis tiempos todo era elegante* / *sin greñudos y sin rock.*

AA: El "sampler" dice "¡Golfas, ya llegó su pachucote!" Es la voz del Tin Tan.

HC: Si van a los conciertos de Maldita, cuando tocan esa canción, cuidado, van a salir sangrientos y sangrientas del mosh pit porque las chavas y los chavos se ponen prendidísimos.

AA: No los asustes. No van a ir a los conciertos.

HC: El tema que sigue a "Pachuco" es "Un poco de sangre."

Poco de sangre roja / *sobre un gran auto nuevo* / *poco de sangre roja* / *sobre un gran auto blanco.* / *Nada más bello,* / *ni más lujoso,* / *tan poderoso* / *como un gran auto nuevo.*

AA: "Un poco de sangre" también está basada un poco en una historia del periódico. Un "yuppie" va en un Cadillac, y pues, no se puede ir a velocidad muy alta en la Cuidad de México, pero tuvo dos cuadras. Cuando llegó a la siguiente esquina, se encontró con un chavo de los que limpian los vidrios y se lo lleva. Entonces, era más o menos la historia del diario, del periódico. Pero era precisamente lo que veíamos si no veíamos que pasaba el auto y lo aplastaba. Había tanto riesgo de eso. Sigue habiendo tantas posibilidades de que eso pase que es muy fuerte ver eso. No sé si ustedes conocen la Ciudad de México, ¿algunos? No sé si recientemente han ido. En diez años la ciudad ha cambiado un no sé qué porcentaje, pero muchísimo, sobre todo, en la calle. La manera en que la gente afronta la miseria o la necesidad, los lleva a todo mundo, a muchos los lleva a algún lado, a muchos los lleva a vender, a otros los lleva a ofrecer servicios, a vender en la calle, a pararse en la calle. Y como hay mucho tráfico en el periférico, entonces, es como si en el "freeway" vinieran caminando con las cervezas para el calor. Hace más de diez años que la ciudad se empezó a llenar de eso, de desempleo, de gente sin recursos y que tiene que ver también con la migración del campo a la ciudad, de las comunidades indígenas que emigran y que en la ciudad no encuentran más que hacer mas que lavar coches, limpiar los vidrios o hacer de jardinero si los dejan.

Pero bueno, "Un poco de sangre" es musicalmente un intento de punk, música para bailar y también es una cuestión que nos hacemos. Estamos haciendo una música para bailar y estamos contando una historia dura, una historia triste, pero de todos modos decidimos contarla, decidimos hacerla, creo que mucho más por lo que nos llevaba la música. La música está planteando momentos y espacios. Hay dos espacios completos y de repente hay un espacio donde hay una especie de rap que dice:

Ahí está en la calle / brilla como el sol. / En su auto nuevo / que orgulloso va. / Vuela por la calle / a gran velocidad. / Todas las personas / lo miran pasar. / Limpiaparabrisas / cruza sin mirar / un niño no puede / el auto esquivar / sólo se oye un grito / golpe y nada más / demasiada sangre / en esta ciudad."

Y algo más fuerte, la canción después dice también:

José trabaja / en una esquina, / limpiando parabrisas. / Corre a un carro, / corre a otro / jabón y trapo / y muy pocas monedas.

Es un poco la historia de esta canción y ustedes si buscan en la letra van a encontrar esta referencia a la ciudad, a la calle y al momento, digamos histórico, que se vive allí.

HC: Hablando de las calles del DF, tocaré "Un gran circo."

Dos por diez, dos por diez, de regalo, de remate, barato, barato. Difícil es caminar / en un extraño lugar / en donde el hambre se ve / como un gran circo en acción / en las calles no hay telón / así que puedes mirar / como rico espectador / te invito a nuestra ciudad.

AA: Eso que se oye allí en la introducción es la calle de México, es un mercado. Son las voces de la gente, son los samplers que nosotros usamos y que habla del mercado del subempleo que viene ya desde hace quince años en México. El subempleo es toda la gente que no tiene espacio en una fábrica, en una empresa, en algo así. Sale a vender, a vender lo que sea. Y lo que sea es poner un mercado en la esquina, algo como el mercadito que tienen aquí pero más grande.

HC: No soy fotógrafo, clase, pero éstas son fotos de la banda, de Aldo y del grupo en Torreón, Coahuila, en el norte de México, en el concierto de la Feria de Torreón, el 17 de septiembre 2002, dos días después de la celebración del Grito. Pueden ver el público que, en realidad, no es muy diferente del público en los conciertos de Maldita en los Estados Unidos. Roco con la calavera en su camisa, esto es antes del concierto. Allí está el Sax, y lamentablemente, no está aquí porque no le dieron permiso de venir a Los Angeles, no lo dejaron pasar. Ese es Pacho en el fondo en la bateria. Pelusa a su lado en percusión. Aldo en bajo entre Pacho y Pelusa. Pato al frente de guitarrista.

Aldo, y ¿"Pata de perro"?

De toda la flota él / era el más jalador. / No había rival / para este gañán. / Pata de perro por aquí. / Pata de perro por allá. / Mario era el nombre / de este buen carnal. / Por todos lados va, / ya no regresará.

AA: "Pata de perro." ¿Alguien sabe qué es un pata de perro?

E: Los viajeros.

AA: Los viajeros. Todos los que estamos aquí de alguna forma somos pata de perro. Creo que el hecho de la posibilidad de viajar, de conocer, de intercambiar y de aprender de los otros, es un buen ejercicio. Es un buen ejercicio y nos ha tocado a nosotros en la vida dar vueltas por el mundo, hacer nuestra música, conocer más amigos, intercambiar ideas, intercambiar conocimientos, juegos. Creo que nosotros en el '89 fue la primera vez que vinimos a Estados Unidos, invitados por MEChA, y fuimos al 5 de mayo a San Francisco. Esa fue la primera vez que nosotros salimos de México a Estados Unidos y que fue un descubrimiento. Fue nuestro primer paso de pata de perro.

Pata de perro se llamó también luego una gira que inventamos, "Gira Pata de Perro." Esta gira nos llevó por cerca de quince países diferentes. Tocamos como 120 shows en como cuatro meses y nos llevó por toda Europa y gran parte de Estados Unidos. Descubrimos todo lo que habíamos contado en esta canción lo íbamos encontrando. Encontramos a los amigos mexicanos en París caminando a mitad de la noche, con su cámara. No había luz, me acuerdo que un día salí a la calle. Salí yo solo para pensar a las dos de la mañana por el Sena. Por allí estaba muy oscuro. Pasé junto a un individuo bien raro, entonces, como a cinco metros después, escucho que dicen: "¡Aldo!" Era un fotógrafo, un mexicano que estaba por allí, pero en la oscuridad, me dije, "cómo puede saber mi nombre este tipo," y además, yo ni lo distinguía. Pues, ése era un pata de perro. Era un tipo que había estado viajando como muchos miles, como nosotros mismos, estaba conociendo, en nuestro caso llevando nuestro trabajo, nuestra música, y ellos, pues, descubriendo, algunos estudiantes, en fin. Nos encontramos a gente en Europa y esta canción es un homenaje a los viajeros, un buen pretexto para agarrar la mochila e irnos a viajar, a conocer.

En esta "Gira Pata de Perro" que inició en '92, finales del '92 y principios del '93, hicimos la gira con 120 fechas, no recuerdo bien, y terminamos en México, en el Auditorio Nacional donde grabamos un disco en vivo. Fue una manera de cerrar esos capítulos de haber viajado mucho, haber hecho estas giras, y un poquito, así como un pretexto para la industria, para dejarnos de lado, no meternos a grabar discos inmediatamente, una serie de cuestiones que no queríamos hacer. Desde un principio, se lo dijimos a la disquera. Y eso hicimos. No vamos a hacer discos como las gallinas. A las gallinas se les prende la luz y ponen huevos. Y nosotros no somos gallinas. De hecho, nuestra música no estaba pensada para la industria, no estaba pensada en función de los discos y las grabaciones. Estaba más en función de lo que nosotros estábamos queriendo decir, de lo que estaba pasando a nuestro alrededor. Entonces, *Pata de perro* es el nombre de ese disco, de la gira también y de esta canción que aún nos lleva a todos lados, todavía nos sigue invitando a viajar.

HC: *¿Baile de máscaras* del '96, Aldo?

AA: Bueno. Nos pusimos tan malos con la industria que nos tocó, nos regresó la bofetada. Y nosotros teníamos desde la "Gira Pata de Perro" nuevo material. Empezamos a trabajar en los camerinos, en los hoteles en Europa, sobre el nuevo material, sobre las experiencias nuevas que estábamos tomando. Llega el momento en el que nosotros preveíamos un poquito lo que estaba pasando en el sureste mexicano. Toda esta situación del levantamiento de los indios en Chiapas. Los zapatistas estaban muy permeables, muy claros, y había situaciones que no podían seguir siendo las mismas. Había cosas que no podían ser sin un cambio, sin una aparición. La aparición fueron los zapatistas en el '94. Para entonces ya estábamos grabando este material que estábamos trabajando primero en un principio.

Grabamos en Nueva York en un estudio que se llama Greenpoint y que nos "producía" entre comillas un cuate que se llama Bill Laswell. Estuvimos varios meses grabando ese disco. Constaba de treinta y dos tracks y teníamos poesía Náhuatl, teníamos sonidos de Lakota, hay cantos del "powwow" con tambores y con muchas cosas, como una fusión musical. Son treinta y dos tracks, son treinta y dos temas. Tuvimos problemas, entre otros, cuestiones políticas y cuestiones económicas con la disquera. Y ese disco nunca salió. Ese disco está todavía archivado en los archivos del señor productor, el cual dice que disque se le debe una lana. Estamos haciendo una colecta para pagarle. Lo malo es que la disquera también es socia de nosotros. No lo vamos a sacar hasta que haya una buena oportunidad. Son treinta y dos tracks que están guardados de los cuales recuperamos seis temas que están incluidos en *Baile de máscaras*.

Baile de máscaras lo grabamos en Memphis, Tennessee en el '95. Los temas, la mayoría, tienen esa relación que es el momento de la historia de México y son los indios y es como los mestizos, como los de nosotros, de fusión de color, de fusión, no somos como, bueno, no sé qué somos. Si ustedes ven el disco hay máscaras huicholas, hay máscaras de la conquista, hay máscaras de la colonia también en el disco. También el arte lo trabajamos nosotros, igual que en los otros discos, trabajamos con artistas clásicos, con pintores, con escultores, y en este caso, pues, pintamos las máscaras y dijimos que era un baile de máscaras. Curiosamente, apareció Marcos encapuchado y el estado se puso su máscara de tolerancia y todos nosotros nos pusimos una máscara de cuestión, de pregunta, ¿de qué está pasando? Ya lo sospechábamos. Los indios se hartaron, se hartaron las poblaciones de campesinos jodidas y olvidadas de la política y de la economía del gobierno. Entonces se levantaron y ese levantamiento fue un poquito lo que originó algunas de las letras y también mucho de, digamos de la temática, no sólo la forma de contar las historias sino de qué estábamos hablando en ese momento. Hablamos, por ejemplo, de un tema que se llama "Saltapa'trás." ¿Alguien sabe lo qué es saltapa'trás? Cuando llegaron los españoles, hubo un pintor que se dedicó a retratar las diferencias de las castas.

Sangre con sangre, / mujeres y hombres. / Poder necesitas de nombres, / temor, divisiones. / Colores y castas: / herencia de segregaciones. / Indio y mestiza/ —coyote, / mestizo con india / —cholo, / negra con zamba / —zambo prieto, / blanco y mulata / —morisco, / blanco con negra / —mulato.

HC: Aldo, la clase tiene una hoja con las diferentes castas. Había unas diecisiete castas que se inventaron en la colonia para ver la congregación de razas, la africana, la indígena y la española y las diferentes mezclas o mestizajes que se podían dar. Este es el siglo dieciocho. Es la respuesta, podríamos decir, del Imperio Español a la Ilustración europea, al pensamiento científico, o sea, la clasificación de razas. El Imperio Español empezó a clasificar a las colonias a base del color de la piel. Tengo tranparencias de los retratos de este pintor famoso de la colonia, Miguel Cabrera. Podrán ver, es una familia, el señor, la señora y el niño: español con indígena produce mestizo. Y siempre es el varón primero y luego la mujer, basado también en el color de la piel, lo blanco primero y luego los demás colores y de allí en adelante. Entonces, esta canción, "Saltapa'trás," es una canción sobre la historia de las relaciones de castas en la colonia, en Nueva España y hoy en México.

Voy por la calle | —¡caco! | me apaña la tira | — ¡tizo! | la greña y tatuajes | —¡naco! | no tengo trabajo | ¡vago! | soy estudiante | —¡rojillo! | uso aretes | —¡joto! | acabo en el tambo | —¡pobre! . . . | Miedo a los otros | a costumbres distintas. | Poder, necesitas de odio, | disfraces y reglas. | Clasificaciones: | vivir entre segregaciones. | Nuestras diferencias somos, | no hay pureza. | No hay pureza.

AA: Sería también muy padre. Yo me imagino que les van a gustar, las pinturas. En fin, en ese disco también viene otro tema que se llama "El dedo."

Juan Charrasqueado y don Emiliano | platican allá en Toniná: |—Uno no gana | para puros sustos, | cada seis años | vuelve a empezar. | Con cada dedazo | todos se van a formar. | El que se mueve no sale en la foto, | con el tapado hay que esperar. | —Se hacen bolas, | se mueven el piso, | parece lo natural, | sabemos lo que vendrá. | —Luego nos dicen que son rete felices. | El pastel se reparten, | no engañan a nadie.

AA: No sé si ustedes saben lo que es el dedazo. El dedazo era, todavía lo es, la designación del siguiente mandatario o de los siguientes funcionarios del gobierno por los anteriores. Es decir, uno dejaba a sus séquitos, a sus amigos, allí en el puesto. Se designaba, pues, por dedazo. Hay una canción que habla del dedo, del dedazo y de las elecciones y de muchos dichos que son muy populares entre los políticos en México, esta idea de que el que se mueve no sale en la foto. Es decir, un año antes de finalizar su sexenio, estas personas preferían evitar meterse, digamos a negociar con otras instancias, digamos con los campesinos o con los estudiantes o con los obreros. Todo para que, bueno, no solucionaran nada antes de este último año porque eso significaba moverse, moverse políticamente, lo cual estaba mal porque si ellos se movían, el año siguiente ya no estaban en la nómina, ya no estaban en la lista de los elegidos. Entonces que la sucesión de la presidencia y de los equipos de burócratas donde "el señor ya no trabaja aquí" se lleva a toda su gente. Llega otro y entonces pone a todos sus amigos, a todos sus allegados, a sus partidarios, por dedazo, por designación. Esto es de lo que habla esta canción.

HC: Y se acuerdan, clase, en *La muerte de Artemio Cruz* (1962) de Carlos Fuentes, aquel momento del '27, en ese capítulo histórico cuando Artemio Cruz entra en la oficina del señor Presidente Plutarco Elías Calles, y la representación es la más negativa que tenemos de un presidente en *La muerte de Artemio Cruz*. Calles fue el primero a iniciar esa sucesión del dedazo; fue Emilio Portes Gil al que escogió para ser el presidente pero en realidad era Calles la fuerza, el poder. Esa es la herencia en México del dedazo.

AA: Que al parecer era más del PRI [Partido Revolucionario Institucional], pero no. Digo no porque no es mucha la diferencia.

E: ¿Va a cambiar el sistema, la economía, con el nuevo gobierno de Fox, del PAN [Partido Acción Nacional]?

AA: No lo va a hacer porque todo el sistema está intacto, el sistema económico, político y social. La cuestión social está muy golpeada por todos lados. Están privatizando todo lo que quedaba de la estructura social, la educación, la salud. Hay cada día menos posibilidades de acceder a educación, a salud y a una serie de cuestiones. No va a cambiar porque es el mismo sistema que están manejando, es la misma operación, digamos, con otras palabras, con otros términos y ya son los mismos. Ya son dos años después de esto, de Fox y siguen siendo lo mismo y no han cambiado y van para atrás.

HC: La tradición se conserva.

AA: Está adentro la corrupción. Es evidente que era muy difícil para este gobierno cambiar todo o cambiar una pequeña parte de las cuestiones, de los reclamos de cualquier partido como el PRI, pero era evidente que no los iban a dejar gobernar un poco holgadamente. Pero sí, mucha gente pensaba que por lo menos una actitud diferente, la actitud de hoy. La política es la misma y ni el asesinato de Colosio ni el asesinato de Juárez. Hay una serie de cuestiones que manejan intereses muy fuertes, económicos y que no van a cambiar tanto por la política exterior del gobierno de Estados Unidos, por la política, digamos la falta de carácter del gobierno. Es muy claro, pues, y también era muy claro que no lo iban a hacer inmediatamente o si no, iban a tardar, pero vamos, hay cosas que van para atrás, muy duras.

Miles de historias / en cada barrio. / Por la calle de Vieyra / viene ya Don Palabras / recitando poesías, / viene canta que canta. / Cierto día Don Palabras / me contó una extraña historia / de cómo nacen las cosas / cada vez que uno las nombra. / El tiempo vive en la memoria.

HC: ¿Cuál es la función, la participación de los artistas, de los medios de comunicación?

AA: Yo creo que hay artistas y hartistas. Hay hartistas con *h*, de hartar. Lo que quiero decir con esto es que hay un aspecto de la cultura de México que no se conoce, que yo creo que es la más rica. Y todo lo que se conoce a través de los medios de comunicación, a través de la tele, del cine mismo, de la radio y de la música misma, generalmente, está llena de balada la música de radio, de balada pop, sonsa, que cuenta una misma historia de amor o una cosa estúpida. En general, eso es lo que ha estado pasando, eso es lo que más difusión tiene porque eso es comercial, porque eso vende. Y esos artistas desde luego no le van a decir al gobierno ni mucho menos a Televisa ni a nadie qué es lo que piensan o qué es lo que sienten aunque podrían hacerlo. Tienen un foro, tienen gente escuchándolos, pero bueno, obviamente, no es una preocupación suya.

Sin embargo, hay escritores, hay fotógrafos que están haciendo cosas muy interesantes, por ejemplo, las fotos de Daniela Rossell. Ella es una amiga muy querida, es una fotógrafa. Hizo un libro sobre ricas famosas [*Ricas y famosas: México 1994–2001* (2002)] que son las herederas de la cuestión. Son las hijas o nietas de los políticos y de los grandes empresarios del priismo retratadas en sus casas con sus tigres y con sus ceniceros de patas de elefantes, cosas que vienen siendo la estética del poder y también del poder del dinero. Ella fue muy criticada por estas gentes precisamente. Simplemente, se dedicó a retratar a estas niñas, a estas mujeres que tienen mucho dinero y que lucen sin problema y sin ningún recato estatuas de negros, estatuas de marfil, una sala llena de oro, cosas brillantes, no. Ella me cuenta que no era su intención ser tan crítica, pero al mismo tiempo estaba jugando con esta crítica y ella lo afrontó de una forma. Todavía no asimila lo que le está pasando. Su libro es uno de los más vendidos de Amazon. Entonces, es muy curioso porque la gente reaccionó a este libro, a estas fotos, de manera muy curiosa. Bueno, es mi amiga, yo la quiero mucho y su trabajo me parece maravilloso porque es el juego de la foto, el juego de fotografiar a esos personajes. Y después, esos personajes cayendo en esta cuestión de "me van a retratar y voy a salir en un libro, voy a ser rica y famosa" pero nunca entendieron que era una crítica vedada. Entonces, cuando se dan cuenta de esto, la empiezan a llamar por teléfono, la empiezan a amenazar, que la van a demandar y hacerle cosas muy fuertes y socialmente es muy interesante porque plantea eso.

Es más o menos lo que pasó con *El crimen del Padre Amaro*. Si ustedes ven la película, no hay una cosa fuerte ni ofensiva en mi manera de ver que haya hecho reaccionar tan fuertemente a la derecha, a la clase retrógrada, a los panistas, sobre todo al Opus Dei, a los jerarcas de la iglesia. Ellos se sintieron agredidos, y en ésta su reacción, ellos provocaron que la película fuese un éxito inusitado de taquilla en México, sobre todo. Ahora todo mundo le dice a Carlos Carrera, quien dirigió la película: "Oye, quiero promoción para mi película." La verdad, ha sido un apoyo excelente, se vende muy bien la película y los discos, el soundtrack y todo, vamos, ¡qué éxito! Pero eso, de manera, obviamente, involuntario. Es como está pasando en México. Hay una serie de absurdos. Cuando el presidente [Vicente Fox] habla y dice algo, no hay quien tenga oídos para eso. Pasan a imaginar otras cosas y ponen en su boca otras cosas que inventan nombres de escritores como José Luis Borgés. ¿O cómo dijo? Sí, así lo dijo, y lo dijo el presidente en España, y lo dijo junto al Rey [Juan Carlos I].

E: El profesor Calderón nos ha dicho que ustedes han leído una gran diversidad de literatura. Y le quiero preguntar cómo les nació la conciencia a ustedes, esa conciencia política. ¿Cómo fue que ustedes se dijeron "nuestra música va a estar politizada"?

AA: No sé si contó Héctor un poquito de los orígenes de algunos de nosotros. Algunos son universitarios, otros venimos de la música desde niños, como el Sax, por ejemplo. Y al juntarnos, nos juntamos para jugar como cuando fuiste a jugar "cascarita" con tus amigos. Y la conciencia, yo creo que eso ya estaba allí como dormido. Lo que es importante también, me parece decir, es que no había tal propósito, no había un línea, es decir, nunca dijimos vamos a hacer letras de protesta o vamos a hacer canciones que digan estas cuestiones del lado politizado. Al contar las historias, nos dimos cuenta que todo tiene que ver con la política. Al empezar a contarnos nosotros las historias, todo era política, todo era economía, todo era momentos, los tiempos de '88, '89, y todo empezó como un juego. Jugamos a acomodar las palabras y, a veces, jugábamos a cambiar las letras de las canciones, a inventar albures, jugar con el sonido. No hubo tal premeditación, nomás hubo alevosía, vamos. Entramos allí a través de las ganas de jugar y descubrimos, nos descubrimos.

La lectura, algunos la hacíamos. Pero sí es importante decir que todo lo que hacemos fuera del grupo, del equipo de trabajo, se retroalimenta, regresa a algo. Es decir, si en mi caso a mí me gusta el cine mucho, yo recurro a esas imágenes para también transformarlo en música, entonces, esto beneficia al grupo de la misma manera. Como le decía hace rato a Héctor, que hay un escritor chileno que se llama Luis Sepúlveda que me gusta mucho y leyendo al argentino Tomás Eloy Martínez o tantos otros, colombianos como el mismo Gabo [Gabriel García Márquez]. Son parte, desde luego, de nuestro acervo, de lo que tenemos como memoria todavía.

HC: Aldo, gracias por venir esta mañana, especialmente, después del concierto en JC Fandango anoche. Cuando te hablé a México de la posibilidad de venir a charlar con la clase, me dijiste, "sería muy chido." Bueno, Aldo, ¡sí, este encuentro ha sido muy chido!

AA: Gracias a ustedes por la paciencia.

Aldo Acuña in his home studio, Colonia Condesa, September 5, 2002. Photo courtesy of author.

Arraigamiento
Contesting Hegemonies in Alfredo Véa Jr.'s
La Maravilla

Ariel Zatarain Tumbaga

Alfredo Véa Jr.'s novel *La Maravilla* (1993) is in great part a negotiation of Mexican and Chicana/o portrayals of the Yaqui nation of Sonora, Mexico. Discourses based on racial and cultural perspectives discernible in *científico* positivism and state *indigenismo* have resulted in the mythification of Yaquis as an innately bellicose and culturally backward people. These discourses appear in the literary representation of Yaquis by important Chicana/o authors, including Rodolfo "Corky" Gonzales, Alurista, and Cherríe L. Moraga, who extend a body of work established by key twentieth-century Mexican writers such as Amado Nervo, Martín Luis Guzmán, and Carlos Fuentes. While historians Alan Knight and Evelyn Hu-Dehart have shed light on the Yaqui history of military and cultural resistance, including the Yaquis' instrumental participation in the Mexican Revolution, scholars have dedicated little research to the cultural significance of these literary portrayals. Anthropologist Edward H. Spicer states that Mexicans "imagined the Yaquis to be fierce warriors who opposed the just authority of European civilization and the righteous truth of Christianity" (1980, 50). Similarly, Chicano scholar George Mariscal, in his *Aztlán and Viet Nam*, points out that Mexican and Chicana/o imaginaries express an essentialist belief in Yaqui warrior prowess (1999, 32).

The trope of the bellicose and backward Yaqui warrior reflects Mexico's accumulated knowledge about the indigenous nation and serves as the foundation for Yaqui Otherness, which is present in many Mexican (and some Chicana/o) literary characterizations. Mexican authors have employed ideologies dealing with the "Indian Problem" and a belief in indigenous racial and cultural inferiority—ideas heavily influenced by the discourses of *civilización y barbarie* and central to the government's program of nation building—to elaborate their Yaqui characters. While literary portrayals of Yaquis also reflect a Chicana/o acknowledgment of their indigenous racial identity—*indigenismo chicano*—a focus on military and cultural resistance and a dearth of references to Yaqui forms of knowledge encourage the persistence of the Yaqui warrior myth. This way of thinking about Yaquis, which is based on colonial Spanish and Mexican perspectives of history and culture, disconnects Yaquis from the traditional origin stories that confront their history of colonial invasion and promote the defense of Hiakim, their ancestral territory.

Véa is part of a community of Chicana/o writers that has turned to Yaqui forms of knowledge, like cosmology, oral tradition, and ethnography, to question previous representations by Mexican authors. These Chicana/o writers relate peculiarly Yaqui accounts of the Chicana/o experiences of immigration and acculturation, and they explore the cultural and social changes that families experience as a result.[1] This essay studies how Véa redeploys literary and anthropological depictions of Yaquis to advance a Yaqui identity. Véa re-creates the traditional links between Yaqui culture, resistance, and ancestral territory—what I have chosen to call *arraigamiento*. He presents an oppositional relationship to US mainstream culture and, at times, he challenges the use of Aztec motifs to represent Chicano nationalism.

Chicana/o and Chicana/o Yaqui Writers

Véa and the community of writers to which he belongs are the daughters and sons of a Yaqui diaspora—the consequence of late nineteenth-century and early twentieth-century *guerras de exterminio*. These Chicana/o Yaqui writers include Miguel Méndez, Luis Valdez, and Alma Luz Villanueva. Their work—novels, poetry, and plays—springs from a distinctly Yaqui epistemic register. They assert a Chicana/o identity and contest nonindigenous perspectives of Yaqui history and culture by adapting ethnographic texts and oral histories and depicting religious practices.

A short illustration will clarify the heterogeneity of this literary community. In *Peregrinos de Aztlán*, Méndez's protagonist, ex-revolutionary "El Yaqui" Loreto Maldonado, recalls the Yaquis' brutal struggle for survival. Dispelling the popular myth of innate Yaqui bellicosity, Loreto criticizes fellow revolutionary-turned-obsessed-insurgent Rosario Cuamea as a man who "se engañaba a sí mismo creyéndose justiciero; como todo idealista fanático" (deceives himself with righteousness, like all ideological fanatics) (1974, 174). At the same time, he recognizes that Frankie Pérez, a Chicano of Yaqui descent, is a frightened boy condemned to service in the Vietnam War instead of a willing warrior. Here, the modern Yaqui's journey into the Aztlán borderlands brings about his own extreme material poverty and psychological degradation, instead of a triumphant return to a pre-Columbian homeland.[2]

Alma Luz Villanueva, in contrast, embraces Yaqui ancestry and warrior history by employing the matrilineal curandera tradition to represent women's agency in her poem "La Chingada." She writes: "I think this poem may have been started with my great-grandmother Isidra. . . . She was a Yaqui Indian converted to Christianity and dared to name her daughter, my grandmother, Jesús" (1985, 140). The poem is Villanueva's response to male oppression of women, including rape. The poetic narrator describes herself as a warrior, walking along a beach, "hooded, masculine parka,/the dog, my knife open in/my hand . . . I/hear my grandmother saying,/'No te dejes'" (145).

In *Mummified Deer* Luis Valdez offers the historical and cosmological knowledge of a living Yaqui nation as an alternative to the Aztec motifs pervasive in Chicana/o literature.[3] Mestizaje and indigenous identity are reinterpreted through a variety of racial origins, all revolving around the protagonist's Yaqui identity. The protagonist, Mama Chu, exhibits the fiery temper typical of the mythical Yaqui warrior. She carries a mummified Yaqui fetus that, writes Jorge Huerta, "becomes a metaphor for the Chicanos' Indio heritage as seen through the lens of his own [Valdez's] Yaqui blood" (2005, x). Her warrior status as a revolutionary *soldadera* is tempered by the presence of a silent Yaqui deer dancer, whose performance represents Yaqui traditional dance and religion and provides a historical contextualization that converts Valdez's Yaqui alternative into a material reality. Significantly, Valdez engages the Chicana/o preoccupation with *vendidos*, or traitors, through the obscene and corrupt clown named Cosme Bravo. Bravo, the proprietor of the "Circo Azteca," is revealed to be a *torocoyori*, a Yaqui who has betrayed his own (50).

In contrast to works by writers of Yaqui descent, Chicana/o literary representations of Yaquis tend to demonstrate a pervasive assimilation of Aztec motifs and a continuing de-emphasis of the cultural links between armed resistance and the origin myths of Hiakim. Among these writers are Rodolfo "Corky" Gonzales, Cherríe L. Moraga, and Alurista. In his seminal 1967 poem, "I Am Joaquín," Gonzales includes Yaquis when referring to wars between indigenous tribes and Mexican troops and to mestizaje: "The chattering machine guns/are death to all of me:/Yaqui/Tarahumara/Chamula/Zapotec/Mestizo/Español" (1972, 39). Chicano poet Alurista quotes from Carlos Castañeda's controversial *The Teachings of Don Juan: A Yaqui Way of Knowledge* in the epigraph to his first collection of poetry: "Fear! A terrible enemy—treacherous, and difficult to overcome" (Alurista 2011, ii). The quote originates from a section in which Don Juan Matus explains the acquisition of knowledge as if it were war: "Every step of learning is a new task, and the fear the man is experiencing begins to mount mercilessly, unyieldingly. *His purpose becomes a battlefield*" (Castañeda 1968, 62, emphasis added).[4]

Similarly, in Moraga's *The Hungry Woman: A Mexican Medea*, the playwright posits her Medea, a Yaqui warrior, in a futuristic Borderlands and surrounds her with a chorus of Aztec female divinities. Medea names her fated sacrificial son Chac-Mool—the stone sculpture used for pre-Columbian offerings. Scholar-director Patricia Ybarra, who directed a performance of the play in 2006, made several decisions so that the set would not appear "more 'classical' and museological than the author intended" (2008, 82–83). Ybarra de-emphasized the Aztec-Greco presence by, for example, excluding Aztec dances and limiting Aztec costume.

By subordinating Yaqui characters to pre-Columbian motifs and separating them from their cultural context, these Chicana/os inadvertently carry the Yaqui warrior myth into the twenty-first century.[5]

Hegemonic Epistemologies and Yaqui Otherness

Key to Alfredo Véa Jr.'s *La Maravilla* is an insidious Yaqui Otherness that relies on a colonial Spanish-Mexican epistemology that interprets the Yaqui homeland, Hiakim, and its people as exploitable resources for mining and farming labor.[6] The Mexican concept of Yaqui history and culture most resembles what cultural critic Walter D. Mignolo has called an "epistemic colonial difference" that has continued to delegitimize indigenous forms of knowledge and history (2005, 43). As Spicer points out, at the root of the Yaqui warrior myth are depictions like those in the colonial missionary literature of Andrés Pérez de Ribas. In *Triunfos de nuestra Santa Fe*, first published in 1645, he documents the 1533 Yaqui victory over the Spanish and reports the words of conquistador Diego Martínez de Hurdaide, who

> salió diciendo, que no había hallado en otras naciones, con quienes había combatido, tal coraje de pelear como el de los yaquis. Porque no

desmayando, como otras, en ver cuerpos muertos de los suyos, y tendidos por el campo; antes haciendo pie sobre ellos, encaraban con más furia sus arcos diciendo: mata, que muchos somos. (1944, 1: 65)

(said that he had never seen a nation fight with as much courage. This was because they did not become faint like others when they saw their comrades' corpses spread all over the field. Rather, they planted their feet firmly on these bodies and arched their bows with even greater fury, saying "Kill, for we are many." And they did not weaken one bit in the fight.) (1: 328)

This colonial document serves as an epistemic foundation for the Yaqui fighter, who is considered a barbarous enemy yet, at the same time, is admired for his skill on the battlefield.

In the early seventeenth century, after overcoming Spain's military efforts, the undefeated Yaquis began to adopt Spanish Catholicism into their traditional belief system. Church stewardship shielded the Yaquis from land grabbing and labor exploitation by miners until the eighteenth century and helped to solidify the Yaqui nation's semiautonomous existence (Spicer 1980, 37). Despite the Jesuit's continued ethnographic work, which at times spoke well of the Yaquis, future representations of Yaquis were often defined by their status as warriors.

By the late nineteenth century the concept of a European-style *civilización* and an indigenous *barbarie* was well rooted among educated and elite Mexicans.[7] President Porfirio Díaz and his followers adhered to the philosophy of *científico* positivism, which promoted a racial paradigm based on the "new truth" about race drawn from the scientific writings of Charles Darwin and Herbert Spencer (Graham 1990, 2). A spectrum of thinkers, from conservative Francisco Bulnes to renowned educator Justo Sierra, accepted social Darwinist rationalizations for the mestizo subjugation of indigenous Others, who were deemed racially or culturally unfit to initiate and carry out the all-important task of national progress (Zea 1988, 409). Bulnes thought that a Yaqui territory, geographically located within Mexican borders and confirming the existence of a Yaqui nation, could not possibly exist, as it would undermine Mexico's national integrity (1952, 67). Díaz moved to colonize the Yaquis' agriculturally promising territory and attempted to convert the Yaquis into wage laborers on their former land. Some sectors of the government considered Yaquis so subhuman that when the Yaquis resisted under the leadership of José María "Cajemé" Leyva, the Mexican government initiated a *guerra de exterminio* that Evelyn Hu-DeHart describes as Yaqui "elimination from

Sonora rather than outright genocide." Yaquis were massacred and entire families were deported to Yucatán, where they were enslaved (1984, 181–82).[8] By 1908 nearly half of the population had been deported while "countless others" escaped deportation by "fleeing across the border to Arizona and other parts of the southwestern and western United States" (188).

When the Mexican Revolution erupted in 1910, Yaquis returned to participate. Entire battalions of Yaquis fought, hoping to retrieve their infringed-upon territory, and this added to the Yaquis' warrior reputation. It is telling that Francisco I. Madero, the intellectual architect of the revolution and revolutionary Mexico's president, cited the oppression of Yaquis as a justification for a revolution and a metaphor for Mexico's catastrophic future under the Porfiriato (2005, 210). Knight has gone so far as to suggest that the Yaquis' participation in the armed struggle was based on their desire for a Yaqui revolution that would produce a Yaqui nation with dominion over Hiakim (1986, 6). Toward the end of the revolution Mexicans found the indigenous nation's resistance to colonization as tenacious as ever, and the "Yaqui campaign" was reinitiated intermittently at the command of Álvaro Obregón until 1928 (Spicer 1980, 230). Despite Madero's proclamation of alliance, the Mexican government continued to oppose the idea of an autonomous Yaqui nation, and Mexicans continued to imagine Yaquis as innately bellicose (Knight 1986, 337).[9]

In *La Maravilla* Véa confronts Yaqui Otherness as it endured under the auspices of the Mexican government's post-revolution indigenismo policies, whose aim was to "elevate" indigenous peoples via their national incorporation economically and culturally—or racially—through mestizaje. Manuel Gamio, considered the "father of indigenismo," promoted the role of anthropology as part of the nation-building process in his landmark *Forjando patria* (first published in 1916). Ever the pragmatist, Gamio suggested the strategy to "Europeanize" indigenous peoples by introducing Western culture via a Mexican rapprochement to indigenous cultures, thereby rendering it less exotic and more comprehensible; but, he warned, "Naturalmente que no debe exagerarse a un extremo ridículo el acercamiento al indio" (Naturally, this approach to Indians should not be exaggerated to a ridiculous extreme) (1982, 96). The one-sided nature of Gamio's *incorporación* philosophy is clear: post-revolution leaders must find innovative ways to make the national Mexican culture, which is primarily European, attractive to indigenous communities so that they can be drawn out of their cultural and social isolation. Gamio predicted that the Yaquis, representative of Mexico's "semi-civilized" indigenous sector, would necessarily have to opt for "fusion" with the dominant race (175).

Mexico's foremost intellectual, José Vasconcelos, revealed an ongoing national racism in his proposal to redeem indigenous people through a project of "aesthetic eugenics," in which Indians would simply vanish through mestizaje, a selective process in which the lower races would be absorbed by those that are more beautiful (2005, 27). Despite the panoply of ethnographic texts dealing with a myriad of topics, writes Alexander S. Dawson, early indigenista works "laid the foundations for the 'state simplifications' that would be central to the mandate of anthropology as an exercise in state making" (2004, 8). Notably, anthropologists researching Yaqui culture, such as Ralph L. Beals (1932, 94), W. C. Holden (1936, 7), Alfonso Fabila (1940, x–xiii), and Carlos Basauri (1940), would frequently refer to colonial and nineteenth-century histories, which were heavily influenced by the discourse of an innate Yaqui resistance to the advanced Spanish and Mexican cultures, as well as to one another's investigations. From this epistemic base, Holden comfortably asserts, "What more war-loving race has there been on the American continent than the Yaqui Indians?" (1936, 114).

This historical and ethnographic literature amounts to what Edward Said has called an influential accumulation of texts whose "referential power" was felt among researchers and eventually "in the culture at large" (1994, 20). Notwithstanding their varied subject matter, the ethnographies contained a repeated emphasis on a nearly innate Yaqui warrior prowess and a particular interest in Yaqui *pascola* and deer dancers (Spicer 1980, 275). Due to the scientific legitimacy of anthropological knowledge, the Yaqui warrior myth—and its exoticized dance component—would find its way into Mexico's popular imaginary and literature.[10] The Yaquis, first depicted as colonial barbarians and evolutionary failures, then as a metaphor for Mexico's oppression, and finally as citizens in need of Mexicanization, have indeed been a "blank page upon which each outside group has the right and the obligation to write its own particular message," as Guillermo Bonfil Batalla concludes about all indigenous nations in Mexico (1996, 126).

Nationalism, Anthropology, and Literary Representations of Yaquis

Véa is an intellectual, an attorney, and a writer who has studied and assimilated Mexican and U.S. discourses on the Yaqui. In *La Maravilla* he reexamines literary stereotypes of Yaqui bellicosity and dance in writings that were influenced by an epistemology that urged the need to "Mexicanize" Yaquis as much as it celebrated their traditional dances. Novels about the Mexican Revolution, a genre that is widely thought to define Mexico's post-revolution identity, includes Yaquis in five of its most representative works: Carlos Fuentes's *La region más transparente* (1958), Gregorio López y Fuentes's *Campamento* (1931) and *Tierra: La revolución agraria en México* (1933), Martín Luis Guzmán's *El águila y la serpiente* (1928), and Rafael F. Muñoz's *¡Vámonos con Pancho Villa!* (1936).[11] Though these literary depictions are mainly adjectival—a way of describing the revolutionary landscape—they share common themes: stoicism, barbarism, a cultural void, and/or an exaggerated warriorhood.[12] These motifs reveal the continuing prevalence of nineteenth-century racist discourses regarding Yaqui backwardness and bellicosity among post-revolution writers.

Indigenista literature follows a similar trend, but for different reasons. Influenced by the anthropological mission of incorporating indigenous peoples into a unified Mexican state, indigenista literature finds inspiration in the ethnographic research published at the time. In 1940, at the Primer Congreso Indigenista Interamericano in Pátzcuaro, Michoacán, anthropologists and fiction writers solidified an alliance in which literature became a means for spreading their understanding of indigenous cultures among fellow Mexicans (Bigas Torres 1990, 50). Roberto González Echevarría has explained how indigenista literature became a simulation of dominant anthropological practices, turning authors into ethnographers who explained each country's "internal Others" (1990, 220). Unlike actual ethnographies, however, literary representations of Yaquis tend to ignore Yaqui cosmology and oral histories about their land, their resistance, and their origins.

"La triste historia del Pascola Cenobio" (1952) is an exemplary indigenista short story written by anthropologist-author Francisco Rojas González, who masterfully weaves ethnography and nationalist discourses didactically into his narratives (Sommers 1966, 222–25). "La triste historia" portrays a violent and mostly backwards Yaqui nation that suppresses a young pascola dancer who breaks with indigenous insular attitudes to better his financial situation so that he can afford to marry a Yaqui woman.[13] The narrative elides the Yaquis' history of massacres and forced deportation when the protagonist's efforts end in violence and ridicule after he transgresses the group's traditional isolationism by working for non-Yaquis. In Rojas González's ethnographically detailed descriptions of the dancer's costume and the Yaqui authorities' traditional organization, somber demeanor, and

Yoeme language, he depicts an aesthetically beautiful, yet hopelessly violent and backwards Yaqui Other.

Regional novelist Armando Chávez Camacho's *Cajeme: Novela de indios* (1948), which focuses on the late nineteenth-century Yaqui insurgent leader José María "Cajemé" Leyva, also describes ethnographically detailed pascola and deer dancers. This book is exceptional in that the author writes from Moisés Sáenz's *pluriculturalista* school of indigenismo (Sáenz 1939) and highlights relationships between ancestral traditions and resistance to the point of including a territorial origin story, "Leyenda yaqui de las predicciones." And after a section describing pascola, coyote, and deer dancers at a religious fiesta, Chávez Camacho concludes that traditional dance "descubre la Fortaleza que caracteriza a los cuerpos y a los espíritus de los indígenas" (uncovers the fortitude that characterizes the corporal and spiritual power of the indigenous people), which sustained their rebellion (1948, 271). While indigenista literature provided more complex depictions of Yaqui culture and history, it frequently perpetuated the discourses of barbarism, senseless cultural resistance, and inflated warrior prowess, suggesting the need to assimilate Yaquis into mainstream Mexican culture.

Like other Chicana/o Yaqui writers, Véa is open about his Yaqui ancestry and readily admits to the autobiographical nature of *La Maravilla*. In an interview the author reveals that the main character's grandparents are based on his Yaqui grandfather and Catholic Spanish grandmother (Aldama 2006, 279). Like Méndez and Villanueva, Véa connects his detailed construction of characters to an oral tradition (283). And similar to Valdez, throughout the novel Véa redeploys Mexican and US anthropological research on Yaquis, filtered through a Yaqui-centered indigenismo chicano. The result of this is a Chicana/o novel written from a Yaqui historical-cultural register that challenges hegemonic epistemologies with what Stacy Alaimo calls "a rootedness to place and an identity tied to history" (2000, 169).

Set in the 1950s, the novel unfolds in a multicultural community named Buckeye Road, Arizona, that defies the US hegemonic ideals of race and culture. Its enclaves of Yaqui, Pima, Black, Okie, Chinese, and other members maintain a harmonious respect despite their prejudices toward one another.[14] The plot focuses on the boy Alberto and the grandparents with whom he lives: Manuel, a Yaqui shaman and refugee of the Mexican guerras de exterminio, and Josephina, an Andalusian immigrant and curandera. Erin G. Carlston proposes that the small squatter community is oppositional to its neighbor, Phoenix, a city that is "white, heterosexual, bourgeois, and utterly divorced from any kind of ethnic, racial, spiritual, or ethical tradition, even England's" (2005, 121). Manuel, a survivor of the Yaqui diaspora and now a marginalized Native American in the United States, is a member of Buckeye Road's community of carnivalesque characters. Poverty stricken and at times overwhelmed by violence, they "cannot be severed from [their] material conditions," which makes it difficult for the nonindigenous reader to become a tourist of these "other" cultures (Alaimo 2000, 166). The novel is filled with indigenous and nonindigenous "visions" and apparitions, as well as incidents that are typical of magical realism.[15] Carlston warns, however, that "Véa's ghosts are as real as history" (2005, 114) and that Yaqui shamanism (like *curanderismo*) presents an epistemic practice that "coincides with a pragmatic political agenda of resistance to oppression" (116).

The Yaquis in *La Maravilla* do indeed oppose the dominant US culture—under the representational umbrella of the Chicana/o immigrant experience—but they also counter Mexican accumulated knowledge about Yaquis. This is evident in the author's redeployment of anthropological research used against the Yaquis. Manuel explains to his grandson that unlike himself, Alberto is Mexican because he is a Yaqui mestizo and that he is Chicano because he is from Aztlán—the Southwest (1993, 35). The idea of indigenismo chicano allows Véa to reconcile the Chicana/o mythological homeland with the simultaneous presence of a living indigenous nation. Nonetheless, he chooses to advance Yaqui identity through his profound knowledge of Yaqui history and culture, as literary critic Roberto Cantú has noted (2001, 40).

In *La Maravilla* Véa draws from a wide nonindigenous epistemology— history, ethnography, literature—to represent oral tradition and cosmology as types of Yaqui knowledge. This knowledge links the Chicana/o Yaqui protagonist's cultural resistance to US mainstream culture through a process of arraigamiento. I use the term *arraigamiento* to define the history of Yaqui military and cultural resistance that is religiously (mythologically) rooted in Hiakim. Yaqui arraigamiento can be found in origin stories like "Yomumuli and the Little Surem People," in which the pre-Columbian deity Yomumuli translates a talking tree's prophecy of the impending conquista and the baptism of the Yaqui people, which led many of the Yaqui ancestors to descend into the earth of the traditional territory. This story is part of a sequence that includes "Leyenda yaqui de las predicciones" and "Omteme," the story of the angry one who, after defending the Yaqui territory by killing the conquistador Christopher Columbus, "descended into the heart of his hill," which to this day is known as Cerro de Omteme (Giddings 1960, 65). Véa follows Mexican indigenista Armando Chávez Camacho, who represents arraigamiento through Yaqui knowledge in *Cajeme*. *Cajeme* incorporates "Leyenda yaqui de las predicciones," a story taken from Alfonso Fabila's ethnography, in which the Yaquis defeat an invading giant serpent through magical intervention and prepare for the inevitable Conquista (Fabila 1940). Both origin stories confront the question of the conquest of Hiakim and endorse its defense, concurrently rooting Yaqui ancestors deep into the Yaqui geography.[16] Here, Yaqui culture, resistance, and sacred territory intertwine.

Arraigamiento, Anthropology, and Chicana/o Yaqui Identity

In *La Maravilla* Véa reappropriates the ethnographic research of Castañeda, Rojas González, and Spicer, who used Yaqui myths and culture for their own works of research or fiction, as well as the indigenista literature of Chávez Camacho and Rojas González, to re-create arraigamiento in Alberto's acquisition of a Yaqui identity.

In sequences dealing with Yaqui peyote rituals, Véa reappropriates facets of Castañeda's *The Teachings of Don Juan: A Yaqui Way of Knowledge* (1968), a US text emblematic of what we know about Yaqui culture. More literature than social science, Castañeda's ethnography conjures sensational images of shamanism and peyote tripping and serves as a ripe source for creative inspiration. In Véa's opening chapter, for example, the old Yaqui sits in a rocking chair after drinking his peyote tea, "riding on that hot air outside," heading with "his tips spread and his neck down toward lost Sonora, the homeland—the lodestone" and the source of his ethnic and spiritual identity (1993, 10). When describing the location of the chair, Véa writes that "his chair rocked under a roof [in his adobe home] instead of in its rightful place, its *spirit place*. . . . The *spot* that faced east and the sunrise" (27, emphasis added). Castañeda's influence in Manuel's depiction as a bird in flight and in the Yaqui's "spirit place" is evident. Castañeda describes his own power spot, or *sitio*, facing "in a southeasterly direction" (1968, 20–21). And like Castañeda's Don Juan, who warns of the perils of this dreamlike state—"A man could be gone for months. . . .The lizards could take a man to the end of the world" (1968, 126)—Josephina recounts an incident in which Manuel "stayed a gila monster for three days, tasting the air with his tongue and crawling on the cracked bones of his heathen

fathers . . . and he couldn't get back here" (Véa 1993, 12). The reference
to flight is repeated when Alberto partakes of an initiation ritual with
his grandfather and his indigenous compadres. After drinking the peyote
tea, Alberto becomes a hawk and sees the other indigenous men as light
(224), just as Castañeda reports that as a crow he extended his wings and
flew, and he saw, with sensitivity to light, "silvery birds!" (Castañeda 1968,
135–36). Unlike Valdez, for whom *The Teachings of Don Juan* symbolizes
a psychedelic hippie acquisition of Yaqui knowledge, Véa reappropriates
aspects of Castañeda's rich text as a type of literary inspiration and a source
for his protagonist's developing Yaqui identity.[17]

Véa also reappropriates the anthropology and literature of Rojas
González—whose works reflect Gamio's philosophy of incorporation—to
construct a positive impression of the use of peyote as an expression of
cultural resistance in Alberto's initiation ritual. In the Arizona desert,
Manuel surrounds his grandson with his compadres: the old "Yoeme"
Salvador; a Yaqui-Tarahumara mestizo named Pascual; and Epiphanio, a
Huichol.[18] Manuel explains the function of peyote as a way to communicate with the supernatural realm: "The genius was an in-between spirit
that could make that communication possible. There are other words for
that genius, *naguales y tonales*, though these words now have many more
meanings" (1993, 222). Véa here refers to Rojas González's 1944 essay
"Totemismo y nahualismo" (1998c), in which the anthropologist-author
describes the concepts of *tona* and *nahual* and notes the many similarities
between the two. The advice that Manuel gives his grandson—to resist
the American mainstream—is also relevant since Rojas González finds that
the tona-nahual concept "tiene como características originales oponer a
las enseñanzas cristianas, la fuerza de las creencias religiosas ancestrales,
reviviendo al efecto las prácticas toltecas" (has as its original characteristics
an opposition to Christian teachings, the power of ancient religious beliefs,
effectively reviving Toltec practices) (86).

Véa and Rojas González agree that peyote use is a form of cultural
resistance, as are the tona and nahual, but the Mexican anthropologist's
intention—the incorporation of indigenous people into mainstream culture—is manipulated by the Chicana/o Yaqui author. In another instance
Véa references Rojas González's 1948 anthropological essay "Jículi ba-ba"
(1998b), as Rojas González does in his short story "Hículi Hualula" (1952b).
In the essay the anthropologist-author describes the use of peyote by the
Tarahumaras and the Huicholes; in Véa's story they are represented by
the characters Pascual and Epiphanio. Rojas González attributes peyote's

most sacred use to the Huichol people (1952b, 32), and it is the Huichol Epiphanio who brings the *hikuli* (peyote) to Manuel (Véa 1993, 220). Later, Epiphanio says, "The Huichol believe that the *hikuli* is God, not just a way to see him. The *hikuli*, the peyote itself, is God. They believe that the deer and the corn and the peyote are one and the same, that the gift of corn and peyote sprang from the head of a deer" (222). Rojas González, noting peyote's close relationship with corn, explains that "los huicholes llaman 'venado' al jículi y lo consideran como tal en el complejo concepto que tienen del cactus y de sus atributos extraordinarios" (the Huicholes refer to the hikuli as "the deer" and consider it as such in their complex concept of the cactus and its extraordinary attributes) (1998b, 101).

Véa's use of Rojas González's ethnography and literature is clear. As Carlston suggests, such supernatural experiences in *La Maravilla* "may, in fact, reflect not only a spiritual belief system but also a historically informed consciousness of the mechanisms of repression and eradication that have been brought to bear on numerous populations in the Americas" (2005, 114). Consuming peyote is an act of cultural resistance not only strictly in the Yaqui sense but also for the Chicano protagonist. As a Spanish Yaqui mestizo—alone among his grandfather's indigenous friends—Alberto "signifies the potential for the mestizo/a to bridge and embrace difference" (Alaimo 2000, 167). Véa may rely on Rojas González for this episode, but the outcome far outstrips the anthropologist's case against a backward Yaqui culture.[19] Instead, the author offers an example of a cultural continuity in which Yaqui ancestral knowledge is congruent with a politicized, counter-hegemonic Chicana/o identity.

In his treatment of Yaqui dance Véa appropriates indigenista literary styles and reworks earlier literary depictions through the lens of indigenismo chicano, thereby shifting discursive emphasis away from assimilation. As in Rojas González's "La triste historia del Pascola Cenobio" and Chávez Camacho's *Cajeme*, Véa employs ethnographic precision to describe Yaqui dancers. For instance, Salvador is described donning his traditional deer dancer costume:

> He wore a skin belt with hooves hanging from it and leggings covered with hundreds of dried cocoons. . . . Over his head he wore a mask, the skin and horns of a deer. Only his mouth could be seen in the open neck stitching that had torn loose over the years. (1993, 220)

Then the Yaqui-Tarahumara, Pascual, is given a similar description as a pascola, whom Véa describes as wearing a strange shirt without a front or a back. He had leather *pantalones* held up by a belt of yellow-white cocoons, and he was placing upon his head a black mask with blood-red cheeks and with goat's hair that sprang from the eyebrows and below the mouth. He wore the mask near the back of his head, as though looking in two directions. He had gourd rattles in each hand. (1993, 220)

Whereas Rojas González depicts a virtuoso pascola dancer who is mainly detached from social obligations, *La Maravilla*'s ethnographically detailed dancers assume their roles in Alberto's acceptance of a cultural legacy.

Arraigamiento and Yaqui Cosmology

Véa's focus on the theme of arraigamiento demonstrates the influence of Edward H. Spicer's *The Yaquis: A Cultural History*, a US anthropological study that explores the links between Yaqui history and religious culture. Still the leading authority on Yaqui ethnography, Spicer's work is removed from racial concerns like those expressed in Carl Coleman Seltzer's study of anthropomorphic measurements (1936, 92), the sensationalism of Castañeda's writings, or the assimilationism of Mexican anthropologists. Still, Spicer has noted his own difficulties in understanding Yaqui culture as a Western scholar. In regard to "El testamento," a flood story delineating the boundaries of Hiakim, Spicer admits his initial unpreparedness "for the interweaving of Christian and pagan names as well as concepts in the mythology" (1992, 115–16). Still, his dedication to linking Yaqui history to culture led him to collect and record information regarding the origins of deer dancers and pascolas, Yaqui Catholicism, and pre-Columbian realms—Yo Ania, Sea Ania—connected to the Huya Ania, the magical wilderness realm. While Valdez alludes to these realms with the presence of the Yaqui deer dancer, Véa employs both the terminology and concepts. Although he does not use the term *Huya Ania*, he nonetheless refers to it when describing Manuel's spirit "spot" outside the house (a la Castañeda), thus meeting the required Yaqui division between the pueblo, a space of human activity, and Huya Ania, where, writes Spicer, "great beings [like the angry one, Omteme] had once lived and perhaps still live" (1980, 64). In this way, Véa subordinates Castañeda's spectacular ethnography by positing it within the less-subjective research of Spicer.

Véa elaborates the three sacred realms in relation to the Yaqui territory by employing Spicer's anthropological theory to secure an alternate

Yaqui homeland and identity for the Chicana/o Yaqui boy. Manuel ties Alberto's initiation ceremony to its territorial origins when he reminds him that "Salvador there is from Potam, and you, Beto, are from Cócorit; your blood, *tu sangre*, is from Cócorit" (1993, 217).[20] He continues: "Something in you will remember a place and time when the smallest, driest seed seemed to grow right when you pressed it into the silt of the [Río] Yaqui. It remembers how *sewam*, the numberless flowers, clogged the banks. . . . It was a flowered world, a seeya-aniya" (217). Manuel connects Cócorit to Yaqui dance and the Sea Ania, the magical flower realm conjured by the deer dancer, who "addresses a mythical deer spoken to as Malichi (Flower Fawn)" (Spicer 1980, 103). Manuel has introduced his Chicano grandson to Hiakim (through Cócorit, one of the eight Yaqui pueblos) as an alternate homeland, in addition to Aztlán, to which he can either voyage, in a spiritual-religious flight, or, perhaps, drive.[21] In a separate moment, Manuel's upset wife recalls an incident pitting her spiritual world against his: "'You see, the evening of the flash flood, it was the Holy Trinity that rescued him from his *yoan-ya*, his crazy religion" (1993, 16). Véa's dreamlike depiction of the Yo Ania is consistent with Spicer's, in which Yo Ania and Yaqui are connected through "the vision, intangible and in fact unidentifiable outside of the dream state" (Spicer 1980, 68).[22]

In a final example, Alberto flies as a hawk during his initiation ceremony to a timeless mythological place in Sonora and encounters his great-grandfather and his grandfather Manuel as a child, who may also be undergoing his initiation. When Alberto asks the boy Manuel if it is true that the return of Apache (the dog) means that he will surely die as his grandmother has predicted, Manuel affirms: "When the singing tree spoke to us so long ago, it told us that death is the gift we must give in thanks for the bounty the world gives to us" (Véa 1993, 227). In this dialogue, Manuel refers to "Yomumuli and the Little Surem People," in which, writes Spicer, "the Tree told the consequences of the acceptance of baptism: those who accepted baptism would ever after be subject to death and those who did not would be immortal" (1980, 67). Those immortal ancestors still survive in the Huya Ania. Véa employs Spicer's research to re-create a Yaqui-peculiar epistemology through dance heritage and cosmology (found in the oral tradition) and to construct a cultural base that will tie traditional, spiritual culture (Yo Ania) to Hiakim (and Cócorit specifically) as the locus of Alberto's identity and his alternate homeland.

The ample nonindigenous epistemology incorporated into *La Maravilla* serves to re-create Yaqui forms of knowledge that are key to Alberto's acquisition of a Yaqui identity and his identification with a Yaqui homeland. Véa challenges the epistemic traditions of *what we know about Yaqui history and culture* that helped spawn the very nationalist and at times racially informed anthropological and literary texts he redeploys. But he also uses these disputable sources of knowledge (the works of Rojas González and Castañeda, for example), and more reliable references, like Spicer's work, for the inspiration to re-create a Yaqui cultural attachment, or arraigamiento, to Hiakim-Cócorit. Hiakim, contrary to nineteenth-century assertions, belongs to a real Yaqui nation whose concepts of knowledge, in the form of cosmology, oral history, and dance, can be defined neither as barbarous nor as in need of rescue by Mexican culture.

Arraigamiento and Acts of Resistance

La Maravilla's Yaqui characters define themselves through an act of cultural resistance that is bound to the Yaqui homeland, Hiakim. Manuel tells his Chicano grandson, "If you follow what is true you will find yourself paying more for every breath, but it's sweeter air. Stay in the gaps, *mijo*. Love for the land is here. *Resistance* is here. The company's better in here" (1993, 221, emphasis added). The "here" in question is an ethnic culture located within Hiakim. It is a source of subaltern identity and resistance on the fringes of mainstream US and Mexican cultures. Here Manuel, "in contrast to the deracinated dominant culture . . . affirms a rootedness to place and an identity tied to history" (Alaimo 2000, 169). During the initiation ceremony, moments before Alberto claims his indigenous identity, he becomes connected to his Yaqui homeland: "It seemed to him that the clay was rising up from the ground beneath him and was somehow claiming him before his time" (Véa 1993, 223). Like the traditional origin stories in which Yaqui ancestors descend into the earth, Alberto becomes affixed to the place of origin, physically through magical experience and metaphorically through the acquisition of Yaqui culture. Resistance and cultural arraigamiento are one. Through his Yo Ania experience Alberto "affirms a rootedness to place and an identity tied to history" (Alaimo 2000, 169). He assumes an active indigenous identity that will allow him to resist assimilation into US mainstream culture.

The theme of cultural resistance allows for the recovery of the mythological Omteme as an archetype of the arraigamiento concept. Omteme, whose name means "he is angry," is recounted as the angry Yaqui who resists European colonization by killing the treacherous Christopher Columbus.

Thereafter, he becomes disillusioned with the prospect of the Conquista announced by the talking tree, and he chooses to become part of the magical wilderness (or Huya Ania) in Hiakim. In *La Maravilla*, Manuel begins his transition into death: "Each rock forward in his chair pushed his eyesight deeper into the earth below the adobe and brought visions from farther and farther away" (1993, 234). He finds himself between life and a mythological plane and, like Omteme, is confronted by one of the Yaquis' greatest enemies:

> He rocked downward into an undying hatred of Porfirio Díaz, instigator of the Yaqui diaspora, the builder of grand *latifundios*. *De repente*, all at once *El Presidente*, *El General* himself stood before Manuel, summoned up by the sheer power of the old man's hatred. The toothless and transparent general strode through the adobe in his Austrian epaulettes and French boots to stand before Manuel. (234)

Continuously recollecting his people's history, Manuel reaches through time to force an encounter with Díaz. Now Manuel is Omteme, for "he is angry." A survivor of the Mexican government's guerras de exterminio, Manuel continues his resistance as he attempts to kill the dictator, knowing full well that "every Yaqui spirit would rejoice if only he could reach the monster's neck" (234). Díaz disappears and, like the mythological ancestor, the old Yaqui shaman performs one final act of arraigamiento: "Now he could taste the *pura tierra mojada*, the pure moist earth of his home" (235).

Finally, Alberto, described as being claimed by the rising "ground beneath him," also becomes an agent of resistance against an overbearing and impending WASP uniformity that threatens from beyond Buckeye Road. When the estranged mother, Lola, returns with her boyfriend to claim Alberto and ridicules the ethnicities of both grandparents, Alberto escapes to Hiakim, his spiritual source: "The boy behind their backs was too far away to hear either of them. He was screeching over ciudad Moctezuma [in Sonora], following the sun-silvered *rio* Yaqui south to Cócorit and Bacum" (297). As his mother's car whisks his body away to California, Alberto dreams/flies from Aztlán (the Southwest) to Hiakim, his alternative homeland. He transforms into a "blinding light in the backseat," visible only to other indigenous people along the desert road. The Chicana/o Yaqui boy's arraigamiento is completed as he becomes, in Alaimo's words, one of those "insurgent knowers who disrupt dominant epistemological paradigms" (2000, 170).

When Alberto establishes a counterhegemonic identity by acquiring a Yaqui knowledge of history and culture, Véa contests the same Spanish-Mexican epistemology used to construct Alberto's Chicana/o Yaqui identity.

The "referential power" of early ethnographies established a Yaqui warrior myth as the main discourse for anthropological, literary, and popular portrayals of Yaquis, as visible in the works of Bulnes and Rojas González. But unlike Bulnes's and Rojas Gonzalez's depictions of a backward Yaqui nation, the pascolas and deer dancers of *La Maravilla* are always reaffirming their religious identity through dance, roles in sacred rituals, and historical memory. Walter D. Mignolo has pointed out that these traditions and rituals are indigenous epistemologies that have been devalued by a Western intellectual tradition (2005, 136).

Indigenous Hierarchies in Aztlán

In *La Maravilla*, indigenismo chicano becomes the site of conflict in which Véa disputes the reliance on Aztec themes in Chicana/o identity by reconciling pre-Columbian motifs with a Yaqui epistemology. The wide acceptance—albeit not without controversy—of what Gaspar de Alba has called "Aztlán aesthetics" in the political and creative texts of the 1960s established the mythological homeland, Aztlán, as a principal motif that was invaluable for the creation of a Chicana/o identity (2004, 114). But the Chicano movement's embrace of mestizaje through "a race toward the Indian" does not necessarily address Native American needs (Pérez-Torres 2006, 16). The function of the mythological homeland of Aztlán has generated heated academic debates. While scholars like Rafael Pérez-Torres and David Cooper Alarcón argue for the preservation of the Chicana/o homeland, others have questioned certain ethnic and cultural implications of indigenismo chicano.[23] In "Who's the Indian in Aztlán?," Josefina Saldaña-Portillo describes the acquisition of indigenous culture by the frequently more-privileged First World Chicana/o, whom she compares to indigenous Mexicans, "the rural subaltern in the Third World" (2001, 404). In particular, she faults a focus on Aztec deities for "ignoring the contemporary Native American inhabitants of the Southwest and their very different mytho-genealogies" (415). Gaspar de Alba questions the value of Aztlán as a basis for a Chicana/o identity, calling it "a 'no place' land, a utopia" (2004, 108). In response to Moraga, Gaspar de Alba notes that "you can't really drive to Aztlán. . . . You can follow a road map to one of the Indian pueblos in New Mexico [other homelands]. But to get to Aztlán, you have to suspend your disbelief" (135).[24]

Without pretending to reach a conclusion on the Aztlán debate, it is nonetheless useful to know that some scholars have recognized the symbolic potential of Yaqui history and culture. Robert McKee Irwin identifies José María "Cajemé" Leyva, the leader of the Yaqui resistance against Díaz, as a cultural icon of a different borderlands, that of the Mexican northwest, in contrast to the notion of a southwestern Aztlán (2007, 189). Yolanda Broyles-González, herself of Yaqui descent, proposes Yaqui religious and historical knowledge, like that of other living indigenous nations, as a rich source for elaborating a Chicana identity (2002, 130)—perhaps more so than the pre-Columbian iconography that Chicana/o authors and cultural critics continue to appropriate.

The counterhegemonic position of Chicana/o literature against discourses that present people of Mexican descent as inferior is evident in *La Maravilla*'s establishment of a Yaqui identity grounded in Hiakim (Saldívar 1991, 17). In an interview, Véa explains that he "would rather be characterized as an author who is Chicano" than a Chicano author because of the expectations placed upon the artist: "Implicit in the concept of 'Chicano' literature is the political agenda rather than the agenda of sighting the artistic bar and endeavoring to surpass it" (Biggers 1999, 34). Instead, opines Véa, "The act of rising [artistically] is political, the result is art." This perspective matters when Véa engages the dominance of pre-Columbian mythology and the academic debates over the utilization of Aztlán as the Chicana/o homeland and the basis for a Chicana/o identity. It is from within indigenismo chicano that Véa embraces the iconography of Aztlán while questioning the utility of a general Aztec identity for Chicana/os through the affirmation of Alberto's, and the author's, Yaqui heritage. Consequently, Véa treats indigenous subject matter with the sensibility displayed by Saldaña-Portillo (1991): he places Chicana/o identity partly under the stewardship of a living Yaqui nation. Thus the protagonist Alberto, because of his mixed blood and place of birth, identifies as Chicano, but he also embodies the acceptance of "different archetypes" of indigenous identity, as the novel puts it (Véa 1993, 304).

In *La Maravilla* we find the conditional acceptance and use of the Aztlán motifs that have dominated Chicana/o cultural production since the Chicano movement's inception. The novel agrees with movement discourses insofar as it identifies the Southwest (here, Arizona) as the location of "Aztlán, this land, right here where the Nahua people began" (Véa 1993, 35)—that is, Alberto's Chicano homeland. Véa employs these motifs to define the way of life of many of the novel's characters. For example, Josephina wrathfully identifies Lola, Alberto's mother, as "Malinche" for abandoning the family and her Catholic and Yaqui traditions (22). Manuel mocks his wife's fanatic

Catholicism after she baptizes Alberto four times, joking, "They are all so scared that Christ will turn out to be Quetzalcóatl" (35). Manuel equates people of any culture—but especially Anglos—whose identities are in question to Xipe Totec: "'They are Xipe,' he said, referring to the ancient god . . . the Aztecs distorted into the God of the Flayed Skin. It was Manuel's word for those people on earth who do not know where they belong" (35). Manuel's view of Anglos challenges US consumer society in the 1950s and the "melting pot" theory, in which immigrants abandon their native culture to become American by assimilation. He appeals to Alberto's Yaqui identity and his relation to Hiakim to forestall Alberto's *becoming* a cultural tabula rasa. Manuel explains: "They have no heroes, just celebrities. . . . The White man has all the rights in this country, but we have the rites, the rituals. Their children see a world without mysteries" (231).[25]

The novel's title also reflects an acceptance of Aztec mythology. When their dog, Apache, returns to claim the old Yaqui's life, Manuel explains it is really Maravilla, "the dog that comes to lead its master to *Mictlan*, the land of the dead, or to the other worlds there" (186). This comingling of Aztec motifs from the past and the Yaqui culture of the present is consistent with the novel's focus on exploring "different archetypes" of culture and knowledge. This is perhaps best illustrated by a statement Josephina makes after Manuel's death: "'The *Mexicanos* and the *Indios* have different *arquetipos* than the *gringos*. Though today, many *Mexicanos* deny their Indian blood'" (304). Here, Véa refers to three groups—Mexicans, indigenous people, and Anglos—each with its own epistemic model. Alberto's dual Chicano and indigenous identity "signifies the potential for the mestizo/a to bridge and embrace difference" (Alaimo 2000, 167). Although every indigenous nation differs markedly from others, Chicana/o mestizaje can extend to non-Aztec indigenous identities, like the protagonist's Chicana/o-Yaqui identity, including the potential Chicana/o-Tarahumara and Chicana/o-Huichol identities in *La Maravilla*, as well as those recognized by Broyles-González (2002, 12–21).[26]

Even though Aztec motifs hold a prominent place in *La Maravilla*, Véa reaffirms a Yaqui epistemology of culture and history that is evident in the culture of the indigenous peoples living in today's Arizona-Sonora borderlands. Ruth W. Giddings, compiler of Yaqui traditional stories, finds that "Yaqui folk literature expresses the tribe's sense of superiority, the sacred and material value of their territory, and the antiquity and distinctiveness of their customs" (1960, 20).[27] *La Maravilla* reflects this sense of ethnic preeminence by re-creating an indigenous hierarchy that places the Yaqui nation at its center and that is typically unknown to the nonindigenous reader. For example, Josephina's longtime marriage to a Yaqui allows her to explain that "the Papagos are more heathen than the Yaquis. . . . But not as dumb as the Pimas. The Pimas let the white man have it all. Then the Navajos stuck it to 'em" (51–52). This perspective is consistent with the one present in the traditional origin story "Leyenda yaqui de las prediccio-nes" (Yaqui legend of the predictions), which exemplifies the arraigamiento concept. The tale takes place "hace muchos siglos, en tiempos remotos, cuando el Yaqui reinaba sobre sus hermanos de las naciones Apache, Euleve, Mayo, Ópata, Pápago, Pima y Seri, siendo centro de la gran confederación india" (many centuries ago, in ancient times, when the Yaqui ruled over the brother nations of Apache, Eudeve, Mayo, Ópata, Papago, Pima, and Seri, and was the great center of the Indian confederation) (Olavarría 1989, 82).[28] Véa's novel represents the continuation of this indigenous hierarchy, in which Yaquis are ethnically superior to other living indigenous peoples. This is clear when the Salvador exclaims, "'Shit, our way is the best!'" (219).

Not surprisingly, Véa creates moments of opposition and even conflict when juxtaposing *lo yaqui* and *lo azteca*, breaking with the Mexican epis-temic tradition that informs indigenismo chicano. To illustrate this point, we can examine the history of Yaqui resistance in *La Maravilla*, when the nation collides with the armies of the Mexican Revolution: "The river people chose to fight just as they had four hundred years before when they turned from fighting the Aztecs to fighting the Spanish." True to arraiga-miento, the unconquered Yaquis are identified by their territory: "The river people, once the best soldiers of the revolution, now fought them all." Véa makes a special point to contrast Yaqui and Aztec identities: "'We were not *Aztecas*,' they howled. 'Now, we are not you'" (9). Yaqui resistance, both cultural and military, is not limited to Spanish, Mexican, or US hegemonies. As the collective Yaqui voice denies the cultural dominance of invading Aztec forces, it executes a "counterhegemonic resistance to the dominant ideology" of Chicano-Aztec aesthetics and identity (Saldívar 1991, 17).[29] The aesthetics of Aztlán, writes Gaspar de Alba, create a homeland that is defined by a Mexican-Chicana/o history that includes pre-Columbian symbols and a heroic iconography spanning *la conquista*, the Mexican Revolution, and the Chicano movement (2004, 114). The shift to a Yaqui historical perspective disrupts the museum-style erasure of a living indigenous people and concomitant praise of Aztec civilization, which questions the foundation of indigenismo chicano (Bonfil Batalla

1987, 54–55). Véa questions the reliance on Aztlán motifs by contesting the post-Revolutionary Mexican belief in the cultural superiority of the Aztecs. The indigenous hierarchy presented by Véa knows no such limitation, as Salvador notes:

> The Yaquis, the Mayos and even the Aztecs in their beliefs are concerned only with the idea of well-being, the health of the universe and the health of the things in it. I tell you, I wouldn't give you a dime for the Aztecs, but they weren't completely stupid. . . . Some say the Aztecs actually harvested the beating heart like a fruit. And they called us the *Chichimeca*, the sons of dogs—the barbarians. (301)

Toward the end of *La Maravilla*, an adult Alberto enters a cemetery only to see "armored Spaniards and feathered Aztecs" who had been "turned back again and again by the barbarians in Sonora, the *chichimecas*" (279).[30] Even the souls of those who had failed to conquer and exterminate the Yaquis—whether Aztec warriors, Spanish conquistadors, or Mexican *federales*—are doomed to an existence that signifies their inferiority to a living Yaqui nation culturally rooted in Hiakim. In spite of the abundance of *La Maravilla*'s Aztec themes, Véa, like Saldaña-Portillo, chooses to confront the pitfall of "ignoring contemporary Native American inhabitants of the Southwest and their very different mytho-genealogies" by positioning Yaqui ethnicity above Aztec culture through a focus on a historical and cosmological indigenous epistemology (Saldaña-Portillo 2001, 415).

Conclusion

Véa responds to the denigration of Yaqui traditional culture in twentieth-century Mexican literature by reappropriating Yaqui culture from literary and ethnographic works that were based on a colonial Spanish Mexican epistemology. The Yaqui warrior myth, created from hegemonic discourses of barbarism and anthropologist-legitimated beliefs in senseless resistance to Spanish and Mexican cultures, collides with a wall of historical contextualization, cosmological stories, and relevant Yaqui rituals. Through recovered Yaqui cultural and historical knowledge, Véa establishes a rendering of arraigamiento—the traditional link between culture, resistance, and ancestral territory—that subverts the colonial and Mexican nationalist portrayals that promote Yaquis as backward internal Others in need of incorporation.

That *La Maravilla* is a Chicano novel, there can be no doubt. The author's deployment of Aztec motifs demonstrates his commitment to the indigenismo chicano established during the Chicano movement, and it is one of the ways through which he explores identity in his work. As a member of a community of Chicana/o writers of Yaqui descent, however, Véa turns indigenismo chicano into a site to contested identity. Alberto is appropriately Chicano: his Yaqui ancestry is combined with what we might call a Chicana/o experience of family life, immigration (or diaspora), assimilation, and a search for identity. Still, the author's desire to transcend a politically determined aesthetic results in an inquiry into alternative Chicana/o paradigms of identity and homeland that privileges Yaqui culture and its pointed peculiarities, yielding a Yaqui-specific narrative of Chicana/o experience. In *La Maravilla* Véa recognizes the importance of the mythological homeland Aztlán at the same time that he acknowledges "the tribe's sense of superiority, the sacred and material value of their territory, and the antiquity and distinctiveness of their customs" (Giddings 1960, 20). This is clear when he juxtaposes lo yaqui and lo azteca to highlight an indigenous hierarchy that upholds the prominence of Yaquis among other living indigenous people and exposes the limitations of a pre-Columbian basis for Chicana/o identity. Focusing on his own Chicana/o-Yaqui identity, Véa redirects Chicana/o identity, if not away from Aztlán, then toward the ancestral knowledge of today's living indigenous nations.

Notes

Editor's Note: From *Aztlán: A Journal of Chicano Studies* 38, no. 1 (2013). The original essay was lightly edited for this collection.

1. I admit to the obvious generalization of what I call "a Chicana/o experience," which must differ for every individual. I do not purposefully ignore questions of class, gender, and race that differentiate these experiences.

2. For a discussion on Méndez's Aztlán as social and material realism, see Luis Leal's "Mito y realidad social en *Peregrinos de Aztlán*" and Francisco A. Lomeli's "*Peregrinos de Aztlán* de Miguel Méndez: Textimonio de desesperanza(dos)," both in Keller (1995).

3. Valdez's play is a particularly ambitious work that follows the protagonist's voyage from the end of the nineteenth century in Mexico to the Yaqui diaspora that followed the Mexican Revolution. The play tracks the Chicana/o experience of migration and labor hardship through the Mexican guerras de exterminio and the Yaqui tendency to cross the US-Mexico border into Arizona and westward.

4. The complete epigraph is: "Fear! A terrible enemy—treacherous, and difficult to overcome. It remains concealed at every turn of the way, prowling,

waiting. And if the man, terrified in its presence, runs away, his enemy will have put an end to his quest" (Alurista 2011, ii). *Floricanto en Aztlán* was groundbreaking for its incorporation of Nahuatl.

5. Other recent literature that I have had to exclude breaks with this pattern. Luis Alberto Urrea's *The Hummingbird's Daughter* (2005) highlights the historical relationship between the Yaquis and a regional saint, Teresita Urrea—a spiritual connection to which Broyles-González also draws attention—and is void of an overarching Aztec theme. Montserrat Fontes's *Dreams of the Centaur* (1997), like Urrea's novel, recounts the Díaz dictatorship's guerra de exterminio and questions the belief in a Yaqui warrior nature. For lack of space, these novels cannot receive the attention and analysis they deserve, and I will reserve them for a future publication.

6. According to Hu-Dehart, in 1562 Haikim resided within the new province of Nueva Vizcaya (1981, 17).

7. This concept's foremost propagator throughout all of Latin America is the nineteenth-century Argentine thinker Faustino Domingo Sarmiento; see his *Facundo o civilización y barbarie* (1986). Pérez de Ribas's complete book title, *Triunfos de nuestra Santa Fe entre gentes las mas bárbaras y fieras del nuevo orbe*, is helpful for understanding how long-standing the belief is. For a study on Yoeme and Mexican epistemologies see Tumbaga (2018).

8. Those surviving the difficult southward trek faced being worked to death in Yucatán's henequen plantations. As a further atrocity, Yaqui women were obligated to reproduce with non-Yaquis. Atrocities by Mexican authorities became commonplace and included massacres, scalping, clandestine drowning and public hangings, and child slavery. See Rosalio Moisés, Jane Holden Kelley, and William Curry Holden's *The Tall Candle: The Personal Chronicle of a Yaqui Indian* (1971) and John Kenneth Turner's *Barbarous Mexico* (1910).

9. In 1937, President Lázaro Cárdenas would decree the land rights of almost all of their territory (Spicer 1980, 265).

10. Thus the addition of the deer dance as emblematic of *mexicanidad* and its induction into the prestigious El Ballet Folklórico de México; see Spicer (1980, 275).

11. Novels *La muerte de Artemio Cruz* (1962) by Fuentes and Brianda Domecq's *La insólita historia de la Santa de Cabora* (1990) differ from the "Novel of the Revolution" and indigenista literature in that they demonstrate a post-indigenista sensibility to Yaqui history. In Fuentes's novel, the character known as Yaqui Tobías not only represents Yaqui participation in the Mexican army's northwestern forces but also the collective history of the guerras de exterminio and deportation. Similarly, Domecq writes about insurgent leader Cajemé from within all his complexity; that is, as a man who was a Yaqui, but who was also looked upon with a degree of suspicion for his participation in the Mexican army and nonindigenous upbringing. Thus, Domecq defers ultimate authority over the Yaqui pueblos to their traditional governors (1990, 39).

12. I am excluding here the short story by Amado Nervo, "La yaqui hermosa (sucedido)" (1921) and Djed Bórquez's *Yórem Tamegua (novela)* (1923), as the former writes as a *modernista* while the latter is an early example of the Novel of the Revolution that is still steeped in nineteenth century writing conventions.

I also do not include in my analysis fiction on other Northern nations, like the Mayos of Sonora—culturally related to the Yaquis—in Emma Dolujanoff's *Cuentos del desierto* (1959) and Nellie Campobello's *Cartucho: Relatos de la lucha en el norte de México* (1931), or the Seris, in the more recent *La visita: Un sueño de la razón* by Agustín Ramos (2000).

13. Ramón Rubín's short story "La mula muerta" (1958) features a bellicose and atavistic Yaqui who mindlessly punishes a Seri family.

14. "Okie," a term used throughout the novel to refer to poor whites, was once a very real racist epithet in the Southwest.

15. In this sense, the novel demonstrates some affinities with Ron Arias's *The Road to Tamazunchale* (1987), in addition to the strong presence of two often oppositional seniors in Arias's novel and the protagonist's deceased-ghost wife.

16. Biggers observes that Véa's "fiction recognizes history as geography, a history that is vital and still breathing life into a world that has not vanished" (1999, 34), an observation consistent with the timeless nature of the cultural connections held by the Yaquis to their traditional territory in *La Maravilla*.

17. Valdez immediately distances his play from the work of Castañeda. In the fictional prologue to *Mummified Deer*, Armida Bravo, a professor of cultural anthropology, mentions Castañeda's work within a US cultural framework: "If it hadn't been for Carlos Castañeda, I never would have known what deep secrets Mama Chu was hiding. In the Spring of 1969, *The Yaqui Way of Knowledge* was a bestseller . . . in Berkeley. . . . With tales of indio sorcerors [*sic*], power spots and peyote hallucinations, Castañeda opened the doors of perception to parallel universes and blew the minds of my hippy generation. . . . But for me, *The Yaqui Way* led back home . . . to reality" (2005, 3).

Right away, Valdez addresses the inevitable presence of Castañeda's Don Juan Matus, the cultural reference for Yaqui culture in the US. Once mentioned, Castañeda's disputed anthropology is quickly forgotten as Armida immediately shifts focus to reality, in the form of a memory of Mama Chu, onstage, "waltzing" to the song "Sonora Querida." For a discussion on Castañeda's academic legitimacy, see Yves Morton's "The Experimental Approach to Anthropology and Castañeda's Ambigious Legacy" in *Being Changed: the Anthropology of Extraordinary Experience* (1994).

18. The choice of the word *Yoeme* comes either from his personal experience, or is the influence of Spicer, since Rojas González uses *Yoreme* instead, which is more often used to refer not only to Yaquis but also to other indigenous *sonorenses* like the Mayos and Seris.

19. Véa demonstrates his knowledge of ethnographic research throughout the novel. In the sixth chapter, the omniscient narrator alludes to a mythological time, an often-cited theme in studies of creation stories: "There is a mythological time; the time of gardens; of Eden and Aztlán. It is a time when all times, past, present and future, may coexist" (1993, 97). This is what allows the warrior Omteme to confront Christopher Columbus, for example. Early on, the narrator refers to the singing tree when expounding on the connections between culture and language (31), and then again when Alberto flies to the mythological Yaqui territory, in Cócorit, to meet his great-grandfather (227).

20. The eight traditional Yaqui pueblos are Cócorit, Bacum, Huirivis, Belem, Torim, Vicam, Potam, and Rahum; the Río Yaqui and what is today Ciudad Obregón also make up part of this territory (Spicer 1980, 27).

21. Here, I am referring to Alicia Gaspar de Alba's response to Cherríe L. Moraga, in which she proposes that Aztlán is not a tangible homeland to which we may, for example, drive (2004, 135).

22. This is also consistent with Alma Luz Villanueva's description of the dreaming taught to her by her Yaqui grandmother (1996, 300).

23. See Alarcón's "The Aztec Palimpsest: Toward a New Understanding of Aztlán, Cultural Identity and History" (1992) and Pérez-Torres's "Refiguring Aztlán" (1997). For the sake of brevity, I have excluded many participants, including *Aztlán: Essays on the Chicano Homeland* by Rudolfo A. Anaya and Francisco A. Lomelí (1989), an essential collection by premiere Chicana/o thinkers, with some poignant criticism toward the concept of Aztlán.

24. In "Queer Aztlán," Moraga calls for a tribal model for the Chicano nation on the grounds that it would be more inclusive of gay and lesbian Chicana/os, rejecting early usages of pre-Columbian culture by males who at times "took the worst of Mexican machismo and Aztec warrior bravado" to oppress Chicana agency (1993, 156–57). In regards to her conception of Aztlán, she alludes to the appearance of the word "Aztlán" on the side of a mountain she drives by and writes that "it had nothing to do with the Aztecs and everything to do with Mexican birds, Mexican beaches, and Mexican babies right here in Califas" (151).

25. The novel also refers to a group called the chemical people, described as African Americans who had mutilated their skin attempting to whiten their faces to conform to 1950s mainstream racial standards. They are also Xipe: "Their skin was blotched black and pink where lye compounds or sulfuric acid mixtures had been applied to whiten the skin" (1993, 88). Alaimo proposes that as "the chemical people attempt to put on the skin of those in power [they represent] cautionary mirror images of how the exchange of identities within oppressive economies becomes a violent and scarring transaction" (2000, 168). Since the controversial practice of cosmetic whitening is beyond the scope of this essay, I recommend Jemima Pierre's "'I Like Your Colour!' Skin Bleaching and Geographies of Race in Urban Ghana" (2008); and, for a US focus, Evelyn Nakano Glenn's "Yearning for Lightness Transnational Circuits in the Marketing and Consumption of Skin Lighteners" (2008). The Aztec divinity of flayed skin is also applied to a group of transgender men known as the *maricones*. But in this instance, their Xipe identity "invokes the more ancient god who represents new life emerging from the old" (Alaimo 2000, 168). Noteworthy is Véa's insistence on the slur "maricones," revealing a realist depiction of transgender people who, while accepted into Buckeye Road's community, remain gendered Others.

26. Poet Lorna Dee Cervantes, for example, openly embraces her Chicana-Chumash heritage.

27. Yaqui ethnic superiority here should not be read as equivalent to Western (US-European) ethnocentrism, fraught with racist science and military justifications of barbaric peoples. Instead, I propose that the Yaqui sense of ethnic superiority be understood as a nationalist tendency through which many populations define

their place among neighboring nations. A further investigation of origin stories of nations big or small would no doubt reveal this to be true.

28. However, Josephina's use of "heathen" is meant to qualify the Spanish curandera's Eurocentric sensibilities as well as engage the concept of *civilización y barbarie*, by which Yaquis have been historically depicted.

29. By "Chicano-Aztec aesthetics," and "the aesthetics of Aztlán," I am referring to the collection of pre-Columbian motifs employed by Chicana/o authors and artists, which amount to what Gaspar de Alba has called "place-based aesthetics, a system of homeland representation that immigrants and natives alike develop to fill in the gaps of the self" (2004, 104).

30. For all the military bravado displayed here, Véa summarizes Yaqui history (as do Nervo, Chávez Rojas González, and Fuentes) early in the novel, writing that the Yaquis "walked away from the Yoris and their wars and their God; walked away from the slave camps in the Yucatán. . . . Men who knelt by the water as farmers and hunters saw homeless guerrillas staring back at them. They saw only sadness" (9). Véa dispels the Yaqui warrior myth, depicting them as peaceful farmers pushed to warfare by Mexican death squads and the victims of slave labor. The Yaquis in *La Maravilla*, meek Arizona laborers, have more in common with Méndez's Loreto Maldonado and Frankie Pérez than with the combatant Yaquis of Gonzales's "Yo soy Joaquín" and Moraga's Medea.

Works Cited

Alaimo, Stacy. 2000. "Multiculturalism and Epistemic Rupture: The Vanishing Acts of Guillermo Gómez-Peña and Alfredo Véa Jr." *MELUS* 25, no. 2: 163–86.

Alarcón, David Cooper. 1992. "The Aztec Palimpsest: Toward a New Understanding of Aztlán, Cultural Identity and History." *Aztlán: A Journal of Chicano Studies* 19, no. 2: 33–68.

Aldama, Frederick Luis. 2006. *Spilling the Beans in Chicanolandia: Conversations with Writers and Artists*. Austin: University of Texas Press.

Alurista. 2011. *Floricanto en Aztlán*. 2nd ed. Los Angeles: UCLA Chicano Studies Research Center Press. First published 1971.

Anaya, Rodolfo A., and Francisco A. Lomelí, eds. 1989. *Aztlán: Essays on the Chicano Homeland*. Albuquerque: El Norte Publications/Academia.

Arias, Ron. 1987. *The Road to Tamazunchale*. 3rd ed. Tempe: Bilingual Press/Editorial Bilingüe.

Basauri, Carlos. 1940. *La población indígena de México: Etnografía*. Mexico City: Secretaría de Educación Pública.

Beals, Ralph L. 1932. *The Comparative Ethnology of Northern Mexico before 1750*. Ibero-Americana, no. 2. Berkeley: University of California Press.

Bigas Torres, Sylvia. 1990. *La narrativa indigenista Mexicana del siglo XX*. Guadalajara, Mexico: Universidad de Guadalajara.

Biggers, Jeff. 1999. "Alfredo Véa, Jr." *Brick: A Literary Journal* 63: 33–35.

Bonfil Batalla, Guillermo. 1996. *México Profundo: Reclaiming a Civilization*. Austin: University of Texas Press.

Bórquez, Djed. 1923. *Yórem Tamegua (novela)*. Guatemala: Sánchez & de Guise, 1923.

Broyles-González, Yolanda. 2002. "'Indianizing Catholicism': Chicana/India/ Mexicana Indigenous Spiritual Practices in Our Image." In *Chicana Traditions: Continuity and Change*, edited by Norma Cantú and Olga Nájera-Ramírez, 117–32. Urbana: University of Illinois Press.

Bulnes, Francisco. 1952. *El verdadero Díaz y la Revolución*. Mexico City: Editora Nacional.

Campobello, Nellie. 1931. *Cartucho: Relatos de la lucha en el norte de México*. Repr., Mexico City: Ediciones Era, 2001.

Cantú, Roberto. 2001. "Diásporas mexicanas en la novela chicana, 1959–1996." In *Y nos volvemos a encontrar*, edited by Alvaro Ochoa Serrano, 35–52. Zamora: El Colegio de Michoacán.

Carlston, Erin G. 2005. "'Making the Margins Chaos': Romantic and Antiromantic Readings of *La Maravilla*." *Aztlán: A Journal of Chicano Studies* 30, no. 2: 113–35.

Castañeda, Carlos. 1968. *The Teachings of Don Juan: A Yaqui Way of Knowledge*. Berkeley: University of California Press. Repr. 1998.

Chávez Camacho, Armando. 1948. *Cajeme: Novela de indios*. Mexico City: Editorial Jus.

Dawson, Alexander S. 2004. *Indian and Nation in Revolutionary Mexico*. Tucson: The University of Arizona Press.

Dolujanoff, Emma. 1959. *Cuentos del desierto*. Repr., Mexico City: Universidad Nacional Autónoma de México. 1972.

Domecq, Brianda. 1990. *La insólita historia de la santa de cabora*. Mexico City: Planeta.

Fabila, Alfonso. 1940. *Las tribus Yaquis de Sonora: Su cultura y anhelada autodeterminación*. Primer Congreso Indigenista Interamericano. Mexico City: Departamento de Asuntos Indígenas.

Fontes, Montserrat. 1997. *Dreams of the Centaur*. New York: W.W. Norton.

Fuentes, Carlos. 1958. *La región más transparente*. Repr., Mexico City: Fondo de Cultura Económica, 1973.

———. 1962. *La muerte de Artemio Cruz*. Repr., Mexico City: Fondo de Cultura Económica, 1998.

Gamio, Manuel. 1982. *Forjando patria*. Mexico City: Editorial Porrúa. First published in 1916.

Gaspar de Alba, Alicia. 2004. "There's No Place Like Aztlán: Embodied Aesthetics in Chicana Art." *The New Centennial Review* 4, no. 2: 103–40.

Giddings, Ruth W. 1960. *Yaqui Myths and Legends*. Tucson: The University of Tucson Press.

Glenn, Evelyn Nakano. 2008. "Yearning for Lightness: Transnational Circuits in the Marketing and Consumption of Skin Lighteners." *Gender and Society* 22 no. 3: 281–302.

Gonzales, Rodolfo "Corky." 1972. *I Am Joaquín/Yo soy Joaquín: An Epic Poem*. New York: Bantam Pathfinder Editions.

González Echevarría, Roberto. 2000. *Mito y archivo: Una teoría de la narrativa latinoamericana*. Mexico City: Fondo de Cultura Económica.

Graham, Richard. 1990. *The Idea of Race in Latin America, 1870–1940*. Austin: University of Texas Press.

Guzmán, Martín Luis. 1928. *El águila y la serpiente*. Repr., Mexico City: Editorial Porrúa, 1998.

Holden, W. C. 1936. *Studies of the Yaqui Indians of Sonora, Mexico*. Vol. 11. Lubbock: *Texas Technological College Bulletin*.

Hu-DeHart, Evelyn. 1984. *Yaqui Resistance and Survival: The Struggle for Land and Autonomy, 1821–1910*. Madison: University of Wisconsin Press.

Huerta, Jorge. 2005. "Introduction." In Valdez 2005, v–xiii.

Irwin, Robert McKee. 2007. *Bandits, Captives, Heroines, and Saints: Cultural Icons of Mexico's Northwest Borderlands*. Minneapolis: University of Minnesota Press.

Keller, Gary D., ed. 1995. *Miguel Méndez in Aztlán: Two Decades of Literary Production*. Tempe: Bilingual Press/Editorial Bilingüe.

Knight, Alan. 1986. *The Mexican Revolution*, Volume 1: *Porfirian, Liberals, and Peasants*. Cambridge: Cambridge University Press.

Leal, Luis. 1995. "Mito y realidad social en *Peregrinos de Aztlán*." In Keller 1995.

Lomelí, Francisco A. 1995. "*Peregrinos de Aztlán* de Miguel Méndez: Textimonio de desesperanza(dos)." In Keller 1995.

López y Fuentes, Gregorio. 1931. *Campamento: Novela mexicana*. Madrid: Espasa-Calpe.

———. 1933. *Tierra: La Revolución agraria en México*. Mexico City: Editorial México.

Madero, Francisco I. 2005. *La sucesión presidencial en 1910*. Mexico City: Editorial Época. First published in 1908.

Mariscal, George. 1999. *Aztlán and Viet Nam: Chicano and Chicana Experiences of the War*. Berkeley: University of California Press.

Méndez, Miguel. 1974. *Peregrinos de Aztlán*. Tempe: Bilingual Press/Editorial Bilingüe. Repr. 1991.

Mignolo, Walter D. 2005. *The Idea of Latin America*. Oxford: Blackwell Publishing.

Moisés, Rosalio, Jane Holden Kelley, and William Curry Holden. 1971. *The Tall Candle: The Personal Chronicle of a Yaqui Indian*. Lincoln: Univeristy of Nebraska Press.

Moraga, Cherríe L. 1993. "Queer Aztlán: The Re-formation of the Chicano Tribe." In *The Last Generation: Prose and Poetry*. Boston: South End Press.

———. 2000. *The Hungry Woman: A Mexican Medea*. Albuquerque: West End Press. Repr. 2001.

Morton, Yves. 1994. "The Experimental Approach to Anthropology and Castañeda's Ambigious Legacy." In *Being Changed: The Anthropology of Extraordinary Experience*, edited by David E. Young and Jean-Guy Goulet, 273–97. Peterborough, ON: Broadview Press.

Muñoz, Rafael F. 1936. *¡Vámonos con Pancho Villa!* Repr., Madrid: Espasa Calpa, 1949.

Nervo, Amado. 1921. "La yaqui hermosa (sucedido)." In *Obras completas de Amado Nervo*, edited by Francisco González Guerrero and Alfonso Méndez Plancarte. Vol. 1. Madrid: Aguilar, S.A. de Ediciones, 1951.

Olavarría, Eugenia. 1989. *Análisis estructural de la mitología yaqui*. Mexico City: Instituto Nacional de Antropología e Historia.

Pérez de Ribas, Andrés. 1944. *Triunfos de nuestra santa fe entre gentes las mas bárbaras y fieras del nuevo orbe por el padre Andres Perez de Ribas*. 2 vols. Mexico City: Editorial "Layac." First published in 1645.

———. 1999. *History of the Triumphs of Our Holy Faith amongst the Most Barbarous and Fierce Peoples of the New World*. Translated by Daniel T. Reff, Maureen Ahern, and Richard K. Danford. Tucson: University of Arizona Press.

Pérez Torres, Rafael. 1997. "Refiguring Aztlán." *Aztlán: A Journal of Chicano Studies* 22, no. 3: 15–41.

———. 2006. *Mestizaje: Critical Uses of Race in Chicano Culture*. Minneapolis: University of Minnesota Press.

Pierre, Jemima. 2008. "'I Like Your Colour!' Skin Bleaching and Geographies of Race in Urban Ghana." *Feminist Review* 90: 9–29.

Ramos, Agustín. 2000. *La visita: Un sueño de la razón*. Mexico City: Océano.

Rojas González, Francisco. 1952a. *El diosero*. Mexico City: Fondo de Cultura Económica.

———. 1952b. "Hículi Hualula." In Rojas González 1952a, 26–34.

———. 1952c. "La triste historia del Pascola Cenobio." In Rojas González 1952a, 6–12.

———. 1998a. *Ensayos indigenistas*. Zapopan: D.R. El Colegio de Jalisco.

———. 1998b. "Jículi ba-ba." In Rojas González 1998a, 93–104. First published in 1948.

———. 1998c. "Totemismo y nahualismo." In Rojas González 1998a, 81–92. First published in 1944.

Rubín, Ramón. 1958. *Segundo libro de cuentos de indios*. Guadalajara: S.E.P.

Sáenz, Moisés. 1939. *México íntegro*. Repr., Mexico City: Consejo Nacional Para la Cultura y Las Artes, 2007.

Said, Edward W. *Orientalism*. 1994. New York: Vintage Books. First published in 1978.

Saldaña-Portillo, Josefina. 2001. "Who's the Indian in Aztlán? Re-Writing Mestizaje, Indianism, and Chicanismo from the Lacandón." In *The Latin American Subaltern Studies Reader*, edited by Ileana Rodríguez, 402–23. Durham: Duke University Press.

Saldívar, Ramón. 1991. "Narrative, Ideology, and the Reconstruction of American Literary History." In *Criticism in the Borderlands: Studies in Chicano Literature, Culture, and Ideology*, edited by Héctor Calderón and José David Saldívar, 11–20. Durham: Duke University Press.

Sarmiento, Faustino Domingo. 1986. *Facundo o Civilización y barbarie*. Edited by María Teresa Bella and Jordi Estrada. Barcelona: Editorial Planeta. First published in 1845.

Seltzer, Carl Coleman. 1936. "Physical Characteristics of the Yaqui Indians." *Studies of the Yaqui Indians of Sonora, Mexico.* Vol. 11. Lubbock: Texas Technological College Bulletin.

Sommers, Joseph. 1966. *Francisco Rojas González: Exponente literario del nacionalismo mexicano.* Xalapa: Universidad Veracruzana.

Spicer, Edward H. 1980. *The Yaquis: A Cultural History.* Tucson: University of Arizona Press.

———. 1992. "Excerpts from the 'Preliminary Report on Potam.'" *Journal of the Southwest* 34, no. 1: 111–28.

Tumbaga, Ariel Zatarain. 2018. *Yaqui Indigeneity: Epistemology, Diaspora, and the Construction of Yoeme Identity.* Tucson: University of Arizona Press.

Turner, John Kenneth. 1910. *Barbarous Mexico.* Chicago: C.H. Kerr & Co.

Urrea, Luis Alberto. 2005. *The Hummingbird's Daughter.* New York: Little, Brown and Company.

Valdez, Luis. 2005. *Mummified Deer.* Houston: Arte Público Press.

Vasconcelos, José. 2005. *La raza cósmica.* Mexico City: Editorial Porrúa. First published in 1925.

Véa, Alfredo, Jr. 1993. *La Maravilla.* New York: Plume.

Villanueva, Alma Luz. 1985. "La Chingada." In *Five Poets of Aztlán,* edited by Santiago Daydí-Tolson, 135–63. New York: Bilingual Press/Editorial Bilingue.

———. 1996. "Alma Luz Villanueva 1944–." In *Contemporary Authors: Autobiography Series 24,* 299–324 (Farmington Hills, MI: Gale).

Ybarra, Patricia. 2008. "The Revolution Fails Here: Cherríe Moraga's *The Hungry Woman* as a Mexican Medea." *Aztlán: A Journal of Chicano Studies* 33, no. 1: 63–88.

Zea, Leopoldo. 1988. *El Positivismo en México: Nacimiento, apogeo y decadencia.* Mexico City: Fondo De Cultura Económica. First published in 1943.

"Putting a Stamp on Racism"

Political Geographies of Race and Nation in the Memín Pinguín Polemic

Kirstie Dorr

On June 29, 2005, the Servicio Postal Mexicano (Sepomex) announced its release of a five-stamp postage series commemorating the internationally known comic book character Memín Pinguín. A racialized caricature of a boy of African descent frequently described as "apelike" and "Sambo-like," Memín was first conceptualized by renowned Mexican artist Yolanda Vargas Dulché in 1943 (Notimex 2005). For over six decades, Memín Pinguín, the eponymous comic series featuring the character, has been sold at newsstands and bookstores throughout the Americas, Asia, and Europe. However, the comic icon only recently gained media notoriety in the United States, following its controversial acclamation by Sepomex.

Issued only weeks after President Vicente Fox's controversial public contention that Mexican immigrants in the United States "are doing jobs that not even blacks want to do" (CNN 2005), the Memín postage series was condemned by numerous US civil rights leaders as an explicit state endorsement of antiblack racism. It sparked public outcry from the membership of US-based organizations including the NAACP, the Rainbow PUSH Coalition, and the Urban League, among others. David Pilgrim, curator of the Jim Crow Museum of Racist Memorabilia at Ferris State University, stated, "I'm disappointed but not shocked. . . . This is consistent with what we in the United States would refer to as a pickaninny image. It's disappointing when you find a government putting its stamp on racism" (Fears 2005a, A01). Such criticisms provoked an equally ardent public defense of the comic character by pro-Memín pundits ranging from Mexican governmental officials to prominent Mexican journalists, with a chorus of fans throughout the hemisphere. Within days of their release, the Memín

Figure 1. The 2005 Memín Pinguín postage series released by Sepomex.

postage stamps catalyzed an enduring international controversy that far
outlasted their relatively brief production life (fig. 1).

Postage stamps are at once a form of legal tender, a collector's
commodity, and an internationalized technology of visual signification.
Accordingly, the controversial Memín stamp series can be read as a text
that invites deeper consideration of the entangled relationships between
modes of cultural production and exchange and processes of racial and
national formation.[1] The Memín polemic brought international public
attention to a set of racial-national projects at work in post-NAFTA
Mexico and the United States, particularly the putative "black-brown
divide" that ostensibly demarcates the African and Latina/o Americas
as discrete, mutually exclusive "temporal geographies" (Brady 2002).[2]
A reading of this international media spotlight, I argue, raises fruitful
questions for scholars of Latina/o and black cultural studies, as it evi-
dences the long-standing, dynamic interaction between such discourses
of race and nation within the hemisphere.[3] By extension, it points to
the need to attend to these as at once *geo-historically specific*—that is, as
emplaced in particular local, regional, and national contexts, as well as
geo-historically relational—that is, as situated within and articulated with
other geographies of racial capitalist formation and networks of cultural
circulation. In this sense, I aim to contribute to the growing body of
scholarship within African diaspora studies that examines the global
"cultural traffic" in blackness.[4] These studies interrogate how translocal
representations of blackness have been shaped by global media industries,
interactive geographies of racial formation, ongoing migrations, and
popular antiracist coalitions.[5]

In this essay, I am interested in exploring how and why the figure
of Memín emerges at the interstices of popular and academic discursive
conceptions of bodies, territories, and economies. To do so, I consider the

336

analytics of national cultural production and the production of cultural nationalisms that the Memín debate encompasses within a critical geographic framework attentive to interactive processes of racial and spatial formation.[6] My aim is to consider the Memín polemic as exemplary of how, today, the materio-discursive borderlands of blackness and *latinidad*—that is, their imbricated visual, linguistic, and symbolic gendered and racialized significations at local, national, and international scales—have become a crucial terrain of struggle for the contradictory processes of racial-capitalist nation building in the context of contemporary global economic restructuring.[7]

Going Postal: The 2005 Memín Controversy

To make sense of the political storm surrounding Sepomex's 2005 release of the Memín Pinguín commemorative postage stamps, one must contextualize this media event within two interrelated geo-historical projects of (national) racial formation. The first concerns a set of public discourses that have together produced an increasingly common and commonsense analytic for decoding socioeconomic friction in postindustrial US urban landscapes: the putative "black-brown divide." From ongoing congressional and popular debates concerning the contentious "immigration question," to working-class conflict over the loss and/or outsourcing of "US jobs" to undocumented immigrants and foreign nationals, to increasingly strained race relations between youth of color in US urban centers, media pundits have cynically narrated the aftermath of the widespread divestment of state capital and resources in urban communities of color as primarily effected by purportedly endemic political tensions and antagonisms between US African American and Latina/o communities.[8] As an interpretive frame constructed and managed through attention to incidents such as the Memín controversy, the "black-brown divide" has become a totalizing script. In this case, it was opportunistically deployed to delimit the racial optics and spatial logics through which the deleterious effects of global economic restructuring can or should be decoded.

The second and related geo-historical project of interest here concerns the meaning and function of blackness within Mexico's current regional and national racial economies. In Mexico, contemporary representations of racial difference in general, and of blackness in particular, have at least two geo-historical antecedents: the institutionalization of the *casta* system as a legal and popular strategy of colonial management in eighteenth-century

New Spain (Delgadillo 2006; Vaughn 2005; Vinson 2005), and, during the postrevolutionary period, the institutionalization of *mestizaje* as the primordial discourse of the modern nation (Vaughn 2005; Vinson 2005). Despite the centrality of African chattel slavery within the political and economic formation of New Spain (Vaughn 2005), these twin racial projects have cyclically contributed to the geo-historical positioning of blackness as corporeally and discursively exterior to *lo mexicano*, or what is quintessentially Mexican. The *casta* system instrumentalized Spanish American settler colonialism by establishing racial matrices that deemed blackness a biological and cultural threat to the national corpus. The adoption of *mestizaje* as a postcolonial anthem both physically absorbed and figuratively expelled *afromexicanos* from the national narrative (Vaughn 2005; Vinson 2005) by repeatedly invoking "the Spanish and Indian dyad" as "the heart of Mexican subjectivity" (Delgadillo 2006, 414).

The 2005 Memín controversy brought these contemporary US and historical Mexican racial projects into conversation and, as a result, marked a turning point in hemispheric American history (Vinson 2005, 6). Previously, such contemporary iterations and past accumulations of contradictions and struggle over the boundaries and meaning of racial and national difference had typically been viewed as separate and independent. However, Memín's arrival on the international public stage made clear that hemispheric histories of racial formation are in fact relational and interdependent (Delgadillo 2006; Dzidzienyo and Oboler 2005).

The Memín Media Wars

Within days of its release, the 2005 Memín postage series—deemed "offensive" for its comic depiction of an Afro-Mexican boy with "oversize lips, exaggerated eyes and an apelike head" (Fears 2005b, A18)—provoked a worldwide fracas. US and Mexican public opinion makers commonly depicted the dispute as the byproduct of "culture wars" between Mexico and the United States (Malkin 2005) and, analogously, between African Americans and Latinos.[9] The purportedly essential and oppositional racial-national character of the pro- and anti-Memín camps was popularized through both Mexican and US press coverage. The *New York Times* and *Washington Post* headlined the controversy: "Fight Grows Over a Stamp US Sees as Racist and Mexico Adores" (Malkin 2005) and "White House Denounces Art on Mexican Stamps; Aide to Fox Says Cartoon Is Cultural Icon" (Fears 2005b). Mexican news conglomerates *El Universal* and *La Jornada* respectively reported that "Memín stamps offend African Americans" (EFE 2005) and "Memín's mischief jeopardizes bilateral relations between Mexico and the US" (Brooks 2005).[10]

Public discourse on both sides of the border spotlighted the aggrieved position of the African American public, largely neglecting or minimizing the scale and import of Afro-Mexican responses to the controversial stamps (EFE 2005; Fears 2005a, 2005b; Goldiner 2005; McKinley 2005). English- and Spanish-language daily newspapers repeatedly emphasized the political demands of US-based civil rights activists and organizations, which sought, among other remedies, a formal apology to African Americans. Taglines featured the opinions of the Reverends Al Sharpton and Jesse Jackson: Jackson condemned the stamps as "comedy with a demeaning punch line," while Sharpton characterized them as a "racial [insult] against African Americans" (Goldiner 2005).

The binational terms in which the dispute was framed set a conceptual stage for the unabashedly statist nationalist platforms put forth by Memín protestors. In a startling performance of US patriotism, Sharpton issued President Fox a July 4 deadline for the stamps' withdrawal (Goldiner 2005). Marc H. Morial, executive director of the National Urban League, joined Sharpton and Jackson in calling upon President George W. Bush and Secretary of State Condoleezza Rice to denounce the stamps. In what could be described as a paradigmatic example of a Gramscian historical bloc produced through a momentary alignment of political contingencies (Gramsci 1992), US civil rights leaders and organizations lobbied Washington for US government intervention.

The Bush administration declined to officially censure the Mexican postal service. Nonetheless, drawing upon the ethical authority ceded to the US state by civil rights leaders, White House Press Secretary Scott McClellan issued a statement urging the Mexican government to recognize that "racial stereotypes are offensive, no matter what their origin." Such images, McClellan concluded, "have no place in today's world" (Malkin 2005). This cooperation among strange bedfellows set the stage for Washington politicians to position themselves, and by extension the US state, as the hemispheric arbiters of racial political rectitude. In the process, Washington's seemingly benign condemnation of anachronistic racial stereotypes became an opportunity for the White House leadership to assign itself a privileged moral (and, by extension, political) authority in the international sphere. Jodi Melamed (2011) demonstrates that the postwar US state has effectively adopted such "official antiracisms" to manage and discipline racial discourse in a manner that bolsters rather than disrupts the expansion of racial capitalism.

This political maneuver was not lost on Mexican governmental officials, who responded to the charges of racism with a vehement condemnation of what they described as the uninformed imposition of a US racial imaginary upon an iconic figure historically and culturally Mexican in origin (Fears 2005b). In a June 30, 2005, interview with Mexican media agency Notimex, President Fox characterized the erupting controversy as a matter of US "ignorance" (Malkin 2005), adding, "all Mexicans love the character" (Lee 2005). Press Secretary Rubén Aguilar declared that Memín is part of the cultural tradition of Mexico and that the stamp would remain in circulation in order to render tribute to the comic figure (Avila 2005). "It shows a complete lack of understanding of our culture," Mexican Foreign Minister Luis Ernesto Derbez told reporters in English, "that people are translating this [character] to their culture with no respect for ours" (Bremer 2005). As these statements illustrate, defense of the Memín postage stamp series by Mexican governmental officials was articulated and rationalized through the sanctified claim of national cultural relativism—that is, the notion that popular texts such as the racialized figure of Memín can and should only be interpreted within the historical, geographic, and linguistic frameworks that popularly define the "culture" of a particular nation.

The Mexican government's call for culturally competent readings of the comic figure was echoed in a number of pro-Memín editorials penned by prominent Mexican and Mexican American intellectuals, fostering the impression that the Mexican public's opinion echoed that of the Fox administration. In a July 12 *Washington Post* opinion piece titled "The Pride in Memín," noted Mexican historian Enrique Krauze charged that US interpretations of the comic series were marred by a lack of familiarity with Mexican history and culture. Mexicans "see the stamp not as a racist slur," Krauze argued, "but as a highly pleasing image rooted in Mexican popular culture. If Memín Pinguín were a person of flesh and blood, I believe he could win the coming presidential election" (2005). Renowned leftist journalist Elena Poniatowska asserted, "During the years of the historieta's existence no one in Mexico felt offended. The image of blacks awakens an enormous fondness, which is reflected not only in personages like Memín Pinguín, but also in popular songs. . . . In Mexico, unlike what occurs in the United States, our treatment toward Blacks has been more affectionate" (Palapa, Montaño, and Mateos 2005).[11]

Like the press statements issued by Mexican government officials, commentators' demands for culturally informed readings of the Memín stamp and series relied upon a conflation of the materio-symbolic terrains of the cultural and the national. Such a conflation is problematic for several reasons. First, it glosses over the ideological contradictions indexed by and expressed through the constitution of what Antonio Gramsci (1992) has called the "national-popular" through contests over racial and national symbols, projects, and meaning-making practices (Hall 1996). Next, this seemingly uncomplicated alignment of the national and the cultural fails to address the embedded nature of commercial visual culture within transnational networks of production and exchange. Numerous scholars of African diaspora studies have argued that global flows of labor, culture, and knowledge have both shaped and been shaped by regional racial and cultural formations (Clarke and Thomas 2006; Delgadillo 2006; Elam and Jackson 2005; Flores 2009; Hall 1993; Pabst 2006; Rowell 2004). Contrary to the statist claims of Memín supporters, then, the nation is better conceptualized as a geopolitical context than as a bounded container of social relations. Finally, pro-Memín editorials consistently argued that the (national) pleasure in consuming racially marked fantasies somehow mitigates the epistemic violence that such (nationalist) consumption unavoidably entails.

On both sides of the US-Mexico border, as well as throughout Latin America and in parts of Europe and Asia, mainstream media discourses surrounding the Memín stamp and comic constituted a polarized debate that worked to simultaneously efface and naturalize the extent to which questions of racial meaning, national sovereignty, and US neoimperialism remain intertwined. On one side of this polemic, critics of the Memín Pinguín caricature found themselves allied with unilateral demands upon the Mexican state and appeals for intervention by the US state. On the other side, opponents of US cultural imperialism, who critiqued the media's centering of American injury and offense, found themselves closely aligned with those who sought to defend or recuperate the racist caricature. Strikingly, neither of these platforms addresses the extent to which both the US imperial and Mexican colonial nations have historically been structured, albeit through distinct geo-cultural nodes and formations, around physical and psychic violence against people of African descent. Equally disturbing is the tendency of Memín apologists and adversaries alike to implicitly suggest that black liberation struggles can or should be subsumed under statist affiliations.

341

Black *or* Latino, Black *and* Latino?

> Memín is not a symbol of racism. . . . In the United States people are
> divided by race and ethnicity, and they are very clear about it. Here [in
> Mexico], this is not the case, here we are all Mestizos.
>
> —Manelick de la Parra, publishing editor of Memín Pinguín
> and son of the character's creator

For nearly two centuries, the postage stamp—a highly portable and widely
dispersed cultural icon—has figured as an important semiotic tool of interregional and international negotiation. As scholars of philately have shown,
postal images are often produced at moments of ideological or economic
crisis, designed to promote and naturalize specific national mythologies,
nationalist "values," and modes of citizenship and belonging.[12] In light
of this, the story of the Memín postage stamp raises several important
questions. How do we make sense of the tendency of contemporary state
makers and other conservative ideologues to garner support and authority
by linking themselves to "national" cultural imaginaries at a moment when
economic and cultural interactions have become increasingly denational-
ized? (Schmidt Camacho 2005). How do these "postnational" nationalisms
align themselves with contemporary processes of racial formation, and what
do such processes reveal about how racialized bodies, communities, and
fields of knowledge are spatially imagined?

Reconsidering the relationship between spatial construction, racial
formation, and state making is of particular value given the frequency with
which the globalization of culture and capital is described in both popular
and academic narratives as a process of "deterritorialization"—that is, the
detachment of sociopolitical and economic structures from their former
"proper" territories, sites, or regions. This misnomer masks the extent to
which globalization is in fact a political strategy of spatial reordering. Far
from being an inevitable or unchartable shift in the geographic flows of
culture and capital, globalization is an always already spatialized process
through which regimes and routes of production, distribution, and consumption are both ideologically and materially reconstituted (Brenner
1999; Sassen 2001). In other words, global economic restructuring has
consistently required the (re)imagination of geographies of racial capitalist exchange and of how the linkages between these different places are
relatively and relationally articulated (Gilmore 2002; Massey 1994; Smith
1993). Encounters between global racial capitalist imperatives and national
state-making strategies are both expressed in and resolved through processes

of geographic differentiation such as the reproduction and/or rearticulation of scale (Smith 1993; Gilmore 2007).

Attention to the binational discourses surrounding the Memín controversy reveals not only practices of spatial construction at work but also the centrality of racial logics to such processes of geographic differentiation. Articulated through Cartesian cartographies of "the national," media discourses on both sides of the border conjointly mapped seemingly stable geopolitical boundaries between African Americans in the global North and (nonblack) Latinos of the global South. Both proponents and critics of Memín anchored their defense of or opposition to the comic in national frameworks that elaborated corollary racial, cultural, and spatial logics. While the ostensible "American" position expressed sympathy for aggrieved US blacks through a language of cultural developmentalism, the constructed "Mexican" stance uncritically recapitulated discourses of biological and cultural *mestizaje*. In voicing these positions, media pundits and cultural workers enabled state actors to opportunistically frame the Memín controversy in terms of competing "national interests" and irreconcilable "cultural differences"—discourses that have been consistently invoked to disavow the binational partnership between US and Mexican politicians that set the stage for the austerity-driven global economic restructuring of the Americas.[13] In the end, the ideological abstractions of race and place described above enabled state actors on both sides of the border to exploit the Memín controversy as an opportunity to call forth their respective citizens in defense of the *cultural* territory of the nation, even as these very subjects experienced increased alienation from that nation's resources, territories, and political franchise.

Reading the Memín controversy as a binational articulation of Mexican and US postnational nationalisms, then, reveals the extent to which neoliberal state-making strategies in both countries have entailed the popularization of an amended geo-cultural imaginary of nation. In both cases, these postnational nationalisms retooled notions of state belonging to inhere not in stable or bounded geopolitical territoriality but rather in abstract and diffuse modes of "modern" and "nostalgic" racial-cultural belonging. These tactics for rationalizing the contradictions of racialized economic restructuring were arguably distinct in content and form. However, they were rooted in similar logics (the strategic management of difference) and deployed through similar strategies (the delocalization of nation). They also pursued similar goals: the garnering of state support and the entrenchment of state authority at a moment when the private interests of transnational corporatism are prioritized over (and often at the expense of) the common interests of impoverished national publics. In the end, these distinctive yet compatible racial-national projects served to obscure the procedures (global economic restructuring) and effects (racialized exploitation) of neoliberal racial capitalism through the concomitant governmental disciplining of difference and reconsolidation of fixed racial-national divides.

One lesson to be drawn from such a socio-spatial reading of the ideological stakes and political consequences of the Memín controversy, then, is the need for antiracist scholars and activists to question the uncritical imposition—and in particular, the oppositional deployment—of essentialized national and racial geographies such as black or brown, American or Mexican, African American or Latino.[14] This is not to underestimate the critical importance of such categories as sites of collective consciousness formation, but rather to emphasize the necessity of cultivating an increased attentiveness in both academic and popular spheres to the political, cultural, and spatial contradictions that are at best silenced, at worst disavowed, through the uncritical promulgation of binaries such as "black or brown." Such attention enables scholars and activists to interrogate how racial-ethnic shorthands such as these not only obfuscate but also actively produce historico-geographic arrangements of power and difference. In other words, we must ask how the racial-spatial organization of political subjectivities not only engenders collective capacities but also constrains them—thus foreclosing, for example, the possibility of *afrolatinidad* as a sociocultural formation.

While the challenge posed by US-based civil rights activists to the stamps demonstrated the crucial role that international critique can play in contesting state-sanctioned antiblack racism, the form and content of this challenge reflected what Naomi Pabst describes as a "not uncommon elision of blackness and African American-ness" (2006, 128). US civil rights leaders and media pundits articulated the Memín controversy as a bipartite racial contest between black people in the United States, on one hand, and Mexicans in Mexico and abroad, on the other. This view was reflected, for example, in political cartoonist Keith Knight's visual juxtaposition of the Sambo-like Memín with a stereotypical racialized image of *mexicanidad* (Knight 2005), and in Al Sharpton's characterization of the Mexican postage stamp as "an insult to African Americans" (Goldiner 2005). Divorced from the broader context of a global African diaspora within which the idea of blackness indexes a range of specific cultural and racial meanings and structural systems, Memín Pinguín's caricatured "blackness" was strategically resignified, located squarely within the territorial boundaries of the United States as the distinguishing racial marker of those dispossessed workers whose denigrated labor was ostensibly being rendered surplus by "brown" Latina/o immigrants.

This reterritorialization of the Memín polemic and of blackness itself both depended upon and fed existing narratives of "race relations" within the United States that depicted an intraclass conflict between two seemingly stable racial groups: on one hand, a US-born "black" community, and on the other, immigrant and US-born Latinos, euphemistically described as "brown." In recent years, the notion of a black-brown divide has been so naturalized as to become both a popular and academic truism. The alacrity with which the US state has embraced this commonsense rhetoric underscores its significant strategic functions. By imposing a stable and predictable racial order upon complex sites and forms of difference, it sutures contested relations of gender, race, and class within racialized communities in the United States through what is at best a disavowal and at worst a cynical leveraging of material conflicts and contradictions that exist within both so-called black and brown communities: interclass or intercultural tensions, urban-rural divides, and strained relations between migrants and citizens. A state-making tactic that anthropologist Allen Feldman (1991) has referred to in another context as "individualizing disorder," public discourses that reinvent socioeconomic crises as conflicts between "black and brown" communities conceal the complicity of the US imperial racial state in producing and managing structural inequalities by reterritorializing the origin of and responsibility for such contradictions from the scale of the nation-state to the scale of individualized raced and gendered bodies.

When examined across space and time, the meaning and boundaries of blackness in the United States and of *afrolatinidad* in Latin America have complex and contested histories that belie simple Manichean constructs of "black" or "brown." Indeed, a critical part of the history of race throughout the American hemisphere has been the strategic policing of the categorical limits of blackness (Fox 2006). Given this, the so-called black-brown divide fails to account for the fluid and overdetermined historical, geographic, political, and linguistic forces that underpin racial-ethnic identities—both imposed and self-fashioned, at home and abroad. Equally important, it works to efface the significant if consistently undercounted populations of people of African descent in (and from) Cuba, the Dominican Republic, and Puerto Rico, as well as the Pacific and Atlantic coasts of Mexico, Central America, and Colombia, the Atlantic coasts of Venezuela and Brazil, the Pacific coasts of Peru, Ecuador, and Chile, and highland and Amazonian regions in Bolivia—in short, everywhere that the African slave trade reached in its 300-year history in the Americas. Thus, as the unfolding Memín Pinguín polemic on both sides of the border contributed to the reification of "black" and "Mexican" as discrete and mutually exclusive *racial* categories, it obscured the enduring presence of Afro-Latinos in Latin America, where the production, circulation, and consumption of Memín comics has traditionally been concentrated.

In positing blackness as a racial-national terrain implicitly (or exclusively) located within the United States, critics of the Mexican state's endorsement of antiblack racism inadvertently reified the representational tactics and state practices that work to disremember and disavow the history and legacies of African chattel slavery in the region. Near the end of the colonial period, Mexico had the largest concentration of people of African descent in the Spanish Americas (Vinson 2000). Yet throughout the nineteenth and twentieth centuries, narrative constructions of the national-popular have repeatedly invoked "the Spanish and Indian dyad" as the collective essence of Mexican subjectivity (Delgadillo 2006). In the postrevolutionary period, *mestizaje*—defined in this instance as an idealized (and often state-engineered) project of corporeal and cultural amalgamation—has persisted as a biopolitical blueprint for state-making strategies (Delgadillo 2006; Hernández Cuevas 2004; Rowell 2004; Rubenstein 1998; Vinson and Vaughn 2004). *Mestizaje's* hegemonic purchase on the national imaginary—a structure of feeling that political theorist Agustín Basave Benítez (1993) has dubbed *mestizofilia*—thus produces ongoing material and imaginative contradictions: the racial-national incommensurability of blackness and *mexicanidad*. The geopolitical consequences of this impasse are equally contradictory. While Afro-Mexicans are rendered hypervisible at the scale of the racially marked body, they remain socially and politically invisible at the scale of the mestizo nation. As a closer look at the history of the publication's content and form illustrates, the Memín comic series was designed to perform the crucial ideological work of equating *mexicanidad* with this notion of *mestizaje* while establishing blackness as the primordial signifier of biological and cultural otherness.

Nationalist Pedagogies, Visual Culture, and the Making of the *Historieta Mexicana*

In postrevolutionary Mexico, relations of popular cultural production constituted a decisive terrain for processes of national formation, including the articulation of a collective identity, the fostering of state legitimacy, and the production of ideal citizen-subjects (Joseph and Nugent 1994; Joseph, Rubenstein, and Zolov 2001). In her examination of Mexican comic book culture from the 1930s to the 1970s, Anne Rubenstein (1998) demonstrates how visual cultural forms—most particularly, *historietas*, or comic books—were an exceptionally popular medium for the rehearsal of national debates. With its relative affordability, its portability, and its hybrid iconic and textual narrative, the Mexican *historieta* commanded a broad readership (Bartra 1994; Rubenstein 1998). Within a decade of its 1934 debut, it had become "as ubiquitous as radio and more common than cinema" (Rubenstein 1998, 13). These "little histories" dramatized in colloquial form the advent and eventualities of midcentury transformations such as rapid urbanization, accelerated industrialization, and widespread emigration. At the same time, *historietas* were exploited as tools for the instruction of nationalist pedagogies; through the alternating use of sponsorship and censorship, state architects harnessed mass media outlets to educate an emergent "national" citizenry about their position and function within the evolving social order (Rubenstein 1998).

Within this history of national cultural formation, the enduringly popular Memín Pinguín served as a powerful mechanism for the comic narration of nation and the making of a national citizenry. In a 2005 interview with *La Crónica*, Memín editor Manelick de la Parra recalled, "In the 1950s and '60s, illiteracy rates were very high, and many Mexicans learned to read by trying to figure out what Memín was saying. [Memín] performed important work and should not fall into obscurity in Mexico."[15] Appearing in print for over six decades, Memín was the bestselling and longest-running series of the comic genre, positioning it as one of "the most durable narratives in Mexican history" (Rubenstein 1998, 177–78 n. 15).

It is undeniable, as Memín advocates have repeatedly asserted, that the comic series and its beloved protagonist are indeed legendary icons of postrevolutionary Mexican national culture. This claim is significant to the extent that it can be read as a call for a historically and geographically situated reading of the popular *historieta*. However, the subsequent relativist position that the comic series can exclusively be understood within a singular and impervious "national" context fails to account for the dynamic, interactive relations of race and space through which such contexts are fabricated. As scholars working within the emergent field of Afro-Latina/o studies have recently shown, and as the history of the Memín *historieta* demonstrates, geographies of racial formation within the Americas are rarely if ever hermetically circumscribed by the national, regional, or linguistic boundaries that most often frame conventional ethnic and area studies approaches. Rather, such geographies are constituted through material and ideological networks that are contingently enabled by and through "transnational cultural contact in the Americas, the significance of African diaspora throughout the hemisphere, and the conceptualization of race within and between nations" (Delgadillo 2006, 407). A reading of Memín as a hemispherically situated national racial project reveals such dynamic processes at work, as the production and transmission history of the publication illustrates the extent to which the inspiration for, the aesthetics of, and the plot innovations of the *historieta* were engendered by and through dynamic local, regional, *and* transnational networks of cultural production and exchange. Such a reading thus demands attention to *relational* as well as regional geographies of racial formation, and to the dynamic relations of capital, culture, and difference that processes of spatial formation both reflect and produce.

Renowned Mexican author Yolanda Vargas Dulché first conceptualized Memín during a visit to Cuba in the early 1940s. According to Vargas Dulché, she was charmed and inspired by Cuban children of African descent whom she met during the trip. She imagined Memín as a novel entry point for a national comic series, given that "en México no hay negritos" (in Mexico there are no blacks) (Malvido and Martínez 2005). While Vargas Dulché's idea was first given visual form by artist Alberto Cabrera in 1943, it was Sixto Valencia Burgos's 1946 overhaul of the character, caricaturing commonly racialized physical features such as eyes and lips and rendering the cartoon figure more akin to monkey than child, that created the highly popular Memín Pinguín of the last half century.

Attention to the comic's international history exposes its ongoing critical function as a national(ist) racial project (Omi and Winant 1994). The affection with which Vargas Dulché remembers the "birth" of Memín—and the corresponding filial love that the cartoon character is depicted as having for his creator—cannot be extricated from the character's simultaneous signification of blackness and foreignness (fig. 2).[16] Indeed, the imagined love between Memín and Vargas on the one hand, and between the nation and Memín on the other, can be understood as a form of what Sumi Cho has described in another context as "racist love" that relies upon perceived racialized otherness. Such love underscores the relative inferiority of ostensibly "domestic" racialized peoples and rationalizes their continued marginalization rather than heralding their

Figure 2. *Yolanda Vargas Dulché appears with Memín in the second installment of the collector's edition of the comic.*

inclusion (Cho 1993). In such a reading, the oft-declared national love for Memín Pinguín might be understood to index the value of Memín's figuration of foreign blackness, which serves to cement the ostensible near-whiteness of mestizo elites while obscuring the marginalization of disenfranchised indigenous peoples through the production of a false national unity rooted in non-blackness.

Cuba was not the only place mined for notions of blackness external to the Mexican nation-state. Ironically, Sixto Valencia Burgos cites renowned New York graphic artist Will Eisner's 1940s comic series *The Spirit*, with its infamous character Ebony White, as the primary influence for his refiguring of Memín (figs. 3, 4).

The obvious physical parallels between the two graphic depictions are indicative of a broader set of similarities and interconnections. While Ebony White's role as sidekick to the Spirit differs from Memín Pinguín's status as protagonist in his "own" series, both characters fill similar critical ideological functions: they are raced and gendered foils to an idealized white—or almost-white—masculinity. Each embodies a comic irrationality in opposition to Western rationalism, a bestial charm in the face of

349

racialized notions of physical beauty, and helplessness in the face of white male potency and action (figs. 5, 6).

To the extent that their mishaps and misfortunes play a critical role in moving plotlines forward by producing crises that can only be resolved through the intervention of their beloved patrons, both Ebony White and Memín Pinguín can be read as cultural descendants of the cast of blackface characters that populated the nineteenth-century US minstrel show.

There are, however, distinct differences in the dialectical means by which Ebony White's and Memín Pinguín's figurations of blackness work to shore up normative notions of whiteness and *mestizaje*. First, while Eisner contrasts Ebony White's stunted or inadequate masculinity to the ostensible virility and potency of the crime-fighting superhero the Spirit, Valencia Burgos's rendering of Memín posits the childlike character as the feminized embodiment of gender deviance against which his adolescent mestizo companions perform a correct incipient adult masculinity. Second, if Ebony White's rendering as a loyal and servile adult embodied the racist fantasy of what Will Eisner

Figures 3, 4. Memín Pinguín and Ebony White show remarkable similarities, from their monkey-like features of oversize lips, wide eyes, and broad noses to their childlike stature and mannerisms.

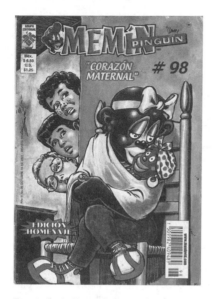 

Figures 5, 6. Figure 5 depicts the character with a yellow bow and shawl, gently cuddling a 8 doll. Figure 6 shows an obliging Memín who patiently allows his older white pals to dress him in women's bridal attire. Taken together, these images demonstrate the comic's perpetual juxtaposition of Memín's gender deviance against the incipient, proper, and virile masculinity of his white and mestizo companions.

has described as African Americans' continuing "slave mentality" (Arnold 2003), then the childlike figuration of Memín as lazy and uneducated, mischievous and dependent, harkens back to what Eric Lott has described as minstrelsy's "romantic racialist thinking," in which a supposedly childlike and innocent black subject serves as the embodiment of a nostalgic longing for a simpler preindustrial past (Lott 1996). In contradistinction to the Jacksonian ideologies embedded in nineteenth-century white working-class minstrelsy, however, the preindustrial simplicity indexed by Memín's madcap adventures is, like Memín himself, both subsumed within and superseded by the progression of the postcolonial modernity project. As a nostalgic figure, Memín represents not a historical legacy that must be reclaimed, but a past that must be supplanted for the good of the nation.

If Memín Pinguín's Mexican locale prohibits the typical spatial marker of romantic racialism in US minstrelsy—the plantation backdrop—it invokes instead an alternative signifier of plantation nostalgia: the figure of the mammy, represented in the series by Memín's mother, Eusafina. As any collector of Latin American consumables can attest, the marketing of and market for products featuring asexual black women caretakers is in no way limited to Memín Pinguín comic books. I would argue, however, that Eusafina's significance to Memín Pinguín as a racial project goes far beyond what the minimal critical attention to her character would suggest. As I have argued elsewhere, if blackness has functioned in the postcolonial Latin American nation as what Patricia Fox (2006) dubs a "contagion," spread through biological and cultural reproduction, then the black female subject represents the seductive danger of contamination that must be contained by reducing her to the role of an asexual reproducer of the mestizo nation. In this sense, Eusafina offers the perfect configuration of black womanhood. Both hypersexual Jezebel and asexual mammy, she simultaneously endangers and nurtures the proper subjects of the mestizo nation (figs. 7, 8).

My observations on the intertextual relationship between the Memín Pinguín comic series and some of the key raced and gendered tropes of the US racial state are in no way meant to suggest that the comic and its characters can be understood solely as exportations of US-based ideologies of antiblack racism across the southern border. Indeed, as Arjun Appadurai (1990) notes, in the case of "global cultural flows," exchanges are neither unilateral nor unidirectional, and the results of such transactions are never identical. Moreover, cultural forms and performances are both

Figures 7, 8. These images show the comic's depiction of Memín's mother, Eusafina, as both domesticated mammy and hypersexual Jezebel—a hybrid portrayal of antiblack racist tropes that have long circulated throughout the Americas.

produced by and productive of their historic and geographic conditions, and thus they constantly remain in the midst of resignification (Dorr 2007). By mapping the complex networks of cultural and ideological reference and exchange within which the figure of Memín is embedded, I have tried to demonstrate that—contrary to the Mexican state's relativist claims of cultural exceptionalism—the history of Memín's inception, the racial imaginaries that he represents, and the racial histories that he is intended to efface betray a simplistic analytical coupling of bounded national and cultural imaginaries. The comic figure of Memín, then, is perhaps better understood a traveling visual narrative that has been redeployed in multiple spatio-temporal contests—from the literature aisles of Walmart to international postal circuits to the gifts shops of Mexico's national airport—to impose, reconsolidate, and/or transgress structures of corporeal and territorial power and meaning.

If the cultural relativist argument made in defense of the Memín commemoration ignored the comic's transnational history, influences, and circulation, it likewise obscured the burgeoning antiracist social movements and coalitions within Mexico that have opposed not only the postage stamp and comic series but also broader institutionalized structures of antiblack racism. For example, an association of black Mexicans, representing the nearly 50,000 Afro-Mexicans living on the southern Pacific coast, submitted a letter to President Fox on July 5, 2005, demanding a recall of the stamp that they condemned as "racist" and "stereotypical" (Reuters 2005b). At the level of state policy, activists under the banner "México Negro" have petitioned the state to include a survey of racial demographics within future census studies in order to press for official recognition of the nation's Afro-Mexican population, which they estimate at nearly 1 million. "We no longer want to be detained by security agents in our own country who say that in Mexico there are no blacks," comments advocate Rodolfo Prudente Dominguez (Okeowo 2010). Coalitions such as México Negro and Comité Afromestizo have begun to internationalize local antiracist struggles by forging transnational political ties with other activist communities throughout the diaspora; the latter has forged ties to African American organizations in Los Angeles and Milwaukee and intends to strengthen these political bonds (Durán 2008). By pursuing strategic alliances that recognize the common histories, struggles, and political aims of dispersed peoples of African descent but that also acknowledge each community's regional and historical specificities, such organizations challenge the state's deployment of cultural relativism to uncritically alibi antiblack racism.

Yet these efforts are all too often undermined on all sides. US-based international critique of antiblack racism in Latin America frequently fails to acknowledge or ally itself with the counterhegemonic political labor of Afro-Latinos throughout the Americas. Meanwhile, Latin American nation-states defend their efforts to produce and maintain hierarchical racial states by leveraging the more sympathetic rhetoric of national autonomy in the face of US imperialism. Indeed, in the final analysis, the Memín Pinguín polemic was produced and defined at the interstices of these conflicting nationalisms. By appealing to the nation-state for support and intervention into the Memín affair, US-based opponents of the Memín stamp legitimated—albeit inadvertently—the discursive capacity of the United States to exert itself as a necessary and natural arbiter of justice within its hemispheric "sphere of influence," temporarily effacing this country's own dealings in the civil, social, and physical death of black people. By framing the defense of Memín Pinguín as a battle against US cultural imperialism and racism, the Mexican state, its national elites, and other Memín supporters disavowed their own complicity in the maintenance of Mexico's racial regimes by conflating political autonomy with the maintenance of mestizo hegemony. As Wendy Brown (1995) has argued, and as the Memín Pinguín polemic illustrates, a rhetoric of ostensible "protection" that encourages subjects to turn to the state for arbitration or redress can afford the nation-state a persuasive materio-discursive strategy of legitimation while obscuring its central role in producing and perpetuating (racialized) violence and (racial) hegemony. In the case of the debates around Memín, the seemingly divergent narratives of the US imperial state and the Mexican postcolonial nation both relied upon common claims of "cultural difference" and national exceptionalism to pursue related, if conflicting, goals: on one hand, obscuring the complicities of each nation in reproducing the racial state, and on the other hand, asserting the right of the racial state to reproduce itself without external interference.

Despite the expansive international media coverage of the Memín Pinguín postage stamp, the controversy surrounding it was relatively short-lived. The 750,000 stamps that were issued sold out in a matter of days, and Sepomex quietly decided to withhold a reissue. At the same time, the media spectacle catalyzed by the stamp continues to have profound implications for the contemporary deployment of Memín as a (trans)national racial project. Circulation of the comic book has been revitalized, as has the figure of Memín himself. As of mid-2005, Memín publisher Editorial Vid reported weekly sales of roughly 100,000 in Mexico alone, as demand for Memín comic issues and memorabilia skyrocketed. Editorial Vid has capitalized on this resurgence of interest by republishing selected issues of the series as collector's editions.

It was one of these collector's editions that briefly appeared in selected US Walmart megastores in the summer of 2008 (Dobuzinskis 2008). The comic series was introduced to stores in California, Texas, and Miami, Florida, as part of the multinational retail conglomerate's effort to increase its Latino market share by reaching out to newly arrived Mexican immigrants.[17] Walmart chose to introduce Memín to US markets through a rereleased issue featuring Memín Pinguín as a presidential candidate in the same month as the Democratic National Convention in which Barack Obama became the first black man to win a major party's presidential nomination—a suggestive decision under any circumstances. But when read as an indirect outcome of the 2005 postage stamp controversy, Walmart's marketing strategy points to the comic icon's transnational exchange value as a flexible signifier of blackness engendered through relational histories of racial and national formation.

If the case of Memín Pinguín demonstrates how state-making capacities and ideologies of white supremacy can simultaneously and symbiotically operate in local, national, and transnational contexts, then the history and future of this controversial figure continues to raise fruitful political questions for scholars working in Latina/o and black diaspora studies. First, the multiscalar nexus of materio-discursive relations that mark the protagonist's circuitous routes of national and international circulation underscores the need for scholars and activists to work across the commonsense racial-ethnic and territorial frontiers of ethnic studies formations. For it is only through such collaborations that we can begin to engage those oft-silenced subjects, sites, and struggles constituted at the interstices of these geographic and disciplinary terrains. Second, this may require embracing and/or deconstructing the numerous tensions that undergird both nationalist and transnational ethnic studies formations: tensions between local resonances and global significations, between visual texts and lived contexts, and, perhaps most important, between racialized and regionalized articulations of national bodies and boundaries.

A turn toward the transnational within ethnic and American studies has opened up new ways of conceptualizing the dynamic interconnectedness of political, economic, and cultural processes occurring both within and between different regions, nations, and communities—from contemporary processes of globalization and economic restructuring to their historical antecedents of colonialism and imperial expansionism. Yet, while attending to ever-changing social processes that are global in scale, US academics and activists must proceed cautiously, retaining a keen awareness of how relations of race, gender, and capital operate across scales, in place-specific ways. As I have argued above, for scholars of ethnic and American studies, this may require honing the theoretical and methodological frameworks capable of transgressing not only territorial boundaries but also those between geo-linguistically defined contemporary fields of racialized and regionalized knowledge production. The necessary intellectual maneuvers may include moving between theoretical trajectories and thematic foci, between Spanish and English, between image and speech, and between ever-shifting conceptions of the local and the global. As we work both across and, at times, against the seemingly dichotomized textual, ideological, and national registries mentioned above, it is my hope that they may begin to wear upon each other in ways that open up new possibilities, configurations, and meanings.

Notes

Editor's note: From *Aztlán: A Journal of Chicano Studies* 39, no. 1 (2014). The original essay was lightly edited for this collection.

1. Here I use Michael Omi and Howard Winant's conceptualization of racial formation, which they define as "the sociohistorical process by which racial categories are created, inhabited, transformed, and destroyed" (1994, 55).

2. See Mary Pat Brady's seminal text, *Extinct Lands, Temporal Geographies* (2002). Brady's title is drawn from her critical reading of Cherríe Moraga's *Heroes and Saints* (1994), which references bodies as "temporal geographies." Brady notes this as one of many examples of the ways in which Chicana theorists have critically acknowledged and debated the mutual imbrication of sociocultural (specifically, linguistic) and spatial relations.

3. While it is my custom to capitalize the term "Black," the term is lowercased here according to the journal's conventions.

4. Kamari Maxine Clarke and Deborah A. Thomas, Theresa Delgadillo, Juan Flores, Trisha Rose, and others have persuasively argued that the historic circulation of captive black bodies through the expansive interregional networks of the slave trade, coupled with long-standing hemispheric networks of cultural, economic, and political exchange in Americas, suggests the importance of theorizing blackness in the New World as a phenomenon that is at once locally situated and globally inflected, materially saturated but equally unstable and mobile.

5. See, for example, Elam and Jackson (2005), Clarke and Thomas (2006), and Flores (2009).

6. Here I am thinking specifically about the ongoing (re)production of hegemonic geographic scales of racial capitalism such as the nation (and by extension, its dominant representations) as well as the body (a highly contested geography of socioeconomic scripts and oppositions to them). For a discussion of the geographic production of scale, see Smith (1993).

7. Karen Barad's (2007) concept of the material-discursive emphasizes the agential capacities of the material world and the undeniably co-constitutive "nature" of material and discursive fields.

8. For a more in-depth discussion of these discourses, see Katerí Hernández (2007). Two striking examples of how such purported antagonisms have been represented can be seen in the media coverage of the 2005 Los Angeles and New York mayoral campaigns. Pundits described as the primary challenge of candidates Antonio Villaraigosa (Los Angeles) and Fernando Ferrer (New York City) the creation of political coalitions that would bring together divided Latina/o and black voting blocks. See, for example, Broder (2005).

9. I use the term "public opinion makers" in sense deployed by Stuart Hall in *Policing the Crisis* (Hall et al. 1978).

10. All translations of quotations from the Spanish-language Mexican media are my own.

11. "Durante los años de existencia de esa historieta, en México nadie se ha sentido ofendido . . . la imagen de los negros despierta una simpatía enorme, que se refleja no sólo en personajes como Memín Pinguín, sino en canciones populares. En México, a diferencia de lo que sucede en Estados Unidos, nuestro trato hacia los negros ha sido más cariñoso."

12. See, for example, Child (2005).

13. Such strategies of global economic restructuring have included, for example, the dismantling of union labor under free trade agreements, domestic and international structural adjustment policies, the privatization of public welfare programs, and the reconsolidation of post–World War II capital accumulation through transnational corporatism.

14. A brief list of scholarly conversations that put forth transnational, relational approaches to the study of racial formation in the Americas (and the function of blackness within such formations in particular) includes those by Jiménez Román and Flores (2010), Gudmunson and Wolfe (2010), Whitten and Torres (1998), and Dzidzienyo and Oboler (2005).

15. "En los años 50 y 60, los índices de analfabetismo eran muy altos y muchos mexicanos aprendimos a leer tratando de saber qué decía Memín, hizo una gran labor, es un gran personaje . . . que no deben perderse en México."

16. The representation of blackness within popular media as the primordial signification of the emergent state's national exterior was a common nation-building strategy in the early republics of Mexico, Central America, and western South America. See, for example, Andrews (2004), Bennett (2010), Fox (2006), and Gudmunson and Wolfe (2010).

17. Following public protest by African American shoppers in Houston, the *historieta* was pulled from US shelves, but it continues to be available at Walmart locations throughout Mexico.

Works Cited

Andrews, George Reid. 2004. *Afro-Latin America, 1800–2000*. New York: Oxford University Press.

Appadurai, Arjun. 1990. "Disjuncture and Difference in the Global Cultural Economy." *Public Culture* 2, no. 2: 1–24.

Arnold, A. D. 2003. "Never Too Late." *Time*, September.

Avila, Antonio. 2005. "Un sello mexicano con un niño negro desata una nueva polémica con EEUU." *El País*, July 1, 6.

Barad, Karen. 2007. *Meeting the Universe Halfway: Quantum Physics and the Entanglement of Matter and Meaning*. Durham, NC: Duke University Press.

Bartra, Armando. 1994. "The Seduction of the Innocents: The First Tumultuous Moments of Mass Literacy in Postrevolutionary Mexico." In *Everyday Forms of State Formation: Revolution and the Negotiation of Rule in Modern Mexico*, edited by Gilbert Joseph and Joseph Nugent, 301–25. Durham, NC: Duke University Press.

Basave Benítez, Agustín. 1993. *México mestizo: Análisis del nacionalismo Mexicano en torno a la mestizofilia de Andrés Molina Enríquez*. Mexico City: Fondo de Cultura Económica USA.

Bennett, Herman L. 2010. *Colonial Blackness: A History of Afro-Mexico*. Bloomington: Indiana University Press.

Brady, Mary Pat. 2002. *Extinct Lands, Temporal Geographies: Chicana Literature and the Urgency of Space*. Durham, NC: Duke University Press.

Bremer, C. 2005. "Mexico, U.S. in Spat over 'Racist' Stamps." Reuters, June 30.

Brenner, Neil. 1999. "Beyond State-Centrism? Space, Territoriality, and Geographical Scale in Globalization Studies." *Theory and Society* 28: 39–78.

Broder, John M. 2005. "A Black-Latino Coalition Emerges in Los Angeles." *New York Times*, April 24.

Brooks, David. 2005. "Travesura de Memín Pinguín pone en jaque la relación bilateral entre México y EEUU." *La Jornada*, July 1.

Brown, Wendy. 1995. *States of Injury: Power and Freedom in Late Modernity*. Princeton, NJ: Princeton University Press.

Child, Jack. 2005. "The Politics and Semiotics of the Smallest Icons of Popular Culture: Latin American Postage Stamps." *Latin American Research Review* 40, no. 1: 108–37.

Cho, Sumi. 1993. "Korean Americans vs. African Americans: Conflict and Construction." In *Reading Rodney King*, edited by Rodney Gooding-Williams, 196–214. New York: Routledge.

Clarke, Kamari Maxine, and Deborah A. Thomas. 2006. *Globalization and Race: Transformation in the Cultural Production of Blackness*. Durham, NC: Duke University Press.

CNN. 2005. "Fox 'Regrets' Remark about Blacks." CNN.com, May 17.

Delgadillo, Theresa. 2006. "Singing 'Angelitos Negros': African Diaspora Meets Mestizaje in the Americas." *American Quarterly* 58, no. 2: 407–30.

Dobuzinskis, Alex. 2008. "Wal-Mart Removes Mexican Comic Criticized as Racist." Reuters, July 9.

Dorr, Kirstie. 2007. "Mapping El Condor Pasa: Sonic Translocations in the Global Era." *Journal of Latin American Cultural Studies* 16, no. 1: 11–25.

Durán, Agustín. 2008. "Costa Chica se organiza en LA." *La Opinión*, February 26.

Dzidzienyo, Anani, and Suzanne Oboler, eds. 2005. *Neither Enemies nor Friends: Latinos, Blacks, Afro-Latinos*. New York: Palgrave Macmillan.

EFE. 2005. "Ofenden estampillas de Memín a afroamericanos." *El Universal*, June 30.

Elam, Harry J., Jr., and Kennell Jackson. 2005. *Black Cultural Traffic: Crossroads in Global Performance and Popular Culture*. Ann Arbor: University of Michigan Press.

Fears, Darryl. 2005a. "Mexican Stamps Racist, Civil Rights Leaders Say; Images Feature Popular Cartoon Character." *Washington Post*, June 30, A01.

———. 2005b. "White House Denounces Art on Mexican Stamps; Aide to Fox says Cartoon Is Cultural Icon." *Washington Post*, July 1, A18.

Feldman, Allen. 1991. *Formations of Violence: The Narrative of the Body and Political Terror in Northern Ireland*. Chicago: Chicago University Press.

Flores, Juan. 2009. *The Diaspora Strikes Back: Caribeño Tales of Learning and Turning*. New York: Routledge.

Fox, Patricia. 2006. *Being and Blackness in Latin America: Uprootedness and Improvisation*. Gainesville: University of Florida Press.

Gilmore, Ruth Wilson. 2002. "Fatal Couplings of Power and Difference: Notes on Racism and Geography." *Professional Geographer* 54, no. 1: 15–24.

———. 2007. *Golden Gulag: Prisons, Surplus, Crisis, and Opposition in Globalizing California*. Berkeley: University of California Press.

Goldiner, Dave. 2005. "Mexico Prez: Cartoon Not Racist." *Daily News* (New York), July 1, 18.

Gramsci, Antonio. 1992. *Prison Notebooks*. Edited by Joseph Buttigieg; translated by Joseph Buttigieg and Antonio Callari. New York: Columbia University Press.

Gudmunson, Lowell, and Justin Wolfe. 2010. *Blacks and Blackness in Central America*. Durham, NC: Duke University Press.

Hall, Stuart. 1993. "What Is This 'Black' in Black Popular Culture?" *Social Justice* 20, nos. 1–2: 104–14.

———. 1996. "Gramsci's Relevance for the Study of Race and Ethnicity." In *Stuart Hall: Critical Dialogues in Cultural Studies*, edited by David Morley and Kuan-Hsing Chen, 411–41. New York: Routledge.

Hall, Stuart, Chas Critcher, Tony Jefferson, John Clarke, and Brian Roberts. 1978. *Policing the Crisis: Mugging, the State, and Law and Order*. London: Macmillan.

Hernández Cuevas, Marco Polo. 2004. *African Mexicans and the Discourse on Modern Nation*. Lanham, MD: University Press of America.

Jiménez Román, Miriam, and Juan Flores. 2010. *The Afro-Latin@ Reader: History and Culture in the United States*. Durham, NC: Duke University Press.

Joseph, Gilbert M., and Daniel Nugent. 1994. *Everyday Forms of State Formation: Revolution and the Negotiation of Rule in Modern Mexico*. Durham, NC: Duke University Press.

Joseph, Gilbert M., Anne Rubenstein, and Eric Zolov. 2001. *Fragments of a Golden Age: The Politics of Culture in Mexico Since 1940*. Durham, NC: Duke University Press.

Katerí Hernández, Tanya. 2007. "Latino Anti-Black Violence: 'Not Made in the USA.'" *Harvard Journal of African American Public Policy* 13: 37–40.

Knight, Keith. 2005. *The K Chronicles* (blog). http://www.kchronicles.com/think.html.

Krauze, Enrique. 2005. "The Pride in Memín." *Washington Post*, July 12.

Lee, Morgan. 2005. "Fox Defends Memín as Beloved Image." *Banderas News* (Puerto Vallarta, Mexico), July. http://banderasnews.com/0507/nr-foxdefends.htm.

Lott, Eric. 1996. "Blackface and Blackness: The Minstrel Show in American Culture." In *Inside the Minstrel Mask: Readings in Nineteenth-century Blackface Minstrelsy*, edited by Annemarie Bean, James Vernon Hatch, and Brooks McNamara, 3–34. Middletown, CT: Wesleyan University Press.

Malkin, Elisabeth. 2005. "Fight Grows Over a Stamp U.S. Sees as Racist and Mexico Adores." *New York Times*, July 2.

Malvido, Adriana, and Teresa Martínez. 2005. "Es mucho lo que ha dejado la historieta como para tratarla mal." *Proceso*, July 3.

Massey, Doreen. 1994. *Space, Place, and Gender*. Minneapolis: University of Minnesota Press.

McKinley, James C. Jr. 2005. "Mexican Stamp Sets Off a New Racial Fracas." *New York Times*, July 1, 2.

Melamed, Jodi. 2011. *Represent and Destroy: Rationalizing Violence in the New Racial Capitalism*. Minneapolis: University of Minnesota Press.

Moraga, Cherríe. 1994. *Heroes and Saints & Other Plays*. Albuquerque: West End Press.

Notimex. 2005. "Aparecerá *Memín Pinguín* en 750 mil sellos postales." *La Crónica*, June 28.

Omi, Michael, and Howard Winant. 1994. *Racial Formation in the United States: From the 1960s to the 1990s*. New York: Routledge.

Okeowo, Alexis. 2010. "Mexico's Hidden Blacks." *1843* (magazine), February 9. https://www.1843magazine.com/content/places/alexis-okeowo/black-mexicans.

Pabst, Naomi. 2006. "'Mama, I'm Walking to Canada': Black Geopolitics and Invisible Empires." In Clarke and Thomas 2006, 112–32.

Palapa, Fabiola, Ericka Montaño, and Monica Mateos. 2005. "Memín Pinguín 'no es el icono popular del racismo en México.'" *La Jornada*, July 1.

Reuters. 2005a. "Mexicans Flock to Buy Stamp Criticized in US." *Washington Post*, July 2.

———. 2005b. "World Briefing, Americas: Mexico: Black Group Protests Stamps." *New York Times*, July 5, 6.

Rowell, Charles H. 2004. "'Todos Somos Primos'/We Are All Cousins: The Editor's Notes." *Callaloo* 27, no. 1: xi–xiv.

Rubenstein, Anne. 1998. *Bad Language, Naked Ladies, and Other Threats to the Nation*. Durham, NC: Duke University Press.

Sassen, Saskia. 2001. "Spatialities and Temporalities of the Global: Elements for Theorization." In *Globalization*, edited by Arjun Appadurai, 260–78. Durham, NC: Duke University Press.

Schmidt Camacho, Alicia R. 2005. "Cuidadana X: Gender Violence and the Denationalization of Women's Rights in Ciudad Juarez, Mexico." *CR: The New Centenial Review* 5, no.1: 255–92.

Smith, Neil. 1993. "Contours of a Spatialized Politics: Homeless Vehicles and the Production of Geographic Scale." *Social Text* 33: 54–83.

Vaughn, Bobby. 2005. "Afro-Mexico: Blacks, Indígenas, Politics, and the Greater Diaspora." In Dzidzienyo and Oboler 2005, 117–36.

Vinson, Ben, III. 2000. "The Racial Profile of a Rural Mexican Province in the 'Costa Chica': Igualapa in 1791." *Americas* 57, no. 2: 269–82.

———. 2005. "Afro-Mexican History: Trends and Directions in Scholarship." *History Compass* 3, no. 1: 1–14.

Vinson, Ben, III, and Bobby Vaughn. 2004. *Afroméxico*. Mexico City: Centro de Investigación y Docencia Económicas.

Whitten, Norman E., Jr., and Arlene Torres. 1998. *Blackness in Latin America and the Caribbean: Social Dynamics and Cultural Transformations*. Bloomington: Indiana University Press.

Model or Menace?
Racial Discourses and the Role of Chinese and Mexican Labor at the US-Mexico Border, 1900–1940

Jayson Gonzales Sae-Saue

This article exposes mutually constitutive racial discourses concerning Chinese and Mexican workers at the US-Mexico border at the turn of the twentieth century. During an era in which the United States racially mystified Chinese as an economic menace to the point of their exclusion from immigration and citizenship, Congress and employers responded to the region's need for low-paid workers by imagining positive racial and social identities for Mexicans so that they could be inserted into the depleted labor market. Yet the racial discourses that structured Chinese exclusion through legislation and rendered Mexican labor an acceptable substitute were never merely contextual. Instead, they were mutually formative, with the vilified Chinese providing a foil against which to invent model social identities for the most readily available workforce after Chinese expulsion: Mexicans.

This twinned relationship enabled a remarkable shift in the labor force on both sides of the US-Mexico border. The discourses regarding Chinese and Mexican workers not only shaped the racial makeup of domestic labor markets, which absorbed Mexicans just as rapidly as they expunged Chinese; they also traversed the US-Mexico border to influence the labor configurations of US economic interests abroad, particularly in the Mexican state of Baja California. There, the US agricultural elite successfully reinvented the Chinese worker as a model of economic production. Most notable among these companies was the Colorado River Land Company (CRLC) of the Mexicali Valley, owned by a syndicate led by Harrison Gray Otis, publisher of the *Los Angeles Times*, and Harry Chandler, his son-in-law, who was a Southern California land developer as well as a *Times* executive. The case of the CRLC illustrates how US industry inverted the racial calculus abroad, giving overwhelming preference to Chinese labor over local Mexicans while it favored Mexicans over Asians in their US-based operations due to the Asian exclusionary laws. This is not to suggest that the inverted racial economic structures in the fertile valley stretching between California and Baja California were representative of labor formations throughout the US-Mexico borderlands generally. Rather, the western end of the border was a key site where ideologies concerning Chinese and Mexican workers functioned relationally across racial differences on the one hand, and transnationally across political borders on the other.

This interracial and transnational dynamic speaks to an important confluence between Chinese and Mexican labor histories. Although this entanglement lasted for nearly four decades of the early twentieth century, it remains underexamined in both Chicana/o and Asian American studies. In order to understand the era that saw one of the largest flows of Mexicans into the United States, we must examine how US industry and government managed Chinese social identities at and beyond the US-Mexico border. To this end, this essay bridges emergent critical interests in cross-racial and transnational formations in Chicana/o and Asian American studies.

In Chicana/o studies, hemispheric models of critical analysis have allowed scholars to investigate broadly the transnational dynamics of Mexican American social, cultural, and economic life.[1] Although the field has developed fresh perspectives that exceed national (and nationalist) paradigms, it is fair to say that it continues to neglect the intimate relations between Mexican and Chinese histories, privileging hemispheric investigations to the exclusion of trans-Pacific ones (Soldatenko 2009, 182–83). Historian Erika Lee makes a similar point about the dominant axes of analysis in Asian American studies, but with a twist. In a special issue of the *Journal of Asian American Studies*, Lee (2005, 235) notes that trans-Pacific perspectives (which are seldom seen in Chicana/o studies) have crowded out hemispheric evaluations in the field, undermining awareness of the messier histories of Asians that cut across the Americas, writ large.

Despite these tendencies, there exists notable scholarship that exceeds the racial and transnational coordinates that have traditionally bounded historical investigation in these fields, particularly in labor studies. As early as 1935, Carey McWilliams's landmark work on migrant farmworkers in California, *Factories in the Field*, spotlighted the interracial dynamics of the state's labor markets, including the racial ideologies that both mirrored and organized its economic structures. Decades later, Tomás Almaguer (1994, 3) showed that racial discourses both reflected and structured economic conditions in California throughout the nineteenth century; he notes that "the simultaneous interaction of both structural and ideological factors . . . shaped the trajectory of the historical experiences" of a range of racial groups. Yet despite their broad racial purview, both writers framed their insights exclusively within US borders, focusing on California in particular.

Although certainly not alone, Robert Chao Romero's *Chinese in Mexico* (2010) boldly traverses this political boundary, taking a specific interest in Chinese historical lives south of the US-Mexico border. This key study broadens the geographic and racial domains of both Chicana/o and Asian American studies by demonstrating how Chinese lives are deeply embedded in Mexico's national past. Instead of recycling models of US-based investigation, Romero frames his study within Mexico proper to articulate a "rich and controversial history of the Chinese of Mexico [that] has been largely . . . forgotten" and that has been "preserved over the years by [only] a handful of Mexican and U.S. historians" (2010, 6–7).

This essay enriches this history by exploring how ideologies structuring Chinese life in Mexico effectively cut both northward and southward across the western end of the US-Mexico frontier. The relational discourses that coded Chinese and Mexican labor in the California–Baja California valley helped secure a divided workforce for US business both domestically and abroad. In moving this discussion forward, this article aims to suture this division by spotlighting the shared regional histories of Chicana/os and Asian Americans—histories that scholars like McWilliams, Almaguer, Romero, and a handful of others have shown can no longer be confined by the racial and national boundaries that traditionally organize ethnic American studies.

Chinese and Mexican Labor: Early Twentieth-Century Abstractions

Chinese began arriving in significant numbers in the US West in the midnineteenth century. They participated actively in the California gold rush and made contributions to regional industries across the former Mexican territories, initially as miners and later as farmers, field laborers, and workers for the Central Pacific Railroad. As a consequence of the low wages Chinese earned in this process of capitalist expansion across the West, US Anglos began to view them as a racial threat to labor markets and to cultural institutions of white society (Almaguer 1994, 6). This led to their exclusion from immigration and naturalization through the Chinese Exclusion Act of 1882.

Afterward, capitalists in the region's thriving economy began recruiting other Asian populations, notably Japanese, to keep wages low and profits high. Like the Chinese, the Japanese impinged on US labor markets by underbidding other workers, and they also began to develop modest farming operations that offered potential competition to Anglo small farmers. It therefore did not take long before US politicians, white labor groups, and US small farming interests redirected racial fears toward the Japanese and other Asians. The Japanese, like the Chinese before them, became subject to federal efforts to curtail their immigration. In 1907 a "Gentleman's Agreement" between the United States and Japan served to restrict Japanese entry into the United States. This was followed by the Immigration Act of 1917, which banned immigration from what it identified as an "Asiatic Barred Zone." The Immigration Act of 1924 (the Johnson-Reed Act) then finalized Asian exclusion from immigration, stipulating that these populations were racially ineligible for citizenship.

In response to this racial legislation, industry leaders in the West began to view Mexican labor as an ideal replacement for the excluded Asian workers. The period of Asian withdrawal from the labor market coincided with a period of intense growth in a number of economic sectors, particularly land development and agriculture. On the heels of the Immigration Act of 1924, C. S. Brown of the American Farm Bureau Federation put the matter bluntly before Congress, warning that the "process of development [in the West] will be stagnated unless we get the kind of labor that in our opinion is the only kind that is in sight—namely, Mexican labor" (US House of Representatives 1926, 33).

And there was plenty of Mexican labor in sight. As the number of Chinese, Japanese, and other Asians in the United States declined steeply under exclusion laws, the number of Mexicans doubled to over 650,000 in a single decade, 1910–20 (Cardoso 1980, 37). In California the Mexican population swelled from nearly 10,000 in 1900 to nearly 200,000 in 1930. In Texas it ballooned from 70,000 to over 260,000 in the same period (Gutiérrez 1995, 56). Nonetheless, US farmers continued to express a dire need for even more workers from the south.

Controls at the US-Mexico border in the early twentieth century largely ignored the Mexican influx into the region. In light of the booming Western economy, and with all the focus on excluding Asians, Mexican nationals were granted permission to cross the border with few formalities so that they could assume railroad and agricultural positions largely vacated by Chinese and Japanese (Ngai 2004, 64). According to Lee (2003, 171), nearly 1.4 million Mexicans entered the country both legally and illegally during the first three decades of the century. Meanwhile, enforcement officials concentrated their efforts almost exclusively on apprehending Chinese seeking illegal entry into the United States from Mexico (Delgado 2004).[2] In this sense, the substantial rise in Mexican immigration marks the Asian exclusion era as a key moment in the Mexican labor diaspora, and it demands an examination of how the legal production of Mexicans as a suitable labor force was imagined against the depiction of Asians as an excludable threat.

The Immigration Act of 1924 exempted Mexico and other countries of the Western Hemisphere from numerical quotas. Furthermore, Mexicans were shielded for a time from immigration restrictions on grounds of their racial eligibility for US citizenship. After the US-Mexican War (1846–48), the United States agreed by treaty to confer citizenship rights on former Mexican citizens living in the areas that had been ceded by Mexico. It therefore defined this population as legally white, since naturalization could only be applied to "free white persons."[3] Partly for this reason, US industry viewed Mexican immigrants as the perfect substitute for Asian labor. Their positive labor value, however, was never only an issue of legal admissibility. It was also affirmed through discursive practices that cast Mexicans as socially constructive to US society and through racial ideologies that imagined them in contradistinction to Asians, particularly Chinese. In other words, while the Asian exclusion acts produced social identities for Asians according to a racial meaning (Ngai 2004), they also established a vocabulary with which to calibrate favorably the labor and social identities of the Mexicans who represented the most available labor force in the US West.

This project of imbuing Mexican labor with positive social value was not easy, however, for Mexicans had long experienced the realities of racial difference in US culture and society. Although they were legally white by default, the social identity of Mexicans in the areas formerly owned by Mexico and of Mexican immigrants seeking entry after the war was hardly equal to that of their Anglo and European counterparts. For Mexican immigrants in particular, their social identity as "other" threatened their legal standing as white and thus jeopardized their racially eligibility for immigration and naturalization. Indeed, in the decades following the United States' acquisition of Mexican territory, individual states and Anglo labor groups regularly sought to restrict Mexican immigration by pushing for exclusionary legislation. In doing so, they often emphasized the Mexicans' indigenous heritage to disprove their status as white and to argue their ineligibility for entry and naturalization.

In re Rodríguez (1897) is perhaps the best-known case in which the US courts deliberated the racial categorization of Mexicans for the purposes of determining their rights to naturalization. When Ricardo Rodríguez of Mexico applied for citizenship in Texas, the Naturalization Board viewed him as Indian and therefore rejected his application on the basis that the United States only conferred citizenship on whites and free blacks. The San Antonio circuit court heard Rodríguez's appeal, and despite viewing him as a person lacking moral character, it upheld his right to naturalization based on international laws cited by the Treaty of Guadalupe Hidalgo. Although Rodríguez won his appeal, his case demonstrates the social perception of Mexicans as racially other, despite their legal standing as white.

The legacy of this racist perspective manifested itself in government-sponsored studies on the social impact of Mexican immigration. For example, the Commission of Immigration and Housing of California, seeking to explain the vast economic inequities between whites and Mexicans at the turn of the century, made plain its racist understanding of these conditions by attributing Mexican poverty to biological essentialisms: "immigrants of this [Mexican] race seem to have a specific gravity which keeps them at the bottom of the district melting pot . . . the Mexicans who come to us are . . . a primitive people, more Indian than Latin" (1916, 143). From Texas to California, the legal categorization of Mexicans as white hardly made them immune to racial discourses that constructed their social identities as "primitive."

Congressman John Box of eastern Texas regularly deployed similar essentialist views during his efforts to restrict Mexican immigration during his tenure in government (1919–31). For more than a decade, he worked feverishly to push legislation that would place immigration quotas on Mexico. However, after the Immigration Acts of 1917 and 1924 banned nearly all immigrants from the Asian continent, the labor shortage in the West became acute. In this context, elite economic actors and select members of the US government began to challenge Box's essentialist views of Mexicans, recalibrating their social identities for the purpose of securing their labor.

This process is made plain by the many congressional hearings on immigration in the years immediately following the exclusionary acts of

1907, 1917, and 1924. For example, on the heels of the Immigration Act of 1924, the Committee on Immigration and Naturalization gathered in 1926 to discuss agricultural laborers from Mexico. In this instance, Congressman Box emphasized before business leaders that the Mexican's "detrimental" and "impure" racial character outweighed his labor value. To prove his point that Mexicans were not sufficiently white, Box opened one session with a racially charged query: "Is it not true that the population of Mexico is overwhelmingly Indian in character? . . . The great part of it is pure-blood Indian and the rest mixed blood" (US House of Representatives 1926, 143). Box repeatedly challenged his listeners to respond to the indigenous elements of Mexico's racial history. Although legally white as a consequence of US expansion, Mexicans were not, Box insisted, racially pure, and he repeatedly asserted the Mexican indigenous lineage as grounds for this group's exclusion.

Faced with severe labor shortages in the West, many business representatives and agriculturalists disagreed with Box. Yet they found themselves compelled to address this economic dilemma within the parameters of a racial discourse that Box and other exclusionists had firmly established prior to their testimony before Congress. Business leaders therefore responded to Box mainly by describing Mexicans not as efficient work hands, but as racially and socially acceptable. For example, E. K. Cumming of the Nogales Chamber of Commerce joined his colleagues from Los Angeles to portray Mexican workers as belonging to a race largely distinct from "Indians." He performed a rhetorical somersault that racialized Mexicans as "Spanish" and therefore European, yet also as a racial and social group similar to ordinary Americans. He stated defiantly, "We have a great many [Mexicans] of our population [in the US West] who are as fine people as a person could meet. . . . Their [character and] mode of living is equally as good as that of the average American family" (US House of Representatives 1926, 138). Members of Congress pressed Cumming and his colleagues to elaborate, asking whether there was "any particular social line drawn between Mexicans and Americans of the same relative class?"—to which Cumming plainly yet powerfully responded: "No" (140).

Cumming's strategy in making a case for Mexican workers was clear: to emphasize their Spanish roots, cast them as racially distinct from "Indians," and equate their social qualities with those of "average Americans" of similar class standing. Central to this was the notion that Mexicans and Anglo Americans shared roots in Europe. In other words, Cumming sought to shift the Mexican racial identity away from its indigenous roots and toward the Anglo American ideal in hopes of bringing more Mexican workers into a depleted labor market. Still, Congressman Box was unimpressed, insisting that "these people down south of the line are Indians" (144). As a retort, Cumming and his partners reminded the congressman from Jacksonville, Texas, a town near the Louisiana border, that those living closer to Mexico "refer to a Mexican as entirely different from what we refer to as an Indian" (144).

Seemingly anticipating Congressman Box's resistance, Cumming's associate from the Los Angeles Chamber of Commerce, Charles Bayer, took a more drastic approach. In his testimony, Bayer imagined Mexican labor as the engine that would drive the national economy forward: "If we do not help build up the surrounding country and the Pacific Southwest [with Mexican workers], we are not going to prosper in Los Angeles, and our people on the outside know that as Los Angeles goes ahead, the surrounding country will also go ahead" (128). Like Cumming, Bayer took a keen interest in refiguring the social identity of Mexican workers. But he also stressed their economic value, casting them as exemplars of the American work ethic and guardians of US economic prosperity. According to Bayer, California is the economic epicenter of the United States, and the nation's financial survival would depend on securing committed Mexican workers, who, he assured Congress, would not be "more of a [public] charge than other nationalities" (132).

These congressional hearings in 1926 were not the first to consider the social and racial qualities of Mexican labor; a number of others had been organized earlier, following passage of the Asian exclusion laws. For example, immediately after the Chinese Exclusion Act became permanent in 1907, the US Immigration Commission was formed to study the social impact of all immigrants. Referred to as the Dillingham Commission after its chairman, William Paul Dillingham, the panel worked from 1907 to 1911 to prepare its findings. Its final report imagines the racial threats posed by a range of "undesirable" immigrants, and in the context of the West, it vividly fantasizes about the hazards that Chinese and other Asians presented for US society.

The Dillingham Commission concluded that immigrants from China in particular posed a serious and credible threat to US society and culture, despite the economic gains to be had from their labor power. In its final report on the Pacific Coast and Rocky Mountain states, the commission acknowledges the economic benefits of Asian workers generally and of Chinese labor specifically: "[In] the beet-sugar industry in several [Western] States and certain other agricultural industries in California . . . many localities have for years relied upon Asiatic labor. . . . Though many ranchers think that for social reasons it would be a mistaken policy to readmit the Chinese, they generally regard Asiatic laborers as indispensible to the prosperity and expansion of the agricultural industries" (US Senate 1911, 667, 672). Yet the report goes on to underscore the racial menace that Asian workers posed due to their alleged inability to assimilate into Anglo American society: "Whatever the capacity of these [Asian] races for assimilation may be . . . a situation has developed which has greatly retarded or prevented the desired end, so that the Chinese who have been here for many years have been assimilated to only a slight extent" (692). The commission therefore recommended, for reasons having more to do with race than economics, that the government make no move to renew Chinese immigration.

Having imagined Chinese workers as an economic force with an unfortunate racial predisposition to social failure, the commission presents a quite different view of Mexican immigrants. Indeed, the Mexicans already seemed a viable replacement for Chinese and other Asian laborers in the booming agricultural industry. The US Department of Commerce and Labor in 1908 described Mexican workers as "docile, patient, usually orderly in camp, fairly intelligent under competent supervision, obedient, and cheap. . . . [The Mexican's] strongest point is his willingness to work for a low wage" (496). The members of the Dillingham Commission concurred with this racial abstraction of the Mexican worker's redeeming social and economic qualities. While underscoring the racial menace posed by Asian labor, the Dillingham report imagined Mexicans as

> providing a fairly acceptable supply of labor in a limited territory in which it is difficult to secure others. . . . [Mexicans'] competitive ability is limited because of their more or less temporary residence and their personal qualities, so that their incoming does not involve the same detriment to labor conditions as is involved in the immigration of other races who also work at comparatively low wages. . . . At present the Chinese laborers are excluded from . . . the United States by law. . . . Elsewhere the Commission has recommended that no change be made in the present policy of the Government as regards the immigration of Chinese. (US Senate 1911, 691)

In an era in which the United States banned Asian immigrants, business and government leaders repeatedly invented favorable "personal qualities" of Mexican workers so that they could be inserted into the nation's racialized economic order. In particular, the Dillingham Commission argued that because they were migratory seasonal laborers, taking up "more or less temporary residence," Mexicans—unlike Chinese—posed no long-term peril to labor or market conditions. It noted that Mexicans could not threaten Anglo businesses because of their "limited" competitive ability relative to Asians, who had begun commercial farming operations throughout the West. And in order to solidify ethnic and cultural distinctions between these labor groups, the US government often stressed that Mexicans, unlike Asians, are Catholic, have European ancestry, and speak a romance language (Almaguer 1994, 8).

These redeeming qualities afforded Mexicans something approaching model status in an Anglo national imagination that was ambivalent about Chinese contributions to US labor and obsessed with the presumed Asian peril to society. E. K. Cumming's and Charles Bayer's testimony on the racial qualities of Mexican workers, coupled with the US Bureau of Labor's and Dillingham Commission's findings of Mexicans as "docile," "orderly," "competent," and "obedient," establish what we might call a *Mexican model minority* discourse. Portrayed as fine workers and as racially and socially virtuous subjects, Mexicans became ideal candidates to fill jobs left vacant by Chinese, Japanese, and other Asian workers in Western fields. The discursive production of Mexicans as a model low-wage substitute for Asians ensured a steady supply of their labor even as it perpetuated the historical production of Asians as a "yellow peril," underscoring the twinned relationship between these groups.

Stuart Hall (1996, 436) describes the ways in which government and industry "harness and exploit [the] particularistic qualities of labour power." In this instance, faced with the demand for cheap workers, the US Congress and American capitalists negotiated multiple levels of racial difference between Chinese and Mexican workers, contributing to their legal and social construction as distinct representations of either antagonistic or model racial otherness. This is an example of how US economic development perpetuates, rather than erases, divisions between workers. While casting Asians as a menace in need of legal exclusion, Congress and employers in the US West responded to the area's need for low-paid labor by imagining Mexicans as obedient and competitively limited, recasting these characteristics as ethnic virtues in the labor market.

The Colorado River Land Company and US Support for Chinese Workers South of the Border

The construction of Asians as a racial menace to US labor and society, and the corresponding invention of Mexicans as model workers for their replacement, helped secure large labor flows from the south. To add to this massive movement of Mexican workers, the US Asian exclusion era coincided with the Mexican Revolution (1910–17), which many Mexicans sought to escape by fleeing across the border. This exodus contributed to a labor shortage in many regions of Mexico's north just as the aggressive neoliberal policies of President Porfirio Díaz (1876–80; 1884–1911) were opening up jobs. During his tenure, Díaz planned to turn Mexico's barren northern borderlands into a profitable, economically vibrant region that would be driven mainly by foreign investment.

To be sure, Díaz imagined this project of northern development as a means to recruit European immigrants specifically. The Mexican president based this preference on three principles: the Europeans' supposedly easy assimilation, their physical beauty, and their value as a counterweight to US influence (Cardiel Marín 1997, 196). In other words, the ideal colonists for Díaz were European, Catholic, and good-looking. Díaz structured his vision according to an ideology of racial mixing that included the *blanqueamiento* (whitening) of the nation in order to dilute its various racial and ethnic differences. Unsurprisingly, Mexico's European ethnocentrism under the Díaz regime viewed Chinese as undesirable. In a move that mimicked US legislative inquiries regarding Chinese influences on US society, Díaz appointed a federal commission in 1903 to study the social and economic value of these immigrants for Mexico. Echoing US findings on the same question, Díaz's commission depicted the Chinese as a threat to the nation based on their racial inability to assimilate, their unfair labor practices, and their menacing cultural influences (Comisión de Inmigración 1911).

However, few European immigrants made their way to northern Mexico, while many of Mexico's own citizens recognized greater opportunities across the border. Facing a labor shortage, the Díaz government therefore allowed Chinese to continue to immigrate in order to provide manpower for its economic modernization plan. This plan was largely propelled by Mexico's Ley de Deslinde y Colonización (Law of Demarcation and Colonization, 1883), which allowed foreign industries to survey huge tracts of land with a guaranteed right to assume ownership of one-third of the areas under inspection. The remainder of the land was then sold in vast strips for prices well below market value (Keen and Hayes 2009, 249).

One US company in particular took great advantage of this favorable proposition. The CRLC, led by Harry Chandler, purchased large tracts of land in Mexico upon the company's founding in 1902, and by 1905 it controlled nearly 850,000 acres of the Mexicali Valley, the extension of California's Imperial Valley lying south of the border. The CRLC was one of the largest US-owned agricultural corporations in northern Mexico. Instead of using local Mexican labor to clear the land for cultivation, the CRLC recruited thousands of Chinese workers who could not gain access to US labor markets. In sum, Mexican migrations northward, Asian exclusion from US immigration, Mexico's liberal economic policies, and US land investments south of the border collectively set the stage for a diaspora of Chinese laborers into Baja California.[4]

The United States had closed its Pacific gateway to Asian labor through its exclusion acts, but it found backdoor access to cheap and productive Chinese workers in Mexico. While US business interests preferred Mexican workers over Chinese for their domestic operations, they inverted this preference abroad, and in doing so recalibrated the economic characteristics ascribed to Chinese labor. Although the US State Department remained ambivalent about thousands of Chinese workers living just miles from the US border, it overwhelmingly supported US businesses in Baja California that hired Chinese and privileged them over local workers.

Indeed, even as the US government continued to condemn Asian immigrants to the point of their formal exclusion in 1924, the US State Department developed a favorable attitude toward the Chinese working in Mexico. For example, the US consul in Baja California portrayed the Chinese as model employees after having witnessed a decade of their work in US industries. In language that bore a striking similarity to the US Department of Commerce and Labor's 1908 portrait of Mexicans in the United States as "docile, patient, usually orderly in camp, fairly intelligent under competent supervision, obedient, and cheap," consul Walter Boyle (1920) described the *Chinese* in Baja California as "supplying an uncomplaining, hardworking, wealth producing subject of exploitation. The favorable condition being that the Chinaman expects to be exploited. . . . [The Chinaman is] quite honest in meeting his commercial obligations." In other words, the Chinese were no longer an inscrutable menace to the market, at least not in Mexico. Instead, they were recognized in the same favorable terms earlier used to describe Mexican laborers in the United States—as "honest" and "hardworking" laborers essential to US economic interests.

Although several US industries in Mexico relied heavily on Chinese workers, perhaps no other US company better exploited their labor in Mexico's north than the Colorado River Land Company. Owing to global demand for cotton, the CRLC began developing the crop throughout the Mexicali Valley, and it relied almost exclusively on Chinese land tenants to do so. Harry Chandler and his business partners were highly familiar with the Chinese work ethic and with the legal situation of Chinese workers in the United States. For this reason, the company explicitly recruited Chinese laborers displaced from US industries to develop its nearly 1 million acres of land in Baja California, while it consigned others directly from Asia (Duncan 1994, 623).

The governor of Baja California, Esteban Cantú Jiménez (1911–20), accommodated the CRLC's demands for Chinese workers. Already a coronel in the federal army by the time he arrived in Baja California in 1911, Cantú relied on his rank and military relations to profit considerably from Chinese labor and CRLC investments. In order to pay for local infrastructure and soldiers, and to ensure his own personal monetary gains, Cantú imposed hefty export tariffs on US companies along with heavy head taxes on Chinese workers entering the district, fees regularly paid by their employers. In light of the economic rewards the Chinese afforded Cantú, the governor provided them his explicit "promotion and protection," and Chinese lessees of the CRLC began to cultivate cotton in the Mexicali desert at unprecedented levels (Cardiel Marín 1997, 215).

With the Mexican Revolution already in full frenzy, the onset of World War I in 1914 further drove up the global and regional demand for cotton. The CRLC and other US cotton growers in Baja California responded by hiring an unprecedented number of Chinese workers to expand production. Carmen Becerra writes:

> Las compañías extranjeras [en Baja California] preferían a los chinos, porque decían que eran incansables en el trabajo—y que muchas veces se les vió trabajar de noche. . . . Ellos trabajaban jornadas hasta 12 horas diarias, se cree que por cada 10 hectáreas abiertas al cultivo había un chino muerto. (Foreign companies [in Baja California] preferred Chinese workers because they were said to be tireless—and often they could be seen working at night. . . . They worked up to twelve hours daily, and it was believed that for every ten hectares of land opened to cultivation, there was one dead Chinese.) (1990, 53)

Although it is most likely hyperbole that one Chinese died for every ten hectares of land cultivated in Baja California, this statement reflects the popular perception of the intense Chinese labor presence in the area. What is certain is that the Chinese were primarily responsible for opening the Mexicali Valley to profit-seeking global agribusiness firms. They did so both as lessees of the CRLC and as planters funded by other US-owned interests, such as the Mexican-Chinese Ginning Company, a business with no Chinese or Mexican ownership. Tax records indicate that by 1915, with the assistance of Chinese labor, cotton became the undisputed principal commodity of Baja California's economy. It was the single most valuable import registered by the Customs Office for the District of Southern California that year, with tariffs totaling over $900,000 (the equivalent of more than $23 million in current prices). This tally represents more than three times that of cattle ($230,000), Mexico's second-largest taxable export into Southern California during the same year (US Customs Service 1915).

Although cotton production in the Mexicali Valley and tariffs for its import into the United States stagnated during the 1920s, the CRLC, along with other US-owned cotton interests, had established a well-organized transnational and interracial economic order in the region. Domestically, this order was sustained by Asian exclusion on racial pretenses and their replacement by Mexican immigrants. In California, Mexicans made up 75 percent of the agricultural workforce by 1920 (Takaki 1989, 30). Furthermore, until the 1930s they were a large contingent in mining, railway, construction, and land development projects throughout the West, including Harry Chandler's real estate ventures in Southern California. Chandler played a major role in developing much of California's San Fernando Valley, largely through a Mexican workforce. In Baja California, however, US industry and the CRLC in particular depended overwhelmingly on Chinese workers instead of Mexicans. As a result of the high profits reaped through Chinese labor, by the mid-1920s the CRLC was invested almost exclusively in plantations leased to Chinese and Japanese farmers, mostly on large-acreage contracts. Owing to the substantial returns to the company on these high-interest, profit-sharing contracts, Chinese held 56 of the CRLC's 95 leases in the mid-1920s, and Japanese lessees held 22. While the company awarded 78 of its 95 contracts to Asians, it awarded only 9 to Mexicans (Duncan 1994, 636). As day laborers, as small investors working with high-interest moneylenders in the United States, or as high-paying tenants of the CRLC, the Chinese alone raised 80 percent of Mexicali's cotton crop in this era (Hu-DeHart 1985–86, 10).

Only a steady increase in the numbers of Mexicans in the United States and a constant flow of Chinese workers south of the border could maintain this transnational and racial economic order. Indeed, between 1920 and 1930 the Mexican population in the United States doubled, reaching well over half a million (Cardoso 1980, 37). Meanwhile, the Chinese population in Mexico also increased significantly. By 1921 the Chinese made up the second-largest foreign-born population in Mexico, behind Spanish nationals (Camposortega Cruz 1997, 41). In the Mexicali

Valley specifically, estimates put the number of Chinese residents in 1921 at 10,000 (Velázquez Morales 2001, 59–60); recent scholarship suggests that this is a modest figure and that there were as many as 20,000 Chinese in the Mexicali Valley by the 1930s (Chang 2010, 10).[5]

The substantial number of Chinese living and working just miles from the US border had already garnered the attention of border agents responsible for apprehending those that might attempt to cross illegally into the United States. Indeed, the shift that placed the Bureau of Immigration under the authority of the Department of Commerce and Labor in 1903 was a direct attempt to "strengthen controls at the Mexican border," given the growing number of illegal Chinese entries in this period (Delgado 2004, 197). Border agents in Southern California also worked to thwart intricate smuggling operations spearheaded by Chinese nationals living in Baja California. Given the availability of jobs in Mexicali, agents remained suspicious of the motives of the Chinese they caught attempting to enter, assuming them to be part of a larger trafficking network that moved whiskey, cigars, and opium into the United States without paying proper tariffs. Chinese who claimed they were crossing in order to "look for work" in the United States immediately raised doubts, for the CRLC and other US-funded cotton operations south of the border had a critical need for cheap workers across hundreds of thousands of acres of the Mexicali Valley.

Luis Chong, a Chinese national from Taishan who had adopted a Mexican name, was caught trying to enter the United States from Mexicali in 1917. During the interview, examining officer A. A. Musgrave dismissed Chong's claims that he was seeking work:

> MUSGRAVE: What is your occupation?
> CHONG: I'm just a farm laborer.
> MUSGRAVE: And where were you going last night when the officers stopped you?
> CHONG: I wanted to go to Brawley California to find work. I couldn't find work in Mexicali, Mexico for two months.
> MUSGRAVE: *The farmers in Mexicali, Mexico state they can't get men enough to do their work, what's the matter?* (Chong 1917; emphasis added)

Although Musgrave and his colleagues eventually put aside their doubts that Chong may have been seeking to move commodities and skirt paying taxes, their disbelief than any "Chinaman" could not find work in Mexicali pervaded their examination of this case and others like it. As early as 1902, years before Chong's arrest, an agent from the San Diego District referred to Mexicali as "the Mecca of Chinese laborers" (Office of the Collector of Customs 1902).

If it was a haven for Chinese laborers, Mexicali was also a place where Mexicans found it difficult to compete for work. This reputation dogged the governors who succeeded Cantú in Baja California after 1920. Furthermore, the Mexican federal government started to pressure the region's leadership to restrict Chinese immigration amid the growing racial emphasis of Mexico's revolutionary-era politics. Transnational shareholding, US funding privileges for Chinese-operated plantations, and US support for Chinese merchants who imported their products almost exclusively from the United States fueled the ire of locals across the Mexican north. The national revolution had already mobilized *movimientos anti-Chinos* (anti-Chinese movements) in other regions of Mexico, and it was only a matter of time before similar campaigns erupted throughout Baja California.

Violent expressions of anti-Asian sentiment first surfaced in Mexico's interior in 1911. In that year, the Mexican revolutionary army massacred over 300 Chinese and a few Japanese in Torreón after taking the city from the federal army and blaming these foreigners for exacerbating poverty in the area (Dennis 1979, 67). The US consul in the region reported that civilian mobs had joined revolutionary soldiers in pillaging businesses and homes while carrying out a series of gruesome murders (Romero 2010, 152). In one case, attackers severed the head of a Chinese resident and tossed it into the street; other Chinese had their bodies cut to pieces with swords. Locals even quartered a Chinese man by attaching his arms and legs to four horses and driving them in different directions. And the young were not spared. One soldier is reported to have grabbed a boy by his ankles and swung his head into a lamppost, shattering his skull (Romero 2010, 152). The Chinese government hired a US law firm specializing in foreign interests in Mexico to investigate the massacre. The law firm Wilfley and Bassett secured a paltry indemnity of approximately $3 million to be paid by Mexico to China in compensation for the lives of its citizens (154–55).

The Chinese massacre marks a sadistic episode of the Mexican Revolution as well as a transition toward violent measures to ensure the expropriation of foreign assets. This incident also signals a shift toward popular struggles that linked the masses and local visions of economic (and racial) autonomy to ideologies emanating from the nation's larger provinces, most of which decried foreign interests. Although the revolution's figureheads held different visions of Mexico's future economic and racial order, the violence in Torreón makes clear the determination to exclude Chinese. It was not long before the momentum of this racial dimension of the revolution shifted northward, and by 1916 more than a hundred Chinese lost their lives in the border state of Sonora alone (Hu-DeHart 1982, 290). Along with physical intimidation and violence, local municipalities also attempted to pass a variety of ordinances levied directly against Chinese interests between 1916 and 1920, including steep hikes in municipal taxes and laws prohibiting Chinese from using leased land for agricultural development. Meanwhile, China had no consular stations in Mexico to support its nationals after the fall of the Qing Empire in 1911, which left the embattled nation with only a few diplomatic representatives around the world.

Responding to the anti-Asian politics in Baja California, both local government officials and US government representatives worked to assist the Chinese labor and merchant groups in the area. To be sure, the US defense of the Chinese in Mexico was less a policy of humanitarian aid than an effort to protect US financial interests, especially those having to do with US exports and rent collections on land leased out by US companies. For these reasons, US consulates successfully pressured senior Mexican officials in Baja California not to cooperate with populist anti-Chinese campaigns, for doing so would disrupt US-Chinese relations expressed in patron-client and landlord-lessee relationships in Mexico's profitable agricultural and trade industries. Seeking to maintain the racialized economic order of the region, the US government worked to safeguard the Chinese in Baja California even as it continued to vilify Asians within its own borders.

The US State Department also recognized that Chinese exclusions in Mexico would almost certainly set off a new wave of emigration northward. For this reason, US consular representatives appealed to the Chinese community to remain in Mexico despite the risks of personal violence and property seizure. In order to prevent a northern exodus of Chinese, US consuls in Mexico frequently provided legal advice on Chinese complaints and informed the Chinese community of its rights under Mexican law. The State Department also brought political pressure on the Mexican national government, threatening a shift in economic relations and a complete pullout of US investments if Mexico chose to support regional anti-Chinese movements.

Expelling the Chinese from Mexico and "Asianizing" Mexicans in the United States

The US support for Chinese abroad, and for Mexicans within US borders, came to an end with the onset of the Great Depression, once again reveal-ing how the racial identities of these groups were built on interrelated economic tropes that cast them as either model or menace. US industries on both sides of the border collapsed, and US government and industry leaders deferred to growing nationalist labor restrictions in Baja California and within US borders. Domestically, rhetoric about the threat of Mexican labor came to a head in the 1930s and once again echoed loudly in the halls of Congress.

Harry Chandler emerged as a key agent committed to maintaining the transnational economy his industries supported. As a principal owner of the CRLC, Chandler sought to maintain a supply of Mexican workers for his US-based operations and to prevent Mexican repatriation from disrupting the Chinese labor schemes of his Mexican-based enterprises. Accordingly, he pleaded with the US Congress to halt the growing number of deportations of Mexicans and Mexican Americans to Mexico, where his company was enjoying twenty years of a near monopoly using Chinese workers. Chandler argued against their deportation by explicitly invoking the US government's racial abstraction of Mexicans expressed only two decades earlier by the Dillingham Commission.

In his 1930 testimony to Congress, Chandler argues that the United States should not deport Mexicans because "the Mexican peon" is an "innocent, friendly, kindly individual. . . . They are not enterprising, of course, like other races, but they are more desirable from our standpoint than any other class of labor that comes, and they create fewer problems" (US House of Representatives 1930). Echoing the Dillingham Commission's favorable yet racialized portrait of Mexican social identity, Chandler stresses that Mexican workers are law-abiding and affable folk. And with the ailing US job market in mind, he repeats the Dillingham Commission's findings that Mexicans have a racial disinclination toward enterprise and thus do not tend to take permanent jobs from Americans or compete with Anglo business. For these reasons, Chandler concludes, Mexican workers represent no permanent peril to the economic and social order of the nation.

Despite his economic clout, Chandler's testimony proved ineffective. In the context of a severely stricken financial market, the United States reassessed the value of Mexican immigration and deported hundreds of thousands of Mexicans and Mexican Americans. In the words of Camille Guérin-Gonzales, during the 1930s over half a million Mexican immigrants and Americans of Mexican descent "became targets of one of the largest mass-removal operations ever sanctioned by the United States government" (1994, 1). Nativists in the US government and business community had inverted the image of the Mexican as a model minority, expressed only decades earlier, by recasting the *same* racial qualities that had previously granted immigration privileges to Mexican laborers as the *very reasons* for their exclusion. Mexican workers, praised as an "acceptable labor supply" by the Dillingham Commission, were now seen as flooding the market; the Mexicans' "limited competitive ability" and lack of enterprising spirit—earlier interpreted as guarantees against a foreign economic take-over—now scripted this population as genetically lazy; and "their more or less temporary residence" now made them vagrants with no permanent commitment to the national community. President Herbert Hoover, who had enthusiastically promoted Mexican workers when he served as the nation's food administrator during World War I, now scapegoated them as one of the primary causes of the economic depression. According to Hoover, Mexicans were un-American and disposable because they took well-paying jobs away from whites and drastically drove down wages in the labor market (Sánchez 1993, 213).

Both in public sentiment and at the highest levels of government, Mexican workers once again assumed identities that were closely linked to their perceived role in the nation's economy. Now that their labor was seen as jeopardizing US economic health, the state used imagined racial qualities to position Mexican workers as a threat to US society, as it had previously done with Asian workers. In effect, the public and government "Asianized" Mexicans, casting them as the latest menace to the market and to white cultural institutions. Mexicans could now be blamed for economic conditions on the base of race and ethnicity alone.

In tandem with the program of mass deportation, enforcement measures effectively closed the border to immigrants from the south (Ngai 2004, 255). Furthermore, the US government urged Mexicans and Mexican Americans already within the nation's borders to leave the country "voluntarily." California officials pressured tens of thousands of Mexicans and their US-born children to leave for Mexico by organizing their transit out of the country and by passing legislation that targeted their work and living places (Hoffman 1974). As a result, as many as 600,000 persons of Mexican descent returned to Mexico in the early 1930s. Many of them had already become naturalized US citizens or had children who were citizens by virtue of their US birth (Gutiérrez 1995, 72).

Mass deportations had a major impact on the Chinese labor and merchant populations in Baja California, where the Mexican population skyrocketed. Between 1930 and 1940 the Mexican population in Baja California increased from 48,000 to nearly 80,000 (Cardiel Marín 1997,

203) This severely increased labor competition and disturbed the region's already delicate race relations. Indeed, the repatriations made the relative success of Chinese operations more conspicuous than they had been in previous decades, thereby refueling local anti-Chinese sentiment and persecutions across Mexico's north. Evoking the rhetoric of early anti-Chinese campaigns, nationalists in northern Mexico once again argued that Americans and Chinese only hired Chinese, hoarded profits, and exported Mexican resources out of the country.

Faced with this new surge of anti-Chinese sentiment, Mexico mobilized its own anti-Asian legislative agenda. In Sonora, the government reinstated anti-Chinese legislation that the US State Department had partially thwarted a decade earlier (Dennis 1979; Hu-Dehart 1982). With the collapse of the regional economy, US representatives could no longer exert political pressure on local governments to rescind anti-Chinese laws. Indeed, the US State Department now sent notes to local consuls informing them of a new noninterventionist approach to Latin American domestic affairs stipulated in the 1933 Good Neighbor Policy (Hu-DeHart 1980, 303). In northern Mexico, where the US government had protected Chinese residents, it now argued that the Chinese government was solely responsible for its nationals living and working abroad.

As the United States dumped hundreds of thousands of Mexicans and Mexican Americans back into the desperate conditions of the northern borderlands, it also exported its legislative model for Chinese exclusion. Following the pattern of the Chinese Exclusion Act of 1882 and the Scott Act of 1888, Mexico passed laws in 1929 that prohibited unskilled Chinese workers from entering the national territory (Duncan 1994, 634). While this national *acuerdo* (agreement) affected all foreign workers, it targeted the Chinese as least desirable on racial grounds, in line with ideological visions of the Mexican nation's future racial formation. The nationalistic doctrine of racial mixture, or mestizaje, had emerged prominently during the Mexican Revolution. While postrevolutionary ideologies differed on the place of indigenous roots in this mixed racial identity, all excluded Chinese. Mexican philosopher José Vasconcelos, in his landmark 1925 work *La raza cósmica*, championed Mexico's racial agglomeration as a "cosmic race" of the future, yet he did so by making explicit warnings about the Chinese threat to Mexico's national identity. Vasconcelos wrote, "If we reject the Chinese, it is because man, as he progresses, multiplies less, and feels the horror of numbers, for the same reason that he has begun to value quality" (1997, 20).

Because of this perceived threat to Mexico's future racial makeup, discouraging mixed-race marriages became a popular means of promoting anti-Chinese ideologies. Mexican senator José Angel Espinoza popularized these views when he published *El ejemplo de Sonora* in 1932, a text that presents racist caricatures of Chinese as diseased subhumans who threaten Mexican women. In this work, images of Mexican women function as a synecdoche for the nation. In one memorable portion of Espinoza's text, a cartoon depicts an imprisoned Mexican bride of a Chinese man and their sickly offspring. The caption calls the child "un escupitajo de la naturaleza" (a spit of nature) (Espinoza 1932, 36). Roberto Ham Chande reminds us that over 97 percent of the Chinese population in Mexico during the first half of the twentieth century consisted of males, 84 percent of whom were small-business owners, agricultural laborers, or day workers (1997, 171–85). Espinoza's caricature exploits these demographics in order to articulate a gendered form of Mexico's anti-Chinese rhetoric, effectively allegorizing the nation's economic health and its future racial identity on the body of a Mexican woman.

To be sure, Espinoza's portrait of an abused Mexican bride contributes to the cult of La Malinche, only here the traitorous Mexican woman is corrupted by sex with a Chinese man, instead of a Spaniard.[6] Robert Chao Romero (2010, 89–96) has shown how cultural representations of Chinese-Mexican marriages developed into popular gendered critiques of economic nationalism throughout Mexico in the twentieth century. This gendered strategy proved effective for purposes of passing anti-Chinese legislation, especially in Mexico's north. Local governments passed bans on interracial marriages and ratified a host of laws that targeted Chinese workplaces and living quarters.[7] Collectively these laws amounted to expulsion. While the Mexican government denies expelling the Chinese from this region, huge tax increases and unreasonable employee quotas forced the Chinese in many instances to leave the region voluntarily.

In Baja California specifically, several anti-Chinese committees eyed the success of the nationalists elsewhere in Mexico and began to recruit their leadership. Among the most influential of these committees was the Partido Nacionalista Pro-Raza, founded in 1933. Using measures similar to those employed in Sonora, this group forced the Chinese to liquidate their assets and to abandon the city of Ensenada by 1934. In Mexicali, restrictionists formed the Partido Nacionalista Anti-Chino in 1932; its president was none other than Alfredo Echeverría, a prominent leader of the successful anti-Chinese campaign in Sonora. Heeding these groups' demands, President Pascual Ortiz Rubio (1930–32) announced the federal government's intention to colonize Baja California with Mexicans being repatriated by the United States. The government would do so by appropriating all foreign holdings in the area, including those belonging to the CRLC.

However, it wasn't until anti-Chinese groups in Baja California secured the assistance of President Lázaro Cárdenas (1934–40) that the federal government managed to nationalize capital. Mexico City had already sent General Abelardo Rodríguez to force Cantú to relinquish his governorship in Baja California in 1920 in order to reassert the central government's authority, years before Rodríguez became president in 1932. Rodríguez's successor, Cárdenas, eventually broke up the CRLC through his agrarian reform policies, which expropriated and redistributed US-owned land, delivering a devastating blow to US industries in the region and to all the Chinese living in the Mexicali Valley. To compound these injuries to the Chinese community, Cárdenas implemented rigid Mexican colonization laws that made it illegal to rent land to Chinese planters. As a result of the shift in the region's labor formation, only 600 Chinese lived in Baja California by 1940 as compared to tens of thousands only decades earlier. Many Chinese residents returned to China, some with their Mexican wives and Mexican-born children (Schiavone Camacho 2012). Others made their way across Mexico's borders to seek work in the United States or in other parts of Latin America.

Conclusion

The Chinese Exclusion Act of 1882, the Scott Act of 1888, and the Immigration Acts of 1917 and 1924 systematically excluded nearly all Asians from US immigration and naturalization. In addition to reducing the number of Chinese and other Asian immigrants working in the United States, these laws also produced social and racial identities for Asians and established a vocabulary with which to recalibrate the labor identities of other immigrant groups in the US West. The Asian exclusion acts thus established a racialized social identity for Chinese and other Asian groups against which to imagine the most readily available labor population in the West after Asian expulsion, namely Mexicans.

US discourses that abstracted the identities of Chinese and Mexican workers during the early twentieth century reveal how their immigration rights were repeatedly redefined in relation to labor market conditions. In both their negative and positive iterations, the racial identities imagined for Chinese and Mexicans were bound up with the perceived threats and benefits of inserting their labor into the regional economy. Reports commissioned by Congress and the Department of Labor, coupled with congressional testimony of agricultural elite such as Harry Chandler, E. K. Cumming, and Charles Bayer, reveal how these institutions and agents calibrated Mexican racial identities in the context of the labor vacancies left by Asian workers and in relation to the alleged threat posed by the Chinese. These discourses influenced the racial formations of domestic labor markets, which quickly took up Mexican workers as they expelled the Chinese. They also influenced the labor market in Mexico, especially in Baja California, where US economic interests benefited from Chinese labor excluded from the United States.

US businesses on both sides of the border, needing cheap workers, harnessed discursive constructions of Chinese and Mexicans as distinct representations of either model or menacing otherness. Industry and the state produced differentiated yet mutually constitutive values for these two labor groups on a transnational scale. The agricultural elite, in tandem with exclusionists such as John Box and William Paul Dillingham, shaped official discourses about Chinese and Mexican immigrants relationally. The effect was to structure a racialized, low-wage economic order throughout the border region, particularly at the California–Baja California border.

The twinned development of Chinese and Mexican racialization teaches Chicana/o studies scholars that in order to understand the history of Mexican immigrants, we must see how US industry and government shaped immigrants' identities relative to other groups—notably the Chinese, at and beyond the US-Mexico border. The construction of Mexican identity has never been strictly a local process. Instead, social discourses script mutually constitutive racialized identities for *distinct yet related* immigrant populations across national boundaries. Studying this process allows us to recognize new historical affiliations in Chicana/o studies that reach across racial boundaries as well as the borders between seemingly distinct academic fields. The imbricated history of Mexican and Chinese workers at the border reveals that these groups are not as unrelated as traditional Chicana/o and Asian American studies would imply. Instead, they share a formative and fascinating interracial past, providing a basis on which to imagine promising and productive interracial relationships for the future.

Notes

Editor's note: From *Aztlán: A Journal of Chicano Studies* 40, no. 2 (2015). The original essay was lightly edited for this collection.

1. While many Chicana/o studies departments and programs have resisted the term "Latina/o studies" to characterize their hemispheric teaching and research, Michael Soldatenko (2009, 182–83) suggests that this shift toward inter-American models of investigation links the field to Latin American studies and makes available its theoretical models, particularly those developed by Enrique Dussel, Walter Mignolo, Maria Lugones, and Ramón Grosfoguel.

2. Erika Lee (2003) and Grace Peña Delgado (2004) have shown how Chinese sought to enter the United States through Mexico to avoid detection at the ports of San Francisco and New York during the exclusion era.

3. Article IX of the Treaty of Guadalupe Hidalgo, which marked the end of the US-Mexican War, reads, "The Mexicans who, in the territories [ceded after the war], shall not preserve the character of citizens of the Mexican Republic conformably with what is stipulated in the preceding article, shall be incorporated into the Union of the United States, and be admitted at the proper time . . . to the enjoyment of all the rights of citizens of the United States according to the principles of the Constitution" (quoted in Tate 1969, 20). Since citizenship could only be conferred on free whites in this era, Mexicans in the annexed territories became white by virtue of the Treaty of Guadalupe Hidalgo. This preserved for all Mexicans their racial eligibility for naturalization, and therefore for immigration, during the early twentieth century.

4. It should also be noted that the traffic between California and Baja California during this period was not unidirectional. Rosario Cardiel Marín (1997, 198) writes that Chinese migration into Baja California "procedía en su mayoría del estado de California, de la Unión Americana; la cercanía entre este estado y el territorio de Baja California motivó un tránsito ilegal constante de este grupo entre ambas fronteras" (Chinese migration into Baja California came primarily from the state of California, and the proximity between California and the Mexican territory of Baja California motivated constant illegal transit of Chinese between both sides of the border).

5. Both the General Census of Mexico 1895–1960 (Censos Mexicanos de población 1895–1960) and the General Archive of the Nation, National Register of Foreigners, Migration, Mexico (Archivo General de la Nación, Registro Nacional de Extranjeros, Migración) tally fewer than 3,000 Chinese in all of Baja California in 1921. However, scholars agree that this figure severely underestimates the number of Chinese in the region.

6. For an examination of the cultural meaning of La Malinche in Mexico, see Paz (1959).

7. Some states such as Sonora forced Mexican women to forfeit their citizenship and assume the nationality of their husband if they married a Chinese man (Cardiel Marín 1997, 211–12).

Works Cited

Almaguer, Tomás. 1994. *Racial Fault Lines: The Historical Origins of White Supremacy in California*. Berkeley: University of California Press.

Becerra, Carmen. 1990. "Presencia de los chinos en el valle de Mexicali." In *La comunidad china del Distrito Norte de Baja California*, 49–59. Baja California, Mexico: Instituto de Investigaciones Históricas del Estado de Baja California.

Boyle, Walter. 1920. "Boyle to State Department, Mexicali, August 25, 1920." RG 59, National Archives and Records Administration. Records of the Department of State Relating to the Internal Affairs of Mexico, 1910–1929. Microcopy 274, 812.00/24495.

Camposortega Cruz, Sergio. 1997. "Análisis demográfico de las corrientes migratorias a México desde finales del siglo XX." In *Destino México: Un estudio de las migraciones asiáticas a México, siglos XIX y XX*, edited by María Elena Ota Mishima, 21–53. Mexico City: Colegio de México.

Cardiel Marín, Rosario. 1997. "La migración china en el norte de Baja California, 1877–1949." In *Destino México: Un estudio de las migraciones asiáticas a México, siglos XIX y XX*, edited by María Elena Ota Mishima, 189–256. Mexico City: Colegio de México.

Cardoso, Lawrence. 1980. *Mexican Immigration to the United States, 1897–1931*. Tucson: University of Arizona Press.

Chang, Jason Oliver. 2010. "Outsider Crossings: History, Culture, and Geography of Mexicali's Chinese Community." PhD diss., University of California, Berkeley.

Chong, Luis. 1917. Preliminary Statement, September 6. Case 619. RG 85, National Archives and Records Administration, Pacific Region, Riverside, CA. Immigration and Naturalization Service, Los Angeles District Office, Chinese Exclusion Acts Case Files, 1893–1943.

Comisión de Inmigración. 1911. *Dictamen del vocal ingeniero José María Romero, encargado de estudiar la influencia social y económica de inmigración asiática en México*. Mexico: A. Carranza e hijos. Bancroft Library, University of California, Berkeley.

Commission of Immigration and Housing of California. 1916. *Second Annual Report of the Commission of Immigration and Housing of California*, vol. 2. San Francisco.

Delgado, Grace Peña. 2004. "At Exclusion's Southern Gate: Changing Categories of Race and Class among Chinese Fronterizos, 1882–1904." In *Continental Crossroads: Remapping U.S.-Mexico Borderlands History*, edited by Samuel Truett and Elliot Young, 183–207. Durham, NC: Duke University Press.

Dennis, Philip A. 1979. "The Anti-Chinese Campaigns in Sonora, Mexico." *Ethnohistory* 26, no. 1: 65–80.

Duncan, Robert H. 1994. "The Chinese and the Economic Development of Northern Baja California, 1889–1929." *Hispanic American Historical Review* 74, no. 4: 615–47.

Espinoza, José Angel. 1932. *El ejemplo de Sonora*. Mexico City.

Guérin-Gonzales, Camille. 1994. *Mexican Workers and American Dreams: Immigration, Repatriation, and California Farm Labor, 1900–1939*. New Brunswick, NJ: Rutgers University Press.

Gutiérrez, David G. 1995. *Walls and Mirrors: Mexican Americans, Mexican Immigrants, and the Politics of Ethnicity*. Berkeley: University of California Press.

Hall, Stuart. 1996. "Gramsci's Relevance for the Study of Race and Ethnicity." In *Stuart Hall: Critical Dialogues in Cultural Studies*, edited by David Morley and Kuan-Hsing Chen, 411–40. New York: Routledge.

Ham Chande, Roberto. 1997. "La migración china hacia México a través del Registro Nacional de Extranjeros." In *Destino México: Un estudio de las migraciones asiáticas a México, siglos XIX y XX*, edited by María Elena Ota Mishima, 167–88. Mexico City: Colegio de México.

Hoffman, Albert. 1974. *Unwanted Mexican Americans in the Great Depression: Repatriation Pressures, 1929–1939*. Tucson: University of Arizona Press.

Hu-DeHart, Evelyn. 1980. "Immigrants to a Developing Society: The Chinese in Northern Mexico, 1875–1932." *Journal of Arizona History* 21: 275–312.

———. 1982. "Racism and Anti-Chinese Persecution in Sonora, Mexico, 1876–1932." *Amerasia* 9, no. 2: 1–28.

———.1985–86. "The Chinese in Baja California Norte, 1910–1934." In *Proceedings of the Pacific Coast Council on Latin American Studies: Baja California and the Northern Frontier*, 9–28. San Diego: San Diego State University Press.

Keen, Benjamin, and Keith A. Hayes, eds. 2009. *A History of Latin America: Ancient America to 1910*, vol. 1. Boston: Houghton Mifflin Harcourt.

Lee, Erika. 2003. *At America's Gates: Chinese Immigration During the Exclusion Era, 1882–1943*. Chapel Hill: University of North Carolina Press.

———. 2005. "Orientalisms in the Americas: A Hemispheric Approach to Asian American History." *Journal of Asian American Studies* 8, no. 3: 235–56.

McWilliams, Carey. 1935. *Factories in the Field. The Story of Migratory Farm Labor in California*. Santa Barbara, CA: Peregrine Smith.

Ngai, Mae. 2004. *Impossible Subjects: Illegal Aliens and the Making of Modern America*. Princeton, NJ: Princeton University Press.

Office of the Collector of Customs. 1902. "Letter to the Secretary of the Treasury, Washington D.C., August 7th, 1902." RG 36, National Archives and Records Administration, Pacific Region, Riverside, CA. San Diego Collection District. Records of the US Customs Service, Letters Sent to the Secretary of the Treasury, 1892–1908 (9L-39).

Paz, Octavio. 1959. *El laberinto de la soledad*. Mexico City: Fondo de Cultura Económica.

Romero, Robert Chao. 2010. *The Chinese in Mexico, 1882–1940*. Tucson: University of Arizona Press.

Sánchez, George J. 1993. *Becoming Mexican American: Ethnicity, Culture, and Identity in Chicano Los Angeles, 1900–1945*. New York: Oxford University Press.

Schiavone Camacho, Julia María. 2012. *Chinese Mexicans: Transpacific Migration and the Search for a Homeland, 1910–1960*. Chapel Hill: University of North Carolina Press.

Soldatenko, Michael. 2009. *Chicano Studies: The Genesis of a Discipline*. Tucson: University of Arizona Press.

Takaki, Ronald. 1989. *Strangers from a Different Shore: A History of Asian Americans*. New York: Penguin.

Tate, Bill. 1969. *Guadalupe Hidalgo Treaty of Peace 1848 and the Gadsden Treaty with Mexico 1853*. Truchas, NM: Rio Grande Sun.

US Customs Service. 1915. *Annual Report of the Customs Business of the District of Southern California, 1915*. RG 36, National Archives and Record Administration, Pacific Region, Riverside, CA. Records of the US Customs Service, Calexico Customs Office (9L-60).

US Department of Commerce and Labor. 1908. *Bulletin of the Bureau of Labor*, no. 78. Washington, DC.

US House of Representatives. Committee on Immigration and Naturalization. 1926. *Seasonal Agricultural Laborers from Mexico*. 69th Cong., 1st sess. Washington, DC.

———. 1930. Statement of Harry Chandler in *Immigration from Countries in the Western Hemisphere: Hearings on H.R. 8523, H.R. 8530, H.R. 8702*. 71st Cong., 2nd sess. Washington, DC.

US Senate. 1911. *Abstracts of Reports of the Immigration Commission, with Conclusions and Recommendations and Views of the Minority*. 61st Cong., 3rd sess. Washington, DC.

Vasconcelos, José. 1997. *La raza cósmica*. Translated by Didier T. Jaén. Baltimore: Johns Hopkins University Press. First published 1925.

Velázquez Morales, Catalina. 2001. *Los inmigrantes chinos en Baja California, 1920–1937*. Mexicali, Mexico: Universidad de Baja California.

Fronteriza Writing in *Nadie me verá llorar*

Cristina Rivera Garza and Other Border Crossers of Yesterday and Today

Carolyn González

In a 1991 lecture delivered at Hampshire College titled "Mexicanas and Chicanas," renowned Mexican writer Elena Poniatowska spoke of her admiration for Chicana writers, who had surpassed Mexicana writers through their lived experiences on "the extreme border" and had "won over class and racial prejudices, social and economic segregation" (1996, 44). She also lamented the disregard that Mexican and Mexicana writers often had displayed for their Chicana/o counterparts and singled out Chicana writers in particular as "an example to Mexican women writers" because of their strength, freedom, and groundbreaking work (47). Poniatowska's lucid and impassioned call for recognition of Chicanas is still strikingly relevant because of the persistent tendency of Mexicana writers to fail to acknowledge the work of Chicanas.[1] A close examination of the work of acclaimed Mexicana writer Cristina Rivera Garza highlights the often overlooked Chicana influence on Rivera Garza's literary production and on contemporary Mexicana literature more broadly.

Mexican Identity on the Border

Cristina Rivera Garza, professor, columnist, historian, poet, novelist, essayist, and short-story writer, has been embraced by Mexican intellectuals and lauded with multiple awards. She is the only author who has won the international Sor Juana Inés de la Cruz Prize twice: once in 2001 for her novel *Nadie me verá llorar*, first published in 1999, and again in 2009 for her novel *La muerte me da* (2007b). For seven years she wrote a weekly column, "La mano oblicua," in the Mexican newspaper *Milenio*, and she currently contributes to *Literal* magazine through her column "Overcast."[2] A public intellectual, Rivera Garza also maintains an active presence on social media and is the author of the blog *No hay tal lugar*.

Born in 1964 in Matamoros, Tamaulipas, Rivera Garza has lived in both Mexico and the United States. Bilingual and bicultural, she is mindful of her Mexican identity on the border, "no sólo porque he nacido en México y me reconozco como elemento de una tradición literaria específica, sino también porque he abrazado una realidad fronteriza y ambivalente donde las raíces relacionales de la identidad y las relaciones sociales en general resultan más patentes, más punzantes" (quoted in Hind 2003, 186) (not only because I was born in México and I recognize myself as part of a specific literary tradition but also because I have embraced an ambivalent border reality where the relational roots of identity and social relationships in general turn out to be more obvious, more keen).[3]

The Lower Río Grande Valley, which includes the Matamoros-Brownsville border area, has produced scholars who have written significant studies of "Greater Mexico." This concept was first introduced by Américo Paredes, considered one of the founders of Mexican American studies, in his PhD dissertation of 1956, which was published in 1958 by University of Texas Press as *"With His Pistol in His Hand": A Border Ballad and Its Hero*. Paredes, like Rivera Garza born and raised on the Brownsville-Matamoros border, coined the term Greater Mexico to refer to Mexico in a cultural sense, beyond political borders. Yet although this idea has gained credence in literary and scholarly circles, the rift between Mexicanas and Chicanas continues, and an institutional border separating Mexican literary studies from Chicana literary studies persists.

Recent scholarly work reflects this still-existing bias. For instance, in her 2007 dissertation "Writing the Past: Women's Historical Fiction of Greater Mexico," Elizabeth Cummins Muñoz includes an analysis of the historical fiction of Rosario Castellanos, Silvia Molina, Rivera Garza, and Alicia Gaspar de Alba, making a clear distinction between the Mexican women novelists and the sole Mexican American (Gaspar de Alba) (iv). She places Rivera Garza in the "dynamic moment of 1990s Mexican intel-lectual feminism and literary activity" (122), noting that Rivera Garza is from the border and expresses her marginality as part of her identity as a Mexican writer. Cummins Muñoz explores this stance, quoting from an interview she conducted with Rivera-Garza,

The author has preferred to maintain a certain distance from the pull of this centrifugal center. She [Rivera-Garza] explains: "Lucho todos los días por mantener esa ex-centricidad. No me interesa ni 'normalizarme' ni 'centralizarme' ni 'desperiferarme,' ni 'desmarginalizarme.' Todo lo contrario" (personal interview 2006). (I battle daily to maintain this ex-centricity. I am not interested in normalizing myself, centralizing myself, leaving the periphery, or demarginalizing myself. All the contrary). This biographical and professional identification with spaces and cultures outside of central, well-defined identities is consistent with Rivera Garza's approach to her intellectual and creative work. (127)

Although Cummins Muñoz cites Héctor Calderón's *Narratives of Greater Mexico: Essays on Chicano Literary History, Genre and Borders* (2004), she neither cites nor uses Paredes's concept of Greater Mexico or his study of Mexican culture on both sides of the Rio Grande. Cummins Muñoz only includes Paredes's term as part of the title of her dissertation to emphasize the divide between writers on one side of the border and those on the other.

US Latina/o Roots of a Mexican Intellectual

Despite this academic divide between Chicana and Mexicana writers, a decidedly Chicana/Latina sensibility informs Rivera Garza's doctoral dissertation, "The Masters of the Streets: Bodies, Power and Modernity in Mexico, 1867–1930" (University of Houston, 1995). Rivera Garza studied at the University of Houston from 1988 to 1995, and her dissertation examines the Mexican working class, prostitutes, and the insane; it would become the genesis of her acclaimed Spanish-language novel *Nadie me verá llorar*. From the 1970s through the 1990s, students of history, sociology, anthropology, and literature in US universities who were concerned with state repression and social control in the emergence of the modern state tended to read English translations of Michel Foucault, Walter Benjamin, Jean-François Lyotard, Mikhail Bakhtin, and Antonio Gramsci, as well as practitioners of the new critical anthropology such as Michael Taussig, James Clifford, George E. Marcus, and Ruth Behar, and precursors such as Américo Paredes. Thus these scholars have contributed to a study of repression and marginalization necessary for the understanding of modern Mexico set forth in Rivera Garza's dissertation.

The years that Rivera Garza lived in Houston also coincided with the emergence of a Chicana/Latina feminist literature. In 1984, the University of Houston's Arte Público Press published Sandra Cisneros's *The House on Mango Street*, centered on US Latina, Mexican American, and Mexican women in Chicago in the late 1960s. An immediate best-seller, *The House on Mango Street* was the first novel by a woman to be published by Arte Público. Cisneros's widely influential collection of short stories, *Woman Hollering Creek and Other Stories*, situated in South Texas and Mexico, was published in 1991. In 1985 Cisneros had relocated to San Antonio, where she wrote the stories of *Woman Hollering Creek* in the late 1980s; it is a collection embedded within the folk and popular cultures of the Texas-Mexico border. In the work of Cisneros as well as in Chicana/Latina feminist scholarship and creative literature more broadly, the Virgin of Guadalupe, also known as Guadalupe Tonantzín, occupies a special place in the redefinition of Mexican femininity. In "*Los* Acknowledgments" to *Woman Hollering Creek*, Cisneros writes, "*Virgen de Guadalupe Tonantzín, infinitas gracias*" (1991, x). And in "Little Miracles, Kept Promises," a story in the collection, Cisneros refers again to the "Virgencita" several times. In her dissertation, Rivera Garza reveals the influence of Cisneros's work on her own scholarship by echoing Cisneros's populist, working-class devotion to Our Lady of Guadalupe. Rivera Garza ends her acknowledgements with "Last, but not least . . . *virgencita de Guadalupe Tonatzin* . . . thanks for the hope" (1995, v). It is important to note that the reference to *la virgencita* using her Spanish and indigenous names is not at all common in Mexican scholarship and creative literature, which is almost always the product of literary elites. This retitling aligns Rivera Garza more closely with Cisneros.

Rivera Garza emphasizes her *fronteriza* identity when she begins her dissertation acknowledgments in a playful bilingual fashion, similar to that of Cisneros, stating, "In this moment of *dar las gracias* I wish to acknowledge . . ." (1995, iii). She later uses code-switching as she thanks "*la* girlfriend" (iv), much as Cisneros did earlier in referring to "*Las* San Antonio girlfriends" (1991, ix). After recognizing Tonantzín, Rivera Garza ends her acknowledgments by thanking "*sup Marcos*" (1995, v), a reference to Subcomandante Marcos of Mexico's Ejército Zapatista de Liberación Nacional (EZLN). Rivera Garza was completing her dissertation during the 1994 indigenous uprising led by the EZLN in Chiapas. Thus Rivera Garza's *fronteriza* identity, with her knowledge of the border and her understanding of the criminalization of the marginal, goes a long way in explaining the crucial moment in her dissertation when she discusses the so-called morally insane in Mexico's infamous asylum, the Manicomio General de la Castañeda.[4] In her chapter titled "The Mad People's Portrait: A Dossier of Terror," she analyzes archived photos of the inmates.[5] She writes:

The immediate, bureaucratic function of these standardized pictures was to provide information, naked information as straight-forward as possible. Yet, in the reduced space of the portrait, the pair of eyes, the mouth, the nose, the hair styles, the shoulders, hats and clothes, also constructed a social identity. The insane were dark-skinned, men often wore peasant hats while long-braided women wrapped themselves with the traditional *rebozo*. These objects and styles laid bare the class and ethnic traits of the insane and clearly delineated as well visual representations of the Mexican working poor. The portraits also constituted illustrations of a mute yet all-encompassing classification of insanity and deviation, of violence and terror. (Rivera Garza 1995, 306–7)

Rivera Garza draws on her bilingual, bicultural border background in her research for her English-language dissertation. She makes a frightening discovery regarding the ethnic profiles of the patients housed in La Castañeda, which was inaugurated by Mexican dictator Porfirio Díaz in 1910.[6] Although Díaz was driven out of power by Francisco I. Madero, leader of the Mexican Revolution, in 1911, the insane asylum continued and was not torn down until 1968, just prior to the Olympics. "Marginal" people, the poor, prostitutes, and the insane, who first lived on the streets of Mexico and later found themselves in the asylum, were a threat to the established order, to *gente decente*, hence the ironic title that they received: "masters of the streets." Despite their powerlessness, Rivera Garza finds agency in the supposed "insanity" of the inmates of La Castañeda. Through her study of extant written records, Rivera Garza discovers that inmates offered critiques of Porfirian Mexico. Doctors could not make sense of the critiques. Yet many years later, scholar Rivera Garza noted the critiques and resistance of inmates, along with their ethnicity, class, and gender. In brief, she is following Chicana/Latina scholars by interpreting writings from the past from the margins, an approach she learned as a graduate student at the University of Houston.

Cristina Rivera Garza and Matilda Burgos: Two Women of the Periphery

Rivera Garza explained the origin of her novel during her participation in the television program *Discutamos México*, where she spoke of coming across an archive at the Archivo Histórico de la Secretaría de Salubridad de Asistencia. She was searching for documents from the Manicomio General de la Castañeda when she found the file of a woman who had arrived at La Castañeda in 1921. Her name was Modesta Burgos. Rivera Garza describes the portrait included in the file as "increíblemente perturbador, una mujer que está a punto de ser recluida, ella no sabe todavía, pero por 28 años en esta institución, está sonriéndole a la cámara en una actitud que a mí me causó estupor" (Gobierno de la República 2010) (incredibly perturbing, a woman who is about to be confined, she has yet to find out, but for 28 years in this institution, she is smiling at the camera with an attitude that astonished me). In a nonfiction Spanish-language book, *La Castañeda: Narrativas dolientes desde el Manicomio General, México, 1910–1930* (2010), inspired by her dissertation, Rivera Garza explains that this file also included notations by doctors who cared for and diagnosed Modesta. These notes were at times revised, and previous notes were crossed out but not erased; this plethora of annotations indicates the presence of several people's voices on one page (Rivera Garza 2010, 260). This file also included a set of personal writings by Modesta, or, as Rivera Garza explains, "una especie de diario que ella llamó sus 'Despachos presidenciales'" (256) (a sort of diary that she called her "Presidential Dispatches"). In these handwritten notes Modesta details the state of the country as well as the mental health facility and her particular perspective on what she calls "la vida real del mundo" (256) (the real life of the world). This woman, Modesta Burgos, would eventually become a character in Rivera Garza's novel *Nadie me verá llorar*. This text, although acclaimed as a Mexican novel written by one of Mexico's most important contemporary female writers, can also be explained and interpreted through its Chicana/Latina and US frame of reference. In general, readers have failed to see the bilingual and bicultural genesis of this novel in relation to Rivera Garza's own marginalization (albeit in a different context, as a writer of the periphery in Mexico and the United States) that she shares with a prostitute judged morally insane.

Rivera Garza uses her dissertation and Modesta Burgos's file as a starting point for *Nadie me verá llorar*. The novel presents the story of the now-fictionalized Matilda Burgos, a patient at La Castañeda, and Joaquín Buitrago, a photographer for the same institution who becomes interested in her story after he recognizes her as a woman he photographed at a brothel years before. He remembers her because of a question she asks him as he takes her picture: "¿Cómo se convierte uno en un fotógrafo de locos?" / "How does one come to be a photographer of crazy people?" (Rivera Garza 2000, 15; 2003, 3). This question leads Joaquín to reflect on his past and to try to figure out Matilda's as well. As both characters' stories are told in a nonlinear narration, with the two lives at times intersecting, partial portraits of the characters emerge along with snippets from the lives of other characters who affect them. The novel's historical time period ranges from the end of the nineteenth century, encompassing part of the Porfirio Díaz dictatorship, or Porfiriato, to Matilda's death in 1958. The novel quotes from, dialogues with, and rewrites various sources, including Federico Gamboa's *Santa* (2002), a bestselling Mexican novel about a prostitute, first published in 1903, which follows the traditional narrative of the fallen woman. Rivera Garza also includes faithful transcriptions of the writings of Modesta Burgos in her work. Thus, *Nadie me verá llorar* is a narrative that successfully merges fiction, nonfiction, and photography. Although the novel does not present actual photographs, it draws from a hybrid document that includes a photograph, and the novel may be read as one that includes and also becomes a series of verbal photographs or images painted in words.[7]

Greater Mexico in a Mexican Novel

Of the verbal images in *Nadie me verá llorar*, some clearly emerged because of Rivera Garza's time in Greater Mexico. She begins the last chapter, "Vivir en la vida real del mundo" (To live in the real life of the world), with the story of Altagracia Flores de Elizalde, a patient in La Castañeda. "[Ella] cree que una pistola cuesta treinta mil pesos y una hacienda sólo cincuenta. *Imaginación excéntrica*. Ama de casa en Aguascalientes" / "[She] thinks that a pistol costs thirty thousand pesos and a hacienda fifty. *Eccentric imagination*. Housewife, Aguascalientes" (Rivera Garza 2000, 243; 2003, 222). This brief description of the patient's beliefs replicates the official discourse concerning Flores de Elizalde. Yet it is significant that the chapter begins with this particular woman. In her dissertation, "Masters of the Streets," Rivera Garza analyzes Altagracia Flores de Elizalde's story and highlights how the doctors are "shocked" and "amazed" at the woman's "delirium" (1995, 317). Writing from a place of marginality, she posits an alternative reading of the woman's story, suggesting that Altagracia's understanding of value was not so different from that of others of the time. Altagracia entered the asylum in 1920, a period of political strife and violence during the Mexican Revolution:

> Altagracia, nonetheless, was by no means the only person making these kind of assertions [that the value of a pistol was greater than the value of a *hacienda*]. *Corridos* of the Mexican Revolution, the ballads and narrative folk songs of the popular armies deeply rooted in a peasant background, frequently described and stressed the positive social value

of rifles and pistols. As in the ballad of Gregorio Cortez, heroic corridos especially evoked a man, pistol in hand, defending his personal and his community rights. . . .

The corrido spread important information through the community. . . . Orally created and transmitted, the overwhelming positive associations of weapons as empowering tools of peasants and other subordinate groups of society thus reached large popular audiences, leaving deep marks in the social consciousness of the poor and the dispossessed. (322–23)

Drawing on Chicano scholarship and the Greater Mexican corrido to prove her point, Rivera Garza offers this alternate analysis of Altagracia's valuation of dwellings and weapons to demonstrate that some of the so-called irrational tales of the inmates of La Castañeda "touch upon some crucial traits of an emerging rational and modernized society, especially when taken out of the walls of the asylum" (324). Rivera Garza's choice to begin the final chapter of her novel in this manner, with a reference to Flores de Elizalde, indicates her desire that Matilda's story as well as her "irrational tales" be understood in a different context, outside the controlling "walls of the asylum."

Encouraging an alternate understanding of Modesta/Matilda's writing, in this final chapter of *Nadie me verá llorar*, Rivera Garza also inserts transcriptions of Modesta's papers, which she called her "Cuerpos Diplomáticos" (1995, 325). This way, at the end of the novel, the reader is allowed to glimpse and interpret the "original" file, now part of Rivera Garza's text, allowing for a new interpretation of Modesta's writing. Like Flores de Elizalde's assertions, Matilda's writings—the writings of a so-called madwoman—also include very lucid critiques of the politics, society, and medical practices of that period. As Rivera Garza posits,

> Although [Modesta's] *Cuerpos Diplomáticos* lacked the style and content of a political banner, her words nonetheless disclosed a person critically reviewing the changing social environment of this era. Terms such as corruption, thievery, abuse of power and plain violence steadfastly, and effortlessly, surfaced in her texts. (1995, 326)

Furthermore, in one of the texts Burgos refers to "estos médicos—los malos y estafadores—perniciosos—que maltratan gente—y que andan de perversos—con todas las cosas en general" / "These bad, chiseling, pernicious doctors that mistreat people and walk around being perverted with things in general" (Rivera Garza 2000, 249; 2003, 228). Through this statement, she labels doctors, rather than herself, as perverse and uses their equally perverse interest in "todas las cosas en general"—and their interest in her—to gain permission to write. As Rivera Garza explains in *La Castañeda*: "A pesar de los diagnósticos, o tal vez gracias a ellos, estas mujeres lucharon, con éxito en algunas ocasiones, por narrar sus historias personales, con lo cual abrieron una puerta invaluable hacia la autointerpretación de las mujeres de México de principios del siglo XX" (2010, 141–42) (Despite the diagnoses, or perhaps thanks to them, these women fought, with success on some occasions, to narrate their personal histories, through which they opened an invaluable window on the self-interpretation of Mexican women at the start of the twentieth century).

Insometidas of Yesterday and Today

Through her novel, Rivera Garza asks the reader to reevaluate women such as these—women dismissed as "mad"—and demonstrates her solidarity and identification with them. And who exactly were these women? In "Masters of the Streets," Rivera Garza explains that in 1872, Dr. Manuel Alfaro, the physician who wrote the first *Reglamento de la prostitución en México*, a series of government regulations to control prostitutes, analyzed the files of 500 registered prostitutes from the time period of 1868–72 (1995, 161). According to Rivera Garza, "The findings and interpretations of Dr. Alfaro uncovered a wide array of sordid realities that de-glamorized the popular image of prostitutes as *daughters of joy, princesses of pleasure* and turned them instead into common members of the urban proletariat of nineteenth-century Mexico" (161). The women described in a report by Dr. Alfaro were

> mostly young, single women lacking family support. The ages of prostitutes varied from 12 to 49 years old. 358 claimed to be orphans, 104 had one or both parents but did not report if they were alive or not, and no information was provided in the remaining 35 cases. 457 prostitutes were single women, 408 were childless and 48 had children. 36 were widows, 19 without offspring and 17 with it. The records revealed one married woman with two children. No information was recorded in the 5 remaining cases. As Dr. Alfaro himself noted, some prostitutes had indeed an ulterior justification for their activities, that is the maintenance of their own children and even elder parents in some cases. (161–62)

According to Dr. Alfaro's report, a great many of these women had been wage laborers with limited options in the job market and low salaries that rarely exceeded twenty-five cents a day; they were often paid half of what men earned for the same job (163–64). With limited options for survival, "becoming a prostitute thus seemed to be a rational decision of survival rather than a moral defect" (164). Dr. Alfaro also judged most of the women to be poorly educated: "Taking into consideration the manners, the speech patterns and clothing of the 134 prostitutes he personally interviewed, he considered that 77 women had no education, 37 had regular education and only 20 showed the traits of a good education" (165). According to Dr. Alfaro's study, when women were asked about the circumstances under which they had become prostitutes, they "alluded to poverty and family dislocation as the main antecedents that brought about their decision to become prostitutes. Yet . . . a great number of women also replied that they had 'proclivity,' that is an ingrained natural tendency for the profession" (166).

In *Nadie me verá llorar*, Rivera Garza illustrates many of these historical findings. Matilda is initially portrayed as having worked for a cigarette manufacturer, one of the few industries, along with cotton mills, that Rivera Garza lists in "The Masters" as having employed women (1995, 164). When Esther (the woman with whom Matilda lives) dies, leaving her children as extra mouths to feed, Matilda finds work as an unregistered prostitute, also referred to as an *insometida*.[8]

> Trabajaba por la noche, y al amanecer regresaba a la vecindad de Balderas, después de quitarse el maquillaje y cambiar de ropas. Los hijos de Esther se abstuvieron de hacerle preguntas y los vecinos, al tanto de sus obvias correrías, la miraban con tristeza y comprensión. Desempleada y con dos hijos ajenos que mantener, Matilda había tomado la única decisión posible. (Rivera Garza 2000, 170–71)

> She worked at night, of course, and at dawn would return home, after first removing her makeup and changing her clothes. Esther's children refrained from asking questions, and the neighbors, aware of her obvious goings and comings, looked at her with sadness and understanding. Unemployed and with another woman's children to support, Matilda had made the only possible decision. (Rivera Garza 2003, 153)

According to *Nadie me verá llorar*, and reiterating information also found in "The Masters," in turn-of-the-century Mexico City "el doce por ciento de las mujeres entre quince y treinta años de edad eran o habían sido prostitutas alguna vez en su vida" / "twelve percent of the women between fifteen and thirty years of age were prostitutes, or had been at some time" (Rivera Garza 2000, 169–70; 2003, 152). Matilda, whom Rivera Garza features in her novel, is one of these women. Moreover, using a feminist sensibility, Rivera Garza writes this character as actively defiant of the government. She is an *insometida*, a woman who is drawn from a multiplicity of historically documented women who contributed to the failure of the government's regulatory system.

Merging Past and Present Resistance

Beyond Rivera Garza's ties to Cisneros, feminism, the border, marginality, and spaces of inconformity and imprisonment, her work is closely aligned with Chicana feminist theory. Sonia Saldívar-Hull argues for a widespread feminism, beyond the constraints of borders and ethnic identities, in her groundbreaking study *Feminism on the Border: Chicana Politics and Literature* (2000), published just a year after *Nadie me verá llorar*. In fact, she takes this idea a step further in her analysis of *Cuentos: Stories by Latinas* (Gómez, Moraga, and Romo-Carmona 1983), in which she explains that the contributing writers "shatter the tradition of silence imposed on them by the pressures of a culture that works against the viability of an oral tradition" (Saldívar-Hull 2000, 46–47). As women of color living in the capitalist United States of the 1980s, Latinas now had the obligation to "write what was once spoken" (47)—in other words, to put on paper the stories of their youth, their families, their ancestors, that were once communicated person-to-person. And although they recognize themselves as part of a diverse group, as Latinas in the United States, the authors of *Cuentos*—a Nuyorican (Alma Gómez), a Chicana (Cherríe Moraga), and a Chilean (Mariana Romo-Carmona)—must unite with other people of color (46–48). Similarly, though for different reasons—death, constraints of time and space—Rivera Garza, like these Latina authors, cannot privilege oral communication and communicate directly with women/people, "others" of the past; instead she must dialogue with writings, images, and historical documents from the past.

In the final chapter of *La Castañeda*, Rivera Garza asks herself a question: "¿es posible entrevistar a un documento histórico?" (2010, 247) (is it possible to interview a historic document?). She goes on to say, "Esta pregunta, a la vez, es sólo otra manera de plantear la posibilidad que tiene o no tiene el lector contemporáneo de establecer una relación dialógica, interactiva, presencial, con información que viene del pasado y desde el pasado en forma escrita" (247) (This question, at the same time, is only another way of raising the possibility that a contemporary author may or may not have of establishing a dialogical, interactive, person-to-person relationship with information of the past, and from the past in written form). She posits that it is indeed possible to "interview" writing and that one can approach writing in more than one way in order to produce the effect of immediacy often attributed to oral interactions (249). In other words, because of the marginality she shares with deceased women of the past, she can and must bring their experiences to light indirectly, through a written dialogue with historical texts. "The written word, then, becomes essential for communication when face-to-face contact is not possible" (Gómez, Moraga, and Romo-Carmona 1983, vii). The beauty of this effort by Rivera Garza to remember the women's names and experiences is that the reader can come to understand that the women of the past are not so different from Rivera Garza, a Mexicana border writer, from the women of Mexico or Greater Mexico, and from the women of today.

With the creation (or re-creation) of her character Matilda, Rivera Garza shows solidarity with Modesta Burgos and resists the burial of this woman and her contemporaries. This type of activism on the author's part, which began with her dissertation, continues in her present-day work. On November 1, 2015, Rivera Garza published an article in the Mexican periodical *El País* titled "El duelo como forma de exigir justicia" (Pain as a way to demand justice). In this article, Rivera Garza addresses the forced disappearance of forty-three students from the Escuela Normal Rural de Ayotzinapa and their parents' demands that they not be forgotten:

> Cuando los padres de los estudiantes de Ayotzinapa nos instaron a no olvidar, a mantener presentes a nuestros muertos, se situaron en esa tradición mesoamericana y católica que nos invita a mantener abiertos los canales a través de los cuales los vivos y los muertos nos damos la cara, nos reconocemos y coexistimos, y tal vez, incluso, nos intercambiamos. (Rivera Garza 2015b)

> (When the parents of the Ayotzinapa students urged us not to forget, to maintain our dead present, they positioned themselves in that Meso-american and Catholic tradition that invites us to maintain the channels through which we the living and the dead face each other, recognize each other and coexist, and maybe, even, interact with each other.)

Rivera Garza reminds the reader that during Day of the Dead, those who have departed "siguen estando" (are still here) on a day of "entre-cruzamiento y comunión" (crossing over and communion). She views Day of the Dead as a way to defeat the act of forgetting, to "no olvidar que vivimos con los muertos" (2015b) (not forget that we live with the dead). Thus, following the disappearance of the students, a horrific event in Mexican history, she urges her reader to enter into solidarity with those marginalized and cast aside by the Mexican government, to feel their pain and their hurt. Rivera Garza points out that in remembering and recognizing the impact of the dead around us, Day of the Dead turns political. When the pain of the dead is felt by the living, this is a demand for justice: "El duelo contemporáneo no es una forma de 'superar' la tragedia, sino esta honda manera comunitaria de exigir justicia" (2015b) (Contemporary mourning is not a way to get over the tragedy, instead it is a deep communal way to demand justice). With the dead crossing borders between one world and another, they are constantly among the living and thus must not be forgotten.[9]

Fronteriza/o Writers of the Future

Rivera Garza has also become increasingly tied to the northern side of the Mexico-US border, and her Texas-Mexican *fronteriza* identity has evolved since her work in graduate school.[10] In an interview during LéaLA, the Spanish-language book fair in Los Angeles, Rivera Garza (2015c) revealed a desire to foster a bilingual conversation with people in the United States:

> I'm talking about taking or borrowing aspects of English, and aspects of Spanish, and combining them in ways that are even to me ways that I'm not necessarily expecting. And what I'm looking at right now is just to start fostering, and to engage actively with, a conversation with the men and women that I live with here in this country. I've been here for such a long time, and it seems to me I've been waiting, I've been slow to react and that's my time right now.

In this way Rivera Garza continues to follow Latina writers in crossing linguistic borders and now fully and openly embraces her bilingual identity.[11]

Another way this *fronteriza* writer's identity has changed is described in an essay titled "Escritura creativa" (2016), featured in *Literal* magazine, in which Rivera Garza announced that after eight years as a professor in the creative writing section of the Department of Literature at the University of California, San Diego, she would be leaving this position and instead working to launch the first doctoral program in creative writing in Spanish at her alma mater, the University of Houston. Rivera Garza thus returns to her beginnings as a scholar and creative writer in order to form a program combining literary analysis with creative writing. In her essay she includes the following statement:

Tampoco nos dejamos engañar: para muchos de los bilingües con-
temporáneos que vivimos en los Estados Unidos, el español y el inglés
van de la mano en nuestras vidas privadas y públicas. No hay razón
alguna para que ese cruce constante, volátil, generativo, no forme parte
también de la producción escritural de esos autores que, sin duda, serán
los autores del siglo XXI.

(Let us not delude ourselves: for many of the contemporary bilingual
people who live in the United States, Spanish and English go hand in
hand in our private and public lives. There is no reason why this constant, volatile, generative crossing cannot also be a part of the written
production of those authors that, without a doubt, will be the authors of
the twenty-first century.)

Rivera Garza is thus looking forward and toward the future of creative
writing. As a multicultural writer and professor, through her writing and
through her work at the university, she will have a hand in shaping the
twenty-first-century writers who are transcending borders. She will be
enabling a new generation of border writers.

Notes

Editor's note: This essay was commissioned for this collection.

1. María Amparo Escandón, best known for her novel *Esperanza's Box of
Saints* (1999), is a Mexicana author who is an exception to this tendency. She
writes bilingually and engages in conversation with writers and readers on both
sides of the US-Mexico border.

2. Her last column, "La mano oblicua se despide," was published on November 5, 2013.

3. Translations are mine unless otherwise indicated. Translations of passages
in *Nadie me verá llorar* are from the published English-language edition of the
novel, *No One Will See Me Cry* (Rivera Garza 2003).

4. During the 1910s, women in the Manicomio General were often diagnosed with "moral insanity" if they went against accepted models of femininity
of the time. The symptoms of this so-called disease were considered particularly
strong in prostitutes (Rivera Garza 2010, 138). For instance, when Modesta, a
patient, arrived at La Castañeda, "The medical personnel at the asylum reported
her current symptoms. Modesta was sarcastic and gross. She made long inco-
herent speeches about her life, notably including florid verbal descriptions of her
beauty. The medical diagnosis elaborated at the same day of her arrival was decisive: Modesta Burgos suffered from Moral Insanity" (Rivera Garza 1995, 324). It
should be noted that diagnoses of "moral insanity" disappeared by 1930 (Rivera
Garza 2010, 148). According to Rivera Garza, "ésta fue, sin duda, una victoria
de las pacientes sobre la psiquiatría porfiriana; es decir, un cuerpo de ideas leales

a los puntos de vista punitivos de la enfermedad mental en los cuales el sexo y la locura estaban vinculados de manera íntima" (148) (this was, without a doubt, a victory of patients over the psychiatry of the Porfirian era; that is to say, a body of ideas that adhered to a punitive notion of mental illness based on an intimate link between sex and madness).

5. Joaquín María Díaz González, a student at the Academia de San Carlos, opened the first photographic studio in Mexico City five years after cameras first arrived in the country in 1839 (Rivera Garza 2010, 189). This studio was the first of many, mostly owned by foreigners, that would photograph the Mexican elite at the end of the nineteenth century for what were called "tarjetas de visita," or visitor cards. These consisted of a portrait mounted on a card, a technique patented by the Frenchman André-Adolphe Disdéri in 1854.

Como detalle de prestigio y lujo, las tarjetas de visita también hacían visibles las imágenes aceptadas de la normalidad individual y familiar en el México porfiriano. Motivados por el estatus de clase tanto del fotógrafo como de la clientela, los primeros retratos exponían las prendas, características y poses que distinguían a los miembros de la élite y de la creciente clase media, con lo cual creaban el perfil visual de un carácter nacional con todo vigor. Los políticos, hombres de negocios, comerciantes, intelectuales, damas acaudaladas y miembros del clero posaban ante los ojos de fotógrafos capacitados y formaban una colección de identidades de poder, una cierta familia de rostros. (189–90)

(As a token of prestige and luxury, the visitor card also made visible the accepted images of individual and family normalcy during Porfirio Díaz's Mexico. Motivated by the class status of the photographer and of the clients, the first portraits illustrated the clothing, characteristics, and poses that distinguished members of the elite and of the growing middle class, with which they vigorously created a visual profile of a national character. Politicians, businessmen, merchants, intellectuals, wealthy ladies, and members of the clergy posed before the eyes of capable photographers, the results forming a collection of identities of power, a kind of family of faces.)

The difference between these "tarjetas de visita" and the photographs taken of patients at the Manicomio General is quite striking: in the latter portraits "we only see faces and nothing else but faces. The insane appeared in isolation, totally dispossessed in the middle of a social vacuum. These men and women are not only *out* of society, they are nowhere. As all aberrations, they had no roots and no future; they appeared, left a visual mark in the lenses of the camera and, then, they disappeared" (Rivera Garza 1995, 314–15).

6. La Castañeda asylum was founded by Porfirio Díaz as part of a commemoration honoring Mexican independence. Located in Mexico City, it was at the time the largest institution of its kind in Mexico (Rivera Garza 1995, 249). In "Diálogos subversivos: Ficción e historia en *Nadie me verá llorar*" (Subversive Dialogues: Fiction and History in *Nadie me verá llorar*), Cristina Elena Magaña Franco explains, "El manicomio no sólo fue representativo de la bonanza del régimen de Díaz, sino que fue también, hasta su demolición en 1968, reflejo de la decadencia y de la falta de cuidado de los regímenes que le sucedieron al de Díaz.

La poca atención no era solamente en cuanto a las instalaciones se refiere, sino también al desamparo en el que dejaron a los enfermos mentales en México, y, en un sentido más amplio, a los estratos más bajos de la sociedad" (2004, 70–71). (The insane asylum not only was representative of the prosperity under the Díaz regime but also, until its demolition in 1968, was a reflection of decline and neglect under the regimes that followed that of Díaz. The lack of attention was related not only to the facilities but also to the abandonment of the mentally ill of Mexico, and of the lowest social strata more broadly.)

7. In the interview "Desde México para Corea: Entrevista a Cristina Rivera Garza," the writer explains that the manuscript had several names before becoming *Nadie me verá llorar*: "Se llamó 'Agujeros luminosos,' un título con el que yo quería aludir a la estructura del libro, pero que fue rechazado por el primer editor que entablé negociaciones debido a su alto contenido 'intelectual'" (Rivera Garza 2007a). (It was called 'Luminous Holes,' a title with which I wanted to allude to the structure of the book, but that was rejected by the first editor with whom I negotiated on account of its overly "intellectual" tone.) This title gestures to the photographic structure of the novel, implying that each scene appears to shine through a lens. In the new prologue to the fifteenth-anniversary hardcover limited edition of *Nadie me verá llorar*, Rivera Garza explains, "Mi regalo hoy, quince años después, es un secreto: el título verdadero. En mi corazón de corazones *Nadie me verá llorar* sigue llamándose *Agujeros luminosos*. Ahora todos estamos al tanto de esto" (2014, 18). (My gift today, fifteen years later, is a secret: the real title. In my heart of hearts, *No One Will See Me Cry* is still called *Luminous Holes*. Now we have all been made aware of this.)

8. As Rivera Garza explains, "By 1871 the Mexican Regulation of Prostitution identified three types of evil female bodies: The public woman, the isolated and the *insometida*" (1995, 147).

9. In the afterword to *Have You Seen Marie?*, Sandra Cisneros (2012) also speaks of the interconnectedness and exchange of feeling between the living and the dead. In her adult fable she shares a deeper understanding of death after her mother's passing and the knowledge that when someone dies, "a part of them is born in you—not immediately, I've learned, but eventually, and gradually. It's an opportunity to be reborn" (89). She also states that "love does not die . . . we can continue to receive and give love after death" (91).

10. Rivera Garza's roots on the US side of the United States–Mexico border are also familial. In the column "Overcast" that she writes for *Literal* magazine, she described a recent personal discovery: "My grandfather, a man after whom I was named, had lived in the United States from 1911 to 1934, crossing the border back and forth many times afterwards. I found the immigration records that proved this to be true at the National Archives in D.C. even later that summer. He had first crossed the border at the age of three, learning English and working as a farmhand or a sharecropper in the cotton fields of southern Texas as time evolved" (2015a).

11. Sandra Cisneros's *fronteriza* identity has also evolved, as the longtime San Antonio resident recently relocated to the Mexican city of San Miguel de Allende.

Works Cited

Calderón, Héctor. 2004. *Narratives of Greater Mexico: Essays on Chicano Literary History, Genre, and Borders*. Austin: University of Texas Press.

Cisneros, Sandra. 1984. *The House on Mango Street*. New York: Vintage.

———. 1991. *Woman Hollering Creek and Other Stories*. New York: Vintage.

———. 2012. *Have You Seen Marie?* New York: Alfred A Knopf.

Cummins Muñoz, Elizabeth. 2007. "Writing the Past: Women's Historical Fiction of Greater Mexico." PhD diss., University of Houston.

Escandón, María Amparo. 1999. *Esperanza's Box of Saints*. New York: Simon & Schuster.

Gamboa, Federico. 2002. *Santa: A Novel of Mexico City*. Edited by Javier Ortiz. Madrid: Cátedra. First published 1903.

Gobierno de la República. 2010. "Discutamos México, XVII Mujeres 117: Mujeres en la historia de México." YouTube, November 19. https://www.youtube.com/watch?v=fMvpXVqD31o.

Gómez, Alma, Cherríe Moraga, and Mariana Romo-Carmona, eds. 1983. *Cuentos: Stories by Latinas*. New York: Kitchen Table/Women of Color Press.

Hind, Emily. 2003. *Entrevistas con quince autoras mexicanas*. Madrid: Iberoamericana; Frankfurt am Main: Vervuert.

Magaña Franco, Elena Alicia. 2004. "Diálogos subversivos: Ficción e historia en *Nadie me verá llorar*." Master's thesis, Universidad de Colima.

Paredes, Américo. 1958. *"With His Pistol in His Hand": A Border Ballad and Its Hero*. Austin: University of Texas Press.

Poniatowska, Elena. 1996. "Mexicanas and Chicanas." *MELUS* 21, no. 3: 35–51.

Rivera Garza, Cristina. 1995. "The Masters of the Streets: Bodies, Power and Modernity in Mexico, 1867–1930." PhD diss., University of Houston.

———. 2000. *Nadie me verá llorar*. Mexico City: Tusquets.

———. 2003. *No One Will See Me Cry*. Translated by Andrew Hurley. Willimantic, CT: Curbstone.

———. 2007a. "Desde México para Corea: Entrevista a Cristina Rivera Garza." Interview by Jung-Euy Hong and Claudia Macías Rodríguez. *Espéculo: Revista de Estudios Literarios* 35 (March–June). http://www.ucm.es/info/especulo/numero35/crisrive.html.

———. 2007b. *La muerte me da*. Mexico City: Tusquets.

———. 2010. *La Castañeda: Narrativas dolientes desde el Manicomio General, México, 1910–1930*. Mexico City: Tusquets.

———. 2014. *Nadie me verá llorar*. Mexico City: Tusquets.

———. 2015a. "The Afterlife of Cotton: Yuma." *Literal: Latin American Voices*, November 10. http://literalmagazine.com/the-afterlife-of-cotton-yuma/

———. 2015b. "El duelo como forma de exigir justicia." *El País*, November 1.

———. 2015c. "This Mexican Author Says Languages Aren't Straitjackets, but Tools to Start a Bilingual Conversation." Interview by Betto Arcos, Public Radio International, May 19.

———. 2016. "Escritura creativa." *Literal: Latin American Voices*, July 4. http://literalmagazine.com/escritura-creativa/.

Saldívar-Hull, Sonia. 2000. *Feminism on the Border: Chicana Gender Politics and Literature*. Berkeley: University of California Press.

Contributors

Tomás Almaguer is professor of ethnic studies and former dean of the College of Ethnic Studies at San Francisco State University. He is the author of *Racial Fault Lines: The Historical Origins of White Supremacy* (2009) and *The New Latino Studies Reader: A Twenty-First Century Perspective*, co-edited with Ramón Gutiérrez (2016). He has held previous academic appointments at the University of California, Berkeley; the University of California, Santa Cruz; and the University of Michigan.

Héctor Calderón is a specialist in Spanish American, Mexican, and Chicano literature and cultures at UCLA, where he was the founding chair of the César E. Chávez Department of Chicana/o Studies (1994). He has also served as director of the Mexico Study Center of the University of California's Education Abroad Program (2004–8), and he was founding executive director of Casa de la Universidad de California en México, AC (2006–8). Calderón's numerous publications concentrate on border studies and the North American Mexican cultural diaspora. His most recent book is *Narratives of Greater Mexico: Essays on Chicano Literary History, Genre, and Borders* (2005). Current research projects include Mexican literature, film, and rock and Mexican American fiction of Los Angeles. He is currently completing a book on Mexico titled "América Mexicana: The Mexican Cultural Diaspora of North America."

Kirstie Dorr is associate professor of ethnic studies and an affiliate of the Critical Gender Studies and Latin American Studies programs at the University of California, San Diego. Her first book, *On Site in Sound: Performance Geographies in América Latina* (2018) examines the hemispheric circulation of South American musics via informal cultural and economic networks to contemplate the dynamic relationship between sonic texts and spatial contexts. Presently, she is conducting research for a new monograph that contemplates the relationship between queer politics, piracy networks, and globalization in the Americas. Dorr's work has appeared in scholarly periodicals including *Aztlán: A Journal of Chicano Studies, Journal of Latin American Cultural Studies, Women's Studies Quarterly,* and *Journal of Popular Music Studies.*

SHIFRA M. GOLDMAN was a social art historian who helped pioneer the study of Latin American art. Before retiring, she taught art history in the Los Angeles area for many years and lectured widely on Latin American and modern art. She began the campaign to preserve the 1932 Siqueiros mural in Olvera Street in Los Angeles in 1968, and she was instrumental in the development of the groundbreaking exhibition *Chicano Art: Resistance and Affirmation,* which opened at the University of California, Los Angeles, in 1990. She authored *Dimensions of the Americas* and *Contemporary Mexican Painting in a Time of Change* as well as many articles that appeared in catalogs, encyclopedias, dictionaries, and major newspapers and magazines. Goldman died in 2011.

GUILLERMO GÓMEZ-PEÑA is a performance artist, writer, activist, radical pedagogue, and artistic director of the performance troupe La Pocha Nostra. His performance work and eleven books have contributed to debates on cultural and gender diversity, border culture, and US-Mexico relations. His artwork has been presented at over nine hundred venues across the globe. A MacArthur Fellow and a Bessie and American Book Award winner, he is a regular contributor to newspapers and magazines in the United States, Mexico, and Europe and is a contributing editor to *The Drama Review.* Gómez-Peña is a senior fellow at the Hemispheric Institute of Performance and Politics and a patron for the London-based Live Art Development Agency. In 2012 he was named Samuel Hoi Fellow by USA Artists.

CAROLYN GONZÁLEZ is assistant professor of Spanish at the College of Idaho and specializes in the study of Mexican and US Latinx literature. She earned her PhD in Hispanic languages and literatures from the University of California, Los Angeles.

AUDREY A. HARRIS teaches in the Department of Spanish and Portuguese at the University of California, Los Angeles. She is the editor of *Nos contamos a través de los muros* (2016), a collection of writings from a Mexican women's prison. Her articles and reviews have been published in *Chasqui, The Paris Review,* and elsewhere. She is the translator of *The Houseguest and Other Stories* by Amparo Dávila (2018).

JUANITA HEREDIA is professor of Spanish at Northern Arizona University, where she specializes in US Latina/o and Latin American literary and cultural studies. She is the editor of *Mapping South American Latina/o Literature in the United States* (2018), author of *Transnational Latina Narratives in the Twenty-first Century: The Politics of Gender, Race, and Migrations* (2009), and coeditor of *Latina Self-Portraits* (2000). She received a post-doctoral fellowship at UCLA to work on her manuscript "Transnational Latinas/os and the City: Negotiating Urban Experiences in Twenty-first Century Literature and Culture." She has published widely on US Latina/o literature and culture in refereed journals and edited collections.

STEVEN LOZA is professor of ethnomusicology at UCLA. He has authored books that include *Barrio Rhythm: Mexican American Music in Los Angeles* (1993), *Tito Puente and the Making of Latin Music* (1999), and *The Jazz Pilgrimage of Gerald Wilson* (2018), and he is editor of the anthology *Religion as Art* (2009). He has been active as a performer and composer and as a producer of major concerts and festivals at UCLA and in Mexico City. He has directed ensembles in the UCLA Department of Ethnomusicology that focus on Latin American music, world jazz, and intercultural improvisation. *All Is One*, on the Merrimack label, is the most recent of three CDs of Loza's music. In 2008 he composed a tone poem titled *America Tropical*, which was premiered by the Mexico City Philharmonic Orchestra.

JULIA MONÁRREZ FRAGOSO is research professor at El Colegio de la Frontera Norte in Ciudad Juárez. Her publications include *Trama de una injusticia: Feminicidio sexual sistémico en Ciudad Juárez* (2009), for which she received the García Cubas Prize for best scientific work. She is also co-editor (with M. Tabuenca) of *Bordenado la violencia contra las mujeres en la frontera norte de México* (2007) and co-editor (with K. Staudt and C. Fuentes) of *Cities and Citizenship at the US-Mexico Border: The Paso del Norte Region* (2010). She offered expert testimony in the Juárez feminicide case at the Inter-American Court of Human Rights in 2009, and she was the recipient of a Fulbright–García Robles award for research at the Chicana/o Studies Department, University of Texas at El Paso, in 2014–15.

AMÉRICO PAREDES is recognized as one of the foremost Mexican American scholars for his teaching and research on corridos, folkloric ballads, and border stereotypes. He received his doctorate in English and folklore studies from the University of Texas at Austin in 1956, and in 1958 he accepted a position at the university, where he spent the rest of his academic career. He was instrumental in the formation of a center for Mexican American studies in 1970, and he was named its first director. Paredes was the recipient of a Guggenheim fellowship, the Charles Frankel Prize, and the Order of the Aguila Azteca and the Order of José de Escandón from the Mexican government. Among his writings are *With His Pistol in His Hand: A Border Ballad and Its Hero*; *Between Two Worlds*; and *Folklore and Culture on the Texas-Mexican Border*. Paredes died in 1999.

RICARDO ROMO is an urban historian and author of *East Los Angeles: History of a Barrio* (1983). Romo is former president of the University of Texas at Austin (1999–2017). In 2002, President Bush appointed him to the President's Board of Advisors on Historically Black Colleges and Universities, and in 2004, former Secretary of State Colin Powell appointed Romo as a US representative to the United Nations Educational Scientific and Cultural Organization. Romo holds a master's degree in history from Loyola Marymount University and a PhD in history from UCLA.

SANDRA RUIZ is an educator and scholar of Spanish language acquisition as well as Mexicana and US Chicana/o and Latina/o literatures, cultures, and histories. She is an assistant professor at West Los Angeles College, where she is working toward building the college's first Chicano/Latino studies program. Ruiz is currently working on a book project on Mexican and Chicana feminist crime narratives.

JAYSON GONZALES SAE-SAUE is associate professor of English at Southern Methodist University. He is the author of *Southwest Asia: The Transpacific Geographies of Chicana/o Literature* (2016). This book examines the significance of Asia and Asians in Chicana/o literature, showing how both are key elements for how Chicana/o texts articulate a transpacific political culture. His articles have appeared in *American Literature*, *The Journal of Transnational American Studies*, *MELUS*, *Comparative American Literature*, and *The Oxford Encyclopedia of Latina/o Literature*.

ARIEL ZATARAIN TUMBAGA is a scholar of Mexican and Chicana/o literature and culture whose research focuses on the representation of indigenous people and race in literature and culture. He holds a PhD in Hispanic languages and literatures from the University of California, Los Angeles, and has published on indigeneity in the novel of the Mexican Revolution, the feminist works of Rosario Castellanos, and Chicana/o literature. His book *Yaqui Indigeneity: Epistemology, Diaspora, and the Construction of Yoeme Identity* (2018) is an indigenous-centered analysis of portrayals of the Yoeme (Yaqui) nation in US and Mexican politics, anthropology, and literature.

Index